I0814106

"This book is brilliant. As someone who loves the Torah and who cares about effective pedagogy, I am so impressed with *Torah Story*. Gary Schnittjer is clearly a master of the subject and treats it faithfully, thoughtfully, and thoroughly, as a Christian who reveres the Hebrew Bible. But he is also clearly a great teacher, who understands how people learn, and he has tailored the book to maximally help students do just that. Beyond that, he has made it superbly flexible for professors to use in whatever way suits them. If you are going to teach or learn about the Torah, this book is absolutely a must-have."

> ***Elizabeth W. D. Groves,*** lecturer in Biblical Hebrew
> Westminster Theological Seminary, Philadelphia

"I have assigned *Torah Story* in my Pentateuch course for many years because of Gary Schnittjer's engaging approach to Pentateuch studies. What I love most are his insightful Readings, attending to theological interpretation and narrative artistry, and his Another Look brimming with fresh observations about interconnections within and between biblical books. Augmenting these strengths, the second edition of *Torah Story* is enhanced throughout with updated research, tables, images, and interactive workshops that make an effective textbook even better for anyone seeking an apprenticeship on the Torah."

> ***Kenneth C. Way,*** professor of Old Testament and Semitics
> Talbot School of Theology, Biola University

"It is difficult to improve on an already superb work, but Gary Schnittjer has done just this in the second edition of *Torah Story*. The introductory chapter, which has been substantially revised and is now even more helpful to the student, explains how to read the Torah in light of how biblical narrative works. Then in the remaining chapters Schnittjer masterfully models his approach to narrative by offering an astute theological reading of the Torah. Throughout the reader finds many invaluable insights into the Torah's literary features and intertextual allusions, which is exactly what we would expect given Schnittjer's expertise in these areas. I cannot recommend *Torah Story* highly enough!"

> ***Benjamin J. Noonan,*** associate professor of Old Testament and Hebrew
> Columbia International University

"Schnittjer's *Torah Story* is a refreshingly unique textbook on the Pentateuch that moves beyond summarizing the content of these books to tracing their literary strategies, intertextual connections, and enduring significance as Christian Scripture. This volume—especially the second edition—offers a new generation of readers a sophisticated, accessible, and indispensable introduction to Scripture's foundational narratives."

> ***Michelle Knight,*** assistant professor of Old Testament and Semitic languages
> Trinity Evangelical Divinity School

"The second edition of *Torah Story* offers an invitation to the reader to become an apprentice of the Pentateuch. As a skilled guide with decades of experience in the classroom, Schnittjer knows how to lead students down the path of discovery through the inductive study of Scripture and shows us how he does it. This volume is ideally suited for professors who want to turn their course into an interactive workshop. Students will enjoy its thought-provoking questions and suggestions for research projects. Highly recommended!"

> ***Gordon Johnston,*** professor of Old Testament
> Dallas Theological Seminary

"This substantially reworked second edition of *Torah Story* brings students to the cutting edge of Schnittjer's research on how biblical writers converse with each other and draws readers effortlessly into the strange but compelling story that stretches from creation to the edge of the land. Students will experience that story in all its varied plot twists and turns and learn how to read the Old Testament with literary, historical, and theological sensitivity. Having engaged this Torah territory, they won't want to leave."

***Matthew Lynch,*** associate professor of Old Testament
Regent College, Vancouver

"Gary Schnittjer's *Torah Story* is a rich resource for studying the Pentateuch, not only in surveying its content and major themes or in providing helpful charts and illustrations, but by teaching readers *how* to read and enjoy the Torah for themselves. *Torah Story* is a superb guide to the abiding message, composition, and literary beauty of the Pentateuch, which I highly recommend for both classroom and personal study."

***L. Michael Morales,*** professor of biblical studies
Greenville Presbyterian Theological Seminary

"This second edition of *Torah Story* retains all the best features of the first edition and makes them better. I value this textbook for how it trains students to read biblical narrative in all of its rich design and intertextuality. The second edition enhances this key characteristic through updated and clarified discussion and bibliographic entries. The additional and higher quality pictures enrich the reading experience, and students will appreciate the slightly shorter text, editing that made the writing clearer without losing any necessary content. Students will find *Torah Story* to be a beneficial resource for study long after their course is over."

***Dr. Megan C. Roberts,*** assistant professor of Old Testament
Prairie College

"Torah is foundational for God's revelation and understanding it accurately provides a crucial basis for understanding and living out the implications of the rest of Christian Scripture. Gary Schnittjer has given the church and the academy a tool that encourages students of all ages and backgrounds to gain greater access and facility in God's Word. With a high view of Scripture, his work provides believers of all times help in grasping Torah. It is readable and relatable to the newer generation of students that need to be challenged and enticed to see the relevance and excitement of building a firm foundation for a life of study of God's Word and the relevance of the Torah for the whole of God's revelation. With that goal, *Torah Story* provides helpful tools to not only understand the broad strokes but also to dig in deeper with some helpful guidance and direction. It introduces the reader to issues, topics, controversies, and how to read the text for what it intends to teach—all concerns that students new to Torah studies and Scripture in general need to recognize and begin to understand. I look forward to using this even more helpful edition in the classroom as I continue to introduce my students to Torah."

***John Soden,*** professor, Bible and theology
Lancaster Bible College | Capital Seminary and Graduate School

"The key word to take away from this book is the word apprentice. The reader is treated to the work of someone who truly believes that all Scripture is God-breathed and profitable for Christians. Yes, even the Pentateuch. The first edition guided readers faithfully through the Torah, both to understand its message and its relevance for life and godliness. This new edition brings nearly two decades of additional experience and insight from Schnittjer's own apprenticeship in the Bible. It is improved in every way, offering additional insights and reflections while maintaining the character that made the first edition such a valuable guide. One encounters not merely a fresh coat of paint but a thoroughly restored model. The introductory chapters prepare the apprentices for their tour of the Pentateuch, and in the rest of the book, Schnittjer guides readers through each book of the Torah. Like the best kind of tour guide, he has clearly retained his love and wonder of the Pentateuch, and his intent is for the apprentice to be shaped by it."

**_Ryan C. Hanley,_** department chair and assistant professor of biblical studies
University of the Cumberlands

"Gary Schnittjer's careful and close read of the Torah effectively captures the big picture supplemented with attention to the priorities of each narrative segment. Gary's exceptional scholarship is complemented by an aesthetically pleasing format that is user-friendly. Content, formatting, and teaching aids combine to make the second edition of the *Torah Story* an easy choice for classroom and personal study."

**_John F. Klem,_** dean, Center for Biblical Studies Seminary
Antipolo City, Philippines

"The first edition of *Torah Story* has always been my go-to recommendation for textbooks on the Pentateuch. I did not agree with every detail, but it combined clarity and organization with deep research, careful exegesis, and useful application. Over the years I had the privilege of closely observing hundreds of students using this textbook and coming to a deeper understanding of God's Word. Now Gary Schnittjer has made a good textbook even better with updated research, expanded illustrations, and extensive resources for teachers. I look forward to seeing how this new edition will build on the substantial legacy of the first, cultivating sincere love for Christ in those who give themselves wholeheartedly to the study of the Torah."

**_Jonathan L. Master,_** president
Greenville Presbyterian Theological Seminary

"Gary Schnittjer skillfully expounds the Pentateuch from a Christian perspective, illuminating its argument, structure, unity, and trajectory. He excels at explaining intertextual connections and literary techniques. This second edition will enrich the next generation for years to come."

**_Mark A. Hassler,_** professor of Old Testament
Virginia Beach Theological Seminary

"If only this book had been available twenty years ago when I was first asked to teach a survey of the Torah course in a discipleship program for young Israeli believers. Schnittjer's apprenticeship approach to the Torah will be a blessing for teacher and student alike. Every page is filled with gems of learning opportunities—not only in terms of its insights about the Torah but also in its insights about how to teach the Torah. It is my sincerest hope that Schnittjer's approach will be applied to every other book in the Bible in future publications as well!"

**_Seth D. Postell,_** academic dean
Israel College of the Bible, Netanya Israel

"With superb literary sensitivity and elegant prose, Gary Schnittjer guides readers through the Pentateuch. His keen insights into the Torah's macrostructure and intertextual connections offer a refreshing alternative to standard introductions and surveys. *Torah Story* is a masterful textbook—clear and engaging for both students and scholars. Its abundant sidebars, illustrations, and questions elevate the book's usefulness and application for learners at all stages."

*Jillian L. Ross*, associate professor of biblical studies
Liberty University

"Gary Schnittjer has distinguished himself as an especially perceptive reader of biblical narrative, which makes him an ideal guide for students of the Torah. In this textbook and companion *Workbook*, he draws from his deep well of insights on the biblical text and his years of classroom experience. My students genuinely thanked me for assigning the first edition. I'm delighted that Schnittjer has taken the time to refresh and shorten the book to communicate even more effectively to future students. I make it a practice not to assign any book that I wouldn't want to reread myself. *Torah Story* remains an excellent choice!"

*Carmen Joy Imes*, associate professor of Old Testament
Biola University

"Kudos to Gary Schnittjer on the Second Edition of *Torah Story*! Schnittjer has taken one of the best textbooks on the Pentateuch and made it even better. I love the new, beautiful look and layout of the book, as well as the continued student friendly interaction. Likewise, in Chapter 1, I find his guidelines on how to read biblical narrative to be extremely helpful. Indeed, here and throughout the book Schnittjer has incorporated the latest in Old Testamament scholarship into his discussions. As a professor I appreciate the additional resources available through Zondervan's TextbookPlus program, as well as the helpful *Workbook* that is available. All in all, this is a great textbook and I highly recommend it!"

*J. Daniel Hays*, professor emeritus at Ouachita Baptist University
and senior professor of Old Testament at Southwestern Baptist Theological Seminary

# Torah Story

SECOND EDITION

# Torah Story

AN

APPRENTICESHIP

*on the*

PENTATEUCH

SECOND EDITION

GARY EDWARD
SCHNITTJER

ZONDERVAN ACADEMIC

*Torah Story, Second Edition*

Published in Grand Rapids, Michigan, by Zondervan. Zondervan is a registered trademark of The Zondervan Corporation, L.L.C., a wholly owned subsidiary of HarperCollins Christian Publishing, Inc.

Requests for information should be addressed to customercare@harpercollins.com.

Zondervan titles may be purchased in bulk for educational, business, fundraising, or sales promotional use. For information, please email SpecialMarkets@Zondervan.com.

---

Library of Congress Cataloging-in-Publication Data

Names: Schnittjer, Gary Edward, 1965- author.
Title: Torah story : an apprenticeship on the Pentateuch / Gary Edward Schnittjer.
Description: Second edition | Grand Rapids : Zondervan, 2023. | Includes bibliographical references and index.
Identifiers: LCCN 2022005473 (print) | LCCN 2022005474 (ebook) | ISBN 9780310112778 (hardcover) | ISBN 9780310112792 (ebook)
Subjects: LCSH: Bible. Pentateuch--Criticism, interpretation, etc.
Classification: LCC BS1225.52 .S35 2023 (print) | LCC BS1225.52 (ebook) | DDC 222/.106--dc23/eng/20220705
LC record available at https://lccn.loc.gov/2022005473
LC ebook record available at https://lccn.loc.gov/2022005474

---

*Cover design: Gearbox Studio*
*Cover photos: © Tanner Mardis; Taylor Wilcox / Unsplash*
*Interior design: Kait Lamphere*

*Printed in the United States of America*

---

25 26 27 28 29 30 31 32 33 34 35 36 37 /TRM/ 18 17 16 15 14 13 12 11 10 9 8 7 6 5

*To Cheri*

*Blessed is the person who finds wisdom.*

*She is a tree of life to the one who embraces her.*

# CONTENTS

# INTRODUCING THIS BOOK

What culminates in the gospel of Messiah begins with the Torah story. There are other ways to frame the thesis of this book. All of them hinge on two elements. The Torah is a story. And the gospel begins in Torah.

The purpose of this Introduction is to explain some things that can help students and professors make the most of this book. Here is what this Introduction includes:

- Abbreviations and Conventions
- Features of this Book
- A Note to Students
- A Note to Professors

## ABBREVIATIONS AND CONVENTIONS

This book uses the New International Version (NIV) for Scripture quotations unless stated otherwise. The NIV has been modified with permission by using Yahweh for "the Lord," Torah or torah as an English loan word for "Law" or "law," and Messiah for "Christ."

Translations marked as "**lit.**" (literal) are mine.

On occasion this book uses translations by Everett Fox abbreviated as **Fox**, the New Revised Standard Version Updated Edition abbreviated as **NRSVue**, the King James Version abbreviated as **KJV**, and the Jewish Publication Society Bible abbreviated as **NJPS**. The Septuagint is abbreviated **LXX**. Certain places refer to the explanatory comments of the New English Translation as **NET note** (available at https://netbible.org/bible/).

The abbreviations **BCE** and **CE** stand for *before the common era* and *common era*, respectively. The student new to biblical studies should note that dates denoted by BCE count down and those denoted by CE count up, in each case moving toward the present. For example, the northern kingdom of Israel fell in 722 BCE, more than a century before the southern kingdom of Judah fell in 586 BCE.

On occasion, when it seems important or seems like it could help, this work includes references to Second Temple Judaic literature like the Apocrypha, Pseudepigrapha, targums, Dead Sea Scrolls, or other writings of late antiquity. I have not explained such references as they are for more advanced readers. Those who are just getting started with their scriptural studies should skip over these references without concern. Those interested can find English translations of all of these in theological and biblical studies libraries.

Sources are cited by author's last name and page numbers by in-line parentheses. The bibliographic details of all citied sources appear in The Next Steps at the end of respective chapters. Alternate citation format is used for e-books without page numbers or similar situations.

This book uses the term **Chapter** with a capital "C" to refer to Chapters in this book and **chapter** with a lowercase "c" to refer to chapters in the Bible.

*How do the questions work that appear between paragraphs?*

Occasionally a ? symbol with a question will appear after a paragraph. If you can answer the question, you probably understand the discussion. If you have difficulty with the question, it is advisable to reread the preceding paragraph before moving on. In a few cases you may have to reread two or three paragraphs.

## FEATURES OF THIS BOOK

This book serves as an invitation and guide—an apprenticeship or part of one—to the Five Books of Moses, to challenge and assist the student. I have tried to package the discussion in an accessible manner, even when engaging complicated and advanced matters. The book is not supposed to do everything. This book is not a commentary. It does not treat every verse, every law, or every problem in Torah. Rather, it provides the tools and path. The apprenticeship on Torah housed in this book is simply a first step, an important step.

I hope the student-apprentice who learns to read the Torah story faithfully will go on to work through advanced matters that bear on the first five books of the Bible. To this end many significant historical and other background matters appear in Sidebars and the Another Look sections throughout the book. These "teasers" offer an invitation to further studies on the Torah.

Each Chapter, except the first one and the final one, has two parts in its main section, plus special features at the beginning and end. The main sections are designated **A Reading**, which is oriented toward the biblical text itself, and **Another Look**, which steps back to consider selected items in relation to broader concerns—historical, chronological, cultural, theological, or (especially) connections to other biblical contexts.

Before moving on it is worth pausing to note the elements in the beginning and ending sections of every main Chapter.

The first section is entitled **Getting Started**. The reader will get more out of the Chapters by using the tools in this first section.

- ***Focus Question(s):*** This question suggests the key issue to think about when reading the Chapter.
- ***Look for These Terms:*** The student should look for these terms in the Chapter and notice how they are defined.

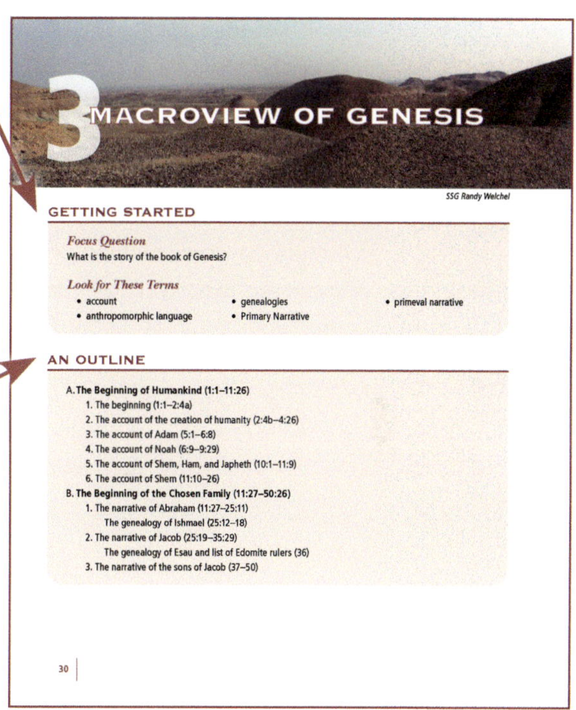

# 3 MACROVIEW OF GENESIS

SSG Randy Welchel

## GETTING STARTED

*Focus Question*
What is the story of the book of Genesis?

*Look for These Terms*
- account
- anthropomorphic language
- genealogies
- Primary Narrative
- primeval narrative

## AN OUTLINE

A. **The Beginning of Humankind (1:1–11:26)**
   1. The beginning (1:1–2:4a)
   2. The account of the creation of humanity (2:4b–4:26)
   3. The account of Adam (5:1–6:8)
   4. The account of Noah (6:9–9:29)
   5. The account of Shem, Ham, and Japheth (10:1–11:9)
   6. The account of Shem (11:10–26)

B. **The Beginning of the Chosen Family (11:27–50:26)**
   1. The narrative of Abraham (11:27–25:11)
      The genealogy of Ishmael (25:12–18)
   2. The narrative of Jacob (25:19–35:29)
      The genealogy of Esau and list of Edomite rulers (36)
   3. The narrative of the sons of Jacob (37–50)

30

***An Outline:*** A broad outline of the biblical material will alert the reader to what A Reading and Another Look sections are introducing. The student will do well to consult the outline when reading the associated scriptural context.

Each chapter ends with an **Interactive Workshop** designed for students. Many of these tools also can benefit individuals or group study.

- ***Chapter Summary:*** A very brief review summarizing the basic contents.
- ***Can You Explain the Key Terms?*** If you have difficulty, it is advisable to review the relevant portion(s) of the Chapter before moving on.
- ***Challenge Questions:*** The reader will find help for these questions in the Chapter, though in most cases the biblical context will need to be read carefully.
- ***Advanced Questions:*** Many of these questions will require advanced reader skills, such as comparing biblical contexts, and will often go beyond what is treated in the Chapter itself.
- ***Advanced Questions with an Asterisk (*):*** These questions provide an opportunity to exercise a variety of Hebrew language skills, some lexical and grammatical, but most are oriented toward semantic and exegetical or theological issues.

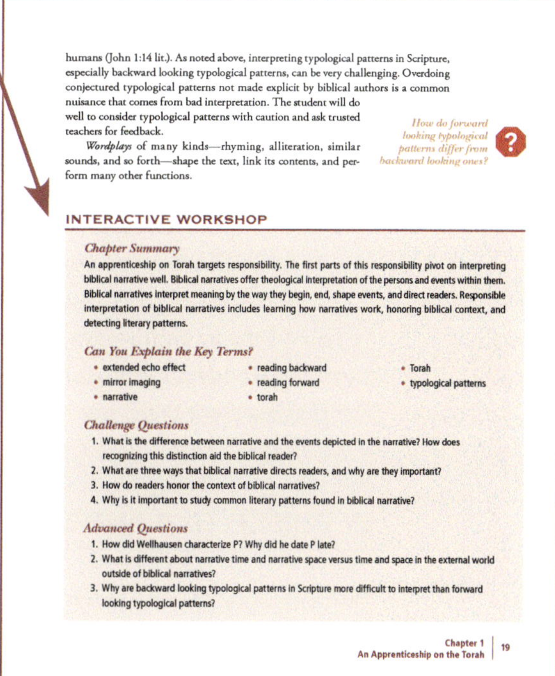

humans (John 1:14 lit.). As noted above, interpreting typological patterns in Scripture, especially backward looking typological patterns, can be very challenging. Overdoing conjectured typological patterns not made explicit by biblical authors is a common nuisance that comes from bad interpretation. The student will do well to consider typological patterns with caution and ask trusted teachers for feedback.

*Wordplays* of many kinds—rhyming, alliteration, similar sounds, and so forth—shape the text, link its contents, and perform many other functions.

*How do forward looking typological patterns differ from backward looking ones?*

## INTERACTIVE WORKSHOP

*Chapter Summary*
An apprenticeship on Torah targets responsibility. The first parts of this responsibility pivot on interpreting biblical narrative well. Biblical narratives offer theological interpretation of the persons and events within them. Biblical narratives interpret meaning by the way they begin, end, shape events, and direct readers. Responsible interpretation of biblical narratives includes learning how narratives work, honoring biblical context, and detecting literary patterns.

*Can You Explain the Key Terms?*
- extended echo effect
- mirror imaging
- narrative
- reading backward
- reading forward
- torah
- Torah
- typological patterns

*Challenge Questions*
1. What is the difference between narrative and the events depicted in the narrative? How does recognizing this distinction aid the biblical reader?
2. What are three ways that biblical narrative directs readers, and why are they important?
3. How do readers honor the context of biblical narratives?
4. Why is it important to study common literary patterns found in biblical narrative?

*Advanced Questions*
1. How did Wellhausen characterize P? Why did he date P late?
2. What is different about narrative time and narrative space versus time and space in the external world outside of biblical narratives?
3. Why are backward looking typological patterns in Scripture more difficult to interpret than forward looking typological patterns?

Chapter 1 | An Apprenticeship on the Torah | 19

***Research Project Ideas:*** Often the first step in pursuing these ideas can be consulting relevant resources listed in "The Next Step."

***The Next Step:*** Please use this list of resources for further study with discernment. I do not necessarily agree with all materials listed here, although I think they are useful in some manner. Most often items listed here are referred to in the Chapter.

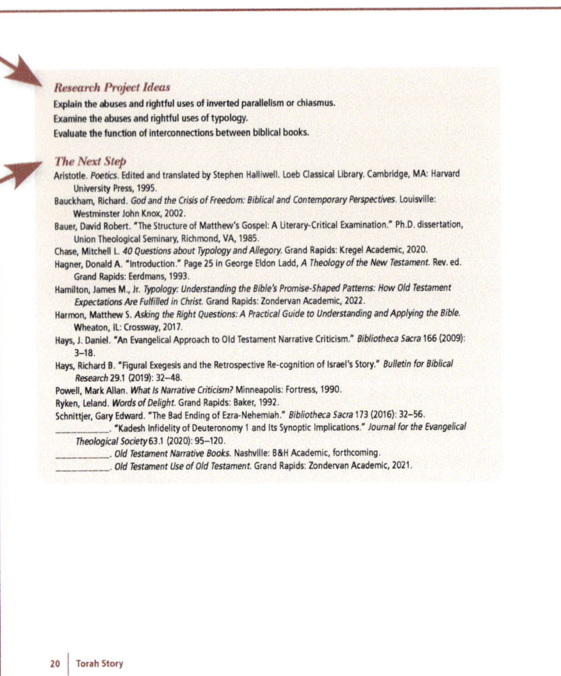

*Research Project Ideas*

Explain the abuses and rightful uses of inverted parallelism or chiasmus.

Examine the abuses and rightful uses of typology.

Evaluate the function of interconnections between biblical books.

*The Next Step*

Aristotle. *Poetics*. Edited and translated by Stephen Halliwell. Loeb Classical Library. Cambridge, MA: Harvard University Press, 1995.

Bauckham, Richard. *God and the Crisis of Freedom: Biblical and Contemporary Perspectives*. Louisville: Westminster John Knox, 2002.

Bauer, David Robert. "The Structure of Matthew's Gospel: A Literary-Critical Examination." Ph.D. dissertation, Union Theological Seminary, Richmond, VA, 1985.

Chase, Mitchell L. *40 Questions about Typology and Allegory*. Grand Rapids: Kregel Academic, 2020.

Hagner, Donald A. "Introduction." Page 25 in George Eldon Ladd, *A Theology of the New Testament*. Rev. ed. Grand Rapids: Eerdmans, 1993.

Hamilton, James M., Jr. *Typology: Understanding the Bible's Promise-Shaped Patterns: How Old Testament Expectations Are Fulfilled in Christ*. Grand Rapids: Zondervan Academic, 2022.

Harmon, Matthew S. *Asking the Right Questions: A Practical Guide to Understanding and Applying the Bible*. Wheaton, IL: Crossway, 2017.

Hays, J. Daniel. "An Evangelical Approach to Old Testament Narrative Criticism." *Bibliotheca Sacra* 166 (2009): 3–18.

Hays, Richard B. "Figural Exegesis and the Retrospective Re-cognition of Israel's Story." *Bulletin for Biblical Research* 29.1 (2019): 32–48.

Powell, Mark Allan. *What Is Narrative Criticism?* Minneapolis: Fortress, 1990.

Ryken, Leland. *Words of Delight*. Grand Rapids: Baker, 1992.

Schnittjer, Gary Edward. "The Bad Ending of Ezra-Nehemiah." *Bibliotheca Sacra* 173 (2016): 32–56.

____________. "Kadesh Infidelity of Deuteronomy 1 and Its Synoptic Implications." *Journal for the Evangelical Theological Society* 63.1 (2020): 95–120.

____________. *Old Testament Narrative Books*. Nashville: B&H Academic, forthcoming.

____________. *Old Testament Use of Old Testament*. Grand Rapids: Zondervan Academic, 2021.

20 | Torah Story

## A NOTE TO STUDENTS

You will do well to carefully read and study the section of Scripture associated with the main Chapters of this book. Some students will want to read the Scriptures under consideration first as a basis to consider the Chapter. Others may wish to read the Chapter first in order to identify elements to look for when reading the Scriptures. Your professor can explain what you should do.

I invite you to have an open copy of the Scriptures on hand as you read the Chapters in this book, to look up passages along the way. Although many scriptural contexts are included in this book, sometimes only Scripture references can be listed. If you compare Scripture as you read, it will strengthen the outcomes of your studies.

## A NOTE TO PROFESSORS

Numerous supplementary materials are available at no cost. Please reach out to your Zondervan Academic representative or see TextbookPlus at ZondervanAcademic.com. Available materials include:

- Quizzes
- Exams
- Visuals
- Teaching synopsis
- Suggested syllabi for courses on the Pentateuch and/or Old Testament with emphasis on the Pentateuch
- American Stories and the Torah Story activities based on old movies or Bible movies—ideally suited for class discussions or individual study assignments
- Also, quizzes on *Torah Story Videos* (see below)

A couple of companion elements to the second edition of *Torah Story* can open up a variety of configurations for designing traditional on-campus courses, online courses, or hybrid courses—the *Workbook* and *Videos* (see below). It may help to first explain that these companion learning tools do *not* cannibalize the Interactive Workshop learning activities at the end of the Chapters in this textbook. I do not mean that there is never partial overlap, but the *Workbook* activities were designed independently and checked against the textbook questions to keep them distinct. One reason is so that the Challenge Questions and Advanced Questions at the end of the Chapters in this book can be used in many different ways. For example, the questions at the end of the Chapters in this textbook can facilitate in-class discussions, online discussion forums, homework study assignments, or exam essay questions, while the *Workbook* can help with study assignments for individual students. There is no "right way" to organize a course. Instead, the activities in the textbook and the *Workbook* offer maximal flexibility that may be applied variously to many different course designs.

The companion *Workbook* for the second edition of *Torah Story* offers several learning activities, with much variety, for every Chapter of the textbook. The activities help students understand the textbook as well as learn from guided case studies in the Torah itself and biblical geography. *Workbook* activities were designed with a view to student outcomes as well as ease of grading. The *Workbook* was tested and adjusted based on critical feedback and re-tested (see acknowledgements therein). An answer key to the *Workbook* is housed in TextbookPlus at ZondervanAcademic.com at no cost to professors.

*Torah Story Video Lectures* do not replicate but complement the content in this textbook. A series of quizzes, available to professors at no cost, have been prepared for the *Videos* (with textbook materials at TextbookPlus at ZondervanAcademic.com).

Some professors use the Enhanced Edition of this textbook that includes the *Videos* in it. As noted above, quizzes on all *Videos* are available at no cost to professors. *Video* quizzes for professors to use are separate from the built-in reading review quizzes in the Enhanced Edition itself.

In summary of the professor resources, learning activities in this textbook, and the *Workbook*, the idea is to over-produce to offer professors options. Though select teaching contexts may lend themselves to assigning everything, most professors will make choices. Professors may desire to use select challenge questions in the textbook one way and select learning activities in the *Workbook* in another way. Certain critical parts of the Torah may require using the full arsenal of learning opportunities for students to really dig in. Here is a comparative summary:

| Interactive Workshops at end of main Chapters of *Torah Story* | Activities in *Workbook* | Selected resources available at no cost in TextbookPlus |
|---|---|---|
| • *Key Terms* are suitable as a basis for short quizzes or minor in class review<br>• *Challenge Questions* primarily focus on the discussion in the respective Chapter of the textbook—suitable for class discussions, online discussion forums, and individual study assignments<br>• *Advanced Questions* lead students to apply the discussion of the respective Chapter of the textbook to case studies in the Torah itself—suitable for class discussions, online discussion forums, and individual study assignments<br>• *Research Project Ideas* | • *Activity 1* in each Chapter focuses on reviewing leading elements of the respective textbook Chapter (without significant overlap of Challenge Questions and Advanced Questions in the textbook itself)<br>• *Activities 2 and following* feature case studies focusing on geography, biblical connections, difficult passages of Torah, and the like<br>• *Making It Our Own Activity* (final activity in each Chapter) provides opportunities for students to work through select implications of their studies | • *Quizzes* on textbook<br>• *Exams* on textbook<br>• *Chapter Summaries* on textbook<br>• Sample *Syllabi for courses using textbook*<br>• *Answer Key* to *Workbook*<br>• *Visual Aids*<br>• *American Stories and the Torah Story* activities based on old movies or Bible movies—ideally suited for class discussions or as individual study assignments<br>• *Quizzes* on *Torah Story Videos* |

# 1 AN APPRENTICESHIP ON THE TORAH

*Paul Venning*

## GETTING STARTED

### *Focus Question*

How should one read the Torah story?

### *Look for These Terms*

- extended echo effect
- mirror imaging
- narrative
- reading backward
- reading forward
- torah
- Torah
- typological patterns

The Torah story is the beginning of the gospel. If the highpoints of the gospel are the teaching, death, and resurrection of Messiah, it all starts with, "In the beginning God created the heavens and the earth" (Gen 1:1). There is no such thing as an adequate grasp of the gospel without an apprenticeship on the Torah.

Messiah taunts his opponents: "If you believed Moses, you would believe me, *for he wrote about me.* But since you do not believe what he wrote, how are you going to believe what I say?" (John 5:46–47, emphasis added). Many Christians have lost a right perspective on the gospel of Messiah by ignoring the Torah of Moses.

Ancient Jews and the earliest Christians studied Torah more than any other Scripture. For many centuries before the earliest Christians, teachers, priests, prophets, poets, sages, storytellers, visionaries, kings, and ordinary people studied the Torah as the word of God. Modern students who do not attend to Torah can only misunderstand songs of the psalmists, messages of the prophets, and teachings of the apostles. Messiah and the New Testament writers do not set aside Torah. They proclaim the gospel by Torah-shaped teachings.

This book is designed to assist with studying the Torah. For most readers this book will be part of an apprenticeship in the form of a course on the Torah or on the Old

Testament with special attention to the first five books of the Bible. This book can be used, however, by any person who wishes to study Torah.

This Chapter offers an introduction to an apprenticeship on the Torah. Here is an overview of the several sections of this Chapter.

Starting Points
Biblical Narrative as Theological Interpretation
Responsible Interpretation of Biblical Narrative
A Case Study
Interactive Workshop

## STARTING POINTS

This section on starting points needs to briefly define a few key terms and concepts. The next three sections explain how a biblical narrative like the Torah works and how to interpret it responsibly, as well as providing a brief case study to illustrate these elements. Many students will want to refer back to these sections in this Chapter as they make their way through the book.

The term **Torah** with a capital "T" is an English loan word from Hebrew that refers to the first five books of the Christian Bible, namely, Genesis, Exodus, Leviticus, Numbers, and Deuteronomy. The term **torah** with a lowercase "t" means instruction or teaching. The next Chapter on Introducing the Torah will explain these issues more fully.

The term **story** or **narrative** refers to telling of characters overcoming obstacles that leads toward resolution (explained more fully below). The terms story and narrative are used identically. Each of the five books of Torah tell a story, and these together form a unified serial narrative—five narratives that together comprise one narrative. The end of Deuteronomy is both the end of the Torah story and a new beginning of the next part of the biblical story line. Within Scripture the Torah story reaches its culmination in Messiah.

The term "apprentice" refers to a person committed to learning a trade or skill in order to gain mastery of a vocational calling. To say **apprenticeship** here seeks to get at attitude as much as calling. The best apprentices own their callings. It defines who they are. The Torah offers much to the diligent apprentice. Torah houses the beginning of biblical redemption even while it reveals the human revolution, the miracle of divine forgiveness, and a pathway toward righteousness. In all of these ways, an apprenticeship on the Torah serves as a gateway to the rest of the gospel.

This book focuses on the Torah itself within its biblical context. Study of historical, cultural, archaeological, literary, and other background contexts offers great value but not at the expense of the scriptural presentation of the story. Part of the reason that this book is oriented toward the biblical story itself relates to learning priorities. Students need to have, first and foremost, a working knowledge of the scriptural narratives themselves, as well as an awareness of how they fit within the larger biblical context (Hays, "Evangelical," 3–18). Too many people know a lot about background matters without possessing a working knowledge of the Scriptures themselves. The history of compositional theories, for example, as important as they are to those who accept and to those who reject them, is not the object of this study (see Sidebar 1-A). Background studies—such as historical, tradition, source, redaction, and canonical criticism—can be best appropriated by those who know the biblical story itself.

### Sidebar 1-A: The Documentary Hypothesis

Many books on the Pentateuch spend a great deal of time stressing the rightness or wrongness of an older theory of how the pentateuchal books evolved into what we have in the Bible. The Documentary Hypothesis—or JEDP, after the supposed four main sources of the Torah, namely, J = the Yahwistic source (J comes from *y* represented in German by *j*), E = the Elohistic source, D = the Deuteronomic source, and P = the Priestly source—dominated pentateuchal studies throughout most of the nineteenth and twentieth centuries. It was thought that what we call the Torah was edited together out of four (or more) sources—written and put together in a particular order, J then E, then D, and finally P—over the course of centuries in the development of Israel's religion (see Friedman, 1992, 2003, 2019). Books and courses on the Pentateuch often focused on isolating pentateuchal sources and determining their historical and theological origin. For example: When and where was the P writer(s) from? How exactly did P get edited together with J and E? Was P first a stand-alone text or is P only additions to JED? and so forth (see Nicholson). As a result, studying the Torah itself was often neglected.

Julius Wellhausen (1844–1918) wrote a book called *Prolegomena to the History of Ancient Israel,* originally published in 1878, that offers the classic and most important expression of the source theory of the Pentateuch. Briefly considering Wellhausen's distinctions between the supposed earliest source, J, and the latest source, P, can help illustrate what is at stake.

Wellhausen found in the older source J the kind of humanistic outlook often valued among modern enlightened European elite. Wellhausen scorned P and, in his view, the dismal Jewish values espoused by P. He often speaks sarcastically when referring to P. The contrast between the older prized ideology of J and the later sanctimonious P shows how, for Wellhausen and others, P practically ruins the Torah with rigid Jewish legalism.

Stated differently and oversimplified, the earliest parts of the Pentateuch—in the "older is better" view of historical criticism—were fashioned in the image of the modern European liberal Protestants who were "discovering" them in the Bible. It is not surprising that one of the significant moves among scholars of source criticism in the post-Holocaust era has been to rehabilitate P and relocate it earlier, during the kingdom period, before or maybe contemporaneous with D. Many debate if classic source criticism of the Pentateuch is anti-Semitic or only anti-Judaic (Silberman). It is one thing to reject the Documentary Hypothesis, as many scholars have; it is another to unpack what these interpretive theories say about the biases of interpreters.

Many scholars have ceased to spend much time talking about the source theories. Part of the reason pivots on the lack of insight such theories produce for understanding the Pentateuch (Goldingay, 8–9).

Friedman, Richard Elliot. *The Bible with Sources Revealed: A New Look into the Five Books of Moses.* San Francisco: HarperSanFrancisco, 2003.

———. "Torah (Pentateuch)." Pages 605–22 in vol. 6 of *The Anchor Bible Dictionary.* Edited by David Noel Freedman. New York: Doubleday, 1992.

———. *Who Wrote the Bible?* New York: Simon & Schuster, 2019.

Goldingay, John. *Genesis.* Baker Commentary on the Old Testament Pentateuch. Grand Rapids: Baker Academic, 2020.

Nicholson, Ernest. *The Pentateuch in the Twentieth Century: The Legacy of Julius Wellhausen.* Oxford: Clarendon, 1998.

Silberman, Lou H. "Wellhausen and Judaism." *Semeia* 25 (1982): 75–82.

Wellhausen, Julius. *Prolegomena to the History of Israel.* 1st German ed., 1878. 2d ed. translated by J. S. Black and A. Menzies, 1885. Reprint, Atlanta: Scholars Press, 1994.

It seems proper that I acknowledge my biases. I am committed to reading the Five Books of Moses as Christian Scripture. This means, first of all, that I am not merely interested in how Torah provides an example of ancient Near Eastern literature or how it sheds light on the religious sensibilities of ancient Hebrew culture. These are very important matters, but only part of studying Torah as the beginning of the Christian Bible. Second, to read Torah as Christian Scripture means it carries the authority of the word of God.

## BIBLICAL NARRATIVE AS THEOLOGICAL INTERPRETATION

Narratives interpret the persons, places, and events that appear within them. Narratives accomplish their interpretive work by how they end, how they interpret everything within them, how they direct readers, and how they begin. The present discussion focuses only on biblical narratives, not narratives outside the Bible and not other literary genres in the Bible. First the building blocks of narrative need to be noted briefly.

Noting the building blocks of narrative such as characters, settings, and plot can begin to show how stories work. A narrative provides a story-shaped framework that explains who **characters** are within the setting and according to the plot. Storytellers carefully characterize the people in their stories. **Settings**—including time, place, culture, and social location—all bear on the characterizations of the people within them. **Plot** refers to key reference points and turning points within a narrative. The drama of a narrative like Exodus presents characters who fit in different social and religious locations within the oppressive setting of ancient Egypt. The plot in this case features a series of divine cosmic terrors like blood, frogs, and darkness while the arrogant pharaoh hardens his heart against the God of Israel. The turning point in the plot is the terror of death to the firstborn. Keeping the building blocks of narrative in mind can help when thinking through how biblical narratives work as theological interpretation.

**Narratives end.** Stories differ from the rest of human life. After winning the big game (or losing it), going on a first date, or getting a new job, people need to wake up the next day. Life has many loose ends and a messiness because it is always incomplete. Stories are different. Stories come to definitive conclusions, even in cases of cliffhangers or open-ended narratives, like Torah.

The ending of a narrative may be thought of as its destiny (Schnittjer, "Bad Ending," 33). Every element, every action, every word of a story makes sense in the light of where the narrative is going (Aristotle, 18.23–28). Whatever happens along the way in a story ultimately takes its meaning in relation to the narrative's resolution. Good examples include the blessing of the sons of Israel in Genesis, the glory coming into the dwelling in Exodus, and the speeches of Moses housed in Deuteronomy in the case of the Torah. These endings play a definitive role in the meaning of everything within Genesis, Exodus, and Torah.

The Torah story has at least two endings that should be noted here. The ending of the Torah itself is a new beginning on the bank of the Jordan River. The next generation of Israel prepares to cross the river to inherit the land Yahweh promised to their ancestors. The Torah story is also the beginning of the gospel story. The teaching, death, and resurrection of Messiah provide the culmination of the gospel narrative that begins in Torah. Both of these endings—the new beginning for Israel and the gospel of Messiah—provide the destinies that explain the meaning of the Torah story.

Scholars affirm the analysis of narrative in Aristotle's *Poetics*, including his well-known emphasis on the way narratives begin and end.

*Everett - Art/Shutterstock.com*

**Narratives interpret.** In what sense do biblical narratives interpret? Because a narrative is an account of an event, it offers an interpretation of the event. A narrative account of an event offers a certain perspective and "spin." The difference between *Jesus died* (an event) and *the Messiah died for sin according to the Scripture* (an interpretation of an event) is all the difference in the world (see Hagner, 25). The opponents of Jesus who watched him die interpreted the significance of his death quite differently from the New Testament authors. For his opponents, and perhaps other onlookers, Jesus simply died a sinner's death.

*How does narrative function as interpretation?*

Both the *degree* and *kind* of spin in a narrative may vary. For example, a security video, eyewitness account, news report, and dramatized motion picture of the same historical event each offer different degrees and kinds of interpretations. The skills that it takes to interpret the meaning and significance of a movie are similar to those that aid the reader of biblical narrative. Reading story comes naturally but, like most other things, can be improved with practice.

In one place, John speaks transparently about the bias and agenda of his gospel narrative. Notice how John shaped his narrative and why:

> Jesus performed many other signs in the presence of his disciples, which are not recorded in this book. But these are written *that you may believe* that Jesus is the Messiah, the Son of God, and *that by believing you may have life* in his name. (John 20:30–31, emphasis added)

John candidly admits he did not use all of his material. He selected certain signs according to his agenda. He told the story he did to persuade his readers of the identity of Messiah in order to evoke a response of trusting in Messiah. Unlike John, most biblical narrators do not explain themselves. As such, determining a story's spin and its point may require careful study.

In what sense is the narrative interpretation of the events theological? Biblical narrative places the human phenomenon within divine perspective. It is, in a real sense, God's story. Biblical story presents the reader with a narrative world that challenges, motivates, and directs. The narrator expects the reader to think and live according to the shape and vision of the story. Biblical narrative is *the story* into which everything, including the world of the reader, fits. This naturally leads to a greater focus on how biblical narratives direct readers.

**Narratives direct readers.** Readers too often are ruled by what they bring to the text. When we hear a song, it can take us back ten years or more and remind us of our younger days. We may say this song means such and such to me. The fact that we associate a given song with part of our own lives has nothing to do with the meaning of the song itself. It is not a big deal to misinterpret popular music. Many, unfortunately, do the same kind of thing with the Scriptures. We may choose to teach or preach on a given passage because of what it meant to us in our own younger days. Thus, sometimes even the selection of texts reflects our bias. There is nothing wrong with the associations between our lives and Scripture, unless we think that our readings of the Scriptures are the meaning. They are not.

"The Bible's total story," says Bauckham, "sketches in narrative form the meaning of all reality" (64). Scripture's story tells us who we are and who we should be (Harmon, 19). It explains the human situation and offers a right view of life in at least three ways. First, biblical story explains the *identity* of all humanity. It narrates the creation and fall of humankind. It situates the human world in relation to its Creator. Readers learn who they are in relation to Yahweh, humanity, the chosen family of Israel, the nations, and the Messiah. Second, scriptural narrative offers readers a view of the *destiny* of humankind and the human world. It points, with the certainty and power of God's own word, to restoration and redemption because of his tenacious love. Third, biblical story defines the *direction* for human life. When we know our identity—*who we are*—and our destiny—*where we are going*—we are in a position to apprehend the direction that our lives should be going. In this way scriptural narratives can motivate faithful readers to serve God and obey his word.

*How do scriptural narratives explain human life?* ?

How should readers relate to scriptural narrative? It is not just the most important book in our lives. Rather, our lives fit within its narrative explanation. For those who read it as Scripture, it is the story of the world in which humankind lives. We apprehend ourselves and envision life from the worldview offered by biblical story.

Biblical narrative is *the story*. The Torah is the beginning of the story. To understand ourselves, the meaning of life—individually and socially—and God himself, we need to devote ourselves to the biblical narrative.

**Narratives begin.** The way stories begin offers readers important clues about the story and its main characters. Genesis begins with creation and rebellion. Since the beginning of Genesis simultaneously stands at the head of the first book of Bible, the Torah, the Old Testament, and the Christian Bible, this profound beginning gets paired with a series of theologically pregnant endings. The beginning of Genesis differs from all other biblical beginnings since nothing comes before *the beginning*.

Other beginnings tell stories within larger narrative frameworks. Exodus starts with the names of Israel's families in Egypt. This begins a new story even while it continues the serial narrative of which it is a part. Leviticus begins with Yahweh calling out to Moses from the dwelling. This starts the story of Yahweh's instructions for worship and holy standards even while it builds on the dangerous situation of Israel because the glory has descended into the dwelling.

In sum, historical narratives should not be thought of as mere facts. An attitude of "just the facts, ma'am" has nothing to do with biblical narratives. Biblical narratives begin and end. These beginnings and endings situate all narrative elements between these guiding frames. All elements between the beginning and ending—characters, settings, plot points—bear on the shape of the narrative's theology and agenda. Every biblical story has a purpose. Biblical narratives offer authoritative divine perspective on the persons and events within them in order to direct readers. The biblical story is God's story.

## RESPONSIBLE INTERPRETATION OF BIBLICAL NARRATIVE

Responsible interpretation starts with a close study of the biblical narrative itself. The present introductory discussion focuses on three aspects of responsible interpretation of biblical narrative: learning how narratives work, honoring biblical context, and detecting literary patterns. Before explaining these activities, it will help to briefly explain the goal.

The reader's goal is not merely to find the moral of the story, to boil it down to a list of propositional ideas, or to outline it correctly according to Western modernist conventions. There is nothing wrong with these activities. But they are not the goal of studying biblical story. The meaning of a particular narrative, for example, is not in discovering five reasons why we should not lie—however valid the reasons—but is the depicted story itself. Leland Ryken says, "The story is the meaning" (88). Responsible interpretation begins with learning biblical narrative itself as the goal. The following elements of responsible interpretation aim toward this goal.

First, responsible interpretation requires learning **how narratives work**. In some respects, thinking through the mechanics of story could be compared to breathing air. People usually do not need to think about breathing air. If they did, in any serious way, there would be many complicated things that would need to be accounted for, like physiological and anatomical features of the human respiratory and cardiovascular systems, the molecular makeup of the earth's atmosphere, the significance of location relative to sea level, and so forth. Most human actions are incredibly intricate if one thinks about them. But, in fact, to breathe air and to read stories is usually easy, normal, natural. We do not study things like breathing and reading narrative to make them difficult. We want to learn to do them better.

A **first reading** of a narrative refers to making sense of given elements based upon what readers know at that point in the story. This might be thought of as reading forward. For example, how should Abraham's actions of having a child with his wife's slave in Genesis 16 be interpreted in a first reading? It is crucial to join Abraham at that moment and think with him in light of his faith in what God has said, along with all of "the givens" of his situation, before second guessing him based on what comes after.

A **second reading** refers to how elements within a story should be interpreted in light of the ending or as a whole. This can also be thought of as reading backward. Anyone who watches a movie for a second time understands the sense of reinterpreting elements based on knowing the ending. In a second viewing of a movie someone may say, "I did not see that before." Of course the person saw it the first time. They mean now they understand what the elements of the story mean in light of the ending.

Responsible interpretation of biblical narrative requires reading all of it forward and all of it backward. Everything needs to be interpreted in light of only what has gone before and then reinterpreted in light of what comes after. Multiple readings and extended consideration of perplexing details can help one move through the stages of learning to be at home in the narratives.

**Narrative time** and narrative space operate at the discretion of the narrator. In the external world, outside of biblical narratives, people might think of time and space as constants of human existence. But biblical narratives operate by different rules. After the flood, it might take Noah years to plant a vineyard, get a harvest, and ferment the wine. But in Genesis it only takes two verses for Noah to get drunk and get naked (Gen 9:20–21). This sort of telescoping of events can be called *jump cuts*. In Noah's case, readers spend many chapters inside the ark for a relatively short period of time that seems long but then jump cut several years to Noah's drunkenness.

In the case of Abraham, as he continues to wait for God to grant him offspring, time slows down. The closer the fulfillment comes, the slower the story unfolds. Abraham is seventy-five in Genesis 12, eighty-six in Genesis 16, and ninety-nine in Genesis 17, but his son Isaac is not born until Genesis 21 when Abraham is one hundred (see Figure 1-B). That is, of the ten chapters of waiting for fulfillment, half of it deals with the last year.

**Narrative space** includes both real places and the symbolic significance they convey. "East of the garden" symbolizes exilic judgment as much as a place. In Torah, Egypt and Canaan are lands where inhabitants worship false gods. Yahweh warns: "You must not do as they do in *Egypt*, where you used to live, and you must not do as they do in the land of *Canaan*, where I am bringing you. Do not follow their practices" (Lev 18:3, emphasis added).

Interpreters need to pay close attention to how the story reshapes every element to its best advantage. In some cases, elements are even narrated out of sequence. Non-sequential narrative elements can be called previews or flashbacks. In biblical studies non-sequential elements are

**Figure 1-B:**
Narrative Time in Genesis 12–21

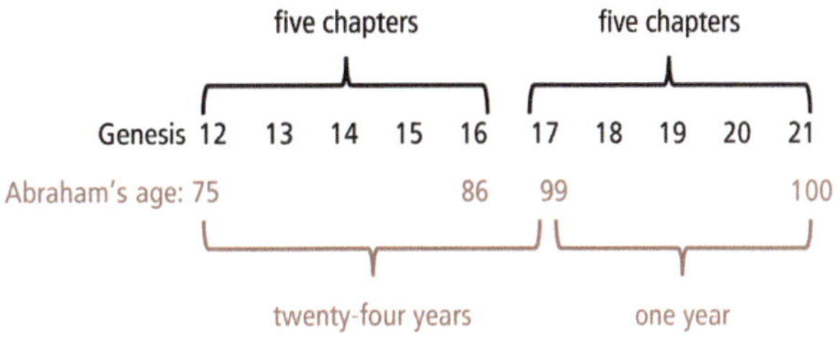

| | five chapters | | | | | five chapters | | | | |
|---|---|---|---|---|---|---|---|---|---|---|
| Genesis | 12 | 13 | 14 | 15 | 16 | 17 | 18 | 19 | 20 | 21 |
| Abraham's age: | 75 | | | | 86 | 99 | | | | 100 |
| | twenty-four years | | | | | one year | | | | |

typically called dischronological narrative. **Narrative sequence** pertains to how events need to unfold for the best advantage of the story (Schnittjer, *OT Narrative*, 10).

Dischronological narrative is very common in Scripture and other ancient literature. In 2 Samuel 5 one of David's most important accomplishments, the capture of Jerusalem, gets fronted immediately following his anointing over all Israel (2 Sam 5:1–10). But the first thing that happened is David's defeat of the Philistines (v. 17). In Luke, John gets arrested before Jesus is baptized (Luke 3:20).

Torah features dischronological narratives in several places. While Israel camps at Mount Sinai, Moses decides on a plan for a hierarchy of judges in Exodus 18 even though the Israelites do not arrive at Sinai until Exodus 19. Thus, the narrative situates a system of judges and then the acquisition of the laws, but the historical sequence is the other way around. This study will highlight dischronological narratives in several places to help interpret Torah (see Chapters 14, 15, and 20).

*What is "dischronological narrative"?*

**Narrative register** gets at many tiny details of literary artistry. The literary finesse of subtle details is on display everywhere in Genesis. Numbers in many ways stands at the other extreme with all manner of historical literary artifacts juxtaposed one against another—lists, laws, worship reports, travel itineraries, and even poems by rival prophets. All of these literary artifacts are arranged amid a series of colorful narratives of the rebellion of Israel in the wilderness.

The point here does not relate to literary appreciation per se. Scripture displays the full range of artistic registers from the literary graces of Genesis, Ruth, and John all the way to the mixtures of literary artifacts in Numbers and Ezra-Nehemiah (Schnittjer, "Kadesh," 103, n. 31; Schnittjer, "Bad Ending," 36). It would be a mistake to judge Numbers or Ezra-Nehemiah as artless in contrast to Genesis or Ruth. Close study of Numbers and Ezra-Nehemiah reveals different kinds of literary art.

**Torah features several great poems** at pivotal transitions. In Broadway shows and cinematic musicals, the songs stand in the foreground and the narrative merely acts as transition from one musical number to the next. While narrative stands in the foreground of Torah, the great poetic blessings of the sons of Jacob in Genesis 49, the Song of the Sea in Exodus 15, the poetic oracles of Balaam in Numbers 23–24, and the Song of Moses and blessings of Moses in Deuteronomy 32 and 33 do more than break up the story. They stand as major transitions in which poetry offers theological interpretation that looks backward and forward.

In sum, responsible interpretation of biblical narrative places a certain kind of demand upon readers. Those who try to impose modern sensibilities or seek to make scriptural narratives fit their readerly agendas fail badly. Biblical narratives need to be studied from both ends. Reading forward and reading backward help place each narrative element in its proper context. Responsible interpretation of biblical narratives requires approaching them on their own terms. This means taking due notice of narrative time, narrative space, dischronological narration, literary register, and large-scale arrangements of story and poetry. All of this takes patience and studied attention to the smallest details as well as wide-ranging patterns.

Second, responsible interpretation of biblical narrative only works by **honoring biblical context**. While biblical stories in many ways work like any other story, with respect to authority they differ dramatically. The narratives of Israel's Scriptures offer an authoritative and permanent interpretation of God's redemptive work. The authority of Scripture affects how readers interpret interconnections within biblical books and between biblical books.

Detecting **interconnections within biblical books** offers one of the keys to responsible interpretation. The running similarities between Noah's drunkenness and the drunkenness of Lot go beyond observing that these are the first two episodes of drunkenness in the Scriptures. The outcome of Noah's inebriation includes the cursing of Canaan. The outcome of Lot's drunken debacle includes the siring of the two cursed rivals of Israel—the people of Moab and Ammon (Gen 9:20–29; 19:30–38; cf. Deut 7:1; 23:3–6). These are the three great cursed peoples of Torah: Canaanites, Ammonites, and Moabites. And the origins of these three cursed peoples stem from the very first accounts of drunken debauchery. This kind of shared pattern indicates a deep continuity extending across Genesis to Deuteronomy.

The first two dances in the Bible appear in Exodus. They could not be more different. Miriam and the women lead a dance of worship after deliverance at the sea (Exod 15:20–21). A few months later Israel immorally dances before the golden calf (32:6, 19). These dances are set at key moments and help contrast Yahweh's faithfulness and Israel's rebellion.

The interconnections within books come from coherence and unity central to the character of biblical narrative. The creation of Israel in Exodus, the reshaping of all of life around the demands of worship and holiness in the shadow of the dwelling in Leviticus, and the last words of Moses on the bank of the Jordan River in Deuteronomy each offer enduring instructions based on the authority of God himself. The power of biblical narratives stems from the authority of inspiration. Torah transcends its moment in history because it offers the word of God.

The **interconnections between biblical books** offer a different kind of interpretive guidance. Responsible interpretation needs to pay close attention to the way scriptural writings interpret other Scriptures. The Torah retains a privileged place at the headwaters of interpretive interconnections among the books of the Christian Bible. The prophets, psalmists, visionaries, and storytellers of Israel all return again and again to Torah. Interpretative interconnections between biblical writing comprise one of the determinative aspects of the progressive revelation of God's redemptive will (Schnittjer, *OT Use*, 848–49, 865–67). The interconnections with Torah by Isaiah, the psalmists, and the letters of the apostles in the New Testament open up new insights into Torah.

Torah should not be sequestered. It needs to be studied in its own right and studied again within the context of the Scriptures to which it is interconnected in hundreds of ways. One of the insights of comparing scriptural teachings interconnected across the Bible is how much of Christian teaching starts in Torah.

The present study will often pause and evaluate interconnections between different parts of Torah as well as interconnections between Torah and other parts of the Christian Bible. These should be seen as case studies of a pervasive, intentional cross-referencing by the biblical authors. These connections are not a surprise. The many interconnections of Scripture demonstrate a deep commitment to the word of God by the authors of Scripture.

In sum of this point, responsible interpretation needs to attend closely to biblical context. Biblical context includes the interrelations within biblical books. Biblical context also includes the larger network of interrelations between biblical writings. The use of Torah by prophets, psalmists, Messiah, and apostles highlights proper ways to interpret and apply Torah.

Third, responsible interpretation of biblical narrative begins by identifying **common literary patterns**. The student will do well to pay careful attention to literary patterns that appear everywhere in biblical narratives. Often these common literary patterns help clarify the meaning of the context.

The importance of a story's structure comes from the importance of the story. Structure serves narrative, not the other way around. Here is a description of several patterns that are typical within biblical narrative (also see Bauer, 8–54; Powell, 32–33):

*Cause to effect* or *effect to cause* links narrative elements together in a specific kind of relationship.

*Climax* is the point to and from which the text ascends and descends. The climax becomes the focal point for considering the narrative function of each part of the story when considering the book as a whole. The books of Genesis and Exodus are good examples of narratives that are oriented toward their respective highpoints (see Chapters 3, 9, and 11).

*Comparison* juxtaposes similar elements. The use of the same or similar elements—words, imagery, and so forth—invites the reader to consider the narrative elements together. Important examples of this phenomenon are discussed as "special words" in Chapter 4 and concerning the term "pledge" in Chapter 9. Also see *repetition* below.

*Contrast* juxtaposes dissimilar elements. The use of contrasting elements—terms, imagery, tenses, and so on—creates irony and/or discontinuity depending on its application by the storyteller.

*Extended echo effect* is the parallel repeated ordering of elements or features in two narrative units. Extended echo effect may include all elements or only some elements.

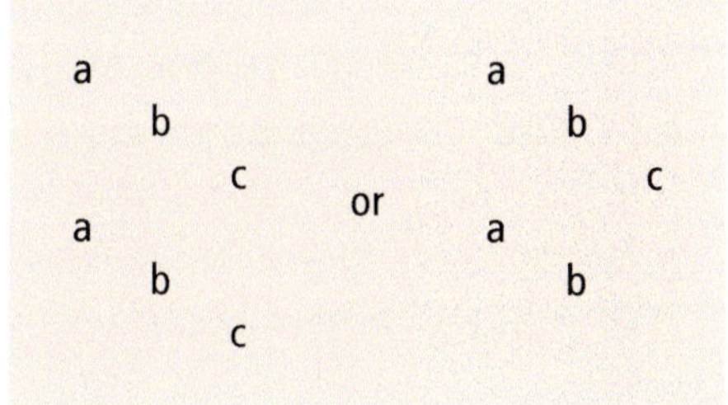


Part of the point of extended echo effect is for readers to see parallel connotations in counterpart contexts. For example, when Noah acts like Adam and Eve after being delivered from the flood, readers detect Adam-and-Eve-like qualities in Noah's behavior. The effects of this kind of parallel in biblical narrative are significant for the reader's view of humanity, God, and faith. The sequential parallels exhibit the sinful bent of humankind. In the Torah narrative, for example, Abraham the deceiver had a son, grandson, and great-grandchildren who were deceivers, caught up in webs of deception. Also, the second generation of wilderness wanderers turned out to be just like their parents' generation, only worse. The repetitions also demonstrate that God's acts in the past are the surest guide of his acts in the future. The major biblical expectations are built on this model—new creation, new exodus, a prophet like Moses, new covenant, and so forth. Thus, lives of faith and prayer are built on trusting that God will once again act as he has. Compare to *mirror imaging* and *typological patterns* below.

*How does extended echo effect work? What are the theological significances of this literary pattern?*

*Ellipsis* occurs when a major element or part is dropped with the expectation that the reader will supply it. Literary ellipsis works exactly the opposite of ellipsis in modern writing in which three dots ( . . . ) signal something intentionally left out because it is not important. Literary ellipsis in biblical narrative draws attention to and emphasizes what is not said (see example of skipping the daughter in Lev 18 discussed in Chapter 19).

*Foreshadowing* suggests elements that will later come to fruition.

*Framing* or *bracketing* (sometimes called *inclusio*) refers to repetition of features or elements at the beginning and end of a unit, causing a framing effect or coming full circle.

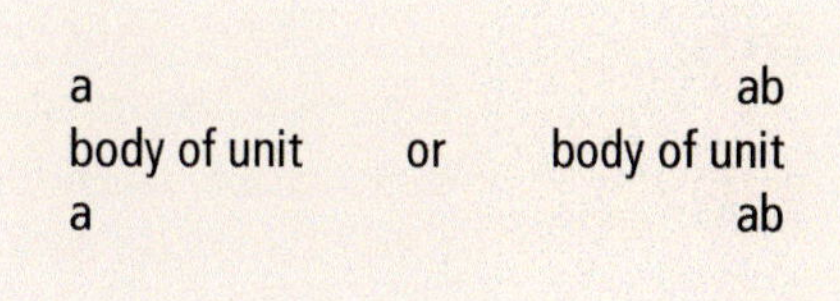


*Generalization* moves from the specific to the general; *particularization* moves in the other direction. The book of Genesis as a whole is an example of narrative particularization. The story moves from a universal context to the story of a particular family. The significance includes setting the story of the chosen family within the framework of all humankind. The meaning of the chosen family cannot be separated from the broader human concerns of the larger story.

*Groupings* or *numbers*—two, three, five, seven, ten, twelve, forty, and so on—are used in literal and symbolic ways (see discussion of "special numbers" in Chapter 4).

*Interchange* employs an alternation of elements that can cause a heightened literary irony, develop comparative imaging, and so forth. The back-and-forth shift between scenes built around Joseph and Judah and his brothers in Genesis 37–45, for example, creates irony and suspense in the story. Readers are invited to consider together both subplots—a readerly perspective not available to any of the characters within the story—creating irony within the ultimately interrelated stories (see Chapter 9).

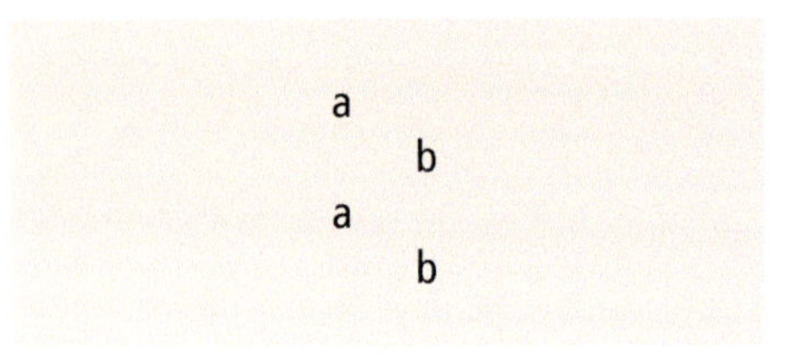


*Janus* is something like a bidirectional turning point, looking back and looking ahead, simultaneously pointing in both directions (see discussion on *turning point* below). This literary term is named after the double-faced Roman god Janus, for which the month of January is named (a month to look back at the old year and ahead to the new). A *janus* may be a small pivot point within an episode, or it may be aptly applied to an entire book (e.g., Deuteronomy). As noted above, the major poems embedded within the Torah—the blessing of Jacob's sons (Gen 49), the Song of the Sea (Exod 15), Balaam's oracles (Num 23–24), and the Song of Moses (Deut 32)—look backward and forward and provide significant poetic-theological interpretation.

*Leading word* is repetition of a key thematic word within a section. Terms such as *eyes, seeing,* and related terms within the Abraham narratives function as a leading word cluster that ties together many of the most significant elements of the story (see especially Gen 22).

*Mirror imaging* has a mirroring effect by repeating elements in reverse order. It is something like looking at a mountain reaching toward the sky and seeing its reflection descending across a lake at the foot of the mountain. The parallel elements may be verbal (exact words), similar words, conceptual, or rhetorical (e.g., biblical quotation); the parallel can be synonymous or antithetical; the center may be a double or single element. Mirror imaging is sometimes referred to as *inverted parallelism* or *chiasmus*, after the Greek letter *chi* (χ), which crosses in the middle. The biggest mistake many people make with mirror imaging is thinking that the main point is always in the middle (for an example of this mistake, see, e.g., Hamilton, 335). Sometimes it is. In narrative, however, the reader needs to realize that story moves between beginning and end. If a middle is important, it only is so as a turning point in a story that continues to reach from its beginning toward its ending. The more common purposes of mirror imaging are to create repetition for emphasis and as a symmetrical organizing device. Mirror imaging is typical of ancient oral literacy contexts to help constituents retain poetry and story lines even when they may never handle the scrolls in their lifetimes

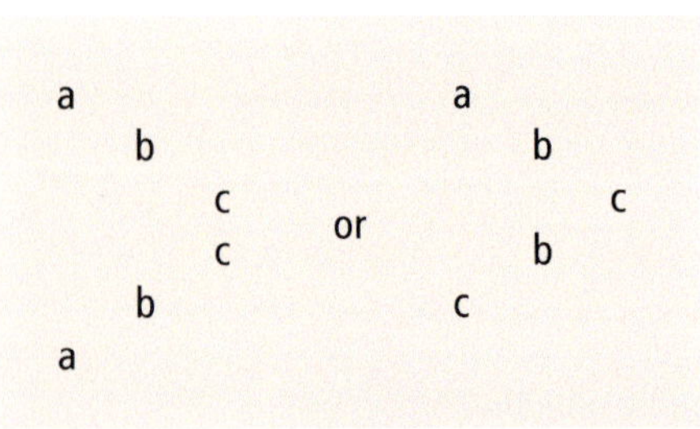

and only hear them read aloud during annual pilgrimage festivals. Mirror imaging may have been so much a part of oral literary conventions that authors and auditors generally did not think about it. In the modern world, mirror imaging (a-b-c, c-b-a) and extended echo effect (a-b-c, a-b-c) appear commonly in children's literature as an oral device to teach literacy. Theodor Geisel may or may not have used an elaborate, incrementally indented outline to plan the progressive extended echo effect of the first half and the mirror imaging of the second half of *The Cat in the Hat*. In either case, children learning to read can safely ignore the mechanics of the structure. Although mirror imaging (a-b-c, c-b-a) and extended echo effect (a-b-c, a-b-c) exhibit similar characteristics on the surface, the significance of these phenomena differs widely. The former encloses and the latter connects its paired counterparts.

*How does mirror imaging relate to narrative?*

Mountain and reflection in Dead Sea

*Photo by נצח פרביאש/ CC BY 2.5*

*Proportion* quantitatively highlights a writing's emphasis. The largest quantities of pentateuchal material are associated with events at Mount Sinai (Exod 19–Num 10) and on the plains of Moab (Num 22–Deut 34). The proportion of material devoted to these events accents the importance of instructing God's people with his word. Likewise, the details of the dwelling for the glory of Israel's God dominates the second half of Exodus, signaling its importance (Exod 25–31; 35–40). The same kinds of observations can be made by discerning the proportional emphases within smaller narrative sections.

## A Case Study

The narrative of Lot and his daughters in the cave of Zoar from Genesis 19:30–38 appearing in the shaded box can serve as a brief case study of several narrative elements discussed in this Chapter.

First, take note of the basic building blocks of the narrative—setting, character, and plot. The setting is not merely a cave but a place without eligible males. The characters are only Lot, his two daughters, and eventually Ben-Ammi and Moab. Although the daughters are singularly focused on childbearing, like many other females in Genesis, there is a sinister irony at work that gets picked up in the third point below. The key plot points pivot on the anxiety of the daughters and what Lot does not know. He is not aware of his daughters' conspiracy or what they do while he is drunk (see two verses marked by letter a and underlined comments of narrator).

Second, note some of the common literary patterns. This passage uses substantial repetition as well as the symmetry of interchange (a-b, a-b) of the two daughters' actions. The repetition of the term "father" eleven times in the space of nine verses establishes a key theme (see bold). All of these events are linked together in a cause-and-effect fashion. Because the daughters are desperate, they resort to a wicked solution of incestuous, unwanted sexual violations—they rape their own father. The major effect is the origins of the nations of Ammon and Moab. Notice how the story is cast as an ancient account of the siring of "the Moabites/Ammonites of today" (see last two verses in shaded box).

**[setting]** Lot and his two daughters left Zoar and settled in the mountains, for he was afraid to stay in Zoar. He and his two daughters lived in a cave.

**[a]** One day the older daughter said to the younger, "Our **father** is old, and there is no man around here to give us children—as is the custom all over the earth. Let's get our **father** to drink wine and then sleep with him and preserve our family line through our **father**."

**[b]** That night they got their **father** to drink wine, and the older daughter went in and slept with her **father**. He was not aware of it when she lay down or when she got up.

**[a]** The next day the older daughter said to the younger, "Last night I slept with my **father**. Let's get him to drink wine again tonight, and you go in and sleep with him so we can preserve our family line through our **father**."

**[b]** So they got their **father** to drink wine that night also, and the younger daughter went in and slept with him. Again he was not aware of it when she lay down or when she got up.

So both of Lot's daughters became pregnant by their **father**.

The older daughter had a son, and she named him Moab; he is the **father** of the Moabites of today.

The younger daughter also had a son, and she named him Ben-Ammi; he is the **father** of the Ammonites of today. (Gen 19:30–38, v. 33 lit.)

Third, we need to briefly take note of connections within this book and between books. Readers of Genesis remember that earlier the daughters' own father had offered them to be gang-raped (Gen 19:8). The would-be victims became sexual predators against their own father. Unfortunately, he taught them the wrong things too well. This helps explain the emphasis on what Lot did not know (see underlining). In addition, as noted earlier, the outcome of this second account of drunkenness in Genesis explains the pair of other cursed people—Moab and Ammon—just as the first drunkenness of Noah explains the cursed Canaanites (9:25). Within the broader biblical context, the reader who knows of the later nations of Moab and Ammon realizes there are two reasons for these nations to be banished from Israel forever. Moab and Ben-Ammi were born of a "forbidden union," namely, incest—which would exclude them according to the law of the assembly: "No one born of a *forbidden union* . . . shall enter the assembly of Yahweh" (Deut 23:2 lit., emphasis added). But that is not why Moab and Ammon are excluded. The next verses in the law of the assembly explain that Moab and Ammon are excluded because of the wretched way they treated the nation of Israel in the wilderness, refusing hospitality and hiring a wicked prophet to damn them (23:3–6). The irony is remarkable. Lot, whose infamous hospitality included offering a mob to freely rape his daughters (Gen 19:8), wound up accidentally siring two nations, by the same daughters, who became cursed for their lack of hospitability to Israel (Deut 23:4). Outside of Torah the most famous Moabitess is the title character of Ruth. She is well-known for her devotion to her mother-in-law from Bethlehem (Ruth 2:11; 3:11). Ruth the Moabitess is a matriarch of king David and the Messiah (4:17, 22; Matt 1:5).

This brief case study on the account of the births of Moab and Ben-Ammi illustrates that narratives do more than relay historical details. Biblical narratives offer theological interpretation of the facts. The narrative patterns in and biblical interconnections with this vignette resemble kindred episodes everywhere in Torah. Students will do well to read and study the Torah according to the elements discussed in this opening Chapter.

*Repetition* refers to the recurrence of similar or identical elements. Whereas *comparison* (see above) is oriented toward relationships between episodes and larger blocks of material, repetition is focused within a given context. In Genesis 4, for instance, the repetition of the word "brother" seven times emphasizes a significant aspect of Cain's crime. This *repetition* should also be *compared* to the rivalry between the brothers of Israel's family at the end of Genesis. Moreover, repetition that extends across several episodes is called *leading word* (see above).

*Summary, statement of purpose*, and *question and answer* each may begin or end a unit. Many chapters in Leviticus begin or end with a statement concerning the purpose of the instructions within the chapter. Question and answer is used for several instructional contexts within Deuteronomy (see Deut 4:32–34; 10:12–13).

*Turning point* (pivot, hinge, or the like) involves a change in direction within the plot—for example, positive to negative or vice versa. The turning point within the sons of Jacob narrative (Gen 37–50) is simultaneously the turning point for the entire book of Genesis (see Chapter 9). The book of Numbers is also narrated around a surprising turning point (see Chapters 20 and 23).

*Typological patterns* refer to expectational similarities of persons, events, or other elements (see Chase, 35–39). Typological patterns operate similarly to extended echo effect (see above) except they include prophetic expectation. Students should take their time with typological patterns because interpretation can be easily abused. In Scripture, some typological patterns are forward looking and others are backward looking (Schnittjer, *OT*, 855–56, 862, 902; as opposed to views that they are always backward looking, Hays, "Figural," 34–36; or always forward looking, Hamilton, 4–5). Forward looking typological patterns include explicit literary signals of expected similarities. Forward looking typological patterns in Torah include the judgment of Israel that will be "*like* the destruction of Sodom and Gomorrah, Admah and Zeboyim" (Deut 29:23, emphasis added). Many of Israel's and Judah's prophets apply this symbol of judgment to the doom of the Hebrew kingdoms (e.g., Hos 11:8; Amos 4:11). Moses becomes a symbol for an expected "prophet *like* [Moses]" (Deut 18:15, emphasis added; cf. 34:10). The earliest Christians were quick to identify the Messiah as the long-awaited prophet like Moses (Acts 3:22; 7:37). Backward looking typological patterns are much more challenging since they only acquire an expectational sense after an authoritative scriptural context connects the later fulfillment to the earlier typological pattern that surprisingly anticipates it. An important example in Torah is the tabernacle. The tabernacle itself is not a forward looking pattern. Yahweh claims he never asked for a temple (2 Sam 7:7). When the glory fills the temple and drives out the priests, this event retrospectively activates the tabernacle as typological when the glory drove out Moses (1 Kgs 8:10–11; cf. Exod 40:34–35). The typological patterns of the tabernacle establish greater fulfillment when Messiah "tabernacles" among humans (John 1:14 lit.). As noted above, interpreting typological patterns in Scripture, especially backward looking typological patterns, can be very challenging. Overdoing conjectured typological patterns not made explicit by biblical authors is a common nuisance that comes from bad interpretation. The student will do well to consider typological patterns with caution and ask trusted teachers for feedback.

*How do forward looking typological patterns differ from backward looking ones?*

*Wordplays* of many kinds—rhyming, alliteration, similar sounds, and so forth—shape the text, link its contents, and perform many other functions.

## INTERACTIVE WORKSHOP

### Chapter Summary

An apprenticeship on Torah targets responsibility. The first parts of this responsibility pivot on interpreting biblical narrative well. Biblical narratives offer theological interpretation of the persons and events within them. Biblical narratives interpret meaning by the way they begin, end, shape events, and direct readers. Responsible interpretation of biblical narratives includes learning how narratives work, honoring biblical context, and detecting literary patterns.

### Can You Explain the Key Terms?

- extended echo effect
- mirror imaging
- narrative
- reading backward
- reading forward
- torah
- Torah
- typological patterns

### Challenge Questions

1. What is the difference between narrative and the events depicted in the narrative? How does recognizing this distinction aid the biblical reader?
2. What are three ways that biblical narrative directs readers, and why are they important?
3. How do readers honor the context of biblical narratives?
4. Why is it important to study common literary patterns found in biblical narrative?

### Advanced Questions

1. How did Wellhausen characterize P? Why did he date P late?
2. What is different about narrative time and narrative space versus time and space in the external world outside of biblical narratives?
3. Why are backward looking typological patterns in Scripture more difficult to interpret than forward looking typological patterns?

## *Research Project Ideas*

Explain the abuses and rightful uses of inverted parallelism or chiasmus.

Examine the abuses and rightful uses of typology.

Evaluate the function of interconnections between biblical books.

## *The Next Step*


Aristotle. *Poetics*. Edited and translated by Stephen Halliwell. Loeb Classical Library. Cambridge, MA: Harvard University Press, 1995.

Bauckham, Richard. *God and the Crisis of Freedom: Biblical and Contemporary Perspectives*. Louisville: Westminster John Knox, 2002.

Bauer, David Robert. "The Structure of Matthew's Gospel: A Literary-Critical Examination." Ph.D. dissertation, Union Theological Seminary, Richmond, VA, 1985.

Chase, Mitchell L. *40 Questions about Typology and Allegory*. Grand Rapids: Kregel Academic, 2020.

Hagner, Donald A. "Introduction." Page 25 in George Eldon Ladd, *A Theology of the New Testament*. Rev. ed. Grand Rapids: Eerdmans, 1993.

Hamilton, James M., Jr. *Typology: Understanding the Bible's Promise-Shaped Patterns: How Old Testament Expectations Are Fulfilled in Christ*. Grand Rapids: Zondervan Academic, 2022.

Harmon, Matthew S. *Asking the Right Questions: A Practical Guide to Understanding and Applying the Bible*. Wheaton, IL: Crossway, 2017.

Hays, J. Daniel. "An Evangelical Approach to Old Testament Narrative Criticism." *Bibliotheca Sacra* 166 (2009): 3–18.

Hays, Richard B. "Figural Exegesis and the Retrospective Re-cognition of Israel's Story." *Bulletin for Biblical Research* 29.1 (2019): 32–48.

Powell, Mark Allan. *What Is Narrative Criticism?* Minneapolis: Fortress, 1990.

Ryken, Leland. *Words of Delight*. Grand Rapids: Baker, 1992.

Schnittjer, Gary Edward. "The Bad Ending of Ezra-Nehemiah." *Bibliotheca Sacra* 173 (2016): 32–56.

———. "Kadesh Infidelity of Deuteronomy 1 and Its Synoptic Implications." *Journal for the Evangelical Theological Society* 63.1 (2020): 95–120.

———. *Old Testament Narrative Books: The Israel Story*. Brentwood: B&H Academic, 2023.

———. *Old Testament Use of Old Testament*. Grand Rapids: Zondervan Academic, 2021.

# 2 INTRODUCING THE TORAH

iStock.com/guter

## GETTING STARTED

### *Focus Question*

What is the Torah? What is the Torah story?

### *Look for These Terms*

- Pentateuch
- torah
- Torah
- Septuagint

## AN OVERVIEW

The Torah is sometimes conceived as a single work, the Torah scroll. Messiah called it the "book of Moses" in Mark 12:26. This single work, the Torah, is comprised of five "books," hence, "Pentateuch" (see Blenkinsopp, 42–47; Childs, 128–32). It is valuable to study each book of the Torah as well as the Torah as a whole (see Fox, "Can?," 31–40; Rendtorff, 22–35). The five books constitute a serial narrative—the Torah story.

*In what sense is the Torah five books and in what sense is it one story?*

The name of each of the five books captures some sense of the book itself. The traditional Hebrew names derive from the opening words of the respective books, and the traditional Christian names are each based on some aspect of the content of the books. The Christian names come from the Septuagint, the ancient Greek translation of the Hebrew Scriptures.

*"In the beginning"* (the traditional name from the Hebrew word *bereshit*)
*Genesis* (meaning "origin") is taken from 2:4 in the Septuagint: "This is the book of the genesis of heaven and earth" (LXX lit.).
*"These are the names"* (*shemot*)

*Exodus* is named for Israel's liberation from slavery and departure from Egypt, the narrative of which is presented in the first part of the book.

*"And he called"* (*vayyiqra*)

*Leviticus* has nothing to do with the Levites. In the ancient Hellenistic world "Levites" meant priests, and the name was given to the third book of the Torah, which presents instructions for the priests and people (see Milgrom, 1).

*"In the wilderness"* (*bemidbar*)

Numbers is named for the censuses in the book (see Num 1 and 26).

*"These are the words"* (*devarim*)

*Deuteronomy* (meaning "second law") stems from a misunderstanding of 17:18 where the term appears in the Septuagint (*deuteronomion*), which actually refers to "a copy of the teaching." Deuteronomy often refers to itself as torah (1:5; 4:8, 44; 29:21; 30:10).

The Torah is set in the ancient Near East. The stories of each book play out from Ur to Egypt in the lands of the Levant (along the eastern seaboard of the Mediterranean Sea) and Mesopotamia (between the Euphrates and Tigris Rivers).

**Map 2-A:**
The Setting of the Torah Story in the Ancient Near East

The books of the Torah are connected together successively. The end of each book dovetails in some fashion with the beginning of the next book (Figure 2-B). Genesis closes with Jacob's blessing of his sons, which looks to the fate of the family line of each of his sons and two of his grandsons. Exodus begins with the twelve families or tribes of Israel. It ends with God's glory filling the tabernacle, and Leviticus opens with Yahweh calling to Moses from inside the tabernacle. Leviticus finishes with a series of regulations for rightly worshiping God, and Numbers starts with the tribes' worship. This book ends and Deuteronomy begins with the Israelites on the plains of Moab preparing to enter the land of promise.

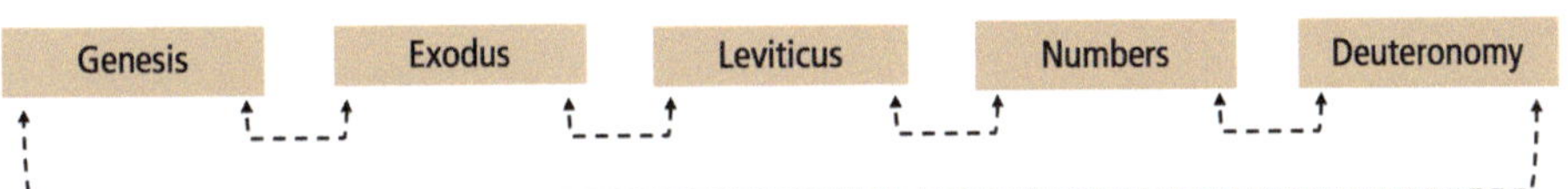


**Figure 2-B:** The Connections between the Books of Torah

In addition to the transitional connections between each of the books of the Torah, there are connections within the Torah as a whole. Put differently, Deuteronomy in some ways functions as a new beginning by challenging Israel for the present and by interpreting the significance of the first four books of the Torah (see Fretheim, 56–63). The imagery of the Song of Moses (Deut 32) echoes imagery from the creation and Sinai narratives. The Spirit of God hovered over the wild and waste of the earth just as he hovered like an eagle over his people in the wasteland of the wilderness (see Table 2-C).

**Table 2-C:** Connections between the Imagery of the Creation and the Redemption

| | | |
|---|---|---|
| When the earth was wild and waste, darkness over the face of ocean, rushing-spirit of God hovering over the face of the waters. (Gen 1:2 Fox, emphasis added) | You yourselves have seen what I did to Egypt, how I bore you on eagles' wings and brought you to me. (Exod 19:4 Fox, emphasis added) | He [Yahweh] found him [Jacob] in a wilderness land, in a waste, a howling desert . . . like an eagle protecting its nest, over its young-birds hovering, he spread out his wings, he took him, bearing him on his pinions. (Deut 32:10–11 Fox, emphasis added) |

The minimal effect of these connections—and there are many others—includes a unified perspective of the Torah as a whole and the oneness of God the Creator and Redeemer. God's activity in both creating and redeeming reveals that he is one in his loving and gracious intentions for humankind (see von Rad, 53–64).

## A READING

The first five books of the Scriptures are known as the Torah or the Five Books of Moses. Many Christians have understood the Hebrew word *torah* too narrowly as "law" because of traditional translations meaning law. It was translated as *nomos* in the Septuagint, *lex* in the Latin Vulgate, and "law" in the King James Version. Although *torah* can be used with legal connotations, this misses the more basic sense of the word. *Torah*, in fact, is better understood as "instruction" or "teaching." The educational overtones of "instruction" aptly capture the expectation that torah would be passed from one generation to the next (see Deut 6:6–9).

*What is the meaning of the Hebrew word* torah?

As noted in Chapter 1, this book uses "torah" of teaching or instruction and "Torah" of the first five books of the Bible. The purpose of the Five Books of Moses was not merely to present the 613 laws embedded within them (see Rabinowitz, 5:761–83). Rather, the Torah—"revealed instruction"—as a whole is story (see Sanders, 9–39). Actually, it is the beginning of *the story*, and as such it offers much to those who seek to read it as God's will.

*What is denoted by "the Torah"?*

The Torah story establishes the larger biblical narrative as the story of God's word and the human revolution against that word. The story may be framed as a question because the matter is still open at the end of the Torah, as well as at the end of the Hebrew Scriptures: *How will God's word prevail over the human revolution?* The question affirms faith in the power of God's word. The answer lies somewhere in the future, beyond the story itself.

*What is the Torah's story?*

Genesis begins with an account of God's speaking the world into existence. God said, "Let there be light," and, indeed, there was light (Gen 1:3). God's word is powerful. It creates and predicts. The prophets preface their oracles with "Yahweh says" to denote the authority with which they claim to speak. When God speaks in the beginning of Genesis, everything listens—everything except human beings. Humans rebel against the single command God gave them. Moreover, humanity as a whole consistently defies God's will. The human exception—whether or not human beings will finally accord with the word of God—forms the problem of the biblical story. Yahweh spoke his answer to Abraham and promised him seed, land, and blessing. Yahweh has spoken and it will be. It is the way Joseph interpreted the events in his story: Even those things intended for evil God used for good to accomplish his word.

Exodus opens with a king of Egypt who had forgotten Joseph, but Yahweh had not forgotten his word to Abraham. Because of the ancient promise, he speaks to Moses from a burning bush and leads his people from slavery to the mountain by his mighty arm. From the mountain Yahweh speaks. The people respond by saying they would obey his voice.

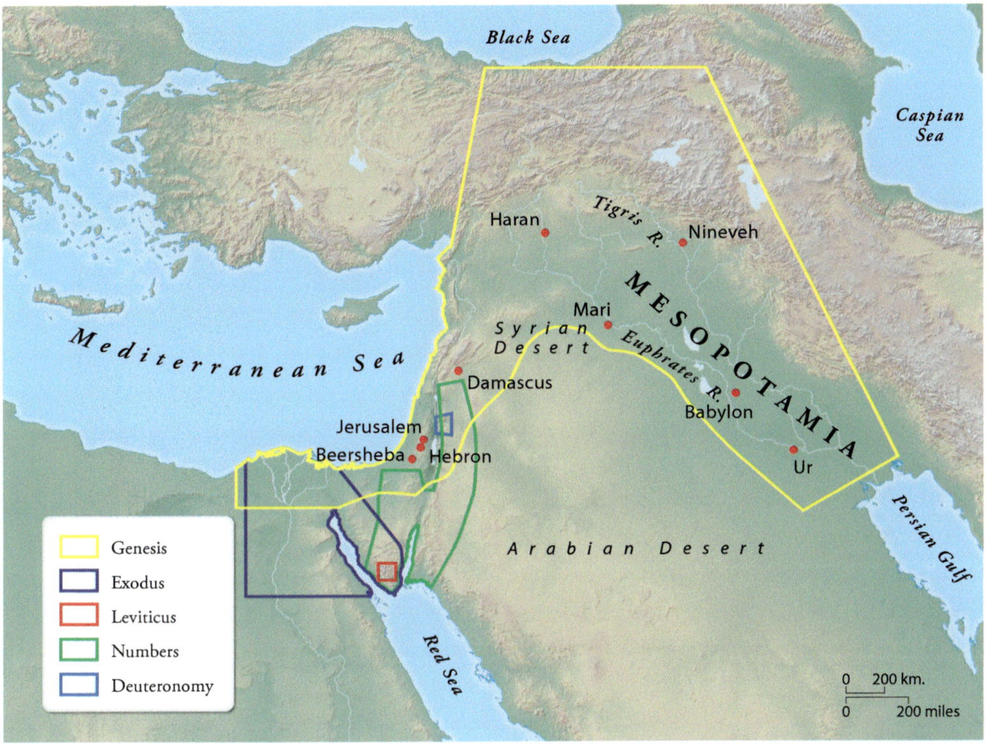

**Map 2-D:** The Geographic Setting of Individual Books of Torah (The settings marked out are for the main story lines and do not include other things like the Table of Nations in Genesis 10.)

Israel, however, proves to be like their ancestors and like all other human beings—sinful and rebellious against Yahweh's will. Yet, in spite of the people's failures, Yahweh's glory descends to the tabernacle and to his people.

Leviticus starts with Yahweh calling out to Moses from the tent of meeting. The book records his instruction for holiness so that his people may continue to enjoy God's presence among them. The other options are unthinkable—he will leave them or his holiness will kill them.

Numbers continues the story of the people in the wilderness. At every turn they succumb to temptation, grumbling, and rebelling against God and his leading. His word is rejected. Even after the first generation is gone, the second proves to have the same dilemma—a propensity toward sinfulness. Yahweh's consistent provision demonstrates, in the end, that the people's problems spring not from the wilderness around them but from their own wickedness. Still, in spite of the failures and rebellions of the second generation, Yahweh will take them into the land he promised their ancestors.

Deuteronomy offers three discourses to you "here today" (e.g., Deut 5:3)—to listeners then and to present readers across the generations. These discourses look both back and ahead, so that the readers do not forget what Yahweh has done when they get to where they are going, namely, the land of promise on the other side of the Jordan River.

The book refers to itself as torah (revealed instruction to its readers). The instruction includes, among other things, the command to love Yahweh with all of oneself and to talk of his word everywhere, all the time. How one passes God's instruction to the next generation reveals the essence of one's devotion to Yahweh.

The Torah looks back and reveals the future. It offers an account of Yahweh's world and Yahweh's word that is a challenge for the next generation. The Torah ends with an expectation for a prophet to come, a prophet like Moses. The future looks like the past. The future hope and the teaching for generations to come are the same: to know God's word and to expect the one who will bring his word to those who need it.

If one can understand the statement "and God said" in Genesis 1:3, then one can understand the entire Torah. Yahweh's will is embodied in his word—Torah.

Torah being lifted up at the Western Wall, Jerusalem
*iStock.com/guter*

## ANOTHER LOOK

What is the function of the Torah? Near the end of the Torah Moses summarizes his pessimistic view of the readers' potential for obedience. "Take this Book of the Torah and place it beside the ark of the covenant of Yahweh your God. *There it will remain as a witness against you.* For I know how rebellious and stiff-necked you are. If you have been rebellious against Yahweh while I am still alive and with you, how much more will you rebel after I die!" (Deut 31:26–27, emphasis added).

The apostle Paul thought that before his conversion he had obeyed the Torah (see Phil 3:5–6). Yet, after his conversion, he came to regard his former interpretation as a misreading (see 1 Tim 1:13, 15). Paul's new reading of the function of the Torah was closer to that of Moses. "Now we know that *the Torah* is good if anyone uses it *the way it should be used.* Knowing this, that *the Torah* does not exist for a righteous person, but for the *torah-less* and defiant, the irreligious and sinful" (1 Tim 1:8–9 lit.). The phrases "*the Torah* is good if anyone uses it *the way it should be used*" and "*the Torah* . . . [is] for *the torah-less*" use wordplays on the Greek word for torah (the italicized terms are each from the Greek word *nomos*).

*What is the function of the Torah?* 

How exactly is the Torah "good" if it demonstrates human sinfulness? Knowing who we are—rebels against God's word—is the beginning of the gospel (see Chapters 24 and 28). Further, the Torah does not speak despair to readers. It offers the story of the word of God. The Torah, therefore, is the beginning of a larger story that explains the meaning of the human situation and the hope for salvation. Torah is life.

## INTERACTIVE WORKSHOP

### *Chapter Summary*

The Hebrew term *torah* literally means instruction or teaching. The Torah story can be framed as a question: How will God's word overcome the human rebellion? Each of the books of the Torah advances the interrelated five-part serial story.

### *Can You Explain the Key Terms?*

- Pentateuch
- Torah
- torah
- Septuagint

### *Challenge Questions*

1. Explain the connection between any two adjacent books of the Pentateuch (include verse references).

2. What is the Torah story, and how does it tie together the Torah with the rest of Scripture?
3. How does the Pentateuch demonstrate the oneness of God as Creator and Redeemer?
4. What is the significance of God's word within the context of the Torah?
5. What evidence demonstrates the need for Torah to be studied in every area of life?

## *Advanced Questions*

1. What are the most important interpretive differences between the Torah as a book of laws versus as story?
2. What difference does it make to interpret one of the books of the Torah as a book versus as a part of the Torah as a whole? Demonstrate this difference with any one of the books of the Torah.

*3. Define the semantic range of the Hebrew word *torah* within the Torah, especially in Deuteronomy.

## *Research Project Ideas*

Explain how any of the five books functions both as a book and as part of the Torah serial narrative (see Fox, "Can?"; Rendtorff).

Define the meaning of the Hebrew word *torah* in the Old Testament and/or the meaning of the Greek term *nomos* in both Testaments (see Downing; Sanders; Byrne).

## *The Next Step*


Blenkinsopp, Joseph. *The Pentateuch: An Introduction to the First Five Books of the Bible*. Anchor Bible Reference Library. New York: Doubleday, 1992.

Byrne, Brendan. "The Problem of *Nomos* and the Relationship with Judaism in Romans." *Catholic Biblical Quarterly* 62 (2000): 294–309.

Childs, Brevard S. *Introduction to the Old Testament as Scripture*. Philadelphia: Fortress, 1979.

Downing, F. Gerald. "Legislation as Social Engineering in the New Testament World." Pages 218–27 in *The Torah in the New Testament: Papers Delivered at the Manchester-Lausanne Seminar of June 2008*. Edited by Michael Tait and Peter Oakes. New York: T&T Clark, 2009.

Fox, Everett. "Can Genesis Be Read as a Book?" *Semeia* 46 (1989): 31–40.

Fretheim, Terrence E. *The Pentateuch*. Nashville: Abingdon, 1996.

Milgrom, Jacob. *Leviticus 1–16*. Anchor Bible 3. New York: Doubleday, 1991.

Rabinowitz, Abraham Hirsch. "Commandments, The 613." Pages 761–83 in vol. 5 of *Encyclopedia Judaica*.

Rendtorff, Rolf. "Is It Possible to Read Leviticus as a Separate Book?" Pages 22–35 in *Reading Leviticus: A Conversation with Mary Douglas*. Edited by John F. A. Sawyer. Journal for the Study of the Old Testament Supplement Series 227. Sheffield: Sheffield Academic, 1996.

Sanders, James A. *Canon as Paradigm: From Sacred Story to Sacred Text*. Philadelphia: Fortress, 1987.

Sparks, Kenton L. *The Pentateuch: An Annotated Bibliography*. IBR Bibliographies 1. Grand Rapids: Baker Academic, 2002.

von Rad, Gerhard. "The Theological Problem of the Old Testament Doctrine of Creation." Pages 53–64 in *Creation and the Old Testament*. Edited by Bernard W. Anderson. Philadelphia: Fortress, 1984.

# Genesis

## IN THE BEGINNING

ויאמר יהוה אל־אברם לך־לך

# 3 MACROVIEW OF GENESIS

*SSG Randy Welchel*

## GETTING STARTED

### *Focus Question*

What is the story of the book of Genesis?

### *Look for These Terms*

- account
- anthropomorphic language
- genealogies
- Primary Narrative
- primeval narrative

## AN OUTLINE

A. **The Beginning of Humankind (1:1–11:26)**
   1. The beginning (1:1–2:4a)
   2. The account of the creation of humanity (2:4b–4:26)
   3. The account of Adam (5:1–6:8)
   4. The account of Noah (6:9–9:29)
   5. The account of Shem, Ham, and Japheth (10:1–11:9)
   6. The account of Shem (11:10–26)

B. **The Beginning of the Chosen Family (11:27–50:26)**
   1. The narrative of Abraham (11:27–25:11)
      The genealogy of Ishmael (25:12–18)
   2. The narrative of Jacob (25:19–35:29)
      The genealogy of Esau and list of Edomite rulers (36)
   3. The narrative of the sons of Jacob (37–50)

## A READING

Genesis opens with the beginning days (1:1–2:4a) and closes with the last days (49:1). It offers, therefore, the framework for the entire story of humankind. As the first book of the Bible, Genesis creates the big story within which the rest of the Bible fits. The remaining Scriptures, with all of their narratives, sermons, songs, prayers, wisdom, and letters, reveal God's relationship with humankind that falls within the narrative context set out by Genesis.

*What is the significance of the beginning and ending of Genesis?*

The beginning and ending of Genesis contain other features that provide the narrative context for interpreting the meaning of the book itself. The story, beginning with the creation of the human world and the revolt against God's word and ending with an expectation for the coming of the Judah-king, has many elements that frame it and give it a sense of literary closure (Table 3-A offers a partial list). Although Genesis is comprised of two sections—the beginning of humankind and the beginning of the chosen family—these two sections are cohesively united in a single book. The story that unfolds between this interrelated beginning and ending needs to be heard within this context. The reader who wishes to hear the story will need to understand from Genesis the significance of the creation and fall and the expectation for the coming of the Judah-king.

**Table 3-A:** Literary Framing in the Book of Genesis

| | |
|---|---|
| the beginning days (ch. 1) | the last days (ch. 49) |
| the creation and fall (chs. 1–3) | the coming of the Judah-king (49:8–12) |
| Adam/Human made from earth, granted life, and exiled from the garden (2:7; 3:24) | Jacob/Israel was returned to the land and buried (50:13) |
| the humans are exiled from the garden (3:24) | the families of Israel leave the land and settle in Egypt (46:8) |
| the snake deceived to incite rebellion (3:4–5) | the lion will rule to secure obedience (49:9–10) |
| the seed of the woman will crush the head of the seed of the snake (3:15) | the Judah-king will, with his hand on the neck of his enemies, secure dominion over them (49:8) |
| God destroyed humankind with a worldwide flood (6:17) | God through Joseph saved the peoples from worldwide famine (41:54) |
| Cain killed his brother (4:8) | Joseph forgave his brothers (50:21) |
| God is the life-giver (chs. 1–2) | God is recognized as the life-taker (50:19; cf. 30:2) |

Genesis tells its story in four parts. The first part, the primeval narrative, narrates the beginning of humankind while the remaining three parts narrate the beginning of the chosen family. The first part relates events across twenty generations over a period of more than 1,600 years, according to the selected details within the text, yet is only eleven chapters in length. The last three parts, making up about three-fourths of the book, cover only four generations over approximately 360 years. The disproportion should not be understood to diminish the account of the beginning of humankind as a mere prologue. Rather, careful attention to the specific narrative of the beginning of the chosen family should foreground their significance within the larger human drama. The human problem conceived in the garden will be finally addressed by the expected descendant of the chosen family.

**Table 3-B:** The Accounts in Genesis

| | |
|---|---|
| 2:4 | the heavens and the earth |
| 5:1 | Adam |
| 6:9 | Noah |
| 10:1 | Noah's sons |
| 11:10 | Shem |
| 11:27 | Terah |
| 25:12 | Ishmael |
| 25:19 | Isaac |
| 36:1, 9 | Esau |
| 37:2 | Jacob |

Genesis makes use of a repeated formula to open sections. The term "account" or "genealogies" (*toledot*) occurs eleven times, five in the first part and six in the latter three parts (see Table 3-B).

The episodes within the first part of Genesis are connected through the use of several genealogies. The two most prominent of these lay out ten generations from Adam to Noah (5:1–32) and ten generations from Noah to Terah, the father of Abraham (11:10–26; see Table 6-A in Chapter 6).

These two ten-generation genealogies close the two panels or narrative cycles within the first section of the book. Genesis 6–11 relates a series of stories that echoes words, themes, and imagery in the same order as the first five chapters of the book (see Table 3-C; for a different view see Clines, 488). The extended echo effect provides the reader with perspective for interpretation as well as important clues to the theological presentation of the story itself (on extended echo effect see Chapter 1). Readers know that the biblical story explains the meaning of their own place in the story because events are like events of the past. That is, the biblical past anticipates the future. Thus, to understand the biblical story is to understand the human phenomenon. Moreover, the God who acted in the past can be expected to act the same way in the future. The biblical story, then, is not merely an accounting of "what happened" but offers readers a view of "why" life happens as it does.

*What is the significance of the extended echo effect in Genesis 1–11?*

The larger component of Genesis tells the story of the beginning of the chosen family. Genesis 12–50 is made up of three major narratives: those of Abraham (11:27–25:11), Jacob (25:19–35:29), and the sons of Jacob (37–50), separated by the genealogies of Ishmael (25:12–18) and Esau (36:1–43).

**Table 3-C:** Repeating Story Sequence in Genesis 1–11

| | |
|---|---|
| water over earth (1:2) | flood (chs. 7 – 8) |
| creation/blessing (ch. 1) | new beginning/blessing (ch. 9) |
| fall/curse (ch. 3) | Noah drunken/Canaan cursed (ch. 9) |
| murder/wander (ch. 4) | tower/scatter (ch. 11) |
| genealogy of ten to Noah (ch. 5) | genealogy of ten to Terah (ch. 11) |

The Negev near Beersheba where the Hebrew ancestors spent much of their lives
*Todd Bolen/ BiblePlaces.com*

There are significant similarities and relationships between these three accounts. Literarily, each uses mirror imaging (or inverted parallelism) to give order to the episodes arranged within them (see outlines at the beginning of Chapters 7, 8, 9, and 10; also see, e.g., Wenham, 262–63). Thematically, the Abraham, Jacob, and sons of Jacob stories are linked by mounting deception. Abraham, the deceiver (12:10–20; 20:1–18), bears Isaac, the deceiver (26:1–11), who in turn bears a son, Jacob, who deceives him (27:1–29) and is deceived by his father-in-law, Laban (29:21–30), who is deceived by his daughter, Rachel (31:17–21, 34–35). Ten of Jacob's sons deceive him (37:31–35; cf. 34:23–24; 38:12–26), which leads to Joseph's deceiving his brothers (42:7). This list gives only the most prominent of many deceptions (see Williams). The repetitions demonstrate the persistence of the human problem, namely, that people, like other creatures, reproduce after their kind (also see 5:1–3).

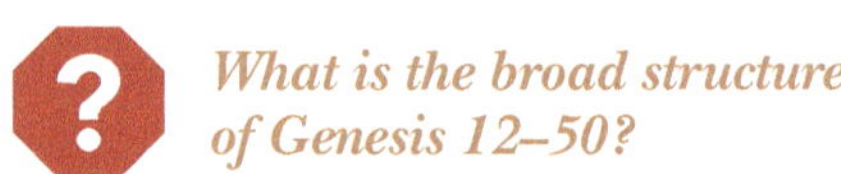
*What is the broad structure of Genesis 12–50?*

The Abraham story opens with Yahweh's call to him. Throughout the narrative Yahweh repeats and expands aspects of this call, which has become known as the covenant or promise to Abraham (see Table 3-D, adapted from Schnittjer, 12). The primary components of the call are land, offspring, and blessing (12:1–3). While these three elements of the Abrahamic promise dominate the rest of the Pentateuch and, indeed, the entire Bible, the Abraham narrative emphasizes the offspring. Abraham has to wait twenty-five years, and the reader ten chapters, before the offspring or "seed" arrives (see Figure 1-B in Chapter 1). Once his son is born, the narrative quickly moves to Abraham's test. Yahweh tells Abraham that he wants him to sacrifice his son. Thus, the story is not about Abraham in any general way but is the story of waiting for and being tested in regard to his offspring. The story closes with Abraham's securing a burial site for his wife and himself and a bride for his son.

**Table 3-D:** Expansions of the Abrahamic Covenant

| Genesis | land | descendants | relationship |
|---|---|---|---|
| **12:1–3** | land deity will show | great nation | families of the earth will be blessed |
| **13:14–18** | all the land Abraham can see forever | like dust of the earth | — |
| **15:16–21** | return when Amorite iniquity complete; from wadi of Egypt to Euphrates | — | — |
| **17:1–16** | land of Canaan | renamed Abraham; sign of circumcision; forever | multitudes of nations; kings |
| **22:16–18** | — | like the sand | all nations of the earth shall be blessed |

At first it may surprise the biblical reader that no cycle of narratives revolves around Isaac. The matter can be seen more clearly when the similarities between his father and his son are juxtaposed to Isaac himself (see Table 3-E; Friedman, 120). The two most important Isaac stories, his near-sacrifice and his blessing on Jacob, are actually parts of the Abraham and Jacob stories, respectively. Genesis 26 presents the only Isaac-focused narratives. The two episodes (Isaac's claiming his wife is his sister and his servants' disputing with Abimelech's servants over various wells) patently demonstrate his likeness to his father, who had already done the same things. The narrator of Genesis, for reasons related to the story he was telling, focused on selected events in the lives of Abraham, Jacob, and the sons of Jacob.

Euphrates River
*Photo by Arian Zwegers/CC BY 2.0*

**Table 3-E:** A Comparison of the Narratives of the Hebrew Ancestors

| Abraham | Isaac | Jacob |
|---|---|---|
| two wives, successively, and one concubine | one wife | two wives simultaneously and two concubines |
| name changed | — | name changed |
| lived and traveled in Mesopotamia and Egypt | — | lived and traveled in Mesopotamia and Egypt |

The Jacob narrative traces his pilgrimage from the land of his ancestors and back, and finally his settling in Egypt. A first reading of Genesis 25–36 offers a picture of a self-centered person with an addiction to deception and a desire for blessing and peace. This picture is true and should not be deflected. At the same time, Jacob grows a little. If one considers Jacob alone, it is hard to see progress because, in many ways, his character remains constant—at the end he is still Jacob-like. Yet, when the reader compares Jacob to any of the other characters with whom he lived—his father, brother, in-laws, wives, or sons—Jacob ends up looking better than they. Again, this is not because Jacob overcame his sinful tendencies. Far from it. Rather, although he manifested particular shortcomings in his character to the end, God met him in visions, wrestled with him, and challenged him. In response to God's continued action, Jacob matured, at least in some ways.

Jacob is as complex a character as any in the Hebrew Scriptures, including David. His contradictory inclinations and behavior make him not only believable but also a beacon of hope. His birth is located at the middle and his death at the end of Genesis. In the end, his new name, Israel, may best describe his significance within the book. Jacob is renamed Israel because he wrestles with God and with humans, and he prevails. This complex character at one time represents both the dilemma and the hope of all humanity. He never fully recovers from the sinful propensities common to all, yet he becomes God's choice as the father of his chosen people. In all these ways Jacob symbolizes both the offspring of the serpent and the offspring of the woman spoken of by Yahweh in the garden in Genesis 3:15:

> And I will put enmity
>     between you and the woman,
>     and between your offspring and hers;
> he will crush your head,
>     and you will strike his heel.

The story of Jacob's sons traverses from Canaan to Egypt—from hatred, grief, and alienation, through hunger and despair, to reunion, momentary peace, and forgiveness. The central plots have been set up by preceding episodes, namely, which brother will receive the birthright and which the blessing. Several factors trick the reader into thinking it will be Benjamin or Joseph, the two youngest sons of Jacob. The narrator is not really trying to trick the reader, but he tells the story with some twists that surprises first-time readers (see Chapter 9). The surprise ending is that while Joseph secures the birthright (a double share of the inheritance), Judah, the fourth-born through Leah, is granted the blessing. Moreover, that blessing includes the expectation that one of his descendants will be a world ruler, the long-awaited offspring.

Genesis closes with the death of Israel. His last words foretell the fate of the families of his sons. He breathes his last and, like Abraham and Isaac before him, is gathered to his ancestors. After Jacob's death, Joseph assures his brothers that he has forgiven them their treachery. His parting words declare that God will one day bring his people from Egypt to the land he promised to Abraham, Isaac, and Jacob.

When the reader looks across Genesis, there appear to be many "accidents," often at significant points in the story. Are the accidents just happy coincidences that the storyteller latches upon? Or are there really accidents at all? Things like the ram caught in the thicket in Genesis 22, providing salvation for Isaac, appear to have been prepared by Yahweh so he could test Abraham. At other times Yahweh reveals that he is at work even when his actions are not sensible to those he is acting upon (see 20:4–6). In the extraordinary case mentioned by Joseph, with which the narrator agrees, God's plan is working through sinful actions committed with evil intent (50:19–20).

What, then, is the supposed relationship between the world of circumstance and the intentions of God? Does the storyteller think that Yahweh only occasionally intervenes so that the key accidents go in the right direction? Or, conversely, is God intimately involved throughout?

The Hebrew ancestors migrated from Lower Mesopotamia
*SSG Randy Welchel*

It is probably too soon to answer these questions, if they can be answered at all. It is useful, however, to raise them and to keep them in mind. When God "remembered" Noah or "came down to see" the tower, the reader does not really imagine that God merely visits the human realm on occasion (8:1; 11:5). No, that is not the story being told. Yet, on the other extreme, the anthropomorphic language, ascribing human features to God, means something. It means something that God remembers Noah and that at a given time, but not sooner, he grants life to the infertile matriarchs (Sarah, Rebekah, Rachel).

The reader's quest revolves around discovering what exactly that something is. The relationship between Yahweh and the story makes all the difference. Besides being a story about ancient events, which it has always been, Genesis is the beginning of Yahweh's story for those who read it as Scripture. In this sense, the narrative world created for readers in this book invites wonder at the relationship of the story and Yahweh.

## ANOTHER LOOK

The book of Genesis is at once a self-contained narrative and the beginning of a larger story. In a real sense, this book has coherence and closure as an individual book. Still, it is the first part of the larger biblical story. We might say it is the beginning of a serial story. In this respect it may be read like a book in a series or be compared to a movie with its related sequels. The issue is interpretive. In what context should the reader place the details of Genesis?

*In what sense is Genesis a stand-alone "book," and how is it related to other biblical narratives?*

What ending fits with the Genesis beginning? It starts the collection of stories that closes with Moses's death and an expectation for the coming of a prophet like Moses. The relationship between the start and finish of the Torah includes not only verbal parallels, like the "hovering eagle" (see Table 2-C in Chapter 2), but also commands that determine life and death (Gen 2:17; Deut 30:11–20). Deuteronomy's forward looking perspective expects the kind of moral failure that characterized the primeval world (Gen 6:5; Deut 31:21, 27).

Genesis also begins the story that ends with the fall of Jerusalem. The Primary Narrative is the nine-book serial narrative from Genesis to Kings, each of which is linked to the previous book (see Chapter 29). This narrative opens and closes with an exile, to the east of the garden and from the land of promise, respectively. The stories within the opening chapters of Genesis also appear to correspond to the experience of Israel recounted in the Primary Narrative. The story comes full circle when Babel, which disappeared from view at the close of the primeval narrative, reappears at the end of the book of Kings as Babylon (see Freedman, ix–x).

Each scroll that was added to the Primary Narrative series reaches across the previous ending and creates a new sense of a whole story with the beginning in Genesis. As a result, Genesis serves as the beginning of many narrative contexts at the same time. To answer the question asked above, it is not that Genesis means one thing by itself and something different as the beginning of the Torah, the Primary Narrative, the Hebrew Scriptures, or the entire Christian Bible. It means something in its own context and means more in the larger contexts of which it is a part.

## INTERACTIVE WORKSHOP

### *Chapter Summary*

The structure of Genesis includes four main parts. The first narrates the beginning of humankind, and the last three narrate the beginning of the chosen family. The book both begins many collections of biblical books and sets the framework for the entire biblical narrative.

### *Can You Explain the Key Terms?*

- account
- anthropomorphic language
- genealogies
- Primary Narrative
- primeval narrative

### *Challenge Questions*

1. Why does Genesis begin as it does rather than simply starting with the call of Abraham?
2. What does it mean for Genesis to set the framework within which the rest of the Bible fits?
3. What are some of the possible reasons why this book gives so much attention to Abraham and Jacob and so little to Isaac?
4. What are Jacob's leading characteristics, and how does he function within the story?

### *Advanced Questions*

1. What are some of the implications of the fact that former biblical stories, in many ways, anticipate later biblical stories?

*2. What does the term "seed" (*zera'*) in Genesis 3:15 refer to within the context of the book of Genesis on the one hand and within the entire Bible on the other?

*3. Can the term *toledot* mean "genealogy" in some contexts and "account" or "narrative" in other contexts of Genesis? In either case, why?

### *Research Project Ideas*

Compare the beginning and the ending of Genesis in terms of literary closure.

Compare the literary structure of the three major narratives of the Hebrew ancestors.

### *The Next Step*

Clines, David J. A. "Theme in Genesis 1–11." *Catholic Biblical Quarterly* 38 (1976): 483–507.

Freedman, David Noel. *The Nine Commandments.* New York: Doubleday, 2000.

Friedman, Richard Elliot. *Commentary on the Torah.* San Francisco: HarperSanFrancisco, 2001.

Schnittjer, Gary Edward. *Old Testament Use of Old Testament.* Grand Rapids: Zondervan Academic, 2021.

Wenham, Gordon. J. *Genesis 1–15.* Word Biblical Commentary 1. Waco, TX: Word, 1987.

Williams, Michael James. *Deception in Genesis: An Investigation into the Morality of a Unique Biblical Phenomenon.* New York: Peter Lang, 2001.

# 4 THE BEGINNING

## *Genesis 1:1–2:4a*

*iStock.com/lermannika*

## GETTING STARTED

### *Focus Question*

In what ways does the beginning set the course for all that follows?

### *Look for These Terms*

- cosmology
- cosmogony
- connotation
- create
- denotation
- image of God
- *ruah*
- Sabbath
- special numbers
- special words

## AN OUTLINE

A. **The Creation of the World (1:1)**

B. **Forming and Filling (1:2–31)**

1. Formless and empty (1:2)
2. The forming (1:3–13)
    a. Day 1—light (1:3–5)
    b. Day 2—water and sky (1:6–8)
    c. Day 3—land and vegetation (1:9–13)
3. The filling (1:14–31)
    a. Day 4—lights (1:14–19)
    b. Day 5—water and sky animals (1:20–23)
    c. Day 6—land animals and humankind (1:24–31)
        i. Animals created according to their kinds (1:24–25)
        ii. Humanity created in the image of God—manifest in dominion and relationship (1:26–31)

C. **Day 7—the Rest (2:1–4a)**

## A READING

The Torah begins with a beginning—"in the beginning." This is most important because it simultaneously serves as the introduction to the book of Genesis, to the Torah, to the Hebrew Scriptures, and to the entire Bible. The reader may wonder, "The beginning of what?" The story that follows reveals that this is the beginning of the human world—the setting for God's story. Whether there are other beginnings or not remains a significant issue. The opening of Genesis, however, tells the story of the beginning of the human realm.

The beginning of the human story in Genesis provides the context for the calling of Abraham and the covenant blessing to the Hebrew ancestors. Within Torah the redemption and creation of Israel makes sense within the framework of the human race and the created realm. This bold choice for beginning with "the beginning" differs from other narrative retrospectives elsewhere in Scripture that often start with the exodus or the Hebrew ancestors (Buster, 13). In this way the creation days help Torah frame the biblical metanarrative—the overarching story line.

Ancient map depicting Babylon as the center of the earth

The reader also may ask, "How did the author learn of this story since there were no people to observe it?" We, as readers, can make guesses. Perhaps the author learned the story from an ancient oral tradition. The author could have imaginatively adapted the narrative as a polemic against an ancient written account like the Babylonian creation story, Enuma Elish (see Sidebars 4-A and 4-B). Perhaps he offered his own interpretation of how it might have been based on his understanding of God, humanity, and creation. Perhaps God revealed it to him in a special way, such as through an oracle or vision. The storyteller does not disclose the source of the Genesis creation story (see Carasik, 5–8). From ancient times, Judaic and Christian believers have embraced Genesis and its account of creation as Scripture—God's word. The other biblical authors found in the Genesis creation narrative an account on which to construct their own writings (e.g., Pss 8; 104).

### Sidebar 4-A: Ancient Near Eastern Cosmologies

The terms "cosmology" and "cosmogony" are closely related. A *cosmology* is a view of the universe and its structure. A *cosmogony* is an account of the beginning of the structured universe.

Scriptural concepts of the physical world are similar, in some respects, to other ancient Mesopotamian cosmologies. This is not to say that there is consistency between different

Egyptian cosmology
*Public Domain*

ancient Near Eastern cultural outlooks (or even within particular societies). Rather, ancient outlooks seem similar to one another when compared, for example, to modern scientific perspectives. It is no surprise that ancient Israel shares many intellectual and social tendencies with neighboring cultures. The word of God to Israel speaks about the world in a way that made sense to readers who possessed an ancient Near Eastern outlook.

Ancient Egyptian cosmology is displayed in The Book of the Dead. It depicts the sky goddess Nut separated from her lover the earth, named Geb, by Shu, the personified atmosphere, holding up his arms. Sometimes it is thought that the celestial lights are on Nut's body, or that Re, the sun god, rides across the sky (Nut) in a boat each day and that the stars are affixed to the udder of a cow. Moreover, sometimes it is thought that Nut gives birth to Re each morning, he rides across her body, and she eats him each evening while giving birth to the cow of the celestial lights.

The view of things held across the two best known ancient Mesopotamian cosmogonies, Atrahasis and Enuma Elish, is the threefold division of the world, namely, heaven is Anu (the gods dwell in the realm of the second heavens), earth is Enlil (humans dwell in this realm), and the lower waters are Enki (or Ea).

Mesopotamians imagined the heavens solid and translucent and able to hold the waters above them (Walton, 155–61). In the ancient temple of Shamash the sun god, worshipers imagine entering into his celestial realm when they enter the temple. An ancient artisan depicted the temple above the celestial waters above the hard sky with the planets within the celestial waters above the solid sky (see image on the left).

Waters above the translucent hard vault of the heavens with celestial lights beneath the sun god in Shamash's temple (888–855 BCE)
*Public Domain*

Though Israel shared many cosmological views with other nations, biblical instruction is largely postured as a polemic against the outlooks of rival nations (see Shinan and Zakovitch, 9–12; Childs, 30–71). The biblical accounts were not merely overcoming the mythical tendencies by means of monotheism but were, in numerous cases, calculated attacks designed to mock those who worshiped other gods (Isa 44:9–20; Jer 10:1–16; Schnittjer, "Idolatry"). In other cases, like Genesis 1:1–2:4a or Psalm 33, the scriptural account defines the power and generosity of Yahweh.

The biblical account depicts all that is as created and sustained by the one true God.

When moderns speak of cosmological realities they use phenomenological (as things appear), poetic language that works at some distance from what people actually think. Moderns say things like "the sunrise was beautiful this morning." No one says: "This morning as the terrestrial sphere rotated toward its star, luminous radiation refracted through the earth's atmospheric gases while the optic membranes on my face captured the light waves and sent neurological signals to my brain, which produced synapses that released chemicals that gave me a pleasing sensation." Moderns never say what they mean about daily cosmic events. Moderns need to be careful not to take ancient poetic ways of speaking too literally. We are not sure how literally ancients regarded their cosmic language.

Notice a selection of poetic cosmological language in Scripture—especially observe the analogical comparison between the heavens and the earth as a woman in Genesis 49:25 (emphases added).

> "So God made *the dome* and separated *the waters that were under the dome from the waters that were above the dome.* And it was so. God called the dome Sky." (Gen 1:7–8a NRSVue)
>
> "*The pillars of the heavens* quake" (Job 26:11a). ". . . *and makes its [the earth's] pillars* tremble." (9:6b)
>
> ". . . *all the fountains of the great deep* burst forth, and *the windows of the heavens* were opened." (Gen 7:11b NRSVue)
>
> "Have you entered *the storehouses of the snow,*
> or seen *the storehouses of the hail.*" (Job 38:22)
>
> ". . . who blesses you with *blessings of the heaven above, blessings of the deep that lies beneath, blessings of the breasts and womb.*" (Gen 49:25b NRSVue)
>
> "For a fire will be kindled by my wrath, one that burns down to *the realm of the dead below* [*Sheol*]. It will devour the earth and its harvests and set afire *the foundations of the mountains.*" (Deut 32:22)


Childs, Brevard S. *Myth and Reality in the Old Testament.* London: SCM, 1960.

Schnittjer, Gary Edward. "The Insanity of Idolatry: Idolatry in Isaiah." *Credo Magazine* 8.2 (2018). https://credomag.com/article/the-insanity-of-idolatry/.

Shinan, Avigdor and Yair Zakovitch. *From Gods to God: How the Bible Debunked, Suppressed, or Changed Ancient Myths & Legends.* Philadelphia: Jewish Publication Society, 2012.

Walker-Jones, Arthur. "Alternative Cosmogonies in the Psalms." PhD diss., Princeton Theological Seminary, 1991.

Walton, John H. *Genesis 1 as Ancient Cosmology.* Winona Lake, IN: Eisenbrauns, 2011.

## Sidebar 4-B: Ancient Near Eastern Creation Myths

The biblical account of creation maintains some similarities with ancient Near Eastern creation myths. Ancient Egyptian myths, for example, sometimes speak of their deities who created by their spoken words. The following excerpt comes from the Hymn to Ra (the sun god) (from Matthews and Benjamin, 7; also see Hymn to Ptah, 4–5). The hymn was developed during the latter part of the third millennium BCE, but the version quoted here was told in the fourth century BCE.

> As the sun dawned, Ra spoke:
> I am Khepri the beetle.
> When I come, the day begins,
> When the almighty speaks, all else comes to life.
> There were no heavens and no earth,
> There was no dry land and there were no reptiles in the land.
> Then, I spoke and living creatures appeared. (col. xxvi:21 and following)

Enuma Elish Tablet I

*© The Trustees of the British Museum*

The most well-known similarities between the Genesis creation narrative and ancient myth are those in Enuma Elish, the Mesopotamian creation myth from the early part of the second millennium BCE. The similarities include the separation of the water into the oceans and the sky, the divine crafting of humans, and the making of chaos into order. The following excerpts from Enuma Elish illustrate the main kinds of similarity between it and the biblical creation narrative (from Pritchard, 60–61, 67, 68).

> When on high the heaven had not been named,
> Firm ground below had not been called by name,
> Naught but primordial Apsu, their begetter,
> (And) Mummu-Tiamat, she who bore them all,
> Their waters commingling as a single body. (Tablet I, lines 1–5)
> The lord [Marduk, the principal god of the city of Babylon] trod on the legs of Tiamat
> [his mother and enemy]
> With his unsparing mace he crushed her skull.
> When the arteries of her blood he had severed,
> The North Wind bore (it) to places undisclosed . . .
> Then the lord paused to view her dead body,

That he might divide the monster and do artful works.
He split her like a shellfish into two parts:
Half of her he set up and ceiled it as the sky. (Tablet IV, lines 129–132, 135–138)
[Marduk declares:] "Blood I will mass and cause bones to be.
I will establish a savage, 'man' shall be his name.
Verily, savage-man I will create.
He shall be charged with service of the gods that they might be at ease!"
(Tablet VI, lines 5–8)

The biblical creation narrative also differs greatly from Enuma Elish and the other ancient Near Eastern creation myths. The ancient myths feature battles and interaction between the gods that establish the human world as a matter of course. Often humankind is merely a sidelight of the struggles of the gods. The biblical account depicts the Creator who creates the human world for the human society as an act of his grace by the power of his word. The human world, far from being an extension of the chaos of the divine realm, is ordered and is granted light and life by the one and only God, Yahweh.

Matthews, Victor H., and Don C. Benjamin. *Old Testament Parallels: Laws and Stories from the Ancient Near East.* Rev. ed. New York: Paulist, 1997.
Pritchard, James B., ed. *Ancient Near Eastern Texts Relating to the Old Testament.* 3rd ed. with supplement. Princeton, NJ: Princeton University Press, 1978.

Biblical readers are free to wonder about the source or sources of the creation account. An apprentice of the biblical writers, especially one who regards their writings as Scripture, needs to put the weight of her or his studies on what the biblical authors have written rather than on what they have omitted. In this case, the author is not primarily explaining in historical or scientific terms the beginning of the human realm. Instead, the opening of Genesis theologically interprets the relationship between God and the human world, namely, that he created it by the power of his word.

According to the storyteller, the world God created in the beginning was unformed and unfilled—wild and waste. The unformed and unfilled state of the earth set up the six creation days—three in which God formed the world and three in which he filled it (see Table 4-C). The relationship between the preformed and prefilled world and the creation days is important for this passage and for the entire Torah (not to mention all Scripture). In the creating days, the power of God's word tamed what was wild and brought to life what was desolate. The Torah closes with the people at the end of a trek through the wild and barren wilderness hoping for

*What is the relationship between the formless and void world and the creation days?*

blessing and life in the land God promised to their ancestors (see Deut 32:9–11; Table 2-C in Chapter 2). What God did at the beginning and in the wilderness he can do again. Indeed, the Torah portrays a gracious God with a powerful voice that all readers need to obey.

"Now the earth was formless and empty, darkness was over the surface of the deep, and the Spirit of God was hovering over the waters" (Gen 1:2).
*plus69 © 123RF.com*

Within these first verses readers are introduced to a distinctive biblical literary style that, in some ways and to varying degrees, was emulated by all later biblical writers. In Genesis 1:2, for example, a "special word" is used, or better, an ordinary word is used in a special way. The Hebrew word *ruah* can signify one of several meanings depending on context. Here it seems to mean spirit—"the *Spirit* of God was hovering over the waters" (emphasis added). In the following chapters, *ruah* is applied in other contexts that at once give it a new sense and invite readers to consider the new use in light of this context.

In Genesis 3:8 Yahweh is said to walk about in the garden in the *ruah* of the day (traditionally, in the "cool" of the day). If *ruah* here means windy, then perhaps cool of the day or evening is appropriate. Still, the reader may easily think of the *ruah* of the day in reference to the *ruah* of God hovering over the waters in Genesis 1:2. The hiding humans and the chaotic empty world provide the contexts in which God is seeking and hovering, respectively.

In Genesis 8:1 God remembers Noah and sends the *ruah* (wind) to make the waters of judgment subside so that Noah can again live on the earth. The fact that *ruah* is sent by God to clear the waters for human life on earth to resume, and that previously the *ruah* of God hovered over the unformed and unfilled world prior to the creation days, invites readers to compare and consider this word in a special way (see Table 3-C).

The dual imagery of the flood and the wind—judgment and new beginning—is similar to the imagery of Israel's salvation from the Egyptians at the sea in Exodus 14 (similarly see Lynch, 76). There God sends an east wind (*ruah*) to provide deliverance to Israel and uses the waters to destroy his enemies.

"And God said, 'Let there be light,' and there was light" (Gen 1:3).
*Dmytro Balkhovitin/ Shutterstock.com*

The narrative of the sea crossing in Exodus uses imagery from Genesis 1 in order to depict the theological significance that God is creating a nation for himself (Gen 1 imagery in italics): "Then Moses stretched out his hand over the sea, and all that night Yahweh drove the sea back with a strong *east wind* [*ruah*] and turned it into *dry land*. The *waters were divided*, and the Israelites went through the sea on *dry ground*, with a wall of water on their right and on their left" (Exod 14:21–22). The imagery here can also be thought of in terms of "denotation" and "connotation." The narrative of the sea crossing *denotes* or refers to the acts of God to save Israel from the Egyptian threat. Yet, the specific language used to tell the story of the sea crossing connects it by its imagery with the account of creation in Genesis. Thus, the sea crossing narrative *connotes* God as the Creator of his nation. Notice how Isaiah makes this connection: "But now, this is what Yahweh says—*he who created you*, Jacob, he who formed you, Israel: 'Do not fear, *for I have redeemed you*; I have summoned you by name; you are mine. *When you pass through the waters*, I will be with you'" (Isa 43:1–2a). Many biblical words are used in special ways that both reveal a need for close reading and show a depth, another dimension, to the text.

In a manner similar to the use of special words, Genesis 1:1–2:4a begins the biblical precedent for special numbers. The seven days set a pattern for a complete week—God finished his work and rested. Thus, in the biblical writings, seven often signifies completion or perfection. In the following chapters of Genesis other numbers become special, such as three, ten, twelve, and forty. The special numbers become part of the fabric of classic biblical style. The use of special numbers invites readers to reflect on the later events in relation to earlier ones. The forty years that Israel was wandering in the wilderness, for example, encourages the reader to compare it to the forty days of rain in the flood narrative.

The use of special words and special numbers are among the many distinctive characteristics of biblical narrative that begin in Genesis 1. The narrative style—somewhere between prose and poetry—displays rhythmic lines, characteristic repetition, symmetrical imagery, the manifold use of "and" to connect lines and scenes, frequent allusions, earthy symbolic language, and so forth. The literary features effectively create a narrative almost poetic with its intertwined realistic and surreal qualities so familiar to biblical readers (on the genre of Gen 1 see Hays, forthcoming). Later biblical narrators emulated, whether by intention or otherwise, many of these literary characteristics, always with their own flair, in such a way that their writings sound like the Bible.

The creating days themselves demonstrate the significance of the entire story. Throughout chapter 1 there is a repetition of "God" plus verb, thirty times in six days. For example, note the fourfold repetition in Day 1: "God said," "God saw," "God separated," "God called" (1:3–5; Schnittjer, 483). The rhythm of God-plus-verb demonstrates several things: the power of God's word; the relationship between God and creation, namely, the dependence of creation on God and God's power over and ownership of creation; God's interest in measuring the character of creation (i.e., "God saw that it was good"); and more. Above all else, the reader is confronted by God the Creator.

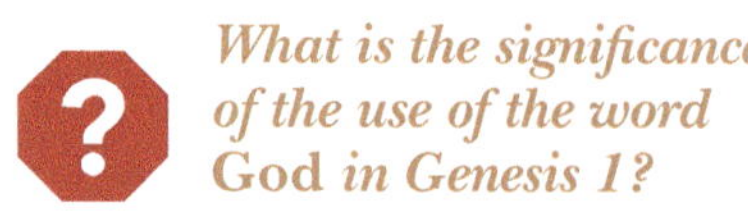


**Table 4-C:** The Creation Days Framework

| Separating the realms | Filling the realms |
|---|---|
| Day 1, light and darkness | Day 4, celestial lights |
| Day 2, heavens and waters | Day 5, birds and fish |
| Day 3, waters and land | Day 6, land animals and humans |

What does it mean to create? Whatever it means, to form and to fill is synonymous with creating in the context of Genesis 1. To understand the Creator, therefore, one must comprehend what it means to form and to fill. In the first three creating days God formed the realms for existence in this world—light and darkness, heavens and seas, land and vegetation. During the next three creating days God filled these realms successively with celestial lights, birds and marine life, and land animals and humankind. The six creation days demonstrate, among other things, the power of God's word to order and to grant life (see Table 4-C).

The first three creation days expose the difference between unformed and formed, chaos and order. The difference is separation. To create, in these cases, is to separate. The light was separated from the darkness, the heavens from waters, and the land from the seas. Without grasping the essence of order as separation, the call to be holy (to be separate toward God) in Leviticus will not be rightly appreciated. Yahweh "separates" Israel from the nations to be holy to himself (Lev 20:26). The holiness required of worshipers is the basic characteristic for relating to the Creator.

The fourth, fifth, and sixth creation days likewise display the difference between unfilled and filled. The difference, in large part, is light and life. To grant life, or to fill realms with light and life, is, in these instances, what it means to create. The realm of illumination was filled with life-sustaining cosmic lights (these lights also function as time separators; thus the fourth day is transitional), the heavens with flying beings, the waters with aquatic creatures, and the land with terrestrial beings. The Creator is the life-giver.

By conceiving of creation as forming and filling, separating and life-giving, the tools are in hand for uncovering the meaning of judgment. To be specific, to die is at once separation and life-losing. Death is the effect of anticreational acts of sin. Death is not separation to form but from form. It does not give but takes life. The death that comes from defying God's commanding word contradicts creation. Life, by analogy, is to accord with the word of God. When the nature of creation and judgment is recognized, the oneness of God as Creator and Redeemer comes into sharp relief.

The story of the creating days not only reveals the relationship of God to the created realm and the meaning of creation itself but also the place of humanity within creation. Creation is viewed in human-centered terms. The created realm itself tells of God's grace toward humankind. The human-centered view of the created world can be seen in the case of each of the six creation days. For example, on the fourth day the entire description of God's creating the celestial lights is geocentric.

The earth-centered viewpoint of the fourth day is the opposite of the modernist perspective of the twentieth and twenty-first

On the third day God created plants of all kinds.

*iStock.com/lermannika*

*iStock.com/Vladimir1965*

*Nailia Schwarz/Shutterstock.com*

*iryna1/Shutterstock.com*

*iStock.com/OLENA SAKHATSKA*

centuries. The "objective" perspective of modernity views the rather ordinary star that is our sun as located in a remote area of the rather unexceptional Milky Way galaxy, which is one of billions of such galaxies. An objective view from "out there" makes the earth seem inconsequential within the universe of planets and stars and galaxies. One of the biblical poets reflecting on Genesis 1, by contrast, marveled at God's grace toward humans given the enormity of the heavens and the celestial lights: "*When I consider your heavens*, the work of your fingers, *the moon and the stars*, which you have set in place, what are mortals that you are mindful of them, human beings that you care for them? . . . You made them rulers over the works of your hands; you put everything under their feet" (Ps 8:3–4, 6, emphasis added; v. 4 lit.).

*What does it mean to create?*

The vantage point of the fourth creating day is that of the earth-dwellers—from here. The great lights are those that rule the earth days and the earth nights, namely, the sun and the moon. Even describing the cosmic lights in terms of "day" and "night" is an entirely earth-centered point of view. Time is measured in earth days and earth years. The stars, moreover, are regarded according to their function of measuring the earth-dwellers' time. "And God said, 'Let there be lights in the vault of the sky *to separate the day from the night*, and let them *serve as signs to mark sacred times, and days and years*, and let them be lights in the vault of the sky *to give light on the earth*.' And it was so" (Gen 1:14–15, emphasis added).

By interpreting creation in a human-centered manner, the stage is set for the entire biblical drama. The story unfolds from this beginning. It is the story of humankind within the human world—both created by God—and their progressive relationship with the God who speaks, creates, evaluates, and gives.

On the sixth day God made land animals after their kind and humankind in his own image and likeness. The phrases "after their kind" for animals and "in his image" for human beings underscore the categorical difference between human beings and all other created beings—the unique ability to relate personally to God. Although God prohibits making images of himself in the Ten Commandments, he made humanity in his image. Human beings reflect and represent God in a special sense. Their creational design defines them according to the Creator. This image is displayed vertically in responsible dominion over the creation and horizontally in mutual social relationships (see Figure 4-D).

> Then God said, "Let us make humankind in our image, according to our likeness; and *let them rule over* the fish of the sea, and over the birds of the air, and over the cattle, and over all the wild animals of the earth, and over all the creatures that move on the earth." So God created humankind in his image, *in the image of God he created it; male and female he created them*." (1:26–27 lit., emphasis added)

The two great commandments—love God and love others—are direct implications of humanity's being created in the image of God. Because humans are created in the image of God, it is their intrinsic responsibility to love him. And because all other human beings are created in his image, it is each person's responsibility to love others as oneself. The great commands of Leviticus and Deuteronomy are the natural extensions of creational design.

*What is the creational basis of the two great commands?*

Beyond the responsibility humans have toward their Creator and toward fellow humans is their responsibility toward the rest of creation. Humankind is related to but distinct from the Creator and the creation at the same time. With respect to being, human beings are creatures among other creatures who live within the created realm. Yet with respect to dominion, humans are responsible to rule over the other creatures by virtue of humankind's distinction of being created in God's image. Humans are creatures, but not like any other because they are like God (see Figure 4-E). The concept of image signifying dominion was part of the ancient Near Eastern idea that statues or images of a king could be used to mark or define the realm of his domain (Kofoed, 19–20). In this sense humankind is the Creator's royal representative ruler on earth. Human beings are the lords of creation because they are specially created in the image of God.

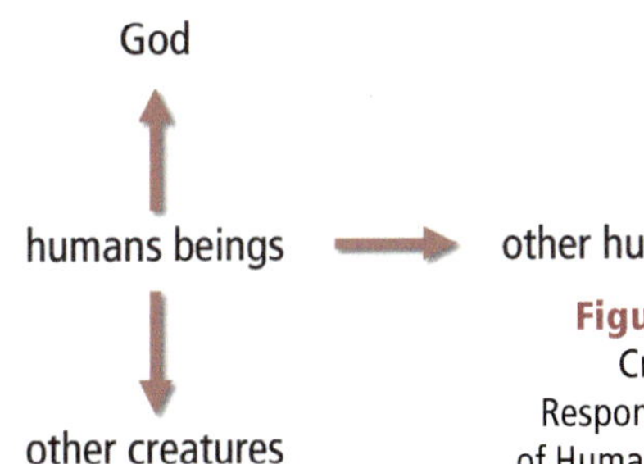


**Figure 4-D:** Creational Responsibilities of Humans in the Image of God

| the distinction between Creator and created | the distinction between rulers and ruled |
|---|---|
| Creator | Creator |
| ———— | humans in his image |
| humans | ———— |
| other creatures | other creatures |

**Figure 4-E:** Humanity as God's Image and as Creature

*What does it mean to be created in the image of God?*

One of the major distinctions between humans and other creatures pivots on the repeated third-person statement "according to their kinds" and the first-person statement "according to our image." The tenfold use of "according to their kinds" regarding plant life, fish, birds, and land animals appears across creation days three, five, and six. Then within day six, a radical shift moves to first-person plural and uses two new terms, "image" and "likeness," instead of "kinds" (van Wolde, 149). The dramatic shift in language—"Let us make humankind in our image"—reinforces that humans are not like any other creature. They are created in the image of God.

The creation of humans on the sixth day seems like a climax, and it is. But there is a surprise higher literary climax after it on the seventh day. In that sense the high point of the sixth day turns out to be the penultimate high point of the creation week (see Figure 4-F). The same pattern appears again in the Abraham stories, seeming to reach a climax in Genesis 21 with the birth of the long-awaited son of promise after twenty-five years and ten chapters (see Figure 1-B in Chapter 1). But the real high point of the story comes in Genesis 22 when Yahweh surprises Abraham by telling him to sacrifice his only son.

**Figure 4-F:** Sixth Day as Penultimate and Seventh Day as Ultimate

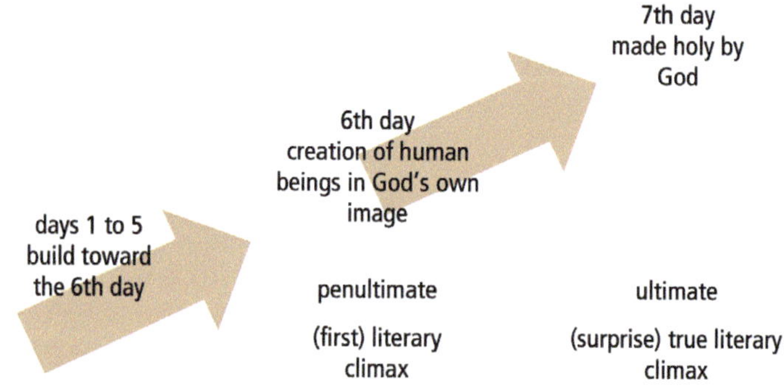


The creation days move in a direction. They move toward the seventh day, the day of God's rest. The nature and significance of time itself is thus defined. Time is measured in earth days and counted in sevens or weeks. Each week moves invariably toward its completion—the Sabbath. The perpetual repetition of celebrating the day of God's rest provides a constant reminder of the human place within the world. Humans live in a world created by God, forever moving toward the day of God's rest.

The story, thus, begins with a beginning. It is the beginning of the human world created by God. Genesis 1 defines the manner in which the story is told and the way to hear and read the story. Moreover, the beginning provides the cosmological backdrop against which the rest of the story—the book of Genesis, the Torah, and the Bible—unfolds. The events narrated in the remainder of the story did not just happen in remote historical contexts. They happened within the context of the entire human world, the world God created by his word. Because the beginning of the story is God's creation of humankind within the human context, the story line is, in some way, about the relationship between God and the creatures in his own image.

## ANOTHER LOOK

After reading Genesis 1, we as modern readers have many questions. We may wonder, for example, why the story differs so much from the theoretically reconstructed interpretations from the biological sector of the scientific enterprise. One of the reasons may be the relative purposes of the biblical over and against the biological interpretations of the human realm. To be specific, biological theorists seek to offer plausible explanation of the facts of nature as we presently understand them. The biblical text also provides an interpretation of the origins of the world. It, however, explains the beginning in a manner that serves as the context for interpreting the story of which it is a part.

A biblical reader may certainly take up scientific-philosophical questions. It is to answer such questions that some have proposed various interpretive readings. In an effort to harmonize a literalistic reading of Genesis 1 with evolutionary theory, some have proposed solutions: that a long gap of time, perhaps billions of years, expired between Genesis 1:1 and 1:2; that "day" in Genesis 1 may refer to an epoch rather than a literal twenty-four hour earth day; that the earth and universe were created with apparent age (e.g., the light from distant stars already touched earth, Adam was created as an adult, and so on); that geological facts that make the earth seem old can be explained by the cataclysmic effects of Noah's flood; and so forth (see Numbers; Young, 20–21; Charles; Collins). Another hypothesis is that God created Adam and Eve in the garden, and after they were cast out, they intermingled with a larger population of humans outside the garden who had arisen by evolution (Swamidass, 24–26). Some interpreters say they interpret Genesis 1 literally but then skip verses, or read them in non-literal ways, like the description of waters above the sky (v. 7; cf. image on p. 42).

The biblical narrative does not attempt to satisfy our curiosity. It says what it says. The selectivity of biblical narrative is determined according to the story itself. We may wonder, for example, what it means for God to create light three days before he created lights. Such a description of creation defies the reader's ability to conjure a mental picture. It nonetheless aptly fulfills the forming and filling strategy of the narrative. Problems occur when readers use the Scriptures to answer their own questions—questions that the biblical text was not designed to answer (Imes, 18). For an apprentice of the Scriptures to become skilled at her or his craft, it is necessary to know when to say, "I don't know."

On another note, the mention of the image of God itself occurs only occasionally in Scripture. According to the New Testament, Messiah is the very image of God in human form (see 2 Cor 4:4; Phil 2:6; Col 1:15; Heb 1:3; cf. John 1:18). The biblical teaching on transformation into the image of Messiah is a return or restoration of humanity to the way it is supposed to be (see Eph 4:24; Col 3:10; Calvin, 1.15.4 [1:183–96]). There is, of course, a qualitative distinction between humanity being created in God's image and the Messiah as the image of God itself. Yet, God condescended in the incarnation to grace fallen humanity with a way to enjoy new life with him, by him, in him, for him. If being Messiah-like or godly is central to the image of God in humanity, then the image of God in humanity is primarily about moral responsibility. This image was perverted through the fall, yet in some sense it remains (see Gen 5:1–3; 9:6; Jas 3:9–10).

# INTERACTIVE WORKSHOP

## *Chapter Summary*

The beginning set the course for all that followed. The Creator formed and filled the human world by the power of his word. Humans were designed in the image of God, which explains the creational shape of the great commandments.

## *Can You Explain the Key Terms?*

- cosmology
- cosmogony
- connotation
- create
- denotation
- image of God
- *ruah*
- Sabbath
- special numbers
- special words

## *Challenge Questions*

1. Genesis 1 offers an account of the beginning of what?
2. Explain the relationship of Genesis 1:2 and the first six creating days.
3. According to Genesis 1, what is the relationship between God and creation?
4. How is humankind related to the rest of creation according to Genesis 1?
5. What does it mean to be created in the image of God?

## *Advanced Questions*

1. What is the relationship between the creation days and the rest of the Torah?
2. Define the human-centered aspects of any of the creation days (other than the fourth day).
3. What is the significance of plurality of genders within the human race?
4. How does the seventh day, the day of God's rest, relate to later pentateuchal teaching on the Sabbath?

*5. What is the significance of *tohu* and *bohu* in Jeremiah 4:23 when compared with the use of the same words in Genesis 1:2?

*6. Trace the uses of *ruah* in Genesis 1–11 and explain the theological significance of each.

## *Research Project Ideas*

Explain the meaning of the image of God in humanity.

Compare the options for interpreting the meaning of God's use of first-person plural pronouns in Genesis 1:26 (see Levine and Brettler, 88–92; Schnittjer, 482; Wenham, 27–28).

Evaluate the gender inclusivity or exclusivity of the Hebrew word for "human" (*'adam*) in Genesis 1:27 (see Clines, 297–310).

## *The Next Step*


Buster, Aubrey. "Sense of a Beginning: The Role of Beginnings in the Israelite Historical Résumés." Pages 3–21 in *For Us, but Not to Us: Essays on Creation, Covenant, and Context in Honor of John H. Walton*. Edited by Adam E. Miglio et al. Eugene, OR: Pickwick, 2020.

Calvin, John. *Institutes of the Christian Religion*. 2 vols. Edited John T. McNeill. Translated by Ford Lewis Battles. Philadelphia: Westminster, 1960.

Carasik, Michael. "Three Biblical Beginnings." Pages 1–22, in *Beginning/Again: Toward a Hermeneutics of Jewish Texts*. Edited by A. Cohen and S. Magid. New York: Seven Bridges, 2002.

Charles, J. Daryl, ed. *Reading Genesis 1–2: An Evangelical Conversation*. Peabody, MA: Hendrickson, 2013. (Five evangelical scholars present their views and push back on the other views. The authors are Richard Averbeck, Todd Beall, John Collins, Tremper Longman, and John Walton.)

Clines, David J. A. "אדם the Hebrew for 'Human, Humanity': A Response to James Barr." *Vetus Testamentum* 53 (2003): 297–310.

Collins, C. John. *Reading Genesis Well: Navigating History, Poetry, Science, and Truth in Genesis 1–11*. Grand Rapids: Zondervan Academic, 2018.

Hays, J. Daniel. *The Pentateuch: Living in the Presence of God*. Brentwood: B&H Academic, forthcoming.

Imes, Carmen Joy. *Being God's Image: Why Creation Still Matters*. Downers Grove: IVP Academic, forthcoming [2023].

Kofoed, Jens Bruun. "Send in the Clones?: The Image of God in Genesis 1 and Ancient Near Eastern Temple Imagery." Pages 11–24 in *Fri och bunden. En bok om teologisk antropologi*. Edited by Johannes Hellberg, Rune Imberg, and Torbjörn Johansson. Göteborg: Församlingsförlaget, 2013.

Levine, Amy-Jill and Mark Zvi Brettler. *The Bible with and without Jesus: How Jews and Christians Read the Same Stories Differently*. New York: HarperOne, 2020.

Lynch, Matthew J. *Flood and Fury: Old Testament Violence and the Shalom of God*. Downers Grove, IL: IVP Academic, 2023.

Numbers, Ronald L. *The Creationists: The Evolution of Scientific Creationism*. Berkeley: University of California Press, 1992.

Schnittjer, Gary Edward. *Old Testament Use of Old Testament*. Grand Rapids: Zondervan Academic, 2021.

Swamidass, S. Joshua. *The Genealogical Adam & Eve: The Surprising Science of Universal Ancestry*. Downers Grove, IL: IVP Academic, 2019.

van Wolde, Ellen. "The Text as Eloquent Guide: Rhetorical, Linguistic, and Literary Features in Genesis 1." Pages 134–51 in *Literary Structure and Rhetorical Strategies in the Hebrew Bible*. Edited by L. J. de Regt, J. de Waard, and J. Fokkelman. Winona Lake, IN: Eisenbrauns, 1996.

Wenham, Gordon J. *Genesis 1–15*. Word Biblical Commentary 1. Nashville: Nelson Reference, 1987.

Young, Davis. "'Let There Be Light': Spectrum of Creation Theories." *Eternity* 38 (May 1982): 20–21.

# 5 THE GARDEN AND THE EXILE

## *Genesis 2:4b–4:26*

*Jon Cooper*

## GETTING STARTED

### *Focus Questions*

What is the relationship between sin and death? What does it mean to die?

### *Look for These Terms*

- *'adam*
- death
- Eve
- tree of life
- woman

## AN OUTLINE

A. **Partners in the Garden (2:4b–25)**
   1. The human and the garden (2:4b–14)
   2. The instruction of the tree of the knowing of good and evil (2:15–17)
   3. The animals and the woman (2:18–25)

B. **Rebellion (3:1–19)**
   1. The conversation of the serpent and the woman (3:1–5)
   2. The fall (3:6–7)
   3. The judgment (3:8–19)
      a. Confronting the rebels (3:8–13)
      b. The judgment of the serpent, the woman, and the man (3:14–19)

C. **Exile of the Humans (3:20–24)**
   1. Naming Eve and getting dressed (3:20–21)
   2. Losing the tree of life (3:22)
   3. Expelled from the garden (3:23–24)

D. **Brothers in Exile (4:1–26)**
   1. Murder and wandering (4:1–16)
   2. Descendants of Cain (4:17–24)
   3. Another brother (4:25–26)

## A READING

The power of the word of God in the story of the beginning days is fear-inspiring. When God speaks, everything listens. Everything responds to God because he speaks—everything except humans. The story of the beginning reveals the power of the word of God and sets up readers for a surprising exception. As it turns out, the highest and most responsible beings in God's creation, the ones patterned after his own likeness, decided early on to rebel against his instruction. The revolution against Yahweh and his teaching was total. The fall propelled humanity from Eden to exile, to wander a path that would lead to Babylon, Golgotha, Auschwitz, Hiroshima, and the Twin Towers. The garden narrative initiated the tragic disability of humankind. The lords of creation began the rebellion of the ages. They rejected Yahweh and his word.

The garden and exile narratives are characterized by the kinds of literary features and symmetries that run through much of the Torah and the rest of the Scriptures. Among the chief examples in this case are mirror imaging, wordplay, and leading word. The most notable mirror imaging may be that which frames the act of rebellion itself (see Table 5-C). Several features of this story will be treated while attending to the meaning of sin and death.

What is the meaning of God's torah to the first humans: "You may certainly eat of any tree of the garden; but of the tree of the knowledge of good and evil you shall not eat, *for on the day you eat of it you shall certainly die*" (Gen 2:16b–17 lit., emphasis added)? The easier observation to make is the relationship between sin and death. Sin is the cause and death the effect. Paul explains, "Sin entered the world through one man, and death through sin, and in this way death came to all people, because all sinned" (Rom 5:12).

The more difficult matter is the meaning of the phrase "for in the day you eat of it you shall certainly die" (lit.). At the literal level the reader finds out that the humans did not *physically die* on that *earth day*. Some interpreters have wrongly deduced that because Adam and Eve did not physically die when they rebelled, this signals mitigation or partial relief of the punishment (e.g., Clines, 488–89).

Bruce Wells compares the narrative in Genesis 2–3 to conditional verdicts in ancient Neo-Babylonian legal contexts. For Wells, since they did not die, Yahweh changed his mind and reduced the penalty (Wells, 657–60). The present discussion can only get at two fatal flaws with Wells's interpretation. First, Wells twists the context to make the comparison fit by saying that Genesis 2:17 is a conditional verdict like those in ancient Neo-Babylonian legal contexts (648). But Genesis 2:17 is not a verdict. It is a command given before the man and woman did anything wrong. Second, of the three uses of "certainly die" in Torah (lit. Gen 2:17; 20:7; Num 26:65), Wells does not note the correspondence between death as perpetual exile in two of the three cases

(652). Just as Israel's death sentence committed them to perpetual wandering outside the land of promise (cf. Num 14:35), so too Adam and Eve's death sentence included permanent exile from the garden and more.

What does it mean to die? The meaning of Yahweh's teaching "you shall die" can be discovered by comparing the human situation before they broke the teaching and their new situation afterward. The difference within the narrative context is what Yahweh means by "you shall die." In this context death has relational significance. Death is separation or exile. The humans were separated from their original situation. Five of the most prominent human relationships that died or were separated that day are summarized in Table 5-A and discussed in turn.

? *How can readers determine the meaning of death in the narrative of the fall of humanity?*

**Table 5-A:** Death as Separation in the Context of the Garden Narrative

| Harmony and peace before | | Separation after |
|---|---|---|
| 2:4–22 | Humanity and God | 3:8–9 |
| 2:25 | Humanity and self | 3:7 |
| 2:15 | Humanity and creation | 3:15, 17–19 |
| 2:23–24 | Humanity itself as society—man and woman | 3:11–16, 20 |
| 2:7, 21–22 | Humanity and life | 3:22–24 |

"[Yahweh] God formed the man from the dust of the ground" (Gen 2:7).
*Andriy Kananovych/ Shutterstock.com*

First, grace, beauty, and love characterized the relationship between God and humanity prior to the rebellion. Starting in Genesis 2:4b, the storyteller presents a close-up view of the creation of the first humans. This story, like many in the Torah and the rest of the Bible, pictures God anthropomorphically, that is, in human terms. He is a potter handcrafting the man from the dust of the ground. A wordplay between ground/*adamah* and human/*adam* highlights the power of the life-giving breath of Yahweh. "Yahweh God formed *the human* from the dust of *the ground* and breathed into his nostrils the breath of life, and the human became a living being" (Gen 2:7 lit., emphasis added). The potter breathed into his clay person, animating him into a living being.

Many have pointed out the significance of the term translated "living being" (*nephesh hayyah*) in 2:7. It is significant in the sense that Yahweh made alive the clay person. The significance of the term, however, has often been overstated in other ways.

It is not exceptional among created beings that the human was a living being, for all the water, sky, and land animals are referred to as "living beings" (1:20, 21, 24; 2:19). The unique relationship between God and humans, distinct from all other earthly creatures, is captured by the story of God personally handcrafting and breathing into the human. But this is not all.

Yahweh located the human in his new home, the garden. The narrator describes the garden of Eden in rich and beautiful dimensions. It is pictured at the center of the most significant tributaries of life in the ancient Near Eastern world, the great rivers. It was stockpiled with precious metals and stones and a stunning array of the best vegetation. The garden was an environmental masterpiece. It was a paradise. It was a gift for the human (Sidebar 5-B).

Yahweh vested the human with the responsibility to take care of his garden home.

## Sidebar 5-B: Life outside the Garden

The Teacher of the book of Ecclesiastes reveals the problem with attempts to create utopian life outside the garden. Although the following passage is dense with language from the garden narrative in Genesis, there is a major difference. The garden of Eden was a gift from God and cannot be manufactured by human self-interest. Notice the egocentric shape of Ecclesiastes 2:4–11.

> **I** undertook great projects: **I** built houses **for myself** and planted vineyards. **I** made gardens and parks and planted all kinds of fruit trees in them. **I** made reservoirs to water groves of flourishing trees. **I** bought male and female slaves and had other slaves who were born in my house. **I** also owned more herds and flocks than anyone in Jerusalem **before me**. **I** amassed silver and gold **for myself**, and the treasure of kings and provinces. **I** acquired male and female singers, and a harem as well—the delights of a man's heart. **I** became greater by far than anyone in Jerusalem **before me**. In all this **my** wisdom stayed with **me**.
>
> **I** denied **myself** nothing **my** eyes desired;
> **I** refused **my** heart no pleasure.
> **My** heart took delight in all **my** labor,
> and this was the reward for all **my** toil.
> Yet when **I** surveyed all that **my** hands had done
> and what **I** had toiled to achieve,
> everything was meaningless, a chasing after the wind;
> nothing was gained under the sun. (emphasis added)

He also gave him a single instruction: God prohibited the human from eating the fruit from the tree of the knowing of good and evil.

The many repetitions of "God saw that it was good" from Genesis 1 may still be ringing in the ears of the reader when God said, "It is *not good* for the man to be alone" (Gen 2:18, emphasis added). The rhetorical force of "it is not good" within this context foregrounds another important and distinct feature in the story of the creation of the human beings. They were created in a manner that demonstrates their companionship. The ideal of human society is illumined by the story of the creation of the woman.

Animal life in the Serengeti

*Marc Veraart/ CC BY-ND 2.0*

God brought before the human all the animals in pairs. By naming them he came to recognize that he was alone. God showed the human his need for society before he created human society. By naming the animal pairs, the human discovered that there was no partner, or counterpart, for him.

After the man came to recognize his need for a partner, God put him to sleep and went to work making the woman. As the man was made from the soil, so God made the woman from the man. Yahweh is pictured as personally making the woman by hand. He designed her to partner with the man, and the human beings together provide the social dimensions that could make humanity good. The handcrafted man points to the life-giving power of Yahweh and the handcrafted woman to Yahweh as the caring society maker.

The creation of the human partnership, along with giving them the garden home, offers a compelling view of the intimate graced relationship the humans shared with their Creator. The close personal bond between the humans and Yahweh was immediately and summarily broken when they rebelled against his word. The humans were separated from Yahweh.

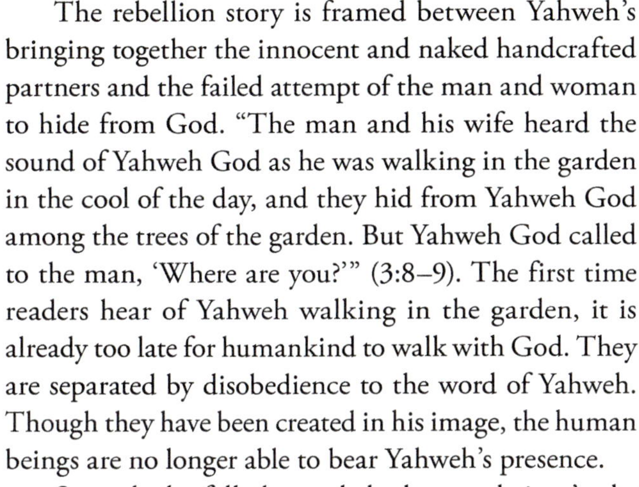

The rebellion story is framed between Yahweh's bringing together the innocent and naked handcrafted partners and the failed attempt of the man and woman to hide from God. "The man and his wife heard the sound of Yahweh God as he was walking in the garden in the cool of the day, and they hid from Yahweh God among the trees of the garden. But Yahweh God called to the man, 'Where are you?'" (3:8–9). The first time readers hear of Yahweh walking in the garden, it is already too late for humankind to walk with God. They are separated by disobedience to the word of Yahweh. Though they have been created in his image, the human beings are no longer able to bear Yahweh's presence.

Jon Cooper

*How did the relationship between humans and God change when the humans sinned?*

Second, the fall changed the human beings' relationship with themselves. The view of the humans before the fall is stated in the negative for post-fall readers: "Adam and his wife were both naked, and they felt no shame" (2:25). They were at home with themselves in a manner that required nothing. After they met the serpent, their self-images changed greatly.

The wordplay between the terms for "naked" (*'arom*) and "crafty" (*'arum*) is partially picked up by one translation: they "were *nude*. . . . now the snake was more *shrewd*" (2:25–3:1 Fox, emphasis added). The serpent asked the woman about God's word. She replied that God had instructed, "You must not eat fruit from the tree that is in the middle of the garden, *and you must not touch it*, or you will die" (3:3, emphasis added). The misquotation of God's word is interesting but not necessarily alarming (see Niehaus, 150–52). Perhaps the woman was flustered by the talking snake and misspoke; she later claimed to be deceived (3:13). Or, perhaps the man put a fence around the torah when he relayed it to the woman, "Do not eat from it or even touch it." The responsibility for the distortion, whether by him or by her, is lost to us since it was relayed offstage. The storyteller may have hidden the basis of the changed wording so that readers would wonder about it and discuss it. I will take up the issue of intentional ambiguity in biblical narrative relative to the sin of Moses in Chapter 22.

The serpent responds by interpreting God's word too literally. When he says, "You will not die" (3:4), he speaks more narrowly than Yahweh had meant. He suggests, not too subtly, that physical life is enough. He also goes on to advertise that they would become "like God" (3:5) in the sense of knowing good and evil. This second deception exudes irony for the reader who knows that they are already like God, more so than anything else in the created realm.

Dragon (compare the equivalence of dragon and serpent in Revelation 12:9) from Ishtar Gate of ancient Babylon on display in the Metropolitan Museum of Art, New York
*Jess Belani*

In the narrative, the moments preceding and following the fall are involved with the looking and seeing, both literally and metaphorically, of the human beings. Table 5-C illustrates the reverse imaging or, better, a reversal in Adam and Eve's perception of themselves and their world. What she had thought was wisdom is foolish. This is the creational starting point for much of biblical wisdom literature. Whereas the fruit had appeared beautiful, now the people suddenly become ashamed of their nakedness.

**Table 5-C:** The Structure of Genesis 3:6–7

| | |
|---|---|
| 3:6 | she saw that the fruit of the tree was good for food and |
| | pleasing to the eye, and also desirable for gaining wisdom, |
| | she took some and ate it . . . and he [her husband] ate it |
| 3:7 | the eyes of both of them were opened, and they realized they were naked; |
| | so they sewed fig leaves together and made coverings for themselves |

They were no longer at home with themselves. Their embarrassment with themselves is so great that they turn again to a tree, but this time to secure clothing. The effect of the fall, in the relationship of the humans to themselves, separates them from themselves. They are now ashamed and wish to hide their nakedness.

Third, the responsible relationship between humankind and creation transformed itself into war. The curse that God pronounced against the serpent symbolizes the rebellion of the creation against its former master as well as provides a real, though ambiguous, promise of hope for humanity. God said to the serpent, "I will put enmity between you and the woman, and between your offspring and hers; he will crush your head, and you will strike his heel" (3:15). The term "offspring," traditionally translated "seed," is a special word. When Abram, and much later David, is promised offspring, Yahweh's pronouncement against the snake echoes in the reader's ears. It is when these later contexts are read along with this context that the original ambiguity of the poetic promise proves to have enough room for the hope of the ages.

*Why is offspring a special word?* ?

The separation between humanity and creation is symbolized further, and more directly, in Yahweh's judgment against the man. The very soil from which the man was made would rebel against him, causing a life of pain and toil (see Figure 5-D). The wordplay between human/*'adam* and soil/*'adamah* demonstrates the reversal and contradiction of sin's effects against creation. The man was sentenced to perpetually struggle against the soil from which he was made. The humans were separated from the creation, of which they were a part and for which they were responsible, in a new anticreational sense because of their rebellion against the word of God.

**Figure 5-D:** From Dust to Dust

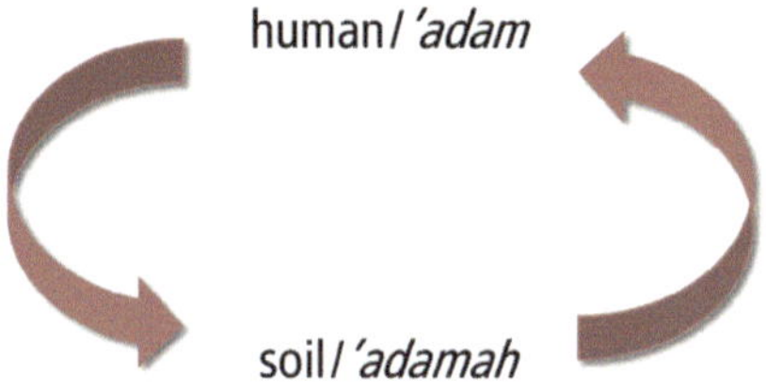

human/*'adam*

soil/*'adamah*

Fourth, the first sin effected division within human society. When the first man met the first woman for the first time, he presented the first poem:

> This is now bone of my bones
>     and flesh of my flesh;
> she shall be called woman,
>     for she was taken out of man. (2:23)

The wordplay between man/*'ish* and woman/*'ishah* complements the relationship the human counterparts shared. They were made of the same stuff, literally, and were created for each other. The man knew he was incomplete without her. When he called her "woman," that was not her proper name. Man and woman were, rather, the identities of the kinds of human beings that belong together. Their initial relationship symbolizes the peace and harmony and love that should characterize a creational human society.

The fall caused an unstoppable separation to open up between humans. When Yahweh holds the man accountable for the shame of his nakedness, the man tries to blame the woman for giving him the fruit. This is a rather shallow plea given his solidarity with her, his listening to her dialogue with the serpent, and his eating the fruit with her. The key issue, for the present line of thought, is that his attempted blame signifies the breach in the once "flesh of my flesh" kind of relationship.

The separation between the humans shows up in the last part of the woman's judgment. Yahweh said, "Your desire will be for your husband, and he will rule over you" (3:16). There appears to be a good measure of ambiguity in this phrase. In what sense will she "desire" her husband? There are a couple of clues in the context that help. We may consider the use of "desire" and "rule" together in Genesis 4. As we will see below, Yahweh uses a graphic figure to explain Cain's problem with temptation: "If you do not do what is right, sin is crouching at your door; *it desires to have you, but you must rule over it*" (4:7, emphasis added). Yahweh personifies sin as a predator ready to pounce. The "desire," in this case, is set against the one who could "master" it. The desire that the woman would have for her husband may be in more than one sense. But in light of the context, it seems one of these senses is desire set against mastery, as in the case of Cain's struggle with sin.

Also, a comparison of the woman's judgment to the man's offers possible help. Because of the fall, the judgment of the man included a lifelong struggle with the soil from which he was made (note mixture of irony and hope in Sidebar 5-E). Perhaps the woman was likewise judged to do perpetual battle with the source of

## Sidebar 5-E: The Gardener

The old woman
works in her garden
even though the world is ending,
and she is not crazy.

Others, younger,
captured by or fleeing the war
stare at her there,
tending flowers at the mouth of hell.

By Bernadette Rule from *Gardening at the Mouth of Hell* (Hamilton, Ont.: West Meadow, 1996), 37. Used by permission.

The poet said that the poem was inspired by a newspaper photograph of a woman gardening in her bombed-out neighborhood; those passing by looked at her with mixed concern and delight. I came across Rule's book at a small college outside Toronto. I have thought many times that the title—as well as the title poem above—is an apt metaphor for the human enterprise after the fall.

herself, namely, the man. Just as the ground (*'adamah*) from which the human (*'adam*) was taken would trouble him with weeds, so too the man (*'ish*) from whom the woman (*'ishah*) was taken would trouble her. The other aspects of their curses are parallel—they both would face pain and suffering. Thus, it may follow that as the man would toil against the land from which he was created, so too the woman would struggle against the one from which she came.

woman ⟷ man
Eve
↓
"the living"

**Figure 5-F:** The Social Orientation of "Woman" versus "Eve"

The division between the man and the woman can also be seen in the proper name he gives her. The name "Eve" itself, meaning mother of the living, is a good name but has a shadow across it. It is a good name because of its creational significance—she bears life—and in particular because the promised offspring would come from her. The shadow on her name as mother of all the living, however, comes from her judgment as suffering in childbirth.

More important, naming the woman Eve also signifies a shift in the human society. The rebellion in Eden had separated the fellowship that the human society had once enjoyed. Before the fall, the man called her woman because of the kind of relationship she had with the man. Her identity as woman foregrounded her partnership and compatibility with the man. Conversely, the proper name Eve highlights her in relation to their offspring (see Figure 5-F). The act of naming Eve itself may reflect the struggle for "mastery" in light of Adam's naming the animals over which he had dominance. The difference between calling her woman and naming her Eve suggests a shift or separation in the human society, or at least a new way to regard her primary function. The name Eve itself symbolizes at once both the hope and trouble of humanity.

*In what ways is Eve a positive name? What dark shadows are cast across this good name?*

Fifth, the humans were separated from "life." God expelled them from the garden and posted winged sphinxes and a flaming sword to prevent them from eating of the tree of life. The present discussion focuses on the immediate context and in Another Look below, a larger context. The fact that the humans were permanently prohibited from eating of the tree of life has always caused readers to wonder several "what ifs."

Ancient Assyrian guardian on display at the Louvre, Paris
*Robert C. Kashow*

Often I get to this passage in class and students raise one or more of the following questions. What would have happened if they ate from both the tree of the knowing of good and evil and the tree of life? What would have happened if they only ate from the tree of life? Would they have died if they did not eat from either tree? The answer to each is: I don't know. Anyone can guess answers to "what if" questions, but there is no way to really know about what did not happen. The first question above—What if they ate from both trees?—is the most important of the hypothetical scenarios because it is exactly what Yahweh wanted to prevent. Yahweh deliberates that the humans must not be allowed to eat from the tree of life "and live forever" (3:22). To prevent this outcome, they are permanently banished from the garden to spend their days in exile.

We are now at the heart of the question. The two issues—What does it mean to die? and What does it mean to live forever?—can be considered together for a moment. What started the present line of inquiry was that the death that was promised when they ate the fruit was not death in the most literal sense—mere physical death. Thus, to "live forever" should not be considered mere physical life. The term "forever" (*'olam*) includes a temporal sense—something like "for all time to come" in this context—yet here signifies entry into a new state of life upon eating from the tree of life. Stated plainly, the first couple did not physically drop dead on the day that they ate from the tree of the knowing of good and evil, but they were exiled from the garden on that very earth day to extinguish the possibility of their eating from the tree of life and the new dimension of life it offered.

A brief summary is useful before moving to the stories of life and death outside the garden. When Yahweh said, "On the day you eat from it you shall certainly die" (lit.), he means, to paraphrase the reading above, "on the earth day itself you will die in the sense that you will be separated from human life as it was created to be." The judgment for eating from the tree of the knowing of good and evil includes separation from God, self, creation, other humans, and life—all effective immediately on that day (see Table 5-A). The certainty of physical death, as well as the impossibility of enjoying the forever life by the tree of life, began on the day of the original rebellion.

When death as separation is seen in the context of the creation days, its true nature comes into focus. The story tells of the Creator separating and granting life. Death is separation in the other direction, away from life and back to chaos. God created by rightly separating or ordering the human realm and filling the spheres with light and life. Humanity sinned against Yahweh's teaching, effecting death and separating every aspect of human life from its proper place. Human beings, made in the image of the Creator, revolted against God, ironically, to become "like God." The effect of the human revolution, therefore, includes humankind becoming a contradiction unto itself.

?

*What does it mean to die in the context of the garden narrative?*

The anticreationality of human sinfulness that came to characterize *the* human problem throughout the rest of the Scriptures, and all of human existence, is typified in the story of the brothers in exile in Genesis 4. The jealousy and murderous rage of Cain strikes readers because he directed it against his own brother, a term used seven times in this chapter. While the jealousy over Yahweh's positive regard toward Abel's sacrifices was the cause of the rivalry, the basis for the problem with Cain's sacrifice is not clear. Yahweh regarded Cain's offering without favor and Abel's offering with favor for reasons not described in the narrative (see Peterson, 154–71). This is an example of the kind of narrative ambiguity that is exhibited in many of the sin stories in the Torah (see discussion on the sin of Moses in Chapter 22).

The story of the first murder contains elements that are particularly notable in light of the preceding context, such as the use of "soil" and "face," the latter of which is a leading word here.

> Cain became exceedingly upset and his **face** fell. Yahweh said to Cain: "Why are you so upset? Why has your **face** fallen? Is it not thus: If you intend good, lift it up, but if you do not intend good, at the entrance is sin, a crouching-predator, toward you his lust—but you can rule over him." Cain . . . killed him [Abel]. Yahweh said to Cain: "Where is Abel your brother?" He said: "I do not know. Am I the watcher of my brother?" Now he said: "What have you done! A sound—your brother's blood cries out to me from the **soil**! And now, damned be you from the **soil**, which opened its mouth to receive your brother's blood from your hand. When you wish to work the **soil** it will not henceforth give its strength to you; wavering and wandering must you be on earth!" Cain said to Yahweh: "My iniquity is too great to be borne! Here you drive me away today from the **face** of the **soil**, and from your **face** I must conceal myself, I must be wavering and wandering on earth." (Gen 4:5–14, Fox, spelling of names altered, emphasis added, v. 7 lit.)

The humanlike imagery applied to inanimate elements within this context is striking. For example, sin is personified as a stalking predator, and the soil, the source of Cain's former livelihood, is depicted as physically grieving after an unwanted drink.

The story echoes the sounds of the first humans' rebellion in the garden (see Table 5-G). The repetitions offer theological as well as literary significance.

**Table 5-G:** Extended Echo Effect in the Stories of the Sin of the Parents and the Sin of Cain

| | |
|---|---|
| "Your desire will be for your husband, and he will rule over you." (3:16) | "Sin is crouching at your door; it desires to have you, but you must rule over it." (4:7) |
| "Where are you?" (3:9) | "Where is your brother Abel?" (4:9) |
| "Cursed is the ground because of you." (3:17) | "You are under a curse and driven from the ground." (4:11, 14) |
| Yahweh God banished him from the Garden of Eden. . . . He placed on the east side of the garden of Eden cherubim. (3:23–24) | Cain went out from Yahweh's presence and lived in the land of Nod [Wandering], east of Eden. (4:16) |

The story of the fall, while unique in various respects, provides the explanation for the sin and death that characterize humanity outside the garden. As the parents, so the children: Sinful parents breed sinful children. Cain's problem with sinfulness sounds like his parents' because the separation of death, the effects of the human rebellion, infects all of humanity.

Genesis 4 goes on to narrate the descendants of Cain. This initiates the pervasive feature of Genesis 1–11, namely, a series of episodes connected by several genealogical lists. The seventh generation from Adam through Cain is Lamech. He is significant not only because he is the first known polygamist but also because he compares his own sin to that of his ancestor, Cain. Lamech uses "sevens" in poetic bragging to his wives. Emphasis in poetic numbering is often achieved by X, X+1 in successive lines; for example, "for three sins . . . even for four" (Amos 1–2; also see, e.g., Prov 6:16–19; 30:18–22). The extravagant X, XX—seven, seventy-seven in Lamech's poem—probably signifies Lamech's haughtiness within the growing spiral of sin:

> I have killed a man for wounding me,
> a young man for injuring me.
> If Cain is avenged seven times,
> then Lamech seventy-seven times. (4:23b–24)

Lamech's song about himself follows the pattern of things coming to their completion in the number seven.

The meaning of human life outside the garden is closely related to the sin that brought death (Toews, 42). Human beings rejected the powerful word of God. They sought another way to gain wisdom and achieve godlikeness. The way they chose was a perversion, an anticreational rebellion. The judgment accorded with God's word: On that day they died. The separation from creational life that began with a revolution in the garden brought death and judgment across the generations of wandering exiles.

## ANOTHER LOOK

Earlier I skipped one of the questions often asked about the tree of life: Did Yahweh prevent the fallen humans from eating of the tree of life as judgment or as grace? Many speculate that it was an act of grace. This line of thinking bases itself on a literal reading of eating of its fruit to "live forever" (3:22). Those who adopt this view think that living forever here refers to mortal life, thus consigning the "spiritually dead" people to this state for all time. As I tried to point out above, viewing death as literal-metaphorical and life as only literal appears to miss the relationship between these ideas. It seems better to regard the banishment from the tree of life as judgment on the sinners. Specifically, losing the possibility of eating of the tree of life resides close to the center of the death sentence for the first sin.

To regard the results of eating from the tree of life—to live forever—in a literal-metaphorical sense (akin to the sense of death that humankind secured by the fall) raises two further questions. First, can "live forever" be defined more specifically? The most helpful material comes from John. The concepts concerning "eternal life" developed in John's gospel should not be read directly into Genesis 3. Still, the concepts are close enough that we can be assisted in understanding "live forever" here.

The purpose of the Fourth Gospel is that readers "may believe that Jesus is the Messiah, the Son of God, and that by believing *you may have life* in his name" (John 20:31, emphasis added throughout). Throughout John's Gospel the terms *life* and *eternal life* (sometimes translated *everlasting life*) are used interchangeably. In the midsection of the gospel Jesus said, "I have come that *they may have life and have it to the full*" (10:10b). The concept of abundant life or full life accents rather than answers the question: Full of what? The answer is not to be found in quantitative categories; instead, the life spoken of is qualitatively different, or more than mere physical living (see Brown, 1:505–8).

In the story of the climactic seventh sign, Jesus has an important dialogue with Martha, saying, "*I am the resurrection and the life.* The one who believes in me will live, even though they die; and whoever lives by believing in me will never die" (11:25–26). To have life is not simply to have a greater amount, even unlimited, of physical life. The resurrection and the life are somehow related directly to the person of Messiah.

In the account of the upper room discourse, Philip said, "Lord, show us the Father and that will be enough for us" (14:8). Jesus responds to Philip in a manner typical of several similar statements he had made previously: "Anyone who has seen me has seen the Father. How can you say 'Show us the Father'?" (14:9). With this and other similar teaching resounding in our ears, we hear the powerful statement of Jesus in his so-called high priestly prayer. "Now *this is eternal life: that they know you, the only true God, and Jesus Messiah*, whom you have sent" (17:3). Whatever else may be said of it, it can be affirmed that the life spoken of in John's Gospel refers to knowing God through a relationship with Messiah. In particular, it seems that the "full life" is life reoriented by and toward faith in the Messiah, the Son of God.

*What is the meaning of life in the Gospel of John?*

Eating from the tree of life was not identical to believing in Messiah. The parallels between the two appear in the effects of eating of the tree of life and/or trusting the Messiah. In both cases the promised results are a different kind of life—to know God. And my guess, and it is no more than that, is that the effects of eating from the tree of life may have brought the humans to a new orientation toward God, to know him in a new way (see Chapter 28).

Second, what is the path to life outside the garden? The tree of life itself only appears in the book of Proverbs metaphorically and in the vision of paradise in the book of Revelation. Still, the possibility for finding life can be seen in the stories of Enoch and Noah, who each avoided the terminal fate of their respective contexts. Torah itself ends with a call for readers to choose between the life and death offered by the word (Deut 30). Thus, the Torah begins with the fateful eating of the tree of the knowing of good and evil bringing death and exile from the tree of life, and it ends by challenging readers to choose life.

## INTERACTIVE WORKSHOP

### *Chapter Summary*

The humans were specially created and placed in their garden home. They disobeyed the word of God and died, meaning they were separated from all creational human relationships—to God, self, creation, others, and life.

### *Can You Explain the Key Terms?*

- *'adam*
- death
- Eve
- tree of life
- woman

### *Challenge Questions*

1. What are the similarities and differences between the stories of the making of the humans and the other created beings?
2. In the context of Genesis 2–3, what does it mean to die?
3. How did the serpent deceive the woman, according to her own testimony in Genesis 3:13?
4. In Genesis 3, what are the similarities between the judgment on the woman and the man?
5. What is the significance of eastward exile from the garden?

### *Advanced Questions*

1. Why does the Torah appear to allow for multiple spouses, in many stories as well as in regulations like Deuteronomy 21:15–17, in light of the teaching in the end of Genesis 2?
2. How did later biblical teachings extend the promise concerning the seed of the woman in Genesis 3:15?
3. What clues do we have, if any, for the problem with Cain's offering?

*4. In Genesis 1–3, which instances of *'adam* should be translated "humanity" or "human being" and which as the proper name "Adam"?

*5. How does the Hebrew term *'olam* ("forever"), such as in Genesis 3:22, differ in its sense from later philosophical notions of eternity?

## *Research Project Ideas*

Compare the creation accounts in Genesis 1:1–2:4a and 2:4b–25.

Explain Paul's interpretation of Genesis 3 in Romans 5:12–21 (Edwards) and/or 1 Corinthians 15.

Evaluate Genesis 2–5 as historical narrative (see Collins).

Discuss the similarities between the creation and garden in Genesis 1–3 and the tabernacle (Hays, 20–27; Morales, 40–42; Imes, 134–37; Kim, 37–56; Weinfeld, 501–12; Hamilton, 229–32).

Compare the fall of the humans and Cain's sin in Genesis 3–4.

## *The Next Step*


Brown, Raymond E. *The Gospel According to John.* 2 vols. Anchor Bible 29 and 29A. New York: Doubleday, 1966.

Clines, David J. A. "Theme in Genesis 1–11." *Catholic Biblical Quarterly* 38 (1976): 483–507.

Collins, C. John. *Did Adam and Eve Really Exist?: Who They Were and Why You Should Care.* Wheaton, IL: Crossway, 2011.

Edwards, Jonathan. *Original Sin.* Ed. Clyde A. Holbrook. Works of Jonathan Edwards, vol. 3. New Haven: Yale University Press, 1970.

Hamilton, James M., Jr. *Typology: Understanding the Bible's Promise-Shaped Patterns: How Old Testament Expectations Are Fulfilled in Christ.* Grand Rapids: Zondervan Academic, 2022.

Hays, J. Daniel. *The Temple and the Tabernacle: A Study of God's Dwelling Places from Genesis to Revelation.* Grand Rapids: Baker Books, 2016.

Imes, Carmen Joy. "The Lost World of the Exodus: Functional Ontology and the Creation of a Nation." Pages 126–41 in *For Us, but Not to Us: Essays on Creation, Covenant, and Context in Honor of John H. Walton.* Edited by Adam E. Miglio et al. Eugene, OR: Pickwick, 2020.

Kim, Brittany. "Stretching Out the Heavens: The Background and Use of a Creational Metaphor." Pages 37–56 in *For Us, but Not to Us: Essays on Creation, Covenant, and Context in Honor of John H. Walton.* Edited by Adam E. Miglio et al. Eugene, OR: Pickwick, 2020.

Morales, L. Michael. *Who Shall Ascend the Mountain of the Lord?: A Biblical Theology of the Book of Leviticus.* New Studies in Biblical Theology 37. Downers Grove, IL: IVP Academic, 2015.

Niehaus, Jeffrey J. *When Did Eve Sin?: The Fall & Biblical Historiography.* Bellingham, WA: Lexham, 2020.

Peterson, Brian Neil. "Cain's Struggle: A Proposed Reason for the Rejection of Cain's Sacrifice." *Bibliotheca Sacra* 177 (2020): 154–71.

Toews, Brian. "Genesis 1–4: The Genesis of Old Testament Instruction." Pages 38–52 in *Biblical Theology: Retrospect and Prospect.* Edited by Scott J. Hafemann. Downers Grove, IL: IVP Academic, 2002.

Weinfeld, Moshe. "Sabbath, Temple, and the Enthronement of the Lord—The Problem of the *Sitz im Leben* of Genesis 1:1–2:3." Pages 501–12 in *Mélanges bibliques et orientaux en l'honneur de M. Henri Cazelles.* Edited by A. Caquot and M. Delcor. Kevelaer: Butzon & Bercker/Neukirchhen-Vluyn: Neukirchener Verlag, 1981.

Wells, Bruce. "Death in the Garden of Eden." *Journal of Biblical Literature* 139.4 (2020): 639–60.

# 6 THE FLOOD AND THE NATIONS
## *Genesis 5–11*



## GETTING STARTED

### *Focus Question*

What is the meaning of the flood?

### *Look for These Terms*

- Canaan
- Enoch
- Lamech
- Nephilim
- sons of God/the gods
- walk with God

## AN OUTLINE

A. **The Genealogy of Ten Generations from Adam to Noah (5)**

B. **The Flood (6–9)**

1. The sinfulness of humankind (6:1–8)
2. Noah and the flood (6:9–8:22) (see Table 6-C)
3. The Noahic covenant (9:1–19)
4. Noah's drunkenness and the curse of Canaan (9:20–29)

C. **The Genealogies of the Sons of Noah: Japheth, Ham, and Shem (10)**

D. **The Tower of Babel (11:1–9) (see Table 6-G)**

E. **The Genealogy of Ten Generations from Noah to Terah (11:10–26)**

## A READING

The human revolution against God's word begins in the garden. God's judgment and the exile of humans from the garden does not put an end to the insurrection. The rebel sinners are broadcast across the lands. The earth that they were to fill with life according to the blessing of the Creator increasingly fills with sin and death. In view of human corruption, God takes drastic measures. He kills the entire human race, along with all other living creatures, except for one family and pairs of all animals. Even through the terrible judgment, he graciously provides a new beginning for humans, a new beginning that looks like the previous one. Individual humans and society at large again rebel immediately and continuously against God and his word.

The stories of the creation and the garden in Genesis 1–4 and those of the Hebrew ancestors in chapters 12–50 are connected by two genealogies of ten generations each and several short narrative accounts. The similarities between the genealogical records in Genesis 5 and 11 suggest that they have parallel functions within chapters 1–11 (see Table 6-A). An overview of chapters 1–11 suggests that the two ten-generation genealogies were conclusions of two narrative panels of macro-level extended echoes (see Table 3-C in Chapter 3). At the same time, the genealogies of Genesis 5 and 11 can be viewed as framing a series of short accounts that connect the creation of the world to the calling of the chosen family. From both vantage points these genealogies, along with those in chapters 4 and 10, provide a meaningful connecting structure, in the form of human generations, to the opening sections of Genesis.

**Table 6-A:** A Comparison of the Genealogies of Genesis 5 and 11

| Genesis 5:1–32 | Genesis 11:10–26 |
|---|---|
| Ten generations from Adam to Noah | Ten generations from Noah to Terah |
| plus Noah's three sons: Shem, Ham, and Japheth | plus Terah's three sons: Abram, Nahor, and Haran |

The stories that appear between the two ten-generation genealogical records (especially the accounts of the flood and the tower of Babel) are universal in scope. The flood brings judgment on the entire human race, making way for a new beginning. The tower builders are referred to as "the whole world" with "one language" (11:1). The account of the tower of Babel is a judgment against humankind.

Genesis 5 opens with a brief rehearsal of certain aspects of the creation of humanity from the end of Genesis 1. Specifically, the humans, male and female, were created in the likeness of God. The first man, Adam, had a son "in his own likeness, in his own image" (5:3). The implication is, to borrow a phrase from Genesis 1, that human beings reproduce *after their kind*. As the parent, so the offspring. God's image in humans means they are his family (Imes, 32). That the image of God in humanity was not lost entirely in the fall of humanity is reinforced in the teaching on capital punishment (9:6).

Following the brief introduction, the narrator presents a genealogical record of ten generations from Adam through Seth to Noah. The genealogy follows a repeated formula only broken with the seventh and tenth generations. Each of the genealogical records ends with the same phrase, "and then he died" (e.g., 5:5). This rhythmic repetition foregrounds the terminal reality of human life outside the garden. Everyone dies. Almost everyone.

The two exceptions within the context of the genealogy of death are the seventh and tenth generations. The seventh generation from Adam through Seth is Enoch. Readers discover only one thing about his life, but it is stated twice: Enoch "walked faithfully with God" (5:22, 24). His record does not end with "and then he died" but with "he was no more, because God took him away" (5:24). Whereas it could be argued that 5:24 uses a euphemism for death to accent the difference between Enoch and the rest, it can as well be interpreted that Enoch did not die (as is stated in Heb 11:5). There is an exception to the universal curse of death, even for someone exiled from the garden.

The brief account of Enoch can be compared to at least two items in the preceding context. First, the phrase he "walked faithfully with God" echoes the account of God's walking in the garden looking for the humans in Genesis 3:8 and shows that people can walk with God outside the garden. In Enoch's case, walking with God gave him an exception to the rule of death.

Second, Enoch, the seventh from Adam through Seth, can be compared with Lamech, the seventh from Adam through Cain. If the number seven carries with it the symbolic significance of completion in this context (because of the completion of creation in seven days), then Lamech and Enoch may signify the full difference between Cain and Seth. Lamech, of course, explicitly noted the magnified relationship of immorality that he shared with Cain. If a parallel relationship is implied for the line of Adam through Seth, then perhaps "walking with God" is an outgrowth of being created in the image of God in its fullest sense. As if to trip up a pristine distinction between a "good line" and an "evil line," there is also an Enoch in Cain's line and a Lamech in Seth's line.

Noah is the tenth from Adam. His genealogical account differs from the others in two ways. First, his record offers an explanation for his name. (The other) Lamech "named him Noah and said, 'He will comfort us in the labor and painful toil of our hands caused by the ground Yahweh has cursed'" (5:29). Noah's name reflects the hope that he will deliver humanity from the effects of the curse. The staggering irony is that his entire generation will be judged even while Noah himself is delivered to a new beginning.

Second, the genealogical record of Noah in Genesis 5 does not end with "and then he died"—another exception. Noah is delivered from the judgment of Yahweh against his generation. He does eventually die, but not until he has been saved from the damning judgment of Yahweh. He functions as a new Adam and Eve with a new beginning for humanity.

The significance of Noah as an exception is that he, like Enoch, "walked faithfully with God" (6:9). The narrator elaborates further here: He was "blameless" and "righteous." What does it mean to walk with God? In the context of ancient nomadic societies, it was natural to think of life on the move. "To walk with God" may mean something like to live in accord with the ways of God through life's journey. In any case, from these early examples, along with Abraham (17:1; see also 13:17), the ideal of walking with God became a recurring image for the life of the godly. In wisdom literature various notions such as the way or path of righteousness, the way everlasting, not going to the right or the left, and so forth are rooted in the pictures provided by the stories of Enoch, Noah, and Abraham in the Genesis narratives. That is, biblical wisdom literature is Genesis-shaped.

*What does it mean to walk with God?*

The genealogy breaks off at the end of Genesis 5 and is followed by two brief narratives. Genesis 6:1–4 is notorious for its difficulty and obscurity and for some unusual interpretations to which this passage has given rise. I will state the chief point of this context, briefly outline the leading interpretive issues, and reaffirm the central premise. The storyteller interprets the events of Genesis 6:1–8 as *signifying the comprehensive wickedness of humankind*. Whatever else these narratives may mean, these verses explain the damnable condition of the human race.

The leading interpretive issues relating to Genesis 6:1–4 are interrelated. The passage says:

> When humans began to multiply on the face of the land, and daughters were born to them, *the sons of God* saw that the daughters of humans were beautiful; and they took wives for themselves, whomever they chose. Then Yahweh said, "My spirit will not abide with humans forever, because they are mortal; their days will be one hundred and twenty years." The *Nephilim* were on the earth in those days, *and also after*, when *the sons of God* came into the daughters of humans, and they bore children to them. *Those were the heroes of old, persons of name.* (lit.)

Who were the "sons of God" or "sons of gods"? The reasons that the term can be translated in the singular or plural is that the Hebrew term *'elohim* often signifies the God of Israel, Yahweh, in the Scriptures. When *'elohim* is used with a singular verb, it is singular, such as "God created [singular] the heavens and the earth" (Gen 1:1). If the term *'elohim* is used with a plural verb or in a context demanding plurality, then it refers to "gods." In Genesis 6:2 it could go either way.

*What is the human condition in Genesis 6:1–8?*

The plural sound of the singular term *'elohim* denotes status. Other terms like "lord" (*'adon*) and "master/owner" (*ba'al*) also appear with plural forms when used in the singular (*'adonim*, *ba'alim*). For example, in Genesis 39:8 both the singular-sounding and plural-sounding form of *'adon* (lord) are used to refer to a man named Potiphar, and in Exodus 21:34 the singular-sounding and plural-sounding forms of the term *ba'al* (master/owner) are used of individual persons. In English often capitalization of a term is used to show status, like the God of Israel versus the god of any other people. The use of plural-sounding singular terms like God (*'elohim*), lord (*ba'alim*), and master (*'adonim*) shows respect for status akin to capitalization in English (see Schnittjer, 496, n. 61). In any case, the use of plural spelling for both the singular and plural terms "God" and "gods"—both spelled exactly the same way—makes it impossible to know for sure if Genesis 6:2 says "sons of God" or "sons of gods."

The three most common answers to the identity of the sons of God/gods in Genesis 6 have been: (1) the sons of God/gods are fallen celestial beings; (2) the sons of God are the men of the line of Seth and the daughters of humans are the women of the line of Cain; and (3) the sons of God/gods are the men of the tyrannical dynasty of Lamech. Each view uses the biblical context for support.

The first view—the sons of God/gods were fallen celestial beings—is based in part on the use of the term "sons of God" for celestial beings in Psalms and Job (see, e.g., Job 1:6; 2:1; 38:7; Ps 89:6). The contrast between sons of God and daughters of humans makes it seem as if the former may not be human. This view was held from pre-Christian times (see, e.g., 1 Enoch 6:1–7; Testament of Reuben 5:6; Jubilees 5:1–2).

## Sidebar 6-B: Nephilim

Who were the Nephilim? The word "Nephilim" is the Hebrew word spelled with English letters that sound similar. The translators of the Septuagint used the Greek word for "giants" (*gigantes*) to translate the Hebrew term *nephilim*. There are several reasons for their decision. The ten scouts called the large-sized Canaanites "Nephilim" (Num 13:33); they were described as "heroes of old, persons of name" (Gen 6:4 lit.), which could give them a legendary sort of stature; and perhaps their fathers were celestial and so they could be physically large (cf. Genesis Apocryphon [1Q20] 2.1). Neither of the first two reasons are adequate. The ten scouts were fabricating a myth in Numbers 13:33 (see Chapter 22), and "heroes of old, persons of name" does not need to be related to physical stature. The third line of reasoning is a hypothesis built on top of another hypothesis; thus, it is weak. Even if the Nephilim were the biological offspring of celestial "men" and human women, there is no way to know whether this would affect their physical stature.

What is the meaning of the phrase "and also afterward" (6:4)? This is a difficult phrase for all of the above combinations of views *because the Nephilim were killed in the flood.* Two of the many ways that this phrase can be interpreted are as follows. (1) This phrase was not original but was inserted by a later copyist-scribe who tried to "correct" the narrative based on the report of the ten scouts in Numbers 13. (2) Though the *Nephilim* themselves were destroyed in the flood, the term later became elastic and could be used to describe the mythic size or wickedness of people like the Anakites (Num 13:33). Either of these may work, but neither are satisfying or solve the difficulties.

Often this view has been combined with the view that the "Nephilim" were giants, the logic being that the offspring of celestial and human relations could be physically large in size (on the Nephilim as giants, see Sidebar 6-B). Proponents of this view argue that celestial beings take on male human bodies in Genesis (19:1–3), while opponents contend that celestial beings do not have the capacity for marital relations (Mark 12:25). Proponents often read 1 Peter 3:19–20 and Jude 6–7 as referring obliquely to Genesis 6.

The second view—the sons of God were men from the line of Seth—is based on the two genealogies, Cain's and Seth's, which immediately precede this context. If Seth is in Adam's likeness because he is Adam's son, and Adam is in God's likeness, then Adam is a son of God and the Sethites are sons of God (Gen 5:1–3). It is thought that the two human lineages, one more wicked and one more godly as typified by Lamech and Enoch respectively, began to intermarry and became corrupt.

The third view—the sons of God/the gods are the tyrannical dynasty of Lamech—was formed by noting the quasi-divine and celestial language often used by ancient peoples regarding royal personages. The description of their offspring as "heroes of old, persons of name" appears, for the proponents of this view, to lend credence to their military or political dominance. Moreover, ancient rulers slept with any women they desired (see 12:14–16; 20:2). In this case, these sons of God/the gods intermarried with the daughters of humans. Some have combined the first and third views and speculated that the "tyrants were demon possessed" (see Waltke, 117) or that the dynastic rulers were viewed in semi-mythic terms (see Clines, 337–50).

What is the meaning of the statement "their days will be one hundred and twenty years"? Many think this means that God was judging humanity and limiting their life span to 120 years, which was achieved as the long lives of persons gradually shortened by the end of the book of Genesis. Others think that God meant he would destroy the sinful human race in 120 years, that is, through the flood.

Many of the "sin stories" in the Torah exhibit a kind of ambiguity as is evident here. Narrative clues seem to lead in different directions simultaneously, thus creating competing readings. It is my thinking that the sin stories have been written with intentional ambiguity to invite readerly study and conversation and to resist conclusive readings. The stories of the sins of Cain, Ham, Aaron's sons, and Moses and Aaron are each debated by interpreters as to what exactly the sins were. I think the sin of Genesis 6:1–4 likewise is hidden by the narrator to invite readers to engage the story through the ages. If so, it worked. I will discuss the rationale for purposeful ambiguity in narrative of the sin of Moses in Chapter 22.

Whoever or whatever the sons of God or the sons of the gods were and whoever the daughters of humans were, the narrator's interpretation of the significance of the situation is clear enough. The wickedness of humankind escalated to such a level that

Yahweh was grieved that he had made human beings and was planning to damn them all (Gen 6:5–7). Yet there was Noah's family. The narrator's view of the problem of human sinfulness is the key issue. Biblical readers are welcome to debate and choose among the various interpretations and/or guesses, but they should not neglect the prevailing wickedness of the human race.

The earth was corrupt and full of violence. Yahweh determined to kill everyone but to save Noah and his family, two of every kind of animal, and seven of each of the clean animals (a distinction made in the book of Leviticus) in order to begin anew. Yahweh instructed Noah to build an ark with three decks, big enough to preserve his family and a remnant of the animal kingdom. Noah obeyed. After they had all entered the ark, Yahweh shut them in (7:16).

The story of the flood was written using reverse mirror imaging (see Table 6-C). The first half tells of building the ark and the flood water coming on all the earth. The second half narrates the receding waters and Noah's building an altar. The numbers 150 and forty each appear on both sides of the central point (see Table 6-E). The point of view of the narrative, especially the section leading up to the turning point, reveals something about Yahweh's judgment. When Noah built the ark and filled it with all the animals, it appears large. For the most part the narrative views the scene from inside the ark with the remnant that was preserved. When the flood water envelops the earth, exterminating all living and breathing beings, the ark appears, during the moment we view it from the outside, as an insignificant speck floating above the raging waters of God's wrath (7:17–24).

*How was point of view used in the story of the flood?*

**Table 6-C:** Mirror Imaging in the Flood Narrative

A God resolves to destroy the corrupt race (6:11–13)

B Noah builds an ark (6:14–22)

C Yahweh commands the remnant to enter ark (7:1–9)

D The flood begins (7:10–16)

E The flood prevails 150 days, mountains covered (7:17–24)

F God remembers Noah (8:1a)

E The flood recedes 150 days, mountains visible (8:1b–5)

D The earth dries (8:6–14)

C God commands the remnant to leave the ark (8:15–19)

B Noah builds an altar (8:20)

A Yahweh resolves not to destroy mankind (8:21–22)

At the central point the story turns because "God remembered Noah" (8:1). When he remembered Noah, he sent a wind to clear the waters for a new beginning. The water covered earth, and the "wind" (*ruah*) of God echoes with the sounds of the beginning when the "Spirit" (*ruah*) of God hovered over the waters (1:2). The flood waters cleared, and the family of Noah left the ark for a new beginning.

"He waited seven more days and sent the dove out again, but this time it did not return to him" (Gen 8:12).

*Ted Rabbitts/ CC BY 2.0*

For his part, God promises never to again destroy all of humankind by flood waters. For the part of Noah's family, God blesses them with a covenant. God commissions Noah much like Adam: "Be fruitful and increase in number and fill the earth" (9:1; cf. 1:28; 9:7). The similarities of the covenant with Noah draw attention to the differences (Harmon, 33–34). Instead of commanding dominion over lesser creatures, they now will be in dread of humans (9:2; cf. 1:28). Instead of food provisions restricted to plants, now people may eat meat with no blood in it (9:3–5; cf. 1:29). And most importantly, the new standard of capital punishment for murder stems from the value of humans made in God's own image (9:6; 1:26).

The symbol of the covenant, the rainbow, uses, for the second time in as many chapters, anthropomorphic language of God. Just as God remembered Noah during the judgment, the rainbow was a reminder so that God would remember not to destroy all of humankind with a flood. Forgetfulness was probably, like most anthropomorphic language applied to God, really about the problem of humanity. The reader gets the sense that it is humans rather than God who are forever reminded of God's patient longsuffering.

Many other societies of the ancient Near East had flood stories. A variety of written accounts of a great flood have survived. The biblical account of the flood is quite different in its character, especially its monotheism, from any other of the flood stories that have been discovered to date. The Akkadian flood myth, in one of the episodes of the Epic of Gilgamesh, has many similarities with the Genesis flood narrative (see Sidebar 6-D). Yet despite the similarities, the differences are great. The fact that various regional traditions remember a flood may reflect the greatness of the deluge.

The flood narrative in Genesis 7–8 uses many chronological details. These pieces of information fit together after overcoming a few challenges, such as the length of months, repetitions, overlapping time references, and the variety of ways of counting time. Table 6-E lists the number of days for each chronological reference as well as a running total of the duration of the flood with respect to each reference.

## Sidebar 6-D: Epic of Gilgamesh

Tablet XI of the Epic of Gilgamesh includes the most famous ancient Mesopotamian flood myth, which may have been written sometime around the turn of the second millennium BCE. Among the numerous ancient flood myths, this version contains the most similarities with the biblical account, even while maintaining significant differences. Among the most notable differences are the childish, egocentric, and rivalist behaviors of the gods in the polytheistic legend (Kofoed, 255).

A hero figure, perhaps Gilgamesh
*Robert C. Kashow*

### *Comparing the Epic of Gilgamesh (tablet XI) and the Biblical Flood Narrative*

#### Similarities

- The flood is divinely instigated.
- The protagonist is instructed about the coming judgment.
- The flood destroys the humans.
- The protagonist, his family, and animals are delivered from the flood in a large boat.
- The protagonist releases birds to find out if the flood has subsided.
- The protagonist performs sacrifices after the flood.

#### Differences

| Epic of Gilgamesh | Biblical Flood Narrative |
|---|---|
| many gods | one God |
| the gods and humans both struggle with the flood | the Creator rules creation |
| to stop the noisy humans | to judge sinful human rebels |

The reader who is familiar with the biblical flood narrative will be able to notice many similarities and differences between it and the following excerpts from tablet XI of The Epic of Gilgamesh.

> Utnapishtim said to Gilgamesh, "I will reveal to you a mystery, I will tell you a secret of the gods. You know the city Shurrupak, it stands on the banks of Euphrates? That city grew old and the gods that were in it were old. . . . In those days the world teemed, the people multiplied, the world bellowed like a wild bull, and the great god was aroused by the clamor. Enlil heard the clamor and he said to the gods in council, 'The uproar of mankind

is intolerable and sleep is no longer possible by reason of babel.' So the gods agreed to exterminate mankind. Enlil did this, but Ea because of his oath warned me in a dream. He whispered their words to my house of reeds . . . 'O man of Shurrupak, son of Ubara-Tutu; tear down your house and build a boat, abandon possessions and look for life, despise worldly goods and save your soul alive. Tear down your house, I say, and build a boat. These are the measurements of the barque as you shall build her: let her beam equal her length, let her deck be roofed like the vault that covers the abyss; then take up into the boat the seed of all living creatures.' When I had understood I said to my lord, 'Behold what you have commanded I will honor and perform.' . . . I loaded into her all that I had of gold and of living things, my family, my kin, the beast of the field both wild and tame, and all the craftsmen. . . . I looked out at the weather and it was terrible, so I boarded the boat and battened her down. . . . For six days and six nights the winds blew, torrent and tempest and flood overwhelmed the world, tempest and flood raged together like warring hosts. When the seventh day dawned the storm from the south subsided, the sea grew calm, the flood was stilled; I looked at the face of the world and there was silence, all mankind was turned to clay. The surface of the sea stretched as flat as a roof-top; I opened a hatch and the light fell on my face. Then I bowed low, I sat down and wept, the tears streamed down my face, for on every side was the waste of water. I looked for land in vain, for fourteen leagues distant there appeared a mountain, and there the boat grounded; on the mountain of Nisir the boat held fast. . . . When the seventh day dawned I loosed a dove and let her go. She flew away, but finding no resting-place she returned. Then I loosed a swallow, and she flew away but finding no resting-place she returned. I loosed a raven, she saw the waters had retreated, she ate, she flew around, she cawed, and she did not come back. Then I threw everything open to the four winds, I made a sacrifice and poured out a libation on the mountain top. . . . When the gods smelled the sweet savor, they gathered like flies over the sacrifice. Then, at last, Ishtar also came, she lifted her necklace with jewels of heaven that once Anu had made to please her. 'O you gods here present, by the lapis lazuli round my neck I shall remember these days as I remember the jewels of my throat; these last days I shall never forget.'"

"The Epic of Gilgamesh." Translated by N. K. Sanders. Pages 41–43 in *The Norton Anthology of World Masterpieces: The Western Tradition.* 7th ed. Edited by Sarah Lawall. New York: W. W. Norton, 1999 (spelling Americanized).

Kofoed, Jens Bruun. "Encoding and Decoding Culture." Pages 240–62 in *Write That They May Read: Studies in Literacy and Textualization in the Ancient Near East and in the Hebrew Scripture, Essays in Honour of Professor Alan R. Millard.* Edited by Daniel I. Block. Eugene, OR: Pickwick, 2020.

The flood narrative counts months as thirty days each, as can be seen by comparing 7:11 and 8:4 with 7:24 and 8:3; in this case, five months (of thirty days each) equals 150 days. The practice of counting a month as thirty days was used in several ancient societies, sometimes alongside lunar-based calendars (see Sarna, 55, 376).

**Table 6-E:** Chronology of the Flood

| | | Noah's age | Month | Day | Number of days | Total days of flood |
|---|---|---|---|---|---|---|
| 7:7 | Entering the ark | 600 | — | — | 7 | 7 |
| 7:11 | Flood begins | 600 | 2 | 17 | — | 0 |
| 7:12 | Forty days of rain | — | — | — | 40 | 40 |
| 7:24; 8:3 | Waters prevail | — | — | — | 150 | 150 |
| 8:4 | Ark grounded | — | 7 | 17 | (5 × 30) | 150 |
| 8:5 | Mountains visible | — | 10 | 1 | (74) | 224 |
| 8:6–7 | Raven sent out | — | — | — | 40 | 264 |
| 8:8–12 | Doves sent out three times | — | — | — | 3 × 7 | 285 |
| 8:13 | Earth drying | 601 | 1 | 1 | (29) | (314) |
| 8:14 | Leaving ark | — | 2 | 27 | (57) | 371 |

After the account of the flood and God's covenant with Noah, the scene shifts immediately to the so-called fall of Noah. Noah plants a vineyard and gets drunk. During this first biblical account of drunkenness, Noah unintentionally was passively involved in a sexual sin of his son Ham. The phrase he "saw his father's nakedness" could mean that he was lusting after his father or was mocking his father (9:22). This interpretation works well in light of the fact that Shem and Japheth looked the other way when they walked backwards with a garment to cover their father. The phrase "his father's nakedness," however, could also be a euphemism for sexual intercourse, either with Noah or with Mrs. Noah. Leviticus 18 uses the phrase "do not uncover the nakedness of X" repeatedly with the meaning "do not have sexual relations with." Leviticus 18:8 says literally, "Do not uncover the nakedness of your father's wife; it is the nakedness of your father" (NJPS), meaning, "Do not have sexual relations with your father's wife; that would dishonor your father" (NIV).

Some interpreters have surmised that the reason that Noah cursed Canaan for Ham's sin was that Ham had gotten his mother pregnant with Canaan (Bergsma and Hahn, 34–36). Whatever the sin was—voyeurism, mockery, homosexuality, incest—it was sexual in nature (on the ambiguity of sin stories in the Torah see discussion of 6:1–4 above and discussion of the sin of Moses in Chapter 22). The outcome of the first account of human drunkenness was a curse on a long-term nemesis of the children of Israel.

*Why has the sin of Ham been interpreted in several different ways?*

The only words that Noah speaks in the Bible are a pronouncement against his grandson Canaan. The curse against Canaan has been interpreted by Christians in sinful ways to justify brutal slavery based on ethnicity (see Haynes, 38–40, 69–74, et passim; Goldenberg, 121–45, 153–59, 207–37). Even imposing so-called "races" is racist since there is only one human race (Williams, 5–7, n. 5, 12–13, n. 3). The curse against Canaan, however, is no license for sin but a judgment of it. Few things are more tragic than when people use the Scriptures to condone hateful actions.

The account of Noah's fall carries an extended echo of the story of the sin of the first humans (Table 6-F; adapted from Sailhamer, 293). Noah was like his sinful ancestors. The time needed to plant a vineyard, grow grapes, produce wine, and let it ferment passes instantly for readers (see Table 18-A in Chapter 18). The story of Noah's drunkenness is placed directly after his salvation from the deadly deluge. One implication is that, although through Noah Yahweh grants a new beginning to the human race, Noah takes the effects of the fall with him in the ark. The flood judges the earlier race of rebels but does not fix the problem of human sinfulness. The human dilemma ultimately calls for a different kind of solution.

**Table 6-F:** A Comparison of the Accounts of the Fall and Noah's Drunkenness

| The Fall | Noah's Drunkenness |
|---|---|
| Yahweh God had planted a garden . . . there he put the man (Gen 2:8) | Noah . . . proceeded to plant an orchard (9:20) |
| And she took some [fruit from the tree] and ate it (3:6) | He drank some of its wine, he became drunk (9:21) |
| And they realized they were naked (3:7) | [He] lay uncovered inside his tent (9:21) |
| And [they] made coverings for themselves (3:7) | They . . . covered their father's naked body (9:23) |
| Then the eyes of both of them were opened, and they realized they were naked (3:7) | When Noah awoke from his wine and knew what his youngest son had done (9:24 lit.) |
| "Cursed are you" (3:14) | "Cursed be Canaan" (9:25) |

Genesis 10 is framed in its first and last verses with a summary statement. In between, the lineages of Japheth, Ham, and Shem are laid out in a patterned manner. In each case there is a heading (10:2, 6, 21–22), an expansion of the heading (10:3–4, 7–19, 23–29), and a comment concerning the families, languages, lands, and nations of each son (10:5, 20, 30–31). One notable expansion relates to the treatment of Canaan in

10:15–19. The sons descended from Canaan are the heads of several of Israel's enemies—like Sidonians, Hittites, Jebusites, Amorites, and so on. The records in Genesis 10 situate Israel internationally within the Torah and the rest of the Hebrew Scriptures.

**Table 6-G:** Mirror Imaging in the Tower Narrative

| | |
|---|---|
| A | The whole world had one language (11:1) |
| B | Settled there (11:2) |
| C | Said one to each other (11:3a) |
| D | "Come, let's make bricks (11:3b) |
| E | Let us build [for] ourselves (11:4a) |
| F | A city, with a tower" (11:4b) |
| G | Yahweh came down to see (11:5a) |
| F | The city and the tower (11:5b) |
| E | The people were building (11:5c) |
| D | "Come, let us go down and confuse (11:7a) |
| C | Their language so they will not understand" (11:7b) |
| B | Scattered them from there (11:8) |
| A | Confused the language of the whole world (11:9) |

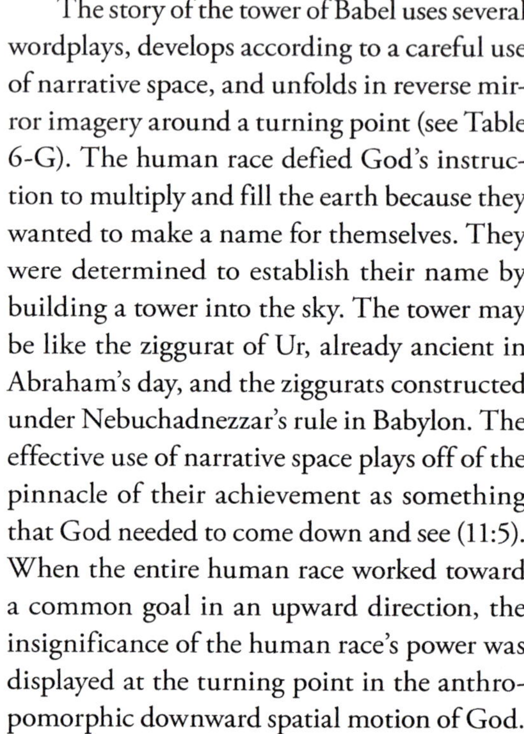

The story of the tower of Babel uses several wordplays, develops according to a careful use of narrative space, and unfolds in reverse mirror imagery around a turning point (see Table 6-G). The human race defied God's instruction to multiply and fill the earth because they wanted to make a name for themselves. They were determined to establish their name by building a tower into the sky. The tower may be like the ziggurat of Ur, already ancient in Abraham's day, and the ziggurats constructed under Nebuchadnezzar's rule in Babylon. The effective use of narrative space plays off of the pinnacle of their achievement as something that God needed to come down and see (11:5). When the entire human race worked toward a common goal in an upward direction, the insignificance of the human race's power was displayed at the turning point in the anthropomorphic downward spatial motion of God.

Yahweh judged human beings by confusing their languages. Thus, they were scattered.

*How is narrative space used in the story of the rebellious tower builders?*

Ziggurat of Ur (late 3rd millennium BCE)
*Donald Cruz*

Stairs of Ziggurat of Ur
*Donald Cruz*

The rhetorical effect of reading this passage in Hebrew includes the semi-tongue twister way in which it was written. The entire passage contains a density of the Hebrew letters *b*, *l*, and *r*. The wordplays within this passage include playing on the name Babel with the Hebrew term for "confounded" (*balal*) (see Holtz, 38; Klitsner, 48–49). Note the climactic wordplay: "Come now! Let us go down and there let us baffle their language . . . Therefore its name was called Bavel/Babble, for there YHWH baffled the language of all the earth-folk" (11:7a, 9a Fox).

The short account of Terah provokes readers to wonder at its tragic incompleteness. Terah takes Abram, Sarai, and Lot and sets out from Ur near Babylon in order to go to the land of Canaan. Terah never makes it to the land of Canaan. He settles in Haran, in the northwest area of the Mesopotamian fertile crescent. Had God called him? Why was he going to the land that Yahweh would promise to his son? These and other questions the text answers with silence.

*Image of drawing of MS 2063 by Andrew George, SOAS University of London, by permission*

*The Schøyen Collection MS 2063, Oslo and London*

## ANOTHER LOOK

Among the most horrifying narratives in the Scriptures is the account of the flood. It is not sensational or particularly graphic, but it places human life in fragile perspective. More specifically, God was willing, if necessary, to kill everyone and start over. A cosmic redo. At the same time, the narrative is not about the flood but about the salvation of Noah and his family from the raging waters of God's wrath. The story of the great deluge, then, is a figure of the wrath *and* the grace of the Almighty.

For good reason, later biblical preachers (namely, Isaiah and Messiah) look to the days

*The Schøyen Collection MS 2063.1, Oslo and London*

The Tower of Babel relief presents a rare image of Nebuchadnezzar II (605–562 BCE) with one of his two ziggurat building projects. The name of the ziggurat of Babylon is E-temen-anki, "House foundation platform of heaven and underworld" (George, 154).

of Noah as a symbol of things to come. For Isaiah the days of Noah offer an image of peace (see Childs, 429; also see 4Q176, 9–11).

> "For a brief moment I abandoned you,
> but with deep compassion I will bring you back.
> In a surge of anger
> I hid my face from you for a moment,
> but with everlasting kindness
> I will have compassion on you,"
> says Yahweh your Redeemer.
> "*To me this is like the days of Noah,*
> *when I swore that the waters of Noah would never again cover the earth.*
> So now I have sworn not to be angry with you,
> never to rebuke you again.
> Though the mountains be shaken
> and the hills be removed,
> yet *my unfailing love for you will not be shaken,*
> *nor my covenant of peace be removed,*"
> says Yahweh, who has compassion on you.
> "Afflicted city, lashed by storms and not comforted,
> I will rebuild you with stones of turquoise,
> your foundations with lapis lazuli.
> I will make your battlements of rubies,
> your gates of sparkling jewels,
> and all your walls of precious stones.
> All your children will be taught by Yahweh,
> and great will be their peace.
> In righteousness you will be established:
> Tyranny will be far from you;
> you will have nothing to fear.
> Terror will be far removed;
> it will not come near you." (Isa 54:7–14, emphasis added)

In his Mount of Olives discourse, Messiah borrows Isaiah's phrase "like the days of Noah" but uses it in an inverted manner. While Isaiah refers to the days of Noah as those days in which God presented his resolve to those who were saved in the ark that he would never again destroy the world with a flood, Messiah refers to the people who were swept away in the flood.

> But about that day or hour no one knows, not even the angels in heaven, nor the Son, but only the Father. *As it was in the days of Noah, so it will be at the coming of the Son of Man. For in the days before the flood,* people were eating and drinking, marrying and giving in marriage, up to the day Noah entered the ark; and *they knew nothing about what would happen until the flood came and took them all away. That is how it will be at the coming of the Son of Man.* Two men will be in the field; *one will be taken* and the other left. Two women will be grinding with a hand mill; *one will be taken* and the other left. Therefore keep watch, because you do not know on what day your Lord will come. (Matt 24:36–42, emphasis added)

According to Genesis 7:21–23 all living beings were destroyed in the flood and "only Noah was left." Similarly, Messiah states that "one will be taken and the other left" (Matt 24:40–41). Moreover, the different terms used for eating and drinking in Matthew 24:38, 49 probably imply surprise, not sinfulness, with regard to the flood story (see Gibbs, 541).

In Matthew's account of the Mount of Olives discourse, it seems that Messiah extends the days-of-Noah imagery into the parables that follow, particularly the story of the virgins. The narrative point of view in Genesis largely follows Noah and his family into the ark—the point of view remains on those delivered (see Fretheim, 106). In Messiah's story, however, listeners follow the foolish virgins to town and back. In the former case, Noah's family was shut in; in the latter, the foolish virgins are shut out (see Balabanski, 47). In both stories, the door symbolizes a sure fate, either salvation or judgment.

> "Put a door in the side of the ark and make lower, middle and upper decks. . . ." The animals going in were male and female of every living thing, as God had commanded Noah. *Then Yahweh shut him in.* (Gen 6:16b; 7:16, emphasis added)

> But while they were on their way to buy the oil, the bridegroom arrived. The virgins who were ready went in with him to the wedding banquet. And *the door was shut.* Later the others also came. "Lord, Lord," *they said, "open the door for us!"* But he replied, "Truly I tell you, I don't know you." (Matt 25:10–12, emphasis added)

Isaiah adapts his use of the Noah narrative based on those who were saved *in* the ark, whereas Messiah draws on the same narrative but focused on those *outside.* Messiah invents a terrible counterpoint of view to both the Genesis story and Isaiah's hope (see Figure 6-H). He interprets together Genesis 6–8 and Isaiah 54 and advances revelation within his forward looking discourse.

**Figure 6-H:** The Image and Reverse Image of the Days of Noah in Genesis, Isaiah, and Matthew

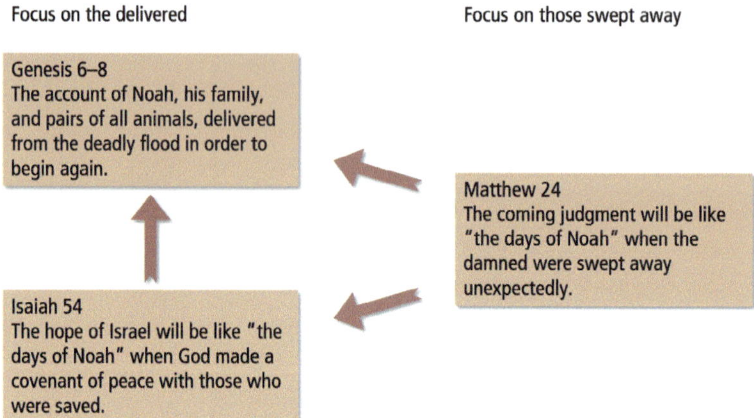


The earth and all of the created order, even the animals, have their collective fate tied into that of humankind. Humanity, created in the image of God, has a unique place and a weighty responsibility for the entire realm of creation. They are the lords of creation, and as they go, so goes their world. When the human society was damned, it brought death to everything that had the breath of life.

Along these lines, yet for opposite effect, Paul personifies the earth and pictures her as a pregnant woman in labor. She waits expectantly for her release, which comes as an effect of the redemption of humankind.

> The creation waits in eager expectation for the children of God to be revealed. For *the creation was subjected to frustration*, not by its own choice, but by the will of the one who subjected it, in hope that the creation itself will be liberated from *its bondage to decay* and brought into the freedom and glory of the children of God.
>
> We know that *the whole creation has been groaning as in the pains of childbirth* right up to the present time. Not only so, but we ourselves, who have the firstfruits of the Spirit, groan inwardly as we wait eagerly for our adoption to sonship, the redemption of our bodies. (Rom 8:19–23, emphasis added)

The hope of creation, then, is that the human revolution against God's word will not finally prevail.

## INTERACTIVE WORKSHOP

### *Chapter Summary*

The human society that grew up in exile from the garden is increasingly characterized by sinfulness and death. The few who "walk with God" are spared the inevitable judgment of the larger society; most notably Noah and his family are saved from the flood to enjoy a new beginning for humankind. Nevertheless, sin against God's word quickly enters the new beginning, as represented by the incident of Noah's drunkenness and the rebellion at the tower of Babel.

### *Can You Explain the Key Terms?*

- Canaan
- Enoch
- Lamech
- Nephilim
- sons of God/the gods
- walk with God

### *Challenge Questions*

1. What is the general structure of Genesis 5–11, and how does this help us understand its meaning?
2. In what ways can Lamech be compared to Cain, and in what ways to Enoch?
3. According to the narrator, what is the point of the story in Genesis 6:1–4?
4. Why are animals killed in the judgment of the human rebels?
5. What are the new features of human society after the flood based on the Noahic covenant (Gen 9)?
6. Why are the tower builders judged? How do languages function as punishment?

### *Advanced Questions*

1. How does point of view affect the narrative interpretation of the events depicted in the flood story?
2. What is the narrative and theological function of genealogies in Genesis 5 and 11? Compare and contrast this to other uses of genealogies elsewhere in the Scriptures.
3. What is the structure and significance of the genealogies of Genesis 10?

*4. Who are the *bene ha'elohim* (sons of God/the gods) in Genesis 6:2, and what controls are used to maintain your interpretation?

### *Research Project Ideas*

Investigate the literary and theological function of genealogies within scriptural narrative and in the Sumerian king list.

Compare, literarily and theologically, the biblical flood narrative to that of tablet XI in the Epic of Gilgamesh or Atrahasis.

Study the exegetical and theological relationship between the Noahic covenant and the original creational order.

Explain the notions of "exile" and "east" in Genesis 1–11 and evaluate the theological significance of these within its larger biblical framework.

## *The Next Step*


Balabanski, Vicky. *Eschatology in the Making: Mark, Matthew and the Didache.* Society for New Testament Studies Monograph Series 97. Cambridge: Cambridge University Press, 1997.

Bergsma, John Sietze, and Scott Walker Hahn. "Noah's Nakedness and the Curse on Canaan (Genesis 9:20–27)." *Journal of Biblical Literature* 124 (2005): 25–40.

Childs, Brevard S. *Isaiah.* Old Testament Library. Louisville: Westminster John Knox, 2001.

Clines, David J. A. "The Significance of the 'Sons of God' Episode (Genesis 6.1–4) in the Context of the 'Primaeval History' (Genesis 1–11)." Pages 337–50 in *On the Way to the Postmodern: Old Testament Essays, 1967–1998.* Vol 1. Edited by David J. A. Clines. Journal for the Study of the Old Testament Supplement Series 292. Sheffield: Sheffield Academic, 1998.

Fretheim, Terrence E. *Creation, Fall, and Flood: Studies in Genesis 1–11.* Minneapolis: Augsburg, 1969.

George, Andrew R. "A Stele of Nebuchadnezzar II." Pages 153–69 in *Cuneiform Royal Inscriptions and Related Texts in the Schøyen Collection.* Edited by Andrew R. George. Bethesda, MD: CDL, 2011.

Gibbs, Jeffrey Alan. "'Let the Reader Understand': The Eschatological Discourse of Jesus in Matthew's Gospel." Ph.D. diss., Union Theological Seminary, Richmond, VA, 1995.

Goldenberg, David M. *Black and Slave: The Origins and History of the Curse of Ham.* Studies of the Bible and Its Reception 10. Berlin: De Gruyter, 2017.

Harmon, Matthew S. *The Servant of the Lord and His Servant People: Tracing a Biblical Theme through the Canon.* Downers Grove, IL: IVP Academic, 2020.

Haynes, Stephen R. *Noah's Curse: The Biblical Justification of American Slavery.* New York: Oxford University Press, 2002.

Holtz, Barry W. *Back to the Sources: Reading the Classic Jewish Texts.* New York: Summit Books, 1984.

Imes, Carmen Joy. *Being God's Image: Why Creation Still Matters.* Downers Grove: IVP Academic, forthcoming [2023].

Klitsner, Judy. *Subversive Sequels in the Bible: How Biblical Stories Mine and Undermine Each Other.* Jerusalem: Maggid Books, 2019.

Sailhamer, John H. *Introduction to Old Testament Theology: A Canonical Approach.* Grand Rapids: Zondervan Academic, 1995.

Sarna, Nahum M. *Exodus.* JPS Torah Commentary. Philadelphia: Jewish Publication Society, 1989.

Schnittjer, Gary Edward. *Old Testament Use of Old Testament.* Grand Rapids: Zondervan Academic, 2021.

Waltke, Bruce K., with Cathi J. Fredricks. *Genesis: A Commentary.* Grand Rapids: Zondervan Academic, 2001.

Williams, Jarvis J. *Redemptive Kingdom Diversity: A Biblical Theology of the People of God.* Grand Rapids: Baker Academic, 2021.

# 7 THE ABRAHAM NARRATIVES

## *Genesis 12:1–25:18*

*A.D. Riddle/BiblePlaces.com*

## GETTING STARTED

### *Focus Questions*

What is the story of Abraham? Why did he have to wait so long?

### *Look for These Terms*

- circumcise
- covenant
- laugh
- offspring
- test

## AN OUTLINE

A. **The Call of Abram (12:1–9)**
  1. The covenant (12:1–3)
    a. The land (12:1)
    b. The offspring (12:2)
    c. The blessing (12:3)
  2. Abram's response (12:4–9)

B. **Waiting for the Offspring (12:10–20:18)**
  1. Abram and Sarai go to Egypt and lie about their relationship and God saves them (12:10–20)
    2. Abram saves Lot (13–14)
      3. The cutting of the covenant (15)
        4. The conception and birth of Ishmael to Hagar (16)
      5. The sign of the covenant (17)
    6. Abraham intercedes for Lot (18–19)
  7. Abraham and Sarah lie about their relationship and God intercedes for them (20)

C. **The Beginning of the Fulfillment of the Promise (21)**
  1. The birth of Isaac (21:1–7)

2. Hagar and Ishmael are banished and God provides water (21:8–21)
3. Abraham secures the well at Beersheba (21:22–34)

**D. The Test of Abraham (22)**

**E. The Passing of the Covenant (23:1–25:11)**

1. The land—purchasing the Machpelah burial plot (23)
2. The offspring—securing a wife for Isaac (24)
3. The blessing—inheritance given to Isaac (25:1–11)

## A READING

The human revolution against God's will continued unchecked even after the catastrophic flood. Yahweh, against this backdrop, acts decisively. He calls Abram. The word of Yahweh to Abram is the beginning of his restoration of humankind and creation. Abram's family is specially chosen to bring blessing to all the families of the earth.

The Abraham stories, covering roughly Genesis 12:1 through 25:11, make up the second of the four major sections of Genesis. It is the first of the three parts that trace the beginning of the chosen family. The book does not begin with the call of Abraham. The beginning of this family is set against the universal concerns of the story of the beginning of humankind (Gen 1–11). The choosing of a particular family, therefore, is not for their personal benefit, but Yahweh selects them in relation to the dilemma shared by humankind. The general human story, especially the problem of sinfulness, offers the correct context in which to interpret the meaning of the chosen family.

The Abraham stories challenge and, in some cases, startle readers. The climactic episode of the narrative, the test, can surprise readers once again, even those who have known it their entire lives. The design of the stories heightens this remarkable event. The storyteller's skill with leading words ("seeing," "eyes," and related terms), mirror imaging (see outline above), and especially narrative time (see Figure 1-B in Chapter 1) is put to good use in the theological challenge that compels readers of this segment of Genesis.

The story begins where Terah failed—even while all of the prominent matriarchs and patriarchs descend from Terah (see Figure 7-A). Terah only gets as far as Haran (Map 7-B). Yahweh called Abram, "Go you!" (lit.), a phrase (*lek leka*) that in this form only occurs in one other place in the Scriptures (22:2; see Table 7-H). The word of Yahweh to Abram includes a threefold promise—land, offspring, blessing—which both sets the scope of the Abraham narratives and presents the theme of the entire Torah.

> Yahweh had said to Abram, "Go from your country, your people and your father's household *to the land I will show you. I will make you into a great nation*, and *I will bless you*; I will make your name great, and you will be a blessing. I will bless those who bless you, and whoever curses you I will curse; and *all peoples on earth will be blessed through you*." (Gen 12:1–3, emphasis added)

The Torah houses the story of the beginning of the fulfillment of the promise to Abraham: the focus through the remainder of Genesis is on the *offspring* (or seed); Exodus and Leviticus underscore the *blessing* in terms of relationship with God; and Numbers and Deuteronomy demonstrate progress to the *land* and offer instruction for living in the land (see Clines, 31–47). Yahweh returns several times and expands upon his threefold promise in the Abraham cycle of stories. The word of God to Abram will be clarified, extended, and looked back upon through the rest of the Torah and, in a real sense, throughout the entire Christian Bible.

*How is God's word to Abram in Genesis 12:1–3 related to the rest of the Five Books of Moses?*

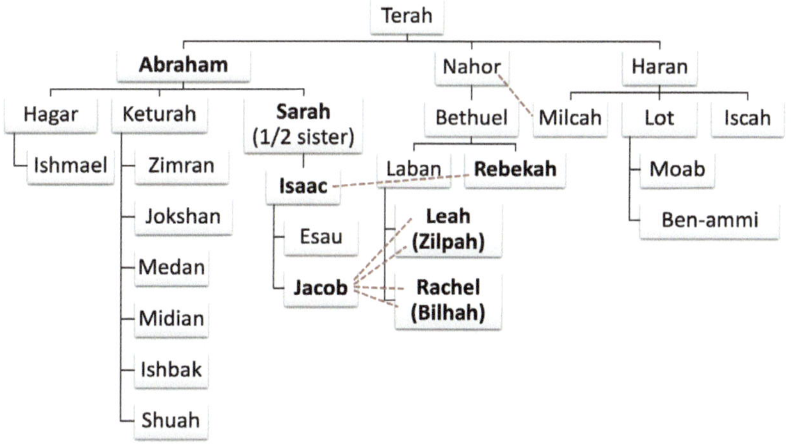


**Figure 7-A:** Family Ties of Hebrew Ancestors[a]

[a]Some of these marriages are illegal by the standards of Leviticus 18. The narrator is aware of this and let readers know anyway. Why? Perhaps because the priority of demonstrating the purity of the line of the ancestors from Terah outweighs other concerns. It is important to marry within the people called by Yahweh.

The promise of making a name for Abram (12:2) foregrounds God's grace in this context. The Nephilim, heroes of old, *persons of name* (6:4 lit.), were exterminated by the terrible flood. The people of Babel sought to *make a name* for themselves (11:4), and God defeated their efforts. But here, to Abram, one of the descendants of Shem (whose name means "Name"), Yahweh chooses to give a name.

The aspect of Yahweh's word to Abram that takes center stage for the next eleven chapters and beyond is the promise to make him a great nation. After Abram responded to God's word and traveled to the land of Canaan, God said even more specifically, "To your offspring I will give this land" (12:7). The term offspring or seed echoes God's word to the serpent in 3:15. Attentive readers may hear the term offspring in the

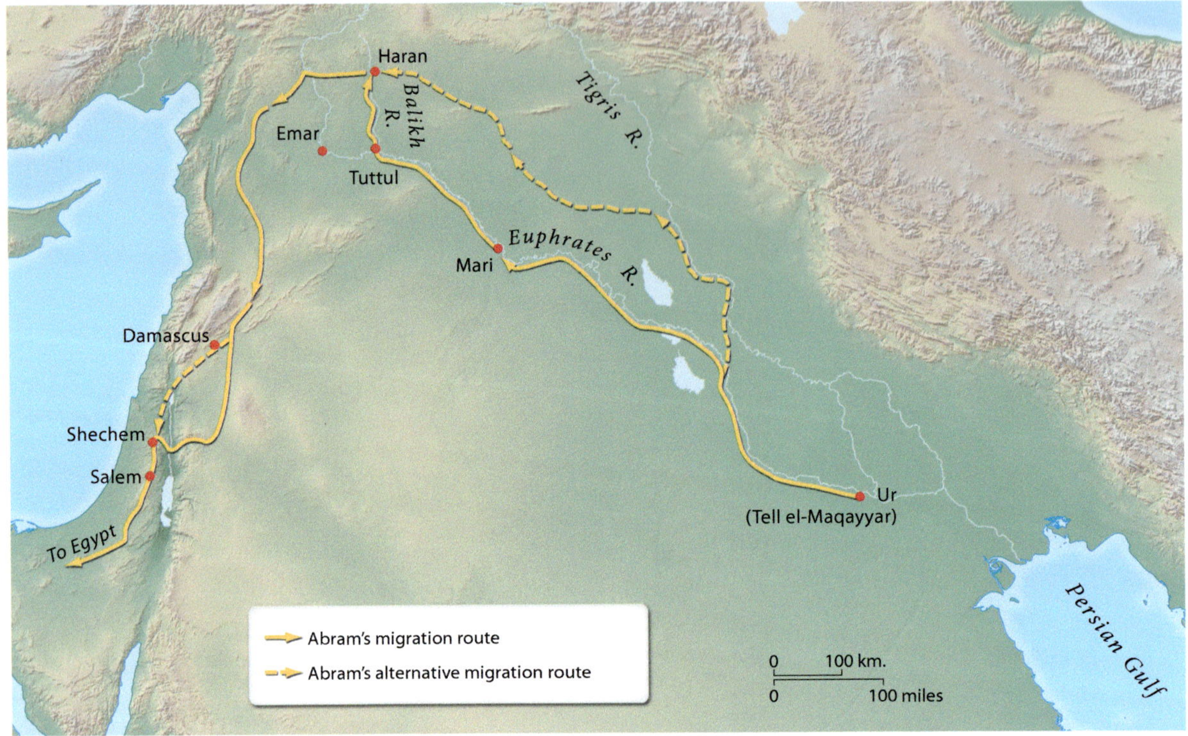


**Map 7-B:** Abram's relocation

promise to Abram and connect it to the word of God for the larger human situation in the poem of judgment on the serpent.

Considering narrative time can help readers appreciate the climactic development of the story. The recounting of selected events in Abraham's life does not accord with the constancy with which time is measured in the external world. Rather, narrative time, marked by Abraham's age (which readers are apprised of routinely), is a function of the story (see Table 7-C and see Figure 1-B in Chapter 1). The story that is dominated by the expectation of the offspring uses time in a way that heightens the drama of the birth of Isaac.

**Table 7-C:** The Age of Abraham between His Call and the Birth of Isaac

| Genesis | Abraham's Age |
|---|---|
| 12:4 (promise) | seventy-five |
| 16:3 | eighty-five |
| 17:1 | ninety-nine |
| 21:5 (Issac's birth) | one hundred |

The story accents Yahweh's grace to Abraham and Sarah as well as the power of the test of Abraham. The nine chapters between the promise and the birth of the offspring span two and a half decades. Yet, halfway through the chapters of waiting, Abraham has already waited for twenty-four years. That is, the closer the reader gets to the birth of the offspring, the slower narrative time passes. The elderly couple was acutely aware of the passing of years. The combination of their faith and their aging led them to find other meanings of God's word of promise.

*What is the relationship between time and the promise of offspring in the Abraham stories?*

After Yahweh called Abram and he responded by relocating to Canaan, he spends only six verses in the land before famine forces him to go to Egypt. The promised offspring seems at risk because of Abram's deceptive tactics to protect himself. Sarai was so beautiful that Abram feared he would be killed by those wanting to take her from him. Abram and Sarai lied and said she was his sister. As a result, pharaoh took her as a bride. Yahweh rescued Sarai by bringing terrible plagues against pharaoh. This short episode anticipates the later and much longer sojourn of the Israelites in Egypt (Table 7-D, adapted from Sailhamer, 142; also see Geoghegan, 16–25, 43–45; Jericke, 141–43; Morales, 22–23; Postell, 16–31). What happened to Abram in Genesis 12 anticipates extended echo effect in the accounts of the Israelites moving to Egypt because of a famine in Genesis 46 and leaving Egypt in Exodus 12–13.

**Table 7-D:** Extended Echoes between Abram's and Israel's Sojourns in Egypt

| Abram in Egypt | Israelites in Egypt |
|---|---|
| There was a famine in the land (Gen 12:10) | There was a famine in all the other lands (Gen 41:54) |
| As he was about to enter Egypt (12:11) | And they entered the land of Goshen (46:28 lit.) |
| He said to his wife Sarai . . . (12:11) | Joseph said to his brothers . . . (46:31) |
| "When the Egyptians see you, they will say . . ." (12:12) | "When Pharaoh calls you in and asks . . ." (46:33) |
| "Say . . ." (12:13) | "Say . . ." (46:34 lit.) |
| "So that I will be treated well for your sake" (12:13) | "You will be allowed to settle in the region of Goshen" (46:34) |
| And when Pharaoh's officials saw her, they praised her to Pharaoh (12:15) | Joseph went and told Pharaoh . . . (47:1) |
| And she was taken into his palace (12:15) | And Pharaoh said . . . "Settle your father and brothers in the best part of the land" (47:5–6) |
| And Abram acquired sheep and cattle (12:16) | "Put them in charge of my livestock" (47:6); They acquired property there and were fruitful and increased greatly (47:27) |

*(continued)*

| Abram in Egypt | Israelites in Egypt |
|---|---|
| But Yahweh inflicted serious diseases on Pharaoh (12:17) | "I will bring one more plague on Pharaoh (Exod 11:1; cf. 4:21–23; 6:1–9) |
| So Pharaoh summoned Abram and said . . . (12:18 lit.) | Pharaoh summoned Moses and Aaron and said . . . (Exod 12:31) |
| "Take . . . and go!" (12:19) | "Take . . . and go" (Exod 12:32) |
| And they sent him on his way, with his wife (12:20) | To send them away (Exod 12:33 lit.) |
| So Abram went up from Egypt to the Negev (13:1) | The Israelites journeyed from Rameses to Succoth (Exod 12:37) |
| Abram had become very wealthy in livestock and in silver and gold (13:2) | And also large droves of livestock (Exod 12:38); silver and gold (12:35) |
| And Lot went with Abram (13:5 lit.) | Many other people went up with them (Exod 12:38) |

In a more specific manner, this same problem will resurface for Abraham in Genesis 20 and for Isaac in chapter 26 (see Table 8-A in Chapter 8).

After Yahweh delivered Abram and Sarai from pharaoh in chapter 12, the next two chapters recount how Abram delivers his nephew Lot. Lot's troubles began when those tending his herds and those tending Abram's herds quarreled because the two had become wealthy with livestock. Abram generously offered Lot the choice of whatever portion of the land he wished, and Abram would move off in the other direction.

Ancient Beersheba
*© Lev Levin/ Shutterstock*

The lush Jordan Valley caught Lot's eye, so he decided to reside near the town of Sodom. After Lot left, Yahweh said to Abram, "Look around from where you are, to the north and south, to the east and west. All the land that you see I will give to you and your offspring forever" (13:14–15). This is the first of several times that God reiterates and expands on his word in chapter 12 (see, for example, 15:5–21; 17:4–8, 12–19; 18:18–19; 22:17–18; 26:2–4, 24; 28:13–15; 35:11–12; 46:3; Exod 3:6–8; 6:2–8; also see Table 3-D in Chapter 3).

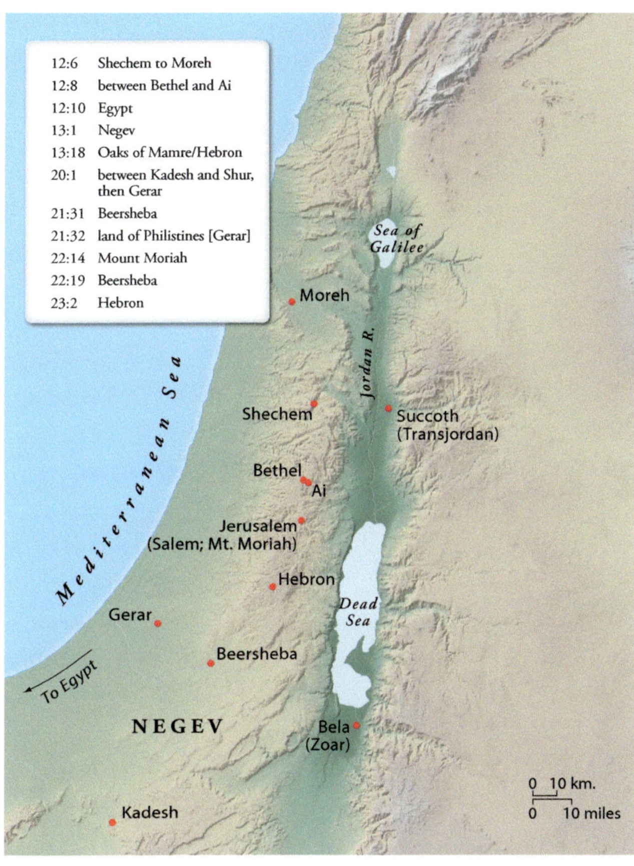


**Map 7-E:** The Journeys of Abraham

Genesis 14 opens with a detailed account of a confederacy of four monarchs of regional eastern kingdoms who joined together to suppress a revolt of five kings of western localized kingdoms from within the lower Jordan River Valley or Dead Sea area. The abundance of detail associated with this military campaign is unique within Genesis. During the course of stopping the revolt, the four eastern kings raided and plundered the cities they re-subjugated to themselves. This military campaign is recorded in Genesis because the kings carried off Abram's nephew, who had moved into Sodom.

Abram then took the 318 trained men of his own household, a symbol of his enormous wealth, joined with three allies, and tracked down the raiding kings who had headed off to the north. Abram defeated the raiders and rescued Lot. The text mentions that Abram and his allies caught up with the four kings at the city of Dan. The fact that this town was not founded until much later gives a clue toward the perspective of the expected readership, or perhaps signifies a later scribal updating for the sake of clarity (Grisanti, 583–84).

As Abram was returning home, he met up with Melchizedek, the king and priest of Salem, short for Jerusalem. Melchizedek blessed Abram by the Most High God. Many suggestions have been made concerning the identity of this king. For example, some have thought that Melchizedek was another name used by Shem; the math in the genealogy of Genesis 11 allows for this. Others have thought that his meeting with Abram was a preincarnate appearance of the Messiah. These, and other views, are possible, but there is no evidence to support or refute them. The Melchizedek traditions within the letter to the Hebrews are related, in large part, to the brief poetic reflection on him in Psalm 110 (Levine and Brettler, 141–47, cf. 160–64). Of significance in the present context is that, whereas Abram gave a tenth of his great wealth to the priest-king of Salem, Abram also flatly refused any form of reward from the grateful king of Sodom, desiring to retain all credit for God.

Genesis 15 provides significant insight into Abram's faith and Yahweh's faithfulness through an extended vision. When Yahweh spoke to him in the vision, Abram responded bitterly that his chief servant Eliezer would be his heir. Yahweh countered that he would fulfill his word to Abram. Abram's heir would be his own biological son. Abram believed the word of God and was counted as righteous.

Yahweh cut a covenant with Abram to guarantee his commitment to his word. One ancient covenantal ritual was to divide an animal in two (in this case three grazing animals and two birds), and each party would pass between, signifying that this should be done to them if they were to break the agreement (see Jer 34:18–20). Yahweh revealed the future enslavement and deliverance of Abram's descendants, thus previewing for readers the account in Exodus as within his plan. When darkness fell, a glowing torch passed between the animals, but Abram did not go between them. The fact that Yahweh alone committed himself to the covenant, symbolized by the torch, suggests that the promise is permanent.

Older discussions of the Abrahamic and Davidic covenants tend to get things confused by discussing whether these covenants are "unconditional." The point seems to be that God will be faithful no matter what, but the term unconditional is a bad fit.

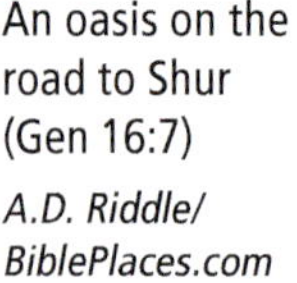

An oasis on the road to Shur (Gen 16:7)
*A.D. Riddle/ BiblePlaces.com*

The prophets make clear that Israel and Judah must obey God's covenantal will or be cast into exile. The permanent or irrevocable covenants come with obligations. But even after Israel and Judah are consigned to exile, the enduring faithfulness of God is demonstrated in his commitment to the irrevocable promises to Abraham (Isa 41:8–10) and David (Jer 23:5–6). The newer approaches helpfully emphasize that though the covenant comes with obligations upon Israel, it is an irrevocable promise of Yahweh's faithfulness (see Block, 2–3, 316; Chisholm, *1 & 2 Samuel*, 218–19, 224–25; Schnittjer, "Your House"; Johnston cited in Schnittjer, "Blessing," 25–26, n. 22).

While Genesis 15 began with Abram's suggesting that Eliezer would be his heir, in the next chapter it was Sarai who offered her servant to bear Abram's child as their heir. The attempts to assign the chief servant and then to have Hagar bear offspring demonstrate, in my view, the faith of both Abram and Sarai. They were seeking to make sense of God's word in light of circumstance. They were, to be sure, wrong in how they were trying to make sense of God's word. But it appears that the attempt to have a child by Hagar was based on God's word concerning an heir. Abram, now eighty-six years old, agreed with Sarai, and Hagar was soon pregnant with his child. Sarai, inflamed with jealousy, mistreated Hagar so that she fled. A messenger brought the desperate woman Yahweh's promise for the eldest biological son of Abram, with whom she was pregnant, and instructed her to return to her mistress.

*How did Abram and Sarai demonstrate their faith in God's word in Genesis 15 and 16?*

Thirteen years after Abram's son was born to Hagar, Yahweh instituted with Abram the sign of circumcision as a symbol of his commitment to the covenant. The rite of circumcision was to be an ongoing physical sign of the parents' commitment. Circumcision, performed on the eighth day of a child's life, was passive for the recipient and would play a significant role in the symbolic and metaphorical use of this ritual. The rite of circumcision demonstrates that mere "physical descent from Abraham is not sufficient to make true Israelites" (Vos, 90).

At this time God also gave Abram and Sarai new names, Abraham and Sarah, as a sign of his continued commitment to give Abraham offspring through his wife. Abraham fell down and laughed because he was almost a century old and Sarah had lived some nine decades. He protested, saying that Ishmael could be his heir. Abraham was seventy-five years of age and Sarah sixty-five when Yahweh first promised him offspring, and twenty-four long years had passed. Moreover, Abraham and Sarah had had a biological son for thirteen years that they had thought was the answer to Yahweh's promise. It was Abraham's faith in Yahweh, along with many years believing that Ishmael was the son of promise, that explains, in part, his response to Yahweh here. Abraham's laughter suggests doubt, as well as, perhaps, the idea that siring a child at his age was funny. Still, the suggestion of Ishmael's being the heir demonstrated

Lot looked up and saw that the whole plain of the Jordan was well watered, like the garden of Yahweh, like the land of Egypt, toward Zoar. (Gen 13:10)
*A.D. Riddle/BiblePlaces.com*

The Dead Sea
*© 2018 Zondervan*

Salt deposits in the lower Dead Sea basin near the location of Sodom and Gomorrah
*Sean Pavone © 123RF.com*

faith—wrong-minded, but faith nonetheless. Abraham believed God's word and came to understand its meaning according to the categories of his life—namely, that he had a biological child when he was eighty-six. Yahweh insisted that, indeed, Abraham and Sarah would have a child who would be the offspring of promise.

Not long thereafter, Yahweh, in a bodily form, and two delegates paid a surprise visit to Abraham. While they ate a hastily prepared feast, which typified Abraham's kind hospitality, Yahweh informed Abraham that Sarah would deliver their son in one year. Sarah, eavesdropping, responded with laughter as her husband had: "After I am worn out and my master is old, will I now have this pleasure?" (18:12). The woman's laughter was foregrounded even further when Yahweh asked why she laughed, and she denied it. He insisted that she had.

The kinship between Yahweh and Abraham can be seen in their parting conversation. God decided not to hide his intentions from Abraham because of the blessing he had pronounced on him. He told Abraham that his two delegates were going to see if the towns of Sodom and Gomorrah were as sinful as they appeared. Abraham asked a question concerning the relationship of God's justice and his mercy: "Will you sweep away the righteous with the wicked?" (18:23). Readers, remembering the fear-inspiring flood, are well aware that Yahweh was willing to go to great lengths in his judgment. Remarkably, Abraham quantified the situation and asked Yahweh if he would relent for fifty righteous. When he agreed to the idea, Abraham negotiated the number down to ten. The storyteller then shifts the scene—from daylight and petitioning Yahweh to night in Sodom with the messengers of doom—so readers can find out if there were even ten.

When the delegates that appeared as men arrived in Sodom, Lot, apparently a prominent citizen who sat in the gate, urged them to stay at his house. After dinner, the men of the town surrounded Lot's house because they wanted to have sex with Lot's guests. Lot's hospitality was raised to new and morbid dimensions when he offered to let the men gang-rape his two daughters if they left the men alone. The response was a mob scene as Lot blocked their way to the house. Lot's guests pulled him in and shut the door—the reader may hear an echo of the ark's door being shut—and afflicted the men of the town with temporary blindness.

The visitors then convinced Lot to leave Sodom. And in a manner akin to his uncle, Lot persuaded his guests to spare Zoar from destruction (19:21; cf. Lynch, 156–57). Though they were instructed not to look back, Mrs. Lot could not resist and immediately was turned into a condiment. As the sun came up, Abraham stood where he had spoken to Yahweh and watched the smoke rise into the sky. There were not even ten. He did not know what the reader knows. What did he think regarding the fate of his nephew? How did this affect his view of Yahweh's wrath and mercy?

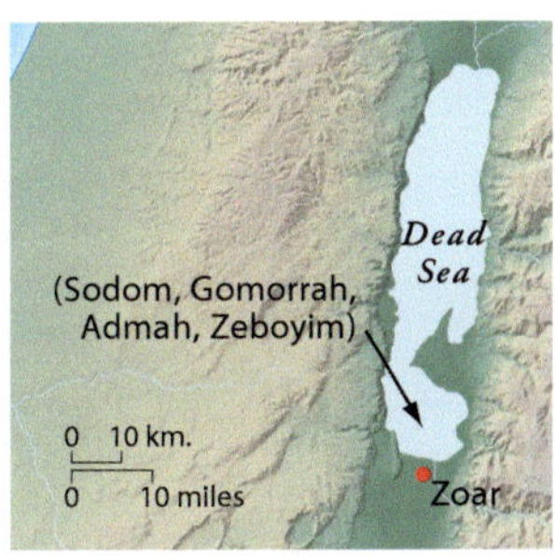


**Map 7-F:** Possible location of the cities of the plain

Meanwhile, Lot and his two daughters made their way to a cave outside Zoar (see Map 7-F). His virgin daughters figured they were in a hopeless situation as far as marriage and children went, hiding out alone with their father. Maybe they reflected on how Lot had offered them to the men of Sodom to rape and realized their relative worth to him. In any case, they got him drunk and raped him on two consecutive nights. Lot unintentionally committed incest with both of his daughters and became the father of his own grandchildren (see Case Study at the end of Chapter 1). Lot's story in this chapter moves between Sodom's perverse lust to his own daughters' perverse solution to their desperate situation (see Letellier, 187, 191). Thus, in the first two accounts of drunkenness in the Bible—Noah and Lot (see Table 7-G)—the three most cursed enemies of Israel were established—Canaan, Moab, and Ammon.

**Table 7-G:** Extended Echo in the Story of the Cities of the Plain

| Noah | Lot |
|---|---|
| the sinfulness of humankind (6:5–8) | the wickedness of the cities of the plain (18:20–21) |
| the door of the ark shut (7:16; cf. 6:16) | the door of the house shut (19:10–11) |
| all beings with breath killed in the judgment (7:21–23) | the wicked cities of the plain destroyed (19:24–26) |
| Noah's family escaped (7:23b–8:1) | Lot and his two daughters escaped (19:30) |
| Noah's drunkenness (9:20–23) | Lot's drunkenness (19:31–35) |
| Canaan cursed (9:24–27) | Moab and Ammon born (19:36–37; cf. Deut 23:3–6) |

The Moabites and Ammonites were not cursed because of their origin but because of their treachery against Israel (see Deut 23:3–6).

*What was similar between the cursed peoples of Canaan, Moab, and Ammon?*

The episode concerning Abimelech in Genesis 20 fits well within the closely related Abraham narratives. The reaffirmation of the promise in Genesis 17 is followed by an account of Abraham's interceding for Lot in chapters 18–19. And now, in chapter 20, God intercedes for Abraham, who, once again, claimed that Sarah was his sister. These sequential connections between episodes complement the symmetrical relationship of the episodes that span Genesis 12 through 20. The symmetry is based on literary framing—that is, the attempts to understand their life situation in accord with God's word in chapters 15, 16, and 17 are framed by Abraham's twice seeking to save his nephew in chapters 13–14 and 18–19, which are framed in turn by Abraham's deceptions concerning his wife in 12:10–20 and chapter 20 (see outline at the beginning of this Chapter).

When Abraham relocated in the western Negev region, he identified Sarah as his sister (see Table 8-A in Chapter 8). The reader may have at least two immediate responses. First, and merely a curiosity, Sarah's perspective of herself was that she was elderly and "withered" (18:12 NJPS). Yet, she was beautiful enough not only for Abraham to fear for himself but for Abimelech, the ruler of Gerar, to seek her in marriage. The narrative depictions of Sarah as strikingly attractive and as a ninety-year-old woman in menopause push against each other. Second, and significant theologically, Abraham made the same blunder two and a half decades earlier. The pattern of deception as the strategy to handle life's challenges is not only a habit for Abraham but becomes the deeply ingrained character of his son, grandson, and great-grandchildren.

After Abimelech had taken Sarah, God came to him in a dream and threatened deadly judgment on him. He responded, "Will you destroy an innocent nation?" (20:4), which echoes the sentiment of Abraham's former question, "Will you sweep away the righteous with the wicked?" (18:23). Abimelech told Yahweh that he did not know that Sarah was married, and besides, he had not touched her. God's response is instructive concerning his manner of directing human affairs: He had prevented Abimelech from touching her. It seems as if Abimelech was unaware of the activity of the spirit of God intervening. The mystery of God's outworking of his designs within the context of the human phenomenon will surface later in Genesis.

When Abimelech confronted Abraham, he found out, as does the reader for the first time, that Sarah was, in fact, his half-sister. As it turns out, each of the leading patriarchs and matriarchs of the chosen family are descendants of Terah (see Figure 7-A). The important issue in the story has been established: Abimelech has not had intimate relations with Sarah. If she conceives a child, it cannot be his.

After twenty-five long years of waiting (and nine chapters for readers), Abraham and Sarah have the offspring of promise in chapter 21. The child is named Isaac—"he laughs" (21:3 Fox)—because of the laughter of joy he brought to Sarah in her old age. The imagery of laughter reveals that Yahweh's power could change the laughter of Abraham's and Sarah's doubts (see chs. 17–18) to laughter of joy. Moreover, the laughter sets up the scene in which Sarah saw Ishmael making fun of Isaac. For this reason she had Abraham expel Hagar and Ishmael into the wilderness. In the latter part of chapter 21, God provided water for the dehydrated woman and her son, and Abraham secured a well of water named Beersheba from Abimelech.

The boy Isaac grew up, and Abraham is tested in the very next chapter. The long waiting followed immediately by a test demonstrates that the story of Abraham is primarily concerned with his response to God's word, especially the promised offspring. The "test" of Abraham rings with sounds that invite readers to compare it with his call. Genesis 12:1 and 22:2 each use threefold emphases of God's word as well as the fact that the construct "leave/go" (*lek leka*) appears only in these two contexts. The threefold qualifications in both the call and the test of Abraham are arranged climactically (see Table 7-H). The parallels between 12:1 and 22:2 and the use of narrative time illumines the test as the climactic episode in the Abraham stories.

*Why does so much time elapse between chapters 21 and 22 when time "goes by slowly" in chapters 12 to 21?*

| The Call—12:1 | The Test—22:2 |
|---|---|
| *Go forth* from | Take |
| your country, | your son, |
| your people, | your only son, |
| your father's house, | whom you love, |
| | and *go forth* |

**Table 7-H:** Comparing the Call and the Test of Abraham

When Yahweh called, Abraham responded. When Yahweh clarified the meaning of his word, Abraham believed, and he was counted as righteous. The testing in Genesis 22 reveals the nature of his obedience and faith. The issue was whether or not Abraham would sacrifice the son of promise, the son he loved, in response to God's word. This test shows the kind of devotion that Abraham had toward God. After Abraham obeyed, the messenger of Yahweh said, "Now I know that you fear God, because you have not withheld from me your son, your only son" (22:12). One may surmise, however, that God already knew his inner heart and that the test actually revealed the depth of Abraham's faith to himself and to readers.

This story pushes hard against the sensibilities of the reader. How could Abraham do such a thing? How could God ask Abraham to do such a thing? Why did God wish to demonstrate that Abraham was willing to kill his own son for the sake of his command? Before I had my own children, this passage made a lot more sense to me. I remember the first time I held my son. I was looking at him, and a question filled my mind: How could Abraham do it? I no longer knew how to make sense of Genesis 22. It is as strange as the most secret place in the Himalayan mountains. It is unthinkable. It exceeds the categories of rationality. It sounds like mental illness. Søren Kierkegaard, the Danish Christian philosopher of the early nineteenth century, in his book *Fear and*

*Trembling*, accented the insane dimensions of this example of Abraham's faith. I have to concur, at least at some level. If one of my students told me that God had told them to sacrifice their child—no matter how sound I usually found their judgment—I would use any means to stop them and get them help. Did Abraham wonder whether it was really God? What could he have been thinking?

The silence of the text itself compels readers toward these and other questions. The unstated aspects of the testing of Abraham episode exemplifies the biblical style of leaving much of the story in the "background" (see Auerbach, 12–14). Almost everything in Genesis 22 is left in the background. Abraham had three days during his travel to the place of sacrifice to think about what he was doing (see Sidebar 7-I). The silence creates tension between, among other things, the story of Abraham's persistent protest and bargaining with God regarding the destruction of Sodom and his quiet obedience in the sacrifice of Isaac (see Boehm).

*Why does biblical narrative leave so much in the background?*

What would he tell Sarah? This is the question hidden in the background that is hardest for me to grasp. I try to imagine the conversation that he might imagine having upon returning home—alone.

"Where is Isaac?" she might begin.

"I probably should have talked to you before I left . . ."

"We can talk later. Where is Isaac?"

"That's the thing. You know how sometimes God talks to me?"

"Yes, I know. Where's Isaac?"

"You are not going to believe what God told me to do."

And that's the thing. How could Sarah, how could anyone, conceive of God telling Abraham to sacrifice his son? Yet, that is exactly the circumstance in which Abraham—and Isaac (What did he say before he let his father bind him?)—obeyed his God. One of the traditional Judaic interpretations holds that Abraham did tell Sarah what he was going to do before he left and that she died of grief, either on the spot or after his leaving. This view takes note that the next chapter begins with her death. All such questions that readers have pondered continue to be answered by the silence of the text. Whatever Abraham was thinking and whether or not he told Sarah—at all—are among the many things that remain in the invisible background of the story.

*The Sacrifice of Isaac* (1602) by Caravaggio
*Public Domain*

## Sidebar 7-I: Road to Godforsakenness

Gerhard von Rad wrote, "Isaac is the child of promise. In him every saving thing that God has promised to do is invested and guaranteed. The point here is not a natural gift, not even the highest, but rather the disappearance from Abraham's life of the whole promise. Therefore, unfortunately, one can only answer all plaintive scruples about this narrative by saying that it concerns something much more frightful than child sacrifice. It has to do with a road out into Godforsakenness, a road on which Abraham does not know that God is only testing him" (244).

Regarding von Rad's comment, R. W. L. Moberly surmises, "The resonances of 'road to Godforsakenness' with Jesus' cry on the cross, 'My God, my God, why have you forsaken me?' (Matt 27:46; Mark 15:34) indicate that von Rad is interpreting Abraham by analogy with Jesus, as one who embodies the dynamics found supremely in the death of Jesus but also more generally in the life of faith" (182).

Moberly, R. W. L. "Living Dangerously: Genesis 22 and the Quest for Good Biblical Interpretation." Pages 181–97 in *The Art of Reading Scripture*. Edited by Ellen F. Davis and Richard B. Hays. Grand Rapids: Eerdmans, 2003.

von Rad, Gerhard. *Genesis: A Commentary*. Rev. ed. Philadelphia: Westminster, 1972.

Traditional site of Cave of Machpelah in Hebron, also known as the Tomb of the Patriarchs
*Library of Congress*

In the foreground the use of the leading word carries the key points of the episode. On the third day Abraham "*looked up and saw*" Mount Moriah in the distance (22:4). When Isaac asked where the lamb was, Abraham responded, "God *will see to* the sheep for his burnt offering, my son" (22:8 NJPS). After the messenger of Yahweh stopped Abraham, who held the knife raised above his beloved son, and commended his devotion to God, "Abraham *looked up, his eye fell upon* a ram, caught in the thicket by its horns" (22:13 NJPS). The ram was slaughtered and his son spared. The place was called Mount Moriah because on the mount of Yahweh "*there is vision*" (22:14 NJPS, emphasis added throughout this paragraph). The emphasis on seeing underlines the provision of Yahweh (see Lyons, 169).

After the climactic account of the near-sacrifice of Isaac, the Abraham narratives wrap up the way they began. When God's word came to Abraham, it included the promise of land, offspring, and blessing. At the close of his story he secures a plot of land (ch. 23), has a bride chosen for his son from Terah's family line (ch. 24), and bestows the inheritance to Isaac, his son of promise (beginning of ch. 25).

The accounts of acquiring the cave of Machpelah near Mamre (Hebron) as a burial plot for Sarah and securing Rebekah for Isaac each have many details. Regarding the former, the purchase of a burial plot is significant because it is the only piece of land Abraham legally owns. Regarding the latter, the threefold repetition in chapter 24 of the account of Abraham's servant finding the right woman—he prayed that she would water

Well and watering trough outside of Beersheba (cf. Gen 24:19–20)

*Dr. Avishai Teicher Pikiwiki Israel/ CC BY 2.5*

the camels (24:12–14), she did water the camels (24:15–21), and he recounted to Laban the prayer for and her watering of the camels (24:42–47)—accents God's providence in bringing together Isaac and Rebekah (see Schnittjer, *OT*, 10–11).

The brief account of Abraham's six other sons (in addition to Ishmael and Isaac) through his second wife and the record of their descendants catch the first-time reader by surprise (25:1–8). The many chapters overshadowed by Abraham and Sarah's infertility, combined with the remarkable nature of his having two sons at ages eighty-six and one hundred, make it startling to consider that Abraham remarried and had a half a dozen sons between 137 and 175 years of age. These sons were sent away, again to the east, to ensure the inheritance of the promise to Isaac. This is followed by a list of twelve sons of Ishmael (see Figure 7-J). These remarkable events are passed over in the space of a few sentences, reinforcing the point that the Abrahamic narrative is not a biography or history in any general sense. Rather, it is the story of Yahweh's word to Abraham and the beginning of his fulfillment of that word, especially as it relates to the son of promise.

Ishmael — Nebaioth, Kedar, Adbeel, Mibsam, Mishma, Dumah, Massa, Hadad, Tema, Jetur, Naphish, Kedemah

**Figure 7-J:** The Family of Ishmael[a]

[a]Ishmael's twelve sons each became tribal leaders like the twelve sons of his half-nephew, Jacob. Whereas Isaac lived to 180 years of age and Jacob 147, Ishmael died at 137 years of age.

## ANOTHER LOOK

The Abraham narratives in Genesis demonstrate the power of God's word and his faithfulness to that word. What is less clear is why Yahweh called Abraham. The clues in the end of Genesis 11 suggest that Abraham was willing and possessed faith to do what Terah did not do, namely, to journey to the land of Canaan. But the question remains: Why did Yahweh call Abraham? Some perspective can be gained by comparing the account in Genesis to the retelling of the same events in the last chapter of Joshua.

At the end of his life, Joshua, the great military leader and successor of Moses, assembled the people to issue them an important challenge. As a set-up to his challenge, Joshua retold the story of the nation of Israel from the calling of Abraham through the conquest of the land of Canaan several centuries later. That is, he summarized in about a dozen verses the entire narrative from Genesis 12 through Joshua 24. In the course of retelling the story, Joshua included two facts—new facts for readers—that were the key points in his challenge, points that were not mentioned in the pentateuchal narratives.

Joshua told the people that Abraham's father, Terah, worshiped other gods and that the Israelites who had lived in Egypt had also worshiped other gods. He began, "Long ago your ancestors, including Terah the father of Abraham and Nahor, lived beyond the Euphrates River *and worshiped other gods*" (Josh 24:2, emphasis added). And he concluded, "Now fear Yahweh and serve him with all faithfulness. Throw away *the gods your ancestors worshiped beyond the Euphrates River and in Egypt*, and serve Yahweh"

(24:14, emphasis added). These details are not recorded in Genesis or Exodus. The differences in Joshua's discourse can, in large part, be explained by the specific purpose for the narrative. He wanted the Israelites to reject the polytheistic practices of their Canaanite neighbors and to serve Yahweh alone. Joshua was right. Their failure to listen to Joshua's challenge would eventually lead to their exile into captivity.

The book of Genesis and the last discourse of Joshua offer two different, though complementary, interpretations of the selfsame events. The different emphases reflect the different purposes of the respective accounts. Joshua includes the detail about Terah's devotion to false deities in order to recommend his listeners to singular devotion to Yahweh (for an example of a later Judaic imaginative extension of Terah's idolatry, see Jubilees 12:1–8, 12–15). Why did the narrator of Genesis decide not to include this detail in his version of the calling of Abraham? Why did he tell the story of Abraham's call as he did?

Genesis gives no reason why Yahweh called Abraham. It could be that the narrator wished to emphasize the mysterious ways of Yahweh. This is probably true, but there also seems to be a more significant theological issue.

Many children, including my own, go through a stage where they ask their parents "Why?" about this or that. The parent explains. The child responds by asking why to the new answer. After several levels of explanation are given and the child continues to inquire, "Why? Why?" the parent may respond, "Just because." Some children are persistent and say, "Because why?" The parent may respond, "Because I said." If the child goes on to ask, "Why did you say that?" the parent may answer, "I said it because I said it."

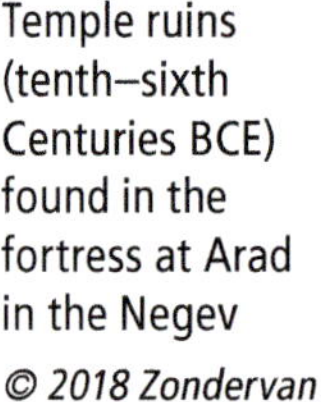

Temple ruins (tenth–sixth Centuries BCE) found in the fortress at Arad in the Negev
*© 2018 Zondervan*

Greater Negev
*Isaiah and Abby Cramer*

In the natural course of things, curious children learn that some things of life are *just because.*

The account of Abraham's call in Genesis is based solely on Yahweh's word. Why did Yahweh choose Abraham? Just because. *That Yahweh called him* is the deepest level of meaning in the Genesis story. The Abrahamic narrative does not point back to the reasons for Abraham's call but forward to Abraham's future. It is about a future that only Yahweh can create by the power of his word. The retelling of the same events by Joshua demonstrates that there are other ways to tell the story. The narrator of Genesis offers a particular interpretation of this event to readers. Yahweh called Abraham.

*What was the reason for the call of Abraham?*

Many aspects of later narratives in the Hebrew Scriptures will come back to the call of Abraham. In the beginning of Exodus, for example, Yahweh decided to deliver the Israelites from the Egyptian bondage because he remembered his promise to Abraham. Later in the book, he decided not to destroy the people after they rebelled with the golden calf when Moses reminded him of his promise to Abraham. The logic of these stories and of many others is ultimately rooted in the faithfulness of Yahweh to uphold his promise. The power of Yahweh's word can be seen in the "just because" theology of the narrative of Abraham's call. Yahweh may have had his reasons, but biblical readers simply hear his word.

The location of the near-sacrifice of Isaac is a point of contact for later biblical stories. Mount Moriah was the future locale of the temple (2 Chr 3:1). This is the place where the name of Yahweh would dwell. Moreover, Christian readers reflect on the fact that many years later, a short distance from Mount Moriah just outside the city of Jerusalem, the Messiah died on a hill known as Golgotha, the Skull. The story of Isaac's would-be sacrifice, as powerful as it has always been, highlights the significance of the death of the Messiah, the Son of God (see Rom 8:32). The close spatial proximity between the near death of one son and the crucifixion of the other son heightens the symbolic relationship between them.

## INTERACTIVE WORKSHOP

### *Chapter Summary*

Yahweh called and Abram obeyed. Yahweh promised him land, offspring, and blessing. The many chapters of waiting unfold the faith of Abraham and Sarah. Demonstrating obedience and faith were not enough, in this case. As soon as they had the son of promise (in narrative time), Abraham was tested—the climax of the story.

### *Can You Explain the Key Terms?*

- circumcise
- covenant
- laugh
- offspring
- test

### *Challenge Questions*

1. What is the significance of Genesis 12:1–3 for the entire Torah?
2. How does narrative time reinforce the main themes of the Abrahamic narrative?
3. How do we determine whether or not the Abrahamic covenant was irrevocable?
4. How does the account of the "test" of Abraham in Genesis 22 relate to his calling and faith?

### *Advanced Questions*

1. Answer the questions raised in Genesis 18 and 20 concerning God's willingness, or lack thereof, to bring judgment on the righteous along with the unrighteous—"Will you sweep away the righteous with the wicked?" (18:23) and "Will you destroy an innocent nation?" (20:4).
2. What evidence explains if it is normative or exceptional that Abimelech was unaware of God's working in his life (20:6)?
3. How can two accounts of the exact same events (like the narratives of the call of Abraham in Genesis 12 and Joshua 24) record different facts for different purposes and yet still both be true and avoid pluralism?

*4. Offer a translation of Genesis 14:18 that emphasizes the themes of righteousness and peace that are not always evident in English translations.

*5. What is the theological significance of the wordplays on "laugh" (*tsahaq* and *yitshaq*) in Genesis 17:17; 18:12–13, 15; 21:3, 9?

*6. Should the Nifal of *brk* in Genesis 12:3d be translated as passive or reflective? Be sure to compare parallels like Genesis 48:20 (see Chisholm, *From Exegesis*, 15, 18) versus Psalm 72:17 (see Schnittjer, *OT*, 491–92).

### *Research Project Ideas*

Investigate how narrative time and symmetrical literary structure reinforce the meaning of the Abraham narrative.

Evaluate the placement and meaning of the Lot stories in the Abraham narrative.

Study the foreground and background of the testing of Abraham narrative (see Auerbach) or interact with Kierkegaard's reading of the poetic silence of Abraham's faith in *Fear and Trembling*.

## *The Next Step*


Auerbach, Erich. *Mimesis: The Representation of Reality in Western Literature.* Translated by Willard R. Trask. Princeton: Princeton University Press, 1953.

Block, Daniel I. *Covenant: The Framework of God's Grand Plan of Redemption.* Grand Rapids: Baker Academic, 2021.

Boehm, Omri. "The Binding of Isaac: An Inner-Biblical Polemic on the Question of 'Disobeying' a Manifestly Illegal Order." *Vetus Testamentum* 52 (2002): 1–12.

———. "Child Sacrifice, Ethical Responsibility and the Existence of the People of Israel." *Vetus Testamentum* 54 (2004): 145–56.

Chisholm, Robert B., Jr. *1 & 2 Samuel.* Teach the Text. Grand Rapids: Baker Books, 2013.

———. *From Exegesis to Exposition: A Practical Guide to Using Biblical Hebrew.* Grand Rapids: Baker, 1998.

Clines, David J. A. *The Theme of the Pentateuch*, 2d ed. Journal for the Study of the Old Testament Supplement Series 10. Sheffield: Sheffield Academic, 1978, 1997.

Geoghegan, Jeffrey C. "The Exodus of Abraham." *Bible Review* 21 (2005): 16–25, 43–45.

Grisanti, Michael A. "Inspiration, Inerrancy, and the OT Canon: The Place of Textual Updating in an Inerrant View of Scripture." *Journal of the Evangelical Theological Society* 44.4 (2001): 577–98.

Jericke, Detlef. "Exodus Material in the Book of Genesis." Pages 137–56 in *Book-Seams in the Hexateuch I: The Literary Transitions between the Books of Genesis/Exodus and Joshua/Judges.* Edited by Christoph Berner and Harald Samuel. Forschungen zum Alten Testament 102. Tübingen: Mohr Siebeck, 2018.

Kierkegaard, Søren. *Fear and Trembling.* Edited and translated by Howard V. Hong and Edna H. Hong. Princeton: Princeton University Press, 1983.

Letellier, Robert Ignatius. *Day in Mamre Night in Sodom: Abraham and Lot in Genesis 18–19.* Biblical Interpretation 10. Leiden: Brill, 1995.

Levine, Amy-Jill and Mark Zvi Brettler. *The Bible With and Without Jesus: How Jews and Christians Read the Same Stories Differently.* New York: HarperOne, 2020.

Lynch, Matthew J. *Portraying Violence in the Hebrew Bible: A Literary and Cultural Study.* Cambridge: Cambridge University Press, 2021.

Lyons, Michael A. "The Aqedah as 'Template'? Genesis 22 and 1 Kings 17–18." *Journal for the Study of the Old Testament* 46.2 (2021): 161–76.

Morales, L. Michael. *Exodus Old and New: A Biblical Theology of Redemption.* Essential Studies in Biblical Theology 2. Downers Grove, IL: IVP Academic, 2020.

Postell, Seth D. "Abram as Israel, Israel as Abraham: Literary Analogy as Macro-Structural Strategy in the Torah." Pages 16–36 in *Text and Canon: Essays in Honor of John H. Sailhamer.* Edited by Robert L. Cole and Paul J. Kissling. Eugene, OR: Pickwick, 2017.

Sailhamer, John H. *The Pentateuch as Narrative: A Biblical-Theological Commentary.* Grand Rapids: Zondervan, 1992.

Schnittjer, Gary Edward, "The Blessing of Judah as Generative Expectation." *Bibliotheca Sacra* 177 (2020): 15–39.

———. *Old Testament Use of Old Testament.* Grand Rapids: Zondervan Academic, 2021.

———. "Your House Is My House: Exegetical Intersection within the Davidic Promise." *Bibliotheca Sacra* (forthcoming).

Vos, Geerhardus. *Biblical Theology: Old and New Testaments.* Grand Rapids: Eerdmans, 1948.

# 8 THE JACOB NARRATIVES

## *Genesis 25:19–36:43*

*Isaiah and Abby Cramer*

## GETTING STARTED

### *Focus Question*

In what sense did Jacob prevail?

### *Look for These Terms*

- birthright
- blessing
- Edom
- Israel
- Joseph
- Judah
- Laban

## AN OUTLINE

A. **Jacob at Home (25:19–27:40)**
  1. The birth and early problems between Jacob and Esau (25:19–34)
  2. Isaac deceived Abimelech and relocated to secure water and peace (26)
  3. Jacob deceived his father to secure the blessing he had for Esau (27:1–40)

B. **Jacob's Vision at Bethel (27:41–28:22)**

C. **Jacob in Laban's House (29–31)**
  1. Jacob came to Laban and made a bargain with him (29:1–20)
  2. Laban deceived Jacob (29:21–30)
  3. The fertility and growth of Jacob's family (29:31–30:24)
  4. The fertility and growth of Jacob's herds (30:25–43)
  5. Jacob deceived Laban (31:1–21)
  6. Jacob left Laban and made a covenant with him (31:22–55)

D. **Israel Wrestled with God (32)**

E. **Jacob Returned to His Homeland (33–35)**
  1. The reunion of Jacob and Esau (33)
  2. Simeon and Levi deceived the Shechemites and upset the Canaanites (34)
  3. Jacob returned to Bethel; the birth of Benjamin and the deaths of Rachel and Isaac (35)

## A READING

The conflict between God's word and the human revolution runs through Jacob's story, primarily within his own person. He wrestled with his own conflicted inclinations. He listened to God and trusted him, yet the painful path of his life offered him many occasions to apply his own ingenuity and deception. Further, Jacob's tendency to destructive favoritism resulted in the defining problem for his wives and children. Nowhere does the conflict between God's word and the sinfulness of humanity intertwine more thoroughly than in the Jacob narratives.

Jacob seems to embody at one time both the human problem and human hope. He wrestled with his brother even before he was born, and he wrestled with God or a celestial delegate when he was old (see Hos 12:3–4a). He was born clutching his brother's heel and was named Jacob (Gen 25:26). It was foretold that his brother would bow down to him (27:29). Thus, Jacob seems symbolically to represent both the offspring of the snake bruising the heel and the offspring of the woman pressing down on the offspring of the snake (3:15). The possible symbolic significance of his story is heightened when it is remembered that Genesis ends with the events related to Israel's death and burial. He is a dominant figure throughout the second half of the book.

*How does Jacob symbolize both the human problem and its solution?*

The most challenging factor in the Jacob narratives is Jacob himself. Jacob is human enough, and his life embodies, at a whole new level, the deceptive tendencies of his parents and grandparents. To the end of his life he never seemed to make progress in relation to his addiction to deception. In several contexts he exhibits enough presumption to make most readers cringe. Yet, it is he for whom Israel is named. Jacob is named Israel because he "wrestled with God and with humans and prevailed" (32:28 lit.). The renaming of Jacob foregrounds the question at the heart of the matter: In what sense did Jacob prevail?

If readers approach the Jacob narratives to understand in what sense he overcame, they are apt to be surprised by their discoveries about the man renamed Israel. There is no need to set aside his sinful tendencies—not at all. Rather, the challenge is to discover the sense in which he prevailed in spite of his sinfulness. If we compare Jacob with each of the main characters within his story, his single positive distinct characteristic becomes increasingly evident. Throughout his life Jacob learned of God, interpreted the significance of his life in light of God, and gave God the credit for his accomplishments. Although he never loosened his commitment to deception as a strategy to deal with the problems of life, Jacob learned of God and grew, a little.

*What is the outcome of comparing Jacob and the other persons in the Jacob narrative?*

The Jacob narratives exhibit many of the same features already evident in Genesis. The sequences of stories use mirror imaging

"So Jacob called the place Peniel, saying 'It is because I saw God face to face, and yet my life was spared'" (Gen 32:30)
Goats near Peniel
*Todd Bolen/ BiblePlaces.com*

(see outline above). Several episodes use leading words from earlier contexts, like "face" (compare the narrative of Cain and Abel, 4:5, 6, 14, 16) and the word cluster "eyes/looking/seeing" (compare the Abraham narratives, e.g., NJPS of 22:4, 8, 13, 14). In the cases of Jacob's two most significant rivals, his brother and his uncle, the narrator uses wordplays on "red" and "white." Jacob also had twelve sons, the names of whom are often wordplays. But the most pervasive element throughout this section of Genesis, as well as the next, is deception.

The crucial aspect of the Jacob narratives, for the meaning of his prevailing, is the development of his character in relation to the other key characters. Isaac and Rebekah struggled with infertility. Unlike the story of Abraham and Sarah, however, readers only have to wait for one verse for Rebekah to get pregnant (25:21). Narrative time instantly passes by the two decades that Isaac and Rebekah waited, in order to focus on the story line (see Table 10-E in Chapter 10). Her pregnancy was difficult because of the twins wrestling within her. She prayed and the word of Yahweh came to her: "Two nations are in your womb, and two peoples from within you will be separated; one people will be stronger than the other, and the older will serve the younger" (25:23). This oracle will prove significant in several ways. The older brother, Esau, was born red and hairy, and Jacob, the heel-grabber, followed, clutching Esau's heel.

The fighting twins were born into a dysfunctional family, and both brothers learned the wrong lessons too well. Isaac loved Esau and Rebekah loved Jacob. Within a paragraph the brothers grow up and Esau trades his birthright to Jacob for a bowl of "red stew" (25:30). The narrator explains the humiliating fact that Esau was called "Edom" ("red") to commemorate forever the red soup for which the Edomites are named. As the people of Israel hear this story, it would perpetually ridicule their bitter enemies the Edomites as the red-soup people.

The parental patterns are a virtual copy of Abraham and Sarah's (see Table 8-A; Ross, 271). During a famine-induced sojourn Isaac and Rebekah told King Abimelech that they were siblings. Abimelech's observation of Isaac and Rebekah "playing" (26:8 lit.) or "caressing" (NIV) caused him to investigate and avoid the mistake he had made with Isaac's parents. Abimelech learned from his mistakes even while the chosen family repeated theirs over and over. The only other thing we are told about Isaac is that his servants, re-digging the same wells Abraham's servants had dug, quarreled with Abimelech's servants, again as Abraham's servants had, until they secured the well at Beersheba. Another déjà vu. Genesis 26 closes with Esau marrying two Canaanite women, which brought grief to Isaac and Rebekah.

**Table 8-A:** Comparing the "She's My Sister" Stories in Genesis‡

| Abram/Sarai—12:10–20 | Abraham/Sarah—20:1–18 | Isaac/Rebekah—26:1–11 |
|---|---|---|
| Famine in the land (12:10) | — | Famine in the land (26:1) |
| Beauty of Sarai (12:11) | — | Beauty of Rebekah (26:7) |
| Deception as "sister" (12:13) | Deception as "sister" (20:2) | Deception as "sister" (26:7) |
| Fear of death (12:13) | Fear of death (20:11) | Fear of death (26:7) |
| Egyptians saw her (12:14) | — | Men of that place asked (26:7) |
| Taken by pharaoh (12:15) | Taken by Abimelech (20:2) | — |
| Wealth to Abram (12:16) | Wealth to Abraham (20:14–16) | — |
| Plagues (12:17) | Warning dream (20:7–8) | Observed by Abimelech (26:8) |
| Abram rebuked (12:18–19) | Abraham rebuked (20:9–10) | Isaac rebuked (26:9) |
| Expulsion (12:20) | Prayer of Abraham and restoration of child-bearing (20:17) | — |

‡Adapted from Alan P. Ross, *Creation and Blessing: A Guide to the Study and Exposition of the Book of Genesis* (Grand Rapids: Baker, 1988), 271. Used by permission.

By chapter 27 Isaac was old and had weak eyes. He was ready to grant his blessing on the son he loved. While Esau, in order to get the blessing, was out hunting game to prepare the dish Isaac liked, Rebekah concocted a scheme to secure the blessing for the son she loved. Perhaps she justified deceiving her husband because of the oracle she was given concerning Jacob before he was born. She disguised Jacob so that he was able to trick three of the four senses of his father that still worked. He sounded like Jacob, but the dish tasted right and he felt and smelled like Esau. The disguise mocks Esau. Rebekah only needed to attach a dead goat to Jacob. Jacob felt like a dead goat and smelled like a dead goat. This convinced his father he was Esau. Isaac "accidentally" blessed Jacob. "May nations serve you and peoples bow down to you. Be lord over your brothers, and may the sons of your mother bow down to you. May those who curse you be cursed and those who bless you be blessed" (27:29).

It is useful to keep this blessing in mind, along with Yahweh's word to Rebekah, when approaching Genesis 37 and 49 and Numbers 24. Many years later Joseph brought Ephraim and Manasseh for Jacob's blessing (Gen 48). Though Jacob's eyes were weak, he could "see" well enough to switch his hands and bless the grandsons as he desired, to the frustration of their father.

*What is the significance of the similarities and differences between Isaac and Jacob?*

When Isaac and the son he loved realized they had been tricked, Esau made a murderous oath. Rebekah again attempted to help fulfill Yahweh's word concerning Jacob by suggesting that her son seek shelter with her brother Laban. She told Isaac, however, that she was disgusted with the Canaanite women that Esau had married and persuaded her husband to send Jacob to his uncle's house with his father's blessing. Meanwhile, readers look over Esau's shoulder as he considered these matters and made the erroneous judgment that marrying one of Ishmael's daughters would correct his situation (28:6–9). So far, the brothers differed only in their predicted futures. Jacob had not yet met God.

## Sidebar 8-B: The Line of Esau

Genesis 36 has several interesting items, of which I will mention four. First, Genesis 36 presents several lists associated with Edom in some way:

- Esau's wives (vv. 1–5)
- Esau's sons and grandsons (vv. 9–14)
- Edomite clans (vv. 15–19)
- Horites in the land of Edom (vv. 20–30)
- Early Edomite kings (vv. 31–39)
- Edomite clans and land area (vv. 40–43)

Second, several persons included in the Edomite lists sound like people mentioned elsewhere in the Scriptures. *Reuel* may be the ancestor of the clan from which Moses's father-in-law hailed (36:4, 13, 17; Num 10:29); *Amalek* is mentioned (Gen 36:12; Exod 17; Deut 25:17–19; 1 Sam 15); some wonder about a possible relationship between *Eliphaz*, father of the Teman clan, and Eliphaz the Temanite (Gen 36:15; Job 2:11) or if *Bela son of Beor* is connected with Balaam son of Beor (Gen 36:32; Num 22:5).

Third, notice the similarity in the description of Esau and Jacob in comparison to that of Abraham and Lot. In both cases the relative outside of the line of promise left for land in the east by his own choice.

> Now Lot, who was moving about with Abram, also had flocks and herds and tents. But the land could not support them while they stayed together, for their possessions were so great that they were not able to stay together. . . . So Lot chose for himself the whole plain of the Jordan and set out toward the east. The two men parted company: Abram lived in the land of Canaan, while Lot lived among the cities of the plain and pitched his tents near Sodom. (Gen 13:5–6, 11–12, emphasis added)

> Esau took his wives and sons and daughters and all the members of his household, as well as his livestock and all his other animals and all the goods he had acquired in Canaan, and moved to a land some distance from his brother Jacob. Their possessions were too great for them to remain together; the land where they were staying could not support them both because of their livestock. So Esau (that is, Edom) settled in the hill country of Seir. (36:6–8, emphasis added)

Fourth, the list of kings in verses 31–39 dates from after the time of Saul. Notice 36:31: "These were the kings who reigned in Edom *before any Israelite king reigned*" (emphasis added). This makes the Davidic era the earliest that the book of Genesis could have come into its final form.

Jacob camped near the town of Luz on his way north to Haran. He had a vision of celestial delegates going up and down stairs reaching into the heavens. Yahweh spoke to Jacob and promised him land, offspring, and blessing, just as he had to his father and grandfather. In addition, Yahweh committed himself to protecting Jacob throughout his life. When Jacob woke up, he anointed his stone pillow—the end of each of the three major sections of the Jacob story (i.e., home, Haran, and home) were marked by a stone monument (see 28:18–19; 31:45–47; 35:14–15; Fokkelman, 47)—and renamed the place Bethel, "house of God," and made a vow to Yahweh. The vow sounds somewhat presumptuous, making his devotion to Yahweh dependent on physical protection. Whatever his motives, the vow at least demonstrated that Yahweh was now part of Jacob's life.

**Map 8-C:** The Journeys of Jacob

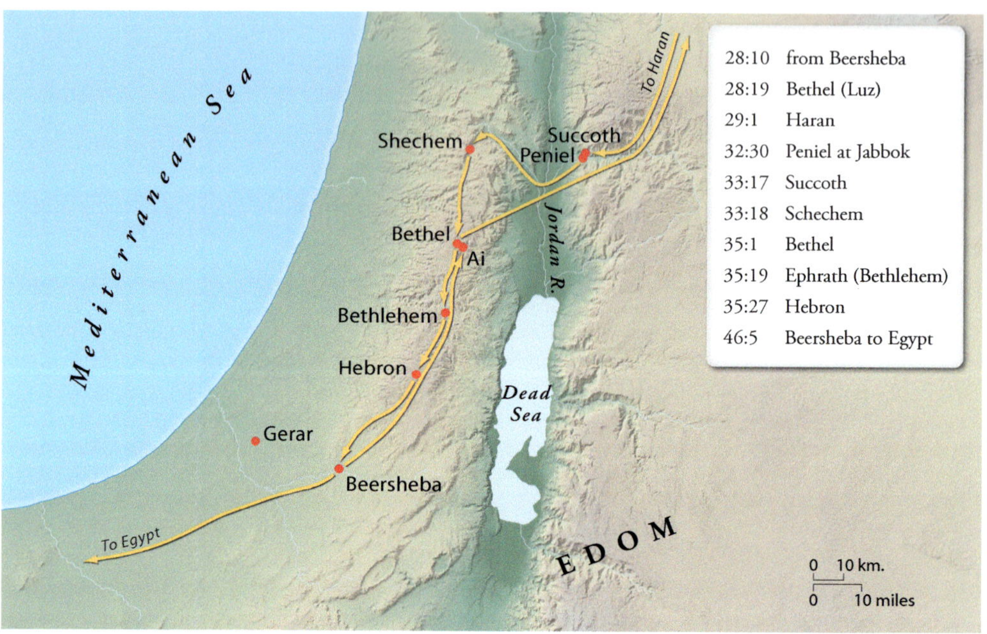

Well at Haran

*Mustafa Çukur © 123RF.com*

Arriving at Haran, Jacob met Rachel, his cousin, at a well and kissed her. She took him to her father, his uncle Laban, who kissed his nephew and said that they were of the same bone and the same flesh. Not only was this true, but it also signaled the mutual deception and mutual presumption that these two would exhibit toward each other. The relationship between Laban and Jacob became that of employer and employee. First Jacob worked for Laban to earn wives and then to earn cattle (see 29:15–18; 30:28–29).

After working for Laban for seven years to earn Rachel as his wife—told in as many verses—Jacob woke up for the first time as a married man and realized he was on the wrong end of a swindle. He had married, accidentally for him and on purpose for his mother's brother, the wrong cousin. The deceitful siblings, Laban and Rebekah, had a way of helping things work out as they thought they should. Jacob spent seven days with Leah before he married her sister Rachel. Then he began another seven years to earn her again. Jacob began his dysfunctional home life along the lines he had learned growing up: He loved Rachel and not Leah.

The storyteller narrates the next thirteen years of Jacob's life in two panels based on the structure of days in Genesis—"and there was evening, and there was morning" (Gen 1; see Table 8-D). The reader stays home with the little harem for seven years, wherein Yahweh grows Jacob's family at home in the evenings. Next, the story goes on the job with Jacob in the daylight for six years; this time God grows his herds. The dominant issue in both narrative panels is the life-giving power of God, thus highlighting his role as the Creator.

**Table 8-D:** A Day in the Life of Jacob for Thirteen Years

| Genesis 29:31–30:24 | Genesis 30:25–43 |
|---|---|
| • evenings at home | • days at work in the fields |
| • procreating with wives and concubines | • breeding cattle |
| • growing family | • growing herds—striped, speckled, spotted |

The narrator explains that Yahweh gave children to Leah but not to Rachel, in counter-direction to Jacob's affections. Leah had Reuben, Simeon, Levi, and Judah. The baby contest between the sisters was on. Rachel in a jealous rage demanded children from Jacob. Jacob asked, "Am I in the place of God?" (30:2), implying, not too subtly, that God alone is the life-giver. He recognized the power of the Creator. In the final chapter of Genesis Rachel's first son would ask the same question, for different reasons, of his brothers.

*Public Domain*

*Viktor Loki/Shutterstock.com*

Mandrakes, like those Leah traded to Rachel for a conjugal visit from Jacob (Gen 30:14–15), were believed to have aphrodisiac powers and were associated with ancient fertility rites.

Jacob's nocturnal responsibilities were expanded when he had relations with Rachel's maidservant Bilhah. At one point the sister wives barter over conjugal relations with Jacob so Rachel could acquire mandrakes (30:14–15). Since ancients could consider mandrakes as an ancient aphrodisiac, Rachel may have thought they could help her infertility. Rachel took credit for the two sons Bilhah bore, claiming, "A struggle of God have I struggled with my sister; yes, and I have prevailed!" (30:8 Fox). The self-proclaimed victory sounded hollow—even to Rachel—in relation to commendation that Jacob would later receive (32:28). Rachel's "victory" was short-lived, for Leah's maidservant, Zilpah, bore two sons, and Leah herself had another two sons and a daughter, Dinah.

Leah and Rachel each demonstrated self-centered motives for having children, in both cases caused by Jacob's favoritism. The children were a means to the sisters' own personal ends. Leah hoped that the sons she bore would cause Jacob to regard her more highly, so she named each son in relation to her desire to gain her husband's affections. She explained, for example, Reuben's name, "It is because Yahweh has seen my misery. Surely my husband will love me now" (29:32), and regarding Levi, "Now at last my husband will become attached to me, because I have borne him three sons" (29:34; also see 29:33; 30:20). The only exception is Judah, whose name reflects gratitude to Yahweh for the son himself: "She conceived again, and when she gave birth to a son she said, 'This time I will praise [*ydh*] Yahweh.' So she named him Judah [*yehudah*]" (29:35a; and see Schnittjer, 17–18).

When God finally remembered Rachel and gave her a son, she named him Joseph because she wanted "another son" (30:24). Her first son was for her, tragically, simply the initial step of catching up to her sister. The morbid irony was that giving birth to the next one would kill her. The mothers of the twelve children, eleven brothers and one sister so far, taught the children, by example, to compete for the affections of their father. They learned the lesson well.

*What were Leah's motives for bearing children? What were Rachel's motives?*

After Joseph was born, the point of view of the narrative shifts from evenings at home with the competing mothers to Jacob's days at work with the mating cattle. Jacob was ready to leave after earning Rachel, but Laban hired him to stay on and earn some animals—those striped, speckled, and spotted. Jacob agreed and used an unusual method of animal husbandry that included putting sticks with white stripes before the strong animals while they were mating. Later Jacob explained to his wives that he had had a vision, which he appears to have applied literally (31:10–13). The trick with the white-striped sticks worked. The strong animals had streaked, spotted, and speckled calves; and the weak animals had plain, weak calves for Laban. The "white" (*lavan*) sticks was a wordplay on Laban's name (*lavan*). Years before Jacob had used red soup to get his red brother's double portion of the inheritance, and in this context he uses white-striped sticks to acquire the better part of "uncle White's" livestock.

After working for Laban for two decades, Jacob decided, for several reasons, that it was time to leave. The dialogue in Genesis 31:1–16 reveals three different interpretations of Jacob's wealth and his duty. First, Jacob overheard his brothers-in-law complaining that he had taken all of their father's wealth. They, like Esau, were losing their inheritance to Jacob. Second, Jacob listened to God's word. Yahweh told him to return to the land of his fathers. Jacob called his two wives out to the field and explained his view of things to them:

> "I see that your father's attitude toward me is not what it was before, but the *God of my father has been with me*. You know that I've worked for your father with all my strength, yet your father has cheated me by changing my wages ten times. However,

*God has not allowed him to harm . . . God has taken away your father's livestock and has given them to me.*" (31:5–7, 9, emphasis added)

Third, Leah and Rachel believed that the wealth that God gave to Jacob belonged to them (31:14–16). The similarity between the views of Jacob, his wives, and his brothers-in-law is that each thought the wealth belonged to them. The difference between the interpretation of Jacob and of Laban's sons and daughters was qualitative. For Jacob, the important point was not that the livestock belonged to him but that they were given to him by God.

Jacob gathered his family and his animals and fled south, back toward Canaan. Laban gathered his family and pursued his nephew. God came to Laban in a dream the night before he caught up with Jacob and instructed him not to interfere with Jacob. Laban, who had commented on their similarity when they first met, fumed, "What have you done? You've deceived me" (31:26). He went on to accuse Jacob of stealing his gods. Jacob retorted with a rash oath, "If you find anyone who has your gods, that person shall not live" (31:32). He did not realize that his beloved Rachel had stolen them. His word of judgment would come to pass soon enough (see discussion of the birth of Benjamin in Chapter 10). Rachel deceived her husband and her father. She had saved the gods at the cost of her own life.

Jacob and Laban faced off and offered diametrically opposed interpretations of Jacob's wealth. Jacob first rehearsed his integrity and hard work and concluded: "*If the God of my father, the God of Abraham and the Fear of Isaac, had not been with me*, you would surely have sent me away empty-handed. *But God has seen* my hardship and the toil of my hands, and last night he rebuked you" (31:42, emphasis added). Laban countered, "The women are *my* daughters, the children are *my* children, and the flocks are *my* flocks. *All you see is mine*" (31:43, emphasis added). Both men were shrewd, had worked hard, and had a stake in the family and livestock. The difference between their viewpoints is striking. Laban claimed as his own all that belonged to Jacob. Jacob gave the credit to God. The two made a covenant and went in opposite directions.

*How was Jacob's view of his possessions different from Laban's view of Jacob's possessions?*

Jacob escaped from Laban. Traveling south, home, he learned that Esau and four hundred men were traveling north from the land of Edom to meet him. The narrative use of space heightens the suspense of Jacob's predicament between his mother's brother and his own brother (see Figure 8-E). He had acquired the wealth of both men, if he could survive. Fearing Esau, Jacob sent him a series of gifts and stayed behind.

The context is dense with wordplays. Jacob/*ya'aqov* was alone at the Jabbok/*yabboq* River until he wrestled/*ye'aveq* with someone in the dark. He wrestled with the mysterious figure until daybreak. Jacob agreed to release his opponent if he received a blessing.

**Figure 8-E:** Jacob Fleeing Esau and Laban

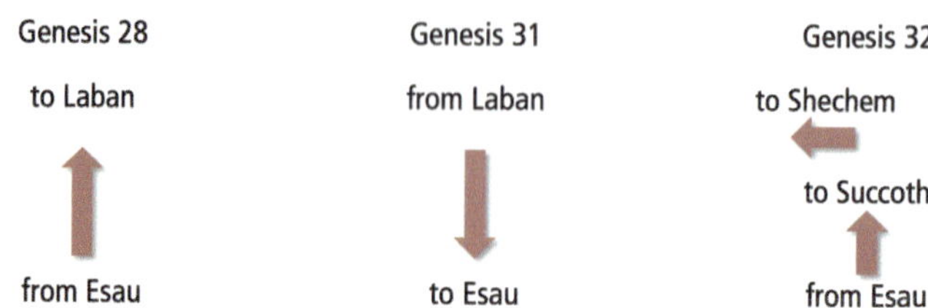


The man responded, "Your name will no longer be Jacob, but Israel, because you have struggled with God and with humans and have overcome" (32:28). Jacob called the place Peniel because "I saw God face to face" (32:30; note that the word for "face" is used five times in the Hebrew of 32:20–21 [vv. 21–22 in Fox/Hebrew]; cf. Zakovitch, 103–4). Later that morning Jacob met Esau and said, "To see your face is like seeing the face of God" (33:10).

Jacob and Esau were both wealthy men. Esau seemed content with what he had. Yet, when Jacob repeated that he had all he needed, he added that God had been gracious to him (33:11). Esau invited Jacob to follow him to the land of Edom. Jacob lied and deceived his brother by assuring him that he would follow, slowly but surely, behind him to Edom. Esau left and headed south, away from the promised land. Jacob turned around and headed northwest to Succoth and later west to Shechem in the land of promise (see Map 8-F).

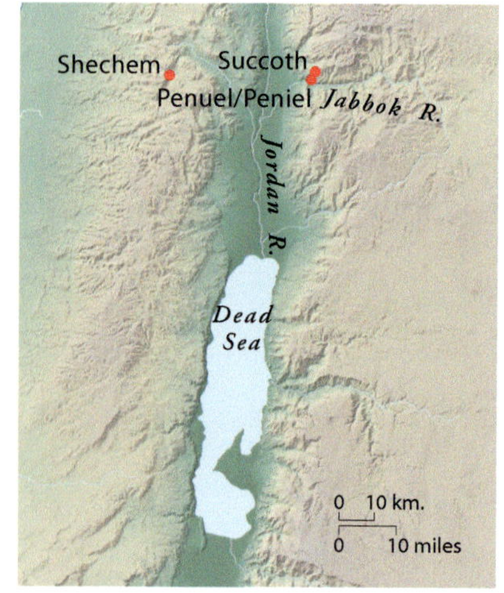


**Map 8-F:** Places Associated with Jacob in Genesis 32–34.

Jacob survived, but the peace he hoped for continued to evade his grasp. He and his family lived near Shechem for several years, maybe up to a decade (see discussion in Another Look in Chapter 10). During this time his eleven oldest children grew up. They had been approximately between the ages of six (Dinah) and thirteen (Reuben) when they left Haran. Shechem, the son of Hamor, the ruler of the area, was attracted to Dinah, who was a young woman by this time. The lack of detail opens itself to several ways to handle the sense of Shechem raping the girl he loved (see Goldingay, 531–33) While the majority view is that he raped her (NIV, NRSVue, NJPS; Peterson, 274), the text focuses on the outcome rather than the action—he degraded her and wanted to marry her (see van Wolde; Richter, 65). Jacob said nothing and did nothing. Two of Dinah's full brothers, Simeon and Levi, deceived the men of Shechem by insisting that they all be circumcised for the marriage to take place. To avenge their defiled sister, the two brothers killed all the men of the city while they were recovering from circumcision. As a result, Jacob was afraid that his sons' vengeance could incite the Canaanites to trouble his family.

Hills and mountains of Edom

*Isaiah and Abby Cramer*

Genesis 35 records several stories, not all in their sequence (the death of Isaac is a clear example). The challenges of the chronological versus the narrative sequence of Genesis 34–35 are treated along with other matters of this sort in Chapter 10 (see especially the discussion related to Tables 10-E and 10-F).

The family traveled south to Bethel, and Jacob built an altar to God. The last time he had left Bethel he met Rachel. This time he lost her. She died while giving birth to Benjamin, near Bethlehem as they were traveling south. Jacob had only his two youngest sons by whom to remember his beloved Rachel. Jacob's love for her, redirected toward her sons, continued to create contention within the dysfunctional family. None of these problems can justify Reuben's incest with (and possibly rape of) his stepmother Bilhah, Rachel's former slave (35:22). Jacob's family is deeply troubled.

*For Jacob, what is the importance of Joseph and Benjamin?*

Chapter 35 closes with a list of Jacob's sons and a report of the death of Isaac. Table 8-G lists the sons by mother, as in 35:23–26, and by birth order, as in 29:31–30:24 (not including Dinah). The sons of Israel are ranked in various ways in the Torah. The arrangement of the tribes around the dwelling of God in Numbers, for example, is affected by the mother of each tribal head as well as by the narrative accounts in Genesis and Exodus (see Chapter 21). In this respect the stories of the ancestors explain even the particular identity of the tribes of Israel.

**Table 8-G:**
The Sons of Jacob by Mother and Birth Order

| | | |
|---|---|---|
| sons of Leah | Reuben | ("the firstborn") |
| | Simeon | (2) |
| | Levi | (3) |
| | Judah | (4) |
| | Issachar | (9) |
| | Zebulun | (10) |
| sons of Rachel | Joseph | (11) |
| | Benjamin | (12) |
| sons of Rachel's servant Bilhah | Dan | (5) |
| | Naphtali | (6) |
| sons of Leah's servant Zilpah | Gad | (7) |
| | Asher | (8) |

*Right:*
Negev
*Isaiah and Abby Cramer*

In sum, Jacob was a deceiver when he lived at home, when he lived away from home, and when he returned to his homeland. To look at Jacob himself one may be tempted to conclude that he had not changed and to ask why God said that he "prevailed" (32:28 lit.). Perhaps it is better to ask: In what sense did Jacob "prevail"? The answer can be seen by reviewing the several similarities and differences between Jacob and each of the other major characters in Table 8-H.

**Table 8-H:**
Jacob and His Relatives Compared

| *Jacob and . . .* | |
|---|---|
| *his parents* | **Jacob** was like **Isaac** who trusted his ability to discern, for the latter through his senses, and like **Rebekah** who used ingenuity and deceit to assist God's word of promise. |
| *his brother* | Whereas both **Jacob** and **Esau** failed early and failed often, **Jacob** learned of God and grew but **Esau** did not. |
| *his uncle* | Whereas both **Jacob** and **Laban** worked hard and acted shrewdly to secure wealth, **Laban** concluded that his belongings were his because of his own efforts, and **Jacob** recognized his earnings as gifts from God. |
| *his uncle, cousins, and wives* | Whereas **Laban**, his sons, and his daughters, **Leah** and **Rachel**, defined their possessions in terms of how much they had acquired, **Jacob** defined his possessions in terms of whom they were from. |
| *beloved wife* | Whereas **Rachel** protected her father's gods and incurred judgment, **Jacob** wrestled with the God of his fathers and secured a blessing. |

Jacob was not a prevailer because he overcame his tendencies toward sin but because he listened to God, interpreted his life in light of God, and sought the blessing of

God. Perhaps the most notable example of Jacob's growth is the faith he demonstrated when he found out his brother was coming to meet him. Jacob prayed and in humility expressed his trust in the word God had spoken to him:

> Then Jacob prayed, "*O God of my father Abraham, God of my father Isaac, Yahweh, you who said to me,* 'Go back to your country and your relatives, and I will make you prosper.' I am unworthy of all the kindness and faithfulness you have shown your servant. I had only my staff when I crossed this Jordan, but now I have become two camps. Save me, I pray, from the hand of my brother Esau, for I am afraid he will come and attack me, and also the mothers with their children. *But you have said,* 'I will surely make you prosper and will make your descendants like the sand of the sea, which cannot be counted.'" (32:9–12, emphasis added)

That night he wrestled with God and was given a new name, Israel.

*In what sense did Israel prevail?*

## ANOTHER LOOK

Biblical stories often sound like previous biblical stories. More accurately, the reader can often hear the earlier stories within the later ones, because later biblical stories were designed to reflect earlier ones. The fact that the Bible sometimes sounds like other parts of the Bible is a phenomenon that is significant to the larger human drama (see discussion of extended echo effect and typological patterns in Chapter 1).

The careful biblical reader will recognize that *something is going on* between stories of Jacob and his family and David and his family. The most notable similarities can be seen by comparing the stories from when Jacob returned to the land, beginning with his wrestling with God, and from when David reigned in Jerusalem, beginning with God's covenant to him.

Negev

*Isaiah and Abby Cramer*

The narrative of the failures of Jacob's four oldest sons has a variety of echoes in the vying for power between four of David's sons, namely, Amnon, Absalom, Adonijah, and Solomon (based on Friedman, 16–17). Reuben sleeps with one and Absalom with ten of his father's concubines. Absalom, like Simeon and Levi, avenges the rape of his sister. In these cases, their once-strong fathers hear but do not act (emphases added).

- Amnon takes Tamar "and since he was stronger than she, *he raped and degraded her*" (2 Sam 13:14).
- Shechem saw Dinah and "he took her, *raped her, and degraded her*" (Gen 34:2 lit.).
- Tamar told Amnon, "*Such a thing should not be done* in Israel! Don't do this wicked thing" (2 Sam 13:12).
- Simeon and Levi were angry "because Shechem had done an outrageous thing in Israel by sleeping with Jacob's daughter—*a thing that should not be done*" (Gen 34:7).
- Both Tamar's rape and Dinah's marriage with the uncircumcised Shechem is said to be a "*disgrace*" (Gen 34:14; 2 Sam 13:13).
- David *said nothing*. Moreover, Absalom tells Tamar, "*Be quiet*" (2 Sam 13:20).

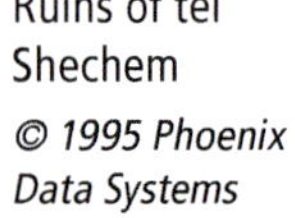

Ruins of tel Shechem

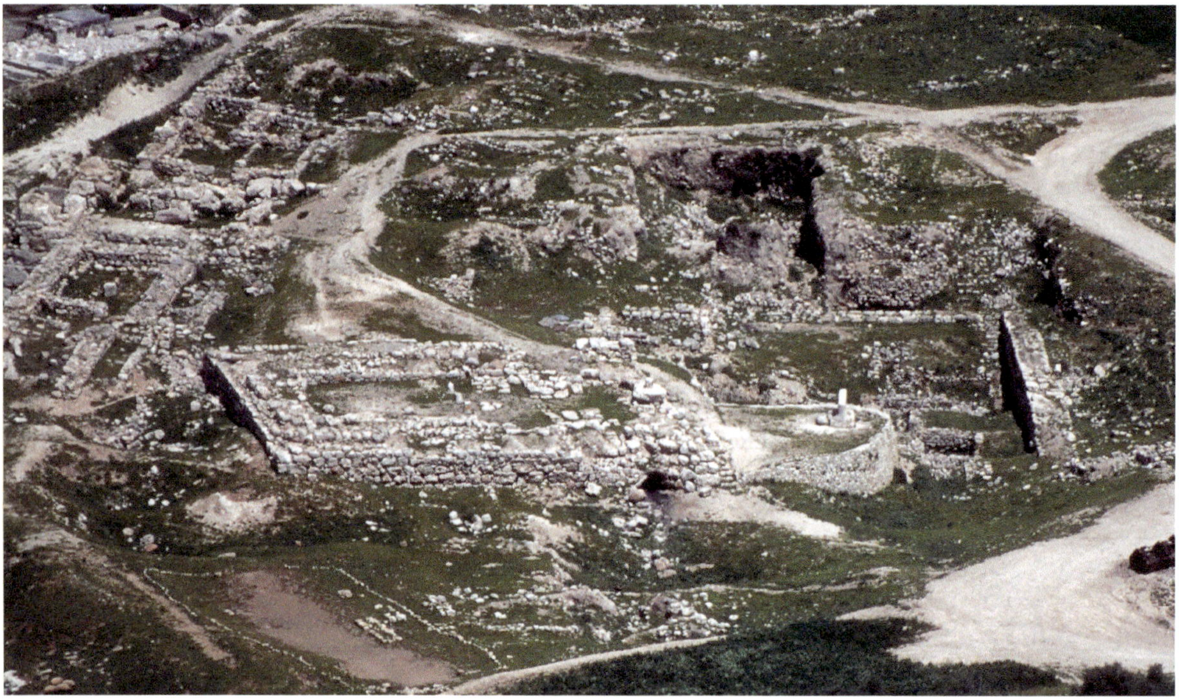

- Jacob *kept quiet* (Gen 34:5).
- Both Amnon and Shechem die violently at the hands of the avenging brothers.
- David knows but does nothing; later he is angry (2 Sam 13:21).
- Jacob knows and does nothing; later he is angry (Gen 34:30–31).

The incident in Shechem robbed Jacob of peace in the land. Absalom's vengeance ultimately led to a civil war. Still, God's promise to Jacob through his father and God's promise to David through the prophet (Gen 27:28–29; 2 Sam 7) were not thwarted but furthered within the context of the tragic and sinful lives of the families of these two men.

The "something" that is going on between the David and Jacob stories should, in part, be thought of in terms of the retrospective comparisons by the later storyteller. It is the storyteller who unfolds the narrative in a manner that lets the reader understand that the past is, in some fashion, a picture of the future. The similarities between the narratives of Jacob and David take on greater significance when the similarities between Judah and David are factored into the comparison. These will be discussed toward the end of Chapter 9.

## INTERACTIVE WORKSHOP

### *Chapter Summary*

Jacob shared many of the sinful characteristics of his relatives, including his parents, his brother, his uncles, and his wives. Jacob, however, was different than them because he listened to God's word and learned gratitude and faith. He was named Israel because he wrestled with humans and with God and prevailed.

### *Can You Explain the Key Terms?*

- birthright
- blessing
- Edom
- Israel
- Joseph
- Judah
- Laban

### *Challenge Questions*

1. How does the meaning of the names "Jacob" and "Israel" relate to the identity of Jacob?
2. Trace the series of deceptions through the Jacob narratives.
3. For what reasons does Jacob, on several occasions, attribute circumstances in his life to the workings of God?
4. What are the steps of Jacob's growth?

## *Advanced Questions*

1. How do the visions of Jacob and Laban function within the narrative?
2. Compare Genesis 32:24–30 with Hosea 12:3–4. With whom did Jacob wrestle?

*3. What is the theological significance of the wordplays on "red" and "Edom" (*'edom*) in Genesis 25 and on "white" and "Laban" (*lavan*) in chapter 30?

*4. What is the semantic range of *panim* ("face") in Genesis 32 and 33?

## *Research Project Ideas*

Explain the function of Isaac, based on his limited role, in Genesis (see discussion in this chapter as well as the explanation of Table 3-E in Chapter 3).

Trace the meaning of the prophetic word as it came to Abraham, Rebekah (Isaac to a lesser extent), Jacob, and Joseph.

Examine the function of Jacob's several visions and other encounters with God.

## *The Next Step*


Fokkelman, J. P. "Genesis." Pages 36–53 in *The Literary Guide to the Bible*. Edited by Robert Alter and Frank Kermode. Cambridge, MA: Belknap, 1987.

Friedman, Richard Elliot. *The Hidden Book in the Bible*. San Francisco: HarperSanFrancisco, 1998, 16–17.

Goldingay, John. *Genesis*. Baker Commentary on the Old Testament Pentateuch. Grand Rapids: Baker Academic, 2020.

Peterson, Brian Neil. "'Jacob's Trouble': The Shechem Fiasco and the Breaking of Covenant in Genesis 34." *Bibliotheca Sacra* 176 (2019): 272–91.

Richter, Sandra L. "Rape in Israel's World . . . and Ours: A Study of Deuteronomy 22:23–29." *Journal of the Evangelical Theological Society* 64.1 (2021): 59–76.

Ross, Alan P. *Creation and Blessing: A Guide to the Study and Exposition of the Book of Genesis*. Grand Rapids: Baker, 1988.

Schnittjer, Gary Edward. "The Blessing of Judah as Generative Expectation." *Bibliotheca Sacra* 177 (2020): 15–39.

van Wolde, Ellen. "Does *'Innâ* Denote Rape? A Semantic Analysis of a Controversial Word." *Vetus Testamentum* 52 (2002): 528–44.

Zakovitch, Yair. *Jacob: Unexpected Patriarch*. New Haven, CT: Yale University Press, 2012.

# 9 THE SONS OF JACOB NARRATIVES
## *Genesis 37:1–47:26*

*Gary Edward Schnittjer*

## GETTING STARTED

### *Focus Question*

What led Jacob to decide to grant the blessing to Judah and the birthright to Joseph?

### *Look for These Terms*

- bad report
- first reading
- leader
- pledge
- second reading
- surprise

## AN OUTLINE

A. **Joseph's Special Coat and Dreams (37:1–11)**
  B. **The Brothers' Crime against Joseph (37:12–36)**
    C. **Judah and Tamar (38)**
      D. **Joseph's Fall and Rise in Egypt (39–41)**
      E. **The Brothers Come Down to Egypt (42)**
    F. **Judah and Benjamin (43–44)**
  G. **The Reunion of the Brothers and the Family of Israel (45:1–47:12)**
H. **Joseph's Rulership of Egypt and Salvation to the Peoples (47:13–26)**

## A READING

Yahweh promised that the offspring of the woman would step on the offspring of the serpent. This is a poetic way to explain that his word will prevail over the sinful revolution. The promise was passed on in increasingly specific terms through the first three generations of the family chosen to bring blessing to all the families of the earth. The last section of Genesis brings these hopes together.

The stories of the sons of Jacob provide the climactic sequence within the epoch narratives of Genesis. The turning point and surprise within the plotline of this section are what make sense of the beginning and ending. Many have approached Genesis 37–50 as though these chapters are the story of Joseph (see Friedemann, 160–68). Though he is a leading figure, the story is arranged around all the sons vying for the birthright and the blessing of Israel, as can be seen at the end of the story (Gen 48–49). Thus, the question of the line of the offspring of Abraham—between Isaac and the other potential heirs of Abraham and between Jacob and Esau—now focuses itself on the twelve sons of Israel. From which of these sons will come the offspring of promise according to God's word?

*Why is it important to approach the last part of Genesis as the sons of Jacob narrative?*

The concepts of "first reading" and "second reading," defined in Chapter 1, can help in approaching this section of Genesis. The dominant feature of the first reading of narrative is the surprise—the twist, turning point, or the like—that resolves the plot. The game of narrative played between storyteller and readers in large part revolves around whether the reader can figure it out or whether the storyteller can surprise. By the time readers get to Genesis 37, the master narrator of this book has set us up for a shocker. The use of second reading—rereading to interpret the elements of the narrative in light of its end or in relation to the whole—helps reveal significance of the resolution.

The Jacob narratives set out the categories for the sons of Jacob narratives. Two things are at stake: the birthright, or double portion of the inheritance, and the blessing, especially who shall rule. In Genesis 48 *Joseph* receives the *birthright*. There will be no tribe of Joseph. His birthright amounts to a double portion, a tribe or family group for both of his sons, Manasseh and Ephraim, within the families of Israel. In Genesis 49, the *blessing*, oriented toward the rulership of a descendant, is given to *Judah*. Therein lies the double twist, the surprise.

*What is a birthright and what is a blessing?*

The narrator sets up readers to expect the birthright and blessing to go to Benjamin by the end of Genesis 37. Just as Jacob acquired both, so too one of his children could also secure both. Three primary features of the set-up continue to be engaged through the sons of Jacob stories (see Table 9-A). First, the pattern of younger over the older is already a recurring theme: Isaac over Ishmael and Jacob over Esau, a pattern by which readers expect Benjamin over his brothers. In the case of Jacob, the pattern was explicit in God's word to Rebekah, "The older will serve the younger" (25:23). This pattern continues to exert itself in Genesis when Ephraim is blessed above Manasseh (48:17–19).

Second, Rachel is special. She is distinct among the four women that made up Jacob's little harem because Jacob loved her. Although he embraced the responsibility of the other women and their children, he only loved Rachel—as far as the reader can tell (29:31–34). But the other significant factor is Rachel's infertility.

| Narrative clues | Where do they point? |
| --- | --- |
| Younger over older | Benjamin is the youngest, then Joseph |
| Rachel is special—loved and infertile | Rachel's sons are Joseph and Benjamin |
| The oldest sons—Reuben, Simeon, and Levi—disqualify themselves through immoral acts | Will the rest of the brothers disqualify themselves? |

**Table 9-A:** Summary of the Narrator's "Set-up" for Heir of the Birthright and Blessing

Sarah and Rebekah had each struggled with infertility. Thus, Rachel's barrenness appears to signal that one of her children, when God finally grants them to her, could be the offspring of promise. Before ever getting to the sons of Jacob story, the combination of Rachel as special and the fact that her two sons are the youngest of the family lead readers to expect Benjamin (or Joseph) to be the one.

Third, the pattern of disqualification, beginning with the oldest brothers, has already begun. In Genesis 34 Simeon and Levi avenged their sister's disgrace in a bloody and deceitful way. Although Jacob remained quiet when his daughter was raped and disgraced, his anger flared up against his two violent sons. Their defiant retort at the end of the chapter, "Should he have treated our sister like a prostitute?" left the matter unresolved. In the next chapter, Reuben committed an act of incest with (and possibly rape of) his stepmother Bilhah. The text ominously notes that "Israel heard of it" (35:22). Thus, the first three of the ten older sons have serious moral failures.

*What three reasons cause the "first-time reader" to expect Benjamin to get the birthright and the blessing?*

In a second reading, these indiscretions are the grounds for passing over Reuben, Simeon, and Levi for the blessing (49:3–7). Jacob rehearses these unresolved sinful events as he proceeds toward granting the blessing to Judah. Later, the Chronicler interpreted the last section of the book of Genesis along these same lines:

> The sons of Reuben the firstborn of Israel (he was the firstborn, but when he defiled his father's marriage bed, *his rights as firstborn were given to the sons of Joseph* son of Israel; so he could not be listed in the genealogical record in accordance with his birthright, and though *Judah was the strongest of his brothers and a ruler came from him, the rights of the firstborn belonged to Joseph*). (1 Chr 5:1–2, emphasis added)

When the reader comes to Genesis 37, the story appears to run along the same lines as those before. Readers are not surprised when Judah is singled out. This appears, in first reading, to extend the established narrative pattern. The three oldest brothers have sinned in ways that put their birthright at risk, and Judah, the fourth brother, commits a great evil. In second reading, however, the repeated attention to Judah (see outline above) can be understood in relation to the pivotal turning point of the Genesis story. Yahweh gave his word to Abraham, to Isaac, and to Jacob. Why would he choose to fulfill it through the line of Judah?

Genesis 37 begins a series of fleeting vignettes to prepare readers for the horrific act of the brotherhood selling Joseph into slavery. Each element—the bad report, the special cloak, and the dreams—converge in motivating the brothers to commit a crime against Joseph (see Figure 9-B). The word for bad report in 37:2 can mean "report of evil things" or "evil motivation of a corrupt report." The term is not used often, but it is used again in Numbers 13. In that context it is the report itself that is bad—that is, the ten scouts distort the facts to turn the people against the views of Caleb and Joshua. Their bad report worked (see Chapter 22). The use of this term in Genesis 37 seems to mean, at first glance, a report of Joseph's brothers' evil (the nature of the problem is not mentioned). The way it is stated, however, especially in light of the other use of this term in Numbers 13, leaves room for a negative interpretation of Joseph's motives. Joseph's attitude toward his brothers can be understood in more than one manner in each of the items mentioned in 37:1–11.

**Figure 9-B:** The Structure of the Opening of Genesis 37

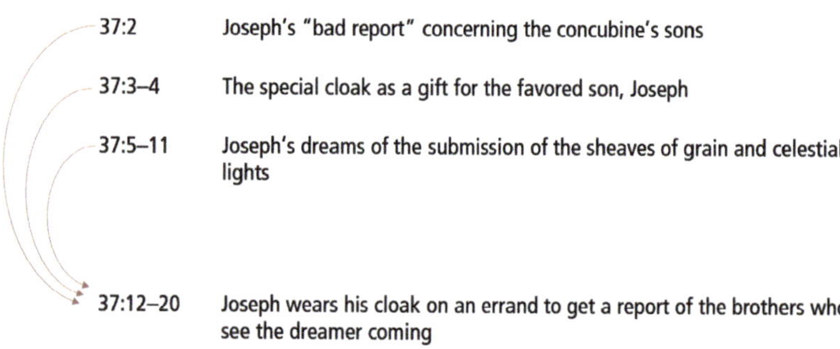


The next issue is Jacob's showing exclusive and observable favoritism to Joseph, the son of "his old age" (37:3), by giving him a special cloak. The favoritism that characterized Jacob's childhood and fueled the bitter competition between the pair of sisters he married now becomes a divisive force among his children. The combination of the bad report and the special cloak as a symbol of his privileged place in Jacob's affections is reason enough for them to resent him—"they hated him" (37:4).

The reader wonders why Joseph repeatedly tells his brothers about his dreams, dreams that suggested their humiliation and his magnification. Is he naïve or mean-spirited? Their sheaves of grain bow to his. They ask, "Do you intend to reign over us?" (37:8), and they hate him all the more. The humble and upright character of Joseph with Potiphar's wife and in the Egyptian prison has led most readers over the ages to regard Joseph as having good, even if naïve, motives in these early episodes with his brothers.

Nevertheless, Joseph demonstrated his shrewdness and cunning in the complexities of running a household, a prison, and a regional empire. He even deceived his brothers in a series of meetings wherein they were unable to recognize him. He used his power to imprison, arrest, and spy on them, listening to their private conversations in their own language. Is it really possible that Joseph, at age seventeen, was unaware that he was aggravating his brothers' jealousy—jealousy arguably justified by their father's flagrant favoritism? Was he righteous, innocent, or vindictive? As in so many other instances in Genesis, the narrative leaves enough in the background to invite readers to wonder (see O'Brien, 447).

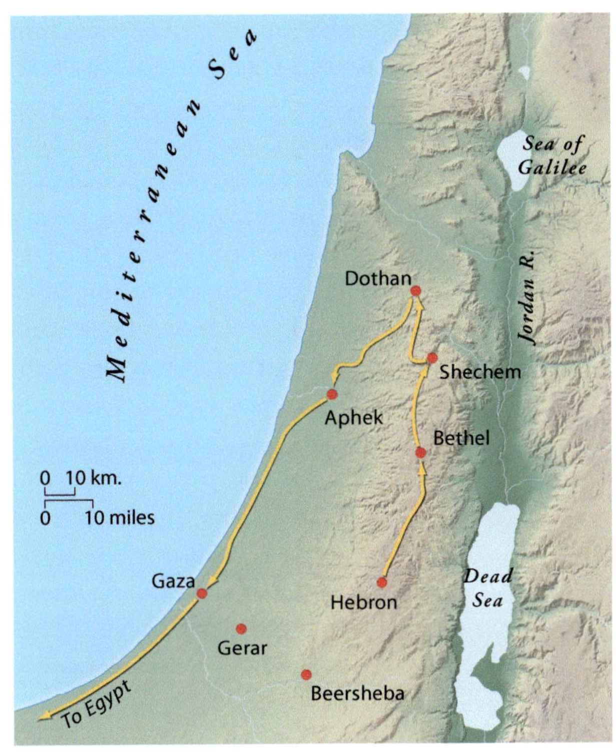


**Map 9-C:** Joseph's Travels from Hebron to Shechem to Dothan to Find His Brothers.

Although the text does not directly disclose Joseph's motives and attitudes, the bitter spirit of his older brothers is accented repeatedly. When Joseph showed up in Dothan wearing his special cloak, intending to take another report back to their father, the brotherhood reacted with the murderous rage that had been building. Reuben persuaded them, for the moment, not to kill their younger sibling. They took his cloak and threw him in a pit. The narrator discloses Reuben's intentions. He wanted to deliver the beloved son and return him to his father. Was Reuben hoping to reacquire a good standing with Jacob and reacquire the birthright and/or blessing? This is not the last time Reuben tries and fails to save the sons that Israel prized.

*What features in the story raise doubts or questions about Joseph's motives?*

Camels in the wilderness
*William Krewson*

When opportunity came in the form of a southbound Ishmaelite caravan, Judah, just as readers expect, answered the call. Judah led his brothers in committing a criminal and inhumane act against their younger brother by selling their brother into slavery. No amount of rationalizing the favoritism and self-aggrandizement, regardless of Joseph's motivations, can excuse this evil act.

The brothers, including Reuben, deceived Jacob by killing a goat and putting its blood on the special cloak. Jacob embraced the idea that an animal had attacked and killed his beloved son—though he still blamed his surviving sons (see 42:36). More than thirty years earlier Jacob had conspired with his mother and, using a butchered goat, deceived his own father. Jacob refused to be comforted. He maintained that he would grieve for Joseph until he himself died. Such protracted grief probably helps explain why his sons continued to live in the shadow of their guilty consciences. More than a decade later, when they had problems in life, they concluded that their troubles were rooted in their sin against their brother (42:21–22). Jacob's love of and his sons' hatred toward the older son of Rachel haunted the family through the years and played a significant part in the relationship of both Jacob and the remaining brothers with Rachel's second son, Benjamin.

Until recently, the relationship of Genesis 38 to its context within the book of Genesis has not been explained well. Many interpreters believed that the story of Judah and Tamar was an interruption (Speiser, 299–300) with "no connection" to the surrounding context (von Rad, 356). The reasons for such a reading included viewing this segment of Genesis as part of the story of Joseph, along with prevalent theories regarding the literary sources of the Torah (see Sidebar 1-A in Chapter 1).

More careful attention to the literary features of biblical narrative has begun to correct the situation. Among the connections between chapters 37 and 38 are that Jacob planned to "go down" to the grave mourning (37:35 lit.) and Judah "went down" from his brothers (38:1); the mourning periods of Jacob, Judah, and Tamar, respectively (37:35; 38:11, 12); and a goat's use for blood and a pledge in the episodes (37:31; 38:17) (see Alter, 1–11). The primary connections between Genesis 37, 38, and 39 are, moreover, based on significant plot points (see Table 9-D; also see Huddlestun, 47–62). The key terms "recognized" and "pledge" recur at high points of the larger narrative (see 38:18; 42:7; 43:9 lit.; 44:32 lit.).

*How does Genesis 38 fit within its immediate context?*

In first reading, the reader may be surprised that chapter 38 spends time recounting another moral failure of Judah. Was it not enough to disqualify Judah for the birthright and blessing by showing his leading role in selling his brother into slavery? In second reading, however, we recognize that Judah, in fact, gets the blessing, and we wonder why. Judah's personal turning point occurs in Genesis 38. Something happens that changes him. Before this he led the way against his own brother.

| 37 | 38 | 39 |
|---|---|---|
| Joseph's special cloak taken (v. 23) | Judah's seal, cord, and staff taken as pledge (v. 18) | Joseph's cloak taken as evidence (vv. 12–13) |
| Cloak recognized (v. 33) | Seal, staff, and cord recognized (vv. 25–26) | Cloak identified (v. 18) |

**Table 9-D:** The Primary Connections between Genesis 37, 38, 39

After this he will lead the way in attempting to save his brother Benjamin. This change within Judah, which took place in the story of himself and Tamar, leads to the climactic twist, which in turn explains why he is given the blessing.

Tamar successively married and became a widow of Judah's two oldest sons, the second as Judah's commitment to Tamar and the line of his oldest son. While Judah's commitment may reflect an ancient Semitic custom, it also anticipates the rules of a widow's brother-in-law—the levirate marriage—given centuries later in the Torah (see Deut 25:5–6; Sidebar 9-E). The narrator explains to readers something that Judah did not know: his two oldest sons died because of their wickedness (Gen 38:7, 10). Judah thought that the problem was related to Tamar and tried to stall giving her to his third and last son. Years later she disguised herself as a prostitute and deceived Judah, who wanted to have sexual relations with her (his wife having died). Because he did not have payment with him, she accepted his seal and its cord and his staff as a "pledge"—that is, as collateral, roughly equivalent in the ancient Near East to driver's license and credit cards. Judah "accidentally" committed incest with his daughter-in-law—he was aiming for a different variety of immorality. Tamar conceived her father-in-law's child and kept his seal and cord and staff.

## Sidebar 9-E: Levirate Marriage in Ancient Near Eastern Context

Hittite Laws (ca. 1500 BCE) say: "If a man has a wife, and the man dies, his brother shall take his widow as wife. (If the brother dies,) his father shall take her. When afterwards his father dies, his (i.e., the father's) brother shall take the woman whom he had" (§193 in Roth, 236).

Middle Assyrian Law (ca. 1200 BCE) says: "If a man either pours oil on her head or brings (dishes for) the banquet, (after which) the son to whom he assigned the wife either dies or flees, he shall give her in marriage to whichever of his remaining sons he wishes, from the oldest to the youngest of at least ten years of age" (§43 in Roth, 169).

After about three months Judah got word that Tamar was pregnant. For him this was good news. He used the opportunity to condemn her to be burned to death for playing the whore, thus freeing himself from giving his youngest son to her. Judah's hypocrisy is extreme. Tamar surprised him by revealing the father's identity with his own seal, cord, and staff. He recognized them and declared, "She is righteous, not I" (38:26 lit.; see Schnittjer, "Blessing," 18–19, n. 8; Patterson, 194). When confronted with his own treachery and double standards, he humbled himself. This self-humiliation, something like repentance or confession of guilt, changed Judah. When he finally saw himself and humbled himself, he became a new kind of person. Tamar, then, is a trickster and a savior of the line of Judah.

In Genesis 39–41, Joseph rose to the head of his master's household under Potiphar, the head of the prison under the warden, and the head of Egypt under only pharaoh. What could have been perceived as bad luck or as a long series of misadventures is interpreted by the storyteller as guided by Yahweh. The narrator does not explain the precise manner of Yahweh's governance of human affairs but repeatedly emphasizes that this is what it was (39:2–3, 5, 21–23). Joseph himself, on more than one occasion, interpreted problems he faced as orchestrated by God (45:5–9; 50:19–20).

? *How does the series of "coincidences" in Joseph's life highlight God's sovereign work?*

Joseph's brothers had taken his special cloak and used it to deceive their father. After Joseph continued to refuse Mrs. Potiphar's aggressive acts of seduction, she used the cloak he left in her hands to accuse him of making unwanted sexual advances toward her. Through these cloaks Joseph went from being the favored son of a wealthy man to slave to prisoner for attempted rape.

During his incarceration Joseph had occasion to interpret the dreams of pharaoh's former cupbearer and baker. Though once he could not state the meanings of his own dreams—meanings that seemed obvious to his own family—now with no difficulty he explained God's message in the dreams of others. The cupbearer would have his head "lifted up" and be restored to his former position (40:13). But the baker's dream meant that his head would be "lifted off" (40:19). Joseph was right about both. After being restored, the cupbearer forgot about Joseph.

Two years after Joseph had explained the meaning of the cupbearer's dream, pharaoh himself was deeply troubled by dreams. The chief cupbearer recommended Joseph, who explained that God would interpret the meaning of pharaoh's dreams. Joseph, apparently acting as a prophet of God, told pharaoh that his dreams, of the seven lean stalks of grain and seven lean cows swallowing up the seven fat counterparts of each, represented seven years of abundance followed by seven years of famine, worldwide. Then, audaciously, the dream-interpreting convict proceeded to give pharaoh advice on how to manage the economic affairs of his kingdom in relation to the coming agricultural disaster (Gen 41:33–36). Pharaoh not only listened but, astonishingly, appointed Joseph—a falsely convicted rapist, slave, foreigner—over the entire Egyptian kingdom to carry out his wide-ranging economic proposal.

When the famine came, Jacob, like everyone else, decided to get food from Egypt. He sent his sons, except Benjamin. Joseph recognized them and remembered his own dreams when they bowed before him "with their noses to the ground" (42:6 lit.). Because they did not recognize him, he was able to deceive them and "test" them. He accused them of spying on Egypt. Whether or not Joseph developed a fuller plan for dealing with his brothers is not included in the story. How far was he prepared to go? Joseph, according to the narrative description of this sequence, cannot be directly reproached. He kept Simeon imprisoned and sent the others back, with their food and their money, to get Benjamin. The brothers interpreted the course of events as a judgment against themselves (42:21–22), and Jacob took the events as "against me" (42:36).

Ancient Egyptian slaves bowing to the ground

*Gary Edward Schnittjer*

Just as Reuben had attempted and failed to deliver Joseph, he now tried to rescue Simeon and Benjamin. It seems as though, in both cases, he wanted to regain what was lost—his birthright and blessing—when he had relations with or raped his stepmother. Reuben offered his own sons' lives if he failed to bring back Benjamin. This offer, while generous and indicative of the level of Reuben's commitment, missed the mark. From Jacob's perspective, if he lost Benjamin, it would help nothing to also kill the children of his oldest son. Reuben failed again.

A year passed and the food was gone. Judah told his father that unless he took Benjamin to Egypt the entire family would soon be dead. Israel revealed his heart when he replied, "Why did you bring this trouble on me by telling the man you had another brother?" (43:6). His angry and fearful question reveals the tenacious grip he still had on his old habit of deceiving. Jacob was incredulous that his sons had not lied! *He interpreted the problem as their failure to deceive.* The reader knows Joseph's secret and hears the sad irony in the family divided and conquered by layers of deception. After Judah explained why they were unable to deceive (readers know that it was because Joseph was deceiving them), he offered himself as a pledge for Benjamin. He took personal responsibility. The use of the term "pledge" echoes the term from chapter 38 and signals Judah's new character (v. 9 lit.; see Mann, 71). Jacob reluctantly accepted Judah's commitment of himself for Benjamin.

*What is the relationship between Judah's commitment in Genesis 43 and his earlier problem with his daughter-in-law in chapter 38?*

The brothers, including Benjamin, returned to Egypt to buy food. They brought the gifts that Jacob wanted them to bring, not unlike the gifts he used to appease his brother some years before (43:11, 26; cf. 32:13–21). After they had dinner with Joseph and obtained the food and Simeon was released, they left. Perhaps they were relieved. If so, it was short-lived, because Joseph's men stopped them and accused them of stealing his sorcery goblet. Just as Jacob had once told Laban that whoever had the household gods would die, not knowing they were with his beloved Rachel (who was probably pregnant with Benjamin at the time; see Table 10-F in Chapter 10), so too the brothers said that whoever had the goblet would die and the rest become slaves. The reader, who already knows where the sorcery goblet has been placed, may wonder how they did not remember the silver that they found in their grain bags the last time they came to Egypt. Although Jacob never realized he had spoken a death oath against Rachel, for she deceived him, the brothers tore their clothes in recognition when the goblet was found in Benjamin's sack.

The sons of Israel, here referred to as "Judah and his brothers" (44:14), returned to stand before Joseph. Joseph told them they could all go free—all except Benjamin. Judah made good on his word and launched into a long, impassioned plea, interweaving details from across the years to persuade the ruler (Schnittjer, *OT*, 11–12; Twiss, 465–71). He concluded: "*Your servant guaranteed [lit. "pledged"] the boy's safety* to my father. I said, 'If I do not bring him back to you, I will bear the blame before you, my father, all my life!' Now then, *please let your servant remain here as my lord's slave in place of the boy*, and let the boy return with his brothers" (44:32–33, emphases added). Twenty-two years earlier Judah had led his brothers in selling Joseph into slavery. Now Judah offered himself in place of Benjamin. The term "pledge" echoes across chapters 38 and 43, and here reaches its climax. Judah is a different person; he has changed.

The high point of the sons of Jacob stories comes when Judah offered himself in place of his brother (see Skinner, 485). This event resolves the two-decade-plus family fracture that resulted from the crime against Joseph and the lie to Israel. The immediate effects were to break Joseph's control over himself and end his deception and manipulation of his brothers. Because of Judah the family had been divided. Because of changed-Judah's self-sacrifice, the family was reunited. Jacob would again see the son of his beloved Rachel. Judah's act ended this particular cycle of deception. He would get the blessing.

*Why did Judah get the blessing?*

The relationship between the story of Judah and Tamar and the larger narrative about the sons of Jacob invites the interpretation that Judah received the blessing because he had stopped the cycle of deception that had been growing through the generations. The connections between the stories exhibit extended echo effect (see Table 9-F; partially adapted from Noble, 235). When Judah finally was honest about himself—confessing his unrighteousness—he gained the moral tools to end the deception, in this case Joseph's, that divided the sons of Israel. His act of substitution reunited the brothers together and Israel with his beloved son. Joseph and Judah are both saviors. Joseph saved the world from starvation and Judah saved the family of Israel from themselves.

**Table 9-F:** Extended Echo Effect between Genesis 38 and Larger Sons of Jacob Narrative

| Judah and Tamar (Gen 38) | The Sons of Jacob (Gen 37–46) |
|---|---|
| A history of bad relationship between Judah and Tamar, including Judah refusing his third son in marriage to Tamar (vv. 1–13) | A history of bad relationship between Joseph and his brothers (37:2–11) |
| Judah's act initiated a lengthy separation between Tamar and his family (v. 11) | Judah led the way in the brothers' crime against Joseph which initiated an extended separation between Joseph and the family of Israel (37:12–36) |
| Judah desired sexual intercourse and met a transformed Tamar—disguised as a prostitute—and did not *recognize* her (vv. 12–16) | The family of Israel needed food and met a transformed Joseph—"disguised" as an Egyptian ruler—and did not *recognize* him (42:1–24) |
| Judah tried but failed to pay for the prostitute's services (vv. 20–23) | The sons of Israel tried but failed to pay for the food (42:25–36) |
| Tamar showed Judah the *pledge* and he confessed his wrongdoing (vv. 18, 25–26) | Judah offered himself as the *pledge* of his brother Benjamin (43:8–10; 44:14–34) |
| Tamar saved Judah's line and bore him twin sons (vv. 27–30) | Judah's act ended the deception and reunited Israel and his beloved son (45:1–3; 46:28–30) |

Fertile land of Goshen (Nile Delta, Egypt)
*Gelia/Shutterstock.com*

**Map 9-G:** Land of Goshen

Everyone except Joseph was shocked. He sent the brothers back to get their father and all of their families and to move to the best part of Egypt—the land of Goshen was near the delta of the Nile River where it entered the Mediterranean Sea (Map 9-G). God's word came to Jacob and assured him that he should go to Egypt, for his family would one day return as he had said to Abraham in Genesis 15 (46:2–4). Judah's role as leader of the family was confirmed when Jacob sent him ahead to meet Joseph and get directions to Goshen (46:28). At last Israel saw his beloved son again: "As soon as Joseph appeared before him, he threw his arms around his father and wept for a long time. Israel said to Joseph, 'Now I am ready to die, since I have seen for myself that you are still alive'" (46:29b–30).

This series of stories began with Joseph's dreams of his rule and ends with a description of the extent of his rule. Under Joseph's rule, he acquired all the wealth and land of all the peoples and saved them from starvation (47:13–26). Joseph was a world savior.

Which story is in the background and which is in the foreground? Are the strife and fraternal competition of the sons of Jacob the backstage view of God's salvation of the peoples through Joseph? Or are the terrible famine and deliverance the background for the reunion of the sons of Israel? The answer may be a matter of perspective. It is, as the second reading reveals, the story of the sons of Jacob that explains why the birthright was for Joseph and the blessing for Judah. The story also highlights the place of Israel in the fate of the nations.

Within the larger context of Genesis, the sons of Jacob stories offer readers a narrative interpretation of why God's word became focused on the expectation of the Judah-king (49:8–12). The surprise that set up the blessing was that Judah changed (see Figure 9-H; Schnittjer, "Blessing," 18–19; also see Giffone, 966–69).

**Figure 9-H:** The Steps in Judah Securing the Blessing

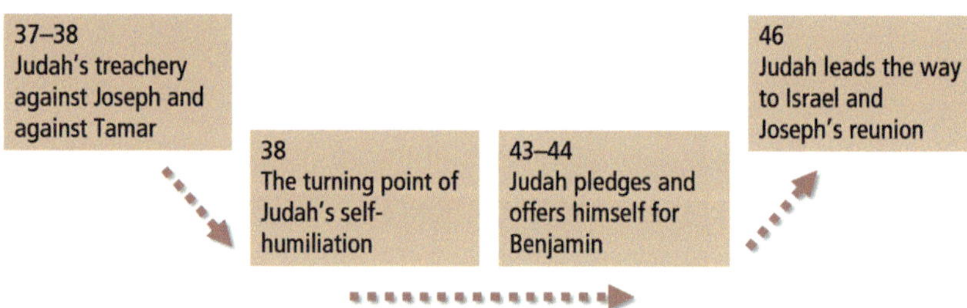

The narrative explanation of Judah's change is written in such a subtle manner—he said, "She is righteous, not I"—that the reader might easily miss it in first reading. That act of repentance that changed Judah could have appeared on its surface as further confirmation that he was immoral. Indeed, he was. When he saw the pledge he had given Tamar, he did not rationalize or deceive himself any longer. Judah's recognition is the significant turning point in the story (see Clifford, 530–32). Later Judah became the leader of the sons of Israel in self-sacrifice and regarded his brothers and father above himself. The reader who recognizes the different way of Judah in Genesis 43 and 44 looks back to see what caused the change. The change was rooted in his self-humbling.

*What is the importance of humility?*

The word of God to Abraham, to Isaac, and to Jacob became focused on the unlikely fourth son of Jacob. Why Judah? Not because he was better than his brothers. Rather, it was because he came to recognize that he was not.

## ANOTHER LOOK

Judah became the leader of his brothers (44:14). Israel sent him ahead to find the way (46:28). Hundreds of years later the clan of Judah was established as the leader tribe. They grew the largest, reflecting the creational blessing of life from God (see Num 1). They led the people through the wilderness and camped on the privileged side of the tabernacle (see Num 2; 10). They were the first tribe in the dedication of the tabernacle (Num 7). Caleb, the representative of Judah, was the first to resolve to obey God and fight the mighty Canaanites—and he did (Num 13:30; Josh 15:14–15; Judg 1:20). After Joshua's death, the Israelites inquired of God who should go first to fight the Canaanites. "Yahweh answered, 'Judah is to go; I have given the land into their hands'" (Judg 1:2). During a civil war, it was Judah that went first to fight the Benjamites (Judg 20:18). The careful reader comprehends how God's chosen king, David of Judah, fits into the larger story.

The closing part of Chapter 8 in this book described some of the similarities between the Jacob and David stories. The David stories were designed to sound like the Jacob stories in order to demonstrate that David and his offspring were in accord with the expectations and word of God to the ancestors. The similarities extend to many messy details of these troubled families. The most significant connection is the similarity between Judah and David. The thing that changed Judah so that he was set apart from his brothers as the leader of the sons of Israel was his self-humiliation, which established his descendant as the object of Israel's blessing. This characteristic was emulated in his descendant David.

Yahweh chose David because he was different from Saul (1 Sam 13:14; cf. Long,

147–148). The storyteller demonstrates this by juxtaposing Saul and David in a way that revealed both similarities and dissimilarities. Saul and David each committed great sins; in this they were similar. The difference was in how they handled their sin. When confronted by the prophet, Saul refused to offer true repentance (1 Sam 15). When God's prophet challenged David with his sin against Uriah, David confessed his guilt. His self-humiliation set him apart from Saul (2 Sam 12). David's poetic confession of his great sin in Psalm 51, therefore, depicts what sets apart Yahweh's chosen one. Notice the similar viewpoints between Joseph and David.

> [Joseph refused the advances of Mrs. Potiphar, saying:] "My master has withheld nothing from me except you, because you are his wife. How then could I do such a wicked thing and *sin against God?*" (Gen 39:9b, emphasis added)

> [David says:] "Have mercy on me O God . . . *Against you, you only, have I sinned* and done what is evil in your sight." (Ps 51:1a, 4a, emphasis added)

Although the sequence is reversed between Judah's self-humiliation and blessing and the Davidic covenant and his confession, humbling is the key common element between the two. The shared feature of self-humiliation for Judah and David sets up the paradigm of humiliation as the basis of exaltation that is featured in the narratives of Jesus the Messiah. "He humbled himself . . . Therefore God exalted him" (Phil 2:8, 9).

To put it all together in light of the blessing of Judah: Judah's act of self-humiliation changed him so that he offered himself in place of his brother, reunited the family of Israel, and acquired the blessing, so that from among his offspring would come a king, a ruler of nations. Judah sounds like David, and in turn, like Jesus the Messiah. The expected king is Genesis-shaped.

## INTERACTIVE WORKSHOP

### *Chapter Summary*

The sons of Jacob were vying for the birthright and the blessing. After the criminal act of treachery against Joseph, he eventually became a world savior and ruler by the subtle workings of Yahweh's grace. After Judah led the sinful acts against Joseph, he acted against his daughter-in-law, Tamar, but finally humbled himself and began to change. When his family was in desperate circumstances, Judah pledged himself in place of his brother Benjamin and thereby broke the chain of deception and reunited the family of Israel.

### *Can You Explain the Key Terms?*

- bad report
- first reading
- leader
- pledge
- second reading
- surprise

### *Challenge Questions*

1. Why does Genesis recount the moral failures of Reuben, Simeon, and Levi?
2. Did Joseph's brothers have good reason to resent him? Hate him? Why?
3. What were the changes in Judah as he progressed through the stories of the sons of Jacob in Genesis 37–46?
4. How did Jacob's favoritism of the sons of Rachel affect the dynamics of the other sons' relationship with their father?
5. What are the similarities and differences, and the significance of these, between Rachel's hiding her father's gods (ch. 31) and the hidden sorcery goblet in Benjamin's sack (ch. 44)?

### *Advanced Questions*

1. Trace out in Genesis 12–50 the pattern of the younger brother over the older and summarize its literary and theological significance.
2. In what ways, especially noting any verbal correspondences, are the narrative presentations of Noah and Joseph similar?
3. How many similarities are there between the stories of the family-saving women (Tamar in Gen 38 and Rahab in Josh 2), and what is the significance of these similarities?

*4. What is the significance of the differences, if there are any, between the use of *dibbah* ("bad report") in Genesis 37:2 and Numbers 13:32?

*5. What is the significance of the two different Hebrew terms used for "prostitute" in Genesis 38—*zonah* (v. 15) and *qadesh* (v. 21)?

### *Research Project Ideas*

Trace out the dreams and visions in Genesis 12–50 and evaluate their significance within this context.
Uncover the web of deception in the sons of Jacob stories and explain its meaning within the context of Genesis.
Compare the sibling rivalry among Israel's sons with the rivalry between their mothers.

## *The Next Step*

Alter, Robert. *The Art of Biblical Narrative*. 2d ed. New York: Basic Books, 2011.

Clifford, Richard J. "Genesis 38: Its Contribution to the Jacob Story." *Catholic Biblical Quarterly* 66 (2004): 519–32.

Friedemann, Golka W. "Genesis 37–50: Joseph Story or *Israel*-Joseph Story?" *Currents in Biblical Research* 2.2 (2004): 153–77.

Giffone, Benjamin D. "Israel's Only Son?: The Complexity of Benjaminite Identity between Judah and Joseph." *Old Testament Essays* 32.3 (2019): 956–72.

Huddlestun, John R. "Divestiture, Deception, and Demotion: The Garment Motif in Genesis 37–39." *Journal for the Study of the Old Testament* 98 (2002): 47–62.

Long, V. Philips. *1 and 2 Samuel*. Tyndale Old Testament Commentaries. Downers Grove, IL: IVP Academic, 2020.

Mann, Thomas W. *The Book of the Torah: The Narrative Integrity of the Pentateuch*. Louisville: Westminster John Knox, 1988.

Noble, Paul R. "Esau, Tamar, and Joseph: Criteria for Identifying Inner-Biblical Allusions." *Vetus Testamentum* 52 (2002): 219–52.

O'Brien, Mark A. "The Contribution of Judah's Speech, Genesis 44:18–34, to the Characterization of Joseph." *Catholic Biblical Quarterly* 59 (1997): 429–47.

Patterson, Todd L. *The Plot-structure of Genesis: "Will the Righteous Seed Survive?"* in the Muthos*-logical Movement from Complication to Dénouement*. Biblical Interpretation 160. Leiden: Brill, 2018.

Roth, Martha T. *Law Collections from Mesopotamia and Asia Minor*. 2d ed. Atlanta: Society of Biblical Literature, 1997.

Schnittjer, Gary Edward. "The Blessing of Judah as Generative Expectation." *Bibliotheca Sacra* 177 (2020): 15–39.

———. *Old Testament Use of Old Testament*. Grand Rapids: Zondervan Academic, 2021.

Skinner, J. *A Critical and Exegetical Commentary on Genesis*. 2d ed. International Critical Commentary. Edinburgh: T&T Clark, 1930.

Speiser, E. A. *Genesis*. Anchor Bible 1. New York: Doubleday, 1964.

Twiss, Paul. "An Overlooked Aspect of Judah's Speech in Genesis 44:18–34." *Journal of the Evangelical Theological Society* 63.3 (2022): 457–71.

von Rad, Gerhard. *Genesis, a Commentary*. Rev. ed. Translated by John H. Marks. Philadelphia: Westminster Press, 1972.

# 10 THE LAST DAYS
## Genesis 47:27–50:26

iStock.com/WLDavies

## GETTING STARTED

### *Focus Questions*

How does the closing of Genesis look back? How does it look forward?

### *Look for These Terms*

- gathered to his people
- Judah-king
- last days
- mummification

## AN OUTLINE

A. **Jacob's Burial Instructions (47:27–31)**
- B. **The Birthright to Joseph—the Blessing of Ephraim and Manasseh (48)**
- C. **The Blessing of Judah and Jacob's Last Words to His Sons (49:1–28)**

D. **The Death and Burial of Jacob (49:29–50:14)**

E. **Joseph's Forgiveness and Death (50:15–26)**

## A READING

Genesis 47:27–50:26 provides closure to both the sons of Jacob section (Gen 37–50) and the entire book of Genesis. The last words of Israel to his sons determine, to a large extent, the significance of their narratives. They provide the end toward which the story has been moving. Whereas Jacob himself acquired both the birthright and the blessing, Joseph was granted the birthright and Judah the blessing. Moreover, the deaths of Israel and his beloved son Joseph signal the end of the ancestors' story. But it is not the end, for Israel's last words offer hope, which reaches past the lives of the Hebrew ancestors toward the last days, especially through the expected Judah-king.

Genesis began with the narrative of the beginning days and concludes with Jacob's blessing for the "last days" (Gen 49:1 lit.; see Table 3-A in Chapter 3). Thus, all other biblical stories fit within its narrative framework. Everything within the human realm fits between creation and the coming of the Judah-king. The storyteller of Genesis, therefore, boldly narrates the context within which to define the meaning of every human being and society. This story explains the origin and destiny of humankind, and readers are expected to interpret the meaning of their own lives within the framework of this theological narrative.

*What is the importance of the reference to the "last days" in Genesis 49?*

The word of God that echoed from the earliest dawning of the human world and came to Abraham, establishing the beginning of the chosen family, is embodied in the last words of Israel. In Genesis the physical world itself is a representation, a response of all that is, to God's word. That word, against which the humans rebelled, is powerful and will prevail. The promise God made to them included an offspring who would step on the biting serpent. God's word came to Abraham and to Jacob, promising them with unbreakable power that the offspring through which all the families of the earth would be blessed would come through them. Israel, then, acts as the prophet of God—speaking his blessing to his sons and for all readers to hear—and proclaims the word of promise. The blessing of the Hebrew ancestors, even if taken by trickery as is the case with Isaac's blessing of Jacob, is irrevocable. A king is coming from Judah.

In Genesis 47 Jacob made Joseph swear an oath to him to bury his remains with his ancestors. In the next chapter Joseph brought his two sons before his father to offer them a blessing. Jacob began by recalling some of the events recorded in Genesis 35 in the same order that appeared there—specifically, the vision of God to Jacob in Bethel and the death of Rachel on the way back from Haran.

Israel had poor vision like Isaac (27:1; 48:10). The similarity between the two provides an opportunity to reveal a difference. Although Jacob and Rebekah were able to con Isaac because he could not see, Joseph could not dissuade Jacob from bestowing the blessing according to his intentions. He crossed his hands, placing his right hand on Ephraim and his left on Manasseh, thus blessing the younger over the older, even though Joseph wanted it otherwise. Though each of Jacob's other sons would have a tribal family named for them in the people of Israel, there was no tribe of Joseph. The birthright, or double portion of the inheritance, was granted to Joseph through two tribal families named for his sons. Many years later during the time of the kings, the two most powerful clans were Ephraim and Judah. When the kingdom was divided north and south, these two tribes came to the fore of the new kingdoms.

The blessing of Joseph's sons included Jacob's personal reflection. When asked his age by pharaoh seventeen years earlier, he expressed a very different perspective on his life. Compare these two personal interpretations of Jacob's life.

> And Jacob said to Pharaoh, "The years of my pilgrimage are a hundred and thirty. *My years have been few and difficult*, and they do not equal the years of the pilgrimage of my fathers." (47:9)

> Then he blessed Joseph and said, "May the God before whom my fathers Abraham and Isaac walked faithfully, *the God who has been my shepherd all my life to this day, the Angel who has delivered me from all harm*—may he bless these boys." (48:15–16a, emphases added)

These two statements do not contradict each other. His life was difficult and God did protect him. The statements reflect different emphases. The different settings, or perhaps the years in Egypt with his reunited family, explain the two viewpoints.

Genesis 49 begins with Jacob calling his sons to his deathbed: "Gather around so that I can tell you what will happen to you in the last days" (49:1 lit.). The things he described were oriented toward each of his sons: first, words for the sons of Leah, then words for the sons of his wives' maidservants, and finally words for the sons of Rachel. The foretold events were given in poetry (see Sidebar 10-B).

Genesis ends with a poetic conclusion, as do each of the major story segments of the Torah (see Table 10-A). Each of the poetic conclusions looks backward and forward. In the case of three of these poetic conclusions—the last words of Israel, the oracles of Balaam, and the Song of Moses—the expression "last days" was used to set the context (Gen 49:1; Num 24:14; Deut 32:29; see Sailhamer, 310). One of the theological functions of the poetic inserts is theological commentary on the narratives themselves (see Watts, 186–93). Moreover, the forward looking poetic conclusions reaching to the last days offer theological commentary of the narratives that envelop the readers. The epoch poems situate readers within the storied world of the Torah.

A vineyard in the land of Judah. The vineyard and wine imagery in Genesis 49:11–12 accords with the vineyards of Judah.

*Todd Bolen/BiblePlaces.com*

**Table 10-A:** Poetic Conclusions to the Major Sections of the Torah

| Beginning: | Exodus from Egypt: | Wilderness Travels: | Preparations for the Land: |
|---|---|---|---|
| Gen 1–50 | Exod 1–14 | Exod 15–Num 21 | Num 26–Deut 34 |
| *last words of Israel (Gen 49)* | *Song of the Sea (Exod 15)* | *oracles of Balaam (Num 23–24)* | *Song of Moses (Deut 32)* |

## Sidebar 10-B: Reading Hebrew Poetry

Hebrew poetry appears enough in Torah to evaluate how it works (see "Poetry in Torah" box). Hebrew poetry is different from English poetry. Hebrew poetry does not make use of meter and rhyming like classic English poetry. Hebrew poetry can be defined as "a type of elevated discourse, composed of terse lines, and employing a high degree of parallelism and imagery" (Berlin, "Reading," 2098). Most lines of biblical poetry are three or four words, but pregnant with imagery, usually causing English translation to be much longer.

### Poetry in Torah

There are five long poetic sections in the Pentateuch—Genesis 49 (blessing of Jacob's sons); Exodus 15:1–18 (Song of the Sea); Numbers 23–24 (Balaam's first oracle: 23:7–10; second oracle: 23:18–24; third oracle: 24:3–9; fourth oracle: 24:15–24); and Deuteronomy 32 (Song of Moses) and 33 (blessing of Moses)—as well as many short poetic sections—Genesis 2:23; 3:14–19; 4:23–24; 8:22; 9:6–7, 25–27; 14:19–20; 16:11–12; 24:60; 25:23; 27:27–29, 39–40; 48:15–16, 20; Exodus 3:14–15; 15:21; 32:18; 34:6–7; Leviticus 10:3; Numbers 6:24–26; 10:35–36; 12:6–8; 14:18; 21:14, 17–18, 27–30.

Berry, Donald. *An Introduction to Wisdom and Poetry of the Old Testament*. Nashville: Broadman & Holman, 1995, 207–9.

Parallelism is one of the most misunderstood aspects of Hebrew poetry. It used to seem important to teach students how to correctly label the supposed types of parallelism. The three main labels were synonymous, antithetical, and synthetic, with many other labels invented and used by various scholars.

*Synonymous*—the related lines repeat or develop similar forms, ideas, and so on.
*Antithetical*—the lines develop opposite or contrasting forms, ideas, and so on.
*Synthetic*—the lines are not balanced in idea or form, as the other two categories.

The labels are not the problem per se, but rather the view of poetry that they represent. Older approaches relied on geometric categories, especially emphasizing equivalence. It was thought that Hebrew poetry was "the practice of saying the same thing twice in different words" (Lewis, 11). This model might suggest a formula: A, and again B. This approach strictly applied hurts almost as much as, perhaps more than, it helps. While assigning labels to the parallel relationship between lines can be helpful for some English readers to appreciate the poetic form, this practice can never be more than an elementary step. Hebrew poetry is not flat and predictable but dynamic and surprising. Most specialists now teach that Hebrew poetry is doing something other than saying the same thing twice.

The newer approaches understand the second or counterpart line, or lines, as developing some feature or idea of the first line (Berlin, *Dynamics*, xvi). This model might suggest a formula: "A, and what's more, B; not only A, but B; not A, not even B; not A, and certainly not B; just as A, so B; and so forth" (Kugel, 13). The dynamic views look for development both vertically—between lines—and horizontally—within lines. "What this means to us as readers of biblical poetry is that instead of listening to an imagined drumbeat of repetitions, we need to constantly look for *something new happening* from one part of the line to the next" (Alter "Characteristics," 616, emphasis added; also see Alter, *Art*, 9–28).

Some scholars go even further and focus on a choice for every individual poetic line. If poetic lines present images, then poetic discourse can be thought of as "image to image progression." As one progresses through a poem, every new line presents the reader with a choice: Is the next line developing the image or introducing a new image (Holmstedt, 630, n. 28)? Another approach stresses the free-rhythm of each poetic line—not pairs of lines—causing balance and imbalance (Grosser).

Ancient Egyptian chariot

*Public Domain*

The metaphorical imagery at the heart of Hebrew poetry is elevated above what is thought of as prose (see "Poetry and Narrative" box). To take poetry as directly referring is to miss its poetic quality. That it literally refers is not a problem so long as it is remembered that it literally refers metaphorically. The narrative of the crossing of the sea in Exodus 14, for example, depicts the sea as coming down upon the Egyptians. Yet, notice how it is presented in the Song of the Sea (Exod 15:1, 4, emphasis added; also see 15:21):

> I will sing to Yahweh, for he is highly exalted.
> Both horse and driver **he has hurled into the sea.** . . .
> Pharaoh's chariots and his army **he has hurled into the sea.**
> The best of Pharaoh's officers are drowned in the Red Sea.

### Poetry and Narrative

The difference between biblical poetry and narrative is not always clear-cut. The priestly benediction is a poetic-narrative proclamation with poetic force similar to what can be called "staircase parallelism," with each line building "steps" on the preceding line—x, x + y, xy + z. The three lines are made up of 3, 5, and 7 Hebrew words, respectively.

> Yahweh bless you and keep you;
> Yahweh make his face shine on you **and be gracious to you**;
> Yahweh turn his face toward you **and give you peace**. (Num 6:24–26, emphasis refers to added steps)

There is a sliding scale between the highly elevated style of poetry and the less highly elevated style of narrative (Kugel, 85; Berlin, *Dynamics*, 5). The different stylistic registers can be overstated to illustrate: from pure narrative to poetic narrative to narrative poetry to pure poetry. The labels are not important except to illustrate the fluid interrelationship between these two modes of discourse. Because biblical narrative is itself elevated language, the difference between it and poetry comes down to the degree of language elevation and the function of the context.

The Song of the Sea's poetry would be considered inaccurate if it was measured along the axes of literal, historical, physical measurement. Yet, it is not wrong at all. Poetry is almost magic in its ability to capture the true theological significance of the event. The Egyptians enraged Yahweh when they threw the Hebrew infants into the river. The poetic interpretation is theologically correct because the event at the sea is seen for what it is, namely, Yahweh bringing justice that is literally poetic—he threw the Egyptian warriors into the sea.

The elevated language of biblical poetry might as easily be termed "elevated vision." In poetic metaphor "two things that do not generally occur together are brought together; they collide, or explode, leaving in their wake a new way of seeing" (Berlin, "Reading," 2102).

The poetic blessing of the sons of Jacob reveals the narrativity of Hebrew poetry and pushes readerly imagination to envision the Judah-king to come. I have labeled the lines of Genesis 49:8 (lit.) with letters so I can discuss them economically.

(a) Judah, you,
(b) your brothers will praise you,
(c) your hand upon the neck of your enemies,
(d) the sons of your father shall bow down before you.

If we were applying traditional parallelism labels, lines b and d would be considered synonymous, while they are simultaneously synonymously related to Judah's rule of line c yet antithetically to the referents of line c (enemies as opposed to brothers). But these labels obscure both the narrativity and the possibility of lines b, c, and d. Whereas "brothers" and "sons of you father" (b and d) are denoting the same persons, it is less clear whether "enemies" (c) gets at the same referents or another. And that is the whole point of poetry. In the immediate context, Jacob looked back in the poetic words to Reuben, Simeon, and Levi, pointing to things in their lives (49:2–7). If lines b, c, and d look back, they appear to reference Joseph's story and his rule over his brothers who hated him when he narrated his dreams of rulership. The blessing, however, is not looking back, and it is not about Joseph. It is looking ahead to a descendant of Judah. Thus, Judah's expected descendant is envisioned according to the shape of Joseph, yet the "enemies" are contrasted to the "brothers" in this future expectation.

Hebrew poetry often uses mirror imaging or chiastic structure, namely, adjacent lines often present the related items in inverted order (Gen 49:9 lit.).

(w) A young lion, Judah,
(x) from the prey, my son, you go up,
(y) he crouches and lies down like a lion,
(z) and as a lioness—who dares rouse him?

*iStock.com/WLDavies*

Notice the reverse order of the elements between lines y and z—(y) posture, animal; (z) animal, posture. The more important point is the way the subsequent lines develop the poem's narrative. The question in line z sounds rhetorical, and maybe it is: Who dares rouse a lion? Yet it is strong irony in light of lines w and x: The lion is roused.

The issue is not that poetic discourse is imprecise and slippery. Poetic discourse is rich, elevated, and surprising. It strikes multiple notes in the reader's ears. It is saying what it is saying and is also pregnant with much more. The Torah and the Scriptures at large use poetry to look back and look ahead and interpret the theological importance of their subject in ways not possible with other modes of discourse.

### *The Next Step*


Alter, Robert. *The Art of Biblical Poetry.* 2d ed. New York: Basic Books, 2011.

———. "The Characteristics of Ancient Hebrew Poetry." Pages 611–24 in *The Literary Guide to the Bible.* Edited by Robert Alter and Frank Kermode. Cambridge, MA: Belknap, 1987.

Berlin, Adele. *Dynamics of Biblical Parallelism.* Rev. ed. Grand Rapids: Eerdmans, 2008.

———. "Reading Biblical Poetry." Pages 2097–104 in *The Jewish Study Bible.* Edited by Adele Berlin and Marc Zvi Brettler. New York: Oxford, 2004.

Grosser, Emmylou J. *Unparalleled Poetry: A Cognitive Approach to the Free-Rhythm Verse of the Hebrew Bible.* New York: Oxford University Press, forthcoming.

Holmstedt, Robert D. "Hebrew Poetry and the Appositive Style: Parallelism *Requiescat in pace.*" *Vetus Testamentum* 69 (2019): 617–48.

Kugel, James L. *The Idea of Biblical Poetry: Parallelism and Its History.* New Haven: Yale University Press, 1981.

Lewis, C. S. *Reflections on the Psalms.* New York: Simon & Schuster, 1961.


Reuben was not given the blessing because of his incestuous relations with his stepmother. Simeon and Levi were passed by because of their violent vengeance on the Shechemites. The blessing was thus given to the fourth son of Leah, Judah. Notice the wordplay marked by underlining and the royal expectation marked by bold. Jacob said:

> Judah [*yehudah*], you,
> your brothers will praise [*yodu*] you,
> your hand upon the neck of your enemies,
> **the sons of your father shall bow down before you.**
> A young lion, Judah, from the prey, my son, you go up,
> like a lion he crouches and lies down, and as a lioness—who dares rouse him?
> **The scepter shall not turn aside from Judah,**
> **nor the ruler's staff from between his feet,**
> **until that which belongs to him comes,**
> **and the obedience of the peoples is his.**
> Binding his jack to the vine,
> his purebred donkey to a choice vine,
> he washes his garment in wine,
> and his robe in the blood of grapes.
> His eyes darker than wine,
> and his teeth whiter than milk. (Gen 49:8–12 lit.; Schnittjer, "Blessing,"16–17)

The royal language of the scepter holds forth a promise for a king from among his offspring. The expectation for the obedience or devotion of the peoples appears to be related to the promise to Abraham and Jacob concerning the blessing that would come to all the families of the earth through their offspring. Israel's blessing of Judah extends Yahweh's word concerning the offspring of the woman, from Abraham, Isaac, and Jacob to the expected descendant of Judah. Later, Balaam makes these connections overt by combining quotations of the Abrahamic promise and blessing of Judah in his third oracle (Gen 12:3//27:29//49:9//Num 24:8–9; cf. 23:22–24; see Schnittjer, "Blessing," 21–22).

"You are a lion's cub, Judah" (Gen 49:9).
*iStock.com/MarieHolding*

What will the rule of the Judah-king look like? The poetic description in Genesis 49:8 builds a picture of the expected Judah-king from the language and narrative of Genesis. The language must be read in the context of the brothers who listen to Jacob and are remined of Joseph's youthful dreams (Schnittjer, "Blessing" 20; also see Emadi, 17–20). In particular, the Judah-king will be something like Joseph as a savior and ruler, who himself, in turn, resembled the blessing given to Jacob. Compare the related passages (emphases added).

> [Isaac blessed Jacob:] "May nations serve you and peoples bow down to you. Be lord over your brothers, and *may the sons of your mother bow down to you.*" (Gen 27:29)

> [Joseph said:] "Listen to this dream I had: We were binding sheaves of grain out in the field when suddenly my sheaf rose and stood upright, while *your sheaves gathered around mine and bowed down to it.*" His brothers said to him, "Do you intend to reign over us? Will you actually rule us?" (37:6–8)

> [Jacob blessed Judah:] "Judah, your brothers will praise you; your hand will be on the neck of your enemies; *your father's sons will bow down to you.*" (49:8)

The description of the descendant of Judah matches the expectation of Jacob's blessing as well as the vision of Joseph that had already come to pass (Kissling, 8–9). For the brothers, the story of Joseph, the ruler and savior, becomes a picture of the expected Judah-king. These connections do not give license to invent wild typological expectations from Joseph's special cloak or any other minor details (contra Hamilton, 270; Lunn, 27–41). Rather, the expectational patterns are limited to the rule, obedience, and worship of the Judah-king spelled out in the blessing of Judah.

*How does Genesis provide the context for understanding the expectation for the coming Judah-king?*

When he finished giving his word for the last days, Jacob instructed his sons concerning his burial. Then Israel died. The narrator's description of the death of Abraham, Isaac, and Jacob must be compared to hear the subtle implications concerning Jacob's death (emphases added).

> Then Abraham *breathed his last* and **died at a good old age, an old man full of years**; *and he was gathered to his people.* (25:8)
>
> Then he [Isaac] *breathed his last* and died *and was gathered to his people,* **old and full of years**. (35:29)
>
> When Jacob had finished giving instructions to his sons, he drew his feet up into the bed, *breathed his last and was gathered to his people.* (49:33)

Each of the three breathed his last and was gathered to his people, but only Abraham and Isaac were old and full of years. Although Abraham and Isaac each lived longer than Jacob (175 and 180 years, respectively), still, at 147 years of age Jacob seems old. The difference may come from Jacob's description of himself to pharaoh: "My years have been few . . . and they do not equal the years of the pilgrimage of my fathers" (47:9). The narrator perhaps reports his death in a manner that reflects Jacob's negative comparison.

The fact that Jacob, like Abraham and Isaac, was "gathered to his people" is a figure of speech, but one that carries significant implications. Through the Torah are various warnings that have the judgment "You will be cut off from your people" attached to them (e.g., Num 15:30–31). The serious warning may have signified that the person would be cast from God's people in this life *and in death* (see discussion of "cut off" in Chapter 17). The other side of the figure of speech is also suggestive: To be gathered to one's people meant that there was something, however vague, beyond this life. Messiah argued that God's self-identification "I am the God of Abraham, Isaac, and Jacob" indicates that the ancestors' "lives" continued in some sense beyond their physical lives, inferring an expectation for resurrection (Mark 12:26–27; cf. Exod 3:6).

*How is resurrection hope inferred in the reports of the deaths of the Hebrew ancestors?*

The funeral and memorial of Israel was extensive both in Egypt and in Canaan. Jacob's remains were embalmed, by physicians not priests, over a forty-day period, and he was mourned throughout Egypt for seventy days. Though mummification was prevalent among those who could afford it in ancient Egypt, the Scriptures only mention Jacob and Joseph as being embalmed (Gen 50:2–3, 26). Jacob was regarded with royal status according to the seventy days of mourning through Egypt.

A large entourage of Egyptian officials went along with Israel's entire family, except the children, to bury him in the cave of Machpelah near Mamre with Leah, Abraham and Sarah, and Isaac and Rebekah. When they arrived at the threshing floor of Atad, they held a seven-day mourning period. The reference to this locale, which was presumably near the cave at Hebron, is noted in an unusual way: "beyond the Jordan" (Gen 50:10 lit.). There are many references to locales beyond the Jordan River in the Torah, such as the plains of Moab, but the phrase "beyond the Jordan" almost always represents an in-the-land perspective that refers to places outside the land. This unusual case referred to a location within the land as "beyond the Jordan." That is, Genesis 50 is addressing readers in exile or outside the land, so that a place near Hebron was beyond the Jordan. Genesis ends with the readers looking across the Jordan toward the land along with the Israelite families living in Egypt. This sets the course for the exilic perspective with which all major collections of Scripture end.

*In what ways does the book of Genesis end with an exilic perspective?*

The brothers feared that with Jacob gone, Joseph might intend to get his revenge. They told Joseph that Jacob had instructed them to ask him to forgive them. It is possible that Jacob did say such a thing. The narrator, however, has not mentioned such a conversation between Jacob and his ten eldest sons. Moreover, the reader might wonder why Jacob would have avoided speaking directly to Joseph about this matter. It appears that the older brothers may have once again resorted to deception as their strategy for handling life challenges. In any case, Joseph was brought to tears, again.

Joseph's response to his brothers contains at least two matters that are theologically significant in relation to Genesis. First, he asked, "Am I in the place of God?" (50:19). This rhetorical question is identical in wording, but in the opposite direction, to the one Jacob had asked Joseph's mother. Rachel had vented her anger at Jacob and demanded that he give her children. He responded, "Am I in the place of God?" (30:2), making the point that all of life is from God. Jacob's conviction that God is the life-giver corresponds with the creational emphasis of Genesis 1. The Creator did not merely create humans and leave the rest to them. Every birth is by the Creator's permission. When God did finally "remember Rachel" (30:22), she bore Joseph.

Joseph's rhetorical question to his brothers reflects a similar view concerning an opposite point. His brothers feared death, and Joseph's question establishes that for him God is the life-taker. Even if Joseph had used his power to have his brothers killed, he believed it could only mean that God had judged them with death. The identical questions from Joseph and his father—"Am I in the place of God?"—accent for readers that every life and every death are always and only God's prerogatives. While things can be explained in human terms, at a deeper level granting life and death belong to God. Readers learn once again that the effects of death and life, whether from the two trees in the garden or from anyone anywhere, point to human responsibility before the Creator.

Second, Joseph stated his conviction that God mysteriously worked his good intentions even through ruthless acts committed with evil intentions: "*You intended to harm me, but God intended it for good* to accomplish what is now being done, the saving of many lives" (50:20, emphasis added). The mysterious interrelationship between human sinfulness and God's grace has rarely been stated so directly. According to Joseph, God's plans are not dependent on the good deeds of the upright, but they were accomplished by his brothers' inhumane acts. The fact that the Genesis storyteller embraced Joseph's conviction is seen in the many narrative comments concerning God's supervision over his life (39:2–3, 5, 21–23; also see 45:5–9). The manner in which God works for good even through human evil is not something that can be explained. But it is a conviction that the storyteller expects readers to embrace.

Joseph's forward looking last words reaffirm the power of God's word to his ancestors concerning the chosen family. "Then Joseph said to his brothers, 'I am about to die. But God will surely come to your aid and take you up out of this land to the land he promised on oath to Abraham, Isaac and Jacob'" (50:24). Genesis records the beginning of the fulfillment of God's word. He had given the offspring of promise to Abraham and had extended, through his prophet Israel, the expectation of the heir of Judah to come. The story of the beginning of humankind and of the beginning of the chosen family endures as a testament to the power of the word of God.

Joseph's last request foreshadows Israel's departure from Egypt more than four centuries later. Before Joseph died, he made the Israelites promise someday to carry his remains out of Egypt with them (Gen 50:25; Exod 13:19; Josh 24:32). They did.

## ANOTHER LOOK

The difficulty in Genesis 49:10, the attention paid to Joseph by later biblical writings, and the relative chronology of the narratives of the last three sections of Genesis will be introduced here. One of the difficulties in Genesis 49:10 is deciding whether to read the Hebrew word *shiloh* as a single word referring to the ancient town of Shiloh or as two Hebrew words, *shi-loh*, meaning either "that which belongs to him," "tribute to him," or the like. Modern committee translations like the NIV and NRSVue typically use one of these in the text and one or more in a textual note. The term *shiloh* in verse 10 is probably not the town of Shiloh since it is never spelled this way in Hebrew elsewhere in Scripture. Based on several technicalities, I favor "until that which belongs to him comes" (see detailed explanation in Schnittjer, "Blessing," 16–17, n. 3). The relationship of this reading to "tribute to him" needs to be explained.

What is *that which belongs to him*? In this poetic context it could refer to the submission of his brothers and enemies (49:8), the scepter (49:10a), or the obedience of the nations (49:10c), or as poetry it can have a broad, imprecise reference that makes the reader consider each of these. Because the coming descendent of Judah will be Joseph-shaped (see explanation of 49:8, above), that which belongs to him may be thought of as "tribute." I agree with the line of interpretation that *tribute* is part of *that which belongs to him*. The Hebrew word for tribute (*minhah*) is not used in 49:10, but it could be an interpretation of *shi-loh* (see de Hoop, 138–39). It appears that later biblical writers expected a ruler to whom the nations would bring tribute. Consider the poetically reinterpreted Genesis imagery in the "of Solomon" psalm of the king (see Table 10-C).

Lion from Ishtar gate of ancient Babylon on display in the Louvre

*Robert C. Kashow*

Also consider the biblical references to the wealth of the nations brought to Solomon and promised to be brought to Jerusalem (see, e.g., 1 Kgs 10:2, 10; Isa 60:4–7; Hag 2:7–9).

| Psalm 72 | Primary Allusions | Secondary Echoes of Genesis |
|---|---|---|
| v. 8, rule ends of earth | Zech 9:10 (cf. 9:9, king coming on a donkey) | **15:18**, land to the Euphrates River (49:11, ruler riding on a donkey) |
| v. 9, lick the dust | Isa 49:23; Mic 7:17 | **3:14**, eat dust |
| vv. 10–11, tribute from kings of Tarshish, distant shores, Sheba, Seba | 1 Kgs 4:21; **Gen 10:4, 5, 7** | **49:10**, that which belongs to him = tribute<br>**10:2, 6**, descendants of Japheth and Ham (who serve the Shem king) |
| v. 17 | **Gen 12:3; 18:18; 22:18** | |

**Table 10-C:** Psalm 72 and Imagery from Genesis[a]

[a]Table based on Schnittjer, *OT*, 489.

Joseph was the first of five major characters in the Hebrew Scriptures to function within the context of a foreign royal court. The stories of the others (Moses, Esther, Daniel, and Nehemiah) each reflect selected aspects of the Joseph narratives. Daniel 2 features many echoes of Joseph explaining pharaoh's dreams in Genesis 41 (see Rindge, 88–90; Philpot, 688–89; Widder, 1112–14). It seems that the book of Esther in Hebrew (there are many differences in the Septuagint's version of this book) often echoes the stories of Joseph in Genesis (see Table 10-D; adapted from Schnittjer, *OT Narrative*, 190).

The well-known fact that God is not mentioned explicitly in Esther appears to be one of the most significant theological points of the book. In Genesis God invisibly works his plans to save the family of Israel as well as many peoples (see Chisholm, 13–14). The narrator emphasizes God's unseen providence (39:2–3, 5, 21–23) in accord with

Joseph's stated convictions (45:5–9; 50:19–20). The book of Esther demonstrates that even what the enemies of Israel meant for evil, God used for good. God can be trusted to be faithful to his word and to protect his people. The invisibility of God within the book of Esther forces readers to believe that he is there even when they cannot see him.

**Table 10-D:** Possible Echoes of the Joseph Narratives in the Book of Esther

| Genesis | Esther |
|---|---|
| Joseph resisted doing the will of Mrs. Potiphar "*day after day*" (39:10) | Mordechai resisted submitting to Haman "*day after day*" (3:4) |
| [Joseph to his brothers:] "*But God sent me ahead of you* to preserve for you a remnant on earth and to save your lives by a great deliverance" (45:7). | [Mordecai to Esther:] "For if you remain silent at this time, relief and deliverance for the Jews will arise from another place .... And who knows *but that you have come to your royal position for such a time as this?*" (4:14) |
| Pharaoh honors Joseph by royal garments and heralds (41:41–43). | Ahasuerus honors Mordechai by royal garments and heralds (6:8–9). |
| [Judah to Joseph:] "*No! Do not let me see* the misery that would come on my father" (44:34b). | [Esther to Ahasuerus:] "*For how can I bear to see* disaster fall on my people?" (8:6a) |
| Joseph elevated as second to pharaoh (41:41). | Mordechai elevated as second to Ahasuerus (10:3). |

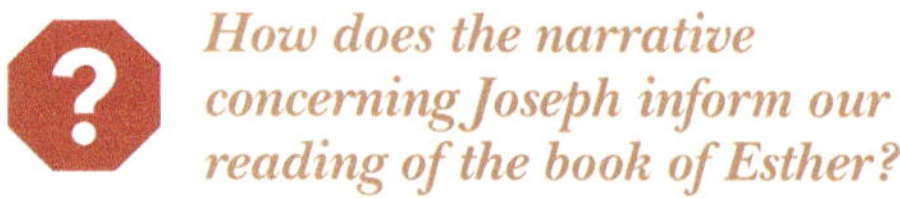


The chronological details of the stories of the Hebrew ancestors have some difficulties, but working through them can help with some of the background issues. The notation of the age of various characters recurs regularly in Genesis. In the closing chapters the references to the age of Jacob and Joseph are given whereby the preceding time markers can be defined, to a certain extent, by counting backward. Genesis provides enough information to correlate the relative chronology of many of the events narrated in relation to the age of the patriarchs and matriarchs. The following two tables present the main correlations between the story line and the leading persons' ages. Some of the ancestors' ages in Table 10-E are inferred (those in parentheses); for example, Jacob's age is counted back from later in Genesis. Table 10-F presents the story line-age correlations related to Jacob and his family.

Three significant difficulties with correlating the stated ages and the narratives should be noted (see Sarna, 364, n. 3; 367, n. 1; 368, n. 17). First, the timing of Joseph's birth could be identified with two different times. When Genesis 30:25–27 is read only in its immediate context, it appears that Joseph was born at the end of the fourteen years of labor for Leah and Rachel but before the six years of work to earn livestock.

| Reference | Narrative Setting | Abraham | Sarah | Isaac | Jacob |
|---|---|---|---|---|---|
| 12:4 | call of Abram | 75 | (65) | | |
| 16:16 | birth of Ishmael | 86 | (76) | | |
| 17:1 | renaming and circumcision | 99 | (89) | | |
| 21:5 | birth of Isaac | 100 | 90 | birth | |
| 23:1 | death of Sarah | (137) | d. 127 | 37 | |
| 24:67; 25:20* | marriage of Isaac | (140) | | 40 | |
| 25:26 | birth of Jacob | (160) | | 60 | birth |
| 25:7* | death of Abraham | d. 175 | | (75) | (15) |
| 28:5 | Jacob leaves home | | | (131) | (71) |
| 35:28 | death of Isaac | | | d. 180 | (120) |

**Table 10-E:** Correlation of the Genesis Storyline and the Ages of Abraham, Sarah, Isaac, and Jacob

*= references listed out of narrative sequence

| Reference | Narrative Setting | Jacob | Joseph | Other Children[a] |
|---|---|---|---|---|
| 29:20 | Jacob began 7 years for Rachel | (71) | | |
| 29:30 | Jacob began to work for Rachel, again | (78) | | |
| 29:31–30:24 | Jacob's growing family (7 years) | (78–85) | | Jacob's 11 oldest children born |
| 30:27* | Jacob began work for cattle | (85) | | |
| 30:25–26; 37:3 | Rachel had a son | (91) | birth | |
| 31:38, 41 | Jacob returned to Canaan | (91) | | (11 oldest children ages 6–13) |
| 37:2 | Joseph worked with brothers | (108) | 17 | |
| 41:46 | Joseph appointed ruler in Egypt | (121) | 30 | |
| 41:50, 53–54 | 7 years of abundance complete | (128) | (37) | (Manasseh and Ephraim born) |
| 47:9 (45:6, 11) | Jacob moved to Egypt | 130 | (39) | |
| 47:28; 49:33 | death of Jacob | d. 147 | (56) | |
| 50:26 | death of Joseph | | d. 110 | |

**Table 10-F:** Correlation of the Genesis Storyline and the Ages of Jacob and His Children

*= references listed out of narrative sequence

[a]The eleven oldest children include ten brothers and Dinah; all the siblings except Joseph and Benjamin.

In another context, however, Jacob rationalized giving the special cloak to Joseph because he was a son of his old age (37:3). This statement does not make sense if Joseph was born about the same time as his siblings. Thus, perhaps the account of Joseph's birth is listed, out of its chronological sequence, with the other birth accounts in Genesis 30 for reasons of theme or plot. Specifically, the narrator may have grouped all the children's births together in the section of Jacob's "evenings" at home, before the section on his "days" at work (see Table 8-D in Chapter 8). Perhaps Jacob's statement in 30:25–26 is given as a forewarning of his departure after all twenty years have passed.

By dating Joseph's birth as I have in Table 10-F, it is much easier to account for the time needed for the events concerning Judah in Genesis 38—sons old enough to marry, much time of waiting for Tamar, his own grieving for his wife (which had taken three years for Isaac, see Table 10-F). If the other reading of 30:25–27 is correct (that Joseph was born in Jacob's fourteenth year with Laban; see above), then Jacob's age from the time he began to work for Rachel the first time to the time he returned to Canaan must be adjusted by six years in Table 10-F; specifically, he would have been seventy-seven years of age at that time, and so on (on this reading see Merrill, 121).

Second, the events of Genesis 34 do not make good sense if they took place immediately after returning to the land of promise. When Jacob returned to his homeland, Dinah was about six and Simeon and Levi approximately twelve and thirteen years of age. The events in this context probably took place a decade or more after the family had left Laban. There are two ways, neither of which is a problem, to account for this. Ten or more years could have passed between living in Succoth (33:17) and then in Shechem, or perhaps the episode recorded in Genesis 34 has been placed out of chronological sequence for thematic, narrative, or theological reasons.

Third, it is difficult to determine the time of the birth of Benjamin. Benjamin's birth and Rachel's death are recorded in Genesis 35 during their travels south from Bethel. It seems that this trip did not take place after the lengthy residency in Succoth and Shechem mentioned above because Jacob later said that she died when he was returning from living with Laban (48:7). The accounts in Genesis 35, therefore, are probably not listed in their chronological sequence but are arranged as they are for other reasons. If this reading is correct, then Rachel was pregnant with Benjamin during their trip from Haran. She lied, then, to hide the household gods on which she was sitting when she told her father she could not get up because she was menstruating (31:35).

The fact that not all of the Genesis story line has been arranged in chronological sequence is not a troubling matter. Many biblical narratives are arranged in nonchronological ways for a variety of reasons (Schnittjer, *OT Narrative*, 10). The Torah itself contains several examples of narratives not arranged chronologically. The advice of the father-in-law of Moses (Exod 18), Moses in the tent of meeting (33:7–11; 34:33–35), and the census of the first generation (Num 1) are each explicitly out of chronological sequence (see Chapters 14, 15, and 20). Biblical narratives are not structured as biographies or histories in any general, or modernist, sense. They are interpreted histories. The materials are not raw facts, as though readers are viewing video recordings from surveillance cameras. The narratives are carefully directed, arranged, and structured as story. They offer the scriptural interpretation of the storied worlds they depict.

*Why do biblical narratives sometimes depart from chronological sequence?*

## INTERACTIVE WORKSHOP

### *Chapter Summary*

Jacob gave a blessing to the two sons of Joseph, thus establishing his reception of the birthright, and then he blessed his own twelve sons. The blessing of Judah instituted a most significant biblical hope, namely, that the Judah-king will one day come and rule the nations. The deaths of Israel and Joseph signaled the end of the story of the ancestors.

### *Can You Explain the Key Terms?*

- gathered to his people
- Judah-king
- last days
- mummification

### *Challenge Questions*

1. Why did Jacob say that Manasseh and Ephraim would be counted as his children (48:5)?
2. Why did Jacob interpret his life in two different ways in 47:9 and 48:15–16 (cf. 48:3–5)?
3. What was the theological significance of the blessing of Judah within the context of Genesis?
4. What was the function of describing the expected Judah-king in language that reflected the rule of Joseph in Genesis?
5. What is the theological significance of Joseph's rhetorical question in 50:19?
6. What evidence from elsewhere in Genesis supports an interpretation that the narrator of Genesis agrees with the view of Joseph in 50:20? What does this mean for readers?

### *Advanced Questions*

1. What is the literary-theological function of the frequent use of poetry within Genesis (e.g., 1:27; 2:23; 3:14–19; 4:23–24; 8:22; 9:6, 25–27; 14:19–20a; 16:11–12; 25:23; 27:27–29, 39–40; 49:2–27)?
2. What is the theological significance of the echoes of the Joseph narrative within the Hebrew book of Esther? How does the Septuagint's expansions of the book of Esther deflect the possible significance of the relationship between the Esther and Joseph stories? (See *Additions to the Book of Esther* in the NRSVue; also see Schnittjer, *OT Narrative*, 194–95).

*3. What is the meaning of *mal'ak* ("delegate, messenger") used in 48:16 within the Jacob narratives?

*4. Was the Hebrew phrase of 49:1, *be'aharit hayyamim*, rightly translated with the Greek phrase *ep' eschaton ton hemeron* in the Septuagint? Explain.

## Research Project Ideas

Trace out how the blessings of the sons of Jacob intersected with the tribes of Israel in years to come.

Define the view of human life after death within the context of the Pentateuch.

Compare the biblical details on the mummification of Jacob with what we know of the Egyptian practice of this era.

Untangle the chronological details of Genesis 34–35.

## The Next Step


Chisholm, Robert B., Jr. "A Rhetorical Use of Point of View in Old Testament Narrative." *Bibliotheca Sacra* 159 (2002): 404–14.

de Hoop, Raymond. *Genesis 49 in Its Literary and Historical Context.* Oudtestamentische Studiën 39. Leiden: Brill, 1999. The review of de Hoop's work by Gary A. Rendsburg is helpful, particularly his interaction with the six sons treated in Genesis 49:13–21; see *Journal of Semitic Studies* 47 (2002): 138–41.

Emadi, Samuel. "Covenant, Typology, and the Story of Joseph." *Tyndale Bulletin* 69.1 (2018): 1–24.

Hamilton, James M. *Typology: Understanding the Bible's Promise-Shaped Patterns.* Grand Rapids: Zondervan Academic, 2022.

Kissling, Paul L. "The Testament of Jacob and the Blessing of Moses: A Narrative Approach." Page 1–15 in *Text and Canon: Essays in Honor of John H. Sailhamer.* Edited by Robert L. Cole and Paul J. Kissling. Eugene, OR: Pickwick, 2017.

Lunn, Nicholas P. "Allusions to the Joseph Narrative in the Synoptic Gospels and Acts: Foundations of a Biblical Type." *Journal of the Evangelical Theological Society* 55.1 (2012): 27–41.

Merrill, Eugene H. "Chronology." Pages 113–22 (esp. Table 3) in *Dictionary of the Old Testament: Pentateuch.* Edited by T. Desmond Alexander and David W. Baker. Downers Grove, IL: InterVarsity Press, 2003.

Philpot, Joshua M. "Was Joseph a Type of Daniel? Typological Correspondence in Genesis 37–50 and Daniel 1–6." *Journal of the Evangelical Society* 61.4 (2018): 681–96.

Rindge, Matthew S. "Jewish Identity under Foreign Rule: Daniel 2 as a Reconfiguration of Genesis 41." *Journal of Biblical Literature* 129.1 (2010): 85–104.

Sailhamer, John H. "The Canonical Approach to the OT: Its Effect on Understanding Prophecy." *Journal of the Evangelical Theological Society* 30 (1987): 307–16.

Sarna, Nahum M. *Exodus.* JPS Torah Commentary. Philadelphia: Jewish Publication Society, 1989.

Schnittjer, Gary Edward. "The Blessing of Judah as Generative Expectation." *Bibliotheca Sacra* 177 (2020): 15–39.

———. *Old Testament Narrative Books: The Israel Story.* Brentwood: B&H Academic, 2023.

———. *Old Testament Use of Old Testament.* Grand Rapids: Zondervan Academic, 2021.

Watts, James W. *Psalm and Story: Inset Hymns in Hebrew Narrative.* Journal for the Study of the Old Testament Supplement Series 139. Sheffield: Sheffield Academic, 1992.

Widder, Wendy L. "The Court Stories of Joseph (Gen 41) and Daniel (Dan 2) in Canonical Context: A Theological Paradigm for God's Work among the Nations." *Old Testament Essays* 27.3 (2014): 1112–28.

# Exodus

## THESE ARE THE NAMES

ויאמר אלהים אל־משה אהיה אשר אהיה

# 11 MACROVIEW OF EXODUS



## GETTING STARTED

### *Focus Question*

What is the story of the book of Exodus?

### *Look for These Terms*

- filling
- Genesis-shaped
- presence
- remember
- tabernacle
- tent of meeting

## AN OUTLINE

A. **From Egypt (1:1–15:21)**
   1. The Egyptians oppress Israel and throw their infant boys into the river (1–2)
   2. The bush (3–4)
   3. The plagues and the Passover (5:1–13:16)
   4. Yahweh throws the Egyptian army into the sea (13:17–15:21)

B. **Through the Wilderness (15:22–18:27)**
   1. Israel's grumbling and God's provision (15:22–17:7)
   2. The Amalekites defeated (17:8–16)
   3. Judges appointed over Israel (18)

C. **At the Mountain (19–40)**
   1. The covenant with the people (19–24)
   2. The dwelling instructions (25–31)
   3. The rebellion and the revelation (32–34)
   4. The dwelling constructed and filled (35–40)

## A READING

Figuring out the story of Exodus is challenging. As the book unfolds, the reader may think, in each subsequent section, this is what the story is. The great acts of God—the exodus, provision in the wilderness, his word at the mountain, the plans for his dwelling place among Israel—are each oriented toward a more basic issue. The account of the rebellion with the golden calf displays the problem. How can Yahweh's presence dwell among a nation of wicked revolutionaries? But that is not quite right. Better, how can sinful rebels bear the presence of the holy Creator? They cannot. That is the problem.

The movement of the story, at least relative to Yahweh and Israel broadly speaking, can be thought of in stages. God brought Israel to the mountain, descended on it, and gave his word and his glory to the people (see Figure 11-A). Each time Yahweh and the people drew closer together, the problem of his presence grew. The stages of the story need to be considered particularly as they situate the problem of Israel in Yahweh's presence.

*What is the significance of the progressive proximity of Yahweh and Israel in the book of Exodus?*

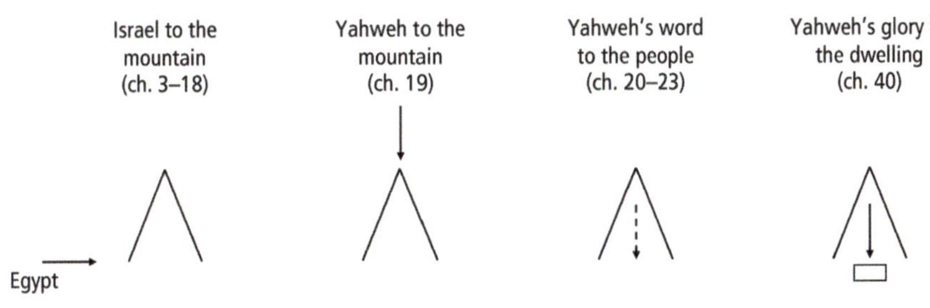


**Figure 11-A:** The Progressive Proximity of Yahweh and Israel in Exodus

First, Yahweh delivered Israel from oppression and brought his people to the mountain. The situation triggering the entire chain of events that constitute the Exodus story was that Israel filled the land of Egypt. This Egyptian problem was actually caused by the creational and covenantal blessing of Israel. They multiplied and became numerous because the people were fulfilling the commission to humanity—be fruitful and multiply (see Gen 1:28; 9:1, 7). Moreover, they were beginning to realize God's word of promise to Abraham (see Table 3-D in Chapter 3). The fruitfulness of Israel became the target of the Egyptian oppression. The Egyptians attacked the life that Yahweh gave his people and in doing so they defied the Creator.

The basis of the salvation of the Israelites from bondage was that God remembered his word to Abraham. "The Israelites groaned in their slavery and cried out, and their cry for help because of their slavery went up to God. God heard their groaning *and he remembered his covenant with Abraham, with Isaac and with Jacob*. So God looked on the Israelites and was concerned about them" (Exod 2:23b–25, emphasis added).

To say God "remembers" does not merely refer to a mental act but an enactment and embodiment of God's faithfulness to his word (Schnittjer, 54). The remainder of Exodus—as well as the Torah and indeed the Bible—is a consequence of the word of promise to Abraham.

*How is the redemption of Israel related to God's word to Abraham?*

Yahweh remembered his word to Abraham and called a deliverer. Moses brought God's terrors against pharaoh. The world God had created became a tool of his judgment against the Egyptians. In Exodus 1 the Egyptian oppression escalated to the point where they attempted to weaken Israel systematically by throwing their infant boys into the river. The judgment of Yahweh against the Egyptians increased through a series of plagues until he killed their firstborn children. Furthermore, in response to pharaoh's pursuing Israel into the wilderness, Yahweh threw the Egyptian army into the sea (see Jubilees 48:13–14; cf. Wisdom of Solomon 18:5).

> Then Moses and the Israelites sang this song to Yahweh: "I will sing to Yahweh, for he is highly exalted. *Both horse and driver he has hurled into the sea. . . . Pharaoh's chariots and his army he has hurled into the sea.* The best of Pharaoh's officers are drowned in the Red Sea." . . . Miriam sang to them: "Sing to Yahweh, for he is highly exalted. *Both horse and driver he has hurled into the sea.*" (Exod 15:1, 4, 21, emphasis added)

The symmetry of Yahweh's wrath against the Egyptians reveals the terrifying power of his word. After God defeated pharaoh, Moses led the people through the wilderness. The one who saw the burning bush on the mountain led the people back to the foot of that same mountain.

Second, Yahweh's glory descended on the mountain and he spoke the Ten Words to Israel. Yahweh's voice terrified Israel. They begged Moses to serve as mediator between them and their God. Moses agreed, and Yahweh approved the arrangement. Moses ascended the mountain to represent the people to God. This act was the beginning of forty long years of pleading the people's case, pleading that God would be merciful to rebellious Israel. Moses received God's word and acted as his prophet speaking his will to the people.

On the mountain Moses received the Ten Words in writing, the various instructions for the "book of the covenant" (24:7—most likely referring to chs. 21–23), and extensive instructions for the dwelling where God's glory would reside in the midst of his people. The instructions for the "dwelling" (traditionally called the "tabernacle" but also called the "tent of meeting"—both terms are used in parallel in 40:34) occupy seven chapters (chs. 25–31). The term *tabernacle* denotes its function as the dwelling place of God's glory, while *tent of meeting* signifies it as the place of the revelatory conferences God held with Moses. The construction of the dwelling fills an additional six chapters,

The sphinx (66 feet high and 240 feet long) and pyramid (40 stories high) were already ancient when Israel served as slaves in Egypt



repeating many details in a slightly different order (chs. 35–40). Exactly in the middle of these thirteen chapters on the dwelling is the remarkable account of the people's rebellion and God's revelation.

*Why was the tabernacle sometimes called the* tabernacle *and sometimes the* tent of meeting*?*

The narrative location of the people's rebellion evokes a grotesque image for readers, falling as it does between the carefully detailed instructions for, and the construction of, the dwelling of Israel's holy God. The holiness of Yahweh mandated that the tent of meeting had to be just so. If his holiness is neglected, even in a small detail, people will die. The depth of the people's audacious sin radiates from its central place within the narrative of the dwelling of God. This stark juxtaposition of his holiness and their rebellion raises the biggest problem of the story. The most serious difficulty is not pharaoh's stubbornness but that of the chosen people. If Yahweh brought his terrors against the defiant Egyptian ruler, then how can Israel avoid his wrath?

*What is the importance of the rebellion with the golden calf?*

The strength of God's word to Israel's ancestors was tested when the people rebelled against him at the base of Mount Sinai. Israel's rebellion incited God's wrath to the point that he intended to wipe them out, excepting only Moses. It was Moses's prayer invoking the promise to Abraham that averted God's judgment:

> "Turn from your fierce anger; relent and do not bring disaster on your people. *Remember your servants Abraham, Isaac, and Israel, to whom you swore by your own self*: 'I will make your descendants as numerous as the stars in the sky and I will give your

> descendants all this land I promised them, and it will be their inheritance forever.'" Then Yahweh relented. (32:12b–14a, emphasis added)

The echo of God's word to Abraham reminds readers that this was the reason for the exodus itself, the reason the people were brought to the mountain. What was at stake at the beginning and the end of the book was the power of Yahweh's eternal word.

It is thus, within this context of extreme opposites, that the wonder of Yahweh's character is revealed. Yahweh forgives. The surprise is that the combination of his holiness and the people's sinfulness does not bring disaster. Rather, Yahweh reveals himself, in part, to Moses. His character toward human rebels is expressed, at his discretion, by the phenomenon of compassion and forgiveness. The Exodus story displays God's wrath against the hard-hearted pharaoh and his grace toward the defiant, disobedient Israelites. The different divine acts cannot be explained by differences between pharaoh and the people. According to the Torah, both were wicked and stubborn. The reasons for his different actions remain hidden from the eyes of mortals, even Moses. The most that we can see, or rather hear, are the effects of God's word to Moses: "Yahweh, Yahweh, the compassionate and gracious God, slow to anger, abounding in love and faithfulness" (34:6b).

Third, the glory of Yahweh filled the tent of meeting. The end of the book echoes the beginning, forming a frame to enclose the story between. The connection between these passages provides the reader with clues to hear the story.

> These are the names of the sons of Israel who went to Egypt with Jacob, each with his family: Reuben, Simeon, Levi and Judah; Issachar, Zebulun and Benjamin; Dan and Naphtali; Gad and Asher. . . . Joseph was already in Egypt. . . . The Israelites were exceedingly fruitful; they multiplied greatly, increased in numbers and became so numerous *that the land was filled with them*. (1:1–4, 5b, 7)

> Then the cloud covered the Tent of Meeting, *and the glory of Yahweh filled the tabernacle*. Moses could not enter the tent of meeting because the cloud had settled upon it, *and the glory of Yahweh filled the tabernacle*. (40:34–35, emphasis added)

The story moves from Israel's filling of the land of Egypt, dwelling in its midst, to the glory of God's presence filling the tent alongside Israel's community.

Exodus closes at the apex toward which the narrative has been moving since chapter 1. Just as the Egyptians could not tolerate Israel filling their land, so too Moses could not remain in the dwelling once Yahweh's glory came upon it. The context of Exodus makes Moses's inability to withstand the presence of Yahweh's glory most remarkable. Moses alone had been chosen by the people to meet with him and hear his voice. Yahweh spoke to Moses uniquely, "face to face, as one speaks to a friend" (33:11). Thus, when Yahweh's glory filled the tent of meeting, forcing Moses out, it symbolized the intensity of his presence (40:34–35). He had condescended in an act of grace to reside with the people.

At first it seemed as if the problems of the Israelites were external—the tyrannical Egyptians and the barren desert. God delivered them from these because of his word to Abraham. He gave them a new word from the mountain and instructions for his dwelling. This caused the real problem. How could these rebels bear the presence of Yahweh's glory? They committed damnable acts against his word even as it was being written. The only way for Yahweh to dwell among his people, therefore, was to condescend to them in grace and forgiveness. He did not relax his standards but forgave Israel in light of the power of his word to the Hebrew ancestors.

Relief of Egyptian beating a slave from door jamb of palace of Merneptah (1213–1204 BCE)

*Matthew Parks*

The progressive movement of the story both reflects and depends on Genesis. The book of Exodus is a complete story, an integrated and interrelated whole, yet it is also the second part of the Torah. As the second book in the series, it needs to be read in light of its prequel. This book is Genesis-shaped. It begins with Israel enjoying the creational blessing of their explosive population growth (see Rendsburg, 129–30). The exodus event itself is based on God's word to Abraham (see Gen 15:13–16). Exodus tells the story of the creation of Israel by the power of God's word. Whereas the Genesis story began with God making a garden for the humans, Exodus ends with Israel making a dwelling place for God. The highpoint of the Exodus narrative is God's coming to dwell with his people. What would it mean for the Creator to reside with Israel? Part of the answer to this question is the book of Leviticus.

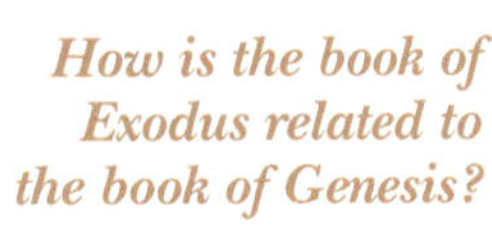

## ANOTHER LOOK

The Exodus narrative itself moves in stages between the Israelites filling Egypt to Yahweh's glory filling the dwelling. God brought Israel to the mountain, descended on the mountain, and gave his word to Israel. Finally, his glory filled the dwelling. The progressive proximity between Yahweh and his people—the plot of the book—correlates with the geographically rooted structure of the book (see Table 11-B).

**Table 11-B:** The Progressive Proximity of Yahweh and His People and the Structure of Exodus

| The proximity of Yahweh and his people within Exodus itself | The structure of Exodus within Torah |
|---|---|
| Yahweh brought Israel to the mountain (1–18) | from Egypt (1:1–15:21) |
| | through the desert (15:22–18:27) |
| Yahweh came down to the mountain (19) | at the mountain (19–40) |
| Yahweh's word to the people (20–24) | |
| Yahweh's glory filled the dwelling (25–40) | |

Within the Torah there is a symmetry in the central section (i.e., Exodus-Leviticus-Numbers). The symmetry is especially seen when Exodus is reread from the vantage point of Numbers, the main connection being Mount Sinai. The people arrive at the mountain in Exodus 19 and camp there through Numbers 10. In the middle of this three-book series is Leviticus, the instruction of Yahweh while the people are encamped at the mountain. The macro-story line, therefore, moves to and from the mountain. The importance of the Sinai event, spanning the middle of the Torah, should not be downplayed (see Milgrom, xvii–xviii; Imes, 14).

The relationship between Exodus and Numbers can be expanded by comparing three parts of each, most importantly the wilderness journeys (see Table 11-C; also see Smith, 205–6). Other comparisons made by Smith between Exodus and Numbers tend to be too general to support a tightly knit mirror imaging.

**Table 11-C:** The Structure of Exodus and Numbers Compared

| Exodus | | | Numbers | | |
|---|---|---|---|---|---|
| from Egypt<br>1:1–15:21 | through the wilderness<br>15:22–18:27 | at the mountain<br>19–40 | the camp at Sinai<br>1:1–10:10 | wilderness journeys<br>10:11–21:35 | plains of Moab<br>22–36 |

The wilderness narratives in Exodus 15–18 and Numbers 10–21 are a special case. The Numbers stories specifically echo many of the incidents recounted in the counterpart Exodus passages (see Table 20-E in Chapter 20). The stories of repetitive grumbling accent Israel's moral shortcomings in the first and the second generation over the course of many years. The cohesion of the wilderness stories through Exodus and Numbers is so great that Deuteronomy often treats all of the wilderness years as a single unit. Note, for example, "From the day you left Egypt until you arrived here [the plains of Moab], you have been rebellious against Yahweh" (Deut 9:7).

? *How is the book of Exodus related to the book of Numbers?*

## INTERACTIVE WORKSHOP

### *Chapter Summary*

The story of Exodus builds in stages and reaches its highest level in the section of the rebellion and the revelation. The sinful people, in the presence of their holy God, are met with forgiveness and grace.

### *Can You Explain the Key Terms?*

- filling
- Genesis-shaped
- presence
- remember
- tabernacle
- tent of meeting

### *Challenge Questions*

1. What is the relationship between the exodus event, the giving of the law, and the larger story of Exodus?
2. What are the main features of the relationship between Exodus and Genesis?
3. What is the significance of placing the account of the golden calf between the instructions for and the construction of the tent of meeting?

### *Advanced Questions*

1. How is interpretation affected by considering Exodus within the Torah as a whole versus regarding Exodus by itself?
2. What is the function of God's word of promise to Abraham, Isaac, and Jacob within Exodus?

*3. What is the meaning of "remember" (*zkr*) within the context of Exodus 2 and 32?

### *Research Project Ideas*

Compare the beginning and the end of the book of Exodus.

Explain the ways that Exodus needs to be situated against Genesis.

Explain the significance of the echoes of Exodus in Numbers.

### *The Next Step*


Imes, Carmen Joy. *Bearing God's Name: Why Sinai Still Matters.* Downers Grove, IL: IVP Academic, 2019.

Milgrom, Jacob. *Numbers.* JPS Torah Commentary. Philadelphia: Jewish Publication Society, 1990.

Rendsburg, Gary A. "The Literary Unity of the Exodus Narrative." Pages 113–32 in *"Did I Not Bring Israel Out of Egypt?": Biblical, Archaeological, and Egyptological Perspectives on the Exodus Narratives.* Edited by James K. Hoffmeier, Alan R. Millard, and Gary A. Rendsburg. Winona Lake, IN: Eisenbrauns, 2016.

Schnittjer, Gary Edward. "The Bad Ending of Ezra-Nehemiah." *Bibliotheca Sacra* 173 (2016): 32–56.

Smith, Mark S. "Matters of Space and Time in Exodus and Numbers." Pages 182–207 in *Theological Exegesis: Essays in Honor of Brevard S. Childs.* Edited by Christopher Seitz and Kathryn Greene-McCreight. Grand Rapids: Eerdmans, 1999.

# 12 THE RIVER AND THE BUSH
## *Exodus 1–4*

Ryan Faas © 123RF.com

## GETTING STARTED

### *Focus Questions*

Why did God call Moses? What does God reveal about himself?

### *Look for These Terms*

- anthropomorphic
- gender-inclusive language
- gender-specific metaphor
- Jehovah
- lord/Lord/LORD
- Masoretes
- Second Temple period
- Tetragrammaton
- Yahweh

## AN OUTLINE

A. **The Egyptians Oppress Israel and Throw Their Infant Boys into the River (1–2)**
   1. Israel fills the land and the Egyptians afflict them (1:1–14)
   2. Two sets of women deliverers and Moses, a would-be deliverer (1:15–2:22)
   3. God remembers his word (2:23–25)

B. **The Bush (3–4)**
   1. The messenger of Yahweh calls to Moses from the burning bush (3:1–10)
   2. The reluctant deliverer (3:11–4:17)
   3. Moses returns to Egypt (4:18–31)

## A READING

The opening sections of Exodus concerning the river and the bush set up the stage-by-stage developing story line of the entire book. Moreover, the elements of these introductory stories show the basis for God's leading the people and preserving them for forty years until they reach the land of promise—that is, the rest of the Torah narrative.

Exodus 1–2 presents the series of problems to be resolved within the book itself, and chapters 3–4 offer readers a view of the dynamic relationship between Yahweh and his people. The redemption from Egypt and the covenant at the mountain, which together create the possibility for the presence of God's glory within the dwelling, were founded on God's promise to the Hebrew ancestors. Exodus is a narrative representation of the effects of God's word to Abraham. His word devastated the Egyptians but preserved the sinful Israelites.

Exodus opens with a list of the sons of Jacob who came down to Egypt generations earlier. Thus, while this book has a beginning, that beginning depends on the narrative of Genesis. The elements within the Exodus narrative make sense within the book itself, but they reach beyond the edges of the book and situate the story within the context provided by Genesis. Even the description of the growth of the families of Israel within Egypt echoes with creational sounds. "The Israelites *were exceedingly fruitful; they multiplied greatly, increased in numbers* and became so numerous that *the land was filled* with them" (Exod 1:7). On the sixth day God said, "*Be fruitful and increase in number; fill the earth* and subdue it" (Gen 1:28). And he said to Noah at the time of the new beginning, "*Be fruitful and increase in number and fill the earth*" (9:1, emphases added).

While readers are invited to regard the narrative in relation to Genesis, a new king of Egypt arose who did not know Joseph (Exod 1:8). When Joseph himself had been forgotten, he remained imprisoned (Gen 40:23). Forgetting Joseph redefined the Israelites as an Egyptian problem. Yahweh, however, had not forgotten.

The Israelites fulfilled the creational blessing within the confines of Egypt and set in motion a series of related events that would ultimately lead to God's presence filling the dwelling in their midst. The land of Egypt was being filled with a minority group, which led to enslavement, oppression, and the systematic extermination of the male infants as a means of control and suppression. The inhuman crimes against the families of Israel and their prayers for help reached God. He remembered his covenant with their ancestors. As a result, he rescued them, established Israel as a nation, gave his word in the form of a covenant, and gave instruction for a dwelling place for his glory. The chain reaction of epic events, culminating in the presence of Yahweh's glory filling the dwelling, began because Israel filled Egypt.

*What is the importance of the creational blessing in the book of Exodus?*

Pharaoh had a twofold approach to the Israelite problem: ruthless enslavement and infant murder. In the former the Egyptians were successful, but the latter strategy failed at first. Pharaoh tried to get the Hebrew midwives to murder the male babies during the birthing process. The midwives disobeyed. When he made them account for not obeying, they lied and said that Hebrew women were different. They said that Hebrew women are "lively," using a term that could be understood as they are "animals" (see note on Exod 1:19 Fox). In any case, their babies were always delivered before the midwives arrived on the scene. God blessed the pair of women deliverers, and the Israelites increased all the more.

Mud bricks
*Vladislav T. Jirousek/ Shutterstock.com*

Semitic slaves (mid-fifteenth century BCE)
*© 2018 Zondervan*

Plan B for dealing with the Israelite problem came in the form of a royal edict to throw all infant Hebrew boys into the Nile River. During the time of this anti-Semitic reign of terror, Moses was born. The deliverer was rescued by women. His mother, from the tribe of Levi, hid him as long as she could and then took a great risk. The language "she saw him that he is good" (2:2 lit.) echoes the creation days when "God saw X . . . that it is good" (Gen 1:4, 10, 12, 18, 21, 25 lit.; Schnittjer, 31). She made a small "ark," the same word used of the large vessel that saved Noah's family and the animals from judgment by water (Rendsburg, 130). "And when she was no longer able to hide him, she took for him *a little-ark* of papyrus, she loamed it with loam pitch, placed the child in it, and placed it in the reeds by the shore of the Nile" (Exod 2:3 Fox, emphasis added). Meanwhile, the child's sister watched.

One of pharaoh's daughters saw the ark and rescued the baby. She gave him an Egyptian name—"Moses"—because she pulled him out of the water. The tradition of Hollywood interpretations stemming from the motion picture *The Ten Commandments* and continuing down to the animated *Prince of Egypt* and others has imagined that her adopted child played a prominent role in the Egyptian royal family. The text of Exodus is silent on the matter; he grew to an adult between verses 10 and 11 of Exodus 2 (forty years passed according to Acts 7:23). The chances are that pharaoh, like most ancient Near Eastern monarchs, had an extensive harem of wives and concubines. The fact that Moses was adopted by one of their daughters put him in an elite class within the ancient Egyptian society but not necessarily in a position to vie for the throne. In any event, explaining the details of Moses growing up within the extended family of pharaoh, beyond the fact that he did, is not a concern of the biblical storyteller.

Moses went out to "his brothers" (2:11), the Hebrews, and saw an Egyptian man beating a Hebrew man. He killed the Egyptian. When pharaoh heard, he tried to put Moses to death. The would-be deliverer fled into desert exile. There he was able to deliver the seven daughters of Jethro, of the Reuel clan, from a band of shepherds. Although earlier in the chapter Moses was referred to as a brother of the Hebrews, Jethro's daughters said he was an Egyptian (2:19). Moses married Jethro's daughter Zipporah and lived in the desert.

The length of time covered by chapter 1 is not specified; rather, it was an indefinite period of enslavement and infanticide. The events of chapter 2 took place over a period of eighty years (see 7:7). In other words, the passing of time moves quickly at the beginning of the book and slows to a near standstill when Yahweh reveals himself on the mountain (see discussion of narrative time in Chapter 1). The chronology of the book of Exodus in Table 12-A can be compared to the larger chronological issues in the books of Exodus, Leviticus, and Numbers (see Tables 14-C and 20-A in chapters 14 and 20, respectively).

**Table 12-A:** Chronology of the Book of Exodus

| Bondage | | Deliverance | Journey to Sinai | The Camp at Sinai |
|---|---|---|---|---|
| Chapter 1 | Chapter 2 | Chapters 3–11 | Chapters 12–18 | Chapters 19–40 |
| Indefinite number of months or years | Eighty years (7:7) | Unspecified number of weeks | Three months (12:1–3; 19:1) | Nine months (40:2, 17) |

Toward the end of Exodus 2 the scene shifts to God. The Israelites cried out and God heard. This passage follows the pattern of the first creation day in the fourfold use of God-plus-verb: "And *God heard* their moaning, and *God remembered* his covenant with Abraham, with Isaac, and with Jacob. And *God saw* the Israelites. *God knew*" (2:24–25 lit., emphasis added; see Fox, 266). Although Exodus 1 focuses on the oppression leading up to the time of the birth of Moses, the mistreatment of the Israelites was forecast as lasting about four centuries in Abraham's vision (Gen 15:13). Even if the oppression is restricted to the eighty years plus in Exodus 1 and 2, it is striking to consider the perspective of the people and that of God. They had been crying out for many generations, and God had not responded. Though it is misguided to think that God was absent and unconcerned because of the long oppression, the narrator is silent on God's reasons for the delay.

The force behind the deliverance God initiated was his word to the Israelite ancestors. The statement "God remembered" should not be thought of as passive reflection, but as in Genesis, when God "remembered," he acted. The anthropomorphic expression (using human language of a deity) plays off a notion of recalling something that spurs action. When God remembered Noah, he sent the wind to clear the water for a new beginning. When he remembered Rachel, she was able to conceive Joseph. The statement in Exodus 2 that God remembered his covenant with the ancestral trio anchors the series of events, beginning with deliverance and leading to the land of promise, entirely on his word. God had spoken a word to Abraham, and he would be faithful.

? *How does the deliverance of God's people relate to his word of promise?*

When Moses saw a burning bush and went to inspect it, he was given the task of rescuing Israel. He had failed as a deliverer in his single attempt many years before. The messenger of Yahweh identified himself, "I am the God of your father, the God of Abraham, the God of Isaac and the God of Jacob" (Exod 3:6). Moses hid his face. He told Moses that he had seen the suffering of his people and intended to rescue them and lead them to the land of promise, and he intended to do it through Moses.

Four figures of Rameses II seated before a temple carved into sandstone cliff at Abu Simbel
*iStock.com/nodostudio*

*Left:* Colossal statue depicts king Rameses II with his daughter Bent'anta (the size difference between the figures is meant to speak to the greatness of the larger figure). *© 2018 Zondervan*

*Right:* Rameses II *© 2018 Zondervan*

The reluctance of Moses, as it seems at first, escalated to rejection of God's will. Yet God prevailed and insisted that Moses obey his word. The progress of the dialogue sketches out the tensions that extend in several directions from the story line. The dialogue consists largely of Moses's questions, excuses, and deflection of God's will and God's revealing response to each. The main exchanges of the dialogue are presented in Table 12-B.

The significance of the dialogue warrants looking briefly at each of the five exchanges. The first exchange revealed that Moses was a prophet of God speaking his word. It was easy enough for opponents of God's prophets to resent or personally hate the prophet himself. The pentateuchal pattern for prophets of Yahweh, however, is that they are mere conduits offering the word of God.

| Moses | Yahweh |
|---|---|
| Who am I? | I will be with you and I sent you (3:11–12) |
| Who are you? | "I am who I am . . . I am has sent you" (3:13–22) |
| What if the people will not believe me? | If they do not believe you, they will believe the signs that I give you—staff into snake, skin disease, water to blood (4:1–9) |
| I am not able to speak well. | I made your mouth and I will teach you what to say (4:10–12) |
| Send someone else. | Yahweh was angry: Your brother Aaron will help you speak (4:13–17) |

**Table 12-B:** The Dialogue between Yahweh and Moses at the Bush

The second interaction reveals the identity of God in terms of his name. The name is associated with the covenantal faithfulness of Israel's God to Israel (see Abba, 326–27). The most likely way to pronounce the four Hebrew letters *yhwh* is "Yahweh" (Freedman, 151–52). When Moses asked God his name, he replied, "I am who I am," or something like "I will be what I will be," a statement that, although difficult to translate, appears to be related to God's proper name, Yahweh (see Grisanti, 1:1025; cf. Advanced Question 5 below). God had not revealed his name to the Hebrew ancestors but preserved this honor for Moses (6:3). The name Yahweh raises some issues for English Bible readers. How should the Hebrew name of God be translated into the languages of the peoples, particularly into Greek and then into Latin and English?

The name of God is holy. Ancient Judaic traditions emerged in the Second Temple era (515 BCE–70 CE) according to which the people stopped using God's name altogether. Since the name of Yahweh dwells in his sanctuary (see below), saying the name began to seem like walking into the holy of holies. The common practice of not saying the divine name extended across New Testament times. When the Hebrew Bible was translated into Greek, the Septuagint translators used the word *kurios* ("lord, master, sir") instead of the name. The same practice was also followed in public Hebrew Scripture reading among Judaic communities. Whenever Judaic readers came to the word *Yahweh* they instead said the Hebrew word for "lord" or "master," *'adonai*. The Great Isaiah Scroll of the Qumran community, for example, features *'adonai* written between lines above the divine name in many places (see Table 12-C; Ulrich, 2:382). In other cases, the Qumran scribes used an old font (paleo-Hebrew) for the divine name while everything else was written in the standard font (Aramaic block letters; see Pesher Habakkuk [1QpHab] column VI, line14). The name of God in the Hebrew Scriptures was spelled with the four consonants, *yhwh*, and eventually became known as the Tetragrammaton (literally, "the four-lettered [name]").

**Table 12-C:** Layout of 28:16a in the Great Isaiah Scroll (1QIsa[a] XXII, 20)

| Hebrew (right to left) | Transliteration of Hebrew (left to right) | English (lit.) |
|---|---|---|
| אדוני | *'adonai* | the Lord |
| לכן כה אמר יהוה | *laken coh 'amar Yahweh* | therefore thus says Yahweh |

The Judaic secretaries responsible for making copies of the Hebrew Scriptures in the medieval period before the printing press was invented were known as the Masoretes. The Masoretes copied the Hebrew Scriptures that had been written with only consonants, and they developed a series of vowel points (dots and dashes placed under or over the consonants to avoid tampering with the condonants themselves) to preserve the ancient pronunciations of the Hebrew words. In the case of the word *yhwh*, the Masoretes put the vowels of the word *'adonai* with it, because readers of the Hebrew Scriptures within rabbinic Judaism read that word instead. The result was that western Christians misread the word as *YeHoWaH* or Jehovah (y = j and w = v based on German influence). The traditional Christian misreading "Jehovah" is not the name of God but the consonants of *Yahweh* combined with the vowels *a* (variant pronunciation of *e* in some cases), *o*, and *a* from *'adonai*.

Most conventional English translations today—such as the New International Version and the New Jewish Publication Society—still follow the ancient practice of substituting the word "lord" for the name of God in the Old Testament, usually capitalized with the other letters in small capitals. In the English Bible, "LORD" refers to the Hebrew word *Yahweh* and "Lord" to the word *'adonai* when referring to Israel's God. The term "lord" in traditional English culture was used as a title to greet one's superior or overlord. This word implies the dignity and social dominion of the person being addressed. For example, to greet a couple respectfully, one might say, "My lord, my lady." Unfortunately, the use of a title ("lord") in modern English translations hides the sense and power of Yahweh as a name (Fretheim, 4:1296).

*How did translations shift to using the word "lord" instead of the name of God?*

Before the exile, ancient Israel probably said the divine name because it is written in Scripture. Since ancient times many strategies have been used to avoid saying the divine name (see Table 12-D). The English word "lord" has lost its traditional meaning within contemporary North American society through disuse and is now a religious word restricted to God. In this book I have chosen to use Yahweh as an English loanword to refer to God's name. While I appreciate the decision of those who choose not to use the name of God out of reverence, I use Yahweh's name in worship and formal writing out of respect for that which is written in Scripture.

| | |
|---|---|
| Hebrew Bible | Yahweh (*yhwh* יהוה) |
| Septuagint | "lord" (*kurios* κυριος) |
| Dead Sea Scrolls | different font for divine name (1QpHab); superscript "lord" (*'adonai*) over divine name (1QIsa[a]) |
| Masoretic Text | consonants of unread *yhwh* with vowels of "lord" (*'adonai*) for reading in synagogue |
| English Bible | the LORD |

**Table 12-D:** Representing the Divine Name

The revelation of Yahweh as the "I am" who sent Moses carried tremendous significance. He revealed himself in his name. The tabernacle (and later the temple) was the place where his name would dwell signifying his ownership and rule (see Deut 12:5; 1 Kgs 8:17–21). Moreover, in this context the name accompanied God's promise to be with Moses (Exod 3:12). Yahweh promised Moses's successor, Joshua, that he would never leave him or forsake him (Deut 31:6; see also Josh 1:6–9). The Exodus story itself was steadily moving toward the climactic revelation of the presence of Yahweh's glory that would dwell with his people in the tabernacle.

The third exchange related to the way in which God's message would be received. God gave Moses a series of signs that manifested the power of his word. The extraordinary acts using ordinary things—stick and snake, horrible skin disease, water and blood—were not the point. The signs were symbols pointing toward the truth and power of God's word through his servant.

The fourth exchange involved the prophet himself. Moses claimed that he could not talk well ("I'm heavy of mouth and heavy of tongue," Exod 4:10, Friedman, 180). Some claim Moses did not know how to speak Hebrew (Exod 4:1, 29–31), and others that he did not know Egyptian (6:12, 30; see Propp, 210–11). However, ancient linguistic evidence suggests that Moses had some kind of speech impediment (Tigay, 57–58). In any case, God had made his mouth and knew his abilities. A natural way to paraphrase Exodus 4:11 is: "If your speech is defective, it is because I have made you that way" (ibid., 62).

Region of upper Midian
*Isaiah and Abby Cramer*

The final interaction was Moses's deflection of the responsibility altogether. He told Yahweh to select someone else. Yahweh's anger burned toward the reluctant, and perhaps defiant, prophet. Yet Yahweh agreed to send Aaron, Moses's older brother, to help him speak to pharaoh and the people. He commanded Moses to go and he went.

Two significant things happened to Moses while returning to Egypt. First, Yahweh spoke to him again. He said that he planned an array of signs against pharaoh but that he would make the king stubborn so that he would refuse to let the Israelites go. He explained why: "Then say to Pharaoh, 'This is what Yahweh says: Israel is my firstborn son, and I told you, "Let my son go, so that he may worship me." But you refused to let him go; so I will kill your firstborn son' " (Exod 4:22–23). God considered the tribes or families of Israel his own. He was a father to them because of his word of promise to their ancestors.

The fatherhood of God to Israel was an anthropomorphic or human metaphor for his relationship to the heirs of his word. There is a sense in which all humans, since they are created in the image of God are his children (see Gen 5:1–3; Acts 18:28). But Israel was the heir, the firstborn son, of God in a fuller sense by covenantal election. Yahweh demonstrated his responsibility to his son Israel by killing the son of his opponent, pharaoh.

It is important in this case to maintain the male orientation of the metaphor, whether applied to males, females, or, as it was, to both together in Israel. The reason for maintaining the male orientation of the metaphor here is the use of other male-oriented metaphors to describe the relationship of Yahweh and his people in the Torah and other Scriptures, especially the use of heart circumcision in Leviticus 26 and Deuteronomy 10 and 30. The hearts Yahweh circumcised, whether physically males or females, were sons of God. Female-oriented biblical metaphors likewise need to retain their gender within their figurative teaching contexts to preserve the meaning prescribed therein. The various biblical teachings on Israel as the wayward wife of Yahweh (e.g., Hos 2; Ezek 16; Jer 3) or New Testament believers as the bride of the Messiah (e.g., Eph 5:25–27; cf. John 14:1–3), for example, apply to males and females alike.

The figurative language in these passages should not, in my view, be neutered to "children" or "spouses" because of the historical social significance of the gender roles in these biblical contexts. Without its gender orientation, theological meaning will be lost. Care should be taken in our gender-conscious day to preserve the full meaning of the historical gender-specific metaphors in biblical teachings concerning the relationship of God and his people—metaphors that apply inclusively to all segments of humankind that are his own. At the same time, when Hebrew words for humans appear they should be presented in gender-inclusive language: "human beings" or "humankind," not man or mankind, again to honor the theological sense of Scripture. Learning to honor the Scriptures over modern cultural trends requires patience and care.

*Why is it important to maintain the gender orientation of some biblical metaphors?*

Second, Moses was saved by a woman, again. During one of the stops that Moses took on his way to Egypt, Yahweh met him and was about to kill him. The event suggests overtones of Jacob's wrestling in the night. Readers have always found this incident unusual and challenging to interpret. Zipporah saved Moses by circumcising their son and touching him with the foreskin. She said, "Surely you are a bridegroom of blood to me," apparently referring to the blood from the hasty circumcision (Exod 4:25). Whereas Moses was on his way to rescue God's son Israel from bondage, he had not expressed his own commitment to a relationship with God by the physical mark of circumcision on his own son. Zipporah delivering her husband from Yahweh also anticipates deliverance by the messenger of death killing the firstborn of Egypt (see Morales, 74–75).

The narrative in which Zipporah rescues Moses (4:24–26) and the one in which Moses delivers Zipporah and her sisters (2:15–22) bracket the dialogue at the bush. Moreover, the story of Moses in Exodus 2–4 is framed by women saving him from death. The entire Moses story, along with the account of God's deliverance of Israel from Egypt, is framed, in addition, by the deliverance of Moses from the river and the song and dance of praise to God by Miriam and the Israelite women because Yahweh had thrown pharaoh's army into the sea. The literary envelope diagrammed in Figure 12-E, along with the account of the savior midwives in Exodus 1, demonstrates not only the courage of the women but also the manifold ways in which God worked to preserve his people. The prophet of God who rescued his people was himself living a life that had been delivered from death by God's saviors.

*Why was there great emphasis on the deliverance of Moses by various women?*

**Figure 12-E:** The Framing of the Accounts of Calling Moses and the Exodus

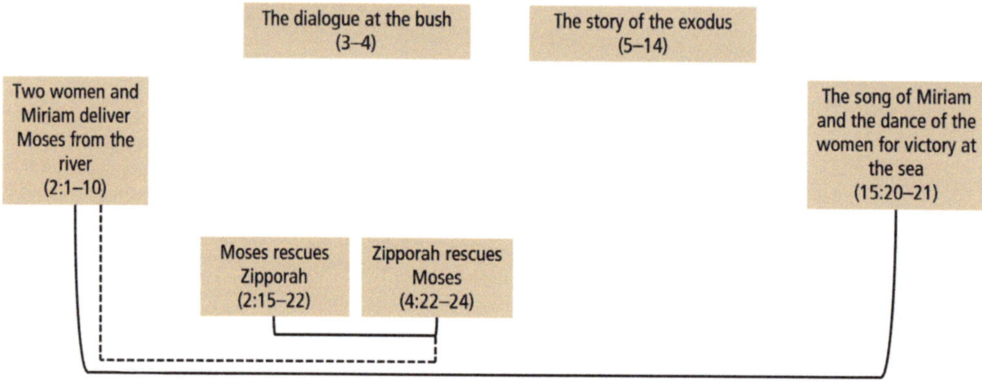


## ANOTHER LOOK

A few literary and theological matters of Exodus 1–4 relative to later Scriptures can be discussed here. First, the Greek term for "lord" (*kurios*) was put to good use by the New Testament writers, especially because of the word's connotation in the Septuagint. *Kurios* was used in the Torah, Prophets, and Writings in Greek both for the Hebrew word for "lord" (*'adon, 'adonai*) and as a substitute for the name of God, *Yahweh*. Jesus himself was called "master" (*kurios*) by his apprentices, the disciples. Thus, when the New Testament letters referred to Jesus as "the Lord" (*kurios*), it signified at one time both his role as the master of those who followed him and his shared identity with Yahweh. He is the divine master.

*What is the double inference of the term* **kurios** *("master, lord, Lord") when used of Jesus in the New Testament?*

Second, all people are children of God because they have been created in his image. The expression "son of God" when applied to Israel signified their heightened relationship with God as father. The metaphorical phrase was used in even more specific ways later in the Scriptures. Yahweh's promise to King David included his commitment to David's son as his own son (2 Sam 7:14). The Davidic heir, the Messiah, then, was Yahweh's son in a fuller sense than Israel. In Matthew 1 the notion of son of God is radicalized from the manner it had been used previously in the Scriptures.

In the case of Jesus there is a literalization of the figurative sense of son of God. To say it anthropomorphically (and not quite right): God is the "biological" or "physical" (that is, somehow, "real") father of Jesus. The intimate proximity between God and the created realm in the virgin's conception of Jesus defies the categories of language to describe it literally without misspeaking. He is the Son of God in a qualitatively different sense from any other son of God.

Third, Joshua 5 has two scenes that echo Exodus 3–4: the circumcision of the second generation of Israelites (vv. 2–9) and the appearance of a messenger of Yahweh causing Joshua to remove his sandals while on the holy ground (vv. 13–15). Moses removed his sandals before the presence of the messenger of Yahweh (Exod 3:5), and Moses's son was given an "emergency" circumcision (4:24–26). The biblical reader may be surprised at first that the Israelites did not circumcise their sons in the wilderness. They failed in one of the same ways that Moses himself had failed. The generation of uncircumcised Israelites raised up under Moses's leadership in the wilderness illustrates that he had not learned from his own near-death experience when Zipporah circumcised their son. The lack of the sign of the covenant also symbolized their sin of unbelief toward the God who had rescued them and patiently provided for their needs.

## INTERACTIVE WORKSHOP

### *Chapter Summary*

The Egyptians oppressed Israel because they were filling the land. God revealed himself to Moses and commissioned him to deliver the people from enslavement in Egypt.

### *Can You Explain the Key Terms?*

- anthropomorphic
- gender-inclusive language
- gender-specific metaphor
- Jehovah
- lord/Lord/Lord
- Masoretes
- Second Temple period
- Tetragrammaton
- Yahweh

### *Challenge Questions*

1. What are the clues from Exodus 1 and 2 that God was working to protect the Israelites, even though he may have seemed absent, during their long bondage?
2. What, according to Exodus, was the motive and rationale for the redemption of Israel from Egypt?
3. What do the series of questions, excuses, and challenges that Moses gave to God in Exodus 3–4 reveal about the future deliverer? What do they reveal about God?
4. What is the significance of the six different female persons involved in rescuing in Exodus 1–4?

## *Advanced Questions*

1. In what ways does Exodus require the narrative of Genesis to make sense of its story?
2. Why does the account of the savior midwives pass over their deceptive tactics without comment and yet affirm the godly motivation for their actions?
3. How did the dialogue of Exodus 3–4 reveal the dynamic tensions that were in the background of the preceding and following narrative sections?

*4. What is the significance of using the same term for "ark" in the account of Moses on the Nile as was used in the Noah narrative?

*5. List and evaluate three of the ways to translate *'ehyeh 'asher 'ehyeh*, the self-identification of God in Exodus 3:14 (see Childs, 50, 60–64; Fox, 270, 273 [on 3:14]; Pannell, 351–53).

## *Research Project Ideas*

Compare the women saviors in Exodus 1–4 with other women saviors in the Hebrew Scriptures like Tamar, Rahab, Jael, Ruth, and so on.

Explain and evaluate the ways Greek and English Scriptures handle the Hebrew word *Yahweh*.

## *The Next Step*


Abba, Raymond. "The Divine Name Yahweh." *Journal of Biblical Literature* 80 (1961): 320–28.

Childs, Brevard S. *The Book of Exodus. A Critical, Theological Commentary.* Louisville: Westminster, 1974.

Fox, Everett. *The Five Books of Moses.* New York: Schocken, 1995.

Freedman, David Noel. "The Name of the God of Moses." *Journal of Biblical Literature* 79 (1960): 151–56.

Fretheim, Terence. "Yahweh." Pages 1295–1300 in vol. 4 of *New International Dictionary of Old Testament Theology and Exegesis.* Edited by Willem A. VanGemeren. Grand Rapids: Zondervan, 1997.

Friedman, Richard Elliot. *Commentary on the Torah.* San Francisco: HarperSanFrancisco, 2001.

Grisanti, Michael A. "היה." Pages 1022–26 in vol. 1 of *New International Dictionary of Old Testament Theology and Exegesis.* Edited by Willem A. VanGemeren. Grand Rapids: Zondervan Academic, 1997.

Morales, L. Michael. *Exodus Old and New: A Biblical Theology of Redemption.* Essential Studies in Biblical Theology 2. Downers Grove, IL: IVP Academic, 2020.

Pannell, Randall J. "I *Would* Be Who *I* Would Be!: A Proposal for Reading Exodus 3:11–14." *Bulletin for Biblical Research* 16.2 (2006): 351–53.

Propp, William H. C. *Exodus 1–18.* Anchor Bible 2. New York: Doubleday, 1999.

Rendsburg, Gary A. "The Literary Unity of the Exodus Narrative." Pages 113–32 in *"Did I Not Bring Israel Out of Egypt?": Biblical, Archaeological, and Egyptological Perspectives on the Exodus Narratives.* Edited by James K. Hoffmeier, Alan R. Millard, and Gary A. Rendsburg. Winona Lake, IN: Eisenbrauns, 2016.

Schnittjer, Gary Edward. *Old Testament Use of Old Testament.* Grand Rapids: Zondervan Academic, 2021.

Tigay, Jeffrey H. "'Heavy of Mouth' and 'Heavy of Tongue': On Moses' Speech Difficulty." *Bulletin of the American Schools of Oriental Research* 231 (1978): 57–67.

Ulrich, Eugene, ed. *The Biblical Qumran Scrolls.* 3 vols. Leiden: Brill, 2013. (Also see high definition images of 1QIsa[a] column XXII at http://dss.collections.imj.org.il/isaiah and 1QpHab column VI at http://dss.collections.imj.org.il/habakkuk.)

# 13 THE PLAGUES AND THE SEA
## *Exodus 5:1–15:21*

*iStock.com/ruvanboshoff*

## GETTING STARTED

### *Focus Questions*

What were God's reasons for his terrors against the Egyptians? How can the hardening of pharaoh's heart be explained?

### *Look for These Terms*

- dialectic
- hard heart
- Passover
- plagues
- Reeds Sea
- sovereignty
- worship

## AN OUTLINE

A. **The Terrors (5:1–13:16)**
   1. The problems of Pharaoh, Moses, and the Hebrew people (5:1–6:27)
   2. Three sets of three plagues (6:28–10:29)
   3. The tenth plague and instruction for remembering it (11:1–13:16)

B. **The Sea (13:17–15:21)**
   1. Travel from Egypt following the pillar of cloud and fire (13:17–22)
   2. The narrative of the crossing of the sea (14)
   3. The Song of the Sea (15:1–21)

## A READING

The story of the exodus from Egypt itself has two main parts: the cosmic terrors and the sea crossing. The challenge between God's messengers (Moses and Aaron) and pharaoh is center stage. Various other minor characters play important roles in the development of the story, such as the supervisors of the Hebrew slaves and pharaoh's wizards. The victory of God in the first part of the story arises from his tenfold terrors against the oppressors of his people. In the second part, Yahweh definitively defeats the oppressors by throwing their militia into the sea. Thus, this segment of the larger story ends with poetic justice for the Egyptian people who once threw Israel's infants into the Nile River.

The conflict between the word of God and the human revolution is in direct view here. Moses spoke God's word, and pharaoh resisted and defied the will of Yahweh. The Creator responded with cosmic terrors, one after another, until he accomplished his purposes.

The account of the plagues contains several items that need careful attention. (1) The rationale for the plagues is a recurring theme. Because of the repetition, and also in light of the way in which these passages present Yahweh's character, the reported reasons for the signs and judgments are of first importance. (2) The matter of the hardening of pharaoh's heart remains a classic example of the puzzle of God's relationship with human beings. Within the account of the first nine plagues the storyteller shines a light inside pharaoh's soul between each of the judgments. (3) The intertwining of the report of the tenth plague and the instruction for Passover celebrations illumines a crucial aspect of the function of the narrative at large.

Locusts

*Left: iStock.com/ ruvanboshoff*

*Right: Holger Kirk/ Shutterstock.com*

First, why did God use these plagues against the Egyptians? Some biblical interpreters see the ten plagues as directed against ten Egyptian gods, effectively embarrassing and defeating them. A summary of the possible gods against which Yahweh battled appears in Table 13-A (adapted from Hannah, 1:120). This reading infers that God was demonstrating his supremacy above the deities of Israel's polytheistic oppressors. I partially agree with this reading.

Torah supports the view that God defied and defeated the gods of the Egyptians *in general*. Referring to the tenth plague God said, "On that same night I will pass

| | |
|---|---|
| *Nile to blood* | Hapi (also called Apis), bull god, god of the Nile; Isis, goddess of the Nile; Khnum, ram god, guardian of the Nile; others |
| *Frogs* | Heqet, goddess of birth, with a frog head |
| *Gnats* | Set, god of the desert |
| *Flies* | Re, a sun god; Uatchit, possibly represented by the fly |
| *Death of livestock* | Hathor, goddess with a cow head; Apis, bull god, symbol of fertility |
| *Boils* | Sekhmet, goddess with power over disease; Sunu, pestilence god; Isis, healing goddess |
| *Hail* | Nut, a sky goddess; Osiris, god of the crops and fertility; Set, god of storms |
| *Locusts* | Nut, a sky goddess; Osiris, god of the crops and fertility |
| *Darkness* | Re, a sun god; Horus, a sun god; Nut, a sky goddess; Hathor, a sky goddess |
| *Death of firstborn* | Min, god of reproduction; Heqet, goddess who attended women at childbirth; Isis, goddess who protected children; Pharaoh's firstborn son considered a god |

**Table 13-A:** Egyptian Gods Against Whom the Plagues Were Possibly Directed‡

‡Adapted from *The Bible Knowledge Commentary OT* by John F. Walvoord and Roy Zuck. 

through Egypt and strike down every firstborn of both people and animals, *and I will bring judgment on all the gods of Egypt*" (Exod 12:12). Reflecting on the exodus as a whole Moses stated, "*Who among the gods is like you*, Yahweh?" (15:11). Also, "Moses told his father-in-law about everything Yahweh had done to Pharaoh and the Egyptians for Israel's sake. . . . [Jethro] said, 'Praise be to Yahweh, who rescued you from the hand of the Egyptians and of Pharaoh, and who rescued the people from the hand of the Egyptians. Now I know that *Yahweh is greater than all other gods*, for he did this to those who had treated Israel arrogantly'" (18:8, 10–11). Again, "They marched out defiantly in full view of the Egyptians; . . . for *Yahweh had brought judgment on their gods*" (Num 33:3–4, emphasis added in all passages).

The fact that Yahweh defeated the gods of the Egyptians in general, however, does not and should not give interpreters license to read into the narrative a specific blow-by-blow list of the supposed deities whom Yahweh defeated. There are historical problems with correlating each plague with a particular ancient Egyptian deity (see Wells, 196). Many of the gods and goddesses had multiple functions or responsibilities, making it difficult to know which deity was being attacked by a given sign. Moreover, according to our present knowledge, many Egyptian deities were only worshiped in certain locales and some only during certain times. There was no group of ancient Egyptians or Israelites, as far as we know, that could have correlated the ten plagues against ten particular Egyptian gods. To add to the challenges, debate continues regarding the date of the exodus itself (see Sidebar 13-B).

*In what sense did the plagues demonstrate Yahweh's superiority over the gods of Egypt?*

## Sidebar 13-B: The Date of the Exodus from Egypt

One of the topics much discussed in older studies was the date the Israelites left Egypt. In the lengthy tradition of the debate, there have been many positions (see Janzen, "Introduction," 20–23; Janzen, "Conclusion," 284–85; Walton, 258–72). In the past few decades many scholars have recognized the limitations of the information we possess and rightly urge caution in chronological matters. Because a few scholars continue to make the same cases, the present discussion interacts with two of the traditional proposals.

The proponents for one of the later dates of the exodus maintain that it occurred sometime around 1250 BCE. An important element for this view is the reference in Exodus 1:11 to the building of the cities of Pithom and Rameses (cf. Gen 47:11; Exod 12:37; Hoffmeier, "Thirteenth-Century," 96–98; Hoffmeier, "Date," 235). The identification of the building project with Rameses II led to the identification of Seti I and Rameses II as the pharaohs of the oppression and exodus respectively (see Table 13-C).

The defenders of an earlier date prefer the year 1446 BCE (Stripling, 29–32). The key issue for them is 1 Kings 6:1, which reports that the exodus took place 480 years before "the fourth year of Solomon's reign over Israel," which we know was in 966 BCE. Accordingly, Thutmose II and Thutmose III or Thutmose III and his son Amenhotep II (depending on difficult issues of Egyptian chronology) would have been the pharaohs of the oppression and exodus respectively (see Table 13-C).

**Table 13-C:** Two Egyptian Chronologies[a]

[a]This table presents two of the ancient Egyptian chronological systems. Difficulties in ancient Egyptian studies prevents an agreed upon chronology. See Lasor, 2:41–44; Kitchen 2:329.

| | Lasor | Kitchen |
|---|---|---|
| *Eighteenth Dynasty* | | |
| Thutmose I | 1526–1512 | 1504–1492 |
| Thutmose II | 1512–1503 | 1492–1479 |
| Hatsheput | 1503–1482 | 1479–1457 |
| Thutmose III | 1482–1450 | 1479–1425 |
| Amenhotep II | 1450–1425 | 1427–1400 |
| *Nineteenth Dynasty* | | |
| Seti I | 1317–1303 | 1294–1279 |
| Rameses II | 1304–1227 | 1279–1213 |
| Merneptah | 1227–1217 | 1213–1203 |

Those who favor the later date explain that the notation of 480 years is not a literal number. It could have been meant schematically—specifically, that about twelve generations had passed between the exodus and the beginning of the construction of the temple. The dozen generations could have translated into a number by multiplying them by the biblical symbolic number for a generation, forty years: 12 x 40 = 480 (Kitchen, 2:702–3; Hoffmeier, "Response," 57–58).

Those who favor the earlier date propose that the name Rameses in Exodus 1:11; 12:37; and Numbers 33:3, 5 did not refer to the great Egyptian pharaoh Rameses II. Some say "Rameses" is a common name even from earlier times (Archer, 49–50). Others say that the references in Exodus could have been the result of later scribal updating so that readers could identify the places (Stripling, 112; Aling, 136–37). Note how Genesis identified the place to which Abram pursued Lot's captors as Dan, even though it was not renamed Dan until much later (see Gen 14:14; Judg 18:29; cf. Gen 47:11).

Proponents of earlier dates and later dates attempted to use different interpretations of archaeological data in Egypt and in the cities of Israel associated with the conquest in order to backdate the exodus by forty years. The complicated multiple interrelated hypotheses associated with the potential archaeological evidence supporting one or another conquest date bred more doubt than confirmation (see Redmount, 77–79; Stager, 94–102).

Many scholars who regard the biblical account of the exodus as referring to historical events do not think the biblical evidence provides enough detail to identify the pharaoh of the exodus or the date of the exodus (Hoffmeier, "Rameses," 281; Hoffmeier, "Date," 226; Merrill, 544; Wells, 210—Merrill and Wells push back against overconfidence with identifying Rameses II as the exodus pharaoh). One reason the historicity of the exodus does not hinge on identifying the pharaoh is that the Scriptures do not name him.

The Merneptah stele celebrates pharaoh Merneptah's (1213–1204 BCE) military victories

*Todd Bolen/ BiblePlaces.com*

One bright spot in recent years is the increased confidence of scholars to regard the Merneptah monument as offering the oldest historical witness to the people of Israel outside the Scriptures. Merneptah succeeded Rameses II and ruled for ten years (see Table 13-C). Israel stands out on the monument since they are referred to as a people rather than a land (see Butler, 127; Pritchard, 378, n. 18). This fact often plays a role in speculations that Merneptah's monument reflects the times of conquest and judges before Israel had settled and established a king (Hoffmeier, "Stela," 2.6 [2:41]; Hoffmeier, "Thirteenth-Century," 105).

*Gary Edward Schnittjer*

The darkened area near the bottom of the Merneptah stele above that mentions Israel is reproduced here. The three vertical strokes under the two figures signify that Israel is a people but not associated with a homeland and the bent throw stick signifies that they are foreigners not Egyptians (see Hoffmeier, "Stela," 2.6 [2:41]).

Aling, Charles F. "The Biblical City of Rameses." *Journal of the Evangelical Theological Society* 25.2 (1982): 129–37.

Archer, Gleason L. "An Eighteenth Dynasty Rameses." *Journal of the Evangelical Theological Society* 17.1 (1974): 49–50.

Butler, Trent C. *Joshua*. Word Biblical Commentary 7A and 7B. 2nd ed. Grand Rapids: Zondervan, 2014.

Hoffmeier, James K. "The (Israel) Stela of Merneptah." Pages 40–41 in *Monumental Inscriptions from the Biblical World*. Edited by William W. Hallo. Vol. 2 of *The Context of Scripture*. Edited by William W. Hallo. Leiden: Brill, 2003.

———. "Rameses of the Exodus Narratives Is the 13th Century B.C. Royal Ramesside Residence." *Trinity Journal* 28.2 NS (2007): 281–89.

———. "Response to Scott Stripling" Pages 53–59 in *The Exodus: Historicity, Chronology, and Theological Implications*. Grand Rapids: Zondervan Academic, 2021.

———. "The Thirteenth-Century (Late-Date) Exodus View." Pages 81–108 in *The Exodus: Historicity, Chronology, and Theological Implications*. Grand Rapids: Zondervan Academic, 2021.

———. "What Is the Biblical Date for the Exodus?: A Response to Bryant Wood." *Journal of the Evangelical Theological Society* 50.2 (2007): 225–47.

Janzen, Mark D. "Conclusion." Pages 283–86 in *The Exodus: Historicity, Chronology, and Theological Implications*. Grand Rapids: Zondervan Academic, 2021.

———. "Introduction." Pages 13–24 in *The Exodus: Historicity, Chronology, and Theological Implications*. Grand Rapids: Zondervan Academic, 2021.

Kitchen, K. A. "Egypt, History of (Chronology)." Pages 322–31 in vol. 2 of *Anchor Bible Dictionary*. Edited by David Noel Freedman. New York: Doubleday, 1992.

———. "Exodus, The." Pages 702–3 in vol. 2 of *Anchor Bible Dictionary*. Edited by David Noel Freedman. New York: Doubleday, 1992.

Lasor, W. S. "Egypt." Pages 41–44 in vol. 2 of *International Standard Bible Encyclopedia*. Edited by Geoffrey W. Bromiley. Grand Rapids: Eerdmans, 1982.

Merrill, Eugene H. "Rameses II and the Exodus: A Case of Mistaken Identity." Pages 533–45 in *Homeland and Exile: Biblical and Ancient Near Eastern Studies in Honour of Bustenay Oded*. Edited by Gershon Galil, Mark Geller, and Alan Millard. Supplements to Vetus Testamentum 130. Leiden: Brill, 2009.

Pritchard, James B., ed. *Ancient Near Eastern Texts Relating to the Old Testament*. 3rd ed. Princeton: Princeton University Press, 1969.

Redmount, Carol A. "Bitter Lives: Israel in and Out of Egypt." Pages 58–89 in *The Oxford History of the Biblical World*. Edited by Michael D. Coogan. New York: Oxford University Press, 1998.

Stager, Lawrence E. "Forging and Identity: The Emergence of Ancient Israel." Pages 94–102 in *The Oxford History of the Biblical World*. Edited by Michael D. Coogan. New York: Oxford University Press, 1998.

Stripling, Scott. "The Fifteenth-Century (Early-Date) Exodus View." Pages 25–52 in *The Exodus: Historicity, Chronology, and Theological Implications*. Grand Rapids: Zondervan Academic, 2021.

Walton, John H. "Exodus, Date of." Pages 258–72 in *Dictionary of the Old Testament: Pentateuch*. Edited by T. Desmond Alexander and David W. Baker. Downers Grove, IL: InterVarsity Press, 2003.

Wells, Bruce. "Exodus." Pages 160–283 in vol. 1 of *Zondervan Illustrated Bible Backgrounds Commentary*. Grand Rapids: Zondervan Academic, 2009.

More significantly, the narrative itself makes no mention of any individual judgment being directed toward any particular god. Each of the above-cited passages concerning the plagues and the gods are generalizations. For historical and literary reasons, therefore, it seems better to take our clues for the meaning of the plagues from the biblical account itself.

How does the biblical narrative interpret the meaning of the ten plagues? Four passages put forward explicit explanations for the judgments (see Table 13-D). The explanations in 4:21–23 and 6:1–9 focus on reasons for the deliverance, albeit by signs of judgment, and those in 6:26–7:7 and 9:14–16 target the reasons for the plagues themselves. These interpretations of God's terrible judgments are embedded within the story and offer the reader the theological meaning of the plagues. The narrative interpretation of the signs against the Egyptians reveals the significance of God's wrath and partially explains the next major issue concerning the hardening of pharaoh's heart.

**Table 13-D:** Reasons for the Plagues

| | |
|---|---|
| 4:21–23 | God would kill pharaoh's son because he would refuse to release God's son Israel even after many wonders |
| 6:1–9 | So that Moses and the people could see God's power;<br>because of God's word to the Hebrew ancestors;<br>so that God would take Israel as his own possession |
| 7:1–7 | The Egyptians would know that Yahweh is God |
| 9:14–16 | God wanted to demonstrate his uniqueness |

Yahweh explained his intention to kill pharaoh's son as the climactic and final plague. Readers, even in first reading, anticipate, therefore, the final judgment and realize that Yahweh will not stop until he kills pharaoh's son.

> Yahweh said to Moses, "When you return to Egypt, see that you *perform before Pharaoh all the wonders I have given you the power to do.* But I will harden his heart so that he will not let the people go. Then say to Pharaoh, 'This is what Yahweh says: "Israel is my firstborn son, and I told you, 'Let my son go, so that he may worship me.' *But you refused to let him go; so I will kill your firstborn son.*"'" (4:21–23, emphasis added)

The main reason for God's hardening of pharaoh's heart, according to this passage, was in order to perform all the terrors and to escalate the confrontation to the point at which God would kill pharaoh's son. This explanation fits with the third point in the second reason (see Table 13-D)—namely, God would use the exodus to claim Israel as his own possession (6:7). In an even more specific way, the tenth plague effectively purchased for Yahweh the firstborn of all of the Israelites for every generation to come (13:2, 12–16; 22:29–30). Later, God chose the tribe of Levi for himself as a substitute for the firstborn of every family in Israel, who were rightfully his own (Num 3:12–13, 45).

God wanted the Israelites and the Egyptians to see his power (Exod 6:1; 7:5). That power manifested itself in the signs of judgment revealed both his faithfulness to his word and his uniqueness (6:3–5; 9:14–16). Yahweh was not merely trying to deliver his people from bondage. He could have done that with a single act of wrath. He chose to deliver his people through the many terrors in order to publicly display his uniqueness. He said:

> Let my people go, so that they may worship me, or this time I will send the full force of my plagues against you and against your officials and your people, *so you may know that there is no one like me* in all the earth. *For by now I could have stretched out my hand and struck you and your people with a plague that would have wiped you off the earth.* (9:13b–15, emphasis added)

It is only partially correct to view the plagues as God's deliverance of his people. The ten sign judgments revealed his mighty power, his uniqueness, and his faithfulness to his word.

*What are the reasons for the plagues?*

Second, what is the significance of the accounts of the hardening of pharaoh's heart? The basic meaning of hard-heartedness is stubbornness and rebellion—the opposite of humility, faith, a circumcised heart, obedience, and so forth. The troubling feature of pharaoh's hard heart is that God hardened it. In order to access the significance of this issue, the context in which it is embedded needs to be understood. Thus, a presentation of the structure of the plagues will precede answering the question.

The ten signs are arranged climactically in three sets of three plagues, escalating toward the predicted tenth plague. The hardening of pharaoh's heart appears before and after the series of plagues as well as in between each of the judgments. The narrative reports regarding the hardening of his heart are the single feature common to all ten plagues. The constant repetition of attention to his heart condition forces readers to ponder the issue. Far from being an embarrassment that should be swept aside, the narrator has located pharaoh's heart as the central concern of the series of judgments that led to the killing of his firstborn son.

An efficient manner of viewing the structure of the first nine plagues is with an outline of the repeated points lined up by indentation. Each of the letters (a, b, c, d) represents a different kind of narrative element that is repeated through the series of plague reports. The detailed outline will be followed by a brief discussion that refers to the layout in Table 13-E.

**Table 13-E:** The Narrative Structure of the First Nine Plague Reports in Exodus

**Signs before Pharaoh**

- b Aaron's staff becomes a serpent (7:8–10)
  - c The wizards performed the same sign, but Aaron's staff swallowed the others (7:11–12)
    - d Pharaoh's "heart became hard" (7:13)

**First Cycle of Plagues**

1 First—Nile turns to blood (7:14–25)
- a Morning warning to pharaoh at the Nile (7:14–18)
  - b The water struck with Aaron's staff (7:19–21)
    - c The wizards performed the same sign (7:22a)
      - d Pharaoh's "heart became hard" (7:22b–25)

2 Second—frogs (8:1–15)
- a Pharaoh was warned of frogs (8:1–4)
  - b Aaron stretched his staff over the waters of Egypt (8:5–6)
    - c The wizards performed the same sign (8:7)
      - d Pharaoh agreed to let the people go sacrifice if the frogs were taken away, but later "he hardened his heart" (8:8–15)

3 Third—gnats (8:16–19)
- b Aaron stretched his staff over the dust and it became gnats (8:16–17)
  - c The wizards failed to produce the sign and acknowledge God's power (8:18–19)
    - d Pharaoh's "heart was hard" (8:19)

**Second Cycle of Plagues**

4 Fourth—flies (8:20–32)
- a Morning warning to pharaoh at the Nile—distinction in Goshen (8:20–23)
  - b The plague came (8:24)
    - d Pharaoh suggested they sacrifice in Egypt close by but later "hardened his heart" (8:25–32)

5 Fifth—death of livestock (9:1–7)
- a Pharaoh was warned (9:1–5)
  - b The plague came (9:6)
    - d Pharaoh saw distinction with Israel's livestock but his "heart was unyielding" (9:7)

6 Sixth—boils (9:8–12)
- b Moses and Aaron threw dust in the air and boils spread on the people and cattle (9:8–10)
  - c The wizards could not come before Moses because they had boils (9:11)
    - d "Yahweh hardened pharaoh's heart" (9:12)

*(continued)*

| Third Cycle of Plagues |
|---|
| 7 Seventh—hail (9:13–25) |
| a Morning warning (9:13–21) |
| b Moses stretched his staff to the sky and the storm began (9:22–26) |
| d Pharaoh confessed his sin and promised to let the people go if the hail was stopped, but later he hardened his heart (9:27–35) |
| 8 Eighth—locusts (10:1–20) |
| a Pharaoh was warned (10:1–6) |
| c Pharaoh's servants asked him to let the men go (10:7) |
| d Pharaoh suggested that the men only go (10:8–11) |
| b Moses stretched his staff over the land and the plague came—none in Goshen (10:12–15) |
| d Pharaoh confessed his sin and asked for the plague to be removed, but later "Yahweh hardened Pharaoh's heart" (10:16–20) |
| 9 Ninth—darkness (10:21–29) |
| b Moses stretched his hand to the sky and darkness fell—except in Goshen (10:21–23) |
| d Pharaoh agreed to let go all the people but not the animals, but later "Yahweh hardened Pharaoh's heart" (10:24–29) |

The structure of the first nine terrors as three sets of three in Table 13-E can be seen by comparing the elements "horizontally" and "vertically" in sets (see Table 13-F). When the sets in Table 13-E are compared horizontally, the first set (1–2–3) features the use of the staff and the presence of pharaoh's wizards. The wizards are able to turn water to blood and produce frogs—just what Egypt needs! They even try to produce gnats during a national gnat infestation. Their failure to produce gnats points toward the incomparability of God's power with the "magic" of pharaoh's wizards. The second set of plague stories (4–5–6) presents the absence of both the staff and the wizards, who only appear in the narrative of plague 6 in order to humorously accent the escalation of the judgments—they cannot come before Moses because they have boils. The third set (7–8–9) again features the staff for plagues seven and eight, but climactically Moses uses his hand for plague nine. When the sets in Table 13-E are compared vertically (see Table 13-F), the first plague in each set (1, 4, 7) comes after a morning warning to pharaoh. The second in each set (2, 5, 8) features pharaoh warned. The third plague in each set (3, 6, 9) simply comes on the Egyptians without warning.

The elements of each of the first nine plague accounts can all be compared together "vertically" (all of the "a" elements, "b" elements, and so on, of Table 13-E). The cumulative effect of each plague on the next is apparent from the appearance of pharaoh's servants in the account of plague 8, where they plead with him to release the Israelites (10:7). Notice too the growing concessions pharaoh offers (see the "d" elements under plagues 4, 8, and 9 in Table 13-E). It is especially noteworthy that pharaoh "confessed his sin" after plagues 7 and 8. His confessions do not appear to represent true repentance because of recognized guilt but mere words to secure relief from physical problems (compare Saul's counterfeit confession in 1 Sam 15:24–25, 30; cf. vv. 15, 20).

**Table 13-F:** Comparing Elements of the First Nine Plague Reports in Exodus

| Horizontal Comparison *(that is, between the three in each set)* | Vertical Comparison *(that is, between the first, second, and third of each set)* |
|---|---|
| 1 2 3 | 1 2 3 |
| 4 5 6 | 4 5 6 |
| 7 8 9 | 7 8 9 |

The fundamental issue of the plague stories is the string of "d" elements in Table 13-E, namely, the series of reports concerning pharaoh's heart (see Wells, 195; Rendsburg, 124–25). Regarding the last plague and beyond, the narrator foregrounds pharaoh's heart another three times along the same lines (11:10; 13:15; 14:4, 8). Readers are afforded a plague-by-plague moral ultrasound image of pharaoh's soul. The fact that both pharaoh and God are each responsible for the stubbornness of pharaoh is no secret. The storyteller wants readers to see this point, repeatedly.

It is true that pharaoh hardened his own heart six times before God did. It is an escape tactic, however, to say that God merely confirmed the stubborn pattern of pharaoh's heart. As discussed above, God was explicit that he was planning to harden pharaoh's heart because he wanted to perform all of his terrifying acts of judgment against the Egyptians (4:21–23; 9:14–16). God did not need to do it this way, but this is the way he chose to do it. Thus, the significance of the hardening of pharaoh's heart in the immediate context is related to the sovereign display of God's power. No one let the Israelites go. It was Yahweh who brought them out of Egypt by his fear-inspiring acts of judgment.

Within the larger context of Exodus the counterpart of pharaoh's hard heart was Israel's stiff neck—two synonymous metaphors of stubbornness (see similar language in Exod 7:3; 13:15 of pharaoh and 32:9; 33:3, 5; 34:9 of Israel; cf. Ps 81:12; 95:8). In the case of the former, God repeatedly hardened the rebellious king's stubbornness and revealed his terrifying judgments for all the reasons he himself explained (see Table 13-D). Those who saw his acts, whether Egyptian or Israelite, knew that he was unique, powerful, and faithful to his word. The case of the stubbornness of Israel and the forgiveness of Yahweh is all the more remarkable within the context of the narrative in Exodus.

Bust of Rameses II on display in the British Museum
*Jon Cooper*

These observations do not answer all the issues involved in God's hardening of pharaoh's heart. The storyteller was aware of how startling readers would find the repeated attention to God's assistance with pharaoh's stubbornness. The narrator did not try to hide it—exactly the opposite. He wanted it to be impossible for readers to simply brush it aside or ignore it. Thus, to soften or explain away God's hardening of pharaoh's heart misses the point. Yahweh is sovereign. Whether or not readers understand why or how, they can read for themselves that judging pharaoh as he did was God's prerogative. He is God. He has the right and the power to rightly and justly make his enemy stubborn in order to display his mighty power in redeeming his chosen people from bondage. This issue will be addressed further in Another Look below.

*Why does the Exodus story prominently display the hardening of pharaoh's heart?*

Third, how does the intertwined narration and instruction of the Passover affect the significance of the biblical story itself? Embedded within the story of the Passover are instructions for commemorating the event by means of the Feast of Unleavened Bread and Passover for the coming generations. The effect of interrupting the story with teaching for the future memorial of the sign is that the last plague was both worship and event (see Table 13-G). The dialectic ("conversation" between elements in tension) is not, however, between the past and the future but between the past and the present. That is, the original readership was already in the future of the narrated past and could enact and remember the work God had done. The power of the event for readers lay, in part, in their participation and ever-renewing representation of the work of God through worship (see Fretheim, 138–39).

*What is the relationship between worship and the story of the acts of God?*

**Table 13-G:** Interchange of Narrative and Instruction in the Account of Passover

| | |
|---|---|
| 11:1–10 | narrative of the event |
| 12:1–20 | instruction concerning commemoration |
| 12:21–39 | narrative of event, including narrative of instruction for future commemoration |
| 12:40–42 | summary |
| 12:43–49 | instructions for commemoration |
| 12:50–51 | narrative of obeying instruction |
| 13:1–16 | narrative of instructions for commemoration |

The importance of the relationship between the narrative representation of the events and the readership is not confined to those passages that contain explicit instruction for ongoing reenactment through worship. Rather, the formal worship instructions make concrete the ordinary participation of the reader through reading the scriptural narratives. Yahweh explained to Moses the function of the narrative for the instruction of the up-and-coming generation: "I have hardened his [pharaoh's] heart and the hearts of his officials so that I may perform these signs of mine among them *that you may tell your children and grandchildren* how I dealt harshly with the Egyptians and how I performed my signs among them, and that you may know that I am Yahweh" (10:1–2, emphasis added). The central importance of instructing the next generation in the word of God will surface again in Deuteronomy.

God led the people out of Egypt with a visible symbol of his presence, a cloud by day and fire by night. The narrator relates God's thinking through the best way to travel from Egypt to the land of promise: "God did not lead them on the road through the Philistine country, though that was shorter. For God said, 'If they face war, they might change their minds and return to Egypt.' So God led the people around by the desert road" (13:17–18a). In light of a second reading, this is an ironic explanation for going the long way. Repeatedly in the wilderness, the Israelites decided that they wanted to go back to Egypt.

The people encamped by a body of water, one large enough to prevent their progress and to drown the Egyptian army. The traditional translation of the name of the body of water beginning with the Septuagint is the "Red Sea" (see also the Vulgate and the King James Version). The meaning of the Hebrew name (*yam suph*), however, is "Sea of Reeds" or "Reeds Sea." Most conventional English translations today retain the Red Sea in the text and give the literal translation in the marginal notes. The variance between the Hebrew and the traditional translations, especially the Septuagint, is among the reasons why it is not certain to which body of water it referred (see Sidebar 13-H).

The salvation at the sea accords with the creation story. The echo of the imagery and language from Genesis 1 and 8 situates the theological location of the narrative of the deliverance at the sea. In Genesis 1:2 God's "Spirit" (*ruah*) hovered over the empty chaos of waters before his word of creation. In 8:1 God remembered Noah and sent his "wind" (*ruah*) to clear the waters of his wrath and grant humanity a new beginning. At the sea God sent an east "wind" (*ruah*) to make a path of life in the midst of the waters (Exod 14:21). The wind that saved Israel became the "breath" (*ruah*) of God that sent the Egyptian army to their watery grave (15:10). Yahweh remained the master of life and death, granting to each as he chose.

The language of the sea crossing has other common imagery with the creation narrative. The "dry land" to grant life (Gen 1:9–10; Exod 14:16, 22, 29; 15:19) in place of the chaos of "the deep" (Gen 1:2; Exod 15:5, 8) connects the imagery of the two contexts. The miracle at the sea, along with the word of God at Sinai, takes form as a Genesis-shaped story of the creation of Israel as his nation (Isa 43:12, 15–16; see Schnittjer, 236).

*What is the importance of the echoes of Genesis in the account of the crossing of the sea?*

## Sidebar 13-H: The Reeds Sea and Mount Sinai

### *What body of water did the Israelites cross in Exodus 14?*

The answer is unclear. Although the Hebrew *yam suph* has traditionally been translated "Red Sea" and identified with the Gulf of Suez, the term means "Sea of Reeds" (see NIV marginal reading for Exod 13:18). But the name of the body of water is not the only problem. Another difficulty is that *yam suph* can refer to other bodies of water, such as the Gulf of Aqabah (Elat) (see 1 Kgs 9:26) or a body of water near Elim (see Num 33:10–11). In spite of this ambiguity, an evaluation of the evidence makes it very unlikely that the sea crossing occurred hundreds of miles from Egypt somewhere along the Gulf of Aqabah (Elat) (Beitzel, 124).

**Map 13-I:** Possible Locations of Sea of Reeds

Scholars have proposed at least half a dozen bodies of water as the location of the sea crossing, like Lake Timsah, the Bitter Lakes, and the Gulf of Suez (Huddlestun, 5:638). It seems likely to many interpreters that the Israelites went through a smaller body of water (it would take a great deal of time for them to cross the twenty-mile width of the Gulf of Suez). The Sea of Reeds in Exodus 14, wherever it is, is a large enough body of water to destroy the Egyptian army (see Map 13-I).

### *Where is Mount Sinai?*

More than a dozen locations have been proposed for Mount Sinai (Davies, 6:48). The traditional view is that Mount Sinai (also called Mount Horeb in Exodus and Deuteronomy) is located in the southern part of what is called the Sinai Peninsula (see Map 13-I). Some evidence points to the region of Midian, though, even if it were correct, the location of the mountain is unknown (Wells, 228–29).

Just as the Scriptures do not identify pharaoh (see Sidebar 13-B), so too evidence is not available to locate the Sea of Reeds or the mountain of revelation. Some suggestions in videos and streaming channels are too clever and lack verifiable evidence. This situation is not new. The historical and theological significance of the exodus does not hinge on making these identifications.

Beitzel, Barry J. *Where Was the Biblical Red Sea?: Examining the Ancient Evidence.* Bellingham, WA: Lexham Press, 2020.

Davies, G. I. "Sinai, Mount." Pages 47–49 in vol. 6 of *Anchor Bible Dictionary.* Edited by David Noel Freedman. New York: Doubleday, 1992.

Huddlestun, John R. "Red Sea (Old Testament)." Pages 633–42 in vol. 5 of *Anchor Bible Dictionary.* Edited by David Noel Freedman. New York: Doubleday, 1992.

Wells, Bruce. "Exodus." Pages 160–283 in vol. 1 of *Zondervan Illustrated Bible Backgrounds Commentary.* Grand Rapids: Zondervan Academic, 2009.

The exodus and the word of God are part of a new beginning for God's people. By redemption, Yahweh created Israel as his people for his own purposes.

The narrative account of the crossing of the sea is presented in a mirror-image fashion that emphasizes the same point at the beginning, middle, and end (see Table 13-J). The reader is struck, first of all, by the panic of the Israelites who should have remembered the terrifying acts of God's salvation and trusted him for deliverance at the sea. The Hebrew people, however, cried out to Moses that they would have preferred to remain enslaved or to have died in Egypt. The structure of the passage also surprises the reader with Yahweh's desire to demonstrate his deity to the Egyptians immediately before they died (see points 1, 6, and 8-a in Table 13-J). The conclusion of the passage reveals that the enduring testimony of God's revelation to the Egyptians, whom he destroyed, is to those who saw it, namely, the Israelites (Exod 14:31).

**Table 13-J:** The Structure of the Narrative of the Sea Crossing

- 1 "The Egyptians will know that I am Yahweh" (14:1–4)
  - 2 Pharaoh chased after the Israelites who left defiantly (lit. "with a high hand") (14:5–9)
    - 3 The people cried out and Moses responded ". . . see the deliverance of Yahweh" (14:10–13)
      - 4 Yahweh's fight
        - a Moses: "Yahweh will fight for you" (14:14)
        - b Yahweh: "Raise your staff" (14:16)
      - 5 On dry ground through the sea (14:16)
- 6 "The Egyptians will know that I am Yahweh" (14:18)
      - 7 On dry ground through the sea (14:22)
      - 8 Yahweh's fight
        - a Egyptians: "Yahweh is fighting for them" (14:25)
        - b Yahweh: "Stretch out your hand" (14:26)
    - 9 The sea closed over the Egyptians when "Yahweh saved Israel" (14:26–30)
  - 10 Delivered by his great hand (14:31)
- 11 They believed in Yahweh (14:31)

Rameses II painted on papyrus
*© 1995 Phoenix Data Systems*

Exodus began with pharaoh's edict to throw the male Israelite infants into the river. This portion of the book closes with a song and dance of celebration because the warrior Yahweh had thrown pharaoh's army into the sea (15:1, 4, 21). The women of Israel, led by Miriam the prophetess and sister of Moses and Aaron, danced, for the first time in the Bible, as an act of gratitude and worship. The second dance, later in Exodus, differs significantly.

The Song of the Sea closes this segment of Exodus with a poetic theological commentary on the redemption of Israel from Egypt (15:1–18). The song was sung before the story was told; thus, the story is a narrative commentary on the events in light of the song. The Song of the Sea marks the closing of the second major section of the Torah's story. The story of the beginning of humankind and the beginning of the chosen family ends with the poetic expectation of the last days (Gen 49), and the story of the redemption of the chosen nation concludes with the Song of the Sea (Exod 15). Both conclusions look backward and forward in poetic theological interpretation.

The Song of the Sea uses graphic imagery to celebrate the victory at the sea. This victory serves as the basis of Yahweh's kingdom of Israel at his holy mountain (vv. 17–18). The song juxtaposes a series of contrasting images—liquid and solid, down and up, trembling and unmovable, death and life. Pharaoh's army is thrown into the sea and sinks like lead. Israel will be led up to God's mountain, his dwelling and sanctuary. The nations will hear and will tremble, but Israel, the object of God's unfailing love, will not be moved. The song defines Israel as a people created by God, separate from and a testimony to the nations.

## ANOTHER LOOK

Later biblical writers often reflect on the narratives of Israel's rescue from Egypt. Israel's prophets infused their messages with terrifying imagery from the account of the plagues along with the fear-inspiring events at Sinai, like thunder and earthquake (Patterson, 385–403). The use of darkness, locusts, blood, and other depictions based on the plagues were common. In several places the series of plagues was remembered or referred to in specific (Pss 78:44–51; 105:23–36; Ezek 5:17; 28:23). In short, the memory of God's devastating judgment on pharaoh and the Egyptians was a leading part of the prophetic imagery of God's judgment.

The parting of the sea foreshadows the parting and crossing of the Jordan River in Joshua 3–4. Crossing the sea symbolized leaving Egypt behind, and crossing the Jordan became a symbol of coming into the land of promise. These two stories bracket the wilderness journeys of the people of Israel (Ps 114:3, 5).

Romans 9 offers an interpretation of the hardening of pharaoh's heart. This reading is important because it deals with the question of God's justice. Also, Paul interprets the matter within the context of Exodus as a book. He sets up the issue with a series of allusions to the Genesis narrative and citations from Genesis 25:23 and Malachi 1:2–3. "What then shall we say? Is God unjust? Not at all!" (Rom 9:14).

Paul answers the question with quotations from Exodus 33 and 9. He first cites part of God's explanation for forgiving the stiff-necked Israelites of their rebellion with the golden calf at Mount Sinai and then quotes part of God's explanation to pharaoh for his role in the plagues (emphases added).

> For by now I could have stretched out my hand and struck you and your people with a plague that would have wiped you off the earth. But **I have raised you up for this very purpose, that I might show you my power and that my name might be proclaimed in all the earth**. (Exod 9:15–16)

> And Yahweh said, "I will cause all my goodness to pass in front of you, and I will proclaim my name, Yahweh, in your presence. *I will have mercy on whom I will have mercy, and I will have compassion on whom I will have compassion.*" (33:19)

> For he says to Moses, *"I will have mercy on whom I have mercy, and I will have compassion on whom I have compassion."* It does not, therefore, depend on human desire or effort, but on God's mercy. For Scripture says to Pharaoh: **"I raised you up for this very purpose, that I might display my power in you and that my name might be proclaimed in all the earth."** (Rom 9:15–17)

*Left:*

Sky goddess Nut above human remains inside a sarcophagus. Ancient Egyptians depicted the afterlife on analogy of this life with the sky above and the earth below (see Sidebar 4-A).

*Jess Belani*

*Right:*

Earth god Geb below human remains inside a sarcophagus

*Jess Belani*

Paul's applied commentary on Exodus juxtaposes the justice of God's hardening pharaoh and forgiving the rebellious Israelites. He is just in his wrath and in his grace. The point is that the one who questions God's justice in judgment must equally challenge his justice in forgiveness.

For Paul, God's relationships with stubborn pharaoh and stubborn Israel are both cases of his divine prerogatives for his own reasons, whatever they are. The God who created humans from the dust of the ground has rights over his creatures. His rights include mercy and stubbornness:

> Therefore **God has mercy** on whom he wants to have mercy, and **he hardens** whom he wants to harden. . . . Shall what is formed say to the one who formed it, "Why did you make me like this?" *Does not the potter have the right to make out of the same lump of clay some pottery for special purposes and some for common use?* (Rom 9:18, 20b–21, emphasis added).

After Paul explains God's rights over humanity within the Creator-creature context, it seems that he returns to the pharaoh-Israelite matter in Exodus. As noted above, Exodus 9:14–16 references that God could have defeated pharaoh and the Egyptians with a single plague (see Table 13-D and related discussion above). God's goal was not simply to win a battle over the Egyptian monarch. He wanted to demonstrate his uniqueness one plague at a time. But there is something more. He wanted to display his grace to those he forgave. Paul interprets or suggests—in hypothetical "if" language—God's reason for making pharaoh stubborn:

> *What if God, although choosing to show his wrath and make his power known*, bore with great patience the objects of his wrath—prepared for destruction? *What if he did this to make the riches of his glory known to the objects of his mercy*, whom he prepared in advance for glory? (Rom 9:22–23, emphasis added).

Paul is arguing, in light of his preceding use of Exodus 9:16, that the plurality of the plagues itself demonstrated God's patience with pharaoh for the purpose of revealing the wonder of his forgiveness to his people.

## INTERACTIVE WORKSHOP

### *Chapter Summary*

God gave several reasons for the plagues. These should be taken into account when considering the hardening of pharaoh's heart. Among the reasons was to testify to his power and grace for generations to come. The acts of God against the Egyptians concluded with the Genesis-shaped deliverance at the sea.

### *Can You Explain the Key Terms?*

- dialectic
- hard heart
- Passover
- plagues
- Reeds Sea
- sovereignty
- worship

### *Challenge Questions*

1. What was the purpose of the plagues on Egypt according to Exodus?
2. Why was the story of the tenth plague intertwined with instructions for commemorating the Passover?
3. Define the theological challenges that face the reader who wishes to understand the hardening of pharaoh's heart in relation to a correct understanding of God. Can these challenges be overcome, and, if so, how?
4. In what respects was the rescue of Israel at the sea Genesis-shaped?

### *Advanced Questions*

1. Explain the use of the plagues against Egypt within Psalm 78, including the different order and omissions.
2. Explain the use of the plagues against Egypt within Psalm 105, including the different order and omissions.
3. Why did God harden pharaoh's heart even after he confessed his sin in Exodus 9:27 and 10:16?
4. In what ways did the Song of the Sea (Exod 15) offer poetic commentary to the preceding narrative of Exodus?

*5. What are the similarities and differences in meaning between the Hebrew idiomatic description of the hardening of pharaoh's heart and Israel as stiff-necked within Exodus?

*6. What is the difference between *ben-nekar* ("foreigner") and *ger* ("residing foreigner") in Exodus 12:43–49?

## *Research Project Ideas*

Evaluate the biblical evidence for the proposed dates of the exodus (see Sidebar 13-B).

Define exegetically and theologically the meaning of the hardening of pharaoh's heart (see Wells, 195; Rendsburg, 119–25).

Evaluate how the account of Passover provides a model for the interrelationship of worship and biblical narrative.

Compare, historically and literarily, the narrative and poetic depictions of the salvation at the sea in Exodus 14–15.

## *The Next Step*


Fretheim, Terence E. *Exodus*. Interpretation. Louisville: John Knox, 1991.

Hannah, John D. "Exodus." Pages 103–62 in vol. 1 of *Bible Knowledge Commentary*. Edited by John F. Walvoord and Roy B. Zuck. Colorado Springs, CO: Chariot Victor, 1985.

Patterson, Richard D. "Wonders in the Heavens and on Earth: Apocalyptic Imagery in the Old Testament." *Journal of the Evangelical Theological Society* 43 (2000): 385–403.

Rendsburg, Gary A. "The Literary Unity of the Exodus Narrative." Pages 113–32 in *"Did I Not Bring Israel Out of Egypt?": Biblical, Archaeological, and Egyptological Perspectives on the Exodus Narratives*. Edited by James K. Hoffmeier, Alan R. Millard, and Gary A. Rendsburg. Winona Lake, IN: Eisenbrauns, 2016.

Schnittjer, Gary Edward. *Old Testament Use of Old Testament*. Grand Rapids: Zondervan Academic, 2021.

Wells, Bruce. "Exodus." Pages 160–283 in vol. 1 of *Zonmdervan Illustrated Bible Backgrounds Commentary*. Grand Rapids: Zondervan Academic, 2009.

# 14 THE WILDERNESS AND THE MOUNTAIN

## Exodus 15:22–24:18



## GETTING STARTED

### *Focus Question*

How did the revelation at Mount Sinai contribute creational shape to the establishment of the nation of Israel?

### *Look for These Terms*

- absolute law (apodictic)
- book of the covenant
- case law (casuistic)
- covenant
- kingdom of priests
- manna
- Sinai covenant
- suzerain treaties
- Ten Words

## AN OUTLINE

A. **The Wilderness (15:22–18:27)**
   1. The water at Marah (15:22–27)
   2. Manna and quail in the wilderness (16)
   3. The water at Massah-Meribah (17:1–7)
   4. The Amalekites defeated (17:8–16)
   5. Judges appointed over Israel (18)

B. **The Mountain (19–24)**
   1. The revelation to the people at Sinai (19)
   2. The Ten Words (20)
   3. The book of the covenant (21–23)
   4. The revelation to the elders at Sinai (24)

## A READING

The story of the journey to and the revelation from the mountain of God is a compact version of the Torah story at large. The people of Israel rebelled against God immediately and continuously. But they had reason to trust him. He had delivered them from brutal slavery by mighty cosmic acts. He provided for their needs throughout the barren wilderness. At the mountain, Yahweh revealed himself in power and glory, and he gave his word to the young nation. Yet every time the people perceived a pause of grace, they protested and fought against their God—through the wilderness and at the mountain.

The creation of the human world included the transformation of watery chaos into a home of beauty and life. The flood that damned the sinful human race was followed by a new beginning with Noah's family and pairs of every kind of animal. The nation of Israel was created by the terrifying acts of Yahweh against the Egyptians, delivering the people through the midst of the sea (see Chapter 13). Each of these three beginnings from deep waters by powerful acts of God was followed quickly by insurrection (see Table 18-A in Chapter 18). We as readers are stunned when we hear the Israelites complain in unbelief every time they face new challenges, yet God continued to provide. The narrator designs, by juxtaposing the accounts of God's powerful and gracious acts and the forgetful and stubborn grumbling of Israel, the story to evoke the reader's criticism against the people.

But what if this pattern is a trick? The storyteller lures readers to pass judgment and shake their heads at the Israelites. But sooner or later, readers get the impression that they are looking into a mirror (cf. Jas 1:22–25). The Israelites were not unusually weak in character. Rather, they represent the best and worst of humanity. They were chosen from humankind for humankind. The irony of the discrepancy between our frustration with the people of Israel and our own moral incompetency essentially arouses self-recognition.

? *Why would the narrator of Exodus want readers to criticize the character of the Israelites?*

**Table 14-A:** Testing on the Journey to the Mountain

| | | |
|---|---|---|
| Exod 15:22–27 | Water at Marah | God tested the people<br>*"Pay attention to his commands and keep all his decrees" (15:26).* |
| 16 | Manna and quail in the wilderness | God tested the people<br>*"Gather enough for that day" (16:4; see also v. 16). Honor the sabbath (16:5, 24–30).* |
| 17:1–7 | Water at Massah-Meribah | The people tested God<br>*"Is Yahweh among us or not?" (17:7)* |

The breathless back-and-forth motion between God's gifts and the people's complaints runs through three stories from Exodus 15:22–17:7. The reader has this, and only this, view of the wilderness journey to the mountain. Whatever else happened along the way remains hidden. The grumbling and quarreling of the Israelites are the only characteristics readers see. In the first two episodes God tested the people, but in the third, the people tested God (see Table 14-A).

First, the people traveled from the sea for three days without finding water. When they finally found water, it was "bitter" (15:23). The bitter water may have been a reminder of the bitter servitude from which they had been rescued (1:14). Yahweh demonstrated his power over the wilderness just as he had over the Egyptians. He made the water sweet.

Second, the people faced hunger as they traveled through the wilderness of Sin. Rather than facing the harsh reality with faith or even with honesty, the people began to creatively use their collective imagination. The Israelites said to Moses and Aaron, "If only we had died by Yahweh's hand in Egypt! There we sat around pots of meat and ate all the food we wanted, but you have brought us out into this desert to starve this entire assembly to death" (16:3). The people's sin was their twofold fictive interpretation. They invented a blessed past in Egypt, at least as far as food went, and they accused God of seeking to deceive and kill them. (The function of creative reinterpretation and self-deception in temptation will be discussed in Another Look in Chapter 22.)

Yahweh responded generously to the people's grumbling. He gave them manna daily and a special provision of quail, a lot of them. Manna literally means something like "What is it?"—the question the people had for the stuff they found on the ground every morning, except the Sabbath, for forty years. The narrator describes this stuff in pleasant terms. The flakes could be gathered and made into cakes. The manna "was white like coriander seed and tasted like wafers made with honey" (16:31b). This positive description demonstrates the depth of Israel's ingratitude when they later became tired of eating the same thing every day. The gift of manna presented Israel with tests (see Table 14-A). Their failure here was merely the beginning of a long line of what is later described as testing God (see Table 22-G in Chapter 22).

Third, after leaving the wilderness of Sin the Israelites again needed water in the arid desert. They immediately, according to narrative time, quarreled with Moses and, once again, created a fictional explanation of their situation. They blamed Moses: "Why did you bring us up out of Egypt to make us and our children and livestock die of thirst?" (17:3b). God instructed Moses to take the staff, with which he had struck the Nile to bring death, and to strike a rock in order to bring life. God said he would stand by a rock on Mount Horeb, which sets up another meeting between God and Moses at a rock on the same mountain in Exodus 34, when Moses will be on the rock with him (17:6; 33:22; see Friedman, 289–90; cf. 1 Cor 10:4).

Moses named this place Testing and Quarreling—Massah and Meribah. Through the entire series of complaints, God seemed patient. His longsuffering in this context eventually gave way to his anger and judgments as Israel persisted in their stubborn sinfulness.

The Amalekites, who remained longstanding enemies of Israel, attacked the people while they camped at Rephidim. God miraculously delivered Israel while Aaron and Hur held up Moses's tired arms. Afterward God commanded Moses to write the account on a scroll, the first place in the Pentateuch that mentions writing the things therein. In this case, ironically, it was to remember forever that the memory of the Amalekites would be completely blotted out (17:14).

**Map 14-B:** Traditional Route of the Exodus

The account of Moses's father-in-law and the establishment of the judges in Exodus 18 is one of the passages of the book that is out of chronological sequence (see Table 14-C). We know it is not in chronological sequence because Moses's father-in-law visited during the Sinai encampment (18:5), but the Israelites had yet to arrive at the mountain (19:1).

Why is this episode placed here, between Exodus 17 and 19? There are several possibilities, neither mutually exclusive nor fully convincing. First, the establishment of judges may have logically set up the need for the law (20–23), yet "decrees and laws" are referred to in the narrative (18:16, 20). Second, it may be located here to bracket the Sinai encampment narrative with the other mention of the father-in-law of Moses (Num 10). Third, the oppressing Amalekites are sometimes mentioned alongside the friendly Midianites/Kenites (see Num 24:20–22; 1 Sam 15:6; cf. Reuel and Amalek descended from Esau in Gen 36:10, 12). Thus, perhaps the assistance of Jethro the Kenite (of the Reuel clan), whose descendants were future neighbors of the tribe of Judah (Judg 1:16), is placed side by side with the defeated Amalekites in Exodus 17 and 18 (see Sarna, 97–98; Milgrom, 78–79).

*Why is it difficult to determine the reason(s) that the account of the appointment of judges has been placed where it is in the Exodus narrative?*

The story of God's revelation at Mount Sinai is of monumental importance. Within the story as a whole—namely, the progressive proximity of God to his people—these

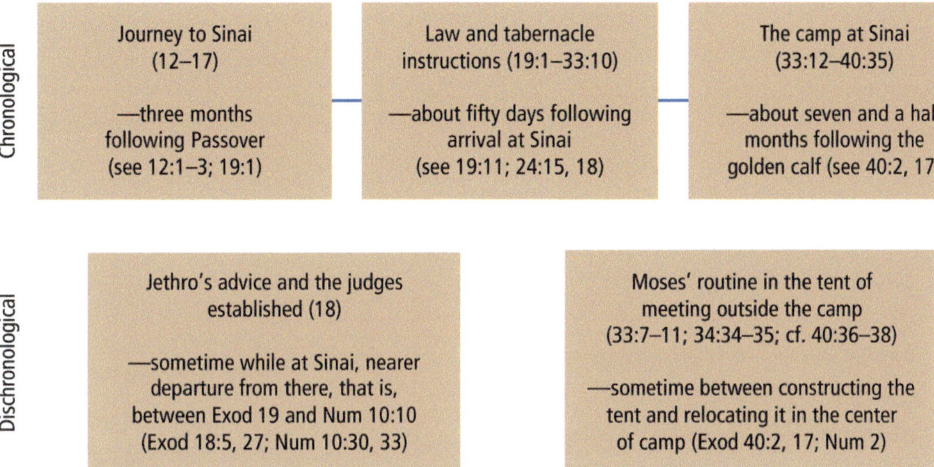


**Table 14-C:** Dischronological Elements of Exodus 12–40[a]

[a] Also note the routine of the cloud, which referred to no particular occasion. See Exod 13:21–22; 40:36–38; cf. Num 9:17–23.

chapters represent two movements of God toward his people (see Figure 14-D). The Ten Words (often called the Ten Commandments or the Decalogue) and the book of the covenant (chs. 20 and 21–23, respectively) are interpreted and reinterpreted in many places in the Torah, including Exodus 34, in several chapters in Leviticus and Numbers, and in Deuteronomy 5–26 (see list in Schnittjer, 32–34; cf. 27).

Yahweh spoke to Israel through Moses, explaining his newly created relationship to them. The redemption of Israel was not based on anything the people had done or would do. It was solely by God's grace because of his word to the Hebrew ancestors (see 2:23–25). The covenant he established with the nation at Sinai was not the basis of their salvation from Egypt but was a result of it. Redemption precedes law. God said:

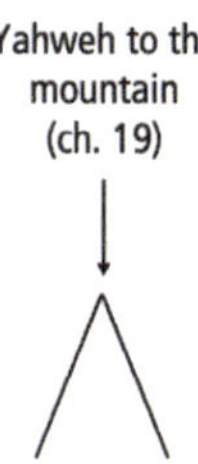

**Figure 14-D:** God Condescended to Israel in Exod 19–23

> You yourselves have seen what I did to Egypt, and how I carried you on eagles' wings and brought you to myself. Now if you obey me fully and keep my covenant, then out of all nations you will be my treasured possession. Although the whole earth is mine, you will be for me a kingdom of priests and a holy nation. (19:4–6a)

The covenant with the nation related to its status among the peoples of the earth. In this sense it was built on the Abrahamic covenant concerning blessing for all the nations. The meaning of "kingdom of priests" seems to highlight this aspect of the Abrahamic covenant. Israel was selected from out of the whole earth that belongs to Yahweh, his because he made it. Thus, the covenant fits within a Genesis-shaped cosmology or creational worldview.

*How did the covenant at Sinai relate to the Abrahamic covenant and the deliverance from Egypt?*

Priests, as we will see later in Exodus and Leviticus, represented their constituents, the people, to God. If Israel as a people was to be a kingdom of priests, then who was the kingdom to represent? The other kingdoms of God's earth. The Sinai covenant, then, was not designed to isolate Israel from the nations but to separate them to serve and represent the nations to their God. They were not chosen for the sake of their being chosen but in order to be a royal priesthood for the nations. (The nature of covenant and its significance will be discussed in Another Look below.)

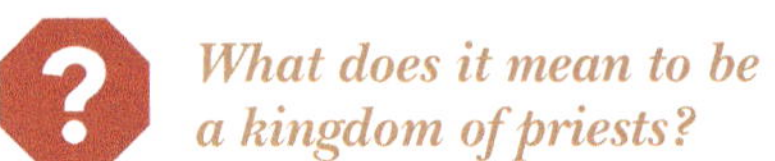


The Ten Words present God's will for his people. Because they were written on two tablets, a twofold division is commonly held (see 34:1). There are different traditional ways to go about this (see Table 14-E). Some regard the first five for Israel because they each include "Yahweh your God," and the final five for all humankind. Others note that the first four concern responsibilities to God and the latter six responsibilities to others (see, e.g., The Heidelberg Catechism, Q&A 93; The Westminster Confession of Faith 19). These traditional views, however, do not take into account what we now know about the kind of ancient Near Eastern treaties to which the Ten Words are often compared (see Another Look below). The parties of such treaties made two copies, one for the god to be placed in a temple and one for the king. Though Israel's theocracy (rule of God) did not yet have a human king, the covenantal structure of Yahweh's relationship with his people signals a need for two copies of the foundational covenant document—one in the ark and one with Moses (Block, 123)

**Table 14-E:** Two Ways to Look at the Ten Words in Two Parts

| Commands for Israel because each includes "Yahweh your God" | Commands regarding proper relationship to God |
|---|---|
| 1 no other gods<br>2 no graven image<br>3 do not bear his name in vain<br>4 remember the Sabbath day<br>5 honor parents | 1 no other gods<br>2 no graven image<br>3 do not bear his name in vain<br>4 remember the Sabbath day |
| **Commands for humankind in general** | **Commands regarding proper relationship to others** |
| 6 do not kill<br>7 do not commit adultery<br>8 do not steal<br>9 do not testify falsely<br>10 do not covet | 5 honor parents<br>6 do not kill<br>7 do not commit adultery<br>8 do not steal<br>9 do not testify falsely<br>10 do not covet |

The first several commands are detailed and focus on the manner in which the people must relate to God, while the latter ones, all brief, relate to others. The commands may follow the creational design of human beings themselves. The image of God in humanity requires devotion and loyalty to God, and living in society with others who are in the image of God requires respect and love (see Chapter 3). The Ten Words begin with "I am Yahweh your God" and end with "your neighbor" (20:2a, 17d).

A closer study of the name commandment offers insight into the Ten Words since it simultaneously embodies who the people of God are and what they need to do. The traditional way of translating and framing the name commandment treats it too narrowly, and somewhat beside the point. The traditional English translation of the third commandment in Protestant enumeration says, "Thou *shalt not take the name of the LORD thy God in vain*; for the LORD will not hold him guiltless that taketh his name in vain" (Exod 20:7 KJV, emphasis added; on counting the Ten Words see Table 26-B in Chapter 26). The sense of "take the name of Yahweh in vain" became identified merely with wrongful speech about God.

The Westminster Larger Catechism takes the ten commandments very seriously, running on for many pages. Consider question 113: "What are the sins forbidden in the third commandment?" Answer: "The sins forbidden in the third commandment are, the not using of God's name as is required; and the abuse of it in an ignorant, vain, irreverent, profane, superstitious, or wicked mentioning or otherwise using his title, attributes, ordinances, or works, by blasphemy, perjury, all sinful cursing, oaths, vows," and so on (261–63). These things are all wrong according to the dozens of supporting Scriptures cited in this question of the catechism. That is not the point. The issue at hand pivots on the sense of the name commandment within Exodus.

Carmen Joy Imes makes a compelling case for reconsidering the sense and scope of the name commandment (*Yhwh's Name*, 113–39). It may help to start with a couple of literal translations focusing on the key verb *nasa'* normally rendered as "lift up" or "carry."

> You *are not to take up* the name of YHWH your God *for emptiness*, for YHWH will not clear him that takes up his name for emptiness. (20:7 Fox, emphasis added)

> You *must not bear (or carry)* the name of Yahweh, your God, *in vain*, for Yahweh will not hold guiltless one who bears (or carries) his name in vain. (20:7 Imes, *God's Name*, 49, emphasis added)

If the commandment amounts to not carrying or bearing Yahweh's name for emptiness or in vain, how does that differ from wrongful talk of the divine name?

Bearing a name refers to ownership. The storehouses of the ancient kings of Judah included containers with seals saying *l-mlk* "belonging to the king" (Lipschits, 337;

Discovery of repurposed horned altar at Shiloh (ca. eleventh century BCE)
*Michael C. Luddeni and Scott Stripling*

Vaughn, 357). The practice of using seals on things runs parallel to ancients branding slaves to signify ownership. Israel had been freed from Egyptian slavery (Exod 20:2) and "entered into the service of Yhwh" (Imes, "Metaphor," 358).

The term "belongs to" is represented by the Hebrew letter equivalent to the letter *L* in English. For example, many psalms of Scripture *belong to* David in some sense and have headings on them such as *le-David*. Some "of David" psalms belong to him by being about him, written as a tribute to him, and some are even authored by him (see 2 Sam 23:1–2). In the same way, those that bear the name of Yahweh belong to him. Notice how Yahweh speaks of Israel at the mountain. Yahweh said:

> "Now if you obey me fully and keep my covenant, then out of all nations you will be *my treasured possession. Although the whole earth is mine, you will be for me* a kingdom of priests and a holy nation." These are the words you are to speak to the Israelites. (Exod 19:5–6, emphasis added)

Because God created all things, he says "the whole earth is mine," that is, it belongs to God. Because God created the nation by redeeming them from Egypt, he says "you belong to me as a treasured possession" and "you will belong to me as a kingdom of priests and a holy nation" (19:5, 6 lit.).

The ideas of "belonging to" and "bearing" need to be brought together. Imes observes that the high priest literally bears the names of the tribes of Israel engraved in the gemstones on his breastpiece (*God's Name*, 50): "Whenever Aaron enters the Holy Place, *he will bear (nasa') the names* of the sons of Israel over his heart on the breastpiece of decision as a continuing memorial before Yahweh" (28:29, emphasis added). In this way, the priest represents the families of Israel by bearing their names before Yahweh. The high priest wears on his head a gold plaque that says "holy, belonging to (*l-*) Yahweh" (lit.), that is, "Make a plate of pure gold and engrave on it *as on a seal*: HOLY *TO YAHWEH*" (28:36, emphasis added). When the priest goes into the inner sanctuary before Yahweh, he belongs to Yahweh even as he represents the people of Israel whose names he bears on his chest (see Imes, *God's Name*, 48–51).

Based upon the context of Exodus, the name commandment gets at the responsibility of the people who belong to Yahweh. Israel bears his name and belongs to him. The name commandment forbids Israel from bearing Yahweh's name in emptiness or in vain. The responsibilities of the name commandment go beyond wrongful talk of God. Yahweh forbids the people who belong to him and who bear his name from misrepresenting him. Or, positively, it means the people of Yahweh need to "represent him well" (Imes, *God's Name*, 52). This includes everything. "So whether you eat or drink or whatever you do, do it all *for the glory of God*" (1 Cor 10:31, emphasis added).

The identity of Yahweh's people runs very close to the covenant formula itself: I am your God and you are my people (see Schnittjer, *Old*, 282). Notice how the heart of the covenant formula fits in Yahweh's redeeming grace to his people:

> I have remembered *my covenant*. Therefore, say to the Israelites: "I am Yahweh, and I will bring you out from under the yoke of the Egyptians. I will free you from being slaves to them, and I will redeem you with an outstretched arm and with mighty acts of judgment. **I will take you as my own people, and I will be your God.** Then you will know that *I am Yahweh your God*, who brought you out from under the yoke of the Egyptians. And I will bring you to the land I swore with uplifted hand to give to Abraham, to Isaac, and to Jacob. I will give it to you as a possession. I am Yahweh." (Exod 6:5b–8, emphases added)

Horn of corner of unlawful cut-stone altar at Shiloh (ca. eleventh century BCE). Altars to Yahweh before he chose a place for his name (Deut 12:5) needed to be made of uncut stone. "If you make an altar of stones for me, do not build it with dressed stones, for you will defile it if you use a tool on it" (Exod 20:25).
*Michael C. Luddeni and Scott Stripling*

Imes summarizes the force of the name commandment: "Israel must see itself as belonging to him, representing him to the world. To bear his name in vain would be to enter into this covenant relationship with him but to live no differently than the surrounding pagans" (*God's Name*, 53).

The Ten Words are followed by the book of the covenant, which appears to be Exodus 20:22–23:19 (see 24:7). These two bodies of law functioned together as the legal and social guidelines for the covenant. The two collections of instruction have distinct character but rightly belong side by side in the covenant.

There are generally two kinds of laws within ancient Near Eastern cultures: absolute laws, known as apodictic, and casuistic or case law. Absolute commands, like those in the Ten Words, are characteristically Israelite, although they can be found occasionally in ancient Mesopotamian cultures (see Marshall, 5–26). Case law, like most of the laws in the book of the covenant, as well as many of the regulations in the "holiness collection" (Lev 19) and the "torah collection" (Deut 12–26), present precedent-setting rules that had to be applied by judges according to the circumstances of individual cases. Case laws start with a contingency followed by legal consequences: If a person does X, then the judgment shall be Y.

*What is the difference between apodictic law and case law?*

The book of the covenant begins and ends with instruction for worship (see Table 14-F). Moreover, the social and religious instructions are intertwined in a way that resists separation. In biblical perspective there was no such thing as "secular" in the modern sense. The place of God within Israelite society was special but also pervasive.

A discussion of each of the laws is beyond the scope of this study, though a few important features will be mentioned briefly (many parallel commands are treated in Chapters 19 and 27). The book of the covenant's instructions concerning worship focuses on holiness and devotion to God alone. The social stipulations in the book of the covenant are generally designed to set proper limits and to protect society, particularly the socially disadvantaged. For example, the law of retaliation—"eye for eye, tooth for tooth" (21:23–25), known as *lex talionis*—is not meant to require vengeance but to restrict it.

*How does the law of retaliation restrict vengeance?*

The legal standards and instructions to Israel come with the authority of the word of God. But Yahweh does not give the laws without explanation. He does not say, "Just do what I say and do not ask questions." The legal collections in Torah feature many explanations and motivations. Yahweh desires more than mere compliance. Yahweh helps his people understand why they need to obey his will. He also offers motivation—some positive and some negative.

A good example of explanation and motivation tied into the laws themselves can be found in the instructions concerning protected classes within the covenant collection:

> Do not mistreat or oppress a foreigner, *for you were foreigners in Egypt.* Do not take advantage of the widow or the fatherless. If you do and they cry out to me, I will certainly hear their cry. *My anger will be aroused, and I will kill you with the sword; your wives will become widows and your children fatherless.* (Exod 22:21–24, emphasis added)

Torah uses different terms for foreigners. The term in Exod 22:21 refers to "sojourners" or "residing foreigners," that is, refugees who

**Table 14-F:** An Outline of the Book of the Covenant

| | | |
|---|---|---|
| I | Worship standards (20:22–26) | |
| II | The judgments (21:1–22:17) | |
| | A | Protections for slaves (21:1–11) |
| | B | Protections for humans (21:12–32) |
| | C | Protections of property (21:33–22:17) |
| III | Additional legal standards (22:18–23:19) | |
| | D | Standards for worship (22:18–20) |
| | E | Protections for the socially disadvantaged (22:21–27) |
| | F | Standards for worship (22:28–31) |
| | G | Protections for the socially disadvantaged (23:1–11) |
| | H | Standards for worship (23:12–19) |
| IV | Mission to settle the land (23:20–33) | |

Interchange: worship and social protections (III, D–H)

seek asylum in Israel. A common denominator between the protected classes is what they lack: widows and orphans lack a man and residing foreigners lack land. Within the framework of a patriarchal agrarian culture, lacking a man and/or land amounts to great social disadvantage (Schnittjer, "Going," 133).

The man-less and/or land-less vulnerable persons belong to Yahweh. He is their man. The land is his. Elsewhere in Torah Yahweh makes clear: "the land is mine and you reside in my land as foreigners and strangers" (Lev 25:23). Yahweh requires Israel to join him in taking care of his people. Anyone who oppresses Yahweh's people will wind up dead, leaving behind their own widows and orphans.

The frequent legal rationale "for you were residing foreigners in Egypt" (Exod 22:21 lit.) carries some irony as well as an important part of Israel's identity. Israel possesses firsthand knowledge of being oppressed as outsiders. Yahweh draws upon Israel's identity as outsiders under pressure as motivation for protecting the vulnerable classes among them.

Notice how the book of the covenant frames Israel's experiential knowledge of being oppressed. "Do not oppress a foreigner; *you yourselves know how it feels* to be foreigners, because you were foreigners in Egypt" (Exod 23:9, emphasis added). The NIV does well to render "you yourselves *know the soul* of the residing foreigners" (lit.) as "you yourselves *know how it feels* to be foreigners" (NIV) (emphases added). The term "soul" here emphasizes the longing that Israel knew when they were outsiders (see Schnittjer, "Going," 134–35).

The motive clause that plays upon Israel's experiences in Egypt may be considered something of a "golden rule." To summarize the logic: protect sojourners because you know what it is like to be mistreated (Kelly, 162–63). And that is just it.

When Israel cried out to Yahweh, he delivered them (2:24; 3:9). The same God who rescued Israel from oppression stands ready to rescue his vulnerable people from the hands of any Israelite who uses their covenantal privilege to oppress those in need.

The final regulations of the book of the covenant concern the three annual pilgrimage feasts and offerings. Three times each year—for Passover, Harvest or Weeks (Pentecost), and Ingathering or Booths—Israelite men were required to travel to the place of worship. They were not to appear before God empty-handed; they were to bring an offering. The three pilgrimage feasts helped constitute the national community aspect of the larger holy calendar required in the Torah (23:14–17; see Tables 19-G and 19-H in Chapter 19).

Many elements of the book of the covenant overlap with ancient Near Eastern legal collections. The similarities between the case laws in the book of the covenant and the law collection, or code, of Hammurabi are well known (Hammurabi was a Babylonian king during the early eighteenth century BCE). These similarities make the differences stand out. One major difference pivots on the relative value in economic versus human priorities. The known ancient Mesopotamian legal standards count breaking and entering and theft as capital crimes (e.g., Collection of Hammurabi §§6, 22). By contrast, crimes against property in the book of the covenant are not punishable by death (though killing intruders in self-defense is permitted, Exod 22:2).

The opposite tendencies may be seen in human values. Notice the relative leniency of merely cutting off a child's hand who strikes the child's father in the Collection of Hammurabi (§195; cf. §193) versus the death penalty in the book of the covenant (Exod 21:15; cf. 21:17; Deut 21:18–21).

The values of the Torah's legal collections with respect to property and humans can be placed in contrast to all of the known ancient legal collections. Ancient norms outside Israel for crimes against property are more severe than crimes against humans. The brackets in Table 14-G mark economic crimes to highlight important differences.

**Table 14-G:** Economic versus Human Value in Scriptural Law versus Ancient Counterparts[a]

| Legal Collection | Financial Penalty | Death Penalty | Other |
|---|---|---|---|
| **Hittite Law**[b] | homicide; assault/ battery causing miscarriage | [theft, bestiality] | no punishment for justified homicide |
| **Middle Assyrian Law**[b] | homicide | [theft] | literal corporal punishment; legalized violence, multiple punishments |
| **Collection of Hammurabi**[b] | bodily injury; accidental homicide | [theft/cheating; adultery (choice of offended party)] | literal punishment; equal measure (*talion*) only for social equals[c] |
| **Torah** | **[property crimes]** | **intentional homicide; some sexual crimes; and religious crimes against God** | **no literal punishment (financial equivalent); equal measure (*talion*) for all free persons (not for slaves)**[d] |

[a]Table adapted from Hayes , "Biblical Law," 23:59. Also see Greenberg, 31–33.

[b]Hittite Laws (ca. 1500 BCE); Middle Assyrian Laws (ca. 1200 BCE); Collection of Hammurabi (ca. 1750 BCE).

[c]For literal measure for measure see Collection of Hammurabi §§196, 197, 200, in Roth, 121. For financial equivalents see Laws of Eshnunna §42 (ca. 1770 BCE), in Roth, 65; Laws of Ur-Namma §§18, 19 (ca. 2100 BCE), in Roth, 19.

[d]See Exod 21:23–25, 26–27; Lev 24:19–20; Deut 19:21.

The differences in valuing humans over property in the legal standards of Torah stem in large part from the divine giving of the law. King Hammurabi himself takes the credit for devising the law when prompted by the gods Marduk and Shamash. Hammurabi says, "When Marduk sent me to rule the people and to bring help to the country, *I established law* and justice in the land and promoted the welfare of the people" (prologue to the Collection of Hammurabi, Harper, 9). The account at the mountain in Exodus underlines the divine origin of the law:

> When Moses went and told the people *all Yahweh's words and laws,* they responded with one voice, "*Everything Yahweh has said* we will do." Moses then wrote down everything *Yahweh had said.* (Exod 24:3–4a, emphasis added)

The divine origin of the law in Scripture supports several implications (indebted to Greenberg, 25–41; Hayes, *Introduction*, 135–46; Hayes, *What's Divine*, 15–24). First, the purpose of the law is sanctification. While biblical law recognizes that obedience may be related to well-being and prosperity, it is more than this. The purpose of law is bringing about holiness and righteousness in the people (see Exod 19:6; Lev 19:2; Deut 6:25).

Second, biblical laws are not simply legal matters but are matters of morality. In Scripture, to break a law is to sin against God. Typically other ancient legal collections kept separate moral values and social responsibilities (like in modern law). In biblical law these are bound together (see Table 14-G).

Third, because biblical law is an expression of God's will, violation of capital crimes cannot be pardoned by human courts (versus cases where it can be in the Collection of Hammurabi, §129).

Fourth, the scope of biblical law collections is much broader and more holistic than ancient counterparts. Biblical law treats moral, civil, and ceremonial legal standards together within God's will. Israel's law concerns all of life. Everything is understood as within God's sovereign rule. Biblical law demands compassion, respect, and charity in matters that cannot be legislated in a court of law (see Exod 23:4; Lev 19:10, 14, 32, 33, 34; Deut 22:6). Many laws that fall outside the state's power to enforce are not too subtly punctuated by "I am Yahweh" or "I, Yahweh, am your God," especially in Leviticus.

The regulations are followed by an explanation in Exodus 23:20–33 of God's commitment to the nation. He will send his messenger before them. In this context, the messenger alternately sounds like a leader, such as Joshua, an angelic being, or God himself. The promises conclude with attention to the land he will give to them, just as he promised to Abraham.

Moses was instructed to write the instruction in the book of the covenant (Exod 24:7). The people spoke their commitment, which was confirmed by the seventy elders who, along with Moses, Aaron, and his sons, ascended the mountain. The group of leaders saw something extraordinary: "Moses and Aaron, Nadab and Abihu, and the seventy elders of Israel went up *and saw the God of Israel.* Under his feet was something like a pavement made of lapis lazuli, as bright blue as the sky. But God did not raise his hand against these leaders of the Israelites; *they saw God*, and they ate and drank" (24:9–11, emphasis added). What exactly did they see? It is traditionally answered that they saw a vision, something like those recorded in Isaiah 6, Ezekiel 1, or Revelation 4–5. In about ten chapters—or forty-seven days later—Moses asked to see God. Yahweh answered, "You cannot see my face, *for no one may see me and live*" (33:20, emphasis added). Whatever the elders saw was something different than what Moses did not see in the revelation of Exodus 34.

The first weeks and months that God spent with the newborn nation are a study in contrasts. Yahweh poured out his grace in provision, gave victory on the battlefield, and revealed his will at the mountain. The people rebelled immediately and consistently. At the mountain God proclaimed his word to the people he had chosen, a kingdom of priests, a holy nation. He established a covenant with them and the people accepted it. Moses ascended the mountain to receive a copy of the law from the hand of God. Before he returned, the people would already break the highest commands of the covenant.

The creation of the nation and the giving of the law itself were each Genesis-shaped. God brought the nation through the waters of the sea and led them to the mountain. As he had spoken the world into existence, now he spoke his word to the people of Israel. The creational structure of the revelation at the mountain was in accord with the separation of the creating days. "Law is a means by which the divine ordering of chaos at the cosmic level is actualized in the social sphere" (Fretheim, 362).

## ANOTHER LOOK

The covenant at Mount Sinai has often been compared to ancient Near Eastern covenant forms. There are several resemblances between the suzerain treaties of the ancient Hittites, a people who lived in what is now Turkey, and the Sinai covenant, as well as other biblical covenants (see Table 14-H; also regarding Deuteronomy see Moskala and Masotti, 93–94). Suzerain treaties were formal agreements between the suzerain (the sovereign or ruler) and the vassal(s) or subjects. The relationship between Yahweh and Israel resembled the relationship between a sovereign and his subjects. Significantly, a Hittite treaty was read aloud to all peoples in Rameses that Israel helped build and elsewhere in Egypt in 1259 BCE as well as published in several versions including its inscription on the walls of the Amon temple in Karnak (Johnston, forthcoming; cf. Table 14-H and discussion in Chapter 24). This explains how Israel could have become familiar with ancient Hittite treaty forms, whether through direct or indirect contact. The ancient treaty form may help establish a general framework that was significantly adapted for the covenant with Yahweh.

| New Hittite Treaties (ca. 1344–1178 BCE) | Egyptian Version of Hittite Treaty: Karnack (ca. 1259 BCE) | Exodus 20–24 | Deuteronomy | Joshua 24 |
|---|---|---|---|---|
| — | introductory frame-text | — | — | — |
| preamble | title/preamble | preamble (20:1) | preamble (1:1–5) | preamble (24:1–2a) |
| historical prologue | historical prologue | historical prologue (20:2) | historical prologue (1:6–3:29) | historical prologue (24:4b–13) |
| stipulations | stipulations I | stipulations (20:3–23:19 | stipulations (4:1–26:19) | stipulations (24:14–15) |
| loyalty oath<br>divine witnesses<br>curses<br>blessing | divine witnesses<br>curses<br>blessings | curses (23:20–21, 32–33)<br>blessings (23:22–31)<br>loyalty oath (24:1–8)<br>divine witnesses (24:9–18) | loyalty oath (27:1–26)<br>blessings (28:1–14)<br>curses (28:15–68; 29:1–30:10)<br>divine witnesses (30:11–20) | loyalty oath (24:16–18, 21)<br>curses (24:19–20)<br>[blessing/curse (cf. 8:24)]<br>divine witness (24:22–28) |
| — | stipulations II | — | — | — |
| — | colophon: royal seals | — | — | — |

**Table 14-H:** Proposed Similarities between Ancient Hittite Suzerain Treaties and Biblical Covenants‡

‡Table adapted and used by permission from: Gordon Johnston, "What Biblical Scholars Should Know about Hittite Treaties," in *TORAH: Treaty, Law, and Ritual in the Hebrew Bible in Its Ancient Near Eastern Environment*, ed. David C. Deuel, et al, Bulletin for Biblical Research Supplement Series (University Park, PA: Pennsylvania State University Press, forthcoming [2023]).

The Israelite collections of laws did not emerge in a vacuum. They stood within the context of many legally ordered ancient Mesopotamian societies. The law collection of Hammurabi contains many notable similarities with certain Israelite legal standards, particularly the book of the covenant. Note selected similarities and differences:

> If a man strike a man's daughter and bring about a miscarriage, he shall pay ten shekels of silver for her miscarriage. (Collection of Hammurabi, §209; Harper, 77)
>
> If people are fighting and hit a pregnant woman and she gives birth prematurely but there is no serious injury, the offender must be fined whatever the woman's husband demands and the court allows. But if there is serious injury, you are to take life for life. (Exod 21:22–23)

If a man destroy the eye of another man, they shall destroy his eye. If one break a man's bone, they shall break his bone. (Collection of Hammurabi, §§196–97; Harper, 73)

But if there is serious injury, you are to take life for life, eye for eye, tooth for tooth, hand for hand, foot for foot, burn for burn, wound for wound, bruise for bruise. (Exod 21:23–25)

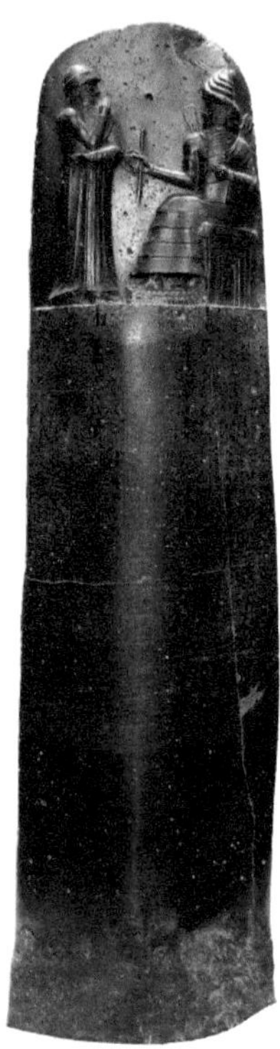

Covenant ceremony for the law of Hammurabi with the king standing before the god Shamash; King Hammurabi ruled Babylon 1792–1750 BCE (on display at the Louvre)
*Mbzt/CC BY 3.0*

If a man's bull have been wont to gore and they have made known to him his habit of goring, and he have not protected his horns or have not tied him up, and that bull gore the son of a man and bring about his death, he shall pay one-half mana of silver. (Collection of Hammurabi, §251; Harper, 87)

If a bull gores a man or a woman to death, the bull is to be stoned to death, and its meat must not be eaten. But the owner of the bull will not be held responsible. If, however, the bull has had the habit of goring and the owner has been warned but has not kept it penned up and it kills a man or woman, the bull is to be stoned and its owner also is to be put to death. (Exod 21:28–29; cf. vv. 30–36)

If a man make a breach in a house, they shall put him to death in front of that breach and they shall thrust him therein. (Collection of Hammurabi, §21; Harper, 17)

If a thief is caught breaking in at night and is struck a fatal blow, the defender is not guilty of bloodshed; but if it happens after sunrise, he is guilty of bloodshed. (Exod 22:2–3a)

The similarities and differences may demonstrate literary relationship (though direct literary adapting is doubtful) or simply signify similar cultural values for certain judicial situations. Divine revelation has been construed within this arena as a legal transformation toward Yahweh's values (Collins, 236–37). The book of the covenant (Exod 21–23) and the Collection of Hammurabi, along with many other law collections like those of Ur-Nammu (ca. 2350 BCE), Lipit-Ishtar (1934–1924 BCE), and Eshnunna (early eighteenth century BCE), are windows into a shared ancient Mesopotamian culture (see Wells, 234, 238–45). Israel's distinctives come into sharp relief within this context (see Table 14-G). There remains no close analog in ancient Near Eastern societies for exactly what we find in the Torah. The nature of monotheism, the Ten Words, and treating devotion to God together with civil matters are unique to biblical revelation.

The shared traits with ancient Near Eastern cultures, as important as they are, should not distract the reader from the distinct voice of the Scriptures themselves. The covenant at Sinai, like the other covenants in the Torah, is situated within a narrative framework. The story as context controls the way readers hear the word of God. The covenant was rooted in the creational worldview and the redemptive acts of God for Israel. That is, the Genesis-Exodus story defines the meaning of the covenant.

Cuneiform case laws inscribed on Law Collection of Hammurabi stele

*Jess Belani*

Whatever Israel shared culturally with her ancient neighbors—and it was a lot—does not and cannot entirely explain the demands of devotion to Yahweh and life according to his will.

There are two contexts under consideration here. When the book of the covenant of Exodus 21–23 is interpreted against its ancient Mesopotamian context, we are privileging the reading that would have been normal for original readers. This is significant and is one of the goals we should have. When we read the biblical law collections, they must also be apprehended within the scriptural context that speaks God's word across every generation and culture.

## INTERACTIVE WORKSHOP

### *Chapter Summary*

The trek through the desert, from the sea to the mountain, was constantly punctuated with the unfaith and grumbling of Israel and the gracious provision of God. When they arrived at Mount Sinai, he established his covenant with them and gave them the Ten Words and the book of the covenant.

### *Can You Explain the Key Terms?*

- absolute law (apodictic)
- book of the covenant
- case law (casuistic)
- covenant
- kingdom of priests
- manna
- Sinai covenant
- suzerain treaties
- Ten Words

### *Challenge Questions*

1. What does the journey through the wilderness in Exodus 15–17 demonstrate about the relationship of God and Israel?
2. Why did God want Moses to write down a permanent memorial regarding the blotting out of the memory of the Amalekites?
3. In what sense is the Sinai law creational?
4. How does the name commandment (third commandment) relate to who the people of God are and how they should live?
5. How do the explanation and motivation of the laws to protect sojourners or residing foreigners (22:21–24; 23:9) make use of Israel's own experiences?
6. What are the implications of biblical laws given by God in contrast to other ancient Near Eastern legal collections?
7. What does it mean that the Israelite leaders "saw God" (24:9–11) in light of the point made later in Exodus that no one can see God (33:20)?

### *Advanced Questions*

1. Why were selected events placed outside of their chronological sequence within historical narrative? Be sure to interact with one of the instances in Exodus.
2. What is the significance of the Mosaic covenant? How does it relate to the Abrahamic covenant?
3. Evaluate the two traditional ways to divide the Ten Commandments into two panels (see Table 14-E) and explain which one is to be preferred.
4. Demonstrate the religious dimension(s) in one of the "social" laws in the book of the covenant (see Table 14-F).
5. In what ways do ancient Near Eastern parallels to the Hebrew Scriptures help us and hinder us in our understanding?

*6. What is the meaning of *segullah* in its context (19:5)?

## *Research Project Ideas*

Compare the grumbling narratives in Exodus 15–17 and Numbers 11.

Compare the narrative context of the Ten Words in Exodus 20 versus the narrative context of Deuteronomy 5.

Define the literary and theological relationship between one of the case laws in the book of the covenant and its parallels elsewhere in the Torah (see Schnittjer, *Old*, 32–34).

Evaluate the similarities between the book of the covenant within the Exodus story and the Collection of Hammurabi (see Matthews and Benjamin, 105–14).

Compare the vision of God in Exodus 24:9–11 and one or more of the other visions of the throne (Isa 6; Ezek 1; Rev 4–5).

## *The Next Step*


Block, Daniel I. "For Whose Eyes?: The Divine Origin and Function of the Two Tablets of the Israelite Covenant." Pages 100–26 in *Write That They May Read: Studies in Literacy and Textualization in the Ancient Near East and in the Hebrew Scripture, Essays in Honour of Professor Alan R. Millard*. Edited by Daniel I. Block. Eugene, OR: Pickwick, 2020.

Collins, C. John. "Divine Action in the Hebrew Bible: 'Borrowing' from Ancient Near Eastern Cultures and 'Inspiration.'" Pages 221–39 in *Write That They May Read: Studies in Literacy and Textualization in the Ancient Near East and in the Hebrew Scripture, Essays in Honour of Professor Alan R. Millard*. Edited by Daniel I. Block. Eugene, OR: Pickwick, 2020.

Fretheim, Terence E. "The Reclamation of Creation: Redemption and Law in Exodus." *Interpretation* 45 (1991): 354–65.

Friedman, Richard Elliot. *Commentary on the Torah*. San Francisco: HarperSanFrancisco, 2001.

Greenberg, Moshe. "Some Postulates of Biblical Criminal Law." Pages 25–41 in *Studies in the Bible and Jewish Thought*. Philadelphia: Jewish Publication Society, 1995.

Harper, Robert Francis, ed. and trans. *The Code of Hammurabi King of Babylon about 2250 B.C.* Chicago: University of Chicago Press, 1904.

Hayes, Christine E. "Lecture 10. Biblical Law: The Three Legal Corpora of JE (Exodus), P (Leviticus and Numbers) and D." YouTube video, 25:39, posted December 6, 2012. https://youtu.be/iJ5qYM24vUA. Hayes discusses many of these details elsewhere without a diagram (see *Introduction*, 135–46, esp. 145–46).

———. *Introduction to Bible*. New Haven: Yale University Press, 2012.

———. *What's Divine about Divine Law? Early Perspectives*. Princeton: Princeton University Press, 2015.

Imes, Carmen Joy. *Bearing God's Name: Why Sinai Still Matters*. Downers Grove, IL: IVP Academic, 2019.

———. *Bearing Yhwh's Name at Sinai: A Reexamination of the Name Command of the Decalogue*. University Park, PA: Eisenbrauns, 2018.

———. "Metaphor at Sinai: Cognitive Linguistics in the Decalogue and Covenant Code." *Bulletin for Biblical Research* 29.3 (2019): 342–60.

Johnston, Gordon. "What Biblical Scholars Should Know about Hittite Treaties." In *TORAH: Treaty, Law, and Ritual in the Hebrew Bible in Its Ancient Near Eastern Environment*. Edited by David C. Deuel et al. Bulletin for Biblical Research Supplement Series. University Park, PA: Pennsylvania State University Press, forthcoming [2023].

Kelly, Joseph Ryan. "The Ethics of Inclusion: The גר and the אזרח in the Passover to Yhwh." *Bulletin of Biblical Research* 23.2 (2013): 155–66.

*The Larger Catechism, with the Assistance of Assembly of Divines at Westminster . . . with the Proofs from the Scripture*. Edinburgh: Alexander Kincaid His Majesty's Printer, 1772.

Lipschits, Oded. "Judah under Assyrian Rule and the Early Phase of Stamping Jar Handles." Pages 337–55 in *Archaeology and History of Eighth-Century Judah*. Edited by Zev I. Farber and Jacob L. Wright. Ancient Near East Monographs 23. Atlanta: SBL Press, 2018.

Marshall, Jay W. *Israel and the Book of the Covenant: An Anthropological Approach to Biblical Law*. Society of Biblical Literature Dissertation Series 140. Atlanta: Scholars Press, 1993.

Matthews, Victor H., and Don C. Benjamin. *Old Testament Parallels: Laws and Stories from the Ancient Near East*. 4th ed. New York: Paulist, 2016.

Milgrom, Jacob. *Numbers*. JPS Torah Commentary. Philadelphia: Jewish Publication Society, 1989.

Moskala, Jiří and Felipe A. Masotti. "The Hittite Treaty Prologue Tradition and the Literary Structure of the Book of Deuteronomy." Pages 73–94 in *Exploring the Composition of the Pentateuch*. Edited by L. S. Baker Jr. et al. University Park, PA: Eisenbrauns, 2020.

Roth, Martha T. *Law Collections from Mesopotamia and Asia Minor*. 2d ed. Atlanta: Society of Biblical Literature, 1997.

Sarna, Nahum M. *Exodus*. JPS Torah Commentary. Philadelphia: Jewish Publication Society, 1991.

Schnittjer, Gary Edward. "Going Vertical with Love Thy Neighbor: Exegetical Use of Scripture in Leviticus 19.18b." *Journal for the Study of the Old Testament* 47.1 (2022): 114–42.

———. *Old Testament Use of Old Testament*. Grand Rapids: Zondervan Academic, 2021.

Vaughn, Andrew G. "Should All of the LMLK Jars Still Be Attributed to Hezekiah? Yes!" Pages 357–62 in *Archaeology and History of Eighth-Century Judah*. Edited by Zev I. Farber and Jacob L. Wright. Ancient Near East Monographs 23. Atlanta: SBL Press, 2018.

Wells, Bruce. "Exodus." Pages 160–283 in vol. 1 of *Zondervan Illustrated Bible Backgrounds Commentary*. Grand Rapids: Zondervan Academic, 2009.

# 15 THE REBELLION AND THE DWELLING

## *Exodus 25–40*

ratpack2 © 123RF.com

## GETTING STARTED

### *Focus Question*

What is the meaning of God's presence with the people?

### *Look for These Terms*

- ark
- attribute formula
- covenant renewal collection
- cubit
- dialogue
- face to face
- golden calf
- image command
- intermarriage
- priestly garments
- transgenerational threat

## AN OUTLINE

A. **Tabernacle Instructions (25:1–31:11)**
  B. **The Sign of the Sabbath (31:12–18)**
    C. **The Rebellion and the Revelation (32–34)**
      1. Golden calf (32)
      2. Presence of God (33)
      3. Covenant renewal (34)
  D. **Remember the Sabbath (35:1–3)**
E. **Tabernacle Construction (35:4–40:38)**

## A READING

The last major segment of Exodus concerns the presence of God with his people. Exodus 25–31 and 35–40 describe the instructions for and the construction of the dwelling or the tabernacle. All aspects of the dwelling and its furnishings were defined with specific detail regarding dimensions, shape, and color. The lengthy repetition establishes the importance of proper detail in everything involved with God's dwelling. The sin with the golden calf presents readers with Israel's devastating rebellion. The shamefulness of the idolatrous incident sounds all the more striking enveloped within the many chapters of tabernacle description.

The rebellion created a crisis that called into question not only the covenant and God's presence with the people, but also their continued existence at all. In Exodus 32–34 the reader moves back and forth between scenes at the base of the mountain and high up on Sinai, close to the presence of God's glory. The dialogues between Yahweh and Moses illumine the tensions between the people and their God. How could the presence of Yahweh's glory dwell amidst the stiff-necked people? Would he leave? Would he destroy them? The surprising dimensions of God's grace can be seen within the dialogues.

This section ends with the highpoint of the book itself—the glory of God coming to dwell with his people. The specificity of the dwelling turned out to be the easier part of the problem. God by his spirit assisted in the construction of his dwelling. The greater issue was the stubbornness of the Israelites. How could they avoid the fate of pharaoh when they shared his foremost characteristic? Of themselves, they could not. That God extended forgiveness, reaffirmed the covenant, and committed himself to dwelling with the people are astonishing revelations of his grace.

The use of mirror imaging heightens the effect of the rebellion. The rebellion of the people and God's revelation is double bracketed—A-B-X-B-A (see outline above). The outside frame contains the instruction for and construction of the dwelling. The details are not given in precisely the same order or with the same emphasis, but the correspondence between the two sections is great (see Table 15-A). The inner frame around the rebellion narrative consists of two teachings concerning the Sabbath. In the first, God explains the holiness of the Sabbath according to the creational pattern of Sabbath as the seventh day (31:12–18). In the second, Moses tells the people the importance of obeying the Sabbath regulations at home because to break these regulations is a capital offense (35:1–3). The location of the rebellion, set within the double envelope of holy time and holy space, makes it all the more obscene.

*What was the effect of placing the account of the rebellion in the middle of the account of the tabernacle?*

The narrative in Exodus 25–31 is an almost static depiction of Moses's forty-day reception of the tabernacle's instruction on the mountain (31:18). The remarkable aspect of the dwelling is the vision of Moses. God instructed him, "Make this tabernacle and all its furnishings *exactly like the pattern* I will show you" (Exod 25:9, emphasis added). The idea of "*according to the pattern* shown you on the mountain" is repeated three more times (25:40; 26:30; 27:8) and "just as Yahweh commanded Moses" several times (31:11; 39:32, 42, 43).

**Table 15-A:** Comparing the Instructions for and Construction of the Dwelling[a]

[a]This table features a narrative layout of the instructions for and construction of the tabernacle. For a synoptic layout that includes the parallels in Leviticus and Numbers and additional details, see Schnittjer, *OT*, 35–36.

**Instructions for the Dwelling**

1 Offerings for the dwelling (25:1–9)
2 The ark (25:10–22)
3 The table (25:23–30)
4 The lampstand (25:31–40)
5 **The dwelling** (26:1–37)
  a Curtains (26:1–6)
  b Tent (26:7–14)
  c Frames (26:15–25)
  d Crossbars (26:26–29)
  e Plan of the dwelling (26:30)
  f Curtain (26:31–35)
  g Entrance to the tent (26:36–37)
6 Altar of burnt offering (27:1–8)
7 Courtyard of the dwelling (27:9–19)
8 Oil for the lampstand (27:20–21)
9 **Priestly garments** (28:1–43)
  a Aaron and his sons (28:1–5)
  b Ephod (28:6–14)
  c Breastplate (28:15–30)
  d Robe (28:31–35)
  e Gold plate (28:36–38)
  f Tunic, turban, sash, undergarments (28:39–43)
10 The consecration of the priests (29:1–46)
11 Altar of incense (30:1–10)
12 The atonement money (30:11–16)
13 Basin for washing (30:17–21)
14 Anointing oil (30:22–33)
15 Incense (30:34–38)
16 Bezalel and Oholiab (31:1–11)

**Construction of the Dwelling**

1 The material for the dwelling (35:4–29)
2 The workers—Bezalel and Oholiab (35:30–36:1)
3 The response of the people (36:2–7)
4 **The dwelling** (36:8–38)
  a Curtains (36:8–13)
  b Tent (36:14–19)
  c Frames (36:20–30)
  d Crossbars (36:31–34)
  e Curtain (36:35–36; see 40:21)
  f Entrance to the tent (36:37–38)
5 The ark (37:1–9)
6 The table (37:10–16)
7 The lampstand (37:17–24)
8 The altar of incense (37:25–29)
9 The altar of burnt offering (38:1–7)
10 The basin for washing (38:8)
11 The courtyard (38:9–20)
12 The cost of the dwelling (38:21–31)
13 **Priestly garments** (39:1–31)
  a Summary (39:1)
  b Ephod (39:2–7)
  c Breastplate (39:8–21)
  d Robe (39:22–26)
  e Tunic, turban, sash, undergarments (39:27–29)
  f Gold plate (39:30–31)
14 Moses inspected the dwelling (39:32–43)
15 Preparing the dwelling (40:1–33)
  a Instructions (40:1–16)
  b Setting up the dwelling (40:17–33)

On the mountain Moses received a vision of the dwelling. The dwelling in the encampment was to be made in accord with his vision on the mountain. The author of the letter to the Hebrews describes the dwelling as a copy and a shadow of what is in heaven (Heb 8:1–5). He believed that Moses saw the dwelling of God, which is in the realm of God. The theological significance of this point relates to matters of worship and relationship with God.

A phrase from the Lord's Prayer captures the spirit of the challenge: "on earth as it is in heaven" (Matt 6:10). Yahweh graciously chose to dwell with the Hebrew community. Once he inhabited it, his glory created a whole new reality for them, explained at length in Leviticus. In this context, we learn that Yahweh would graciously condescend to dwell with his people as the featured part of their community, but they needed to prepare him a place that accorded with his own place. He compensated for their inability by granting Moses a vision of the dwelling and, when it came to its construction, his own assistance.

*How did the dwelling of God change Israel's way of life?*

Below is a brief description of several key aspects of God's instruction for the dwelling. My main concern here is function, but some attention will be given to the physical appearance. All of the dimensions are given in cubits. A cubit was about eighteen inches long, the approximate distance between the elbow and end of the fingers. The dwelling had four pieces of furniture within it.

The *ark*—often referred to as "the ark of the covenant" or "the ark of testimony"—provided the special locale for God's glory. It seems that it, or the winged sphinxes on it (traditionally called cherubim), served as his place of residence or his throne. The ark itself was a gold-covered box with a unique gold lid. Later pentateuchal passages explained that the Ten Words (the second stone copy), a jar of manna, and Aaron's budding staff were each kept in the ark itself and that a copy of the torah was kept in front of it (Exod 16:33; 25:16; 40:20; Num 17:10–11; Deut 10:5; 31:26). The ark was two and a half, by one and a half, by one and a half cubits. The faces of the winged sphinxes were bowed and their wings spread out over the ark. The ark had rings mounted at its bottom corners, which permanently held the gold-covered wood poles for transporting it.

The *table* was two by one and a half by one and a half cubits. It was made of acacia wood and covered with gold just like the ark. The bowls and utensils for the table were made of gold. The table was also fitted with rings through which gold-covered poles were inserted for transporting it. Unlike the ark, however, the rings were located higher up on the legs and the poles were only inserted during relocation of the dwelling.

Winged sphinx guardian of ancient Assyrian throne room on display in British Museum
*Jon Cooper*

The seven-branched *lampstand* or menorah was made of pure gold and detailed with almond flowers and buds.

The *incense altar* was one by one by two cubits, also made of wood, covered with gold, and fitted with rings for transportation poles. The incense altar was outfitted with horns at each of its upper corners thus resembling the large altar in the courtyard of the dwelling.

*Left:*
Acacia tree
*Shutterstock.com/ slavapolo*

*Right:*
Arch of Titus in Rome constructed in 81 CE to celebrate the looting of the Second Temple of Jerusalem in 70 CE including its lampstand (menorah)
*© 2015 Zondervan*

Each of the last three items functioned for the ongoing worship of Yahweh. The table was always to have bread of the presence on it and the lampstand was to remain lit. The high priest was instructed to burn incense on the incense altar every morning and evening at twilight.

The dwelling was a tent or tabernacle designed to house the presence of Yahweh's glory. The dwelling was sometimes called the tent of meeting because God met there with Moses to give him instructions for the people (Exod 25:22; Num 7:89). Both names—tent of meeting and tabernacle—are also used together (Exod 40:34). The tabernacle is sometimes pictured as outside and at other times inside the Israelite encampment. These two locales have led to many suggestions, including the idea that the dwelling and the tent of meeting were two different things. Others think that Moses and the priests went "outside" the camp to go to the dwelling located in the center but some distance from the camp. It seems better to regard the dwelling as originally located outside and then relocated to the center of the camp (see Exod 33:7–11; Num 2:2).

The instructions for *the dwelling itself* describe two chambers, the holy and the holy of holies (the Holy Place and the Most Holy Place in the NIV), which were twenty by ten by ten, and ten by ten by ten cubits, respectively, for a total size of thirty by ten by ten cubits. Figure 15-B depicts a traditional view of the dwelling with the furnishings placed therein (Fox, 491).

The *courtyard* around the dwelling was one hundred by fifty cubits (exactly one quarter the size of an American football field), with curtains five cubits in height. Thus, the actual dwelling could be seen rising above the courtyard curtain by those living in the encampment.

The courtyard was outfitted with a bronze *basin* for washing and a large *bronze altar*, five by five by three cubits, for sacrifices. The altar had horns on each upper corner like the altar of incense. It was outfitted with rings and bronze-covered wooden poles for carrying, as well as bronze utensils. The ark and the altar were located in the centers of the two large squares that comprised the dwelling complex. All of the furnishings were designed in a two-to-one ratio relative to symmetrical proportion except the ark and the bronze altar. The difference in symmetry along with their physically central positions within the tabernacle complex symbolized the centrality of the ark and the altar for the Israelite wilderness community (see Figure 15-B).

**Figure 15-B:** The Floor Plan of the Dwelling Complex

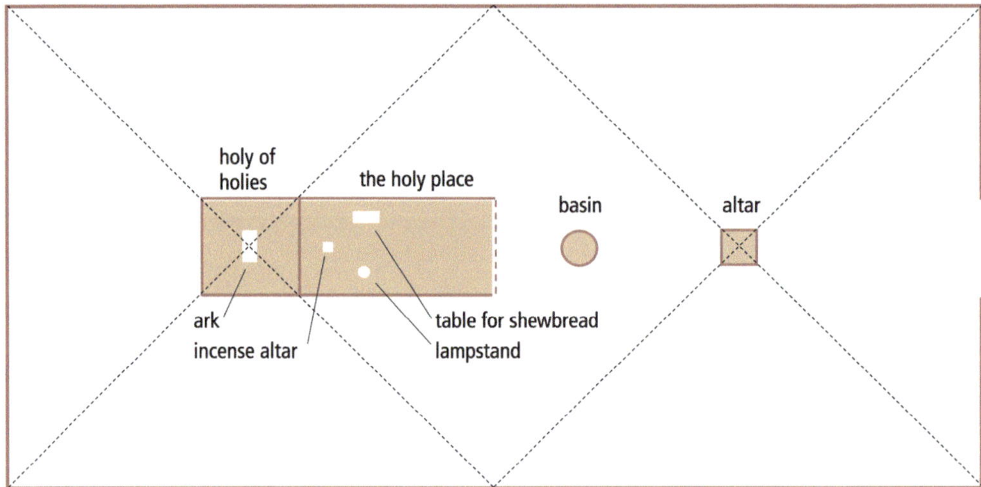


The dwelling represented the concept of sacred space within the encampment. The presence of God's glory dwelt with Israel "physically." The closer to his presence, the more holy the space and the fewer people who could be there less often. The proximity of the entire Israelite encampment with the dwelling made the nation holy compared to any other people. Living within increasingly holy proximity to God carried with it new responsibilities (see Leviticus). The visible and physical sacred space in the wilderness, and later in the land of promise, tangibly revealed the larger issue of the need for spiritual holiness to enjoy relationship with God. The holy space in the encampment along with holy time, weekly on the Sabbath and annually in the feasts, defined the dimensions that literally and physically encompassed all of life as worship.

*How was graduated holiness applied to space in the camp?*

*The clothing of the high priest* was highly symbolic in its colors and design. The priest's garments corresponded to the tabernacle curtains and furnishings in many ways (Imes, "Between," 37). The priestly garments and tabernacle were made from the same materials (see esp. Exod 26:1; 28:5). The priest dressed up in tabernacle-like robes in order to come before the deity (see Erickson, 22). That is, the high priest was a microcosm (small-scale analogy) of the tabernacle

The altar and the basin of the tabernacle
*Shutterstock.com/graceenee*

(see Chapter 16). As the people's representative, the high priest is a bridge between two worlds (Imes, "Between," 62).

The priestly garments included the names of the tribal families of Israel engraved on onyx stones emblematic of the people whom the priest represented before God. The high priest needed to wear holy undergarments (28:42–43) to insure he was not exposed under his robe according to the prohibition against elevated altars (20:26). The logic seems to be to cover the parts of their body that emit human waste corresponding to the need for military personnel to cover their excrement when Yahweh walked around the camp (Wells, 55; cf. Deut 23:14).

**Table 15-C:** The Layers of Holy Clothing of the High Priest

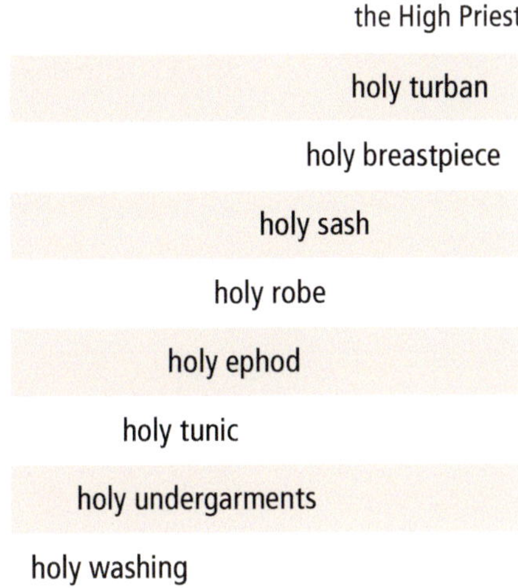

| |
|---|
| holy turban |
| holy breastpiece |
| holy sash |
| holy robe |
| holy ephod |
| holy tunic |
| holy undergarments |
| holy washing |

Perhaps the most important symbolic feature of the high priest's garments was the layer upon layer of "holy clothing" (28:2 lit.) he had to wear to minister before the presence of the glory (see Table 15-C). Aaron, the high priest, wore the names of the tribes of Israel on the breastpiece over his heart whenever he entered the dwelling. He also kept the Urim and Thummim, objects for making decisions, in the breastpiece over his heart. On his head, fastened to the turban with a blue cord, he wore a solid gold plate that said: "Holy to Yahweh."

The function of the priestly garments typifies the larger function of the dwelling and the religious rituals associated with it. Many layers of holy attire could not fix or hide the unworthiness of the priest or the people he represented. The human problem was not physical and could not be covered by many layers of holy clothing. The holy garments were not so much for Yahweh as for the priest and the people. The holy garments of the priests acted like a visual dictionary of Yahweh's holiness every time they put them on (Imes, "Between," 50).

In the end, the reason the priests could minister before Yahweh was not because of their wardrobe. It was grace. The same is true for the entire dwelling and all the instructions related to it. Following these teachings did not solve the problem of human sinfulness. Rather, it was, all of it, a symbol of Yahweh's grace. Yahweh accepted the priest and the worship regulations as "good enough," though not because they actually were good enough. They never could be. The high priest, the tabernacle, and all of the worship rituals stood as a visible sign of Yahweh's grace to his people.

*Why is it important to apprehend the tabernacle regulations as an act of God's grace?*

During the forty days in which Moses was on the mountain acquiring the Ten Words (in writing on stone) the people revolted against the covenant. The rebellion took the form of defiantly breaking the first two commandments. The people persuaded Aaron, whose role in the episode is ambivalent and vexing, to make them a golden calf.

What was the significance of the golden calf? The golden calf was said to be an image of Israel's God. The idols and images used in ancient Near Eastern religious practices were not the gods themselves but representations of the deities. In this case, the golden calf was an image of the god (or gods) that had delivered the people from Egypt, that is, Yahweh.

Sometimes biblical readers have the idea that the ancients considered the image itself the god. These notions may come from reading passages like Isaiah 42–48 in a literalistic manner rather than according to its sarcastic and ridiculing purposes. Generally, the idol itself was not the deity but an image of the imagined deity (Schnittjer, "Idolatry," in section on "Irony," paragraph 4). Therein lies half of the problem in Exodus 32: the people had broken the image commandment. God had chosen to make humans in his image, but his people were not permitted to make any other representations of God. An image of a bull, even if it was supposed to represent worthy ideals like strength or virility, was blasphemous because it depicted God by a creation.

Ancient Egyptian goddess Hathor

*Dave Primov © 123RF.com*

The other part of the problem with the golden calf was how it resembled some of the prominent deities of Egypt and Canaan. Israel was supposed to reject the practices of the Egyptians, from whom they were delivered, and of the Canaanites, who lived where they were going (Lev 18:3). The depiction of Israel's God as a golden calf suggests that they were also worshiping a different god—they broke the first commandment (see Ps 106:19–21).

*How did the rebellion with the golden calf break the first and second commands?*

The Israelites' statement, "These are your gods, Israel, who brought you up out of Egypt" (32:4), is also puzzling because there was only one golden calf. Perhaps the Israelites considered their golden calf, which they claimed represented God, as inherently plural, as gods. Against such a perspective is the great command: "Yahweh our God, Yahweh is one" (Deut 6:4). But note too that Moses referred to the "gods of gold" the people had made (Exod 32:31).

Whatever the people thought when they referred to the golden calf as their gods, this exact phrasing was used by the first king of the northern kingdom when he set up a worship system to compete with the temple of Yahweh in Jerusalem. King Jeroboam had two golden calves made and placed at the southern and northern reaches of his kingdom (Bethel and Dan) so that his constituents would not worship in Jerusalem and possibly return to Rehoboam king of Judah (see Map 15-D). If these two golden calves were counterparts to the golden cherubim/winged sphinxes in the temple's holy of holies, then the calves may have been considered God's throne, which extended across all of the northern kingdom (see Friedman, 32).

Altar at tel Dan
*© 2018 Zondervan*

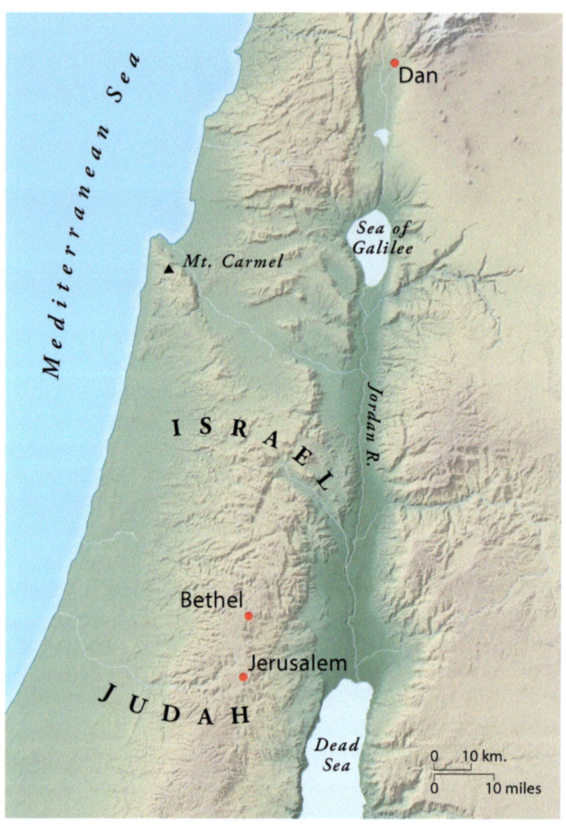


**Map 15-D:** Worship Centers of the Competing Hebrew Kingdoms

*Right:* Image of the Canaanite god El (from Hazor ca. fourteenth century BCE) *William Krewson*

In any case, Jeroboam declared, identically with Aaron in Exodus 32, "Here are your gods, Israel, who brought you up out of Egypt" (1 Kgs 12:28). The constituents of the northern kingdom of Israel accepted the golden calves and followed in the rebellion of their ancestors at Mount Sinai. There are approximately twelve parallels between the accounts of Aaron and Jeroboam and their golden calves (see Aberbach and Smolar, 129–34). The rebellion of the northern kingdom, therefore, is told in a way that demonstrates continuity between the two insurrections.

What was the nature of the worship of the calf in Exodus 32? The people made sacrifices to the golden calf and then had a feast to celebrate: "They sat down to eat and drink and then got up to play" (Exod 32:6b lit.). Their "play" could be called "dancing" (see 32:19). A minority opinion views the Israelite activities as proper behavior for a religious festival (Sasson, 151–59). Most interpreters, however, have understood the revelry as wild, drunken, and sexual. Whereas the Septuagint translated Exodus 32:6 in a neutral manner, the ancient Aramaic translations known as Targums read it in the second sense (see Targum Neofiti and Pseudo-Jonathan). Moreover, Abimelech realized that Isaac and Rebekah were not brother and sister when he saw them "playing" (Gen 26:8 lit., "caressing" NIV, "fondling" NJPS; cf. 39:14, 17). In this context it seems that the Israelites used the worship of the golden calf as a pretext for sexual misconduct.

The difference between the first and the second dances in the Scripture could not be greater. Approximately four months earlier, the women of Israel had danced to exalt Yahweh as their savior (Exod 15:20–21). And only about six weeks earlier, the people had promised to obey the word of God (19:8). Now at the base of the mountain on which Moses was getting the Ten Words and instruction for the tabernacle, the people were defying God in their lust even as they paid homage to a golden calf for delivering them from Egypt.

Meanwhile, at the top of the mountain, readers are able to listen in on the exchange between Yahweh and Moses. Yahweh could have simply

View from Mount Sinai
*iStock.com/ boygovideo*

acted against Israel. He did not have to tell Moses his deadly intentions. This case is similar in a few respects to Genesis 18, in which Yahweh chose to explain to Abraham his intention to judge the cities of the plain, including Sodom, where Lot was living. Yahweh opened himself to Abraham's negotiations and persistence. Here, Yahweh said to Moses that the people are "*your* people" that "*you* brought up out of Egypt" (32:7, emphasis added). Yahweh told Moses to leave him alone so that his anger could grow in order to destroy Israel. If that had been what he wanted, then he did not need to say anything. Instead of excusing Moses, he expressed his inclination, thus inviting dialogue (see Childs, 567).

*Why did Yahweh tell Moses he intended to destroy Israel?*

Moses reminded Yahweh of his prior commitment to his reputation before the Egyptians. That is one of the reasons God had delivered them (cf. Table 13-D in Chapter 13). Moses turned the conversation, "Why should your anger burn against your people, whom you brought out of Egypt with great power and a mighty hand?" (32:11).

Moses's second basis for pardon strikes a deeper chord. He reminds God of his word to Abraham, Isaac, and Israel. The word of Yahweh to the Israelite ancestors was the starting point for the exodus itself. Moreover, praying God's word to God is basic to biblical faith and prayer. God responds to those who trust his word.

Before moving on, the theological significance of Moses's prayer and Yahweh's change of direction needs to be considered. The apparent give-and-take of Yahweh provides an opportunity to reveal his character (see Master, 588). The difference between pharaoh and Israel was not intrinsic to their respective souls—they were both stubborn. The difference was in the word of God. Moses pressed him about the covenant. Yahweh would be faithful to his promise to Abraham and the ancestors.

When Moses arrived back at the camp, he was overcome with fury. He burned the calf, ground it to dust, and threw it into the water. He made the Israelites drink the object of their blasphemous devotion. When questioned, Aaron implied that the image of a calf was produced by accident! This further enforces the ambiguity that started when Aaron said regarding worship before the golden calf, "Tomorrow there will be a festival to Yahweh" (32:5; see Childs, 566). Readers are left mystified by the relative moral ambivalence of the high priest.

Moses commissioned the other Levites to take their swords and kill the rebels. The men of the tribal family of Levi meted out bloody justice on about three thousand people. The Levites killed sexual sinners in the tradition of their ancestor Levi (Gen 34:25). After this deadly purging, Moses informed the people that he needed to return to Yahweh to make atonement for their sin.

The reader, in short order, finds out that by "atonement" Moses has in mind offering up his own damnation. Whereas God considered killing all of Israel except Moses—which would have made him a new Abraham figure—Moses offered himself in judgment so God would forgive the people. When Moses said, "Blot me out of the book you have written," he meant eternal judgment because God's word has no end (Exod 32:32). God responded that he would blot out of his book only those who sinned against him.

As an act of mercy, Yahweh decides he cannot go with Israel any longer or he will kill them all. Readers know that Yahweh has high expectations, and he is willing to kill everyone as he did in the flood of Noah. Yahweh says:

> I will send an angel before you and drive out the Canaanites, Amorites, Hittites, Perizzites, Hivites and Jebusites. Go up to the land flowing with milk and honey. **But I will not go with you**, because you are a stiff-necked people and **I might destroy you on the way**. (Exod 33:2–3, emphasis added).

But Moses stops Yahweh from leaving Israel in the hands of a messenger. Moses insists that Yahweh himself remain with his people as a full manifestation of the covenant. Readers recognize the situation. Yahweh's presence puts rebels in grave danger, but his presence also fulfills the ideals of a covenant relationship. The dramatic set of conversations between Moses and the God of Israel succeeds in securing Yahweh's enduring presence with his people. This is blessing. This is danger.

At this point the narrative is briefly interrupted. Exodus 33:7–11 tells a generalized story, not of a particular occasion but of Moses's habit of meeting with God.

The meetings took place outside the camp in the tent of meeting. The dwelling was not finished until the end of Exodus, so this "sometimes" account—of no particular time—was placed in this narrative sequence even though it refers to a later pattern of meetings (see Table 14-C in Chapter 14). But why is a typical habit, of no particular individual event, discussed at all? And why must it be inserted here out of chronological order?

The reader finds a clue regarding the placement by the phrase "face to face": "Yahweh would speak to Moses *face to face*, as one speaks to a friend" (33:11a, emphasis added). Thus, the nonspecific story, relocated from its temporal context, has been placed here to set up readers to rightly interpret the next episode. Within a few verses God denied Moses's request to see him: "*You cannot see my face*, for no one may see me and live" (33:20); and again, "*My face must not be seen*" (33:23b, emphasis added). By placing the routine, but no time in particular, tent of meeting story in its present location, readers are forced to deal with a contradiction—at least what sounds like one. How could Moses talk to God face to face and yet not, under any circumstance, be able to see his face?

*Why was the story of Moses's talking to God in the tent of meeting placed in Exodus 33 out of its chronological sequence?*

The juxtaposition of these stories creates the need for both contexts to be read with finesse. The reader must first reconsider the meaning of Moses's speaking to God face to face. The expression "face to face" could mean physically face to face, but it must also mean something else. Previously, Jacob had claimed, "I saw God face to face, and yet my life was spared" (Gen 32:30). In that case, the reader is not sure that Jacob saw anything physically because it was dark. The Exodus narrator, after telling of the vision of God on Mount Sinai by Aaron, Nadab, Abihu, and the seventy elders, had also noted that "God did not raise his hand against these leaders of the Israelites; they saw God, and they ate and drank" (Exod 24:11). They saw something, but it could not have been the face of God because neither Moses nor any human being could live through that. The something they saw may have been a vision. In the present context, the fact that Moses talked to God face to face must be defined by the qualifying phrase, namely, as one speaks to a friend. Simply put, Moses had a close, personal, and uncommon relationship with God.

After the interruption to the story line, readers again get a closeup of Yahweh's revelation to Moses. While the continuing story line in Torah grows directly out of the blessing and danger of Yahweh's relational presence with his people, Moses presses his God for more. The result is one of the richest set of revelations of who God is and what it means to be his people in all of Scripture.

Satellite image of northern Egypt and the Sinai Peninsula from the International Space Station (see maps in Chs. 13 and 14).

**Table 15-E:** Requests Leading to Revelations

Table 15-E illustrates how Moses uses his role as an advocate to press Yahweh for more. Yahweh reveals his mercy.

| The advocate's requests | Yahweh's revelations |
|---|---|
| Moses said to Yahweh, "You have been telling me, 'Lead these people,' but you have not let me know whom you will send with me. You have said, 'I know you by name and you have found favor with me.' If you are pleased with me, **teach me your ways so I may know you and continue to find favor with you.** Remember that this nation is your people." (33:12–13) | Yahweh replied, "My Presence will go with you, and I will give you rest." (33:14) |
| Then Moses said to him, "If your Presence does not go with us, do not send us up from here. How will anyone know that you are pleased with me and with your people unless you go with us? **What else will distinguish me and your people from all the other people on the face of the earth?**" (33:15–16) | And Yahweh said to Moses, "I will do the very thing you have asked, because I am pleased with you and I know you by name." (33:17) |
| Then Moses said, "Now **show me your glory.**" (33:18) | And Yahweh said, "I will cause all my goodness to pass in front of you, and I will proclaim my name, Yahweh, in your presence. I will have mercy on whom I will have mercy, and I will have compassion on whom I will have compassion." (33:19) |

The significant set of revelations of the kind of God Yahweh is shows readers how divine power extends compassion to rebels. Yahweh will go with his people. He knows them by name. He exercises mercy according to his sovereign will. This is who Yahweh is. But there is more.

The revelation of God and renewal of the covenant is an unprecedented moment. The reader, like Moses, can only see the effects of his glory phenomenally—according to the functional character of his being. In Exodus God is known by his acts. On the mountain God said, "I will cause all my goodness to pass in front of you, and I will proclaim my name, Yahweh, in your presence. I will have mercy on whom I will have mercy, and I will have compassion on whom I will have compassion" (33:19). After Moses prepared for the meeting, the storyteller depicted it for readers in what is called the attribute formula:

> Then Yahweh came down in the cloud and stood there with him and proclaimed his name, Yahweh. And he passed in front of Moses, proclaiming, "Yahweh, Yahweh, the compassionate and gracious God, slow to anger, abounding in love and faithfulness,

> maintaining love to thousands, and forgiving wickedness, rebellion and sin. Yet he does not leave the guilty unpunished; he punishes the children and their children for the sin of the parents to the third and fourth generation." (34:5–7)

Neither the readers nor Moses can know Yahweh as he is in himself, but only according to his revelation of himself in grace and judgment.

The extraordinary revelation of God to Moses was bound up with the reestablishment of the covenant. The revelation symbolized Yahweh's commitment to extend his presence to his people, Israel. Moreover, God rewrote the Ten Words and reiterated many of the teachings from the book of the covenant in the covenant renewal collection of Exodus 34:11–26 (see Table 15-F). The fact that God instructed Moses to "write down these words, for in accordance with these words I have made a covenant with you and with Israel" (34:27) signified that he was reestablishing his covenant with the people. The multiple re-presentations of Yahweh's covenantal laws, far from being a burden, reveal his forgiveness of and mercy to his people.

**Table 15-F:** Covenant Renewal Collection and Parallel Legal Instructions[a]

| previous regulations | covenant renewal collection | later regulations |
|---|---|---|
| **Exod 20:5; 23:23–24, 32–33** | 34:11–16, prohibition against covenant and intermarriages with nations of Canaan | **Deut 7:1–6** |
| Exod 20:4–6; cf. 32:4, 8 | 34:17, no idols | |
| Exod 12:10–20; 13:3–13; **23:15** | 34:18–20, regulations concerning passover | Lev 23:5–8; Num 9:1–14; 28:16–25; Deut 16:1–8 |
| Exod 20:8–11; 23:12; 31:12–17; 35:1–3 | 34:21, Sabbath rest | Deut 5:12–15 |
| **Exod 23:14–17** | 34:22–24, pilgrimage festivals[b] | **Deut 12:21; 16:16–17** |
| **Exod 23:18** | 34:25, regulations concerning leaven and fat of sacrifice | |
| **Exod 23:19a** | 34:26a, firstfruits | Lev 23:9–14; Num 15:17–21 |
| **Exod 23:19b** | 34:26b, prohibition against boiling kid in its mother's milk | **Deut 14:21b** |

[a]Bold in columns one and three signifies substantial verbal parallels with legal standards in middle column. Table adapted from Schnittjer, *OT*, 27.

[b]For additional biblical references of Israel's holy calendar see Table 19-H in Chapter 19.

Pausing to look at the first prohibition in the covenant renewal collection can illustrate how legal standards teach about who God is and about his redemptive relationship with his people.

The threat of transgenerational punishment in the second commandment has always been challenging, even in Exodus itself. Notice the threat clause of the image command: "You shall not bow down to them or worship them; for I, Yahweh your God, am a jealous God, *punishing the children for the sin of the parents to the third and fourth generation* of those who hate me" (Exod 20:5, emphasis added). Exodus 34 offers help by focusing the threat clause in two ways. Whereas the image command identifies Yahweh as a "jealous God" (20:5), the attribute formula reveals that he is a "compassionate and gracious God" (34:6). But this cherished revelation is followed up by a strengthening of Yahweh's jealousy: "Do not worship any other god, for Yahweh, whose *name is Jealous*, is a jealous God" (34:14, emphasis added). This strong emphasis on a God named Jealous appears in the first command of the covenant renewal collection. Investigating the details can help make sense of the transgenerational threat.

The covenant renewal collection begins with a prohibition against Israel's unfaithfulness (34:11–16). Yahweh worries that people will seek to help their children with "beneficial" marriage matches when they get to the land of promise. The people have long suffered as outsiders in Egypt, and they are wanderers in the desert. Many people will want to help their children move up the economic and social ladder by arranging favorable marriages. These marriages with the established peoples of Canaan could help their children with financial stability and a standing in the local community. Ancient people wanted to help their children, and arranging for their children to "marry up" could make a whole new life for them. These strong motives begin to explain why intermarriage is a persistent problem throughout the Hebrew Scriptures.

The problem with "marrying up" is that it comes by "marrying out" (for these terms see Smith-Christopher, 158–61). The prohibition against intermarriage comes with very strong language. Notice how two translations try to handle the sense:

> And when you take wives from among their daughters for your sons, their daughters will lust after their gods and *will cause your sons to lust after their gods*. (34:16 NJPS)

> And thou take of their daughters unto thy sons, and their daughters go a whoring after their gods, and *make thy sons go a whoring after their gods*. (34:16 KJV)

If the daughter-in-law remains committed to her gods, she will compel her husband from Israel to "lust," or more accurately "go a whoring," after the gods of her people. This warning clause in the prohibition against intermarriage goes a long way in explaining the transgenerational threat. The parents are responsible for putting their sons on a path to worship images and the sons are themselves guilty of whoring after other gods. And sons and daughters-in-law who worship other gods will likely have children who worship other gods. Thus, the transgenerational threat does not need to speak to judgment of innocent sons and grandsons but to sons and grandsons who have given themselves over to false worship. Turning to images by intermarriage is not an individual but a transgenerational sin (Schnittjer, "Bequeathing").

*How does the prohibition against intermarriage help explain the transgenerational threat of the image command?*

Readers may wonder if the prohibition against intermarriage applies to daughters. This is not a modern question but of interest within Torah. An enhanced version of the prohibition against intermarriages with the peoples of the land in Deuteronomy makes the gender-inclusive sense of the law clear: "Do not intermarry with them. *Do not give your daughters to their sons or take their daughters for your sons*, for they will turn your children away from following me to serve other gods, and Yahweh's anger will burn against you and will quickly destroy you" (Deut 7:3–4, emphasis added; cf. Ezra 9:12; Neh 10:30; 13:25).

After the revelation on the mountain, Moses returned to the camp with a physical radiance. The people were afraid. He gave the word of God to the people. The narrator then inserts another generalized (that is, referring to no particular occasion) story of Moses and the veil (Exod 34:34–35). Moses used to remove the veil whenever he met with God and put it back on when he was finished. The mediator had become better friends with Yahweh, at least in the face-to-face way, than with human beings.

Mount Sinai
*IGOR ROGOZHNIKOV/ Shutterstock.com*

After the rebellion and the revelation, the book of Exodus returns to the construction of the dwelling. The last six chapters of Exodus rehearse for readers most of the detailed information from chapters 25–31. The order is slightly modified, but the focus is similar (see Table 15-A).

God granted his Spirit to the skilled workers, enabling them to make his dwelling. Two workers are singled out, one from Judah and one from Dan:

> Then Moses said to the Israelites, "See, Yahweh has chosen Bezalel son of Uri, the son of Hur, of the tribe of Judah, and *he has filled him with the Spirit of God*, with wisdom, with understanding, with knowledge and with all kinds of skills—to make artistic designs for work in gold, silver and bronze, to cut and set stones, to work in wood and to engage in all kinds of artistic crafts. *And he has given* both him and Oholiab son of Ahisamak, of the tribe of Dan, the ability to teach others. *He has filled them with skill to do all kinds of work* as engravers, designers, embroiderers in blue, purple and scarlet yarn and fine linen, and weavers—all of them skilled workers and designers." (35:30–35, emphasis added; cf. 31:1–6; 36:1–2; 38:22)

The Spirit of God with the craftspersons paints this segment with creational imagery. God's Spirit hovered over the heavens and the earth before he separated it to proper order and filled it with life. The humans, the creatures in his own image, were handcrafted lastly and commissioned to fill their world. The Spirit-empowered workers made the holy dwelling in accord with the design Moses had seen on the mountain. When it was finished, Yahweh filled it with the presence of his glory.

The present story not only echoes creation, but it also brings closure to the narrative that was triggered by the families of Israel fulfilling the creational blessing to fill the earth. They were fertile and fruitful and filled the land of Egypt. The fact that they filled Egypt initiated the problem that effected a chain of events—oppression, deliverance, journey, the covenant, the rebellion, the revelation, the dwelling—each building up to the moment when God's glory filled the dwelling. Yahweh condescended to tent with his people.

The context of Moses's relationship with God is necessary for grasping the magnitude of God's glory filling the dwelling. Because Moses's ability to spend time with God in the tent of meeting had been previewed in Exodus 33–34, readers are set up for the moment when Yahweh's glory first fills the tent. Moses had an unusual ability to withstand proximity to Yahweh's glory (also observed by Morales, "Dwelling," 111). The presence of that glory was so intense that Moses had to remain outside the dwelling:

*How is Moses's inability to enter the tabernacle when God indwelt it heightened in the context of Exodus?*

> Then Moses set up the courtyard around the tabernacle and altar and put up the curtain at the entrance to the courtyard. And so Moses finished the work. Then the cloud covered the tent of meeting, and the glory of Yahweh filled the tabernacle. *Moses could not enter the tent of meeting because the cloud had settled on it, and the glory of Yahweh filled the tabernacle.* (40:33–35, emphasis added)

## ANOTHER LOOK

The dialogue of prayer and forgiveness in Exodus 32, which demonstrated the grace and compassion of Yahweh in chapters 33–34, is engaged often by later biblical writers (e.g., Pss 78:38; 86:15; 103:7–8; 145:8–9; Joel 2:13). Two of the most prominent examples of biblical reflections on this context are in the book of Jonah and in Romans 9 (the latter was treated in Another Look in Chapter 13).

In Jonah 4 readers get a retrospective interpretation of the preceding narrative from the prophet's own point of view. In Jonah's dialogue with God, the reader receives a remarkable view of one of Israel's prophets and encounters a startling prayer. Jonah is angry, enough to die, because of Yahweh's compassion and grace:

> But to Jonah this seemed very wrong, and he became angry. He prayed to Yahweh, "Isn't this what I said, Yahweh, when I was still at home? That is what I tried to forestall by fleeing to Tarshish. *I knew that you are a gracious and compassionate God*, slow to anger and abounding in love, a God **who relents from sending calamity**. Now, Yahweh, take away my life, for it is better for me to die than to live." But Yahweh replied, "Is it right for you to be angry?" (Jonah 4:1–4, emphasis added)

In a first reading of the story of Jonah, the reader realizes only now why the prophet and God acted as they had at the beginning of the story. This dialogue offers commentary on Jonah's rebellion, even to the point of his attempting suicide rather than obeying when he requested to be thrown into the raging sea.

The exchange also presents commentary on the nature of God toward sinful gentiles, enemies of his own people. Jonah had known from the beginning that God was "*a gracious and compassionate God, slow to anger and abounding in love, a God who relents from sending calamity*" (Jonah 4:2). He knew it from the account that followed the rebellion of the golden calf in Torah: "*Yahweh, Yahweh, the compassionate and gracious God, slow to anger, abounding in love* and faithfulness" (Exod 34:6)—character that was demonstrated already when "Yahweh **relented** and did not bring on his people the **calamity** he had threatened" (32:14 lit., emphasis added in all cases; cf. Jonah 3:9). Jonah understood that the rebellion narrative in Exodus applied to the Ninevites of Assyria as much as to the Israelites in the wilderness.

*How does the angry prayer in Jonah 4:2 explain the book of Jonah in relation to Exodus 32–34?*

Therein is the rub. The prophet did not want to threaten the people of Nineveh with doom and invite opportunity for repentance and forgiveness. He wanted the judgment to come on the enemies of his people, even if it meant he himself had to die. Moreover, after God did exactly what Jonah expected from his reading of Exodus—namely, forgave the people of

Nineveh—Jonah wanted to die, again (Jonah 4:3). This recurring death wish is both trivialized and put in perspective when the prophet wished for death because a worm had killed a plant that had given him shade while he pouted (4:9).

Yahweh asked identical rhetorical questions concerning the forgiveness of Nineveh and the shade plant that had died: "Is it right for you to be angry?" (4:4, 9). In the case of the question regarding the dead plant, the prophet actually answered, with the wrong answer, providing Yahweh opportunity to explain further his gracious and compassionate relationship toward the people of Nineveh. The book of Jonah, then, is in large part a narrative-theological commentary on the account of the rebellion in Exodus. If Yahweh judged the stubborn pharaoh, he could judge the stubborn Israelites. If God forgave sinful Israel, he could forgive sinful Nineveh.

## INTERACTIVE WORKSHOP

### *Chapter Summary*

The lengthy description of the instructions for and construction of the tabernacle encloses the climactic narrative of the rebellion and the revelation. Although Israel is sinful and stubborn like the pharaoh, God forgives them and condescends to tent among them.

### *Can You Explain the Key Terms?*

- ark
- attribute formula
- covenant renewal collection
- cubit
- dialogue
- face to face
- golden calf
- image command
- intermarriage
- priestly garments
- transgenerational threat

### *Challenge Questions*

1. What is the importance of the relationship between what Moses saw on the mountain and the tabernacle's design?
2. What was the function of the priestly garments?
3. Explain how God did or did not change his mind in Exodus 32.
4. What was the significance of the role of God's Spirit in the construction of the dwelling?
5. In what way is Yahweh's glory filling his dwelling the climactic point of Exodus?

### *Advanced Questions*

1. How does prayer work in the case of Exodus 32?
2. What does it mean that Moses could not see God's face (Exod 33:20; cf. v. 11)?

3. Why did the prophet Jonah think that the forgiveness God had extended to Israel after the incident with the golden calf might be applicable to Nineveh as well?
4. What are the similarities between Moses's and Elijah's experiences on Mount Sinai/Horeb as told in Exodus 33:12–34:7 and 1 Kings 19:9–18?

*5. What is the meaning of *nhm* (Nifal) within the context of Exodus 32:12, 14?

## Research Project Ideas

Evaluate the theological significance of biblical prayer, using prayers of Moses in Exodus 32 or 33 as a case study.

Compare, exegetically and theologically, the tabernacle and the creation (see Morales, *Who*, 40–42; Imes, "Lost," 134–37; Kim, 37–56; Walton, 1:22, 24; Wells, 249).

## The Next Step


Aberbach, Moses, and Leivy Smolar. "Aaron, Jeroboam, and the Golden Calves." *Journal of Biblical Literature* 86 (1967): 129–40.

Childs, Brevard S. *The Book of Exodus: A Critical, Theological Commentary*. Louisville: Westminster, 1974.

Erickson, Nancy. "Dressing Up: Role Playing in the Egyptian *wpt-r* Ritual and a Contextualized View of the Biblical Priesthood." *Advances in Ancient Biblical and Near Eastern Research* 1.3 (2021): 11–27.

Fox, Everett. *The Five Books of Moses*. New York: Schocken, 1995.

Friedman, Richard Elliot. *Who Wrote the Bible?* 2nd ed. San Francisco: HarperSanFrancisco, 2019.

Imes, Carmen Joy. "Between Two Worlds: The Functional and Symbolic Significance of the High Priestly Regalia." Pages 29–62 in *Dress and Clothing in the Hebrew Bible: "For All Her Household Are Clothed in Crimson."* Edited by Antonios Finitsis. Library of Hebrew Bible/Old Testament Studies 679. New York: T&T Clark, 2019.

———. "The Lost World of the Exodus: Functional Ontology and the Creation of a Nation." Pages 126–41 in *For Us, but Not to Us: Essays on Creation, Covenant, and Context in Honor of John H. Walton*. Edited by Adam E. Miglio et al. Eugene, OR: Pickwick, 2020.

Kim, Brittany. "Stretching Out the Heavens: The Background and Use of a Creational Metaphor." Pages 37–56 in *For Us, but Not to Us: Essays on Creation, Covenant, and Context in Honor of John H. Walton*. Edited by Adam E. Miglio et al. Eugene, OR: Pickwick, 2020.

Master, Jonathan. "Exodus 32 as an Argument for Traditional Theism." *Journal of the Evangelical Theological Society* 45 (2002): 585–98.

Morales, L. Michael. "How the Dwelling Becomes a Tent of Meeting: A Theology of Leviticus." *Unio cum Christo* 5.1 (2015): 103–19.

———. *Who Shall Ascend the Mountain of the Lord?: A Biblical Theology of the Book of Leviticus*. New Studies in Biblical Theology 37. Downers Grove, IL: IVP Academic, 2015.

Sasson, Jack M. "The Worship of the Golden Calf." Pages 151–59 in *Orient and Occident: Essays Presented to Cyrus H. Gordon on the Occasion of His Sixty-fifth Birthday*. Edited by Harry A. Hoffner, Jr. Neukirchener: Butzon & Berker, 1973.

Schnittjer, Gary Edward. "Bequeathing Wrath: Exegetical Use of Scripture in Exodus 34." In Title TBD. Edited by Helen Paynter and Trevor Laurence. Sheffield: Sheffield Phoenix Press, forthcoming.

———. "The Insanity of Idolatry: Idolatry in Isaiah." *Credo Magazine* 8.2 (2018). https://credomag.com/article/the-insanity-of-idolatry/.

———. *Old Testament Use of Old Testament*. Grand Rapids: Zondervan Academic, 2021.

Smith-Christopher, Daniel L. *A Biblical Theology of Exile*. Overtures to Biblical Theology. Minneapolis: Fortress, 2002.

Walton, John H. "Genesis." Pages 2–159 in vol. 1 of *Zondervan Illustrated Bible Backgrounds Commentary*. Edited by John H. Walton. Grand Rapids: Zondervan Academic, 2009.

Wells, Bruce. "Exodus." Pages 160–283 in vol. 1 of *Zondervan Illustrated Bible Backgrounds Commentary*. Grand Rapids: Zondervan Academic, 2009.

# Leviticus

## AND HE CALLED

ואהבת לרעך כמוך אני יהוה

# 16 MACROVIEW OF LEVITICUS

© Idan Ben Haim/Shutterstock

## GETTING STARTED

### *Focus Question*

What are the major factors in approaching the book of Leviticus?

### *Look for These Terms*

- community
- holy
- microcosm
- storied framework

## AN OUTLINE

A. **Worship (1–16)**
   1. The sacrifices (1–7)
   2. The consecration of the priests (8–10)
   3. Ritually clean and ritually unclean (11–15)
   4. Day of Atonement (16)

B. **Holiness (17–27)**
   1. Blood and worship (17)
   2. Regulations for people (18–20)
   3. Regulations for priests (21–22)
   4. The religious calendar (23)
   5. Further regulations for priests and people (24)
   6. Regulations for the land (25)
   7. Blessings and curses (26)
   8. Regulations for tithes and vows (27)

## A READING

The beginning of Genesis told the story of God's creating a home for humankind. The earth is the place in which the humans, above all other created beings, represent God by their design and in their responsibilities. The closing portions of Exodus report the story of Israel's making a dwelling for Yahweh's glory. Just as living in the garden carried with it responsibility and accountability, so too are the demands, though much higher, for the privilege of having God dwell in the encampment. Leviticus is the story of Yahweh's instruction for survival in the newly established holy space and holy life of the kingdom of priests.

The traditional Greek-Latin-English name of the third of the Five Books of Moses is the most problematic of the five. The book of Leviticus named for Levites has almost nothing to do with the Levites. It is comprised of teaching for the priests and the people regarding their responsibilities now that the glory of Yahweh had come to dwell with them. Each of the other books of the Torah deals more with the Levites than this third book (they are only mentioned in 25:32–34).

The glory of Yahweh in his dwelling with Israel's encampment transforms Israel into potential worshipers. Worshipers need to ever prepare to come before the courts of Yahweh in worship. Leviticus views all of life as it pertains to preparing to enter the courts of Yahweh (Schnittjer, 18, 39–40). Because Yahweh is holy, Israel has much to do to get themselves ready to come before him. The holiness of Yahweh's glory changes everything. The instructions of Leviticus are Yahweh's gracious gift to priests and people to prepare them for worship.

Four issues need to be examined: holiness, story of instruction, and each of the two halves of Leviticus.

First, the meaning of holiness can be considered from more than one direction. Yahweh's holiness as a phenomenon toward human beings is, in essence, dangerous. There is no greater danger for sinful humans than getting close to the glory of Yahweh's holiness (see Savran, 190–203). Yahweh brought the people to himself, then he came down and spoke to them on the mountain, and finally he filled the dwelling with his glory. This new relationship between Israel and Yahweh created increasingly holy, and thus increasingly dangerous, space the closer one moved toward the dwelling. The two narratives proper within Leviticus, the establishment of the priesthood and the execution of a blasphemer, each present accounts of the death of rebels.

*What is the danger of God's holiness?*

"Holy" means a cut above, separate, other, different, unique. It involves both separation from ungodliness and, more significantly, separation toward God. Separation or differentness is, of itself, no virtue. Whatever is holy is only holy because it is set apart *to* or *toward* God. Therein lies the problem. Moving closer to God, whether metaphorically or spatially, increases the degree of holiness and danger. The extraordinary element of Exodus, Leviticus, and Numbers is that the degrees of holiness were literal and physical because the glory of Yahweh took up residence with Israel's mobile neighborhood.

*What does it mean to be holy?*

In Deuteronomy and in most later biblical narratives, the tent dwelling and later the temple were places where the name of Yahweh dwelt. In Exodus through Numbers, however, the presence of God's glory had some kind of physical manifestation. Leviticus thus tells the story of the literal problem of God's holiness bearing down on Israel's encampment. Whereas Exodus tells the story of Israel's deliverance from the sins of others, Leviticus, especially the teaching on the sacrifices, tells the story of the instruction for deliverance from the community's own unworthiness.

The predicament of God's holiness increases by the prerequisites for holiness in terms of the clean/unclean regulations (see Lev 11–15). Ritual defilement was unavoidable for the citizens of the encampment. Regardless of intentions or efforts, "everyone and anyone at any time" was liable to ritual pollution (see Douglas, 96). The instructions for holiness in Leviticus demonstrated the inability of humanity to live uprightly before Yahweh who is holy.

The reader who thinks that the holy requirements of living in the camp, or in the land under the covenant, were unique to that time and people has missed the creational context exhibited by Leviticus. The creational order of Genesis 1–3 resounds through Leviticus (Morales, "Levitical," 15–18). Yet it is not simply that life with the holy dwelling sounds like the world God created for humans but that the tabernacle is a microcosm—a small-scale model, albeit one pregnant with symbolism—of the creation. The tabernacle in the camp is the universe writ small.

Second, Leviticus as a whole is the story of Yahweh's instruction concerning his holy demands for Israel. For example, nearly every chapter opens with "Yahweh said to Moses. . . ." This feature is important everywhere, but particularly in the opening of the book. The relationship between story and law in this book should be recognized to hear it correctly. Leviticus and Deuteronomy are largely comprised of teaching, especially legal instruction, even while both books contain a few short narratives.

Nevertheless, the ruling genre of neither book is law itself. In both cases the legal instruction is encased in story. Leviticus is the story of Yahweh's instruction for worship and holy living. Exodus ended with Yahweh's glory filling the dwelling. Leviticus, for which the traditional Hebrew name is "And he called," opens with Yahweh calling out to Moses from the tent of meeting. The effect of this brief opening is to situate the teaching of the book within the context of the wilderness narrative that runs from Exodus 15 through Deuteronomy. Even with the two narrative interludes—the institution of the Aaronic priesthood (Lev 8–10) and the young blasphemer condemned (24:10–23)—the book as a whole effectively functions as the story of

Yahweh's instruction for Israel delivered to Moses from the tent of meeting.

The story of Yahweh's instruction in Leviticus is closely related to the story of the instructions for the tabernacle in Exodus 25–31. This includes shared language and also narrative versions of the tabernacle instructions, much in line with the tabernacle construction narrative of Exodus 35–40. Examples include the narrative fulfillment of the dedication of the priests (Exod 29:1–37//Lev 8:1–36) and the ever-burning lights (Exod. 27:20–21// Lev 24:1–3) (see Schnittjer, 53–54, 55). The place of Yahweh's instructing Israel moved from Sinai to the tent of meeting. The Torah story shapes the way we need to hear the instructions within this context.

Tabernacle reconstruction

*Becky Weolongo Booto/BiblePlaces .com*

Failure to appreciate the storied framework of Leviticus will distort it. The book is not naked instruction. It is not presented as timeless regulations applicable to everyone everywhere. Rather, the book maintains an ongoing function to all readers everywhere according to its narrative framework. The leading aspects of the storied framework can be summarized in several points. First, Leviticus is the story of the teaching from the tent of meeting. Next, this book makes sense within the new spatial orientation of Yahweh and his people, namely, that God has condescended for his glory to dwell with them. Next, Leviticus is situated against the story of Exodus, especially in relation to the covenant relationship established at the mountain. Finally, the book fits within the three-part wilderness series of books within the Torah (Exodus-Leviticus-Numbers). In this perspective the story of the teachings of Leviticus are encased within the broad framing effect of Exodus and Numbers. In sum, we as readers do not hear the instructions in the book as spoken to us. But we do hear for ourselves the story of the teachings to the wilderness community.

*What is the significance of the narrative context for hearing the instruction of Leviticus?*

The teaching of Leviticus is theological. Yet the theology is not stated in terms of logical facts, according to the standards of modernist rationality. Rather, the theological meaning of the regulations is bound up with the rituals themselves. The way that the symbolic meaning is embedded within the worship practices can be called analogical. The theological significance of particular rituals only makes sense within the symbolic system of worship described within the context of the book. The analogical or microcosmic style of relational thinking will be taken up in Chapter 17, particularly as it relates to sacrifice (see Table 16-A).

Third and fourth, Leviticus is made up of two halves, each of which, in somewhat different manners, speaks to the community rather than to individuals. This aspect of the book may be the most challenging for modern readers. Moderns characteristically read and think as individual persons. Leviticus is concerned with Israel as a holy nation.

**Table 16-A:** Topics Introduced in This Chapter That Are Developed Elsewhere

| | |
|---|---|
| Chapter 16 | Narrative framework of Leviticus |
| Chapter 17 | Microcosmic or analogical thinking |
| Chapter 18 | Clean/unclean, holy/common, literary framing |
| Chapter 19 | Holy living, literary framing |

The first half of Leviticus (chs. 1–16) focuses on purity for the dwelling within the community. Specifically, the purity of the encampment was sustained by the prescribed worship—sacrifice, priesthood, ritual purification, and the Day of Atonement. The fact that Yahweh's glory took up residence within the dwelling made it sacred space, which could be polluted by sinfulness, profane things (that is, unholy or common), and ritually impure situations. Thus, the first half of the book explains the necessary regulations for maintaining the purity of the dwelling within the community of Israel. The goal is not the ritual purity of the people for their own sakes but to avoid ritual pollution of the tabernacle.

Exodus 33 provides the context motivating the necessary ritual purity. Yahweh said:

> "But *I will not go with you*, because you are a stiff-necked people *and I might destroy you on the way*." When the people heard these distressing words, they began to mourn and no one put on any ornaments. For Yahweh had said to Moses, "Tell the Israelites, 'You are a stiff-necked people. *If I were to go with you even for a moment, I might destroy you*.'" (Exod 33:3b–5a, emphasis added)

The problem of God's holiness and Israel's stubbornness was bidirectional. Either he would not go with them or he would kill them. Both were unthinkable. The people wanted and needed the presence of Yahweh's glory, yet this put their lives at great risk. Leviticus can be seen as the story of Yahweh's gracious teaching. The first half of the book, in particular, presents his compassionate provision for worship to maintain the purity of the community and to sustain his presence with them without killing them. The instructions of Leviticus are a gift from Yahweh.

The role of the priests as teachers both connects the two halves of Leviticus and sheds light on how purity and holiness interrelate to worship and obedience. Priests must be sober when serving at the tent of meeting "so that you can *distinguish between the holy and the common, between the unclean and the clean*, and so you can teach the Israelites all the decrees Yahweh has given them through Moses" (Lev 10:10–11). These two areas relate to the legal instructions of the ritually pure and impure in Leviticus 11–15 and holiness in life and worship in 17–26 (see Figure 16-B; Morales, "Dwelling," 113).

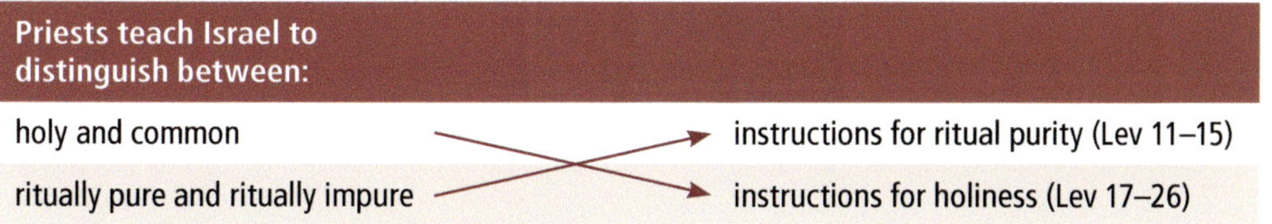


**Figure 16-B:** Areas of Priestly Teaching and the Structure of Leviticus

The second half of Leviticus (chs. 17–27) is oriented toward holiness for persons within the community. At first the teachings may seem individualistic because they are largely instructions for individual persons. It is not a series of regulations to individuals as individuals, however, but for individuals as part of the chosen people. The goal of faithful obedience to the instructions for holiness was not personal holiness but the holiness of the community of God's people. Thus, while both halves of Leviticus are concerned with the community, neither is concerned with the community itself per se. The first half of the book relates to the community responsibility in relation to the ritual purity of Yahweh's dwelling and the second half to the personal requirements of the holy community's constituents.

Among the dominant literary features of Leviticus, both for this book within Torah and within the book itself, is framing effect. Some interpreters question the idea of Leviticus as a "book" (see Gerstenberger, 2–6; Rendtorff, 22–35). It possesses the literary features to be read as a scroll or book within the pentateuchal series. That is, Leviticus is part of the Torah serial narrative. As noted elsewhere, Leviticus is flanked by the mirror imaging of Exodus and Numbers, especially in the wilderness sections (Table 11-C in Chapter 11). One of the effects of this bracketing is to push the holy instruction of Leviticus to the foreground. Because the wilderness series (Exodus-Leviticus-Numbers) falls between the backward looking book of Genesis and the forward looking book of Deuteronomy, Leviticus emerges as the central panel of the Torah.

The use of framing dominates the broad literary features across Leviticus as well. There is some merit to views that promote detailed inverted parallel schemes, or macro-level chiastic arrangements of Leviticus (some essays in Sawyer are devoted to this issue). Yet, it is the framing effects that exert the strongest rhetorical force in the context of the book itself. The major framing effects of Leviticus are summarized in Figures 16-C and 16-D and will be discussed further in the following Chapters. More tentative frames are depicted with dotted lines.

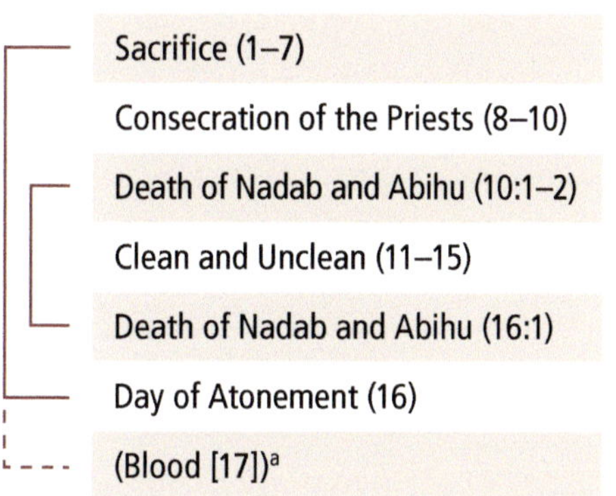


**Figure 16-C:** The Major Framing Elements in Leviticus 1–16

[a]Leviticus 17 in figure in parentheses because of its hinge position in the book—it is a janus (see Chapter 1)—though it properly fits with the second half.

**Figure 16-D:** The Major Framing Elements in Leviticus 17–27

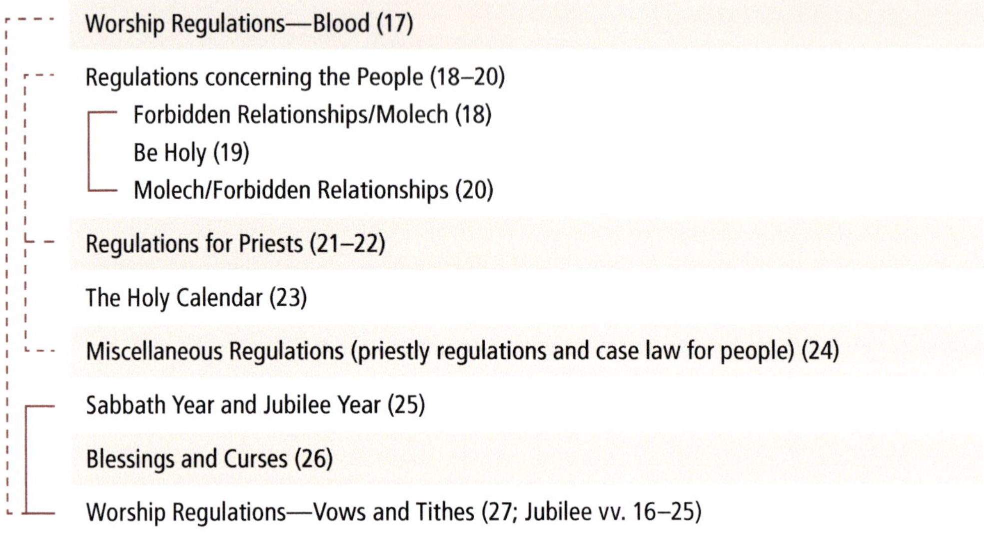


## ANOTHER LOOK

Leviticus needs to be heard within its Torah context, most importantly the creational and tabernacle contexts. These contexts from Genesis and Exodus provide the theological framework for interpreting Leviticus. Considering its teachings in relation to the creation and the tent dwelling helps make sense of the instructions for holiness. The dwelling is a microcosm of creation. Both make order from chaos, albeit the chaos of the waters or the wilderness, by the Spirit of God (Gen 1:2; Exod 31:3; 35:31).

There are many basic commonalities between creation and the holy instructions for dwelling with God. On the fourth creating day God made the celestial lights to mark the times and seasons, and in Leviticus time is segmented into its sacred units (Gen 1:14–19; Lev 23:2, 4). The animals are made according to their kinds and were thus distinguished for the ritual diet of God's people (Gen 1:20–25; Lev 11). Yahweh created the earthly realm and gave it to the humans, along with the responsibility to govern it. So too he functioned as the landlord of the land of promise and Israel is his servant.

> The land must not be sold permanently, because **the land is mine and you reside in my land** as foreigners and strangers. (Lev 25:23)
>
> Because **the Israelites are my servants**, whom I brought out of Egypt, they must not be sold as slaves. (25:42, emphases added)

The first four days of creation describe the separating (based on the Hebrew root, *b-d-l*) work of God in order to make the space he would fill with life (Gen 1:4, 6, 7, 14, 18). The priests were to make distinctions (*b-d-l*) and thus reinforce the word of Yahweh for holiness (Lev 10:10–11).

After the humans rebelled against God, he drove them out from the specially constructed garden to the east. The way to the garden and the tree of life was guarded by winged sphinxes and a flaming sword. The holy of holies was covered from the east by a veil embroidered with winged sphinxes (Exod 26:31–34). The gap between the holiness of God and the ritually and sinfully contaminated people made the holy of holies a no trespassing zone. Fire from Yahweh killed those who approached him wrongly (Lev 10:1–2; 16:1–2). The winged sphinxes of the veil marked off the most holy space where Yahweh's glory was enthroned above the winged sphinxes of the ark. The life of the people who lived with their holy God was sustained by his grace, for he allowed the high priest alone to enter the holy of holies one time each year to purify the dwelling, the camp, the priesthood, and the people on the Day of Atonement.

*In what manner is the book of Leviticus Genesis-shaped?*

Leviticus is the story of Yahweh's word to the Israelite rebels. The word of grace provides the instruction for worship and holiness. The Genesis-shaped story functions as warning and as invitation to those who wish to approach the almighty Creator.

## INTERACTIVE WORKSHOP

### *Chapter Summary*

Leviticus is the story of Yahweh's instruction for Israel to dwell with him. The grace-based instructions explain worship and holiness for the camp.

### *Can You Explain the Key Terms?*

- community
- holy
- microcosm
- storied framework

### *Challenge Questions*

1. How did the presence of Yahweh's glory transform Israel?
2. What is the basic meaning of "holy"?
3. In what ways is the traditional Hebrew title of Leviticus—"And he called," from the opening verse of the book—an appropriate heading for the book?
4. How does the use of framing effect at the macro level of Leviticus inform interpretation?
5. Why do the only two stories within this book (chs. 8–10; 24:10–23) tell of the death of sinners?

## *Advanced Questions*

1. How does the story of Yahweh's instructions for holiness function differently than the instructions would alone?
2. How does the collective focus of Leviticus effect its significance to readers?
3. What is the theological significance of reading Leviticus within its Torah context?

*4. How should *qadosh* be defined according to its use in Leviticus?

## *Research Project Ideas*

Examine the structure of Leviticus, including genre, framing, first versus third person, and so forth.

Define the meaning of Yahweh's holiness within Leviticus.

Compare the creation and the book of Leviticus (Morales, "Levitical," 15–18).

## *The Next Step*


Douglas, Mary. "Sacred Contagion." Pages 86–106 in *Reading Leviticus: A Conversation with Mary Douglas.* Edited by John F. Sawyer. Journal for the Study of the Old Testament Supplement Series 227. Sheffield: Sheffield Academic, 1996.

Gerstenberger, Erhard S. *Leviticus: A Commentary.* Translated by Douglas W. Stott. Louisville: Westminster John Knox, 1996.

Morales, L. Michael. "How the Dwelling Becomes a Tent of Meeting: A Theology of Leviticus." *Unio cum Christo* 5.1 (2015): 103–19.

———. "The Levitical Priesthood." *Southern Baptist Journal of Theology* 23.1 (2019): 7–22.

Rendtorff, Rolf. "Is It Possible to Read Leviticus as a Separate Book?" Pages 22–35 in *Reading Leviticus: A Conversation with Mary Douglas.* Edited by John F. Sawyer. Journal for the Study of the Old Testament Supplement Series 227. Sheffield: Sheffield Academic, 1996.

Savran, George. *Encountering the Divine: Theophany in Biblical Narrative.* Journal for the Study of Old Testament Supplement Series 420. New York: T&T Clark, 2005.

Sawyer, John, ed. *Reading Leviticus: A Conversation with Mary Douglas.* Journal for the Study of the Old Testament Supplement Series 227. Sheffield: Sheffield Academic, 1996.

Schnittjer, Gary Edward. *Old Testament Use of Old Testament.* Grand Rapids: Zondervan Academic, 2021.

# 17 SACRIFICE

## Leviticus 1–7

Hanna Kim © 123RF.com

## GETTING STARTED

### *Focus Questions*

What is the meaning of sacrifice? How did the sacrifices function?

### *Look for These Terms*

- analogical reasoning
- ascension offering
- cut off
- fat
- graduated holiness
- intentional sin
- microcosmic depiction
- purification offering
- reparation offering
- sacrifice
- silence
- unintentional sin

## AN OUTLINE

A. **Sacrifice Instructions for the People (1:1–6:7)**
   1. Burnt offering (1)
   2. Grain offering (2)
   3. Well-being offering (3)
   4. Purification offering (4:1–5:13)
   5. Reparation offering (5:14–6:7)
      a. For sins against the Lord (5:14–19)
      b. For sins against a neighbor (6:1–6:7)

B. **Sacrifice Instructions for the Priests (6:8–7:38)**
   1. Burnt offering (6:8–13)
   2. Grain offering (6:14–23)
   3. Purification offering (6:24–30)
   4. Reparation offering (7:1–10)
   5. Well-being offering (7:11–38)

## A READING

The sacrifices stand at the intersection of the word of God and human unworthiness. The sacrifices were Yahweh's gracious provision to sustain worship and forgiveness for Israel. Grasping the meaning of sacrifice can be challenging, yet understanding them is crucial for the larger task of apprehending the relationship of God and his people.

A couple of issues make it difficult to understand the meaning of the sacrifices in Leviticus. On the one side, the dwelling (or the temple) is something that is not operating presently. It is, for us, an exercise in imagination. We cannot talk about our own perspective as practitioners within a working religious system that includes animal sacrifices. Our viewpoints are hypothetical, and we debate with other hypothetical positions. None of this means that interpretation of Leviticus 1–7 is unimportant. Rather, because no one has intuitive understanding or personal experience, we need to work all the harder.

On the other side, some overinterpret pentateuchal texts regarding Israel's worship instructions. Many sermons and books use over-imaginative ways that the tabernacle or the sacrifices might prefigure the Messiah (some students refer to such overly zealous interpreters as "hyper-typers"). There is nothing wrong with responsible and careful figural or typological interpretation. Many biblical writers use this sort of reading—in fact, we need to read at this level. But we can abuse a good thing (see discussion of typological patterns in Chapter 1). The approach here will be to try to read Leviticus 1–7 within its pentateuchal setting. Then in Another Look below, I will view the sacrifices from the retrospective viewpoint of the entire Bible.

Beyond the two difficulties mentioned above, understanding the meaning of the sacrifices is challenging because the enterprise is based on a different way of thinking altogether. The point is not that sacrificial logic is flawed, just that it is different. I am not here referring to the old-fashioned (and wrongheaded) view that overstressed the supposed difference between the way the Hebrews and Greeks thought. I am referring to something more like the basic logic that allows for balanced symbolic-literal reading of sacrifice. These different ways of thinking can be called analytical and analogical (see Douglas, 13–65). Analytical refers to the kind of linear rationality, whether inductive or deductive, excessively privileged by modernity. Anyone who has taken English Comp knows that the points of the paragraphs of an essay together support the thesis statement. Besides English Comp, the same kind of analytical rationality dominates many realms of modern thinking. Analogical refers to that logic or kind of rationality that governed the meaning of the sacrifices in Leviticus. Many cultures in the ancient Near East and elsewhere approached the world according to an analogical way of thinking.

Analogical reasoning can be defined this way: "One concept stands for another with similar though not identical features . . . indicating a similar and significant resemblance between physical reality and the spiritual reality of which it is the figure"

(Frei, 25; see also Auerbach, 49–60). The pattern for this way of viewing the world was already established at Mount Sinai. The context for the teachings of Leviticus is the narrative of the mountain and making of Yahweh's dwelling in Exodus. The tabernacle is analogically related to the mountain. The medieval Judaic scholar known as Ramban (Rabbi Moshe ben Nachman) noted the parallels between the tabernacle and the mountain within the narrative context (see Scherman, 726).

The three-tiered graduated holiness of the dwelling perpetually commemorated the events at Sinai. The mountain and the dwelling each had three zones that became more holy as proximity to the presence of God's glory increased (see Table 17-A; Sarna, 105, 250, nn. 13–23). The set of analogical relations established by tabernacle worship were later extended and expanded in many ways. For example, in Numbers the dwelling was situated in the very center of the encampment. Thus, the graduated holiness, or increasingly sacred space, was applied not only to the dwelling itself but was depicted by the tabernacle-camp-wilderness arrangement, as well as by other symbolic depictions of graduated holiness (see Jenson, 101–14, 147–48, 180–81). The graduated concentric holiness was, during the Hebrew kingdom, embodied in the holy of holies, temple, Jerusalem, land, outside the land (exile).

**Table 17-A:** Graduated Holiness of Mount Sinai and the Dwelling

| The Mountain | The Dwelling |
|---|---|
| the presence descended in smoke (Exod 19:9, 11, 16, 18, 20; 20:21; 24:15–18) | the presence descended in smoke (Exod 40:34–35) |
| the summit—Moses alone (19:22, 24; 24:2, 12–13, 15) | holy of holies—the high priest alone (Lev 16) |
| partway up—the priests and elders (24:1–2, 9–11) | holy place—the priests (Exod 28) |
| foot of the mountain—the people and the altar (24:4–5) | courtyard—the people and the altar (27:1–8) |

The sacrifices also bear an analogical relation within the priestly worldview. That is, the sacrifices themselves are microcosmic (small-scale models of the universe) representations of the universe (see Douglas, 66–86). The worldview depicted by the worship system was pictured in each animal sacrifice. Microcosmic thinking used analogies to correlate the symbolic meaning of sacrifice and worship. The meaning of life was not described by rational discourse and abstract reasoning. Rather, the philosophy of life was enacted through the system of worship, from the structure of the sacrifice. In this way every sacrifice celebrates the holiness and sovereignty of Yahweh.

*What is the significance of the analogical or microcosmic representation of the sacrifices?*

The animal sacrifice cannot be viewed correctly by imposing a modern scientific vantage point. The instructions regarding the parts of the sacrifice, such as the fat covering the kidneys and the lobe of the liver, should not be pictured separated out

as they might be in a modern zoological anatomy textbook (as they were in Driver, 5). Instead, the reader should consider the details from the perspective of a butcher or a priest (see Douglas, 72). After the animal was killed and the blood was drained, it had to be turned over to extract the various parts in the manner instructed in Leviticus 1–7. Thus, the priest's viewpoint from the upturned lower side of the animal controlled how the animal parts related together. The way to think through the meaning of the sacrifice, therefore, is a different kind of normal.

*What is the priestly normal view of the animal sacrifices?*

Imposition of modern analytical viewpoint on the details of animal sacrifices in Leviticus by images in Driver's commentary on Leviticus (5).

*The Book of Leviticus with Explanatory Notes (S. R. Driver). New York: Dodd, Mead, and Company, 1898. Public domain.*

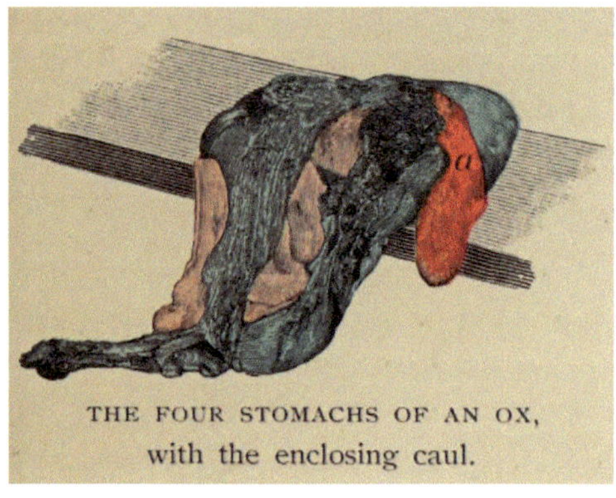


THE FOUR STOMACHS OF AN OX, with the enclosing caul.

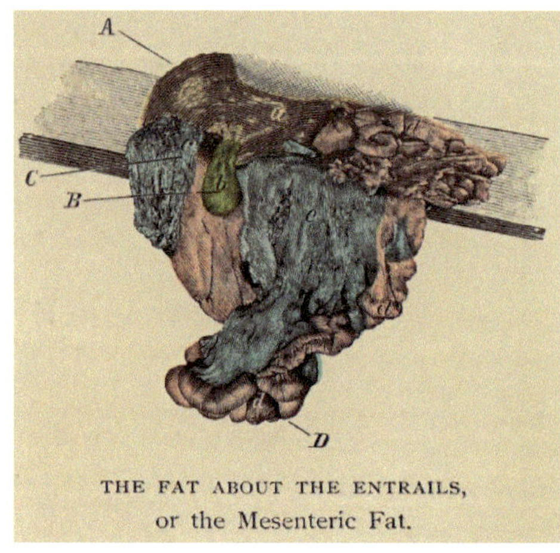


THE FAT ABOUT THE ENTRAILS, or the Mesenteric Fat.

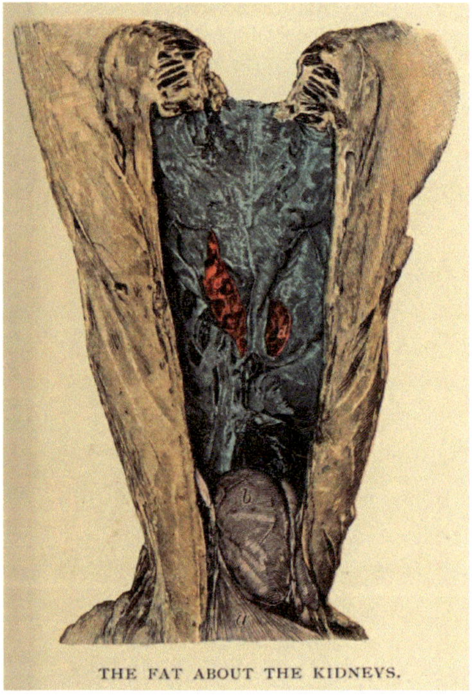

THE FAT ABOUT THE KIDNEYS.

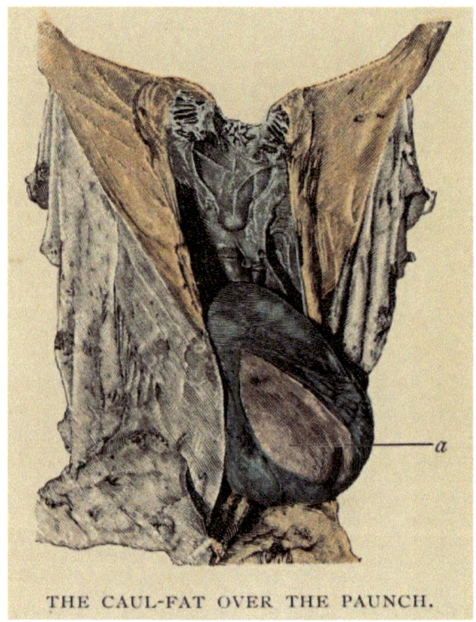


THE CAUL-FAT OVER THE PAUNCH.

*Left:* Inverted animal sacrifice butchered by Assyrian priest (early ninth century BCE)
*Kim Walton/Walton Image Supply*

*Right:* Inverted animal butchered by ancient Egyptians (early twenty-first century BCE)
*Gary Edward Schnittjer*

The instructions concerning the burnt offering and well-being offering can be read together to understand animal sacrifice (these are either repeated or implied in the other animal sacrifice instructions). Animal sacrifices had three parts. We can start with the middle part first and then get to the two parts that it separated.

First, "all the fat is Yahweh's" (3:16c). The fat here does not denote the blubber with the meat but rather the hard suet fat that encased the kidneys. The hard suet fat and the organs it covered (the kidneys and the lobe of the liver) belong to God—"both kidneys with the fat on them near the loins, and the long lobe of the liver, which you will remove with the kidneys" (3:15). It was a serious violation of God's instructions to take his fat. This was part of the grievous sin of the sons of Eli (see 1 Sam 2:15–17, 29).

Why did God want the hard suet fat and the kidneys and liver lobe enclosed therein? The symbolism is significant. The Hebrew term for the physical "kidneys" (*kelayot*) was also used metaphorically to refer to the seat of life, the most secret part of human beings (see Noonan, 307). For example, "You created my inmost being [*kelayot*]; you knit me together in my mother's womb" (Ps 139:13). The kidneys could also function parallel to the heart and be translated as "mind": "The heart is deceitful above all things and beyond cure. Who can understand it? I Yahweh search the heart and examine the mind [*kelayot*]" (Jer 17:9–10a; also see, e.g., 11:20; Ps 16:7). Thus, just as the dense fat hides the inmost secret organs (the kidneys and the lobe of the liver), so too the secret and inmost part of the human soul is hidden from all except God. The suet fat and the vital organs it enclosed in the sacrificial animals belonged always and only to Yahweh.

*What is the symbolic value of always giving the dense fat of animal sacrifices to Yahweh?*

The fat that enclosed the kidneys and liver lobe was in the middle zone that divided the other two parts of the

The altar in the courtyard of the tabernacle
*Hanna Kim*
*© 123RF.com*

sacrifice from each other. Below the fat was the head and body of the animal. The lower portion of the (upside-down) animal sacrifice was placed on the altar first. In those cases in which the sacrifice could be eaten by the priest and/or the people, such as the well-being offering, this was the part of the animal to which they were given access.

The third section of the animal sacrifice was the portion above the middle zone of suet fat, kidneys, and liver lobe, namely, the entrails, reproductive organ, and legs or hind legs. "Aaron's sons the priests shall arrange the parts, with the head and the suet, on the wood that is on the fire on the altar; but its entrails and its legs shall be washed with water. Then the priest shall turn the whole into smoke on the altar as burnt offering, an offering by fire of pleasing odor to Yahweh" (Lev 1:8–9 NRSVue modified).

Presumably the entrails and company were washed to remove the dung. For this reason, some interpreters have thought that the legs referred only to the hind legs. Mary Douglas understands the "legs" as a euphemism for the reproductive organ (76–78). Sometimes the term for feet was used in this manner, possibly in the case of Genesis 49:10 as she suggests (so also Gen 49:10 NET note). In any event, the part of the sacrifice above the suet fat included the entrails, reproductive organ, and shins or legs (or hind legs) (see Milgrom, *Leviticus 1–16*, 159–60). This part of the animal, especially the reproductive organ, symbolized fertility and life. After it was washed, it was placed on the top of the sacrifice, depicting the Creator's life-giving power.

? *What are the symbolic values of the entrails, reproductive organ, and legs of the animal that were placed on top of the sacrifice?*

**Table 17-B:** Graduated Holiness of Animal Sacrifice in Relation to Mount Sinai and the Dwelling

| The Mountain | The Dwelling | Animal Sacrifice |
|---|---|---|
| the summit—Moses alone | holy of holies—the high priest alone | entrails, intestines, reproductive organ, and legs (or hind legs), washed and placed on top of the other parts of the sacrifice |
| partway up—the priests and elders | holy place—the priests | middle zone of dense fat covering the kidneys and liver lobe—secret seat of life—belonging to God |
| the foot of the mountain—the people and the altar | the courtyard—the people and the altar | head and body, access to meat as food for priests and people |

In summary, animal sacrifices were microcosmic depictions of the entire universe. Every time a sacrifice was brought to the tent dwelling, it celebrated the view of the world established at the mountain. Table 17-B summarizes the symbolic aspects of animal sacrifices in relation to the graduated holiness of the mountain and the tabernacle (see Douglas, 79; also see 62–65, and Table 17-A above).

Three other matters applying to sacrifice in general need to be considered before turning to the specific function of the five kinds of sacrifices. First, the Hebrew verb "turn to smoke" (*hiqtir*) used in sacrificial contexts is not the same as the term for "to burn" (*saraph*) used in nonsacrificial incineration. The notion of "turn to smoke" is of transformation to a new kind of existence, to God himself (see Milgrom, *Leviticus 1–16*, 160–61; Morales, 33–36).

Second, the instructions for the sacrifices include alternate sacrifices for those who could not afford the more expensive animal. In each case the instructions are structured from most to least costly. The significance of the less expensive alternates was to make worship accessible to all people. But worship costs everyone something. No one was to come before Yahweh empty-handed (see Exod 23:15; 34:20; Deut 16:16). These are gracious measures of Yahweh to reach out to the disadvantaged.

Third, the sacrifices of Israel, unlike other ancient religions, were conducted without incantations. There are two main lines of thought on the significance of the silence (see Milgrom, *Leviticus 1–16*, 59–60). Some understand it as a polemic against the magical incantations of the sacrificial rites of other nations. Israel's religion did not have magical elements that gave rise to general tendencies toward mythologization. To others, the silence evoked a solemn awe before God. This has sometimes been pushed too far by insisting that psalm singing and prayer were forbidden in the tabernacle and temple areas. The high priest blessed the people at the dedication of the dwelling (Lev 9:23). Worshipers could have praised Yahweh without the priest resorting to magic spells. Moreover, some of the sacrifices required confession. David eventually formalized Levite-led praise of Yahweh (1 Chr 16:4–6; 23:5, 30).

Five kinds of sacrifice did not have any set time (for sacrifices in the religious calendar, see Lev 9; 16; 23; Num 28–29). Leviticus 1:1–6:7 presents the instructions for the sacrifices from the perspective of the people and 6:8–7:38 re-explains them relative to the priests.

First, Leviticus 1 offers instructions for the *burnt offering*, or the *ascension offering* to get at its upward or "Godward" sense (Morales, 28, 36; Watts, 184–85). The offering was a male animal from the herd. If the participant did not have the means for a bull, then a male from the flock (a sheep or a goat) was to be offered. If the person lacked means for a sacrifice from the herd or the flock, then a turtledove or pigeon could be substituted. The meaning of "burnt offering" (*'olah*) is "that which ascends." Yet the verb "offer up" in its causative stem can be used of "kindling" or "lighting" the lamps as well as offering up the burnt offering (e.g., Exod 40:25, 29; see Milgrom *Leviticus 1–16*, 173). The animal was to be completely incinerated on the altar, except the skin (Lev 7:8). This offering was optional and produced "an aroma pleasing to Yahweh"—these points probably signified the gratitude and worship it symbolized (1:17).

*Why is it important that the sacrifices demonstrating gratitude and thanksgiving were optional?*

Second, Leviticus 2 gives the instructions for the *grain offering*, sometimes called cereal or meal offering. The fact that these instructions followed those for the burnt offering suggests that they may have been related. In the case of the purification offering (see below), the person who lacked the means for a bird were to make an offering of grain. The grain offering had to be unleavened and was mixed with oil and frankincense. Part of the offering was burned at the altar and part was reserved for the priests. The grain offering was optional.

Third, Leviticus 3 gives the directions for the *well-being offering*, also known as the peace offering or fellowship offering. The offering of well-being, like all of the animal sacrifices, included the division of the animal into its three parts (as discussed above). The blood was poured on the ground around the altar. The sacrifice was either male or female from the herd, without blemish as with all animal sacrifices. If the donor did not have means for an animal from the herd, a male or female from the flock was permissible.

When the animal was brought to the tabernacle, the person offering it placed a hand on the head of the offering, symbolizing the gift. In the case of the well-being offering, some of the meat was eaten by the worshiper—thus the name fellowship offering. The provision of meat was the primary function of the well-being offering, unique among the sacrifices, and thus the animal could be male or female. No provision was made for bird sacrifices. This offering was voluntary and was a "pleasing aroma" (3:16).

Fourth, Leviticus 4:1–5:13 presents regulations for the *purification offering*, traditionally known as the sin offering. This traditional name has long created problems for understanding the meaning of this offering.

The problem with the English word "sin," in this case, is that it says too much. The things requiring the purification offering include becoming ritually disabled by touching a carcass, childbirth, male discharge, female discharge, and unintentional touching of ritual impurity (5:2–4; 12:6; 15:15; 15:30). These are not sins. Even the idea of accidental commission (4:2, 13, 27) does not fit with the idea of sin resulting in judgment. It was not a sin to have a baby, for example, but the worshiper needed to bring a purification offering. No Christian reader would consider it a sin that Mary gave birth to Jesus. Thus, the offering she and Joseph brought to the Second Temple in Luke 2:22–24 is better understood as a ritual purification offering.

*Why is "sin offering" a problematic translation of the purification offering?*

The animal varied, depending on for whom it was offered: bull for a priest or the whole community, male goat for a leader, female goat for a member of the community, female lamb if the person lacked means, two doves or two pigeons if the person lacked means for a lamb, or grain offering if the person lacked means for the pairs of birds. Some blood was put on the horns of the altar and the rest was poured on the ground.

The purpose of the purification offering is not to purge or purify the person for their own sake but to ritually decontaminate the sanctuary. Violations of ritual standards cause ritual contamination to build up on the dwelling of Yahweh that needs to be purified. The blood of the purification offering is not applied "to" persons but "on behalf" of persons (see Milgrom, "Sacrifices," 766). The purification offering ceremonially decontaminates the sanctuary so that Yahweh's wrath will not break out.

The personal responsibility for the purification offering was grounded on the collective identity of God's people in which individuals participated. The purification offering purged the person, the camp, and especially the dwelling itself of the metaphorical but real contaminants created by the holy presence within the ritually impure encampment (see Wenham, 94–96). The purification offering was necessary to maintain the holiness of the dwelling so that Yahweh's glory could both stay and not bring death to the people. The purification offering is required.

*What was purified by the purification offering?*

Fifth, the *reparation offering*, traditionally referred to as the guilt offering, is explained in 5:14–6:7. The term "reparation" helps get at the function of the offering to repair damaged relations between persons and between the offender and Yahweh. The two terms that are traditionally translated as sin offering and guilt offering are so troublesome that one translation did not translate them into English but simply used the Hebrew words—*hattat* and *asham*—thus leaving the creation of meaning up to the context (see Fox, 520 [Lev 4:3], 529 [Lev 5:19]). Although awkward for reading, being forced to conjure the meaning from the context is a helpful theological exercise for understanding the meaning of these sacrifices.

What kinds of offenses required the person to bring a reparation offering? Primarily sins between human and human that needed to be "repaired." Specifically, the offender had to repay the offended party and add another 20 percent. The various types of offenses caused monetary or measurable damage against another. In addition, the violation was against Yahweh: "If anyone sins *and is unfaithful to Yahweh* by . . ." (6:2a, emphasis added).

Was the sacrifice for unintentional sins only or for intentional sins as well? Reparation offerings were a provision for unintentional violations against the holy things of Yahweh or against Yahweh's commands (see 5:14–19). But whether or not the sacrifice was also a provision for intentional sins is sharply debated. Asked differently, what is the common denominator of the representative offenses listed at the beginning of Leviticus 6? Some interpreters say they are all potentially accidental actions.

> Yahweh said to Moses: "If anyone sins and is unfaithful to Yahweh by *deceiving his neighbor* about something entrusted to them or left in their care or about something stolen, or if they *cheat their neighbor*, or if *they find lost property and lie about it*, or if *they swear falsely about such sin that people may commit. . . .*" (6:1–3, emphasis added)

Although possible, it is difficult for many people, myself included, to think that deceiving, stealing, cheating, and lying make up a list of unintentional offenses. But it is possible to imagine scenarios in which a person accidentally steals or cheats. The judicial nature of "swear falsely," that is, before God, seems to require intentionality. Readers from ancient times have believed that the reparation offering was a provision for intentional or willful sin. The Septuagint interpreted it: "the soul *that sinned and willfully overlooked* the commandments of the Lord" (6:2a lit.; see Wevers, 65).

Implements of sacrifice
*William Krewson*

The chief reasons for reading this list as examples of unintentional offenses are not found in this passage. They are based on other passages, especially the teaching on high-handed sin in Numbers 15. Others who hold certain views of sanctification (Wesleyan, Keswick, and others) believe that willful sin has no place in Christian living (a key passage for these views is Heb 10:26, read in line with their thinking).

The meaning of "high-handed" is bold or defiant. The Israelites left Egypt in a bold or high-handed manner (Exod 14:8; Num 33:3). The teaching on high-handed sin contrasted it to unintentional violation:

> But if just one person sins unintentionally, that person must bring a year-old female goat for a sin offering. The priest is to make atonement before Yahweh for the one who erred by sinning unintentionally, and when atonement has been made, that person will be forgiven. One and the same law applies to everyone who sins unintentionally, whether a native-born Israelite or a foreigner residing among you. *But anyone who sins defiantly [with a high hand]*, whether native-born or foreigner, *blasphemes Yahweh and must be cut off from the people of Israel*. Because they have despised Yahweh's word and broken his commands, *they must surely be cut off; their guilt remains on them*.'" (Num 15:27–31, emphasis added)

The unambiguous point is that there is no provision for high-handed sin.

Was there ever provision for intentional sin? Leviticus 19 presents an example of the kind of sin for which the reparation offering was designed—expanding the list from Leviticus 6:

> *If a man sleeps with a female slave* who is promised to another man but who has not been ransomed or given her freedom, there must be due punishment. Yet they are not to be put to death, because she had not been freed. The man, however, must bring a ram to the entrance to the tent of meeting for a *guilt offering [reparation offering]* to Yahweh. With the ram of the *guilt offering [reparation offering]* the priest is to make atonement for him before Yahweh for the sin he has committed, *and his sin will be forgiven.* (19:20–22, emphasis added)

The sin in this context is definitely intentional, no matter how one interprets the social status distinctions. Fornication cannot be committed by accident. In this case provision was made by means of the reparation offering for forgiveness and restoration.

If there was no recourse for high-handed sin, then how can the reparation offering be viewed as a provision for intentional sins like fornication, lying, cheating, and stealing? The key element is the attitude or spirit of the offender. Leviticus 6:4 explains the occasion for the offender to bring the reparation offering as "when he thus sins and becomes guilty" (NIV), or "when one has thus sinned and, realizing his guilt" (NJPS), or "in the day one was convicted" (LXX lit.). It refers to the personal realization and acknowledgment, voluntary admission, or remorse for the offense.

Jacob Milgrom translates this passage "when one has thus sinned and, *feeling guilty*" to stress the psychological feature of the context (*Leviticus 1–16*, 319; also see 50, 368). He considers, I think rightly, that the instruction for the reparation offering was the origin of the biblical ideal of repentance (377; also see Wenham, 109–11). Philo, an ancient Judaic biblical interpreter from Alexandria, Egypt (ca. 20 BCE–ca. 50 CE), wrote similarly that if one "shall himself become his own accuser, *being convicted by his own conscience residing within*, and shall reproach himself . . . and shall come and openly confess the sin which he has committed, and shall implore pardon; then pardon shall be given to such a man, who shows the truth of his repentance" (*Laws* 1.235–36 [p. 556], emphasis added). He describes the basis of the confession as "the conviction of the soul" (1.237 [pp. 556–57]).

More significantly, notice the further explanation of the offender's response in the reparation offering in Numbers 5:5–7: "Yahweh said to Moses, 'Say to the Israelites: "Any man or woman who wrongs another in any way and so is unfaithful to Yahweh *is guilty and must confess the sin* they have committed. They must make full restitution for the wrong they have done, add a fifth of the value to it and give it all to the person he they have wronged"'" (emphasis added). Confession denotes the kind of attitude or spirit required of the sinner.

How exactly does the repentant attitude of the offender answer the question regarding the relationship between the unforgivable high-handed sin and the reparation offering for intentional sins? Milgrom suggests that the intentional, unforgivable, high-handed sin was changed to unintentional in value by remorse and confession (see *Leviticus 1–16*, 369–73, 486; cf. evaluation in Shepherd, 86–88). I would rather say the sinner changed, not the value of the sin. When the sinner realizes and acknowledges guilt, the offender changes her or his orientation toward the sinful act. Elsewhere Milgrom says more helpfully that "the priestly system prohibits sacrificial atonement to the unrepentant sinner, to the one who 'acts defiantly (RSV "with a high hand")'" ("Atonement," 81).

In other words, high-handed sin for which one could not be forgiven was one for which the sinner refuses to repent (similarly see Noonan, 295–97). The sin was committed purposefully as a defiant act against the instruction of Yahweh. If one felt remorse and confessed that sin and brought the reparation offering, then that one was not caught in a high-handed sin. She or he may have committed it with a high hand but metaphorically lowered the hand in making reparation with a neighbor and bringing the offering. The high-handed sin was not merely intentional but "blasphemes Yahweh" because the offender refused to repent (Num 15:30). The one who would not repent and confess sin but defied the word of God was cut off from one's people.

*What was the difference between the unforgivable high-handed sin and the intentional sin for which one could bring a reparation offering?*

Finally, the oft-repeated judgment of being "cut off from his people" is used in Leviticus in 7:20–21 (cf. Num 15:30–31 on high-handed sin, quoted above). The meaning of the phrase is difficult. The idea of being "cut off" often was used by the prophets according to the figure of cutting a tree down (see, e.g., Isa 14:8; Jer 11:19; Ezek 31:12). In that case, the idea could be associated with death—that is, being cut off from the source of life. This is probably part of the idea of being cut off from God's people. The more basic idea of this judgment in the context of the Torah was to be banished from the community (Exod 31:14). Anyone exiled from Yahweh's people, symbolized by being expelled from his people to the wilderness, had no access to Yahweh. The loss of access to Yahweh was not only about holiness but also concerned the life he granted to his people.

The high priest in full garments
*Sky Light Pictures/ Lightstock.com*

The more terrifying aspect of the idea of being cut off from Yahweh's people is the manner in which this affected persons after the bounds of their mortal lives. Abraham, Isaac, and Jacob were each gathered to their people (Gen 25:8; 35:29; 49:33). If one was cut off from Yahweh's people, the person would not be among Yahweh's people at the resurrection (see comments on "gathered to his people" in Chapter 10).

It is useful to summarize the meaning of the sacrifices in general as well as each of the five kinds of sacrifices presented in Leviticus 1–7. First, the meaning of the sacrifice in general is wrapped up with the symbolic function of the sacrifice. The animal sacrifice itself symbolically represented the biblical worldview. Participants embraced the biblical understanding of the relationship between God and his people whenever they presented sacrifices. Each animal sacrifice testified to the boundaries between Yahweh and his people in terms of graduated holiness. The presence of Yahweh's glory created sacred space that became increasingly more holy. The animal sacrifices demonstrated this reality by their threefold arrangement on the altar (see Table 17-B).

*What is the meaning of sacrifice?*

Second, the significance of the different kinds of sacrifices was also symbolic. The first three kinds of sacrifices—burnt, grain, and well-being offerings—were voluntary and were each designed for positive expression of gratitude by the worshipers toward their God. The last two kinds of sacrifices—purification and reparation—were mandatory and provided the necessary means for life within a community that literally included the presence of Yahweh's glory. Table 17-C summarizes specific functions of the five offerings.

**Table 17-C:** A Comparative Summary of the Offerings of Leviticus 1–7

| Offering | Sacrifice | Instruction and Significance |
|---|---|---|
| *Burnt or Ascension* | bull (alternates: male goat, male sheep, dove or pigeon); unblemished | blood drained and splashed against altar; fat, kidneys, and liver lobe removed for Yahweh and placed on top of head and body on altar; and entrails, reproductive organ, and legs placed on top—**a pleasing aroma of gratitude (optional)** |
| *Grain* | grain (often prepared with oil and/or frankincense) | unleavened grain mixed with oil and incense and burned on altar or cakes mixed with oil for altar and priests—**a pleasing aroma of gratitude (optional)** |
| *Well-being* | male or female from herd or flock, goat or sheep; in each case they may have some imperfections | blood drained and splashed against altar; fat, kidneys, and liver lobe removed for Yahweh and placed on top of head and body on altar; and entrails, reproductive organ, and legs placed on top—**a pleasing aroma of gratitude and fellowship by those who ate it (optional)** |
| *Purification* | bull for priest or nation, male goat for leader, female goat or lamb for citizen, bird or grain for poor; unblemished | offender placed hands on head of animal; blood drained and sprinkled seven times before Yahweh and put on horns of altar and then poured out at altar; fat, kidneys, and liver lobe removed for God and placed on top of head and body on altar; and entrails, reproductive organ, and legs placed on top—**for unintentional transgression (mandatory)** |
| *Reparation* | ram (male lamb for Nazirite vow or person with skin disease); unblemished | offender paid back victim plus 20 percent; confessed sin (Num 5:5–7); placed hands on head of animal; blood drained and splashed against altar; fat, kidneys, and liver lobe removed for Yahweh and placed on top of head and body on altar; and entrails, reproductive organ, and legs placed on top—**for unintentional transgression and intentional sin (mandatory)** |

## ANOTHER LOOK

It is often said that the sacrifices temporarily covered sin until the death and resurrection of Jesus the Messiah. Such a statement, while partially correct, conveys a fundamental error concerning the nature of sacrifice. Thus, the mistake also distorts the way in which the sacrifices prefigure the Messiah. I presume that the oft-said view refers to the sacrifices of purification and reparation, that is, the mandatory offerings. The common view is correct in that mandatory sacrifices were temporary, but even this partial truth has problems. The mandatory sacrifices were temporary, not in their covering of sin but in the fact that they had to be repeated without end. The offerings never, of themselves, mitigated the judgment for sin.

Two Davidic psalms are especially important as early biblical commentary on the meaning and function of the sacrifices, especially those for sin. Psalm 51 is associated with David's confession after Nathan confronted him with his sin against Bathsheba and Uriah. David presents the real issue as repentant humility before God, of which the sacrifice was a mere symbol. For David, there was nothing wrong with the sacrifices themselves so long as their true meaning was kept in view. Compare his psalm with the storyteller's interpretation of the same event.

> You do not delight in sacrifice, or I would bring it;
> you do not take pleasure in burnt offerings.
> *My sacrifice, O God, is a broken spirit;*
> *a broken and contrite heart*
> *you, O God, will not despise.* (Ps 51:16–17, emphasis added)

> Then David said to Nathan, "*I have sinned against Yahweh.*"
>
> Nathan replied, "*Yahweh has taken away your sin*. You are not going to die. But because by doing this you have shown utter contempt for Yahweh, the son born to you will die." (2 Sam 12:13–14, emphasis added)

Sacrifice is a function of repentance.

The other psalm is Psalm 40:6. "*Sacrifice and offering you did not desire*—but my ears you have opened—*burnt offerings and sin offerings you did not require*" (emphasis added). This passage along with its context is quoted in Hebrews 10. The author of the letter interpreted, apparently from Psalm 40 and perhaps other passages, the meaning and function of sacrifice. "But those sacrifices are an annual reminder of sins. *It is impossible for the blood of bulls and goats to take away sins*" (Heb 10:3–4; cf. 9:12, emphasis added).

These two Davidic psalms, therefore, interpret the meaning of the sacrifices themselves as symbolic. That is, the sacrifices functioned as three-dimensional symbols of the humility and repentance that they were to represent. Many prophets in the Bible applied similar interpretations against their listeners and readers who were bringing sacrifices without the corresponding repentance, faith, and obedience that they were supposed to represent (see, e.g., 1 Sam 15:22; Isa 1:10–20; 29:13–14; Jer 6:20; 7:22–23; Hos 6:6; Amos 5:21–24; Mic 6:6–8).

The significance of the different kinds of sacrifices is also symbolic. It was not the sacrifice itself that possessed intrinsic value. The importance of the offerings was entirely in their value as symbols. This holds true for both the optional and mandatory sacrifices. In other words, the purification offering, for instance, did not purify the camp or the tabernacle. Rather, the offerings represented the faith and obedience of the participants, and Yahweh accepted the sacrifice as a symbol of their faith and effected purification. The most significant example is the reparation offering. It was not the offering itself that was of value but the repentance it represented.

During the exile when there was no temple, Yahweh could forgive the sin of the repentant with no sacrifice at all. The animal sacrifices themselves, in the case of the purification and reparation offerings, were not necessary to effect forgiveness other than as symbols of repentance and faith. God has always and only forgiven sin on one basis—the death of his son Jesus the Messiah, whose sacrifice is effectual. According to Paul, "in his forbearance he had left the sins committed beforehand unpunished" (Rom 3:25b). Salvation from sin and judgment were and are a gracious gift based on the "sacrifice of atonement, through the shedding of his blood—to be received by faith" (3:25a).

## INTERACTIVE WORKSHOP

### *Chapter Summary*

The sacrifices, optional and mandatory, functioned as microcosmic depictions of the biblical worldview. Each sacrifice pointed beyond itself to the graduated holiness of worship and the heart conditions of the worshiper.

### *Can You Explain the Key Terms?*

- ascension offering
- analogical reasoning
- cut off
- fat
- graduated holiness
- intentional sin
- microcosmic depiction
- purification offering
- reparation offering
- sacrifice
- silence
- unintentional sin

## Challenge Questions

1. What is the possible significance of the fat that belonged to God?
2. Why were some of the sacrifices optional?
3. What are the problems with referring to the first mandatory sacrifice as the "sin" offering?
4. What biblical evidence supports the reparation offering as for unintentional and intentional sin?

## Advanced Questions

1. Why are the animal sacrifices of Leviticus considered according to analogical versus analytical logic?
2. Why did God require sacrifices that were merely symbolic in value?

*3. What is the meaning of *'asham* in Leviticus 6:4?

*4. Based on various biblical uses of *kelayot* (lit. kidneys), what is its possible significance in the sacrifices of the opening chapters of Leviticus?

## Research Project Ideas

Evaluate the social significance of the less expensive sacrifice substitutes in Leviticus 1–7.

Explain the meaning of the optional sacrifices.

Describe, exegetically and theologically, the function of the reparation offering.

## The Next Step


Auerbach, Erich. "Figura." Pages 11–76 in *Scenes From the Drama of European Literature: Six Essays*. Gloucester, MA: Peter Smith, 1973.

Douglas, Mary. *Leviticus as Literature*. New York: Oxford University Press, 1999.

Driver, S. R. *The Book of Leviticus with Explanatory Notes*. London: James Clarke & Company, 1898.

Fox, Everett. *The Five Books of Moses*. Vol. 1. Schocken Bible. New York: Schocken, 1995.

Frei, Hans W. *The Eclipse of Biblical Narrative: A Study in Eighteenth and Nineteenth Century Hermeneutics*. New Haven: Yale University Press, 1974.

Jenson, Philip Peter. *Graded Holiness: A Key to the Priestly Conception of the World*. Journal for the Study of the Old Testament Supplement Series 106. Sheffield: Sheffield Academic, 1992.

Milgrom, Jacob. "Atonement in the OT." Pages 78–82 in *Interpreter's Dictionary of the Bible: Supplementary Volume*. Edited by Keith Crim. Nashville: Abingdon, 1976.

———. *Leviticus 1–16: A New Translation with Introduction and Commentary*. Anchor Bible 3. New York: Doubleday, 1991.

———. "Sacrifices and Offerings, OT." Pages 763–71 in *Interpreter's Dictionary of the Bible: Supplementary Volume*. Edited by Keith Crim. Nashville: Abingdon, 1976.

Morales, L. Michael. "Atonement in Ancient Israel: The Whole Burnt Offering as Central to Israel's Cult." Pages 27–39 in *So Great Salvation: A Dialogue on the Atonement in Hebrews*. Edited by Jon C. Laansma, George H. Guthrie, and Cynthia Long Westfall. Library of New Testament Studies 516. New York: T&T Clark, 2019.

Noonan, Benjamin D. "On the Efficacy of the Atoning Sacrifices: A Biblical Theology of Sacrifice from Leviticus." *Bulletin for Biblical Research* 31.3 (2021): 285–318.

Philo, *The Works of Philo*. New ed. Translated by C. D. Yonge. Peabody, MA: Hendrickson, 1993.

Sarna, Nahum M. *Exodus*. JPS Torah Commentary. Philadelphia: Jewish Publication Society, 1991.
Scherman, Nosson, ed. *The Chumash*. Brooklyn: Mesorah, 1993, 1994.
Shepherd, Jerry E. *Leviticus*. Story of God Bible Commentary. Grand Rapids: Zondervan Academic, 2021.
Watts, James W. *Leviticus 1–10*. Historical Commentary on the Old Testament. Leuven: Peeters, 2013.
Wenham, Gordon J. *The Book of Leviticus*. New International Commentary on the Old Testament. Grand Rapids: Eerdmans, 1979.
Wevers, John William. *Notes on the Greek Text of Leviticus*. Atlanta: Scholars Press, 1997.

# 18 PURITY AND WORSHIP
## *Leviticus 8–16*



## GETTING STARTED

### *Focus Question*

What were Israel's responsibilities in order to maintain the purity of the tabernacle?

### *Look for These Terms*

- Azazel
- "clean" and "unclean"
- Day of Atonement
- holy and common
- messiah
- moral responsibility
- scapegoat
- skin disease
- unauthorized fire

## AN OUTLINE

A. **Consecration of the Priests (8–10)**
   1. The priesthood established (8–9)
   2. The death of Nadab and Abihu (10)

B. **"Clean" and "Unclean" (11–15)**
   1. Animals (11)
   2. Childbirth (12)
   3. Fungus and skin disease (13–14)
   4. Discharges (15)

C. **Day of Atonement (16)**
   1. The death of Nadab and Abihu (16:1)
   2. Instructions for the Day of Atonement (16:2–34)

## A READING

The sinful Israelites were faced with the dangerous reality of Yahweh's holy presence in the tabernacle. The people's sin, along with their ritual pollution, placed them in grave danger. In this context, the people were responsible for the purity of the tabernacle. The word of God provided the instructions for life by grace.

The instructions concerning sacrifice in Leviticus 1–7 are connected with the narrative and teaching in chapters 8–17. The teaching regarding the sacrifices, along with the instructions regarding the Day of Atonement in chapter 16 and blood in chapter 17, work together to frame the first half of the book (see Figure 16-C in Chapter 16).

Within this outer frame, the story of the death of Aaron's sons Nadab and Abihu (10:1–2; 16:1) creates a second bracket around the instructions concerning clean and unclean. The framing here is not so much to highlight what is in the central panel but to demonstrate the connectedness of these interrelated matters. Worship at the dwelling, the priesthood, and the camp were interdependent in terms of ritual purity. The pollution of the tabernacle presented great danger as typified in the account of the death of Aaron's sons. The purity of the dwelling and safety of the people from Yahweh's wrath depended on the careful obedience of the instructions regarding sacrifice, ritually clean and unclean, and the Day of Atonement. The great privilege of the presence of Yahweh's glory dwelling with the people carried with it the dangerous responsibility of close proximity to his holiness.

The institution of the priesthood is one of the two narratives within Leviticus. This book itself is a narrative, but it is the story of instructions for worship and holiness. The only two passages not instruction-oriented in form are the narratives of the death of Aaron's sons and the execution of the blasphemer in chapter 24. The fact that the only two narratives in Leviticus record the death of rebels should not be missed. The instructions for worship and holiness were mortally serious.

Ancient Egyptian god anoints a public figure

*Gary Edward Schnittjer*

The account of the institution of the Aaronic priesthood in chapters 8–9 gives the details of the consecration of the tabernacle and of Aaron as well as the sacrifices offered for the priests and the people. Some of the instructions for the anointing of the tent dwelling and the priests were given in Exodus 28–30 and 40, but the story occurs here.

Aaron is the first "messiah" in the Scriptures. The Hebrew term *mashiah* is equivalent to the Greek word *christos*, and both terms (*messiah* and *christ*) have been preserved as words in English. Messiah is a verbal noun that means "anointed one," referring to the oil poured on the head of persons publicly recognized to serve God in a given capacity. The ceremony of Aaron's anointing sets the pattern for the human recognition of Yahweh's selection. The old ideal of referring to one's life work or vocation as one's "calling" is a somewhat parallel idea.

Within biblical Israel kings were often ratified with public anointing by a prophet. The anointing was the formal public recognition of God's selection of the individual for the given post (see Talmon, 89). There were many messiahs within ancient Israel's society. During the exile and postexilic period when the people began to look forward to the restoration of Israel, their expectations, especially within certain circles, began to center on the coming of a particular messiah in accord with the hopes set out in the Hebrew Scriptures. The hope for a deliverer of Israel began to be expressed by looking for the coming of *the* messiah.

The wide variety of messianic hopes can be seen in places like the Dead Sea Scrolls and among the characters within the Gospel narratives. For example, notice the civil (Davidic) and priestly messiahs together in 4Q174 (1.1.11, 17–19 in Martínez and Tigchelaar, 1:352–55), a conquering military messiah in Psalms of Solomon 17 and 18 (Gurtner, 346–47), as well as a variety of competing expectations voiced by different persons in John 7. Thus, the term "messiah" was an ordinary word that became increasingly special for biblical readers as they looked for God to fulfill his promises.

*What is the ordinary meaning of the term "messiah," and what is the meaning of the messiah?*

While the primary function of the account of the institution of the priesthood relates to the teachings within the first half of Leviticus, the account also interrelates with the instructions for the priestly garments in Exodus 28 and 39 and the other "beginning of" stories in Genesis and Exodus (see Table 18-A). The similarity between the stories of the beginnings of new institutions in the Torah is the almost immediate sinful failure of the human constituents in every case. The beginning of the priesthood matches the predictable results of human failure in the face of every new vehicle for relationship with God. The priests rebelled. The same pattern of early tragic failures can be seen in later narratives as well, such as Achan (Josh 7), Uzzah (2 Sam 6), and Ananias and Sapphira (Acts 5).

The failure of Nadab and Abihu brought swift judgment from Yahweh. The suddenness of the judgment may be because of the increased responsibility of the priesthood and/or the new intimate proximity between Yahweh's glory and his people. In either case, their fiery death definitively demonstrated the danger of Yahweh's presence.

What was the sin of Nadab and Abihu? The text does not spell it out. "Aaron's sons Nadab and Abihu took their censers, put fire in them and added incense; and *they offered unauthorized fire* before Yahweh, *contrary to his command*. So fire came out from the presence of Yahweh and consumed them, and they died before Yahweh"

**Table 18-A:** New Institutions and Human Failure in Genesis, Exodus, and Leviticus

| Beginning of . . . | The Failure | Time and Length of Narrative Elapsed |
|---|---|---|
| *the Garden* | the fall (Gen 3) | time unspecified/first six verses after creation of human couple |
| *Noahic Covenant* | Noah's fall (Gen 9) | time enough to cultivate a vineyard and make wine/one verse |
| *Post-flood Civilization* | the tower at Babel (Gen 11) | time unspecified/one chapter |
| *Abrahamic Covenant* | Abram left land of promise for Egypt and lied about Sarai (Gen 12) | time unspecified/ten verses |
| *Mosaic Covenant* | the golden calf (Exod 32) | within forty days/six chapter interlude |
| *Aaronic Priesthood* | the strange fire of Nadab and Abihu (Lev 10) | time unspecified/one verse after the consecration ceremonies |

(10:1–2, emphasis added). Commentators have offered many suggestions, such as their practice with the fire may have been associated somehow with the worship of false gods. Although their deaths are referred to several times, no further details are given (Num 3:2–4; 26:60–61; 24:1–2; for a discussion of intentional ambiguity in the sin stories of the Torah, see Chapter 22).

Toward the end of Leviticus 10 the priests made an error in their practice, but they were not consumed by fire (10:16–20). The difference between the problems at the beginning and end of this chapter may have been intentional and defiant versus accidental and repentant. The narrative seems more focused on the significance of approaching Yahweh than on the particular failure of Aaron's sons. Immediately after their deaths Moses said to Aaron, "This is what Yahweh spoke of when he said: 'Among those who approach me *I will be proved holy*; in the sight of all the people *I will be honored*.' Aaron remained silent" (10:3, emphasis added). Moses connected their deaths with the holiness of God.

The death of Aaron's sons provided an opportunity for further instructions regarding rightly approaching priestly responsibilities. In light of the deaths of Nadab and Abihu, the repeated terminal consequences are strongly accented in this context:

> Then Moses said to Aaron and his sons Eleazar and Ithamar, "Do not let your hair become unkempt and do not tear your clothes, *or you will die and Yahweh will be angry with the whole community*. . . . Do not leave the entrance to the tent of meeting *or you will die*, because Yahweh's anointing oil is on you." So they did as Moses said.

> Then Yahweh said to Aaron, "You and your sons are not to drink wine or other fermented drink whenever you go into the tent of meeting, *or you will die*. This is a lasting ordinance for the generations to come." (10:6a, 7–9, emphasis added)

The danger of Yahweh's holiness provides a powerful undercurrent for the teachings on ritually clean and unclean in Leviticus 11–15, sandwiched between the account of the death of Aaron's sons in chapter 10 and its brief rehearsal at the head of chapter 16. The present discussion will briefly summarize the teaching on clean and unclean, then explain the meaning of this designation in general and as it relates to the ideas of holy and common and righteousness and sin. There is a progression in Leviticus 11–15 from the external to the internal (see Table 18-B). These chapters move toward and serve as a prelude to the ritual decontamination of the tent dwelling on the Day of Atonement (ch. 16)—the innermost place in the community (see point C in Table 18-H).

**Table 18-B:** Progression from External to Internal in Leviticus 11–15

| | Ritually pure/ritually impure regulations concerning. . . . |
|---|---|
| *things outside* | animals |
| *things that touch* | touching dead bodies |
| *things from a person* | childbirth |
| *things on a person* | skin disease |
| *things from inside a person* | discharges, male and female |

Students will do well to pay close attention to the instructions regarding ritually pure and ritually impure in Leviticus. The terms "clean" and "unclean" are often mistakenly understood literally as though they relate to dirt or good health. This misunderstanding is unfortunate since these matters offer insight into some of the things Messiah accomplished in his teaching, death, and resurrection. The relationship of God and his people and the significance of worship pivot on Messiah making all things ritually pure. Other obstacles to learning of ritual instruction come from modern biases (see Sidebar 18-C).

The distinction between clean and unclean animals goes back to Noah's taking seven clean and only two unclean of each kind of animal on the ark (Gen 7:2–3). Leviticus 11 presents a list of the clean and unclean animals, an abbreviated form of which appears in Deuteronomy 14:3–21 (see Table 18-D). The criteria for clean land animals are split hooves and cud chewing; for water animals, fins and scales; for swarming insects in Leviticus 11, joined legs. There is no general criterion for permitted birds.

## Sidebar 18-C: Missing the Point of Ritual Purity Regulations

North American readers often struggle with the seemingly bizarre ritual purity instructions in Leviticus. The problem partially stems from the modern failure to apprehend ancient religious culture.

In the early days of modern biblical scholarship, conceptions of defilement were treated with outright scorn. James Frazer (1854–1941) and William Robertson Smith (1846–1894), two founders of modern anthropology, could barely conceal their disgust for the avoidance behaviors of the Bible. Smith, Frazer, and others approached purity rules as if they were a random collection of primitive taboos. Their origin lay in savage fears of blood and demons; their preservation by Israel was simply a matter of perpetuating ancient custom. Making matters worse, Sigmund Freud (1856–1939) in *Totem and Taboo* famously compared religious avoidances with the obsessive behavior of psychotics. Whether they were seen as the products of primitive fears or primeval obsessions, ritualized avoidances were dismissed by many as irrational, pointless, and just plain foolish (Klawans, 2041).

Klawans, Jonathan. "Concepts of Purity in the Bible." Pages 2041–47 in *The Jewish Study Bible*. Edited by Adele Berlin and Marc Zvi Brettler. New York: Oxford University Press, 2004.

**Table 18-D:** An Outline of Leviticus 11 and Deuteronomy 14[a]

[a]For a detailed comparison of the dietary regulations in Lev 11 and Deut 14, see Schnittjer, 120–21.

| **Leviticus 11**<br>*Ritually clean and unclean animals* | **Deuteronomy 14**<br>*Ritually clean and unclean animals* |
|---|---|
| A Regulations concerning living creatures (1–23)<br>1 Permitted land animals (1–3)<br>2 Prohibited land animals (4–8)<br>3 Water animals (9–12)<br>4 Flying animals (13–19)<br>5 Swarming insects (20–23) | A Regulations concerning living creatures (3–20)<br>1 Permitted land animals (3–6)<br>2 Prohibited land animals (7–8)<br>3 Water animals (9–10)<br>4 Flying animals (11–18)<br>5 Swarming insects (19–20) |
| B Contamination from dead animals and ground animals (24–43)<br>1 Animal carcasses (24–28)<br>2 Eight unclean animals (29–31)<br>3 Animal carcasses (32–40)<br>4 Animals that move on the ground (41–43) | B Contamination from dead animals (21a)<br>C Prohibition against cooking a young goat in its mother's milk (21b) |
| C The principle regarding clean and unclean (44–47) | |

The dietary regulations place the entire animal realm within the framework of worship. All animals are defined in one of four categories (see Table 18-E). The distinctions are not about the animals of themselves but about their relative function within Torah-shaped worship, that is, the dietary regulations of Yahweh's people.

**Table 18-E:** Classification of Animals for Yahweh Worshipers[a]

[a]See Wenham, 433.

| Ritually clean | | Ritually unclean | |
|---|---|---|---|
| *suitable for sacrifice* | holy, that is, clean and unblemished | *inedible* | unclean, that is, ritually polluting to eat |
| *suitable for eating* | clean | *inedible and untouchable* | dead, that is, polluting to touch regardless of class when alive |

The designations clean and unclean (*tame'*) have nothing to do with dirt or other repugnant features, or the lack thereof, of animals. It is a question of whether they were ceremonially fit or ritually polluted (see below). From ancient times interpreters have proposed many views as to the common denominator or organizing principle for the dietary classifications. The proposals have included religious taboos (e.g., eating blood) and a measure to prevent the indiscriminate killing of animals (that is, a type of ancient endangered species list). The most repeated suggestion is that the dietary regulations, along with the entire set of clean and unclean teachings, fostered good health and hygiene. But health risks for some of the clean animals offsets this errant deduction (Croteau and Yates, 58). None of these suggestions works out in all cases (Sklar, *Leviticus*, 166–68).

The traditional view, which I regard as correct, holds that the distinctions are arbitrary from the standpoint of human logic. There is no intrinsic reason why the clean are clean. That is, the clean are clean and the unclean are unclean *because God said so.* The instruction regarding new mothers in chapter 12, for example, declares that mothers are unclean whenever they have babies, but twice as long in the case of having female babies. It is irrational to argue, based on the views proposed to date, that new mothers are unsanitary for twice as long after delivering female babies.

Leviticus 13–14 presents lengthy directions for examining and purifying skin disease and fungus. The traditional translation of the Hebrew word for skin disease (*tsara'at*) is "leprosy," from the Greek word *lepra*, beginning with the Septuagint and continuing up to the present. The skin condition of Leviticus 13–14, thus, has been traditionally associated with the incurable condition now known as Hansen's disease. This is an error. A general outline of chapters 13–14 reveals the problem: (1) examination of people (13:1–46); (2) examination of garments (13:47–59); (3) purification of people (14:1–32); (4) purification of homes (14:33–53); (5) purpose (14:54–57). Garments and homes do not get the disease known as Hansen's disease.

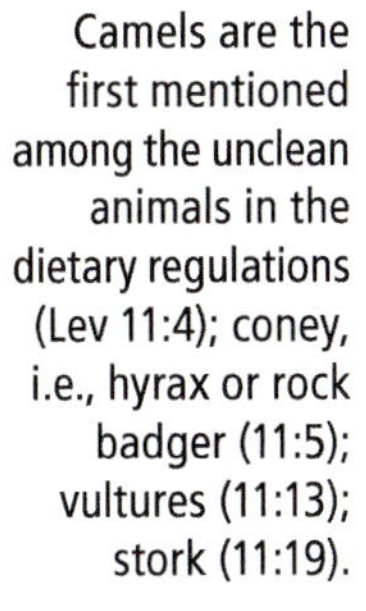

Camels are the first mentioned among the unclean animals in the dietary regulations (Lev 11:4); coney, i.e., hyrax or rock badger (11:5); vultures (11:13); stork (11:19).

*Top left:* *Isaiah and Abby Cramer*

*Top right:* *iStock.com/ Shadow_Hawk*

*Bottom left:* *svarshik/ Shutterstock.com*

*Bottom right:* *iStock.com/ SingerGM*

Hansen's disease is one of the conditions that falls within the category of *tsara'at* or skin disease in Leviticus 13–14, but the category is much broader. Whereas Hansen's disease is incurable, there are regulations to reenter the general populace for the once-banished person who recovers from a skin disease (Olanisebe, 122–25). Also, clothes and houses can be *tsara'at*—apparently affected by certain kinds of fungus. Therefore, some kinds of skin disease that caused ritual impairment and banishment were incurable, while others might go away. In some biblical contexts skin disease is the result of divine judgment; in others it is a biological ailment (Shepherd, 178–81).

Leviticus 15 explains the innermost kind of uncleanness of which humans are susceptible. Both male and female persons may have discharges, normal or abnormal, that will cause ceremonial uncleanness. The chapter, like the two chapters on skin disease, is structured symmetrically (see Table 18-F). The normal discharges were nocturnal emission and menstruation, and the abnormal discharges were the result of infection.

The kinds of adorational disability explained in Leviticus 11–15 were handled in different manners. The manner in which one was ritually re-enabled varied depending on the

**Table 18-F:** The Structure of Leviticus 15

| Discharges causing uncleanness (15) | | |
|---|---|---|
| 1 | Male (vv. 1–18) | |
| | a | Abnormal discharges (vv. 1–15) |
| | b | Normal discharges (vv. 16–18) |
| 2 | Female (vv. 19–30) | |
| | b | Normal discharges (vv. 19–24) |
| | a | Abnormal discharges (vv. 25–30) |
| 3 | Purpose (vv. 31–33) | |

degree of adorational disability. For example, nocturnal emission, menstrual flow, giving birth, and skin disease required, respectively, one day and washing, seven days, seven days or fourteen days (depending on the gender of the baby) plus washing and sacrifice, and moving outside the camp.

In many cases, to become ritually impaired—even intentionally—was not necessarily sinful. Sexual intercourse, for example, caused the married couple to have a ritual disability for a day (15:18). Is sex sin? No. One of the basic human injunctions is to "be fruitful and multiply" (Gen 1:28; 9:7). Moreover, conception in the Hebrew Scriptures was interpreted as a gift from God. Thus, sinfulness, in the case of the clean/unclean regulations, related to persons' intentions toward God's word. Did people listen to and obey his instruction concerning ritual purity? If a couple ignored or rejected the regulations concerning ritual purity after marital relations, that would be sin. It is sinful to reject or ignore the instruction of God concerning ritual purity.

*Was it always sinful to become unclean intentionally? If not, when? Was it ever acceptable to disobey God's instructions regarding ritually clean and unclean states? Why or why not?*

The concept of unclean does not mean physically dirty but rather ceremonially polluted or ritually contaminated or adorationally disabled—perhaps "ritually challenged" in politically correct terms (see Fox, 497–98, 525). Moreover, it is related to, but not identical with, the concepts of holy and common, and righteousness and sin. In a few places clean/unclean and holy/common appear together:

> I am Yahweh your God; consecrate yourselves and *be holy, because I am holy. Do not make yourselves unclean* by any creature that moves along the ground. I am Yahweh, who brought you up out of Egypt to be your God; therefore *be holy, because I am holy.*
>
> These are the regulations concerning animals, birds, every living thing that moves about in the water and every creature that moves along the ground. *You must distinguish between the unclean and the clean*, between living creatures that may be eaten and those that may not be eaten. (Lev 11:44–47, emphasis added; cf. 10:10–11; Ezek 22:26; 44:23).

The difference between being ritually clean and ritually unclean was not based on the intrinsic character of the matters so defined but was so because God said so. Both the holy and the ritually unclean are dynamic, meaning they could be transferred by touch, while the ritually pure is static (Liss, 342). To be holy was to be set apart toward God and was the opposite of commonness. Conversely, to be clean was not necessarily to be holy. Holiness before God required ritual cleanness but was more than that: It meant to be set apart unto God. At the same time, one could be holy *in the categorical sense* of being an Israelite, Levite, or priest and suffer the state of ritual uncleanness. Yet, *in the relative sense* of holiness required to worship, ritual cleanness was an essential prerequisite

| Clean/Unclean | Holy/Common | Holy/Common | Righteous/Sinful |
|---|---|---|---|
| referred to persons, animals, things, and places | *in the categorical sense* of a set-apart status, which was not lost by an unclean state, referred to persons, animals, things, places, and times | *in the relative sense* of the ability to approach God in worship referred to persons | can only refer to persons, that is, those who are morally responsible |

**Table 18-G:** Comparing Ritually Clean/Unclean, Holy/Common, and Righteous/Sinful

(see Table 18-G). The ritually unclean person was banned from coming to the dwelling of God.

*What is the difference between categorical and relative holiness?*

Neither the concept clean/unclean nor holy/common, considered individually or combined, was identical with the righteous/sinful distinction. We see this most clearly if we consider to whom or to what each category could be applied (Table 18-G; and see Averbeck, 4:481). Persons can be sinful in thought, attitude, and/or deed, either by omission or commission. A key factor in sin-innocence-righteousness is intentionality. If a person was unclean, this said nothing, of itself, about his or her moral condition. A person, for example, who had a biological skin disease or menstrual flow was not in sin on this basis. The way one responded to the ritually clean/ritually unclean teachings of Leviticus determined righteousness and sin.

In the same way, one who was holy *in the categorical sense* of being of the nation of Israel or of the tribe of Levi, and so forth, could be either sinful or righteous. Levites, for example, were not removed from their tribal identity because of either ritual impurity or sin; they remained Levites. Exceptions include high-handed sin and other sins for which one was expelled from the assembly. No one was holy *in the relative sense* of being able to approach God in worship if they were ritually impaired and/or in sin. Persons could be holy in the categorical sense of being an Israelite but ceremonially unclean and thus unholy in the relative sense of being unable to approach God in worship. Other persons could be ritually unclean and obedient and thus without sin relative to these instructions. The holiness required to approach Yahweh necessarily required ritual purity, categorical holiness (only his people had access to the dwelling), and forgiveness of sin.

*What was the difference between clean/unclean and righteous/sinful?*

Before moving on one tricky area needs to be noted. Clean/unclean language can be used for ritual impurity and metaphorically of moral impurity (Klawans, 22–31; Sklar, "Prohibitions," 178). Ritual impurities are not forbidden and they are not sinful—such as marital relations, childbirth, bodily flows, corpse contact, and so on (Sklar, *Sin*, 141–53). Moral impurities are forbidden and they are sinful—such as idolatry, murder, illicit sexuality, and so on (Lev 18:20, 24–30; 19:31; 20:1–3; cf. list of biblical references in Wright, 6:734–35). The metaphorical use of impurity language for sinful attitudes and behaviors is carried over to the New Testament (Rom 6:19; Gal 5:19; 1 Thess 4:7). In Leviticus though marital relations and menstruation cause ritual, not moral, impurity (Lev 15:18, 19–24), marital relations during menstruation is forbidden, making it a special case of both ritual impurity in Leviticus 15:24 and moral impurity in 18:19; 20:18 (Rosenberg, 456–64).

One of the communal problems was the pollution of the tabernacle. If the dwelling became polluted through uncleanness or sin, Yahweh would either kill the people or leave (Exod 33:3). The centerpiece of the Day of Atonement is a purification offering. The purpose of the purification offering was not to atone for the offerer but for the tabernacle and its furniture (Milgrom, "Sacrifices," 766). The ritual disabilities, inadvertent sins, and unconfessed intentional sins were "attracted magnet-like to the sanctuary" (Milgrom, "Atonement," 79). The ritual contamination of the tabernacle put the people in danger of Yahweh. Thus, there was an acute need for an annual Day of Atonement to ritually decontaminate the dwelling, the priests, the people, and the camp (Table 18-H; partially indebted to Averbeck, 2:699–700). The Day of Atonement purified all that was necessary, including unknown unintentional sin and unconfessed defiant sin within the community, so that Yahweh could continue to dwell with the people.

**Table 18-H:** The Structure of Leviticus 16—Day of Atonement

A Review of the death of Nadab and Abihu (v. 1)

B Instructions for the high priest's preparation (vv. 2–10)

C Linear description of wiping away impurity from . . .
- 1 the holy of holies (vv. 11–15)
  - 2 the holy place (vv. 16–17)
    - 3 the courtyard (vv. 18–19)
      - 4 the community by means of the scapegoat (vv. 20–22)

D Closing rituals (vv. 23–28)

E A lasting ordinance (vv. 29–34)

The rehearsal of the death of Aaron's sons at the beginning of Leviticus 16 plays a dual role. On the one hand, it connects with the account in chapter 10 and serves to frame the clean/unclean regulations. On the other hand, it accents the need of the priest and people for the purification of the Day of Atonement to avoid Yahweh's deadly wrath.

The Day of Atonement was a significant annual ceremony. Within the context of the community in the wilderness it made possible their ability to dwell with the presence of God's glory and survive. The alternatives were unthinkable—death or his departure from them. The Day of Atonement was the definitive necessary ritual decontamination for the relationship. As noted in point C of Table 18-H, the motion of verses 11–22 depicts the purification from sin and uncleanness, beginning in the innermost part of the camp—the holy of holies—and extending across all of the borderlines of graduated holiness. The scapegoat bore the sin of the chosen people and was expelled outside the limits of the community (see Sidebar 18-I). The annual commemoration reinforced the symbolic and real differences between the holiness within the community and the hostile wilderness within which the people lived.

At the heart of the Day of Atonement practices were two goats. As determined by casting lots, perhaps similar to dice, one goat was slaughtered and the blood was sprinkled on and before the mercy seat of the ark—the lid with the humble winged sphinxes. The other was the scapegoat, a term aptly coined by the early English translator William Tyndale and used in the King James Version. The idea of the term scapegoat follows the Septuagint translation of the Hebrew word *'aza'zel* as "the one sent away."

The term *'aza'zel* is used in two different ways in Leviticus 16. It is used of the scapegoat itself, which was sent into the wilderness, and it was used of the one to whom the goat was sent:

> He will take two goats and set them before Yahweh at the entrance of the tent of meeting. Aaron will cast lots for the two goats, one lot for Yahweh and *the other for the scapegoat [or Azazel]*. Aaron will bring near the goat whose lot fell for Yahweh and offer it as a purification offering. But the goat which the lot designated for *the scapegoat [or Azazel]* fell will be presented alive before Yahweh to make atonement by sending it *to Azazel* into the wilderness. (16:7–10 lit.)

The scapegoat
*Public Domain*

**Map 18-J:** Topography of Jerusalem

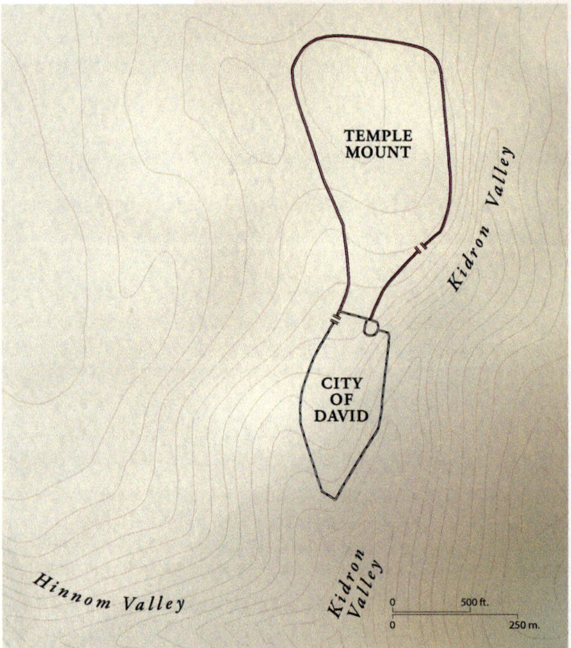

Jerusalem 1931. The temple mount platform (upper right) was built on Mount Moriah where Abraham nearly sacrificed his son of promise, Isaac.

*Library of Congress, Prints & Photographs Division, LC-USZ62-137054*

## Sidebar 18-I: "Outside" Imagery

The idea of "outside" the encampment accords with the growing analogical relations in the biblical worldview. Chapter 17 discussed the analogical or microcosmic thinking exemplified in the sacrifices, dwelling, and Mount Sinai. The outside-oriented imagery, especially regarding the banishment of the scapegoat in Leviticus 16, extends the analogical depiction of the world in an important direction.

In Genesis the concept of outside is sometimes used in terms of death and judgment. The first couple was expelled from the garden and the tree of life. The entire human race, except for one family of humans and one set of animals, was condemned by the flood outside the ark. The less forceful but equally symbolic idea of exile was also reinforced repeatedly, as in the case of Cain, Abraham, Jacob, and the sons of Israel. The depiction of the wilderness outside of the encampment in Leviticus builds upon the ideas of exile, judgment, and death.

The wilderness as the place to expel the scapegoat reinforces the biblical worldview of graduated holiness centering in the holy of holies, progressively diminishing as one moved away from the presence of Yahweh's glory. The scapegoat symbolically carried the sin and ritual defilement of the people into the realm of wandering and judgment. The counterpart to the wilderness encampment was Jerusalem of the Hebrew kingdom. The city was the place of the temple, the house of Yahweh, in which his glory dwelled. Outside the city on the southwest and east were the Hinnom and Kidron Valleys. The western valley that extended around the southern part of the city was known in Hebrew as *ge-ben-hinnom* (lit. "valley-of-son-of-Hinnom") and as *geenna* in Greek. Thus, the Greek word that refers to the literal place known as the Hinnom Valley is the word translated as "hell" in English (*gehenna* in the Latin Vulgate).

How did the valley along the west and south of Jerusalem come to be identified with hell? During the days of the southern kingdom of Judah, in the time of Kings Ahaz and Manasseh, the Hinnom Valley was the site for the sacrifice of children (2 Kgs 16:3; 21:6; see discussion of Molech in Chapter 19; Schnittjer, 809–10). The prophet Jeremiah pronounced threats of doom over the valley (see Jer 7:29–34; cf. 19:6–9; Isa 66:24). Moreover, in Second Temple Judaic literature before the time of the New Testament, the valley began to be seen as the place of the final judgment (see, e.g., 1 Enoch 27:1–2; 54:1–6 [also, Azazel here referred to as a demonic leader]; 90:26; 4 Ezra 7:36; 2 Baruch 59:10; 85:13; Sibylline Oracles 1:103; 2:291; 4:186).

By New Testament times the Hinnom Valley symbolized the place of judgment (see Jeremias, 1:657–58; see also Watson, 3:202–3). Some have said that in late antiquity the Hinnom Valley was a place where fires burned to dispose of trash. Perhaps. But more importantly, ancient Judaic interpreters extended the associations from Isaiah with Jeremiah's preaching against child sacrifice and his judgment of casting the dead into the Hinnom Valley (see Watson, 2:926–928; also see Scripture and other references above). The analogical relationship between the camp and the city was then extended to the ultimate ends of the new Jerusalem and the eternal lake of fire—heaven and hell.

The Encampment, the City, and the New Jerusalem

| the camp | Jerusalem | New Jerusalem |
|---|---|---|
| the wilderness | Hinnom valley (*Gehenna*) | the lake of fire |

The term *'aza'zel* sounds as if it could have referred to the scapegoat (see NIV), or it could have been the name or title of a desert demon (see NJPS; Shepherd, 212–13). The Bible occasionally makes references to the desert as a place of devils (see Matt 12:43; also Lev 17:7). Later Judaic apocalyptic writings sometimes developed imagery and traditions concerning a demonic leader named Azazel (see 1 Enoch 10:4–6; also see, e.g., 8:1; 9:6; 10:8; 13:1; Testament of Solomon 7:7–8; Apocalypse of Abraham 13:6–14; 14:5; 20:5–7; 22:5). The possibility that Azazel was the name of a desert demon may partially explain why some of the goat imagery later became associated, sometimes indirectly, with views of the devil (see Grabbe, 153–61, 166–67).

The regulations regarding the Day of Atonement and the blood of animals in Leviticus 16 and 17 serve as a kind of a hinge or janus in the book. The concerns of these chapters are the purity of the dwelling and the lifeblood of animals. These things look back to the major concerns for sacrifice, purity, and worship in the first half of the book and look ahead to the need for holiness in the community. The instructions regarding the blood in chapter 17 will be taken up in the next Chapter, which focuses on the second half of Leviticus as a call to holiness.

The teachings of Leviticus 1–16 are God's word for the worship of the community. When the presence of Yahweh's glory filled the tabernacle, Israelite life was radically altered. The close proximity of Yahweh's glory and his people redefined their lives entirely. All of life was viewed from the vantage point of the courts of Yahweh. Israel had a new set of weighty responsibilities that were necessarily attached to the privilege of the glory's presence with them. The deaths of Nadab and Abihu accentuated the danger of not fulfilling Yahweh's requirement. The fact that Yahweh's glory tented with the wilderness community was an act of grace. The gift created the responsibility for comprehensive worship to maintain the sanctity of the dwelling, the priesthood, the people, and the camp. The opening chapters of Leviticus explain the life of Israel in terms of ever preparing to enter into the courts of Yahweh.

## ANOTHER LOOK

The categories of clean and unclean were ceremonial. There was nothing intrinsically dirty about the things so designated as ritually unclean; as such, these categories were symbolic. While the matters of ceremonially clean/unclean were figurative, the demand for obedience by the covenant people was real. Because the teachings were based on symbolic designations, later torah could reinterpret or adjust their significance. The word of God never changes. It stands forever. The way that readers are oriented toward the significance of certain teachings can be reinterpreted by later instruction of the word of God.

Messiah proclaimed new torah regarding ritually clean and ritually unclean by the authority of his word (contra Ehorn, 229–30, who fails to observe that Rom 14:14 builds on the event in Mark 7:18–19; see below). After debating with some religious scholars concerning the relationship between the tradition of the elders and God's word, Messiah spoke his teaching on these matters in a riddle to the crowds and again to his followers. The record of that teaching in Mark 7 includes a brief commentary by the narrator, making explicit the meaning of Messiah's new torah. "'Are you so dull?' he asked. 'Don't you see that nothing that enters a person from the outside can defile them? For it doesn't go into their heart but into their stomach, and then out of the body.' (*In saying this, Jesus declared all foods clean*)" (Mark 7:18–19, emphasis added). The word of Messiah set a new precedent.

Paul applied the new teaching of Messiah to the holy/common distinctions of those things that do not have moral responsibility. Specifically, he challenged the view that some times were more holy than others. "One person considers one day more sacred than another; another considers every day alike. *Each of them should be fully convinced in their own mind*" (Rom 14:5, emphasis added). Within the context of the Mosaic covenant there was no latitude for personal discretion concerning sacred time. The Sabbath—one of the Ten Words—and the annual commemorative events were not open to personal inclination; they were law. It appears that Paul based his reinterpretation of the regulations for holiness on the new torah of Messiah referred to above. "I am convinced, being fully persuaded in *the Lord Jesus, that nothing is unclean in itself.* But if anyone regards something as unclean, then for that person it is unclean" (14:14, emphasis added; see 14:20).

*How did Messiah's new instruction on the dietary regulations reorient believers to these biblical teachings?*

The matters of clean/unclean and holy/common that once applied to animals, places, things, and time (see Table 18-G) have a different significance because of the teaching of Messiah. God is still holy and his people must continue to be holy. Matters of holiness are now based only on the category of moral responsibility, that is, the sinfulness or righteousness of those beings created in God's own image.

It is often thought that the distinction between ritually clean and ritually unclean was reinterpreted in Peter's vision of Acts 10. Visions, however, are not about what they are about; they have to be interpreted. Visions were God's figurative manner of communicating with certain persons (Num 12:6). He taught them one thing by means of a figure of another. In the case of Peter's vision, the point is not that God was now declaring all foods clean, for Messiah had already done that. Rather, the new teaching concerning the dietary regulations effectively removed one of the visible and social differences between Jews and gentiles. Through his vision Peter learned that he should preach the good news to Cornelius because God's word is going out to the gentiles.

## INTERACTIVE WORKSHOP

### *Chapter Summary*

The institution of the priesthood and tabernacle worship was quickly followed by the deadly judgment of Aaron's sons, thus accenting the seriousness of the responsibility of Israel's relationship with God. The people were required to obey the ritually clean and ritually unclean regulations. The Day of Atonement purified the tabernacle and the community each year so that Yahweh could continue to dwell with his people without killing them.

## *Can You Explain the Key Terms?*

- Azazel
- clean and unclean
- Day of Atonement
- holy and common
- messiah
- moral responsibility
- scapegoat
- skin disease
- unauthorized fire

## *Challenge Questions*

1. How did the act of anointing set apart a messiah for God's service?
2. What clues does Leviticus give regarding the nature of the offense of Nadab and Abihu?
3. Define, according to Leviticus, the similarities, differences, and interrelationship between the categories of ritually clean/unclean, holy/common, and righteous/sinful.
4. What was the significance of the two goats for the Day of Atonement rituals?

## *Advanced Questions*

1. How does the narrative of the institution of the priesthood (chs. 8–10) function within Leviticus?
2. Why were new mothers ritually unclean twice as long when they gave birth to a female as opposed to a male (see Lev 12)?
3. Compare the degrees of ritual uncleanness regarding the matters mentioned in Leviticus 12–15.

*4. What is the meaning of *tame'* ("unclean")?

*5. What is the meaning of *tsara'at* (traditionally "leprosy")?

*6. How should each of the occurrences of *'aza'zel* in Leviticus 16 be translated?

*7. Does the use of *hilasterion* in the Septuagint's translation of Leviticus 16:13–15 stand behind Paul's use of the term in Romans 3:25? Explain.

## *Research Project Ideas*

Evaluate the viability of the leading interpretations of the sin of Nadab and Abihu.

Evaluate the traditional interpretations of the organizing principle, or common denominators, of the ritually clean and unclean regulations (on dietary regulations see Croteau and Yates, 58–62).

Evaluate the effect of the Septuagint's translation of skin disease as "leprosy."

Explain, exegetically and theologically, the meaning of the Day of Atonement.

Describe and evaluate the history of interpretation on Azazel and the scapegoat.

## *The Next Step*


Averbeck, Richard E. "Clean and Unclean." Pages 477–86 in vol. 4 of *New International Dictionary of Old Testament Theology and Exegesis.* Edited by Willem A. VanGemeren. Grand Rapids: Zondervan Academic, 1997.

———. "כפר." Pages 689–710 in vol. 2 of *New International Dictionary of Old Testament Theology and Exegesis.* Edited by Willem A. VanGemeren. Grand Rapids: Zondervan Academic, 1997.

Croteau, David A. and Gary Yates. *Urban Legends of the Old Testament: 40 Common Misconceptions.* Nashville: B&H Academic, 2019.

Ehorn, Seth M. "Jesus and Ritual Impurity in Mark's Gospel." Pages 217–33 in *For Us, but Not to Us: Essays on Creation, Covenant, and Context in Honor of John H. Walton*. Edited by Adam E. Miglio et al. Eugene, OR: Pickwick, 2020.

Fox, Everett. *The Five Books of Moses*. New York: Schocken, 1995.

Grabbe, Lester. "The Scapegoat Tradition: A Study in Early Jewish Interpretation." *Journal for the Study of Judaism in the Persian, Hellenistic, and Roman Periods* 18 (1987): 152–67.

Gurtner, Daniel M. *Introducing the Pseudepigrapha of Second Temple Judaism: Message, Context, and Significance*. Grand Rapids: Baker Academic, 2020.

Jeremias, Joachim. "γέεννα." Pages 657–58 in vol. 2 of *Theological Dictionary of the New Testament*. Edited by Gerhard Kittel. Translated by Geoffrey W. Bromiley. Grand Rapids: Eerdmans, 1964.

Klawans, Jonathan. *Impurity and Sin in Ancient Judaism*. New York: Oxford University Press, 2000.

Liss, Hanna. "Ritual Purity and the Construction of Identity: The Literary Function of the Laws of Purity in the Book of Leviticus." Pages 329–54 in *The Books of Leviticus and Numbers*. Edited by Thomas Römer. Leuven: Uitgeverij Peeters, 2008.

Martínez, Florentino García, and Eibert J. C. Tigchelaar, ed. *The Dead Sea Scrolls Study Edition*. 2 vols. Leiden: Brill/Grand Rapids: Eerdmans, 1997, 1998.

Milgrom, Jacob. "Atonement in the OT." Pages 78–82 in *Interpreter's Dictionary of the Bible: Supplementary Volume*. Edited by Keith Crim. Nashville: Abingdon, 1976.

———. "Sacrifices and Offerings, OT." Pages 763–71 in *Interpreter's Dictionary of the Bible: Supplementary Volume*. Edited by Keith Crim. Nashville: Abingdon, 1976.

Olanisebe, Samson O. "Laws of *Tzara'at* in Leviticus 13–14 and Medical Leprosy Compared." *Jewish Biblical Quarterly* 42.2 (2014): 121–27.

Rosenberg, Michael. "The Conflation of Purity and Prohibition: An Interpretation of Leviticus 18:19." *Harvard Theological Review* 107.4 (2014): 447–69.

Schnittjer, Gary Edward. *Old Testament Use of Old Testament*. Grand Rapids: Zondervan Academic, 2021.

Shepherd, Jerry E. *Leviticus*. Story of God Bible Commentary. Grand Rapids: Zondervan Academic, 2021.

Sklar, Jay. *Leviticus*. Tyndale Old Testament Commentary. Downers Grove, IL: IVP Academic, 2014.

———. "The Prohibitions against Homosexual Sex in Leviticus 18:22 and 20:13: Are They Relevant Today?" *Bulletin for Biblical Research* 28.2 (2018): 165–98.

———. *Sin, Impurity, Sacrifice, Atonement: The Priestly Conceptions*. Sheffield: Sheffield Phoenix, 2005.

Talmon, S. "The Concepts of Messiah and Messianism in Early Judaism." Pages 79–115 in *The Messiah: Developments in Earliest Judaism and Christianity*. Edited by James H. Charlesworth. Minneapolis: Fortress, 1993.

Watson, Duane F. "Gehenna." Pages 926–28 in vol. 2 of *Anchor Bible Dictionary*. Edited by David Noel Freedman. New York: Doubleday, 1992.

———. "Hinnom Valley." Pages 202–3 in vol. 3 of *Anchor Bible Dictionary*. Edited by David Noel Freedman. New York: Doubleday, 1992.

Wenham, Gordon J. "Why Does Sexual Intercourse Defile (Lev 15:18)?" *Zeitschrift für die alttestamentliche Wissenschaft* 95 (1983): 432–34.

Wright, David P. "Unclean and Clean (OT)." Pages 729–41 in vol. 6 of *Anchor Bible Dictionary*. Edited by David Noel Freedman. New York: Doubleday, 1992.

# 19 HOLY LIVING
## *Leviticus 17–27*

iStock.com/pamela_d_mcadams

## GETTING STARTED

### *Focus Question*

What does it mean to be holy?

### *Look for These Terms*

- blood
- circumcision of the heart
- ellipsis
- euphemism
- Jubilee
- nakedness
- personification
- Sabbath year

## AN OUTLINE

A. **Blood (17)**
B. **Regulations for People (18–20)**
    1. Forbidden relationships (18)
        a. Purpose (18:1–5)
        b. Relationships (18:6–23)
        c. Results (18:24–30)
    2. The call to holiness (19)
    3. Crimes requiring capital punishment (20)
C. **Regulations for Priests (21–22)**
D. **Religious Calendar (23)**
E. **Further Regulations for Priests and People (24)**
    1. Concerning the oil and the bread (24:1–9)
    2. The narrative of a blasphemer condemned (24:10–23)
F. **Regulations for the Land (25)**
    1. Sabbath years (25:1–7)
    2. Jubilee (25:8–55)

G. **Blessings and Curses (26)**
   1. Regulations (26:1–2)
   2. Blessing (26:3–13)
   3. Judgment (26:14–46)

H. **Regulations for Tithes and Vows (27)**

## A READING

The call to holiness requires Yahweh's people to accord with his word. When he says, "Be holy because I, Yahweh your God, am holy," the beginning and the end of the matter are set out (see Lev 19:2). The call to holiness crashes into the human revolution. It demands that sinners listen to his instruction. The instructions, however, anticipate the failure and exile of Israel. But that is not the end, for Yahweh will remember his word to Abraham.

The theme of Leviticus 17–27 is the pursuit of holiness. Whereas the first half of this book is oriented toward worship and ritual purity for the tabernacle within the community, the second half targets holiness for persons of the community. The objective is not the individual. The instructions for holiness are aimed at the necessary character of Israel as a people. The common denominator of both halves of Leviticus is helping Israel live as potential worshipers who need to be ever ready to enter the courts of Yahweh.

*What is the community nature of the call to holiness?*

Leviticus 17–26 has been referred to as "the holiness collection" (many regard chapter 27 as an appendix of sorts based on the closing in 26:46). The holiness collection bears resemblance in its general form to other collections of commandments in the Torah, as shown in Table 19-A (based in part on Levine, 111). The covenantal form of these segments of Scripture, as well as other passages such as Joshua 24, has often been compared to the ancient Near Eastern suzerain-vassal treaties (see Table 14-H in Chapter 14).

**Table 19-A:** Comparing the Structure of the Legal Collections of Torah

| | **Book of the Covenant** *Exodus 20–23* | **Holiness Collection** *Leviticus 17–26* | **Torah Collection** *Deuteronomy 12–28* |
|---|---|---|---|
| Offerings | 20:22–26 | 17 | 12 |
| Commands | 21:1–23:9 | 18–25 | 13–26 |
| Land duties | 23:10–11 | 19:9–10, 23–25 | 15; 24:19–22; 26 |
| Sacred calendar | 23:12–19 | 23 | 16:1–17 |
| Blessings and curses | (23:20–33) | 26 | 27–28 |

Among the teachings in Leviticus 17–27, chapters 19 and 26 have attracted much attention from later biblical writers. Chapter 19 was the portion of the book most often quoted by New Testament writers, especially the instructions to be holy and love thy neighbor (19:2, 18b). The letter of James, for example, shows a marked interest in Leviticus 19 (see Johnson, 391–401). Many later contexts in the Hebrew Scriptures relied on the teachings of Leviticus 26 to explain the causes of and reasons for the fall of the Northern and Southern Kingdoms (see, e.g., 2 Kgs 17; 2 Chr 36; Pss 78; 79; Ezek 20 and many other contexts of Ezekiel; also see Ezra 9; Neh 1; Dan 9; Baruch 2).

The primary structural element of the second half of Leviticus is framing, between chapters and sometimes within the chapters themselves (see Figures 16-C and 16-D in Chapter 16). It is widely recognized that Leviticus 18 and 20 frame the holiness chapter (ch. 19). Leviticus 18 lists forbidden relations and prohibits Molech worship while chapter 20 pronounces capital punishment for Molech worship and illicit sexual relations. Chapters 25 and 27, by referring to the year of Jubilee, bracket the so-called blessings and curses (ch. 26). Far more subtle is the possible framing of Leviticus 23 (Master, 420–24). If chapter 23 is, in fact, framed, it is so by the double bracket of people-oriented teachings in chapters 18–20 and 24:10–23 and priestly instructions in chapters 21–22 and 24:1–9 (i.e., A-B-X-B-A). An alternate view sees chapters 23 and 25 bracketing 24 (Morales, 106–7). Whether or not these literary frames are accepted, the dominant theme of the need for holiness binds together Leviticus 17–26.

The following discussion will briefly introduce each section of teaching with special attention to the stated rationale for the instructions, beginning with Leviticus 17. This chapter offers the command and rationale concerning animal blood. The prohibition against ingesting blood is not new. Along with the clean/unclean distinction among the animals, it was noted in the Noah story: "You must not eat meat that has its lifeblood still in it" (Gen 9:4).

In Leviticus 17:10–12 the rationale for the prohibition was announced:

> "I will set my face against any Israelite or any foreigner residing among them who eats blood, and I will cut them off from the people. *For the life of a creature is in the blood*, and I have given it to you *to make atonement for yourselves on the altar*; it is the blood that makes atonement for one's life. Therefore I say to the Israelites, 'None of you may eat blood, nor may any foreigner residing among you eat blood.'" (emphasis added)

The term for "life" (*nepesh*) here is the same one used in Genesis 1 and 2 regarding the life or soul of animals and human beings (see Gen 1:21, 24, 30; 2:7, 19; cf. 7:22). Whereas in Genesis 1–2 the life was associated with the breath of living creatures, in Leviticus 17 it is identified with the blood.

Breath and blood were each effective symbolic representations of life. The literary term *metonymy* refers to a figure of speech in which the part stands for the whole. The blood of animals is only one part of their life, as is breath. But the identification of blood with life is seen in that as the blood is drained from the animal, its life is extinguished. The blood, therefore, serves as a three-dimensional metonymy of life for the Israelites. Life is precious. Life belongs to God alone. No person is permitted to ingest blood, for life belongs to the Creator (see Hartley, 273–78). Moreover, the blood of animals, while not intrinsically meritorious for atonement, is the vehicle or authorized symbol for the faith of participants (see Chapter 17). Yahweh accepted for atonement the faithful sacrifices of his people.

Leviticus 18 begins with the rationale for obeying God's instruction. Notice the details of this opening with emphases added to consider four observations:

> *Yahweh said to Moses*, "Speak to the Israelites and say to them: '**I am Yahweh your God**. You must not do as they do in Egypt, where you used to live, and you must not do as they do in the land of Canaan, where I am bringing you. Do not follow their practices. You must obey my laws and be careful to follow my decrees. **I am Yahweh your God**. Keep my decrees and laws, for the person who obeys them will live by them. **I am Yahweh**.'" (18:1–5)

First, italics mark the way the narrator begins by signifying that Yahweh is speaking to Moses what he should relay to the people. This follows the framework of nearly every chapter, in that it is the story of Yahweh's instructions. The storied framework emphasizes Yahweh's sovereign authority and goodness in giving instructions to his people.

Second, the instructions throughout this half of Leviticus are frequently punctuated by the declaration, "I am Yahweh your God," as marked by bold. The relationship between Yahweh, holiness, and the ethical demands on his people is intrinsic.

Third, the nature of Israel as a holy nation is accented by their distinction from the peoples of both Egypt and Canaan—marked by broken underlining. They are called to be different from those where they came from and from those where they are going. The place of the people at the mountain of God's revelation between Egypt and Canaan reinforces the ethical dimension of the call to holiness.

Fourth, the statement marked by underlining that "the person who obeys [the decrees] will live by them" needs to be qualified (18:5). This is not a mechanistic cause and effect. Rather, the obedience implies faith, and the life is the graced kind of life depicted in 26:3–13. Paul uses the passage, in an ironic way, to challenge what he believed was a misreading concerning life based on works of the law (Rom 10:5; Gal 3:12). The exilic prophet Ezekiel repeated the phrase "the person who obeys them will live by them" to reinforce Israel's failure to abide by God's commands, thus forfeiting his blessing (Ezek 20:11, 13, 21).

The rest of Leviticus 18 lists a variety of regulations using several figures of speech to forcefully and graphically instruct the readership. Verses 6–23 repeatedly use the gentler phrase "do not uncover the nakedness of" (lit.) with the meaning "do not have sexual relations with" (NIV). The use of a gentler expression for a more explicit idea is called *euphemism*. This passage prohibits a variety of incestuous sexual relationships as well as adultery, same-sex relations, and bestiality.

The listing of prohibited incestuous relations makes use of *ellipsis* by not including one of the forbidden relationships. *Ellipsis* is a literary device whereby something is skipped in order to emphasize it. Ellipses in modern quotations are signaled by typing three dots ( . . . ). The function of modern quotation ellipses—to hide the skipped portion—is exactly opposite of ellipsis as a literary figure of speech—to draw attention to what is not said. The implication behind ellipsis is that all readers will notice the omission and be perplexed over it. This is true in Leviticus 18 when the father-daughter relationship is not mentioned in the prohibited incest list. No one thinks that father-daughter incest was allowed, and identifying the ellipsis means that it was not forgotten by accident. This most serious crime is accented by elliptical omission, forcing readers to fill in the blank themselves. Leviticus 18:6 says "any close relative." Who are they? Leviticus 21:2 states that the close relatives are mother, father, son, daughter, brother, and sister. Thus, mother, daughter, and sister are automatically forbidden in 18:6 (see Rattray, 542; for other ways to reach this conclusion, see Mohrmann, 70; Miller, 42–43). The use of ellipsis demonstrates the biblical view that the Scriptures need to be studied and pondered.

*How does Leviticus 18 use ellipsis?*

A secondary inference of the prohibitions from sexual relations of family members is a definition of the basic family structure. Figure 19-B graphically illustrates the basic family structure deduced from the incest prohibitions of Leviticus 18,

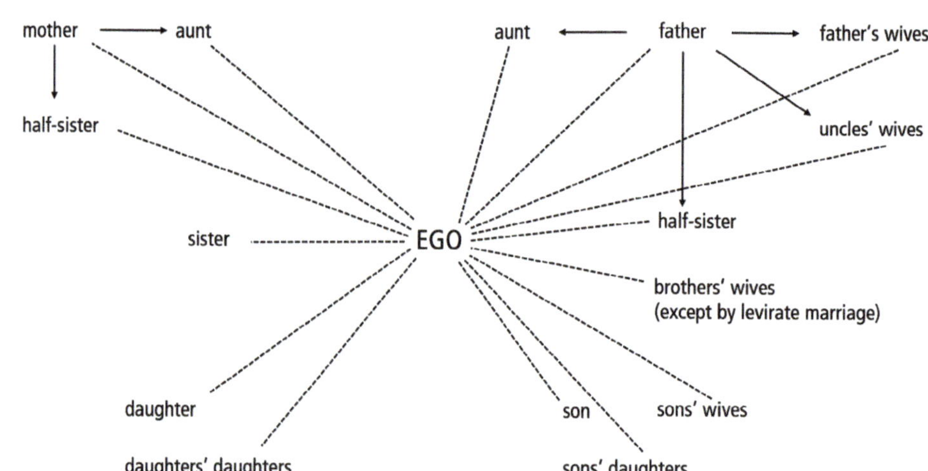


**Figure 19-B:** Basic Family Structure Inferred by Prohibited Sexual Relations of Leviticus 18[‡]

[‡]Adapted from Baruch A. Levine, *Leviticus*. JPS Torah Commentary (Philadelphia: Jewish Publication Society, 1989), 255. Used by permission.

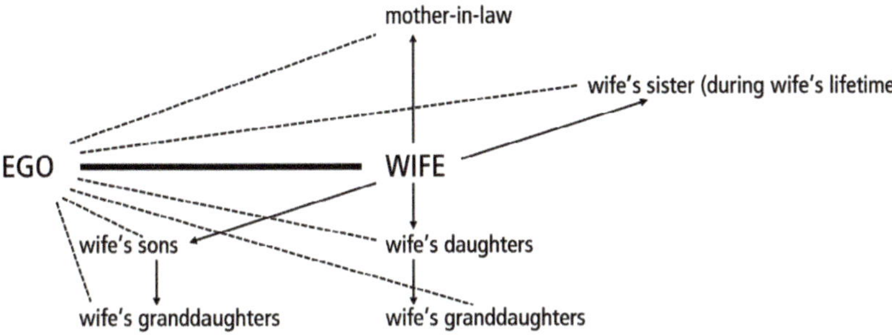


**Figure 19-C:** Basic Extended Family Structure Inferred by Prohibited Sexual Relations of Leviticus 18‡

‡Adapted from Levine, *Leviticus*, 255. Used by permission.

and Figure 19-C depicts the extended family of the married individual. The laws of forbidden degrees or incest alert readers to a couple of illegal relationships by these standards among the Hebrew ancestors (Sarah was Abraham's half-sister and Rachel was sister to Jacob's first wife; see n. a of Figure 7-A in Chapter 7).

Leviticus 18–20 focus on relational purity and righteousness. Besides incest, these three chapters mention six other sexual crimes and their punishments. Three of the offenses do not feature capital punishment, namely, sexual relations during menstruation results in being cut off from the people (18:19; 20:18); fornication with a slave betrothed to another person requires monetary compensation and a reparation offering (19:20–22); and fornication with a prostitute ritually pollutes the land (19:29). These crimes each have social factors that make them lesser crimes. Focus for a moment needs to turn to the three sexual capital crimes besides incestuous relations. Of these three, controversies over same sex relations have led to over twenty views of Leviticus 18:22 and 20:13 (Stone, 212). Treating this violation differently is part of the problem.

Many interpreters have drawn false inferences from the use of "abomination" (*to'evah*) (KJV, NRSVue) in the prohibition against same sex relations (18:22; 20:13). The tendency among interpreters to use this term as a basis to treat certain sexual sins as worse than others must read against the sense of the text because the term "abomination" is applied to all of the sexual violations in Leviticus 18:26, 27, 28, 29 (note the use of "all/any" [*kol*] in three of these four verses). More importantly, adultery, same sex relations, and bestiality are each capital crimes (18:20, 22, 23; 20:10, 13, 15–16). Leviticus views these illicit relations as violations worthy of equal penalties.

*What do the instructions and penalties in Leviticus 18 and 20 teach about the importance of sexual purity?*

The Creator calls for sexual purity, as is his right. The instructions in Leviticus 18 and 20 point toward the importance of sexual purity and righteousness. Whether or not one believes there are biblical grounds for considering some sexual sins worse than others, the treatment of persons who practice different kinds of sexual misconduct should not be driven by hateful prejudice.

Sexual purity in Leviticus includes procreative and creational bases (Sklar, 187–95; Wenham, 363). Yahweh calls Israel to a life of holiness (19:2; 20:7, 26) and obedience (18:4; 19:37; 20:8), set apart from the practices of Egypt and the nations of Canaan (18:3, 30; 20:24, 26). Just as worship and ethics in Leviticus are Genesis-shaped, so too Messiah grounds the ideal of monogamous marriage between a male and a female on Genesis 1:27 and 2:24 (Matt 19:4–5).

Leviticus 18 closes with a memorable use of *personification*, the figure of speech that applies human attributes to inanimate or subhuman life, such as vegetation or animals. In chapter 18 the rationale for sexual prohibitions is, in part, to protect the land from becoming defiled. Just as the purity of the tabernacle is a major concern of the first half of Leviticus, the pollution of the land is a recurring theme that binds together the second half of Leviticus. The symbolic relationship between the tabernacle and the land is another example of analogical reasoning or microcosmic logic (see Chapter 17):

> Do not defile yourselves in any of these ways, because this is how the nations that I am going to drive out before you became defiled. *Even the land was defiled; so I punished it for its sin, and the land vomited out its inhabitants.* But you must keep my decrees and my laws. The native-born and the foreigners residing among you must not do any of these detestable things, for all these things were done by the people who lived in the land before you, *and the land became defiled. And if you defile the land, it will vomit you out as it vomited out the nations that were before you.*" (18:24–28, emphasis added)

Moral defilement relates to those under moral responsibility—that is, human beings, because they are created in God's image (see Chapter 18). Thus, the figural language graphically points out that severe consequences extend to those who disobey Yahweh's word.

Two other implications of Leviticus 18 must also be considered. First, Israel is regarded in relation to the Canaanites within the logic of this context. Just as the inhabitants of Canaan are to be vomited out, so too Israel will be for her rebellion. This Torah context offers rationale for later biblical narrators and prophets to theologically interpret historical, political, and military events. The reason why the Canaanites will be defeated and driven from their homeland is not Israel's military prowess or racial prejudice against Canaanites. The Canaanites will be judged for their sin (Gen 15:16).

The other side of this issue is also true. Israel will not inherit the land because of anything they deserve (Deut 9:3–6). The fate of nations is explained in relation to God's word. The judgment of the Canaanites and the blessing and judgment of Israel are each because of their response to God's instruction. Israel enjoyed whatever success it did because of the word of Yahweh to their ancestors.

Second, the personification of the land is developed in different ways in several of the following chapters. In 19:23–25, the personification of the defiled land extends to fruit-bearing trees:

> Now when you enter the land, and plant any-kind of tree for eating, you are to *regard its fruit (like) a foreskin, a foreskin*. For three years *it is to be considered-foreskinned for you*, you are not to eat (it). And in the fourth year shall all its fruit be a holy-portion, (for) jubilation for YHWH; in the fifth year may you eat its fruit, to add for you its produce, I am YHWH your God! (Lev 19:23–25 Fox, emphasis added)

Some interpreters consider the disposal of the first three crops as trimming the tree's foreskin (see 19:23 Targum Pseudo-Jonathan; Targum Onqelos; Vulgate; also see Levine, 131). Leviticus 20:22 reinforces that obedience was the necessary measure to prevent the land from vomiting out the people (see Num 35:33–34). According to chapter 25, the land was to be granted Sabbath every seventh year. Part of the logic for the punishment of the people by exile was to provide the Sabbaths for the land (see Sidebar 19-D). The personification of the land vividly depicts the sinfulness of the people in these contexts.

*What is the significance of the personification of the land of promise in the second half of Leviticus?*

If the covenant collection of Exodus 21–23 spoke to individual and collective responsibilities based on the revelation at the mountain, the holiness collection of Leviticus 17–26 regulates all Israel in relation to preparing to enter the courts of Yahweh (see Morrow, 11, 253; Knight, 4). Viewing all Israel as potential tabernacle worshipers naturally gives rise to demands for holiness.

The instructions for holy living in Leviticus 19 have often been compared to the Ten Words. Leviticus 19, like the Ten Words, is a high point in the Torah's instruction. Moreover, many interpreters regard Leviticus as the center of the Torah and chapter 19 as the center of the book (see Auld, 40–41; Milgrom, *Leviticus 17–22*, 1364–67). Various ancient, medieval, and modern commentators have suggested that each of the Ten Words have parallels in Leviticus 19. These attempts, according to Milgrom, are built on "exegetical quicksand" (*Leviticus 17–22*, 1600). What can be demonstrated is the framing of the chapter by commands five, four, one, and two in verses 3 and 4 and commands four, five, two, and one in verses 30 to 32.

> Each of you must *respect your mother and father, and you must observe my Sabbaths. I am Yahweh your God. Do not turn to idols or make metal gods for yourselves.* I am Yahweh your God. . . . *Observe my Sabbaths* and have reverence for my sanctuary. I am Yahweh. Do not turn to mediums or seek out spiritists, for you will be defiled by them. I am Yahweh your God. Stand up *in the presence of the aged, show respect for the elderly and revere your God. I am Yahweh.* (19:3–4, 30–32, emphasis added)

## Sidebar 19-D: Neglecting Sabbath Years and Seventy Years of Exile

The Chronicler makes an interpretive blend of two scriptural passages, one from Leviticus and the other from Jeremiah, to explain why the captivity of Judah lasts seventy years. Notice the way the Chronicler deduces the reason for seventy years (added emphases signify allusions):

> Then the land **shall pay its sabbaths** all the days of **its desolation**, and you are in the land of your enemies, then the land **will rest** and **shall pay its sabbaths**. . . . If then their uncircumcised heart humbles itself, and then they **pay** for their iniquity. . . . And the land will be abandoned by them and it **shall pay its sabbaths** while it lies **desolate** without them, and they **pay** for their iniquity, because they rejected my rules and their soul spurned my statutes. (Lev 26:34, 41b, 43 lit.; cf. 25:2)

> All of this land will become a ruin and a waste, and these nations will serve the king of Babylon seventy years. And it will be when seventy years are fulfilled I will punish the king of Babylon, and that nation, declares Yahweh, and the land of the Chaldeans, and I will make it an everlasting waste. (Jer 25:11–12 lit.; cf. 29:10)

> And he took into exile the remnant from the sword to Babylon, and they were for him and for his descendants slaves until the reign of the kings of Persia, to fulfill the word of Yahweh by the mouth of Jeremiah until the land **paid back its sabbaths**, all the days of **its desolation** it **rested**, to fulfill seventy years. Now in the first year of Cyrus king of Persia to accomplish the word of Yahweh by the mouth of Jeremiah, Yahweh instigated the spirit of Cyrus king of Persia, and he announced in all his kingdom and even in writing, saying, "Thus says Cyrus king of Persia, 'All the kingdoms of the earth Yahweh the God of the heavens has given to me, and he has appointed me to build for him a house in Jerusalem which is in Judah. Whoever among you from all his people, may Yahweh his God be with him, and let him go up.'" (2 Chr 36:20–23 lit.)

The Chronicler in essence "does the math," showing that the seventy years of captivity work like back pay to make up for Israel neglecting seventy Sabbath years (490 years of rebellion ÷ 7 for neglected Sabbath years = 70 years of captivity). In this way the Chronicler worked with Leviticus 26 and the seventy years of Jeremiah to explain the exile (Schnittjer, "Individual," 128–30). Tragically, the exile did not bring about the needed change in Israel.

The captives who returned to their ancestors' homeland rebelled against Yahweh in every way as their ancestors did (see Ezra 9; Neh 13; Schnittjer, "Bad," 55–56). Since the exile did not work to change Israel, Yahweh would need to fulfill his covenantal word in another way. This leads to the coming of Messiah from Nazareth.

Schnittjer, Gary Edward. "The Bad Ending of Ezra-Nehemiah." *Bibliotheca Sacra* 173 (2016): 32–56.
———. "Individual versus Collective Retribution in the Chronicler's Ideology of Exile." *Journal of Biblical and Theological Studies* 4.1 (2019): 113–32.

The bracketing of the chapter with these commands from the Ten Words signals the significance of obedience to God's word for holiness.

The framing of Leviticus 19 is doubled, before and after the allusion to the four commands in verses 3–4 and 30–32, by the declaration of Yahweh's right to Israel's devotion. "Yahweh said to Moses, 'Speak to the entire assembly of Israel and say to them: "Be holy because I, Yahweh your God, am holy. . . . I am Yahweh your God, who brought you out of Egypt. Keep all my decrees and all my laws and follow them. I am Yahweh"'" (19:1–2, 36b–37). Figure 19-E provides an overview of the contents of Leviticus 19 that can help with the following survey of selected instructions. The phrase "I am Yahweh (your God)" appears sixteen times amid the fifty-two laws of chapter 19, in each case with prohibitions that could be violated in secret (see Milgrom, *Leviticus 17–22,* 1374–75).

**Figure 19-E:** Contents and Framing of Leviticus 19

1 The command (vv. 1–2)

2 The requirements (vv. 3–36a)
- a concerning parents (v. 3)
- b concerning idols (v. 4)
- c concerning offerings (vv. 5–8)
- d concerning the harvest (vv. 9–10)
- e concerning neighbors (vv. 11–18)
- f concerning mixing (v. 19)
- g concerning female slaves (vv. 20–22)
- h concerning "uncircumcised fruit" (vv. 23–25)
- i concerning pagan practices (vv. 26–28)
- j concerning prostitution (v. 29)
- k concerning Sabbath (v. 30)
- l concerning spiritism (v. 31)
- m concerning elders (v. 32)
- n concerning residing foreigners (vv. 33–34)
- o concerning honesty (vv. 35–36a)

3 The reason (vv. 36b–37)

Notice the collective undercurrents even in seemingly individual-oriented instructions. The commands to honor parents and older persons cited above are complemented by the accountability for one's offspring within the community. "Do not degrade your daughter by making her a prostitute, or the land will turn to prostitution and be filled with wickedness" (19:29). The responsibility for prostitution is not stated here in terms of the individual but from the perspective of the parent. Moreover, the issue is not merely personal, involving the female prostitute

"When you reap the harvest of your land, do not reap to the very edges of your field or gather the gleanings of your harvest. Leave them for the poor and for the foreigner residing among you. I am Yahweh your God" (Lev 23:22).
*Shutterstock.com/ Gianni Dagli Orti*

and her clients, but is a community concern. The bidirectional responsibility to the older and younger generations relate to the community at large. The interconnected logic of these instructions for holiness is far removed from the decidedly egocentric interpretations of the "common good" in the modern world.

Different kinds of teachings are associated together within the call to holiness by shared imagery. The matter of care for the poor and avoidance of idolatrous practices each include regulations concerning "edges":

> When you reap the harvest of your land, *do not reap to the very edges of your field* or gather the gleanings of your harvest. Do not go over your vineyard a second time or pick up the grapes that have fallen. Leave them for the poor and the foreigner. I am Yahweh your God. . . . Do not practice divination or seek omens. *Do not cut the hair at the sides of your head or clip off the edges of your beard.* Do not cut your bodies for the dead or put tattoo marks on yourselves. I am Yahweh." (19:9–10, 26b–28, emphasis added)

Perhaps the most significant observations concern Leviticus 19:18b. Messiah taught that the command to love "neighbors" included even enemies (see Matt 5:43–48; Luke 10:25–37; Harmon and Schnittjer, *Seven*, ch. 8). Although Messiah used extreme rhetorical elements, his emphases appear more like exegetical recoveries and moderate enhancements than brand new inventions. There is a difference in meaning between neighbor and residing foreigner (*ger*), so that using these terms together implies that a neighbor is a fellow Israelite.

The important command to "Love thy neighbor" comes as the culmination of a series of interpretive advances within Torah itself (see Schnittjer, *Old*, 42–44; Schnittjer, "Going," 116, 136–37). Leviticus 19:33–34 blends together two laws from Exodus. The Passover regulation required that circumcised residing foreigners participate just as any native-born of Israel (Exod 12:48). One of the prohibitions in the covenant collection protected residing foreigners from mistreatment (22:21). These laws are combined and enhanced within the holiness collection. Notice that in both Exodus and Leviticus the laws are addressed to Israel in second person and refer to residing foreigners in third person (emphases added):

When a **residing foreigner** residing among you who wants to celebrate Passover to Yahweh must have all the males in his household circumcised; then he may take part as a native-born of the land. No uncircumcised male may eat it. (Exod 12:48 lit.)

**Do not mistreat** or oppress **a residing foreigner**, **for you were residing foreigners in** the land of **Egypt**. (Exod 22:21 lit.)

When a **residing foreigner** resides among you in your land, **do not mistreat** them. The residing foreigner residing among you must be treated as your native-born. Love them as yourself, **for you were residing foreigners in Egypt**. I am Yahweh your God. (Lev 19:33–34 lit.)

The interpretive advancement of Leviticus 19:33–34 builds on the same logic as the prohibition in the older covenant collection. Israel knows how hard it is to be residing foreigners because they had long been residing foreigners in Egypt. The category of residing foreigner is broad enough to include Israel's time as free guests and as slaves in Egypt. To be residing foreigners means they enjoyed asylum as others yet without inheriting land or any other benefits of full citizenship.

The command in Leviticus 19:33–34 goes beyond protection. The new, enhanced version of the law calls upon citizens of Israel to treat residing foreigners as if they were native-born Israelites. And then, even further, treat residing foreigners the way you yourself want to be treated.

From the command to "love the residing foreigner as yourself," it is a small yet critical step to the obligation to "love thy neighbor." Advancements from the lesser to the greater can be found in many places in Scripture (e.g., cf. Exod 23:4–5; Deut 22:1–4). The logic goes something like: If you must treat them as yourselves, then you certainly must treat yourselves as yourselves. Although the terms "love" and "as" are very common, the only two places Leviticus says "as yourselves" are in the two commands compared here.

When a residing foreigner resides among you in your land, do not mistreat them. The residing foreigner residing among you must be treated as your native-born. **Love** them **as yourself**, for you were residing foreigners in Egypt. I am Yahweh your God. (Lev 19:33–34 lit., emphasis added)

Do not seek revenge or bear a grudge against anyone among your people, but **love** your neighbor **as yourself**. I am Yahweh. (19:18, emphasis added)

Even a profoundly important law like "love thy neighbor" did not drop out of the sky. It is a culmination of an important teaching within Yahweh's progressive revelation to Israel.

Unlike ancient Israelites, modern Christians do not know what it is like to live as outsiders in ancient anti-Semitic Egypt. Like ancient Israelites, all Christians know what sort of treatment they hope for themselves. And anyone who has ever felt like an outsider has a sense of what the commands in Leviticus call for. Yahweh's people are called to treat outsiders as native-born and to love them as themselves.

*What are the building blocks from Exodus and Leviticus of the command to love thy neighbor in Leviticus 19:18b?*

The instructions of chapter 19 for holiness are followed in Leviticus 20 by the penalties for many of the violations enumerated in chapter 18. Leviticus 20 opens with the punishment for Molech worship, which involved child sacrifice. The penalty for this criminal act was death by stoning and being cut off from Yahweh's people (see Chapter 17). Moreover, Yahweh promised to cut off any who "closed their eyes" (20:4) to Molech worship, thus emphasizing the corporate responsibility of the personal commands. Those who do not stop their neighbors from child sacrifice are guilty. Leviticus 20 goes on to stipulate capital punishment for illegal sexual relations as well as other regulations. Yahweh explained, "Consecrate yourselves and be holy, because I am Yahweh your God.

Molech (or Molek) worship was a community offense. "If the members of the community close their eyes when that man sacrifices one of his children to Molek and if they fail to put him to death, I myself will set my face against him and his family and will cut them off from their people together with all who follow him in prostituting themselves to Molek" (Lev 20:4–5, emphasis added).

*Public Domain*

Keep my decrees and follow them. I am Yahweh, who makes you holy" (20:7–8). The last phrase is significant because it explains the source of human holiness, namely, "I am Yahweh, *who makes you holy*" (emphasis added).

The same idea is stated at the end of Leviticus 22 in conclusion of two chapters of stipulations for priests. "Keep my commands and follow them. I am Yahweh. Do not profane my holy name, for I must be acknowledged as holy by the Israelites. I am Yahweh, *who made you holy* and who brought you out of Egypt to be your God. I am Yahweh" (22:31–33, emphasis added). The priesthood was held to high standards that included spouses, grooming, and physical blemishes. If any among Aaron's descendants were physically disabled in certain ways, they were excluded from priestly duties before God.

The disqualification for physical disability is not based on moral failure. The priests—in a way similar to animal sacrifices and the tabernacle itself—were microcosms of the entire universe. As the priests, so the sacrifices were to be without blemish—another case of analogical worship regulation (see Chapter 17). The twelve animal blemishes (four, two, and six blemishes) of 22:22–24 are arranged in relation to the priestly blemishes (six, two, and four blemishes) of 21:17–21 (Table 19-F; see Milgrom, *Leviticus 17–22,* 1876). The common denominator of the blemishes listed for the sacrifices is that each was visible to the observer. In the case of the twelve blemishes that disqualified one from priestly service, each was visible except a crushed testicle (ibid., 1836–40). Moderns rightly strive for equal opportunity. The persons that serve in the sanctuary and the animals offered in sacrifice are held to higher standards than Israel in its civil affairs. At the same time Leviticus 21:22 affirms that priests with physical disabilities remain priests. They even retain the privilege and responsibility above others in Israel of eating the most holy food (Fuad, 297).

**Table 19-F:** Twelve Deformities that Disqualify Priests and Animals

| Priests | Animal Sacrifices |
|---|---|
| No man who has any defect may come near: | When anyone brings from the herd or flock a fellowship offering to Yahweh to fulfill a special vow or as a freewill offering, it must be without defect or blemish to be acceptable. |
| [4] no man who is **blind** or **lame**, **disfigured** or **deformed**;<br>[2] no man with a **crippled foot** or **hand**,<br>[6] or who is a **hunchback** or a **dwarf**, or who has any **eye defect**, or who has **festering** or **running sores** or **damaged testicles**. (21:18–20) | [6] Do not offer to Yahweh the **blind**, the **injured** or the **maimed**, or anything with **warts** or **festering** or **running sores**. Do not place any of these on the altar as a food offering presented to Yahweh.<br>[2] You may, however, present as a freewill offering an ox or a sheep that is **deformed** or **stunted**, but it will not be accepted in fulfillment of a vow.<br>[4] You must not offer to Yahweh an animal whose **testicles are bruised**, **crushed**, **torn** or **cut**. You must not do this in your own land. (22:21–24) |

"When anyone brings from the herd or flock a fellowship offering to Yahweh . . . , it must be without defect or blemish to be acceptable" (Lev 22:21).
*Public Domain*

Leviticus 23 enumerates the cycle of commemorative events. The Sabbath was weekly and the others were annual memorial events attesting and celebrating various aspects of the relationship between Yahweh and his people. The significance of the teaching is the rationale concerning all of the appointed times at the head of the chapter: "Yahweh said to Moses, 'Speak to the Israelites and say to them: "These are *my appointed festivals, the appointed festivals of Yahweh*, which you are to proclaim as sacred assemblies. . . . *These are Yahweh's appointed festivals*, the sacred assemblies you are to proclaim at their appointed times"'" (23:1–2, 4, emphasis added).

This provides the narrative framework—the controlling context—of the instructions. The times belonged to Yahweh. Thus, the chapter explains the holy time that enveloped his people. Every week moved toward its destiny in the Sabbath, the holy day of rest unto Yahweh. The weeks themselves were always building toward the next annual event dedicated to Yahweh. The key aspects of the annual events are summarized in Table 19-G (Table 19-H provides a summary of biblical references for further reading on the holy calendar). In comparison with the other biblical collections of instruction for commemorative events, Leviticus 23 focuses almost entirely on individual laypersons and farmers rather than priests (cf. Exod 23:14–17; 34:21–23; Deut 16:1–17). The dates in Leviticus 23 are relative to the redemption from Egypt; other dating systems were used within later biblical contexts.

? *What is the significance of holy time?*

Leviticus 24 presents priestly regulations and the second of two narratives within the book. The first priestly regulation concerns the perpetual duty of keeping the dwelling's lampstand lit through the night. This responsibility was sometimes carried out by the priest's apprentice (see 1 Sam 3:3; cf. Exod 27:20–21). The other priestly regulation concerns the bread of the presence that had to be arranged every Sabbath. This may clarify the teaching about continually providing the bread of the presence in Exodus 25:30 (see Noth, 178; Rhyder, 728).

The inclusion of the narrative of the execution of the blasphemer in the latter section of the chapter has long perplexed interpreters. Why is it located here? Why is this story included in Leviticus at all? One of the possible answers to the first question is that the story may be part of a framing effect (see Figure 16-D in Chapter 16). The second question is more difficult. Two possible parts of answers can be mentioned here.

**Table 19-G:** A Summary of the Holy Calendar in Leviticus 23

| | | |
|---|---|---|
| Passover and Unleavened Bread | first month, fourteenth day, for eight days | to remember God's deliverance of the people from Egypt (pilgrimage feast, see Exod 23:15) |
| First fruits | the day after Passover and Unleavened Bread | an act of gratitude and devotion to God giving him the first produce |
| Weeks | seven Sabbaths and one day after First Fruits | the seven weeks plus one day makes fifty days (thus, Pentecost); note parallel to Jubilee in Leviticus 25 (pilgrimage feast, see Exod 23:16a) |
| Trumpets | seventh month, first day | trumpet blast to signal the coming pilgrimage feast in two weeks (later this became the Jewish New Year, Rosh Hashanah; cf. literal reading of Ps 81:3) |
| Day of Atonement | seventh month, tenth day | to purify the holy of holies, the altar, the dwelling, the priesthood, and the entire encampment (see Lev 16) |
| Booths | seventh month, fifteenth day, for eight days | live in booths to commemorate the temporary shelters when the people left Egypt, also referred to as "Ingathering," the third of three pilgrimage feasts listed in Exodus 23:14–17 |

**Table 19-H:** A Summary of Key Biblical References concerning the Holy Calendar

| Pentateuchal | |
|---|---|
| Sabbath | Exod 20:8–11; 23:12; 31:12–17; 34:21; 35:2–3; Lev 23:3; Deut 5:12–15; cf. Gen 2:1–3; Exod 16:22–30; Num 15:32–36 |
| Passover and Unleavened Bread | Exod 12:1–20; 13:3–10; 23:15; 34:18; Lev 23:5–8; Num 9:1–14; 28:16–25; Deut 16:1–8 |
| First fruits | Lev 23:9–14 |
| Weeks (Pentecost) | Exod 23:16; 34:22; Lev 23:15–21; Num 28:26–31; Deut 16:9–12 |
| Trumpets | Lev 23:23–25; Num 29:1–6 |
| Day of Atonement | Lev 16; 23:26–32; Num 29:7–11 |
| Booths (Tabernacles, Ingathering) | Exod 23:16; 34:22; Lev 23:33–43; Num 29:12–34; Deut 16:13–15 (Zech 14:16–19; Neh 8:13–18; 1 Kgs 8:2; Ezra 3:1; Neh 7:73) |
| Sabbath Year | Exod 23:10–11; Lev 25:1–7 |
| Jubilee | Lev 25:8–55; 27:17–24; Num 36:4 |

*(continued)*

| Post–Pentateuchal | |
|---|---|
| Purim | Esth 9:18–32 |
| Dedication (Hanukkah, Lights) | 1 Maccabees 4:52–59; 2 Maccabees 2:16; John 10:22 |
| Fasts | Four fasts are listed in Zech 8:19; 7:5, namely, "the fasts of the fourth, fifth, seventh and tenth months." The fasts: "fourth" lamented the breaking into Jerusalem by Nebuchadnezzar (2 Kgs 25:3–4; Jer 39:2; 52:6–7); "fifth" mourned the burning of the temple (2 Kgs 25:8–10; Jer 52:12–14) (according to Judaic tradition both temples were destroyed on the Ninth of Av, the first by the Babylonians in 586 BCE and the second by the Romans in 70 CE); "seventh" marked the assassination of Gedaliah (2 Kgs 25:22–25; Jer 41:1–3); "tenth" commemorated beginning of Nebuchadnezzar's siege of Jerusalem (2 Kgs 25:1; Jer 39:1; Ezek 24:1–2). |

First, the narrative is precedent-setting. Moses inquired of Yahweh what should be done with the blasphemer, and God pronounced the death sentence (see Chavel, 78–79). In this way, the story reinforces the capital punishments prescribed for various sins listed in Leviticus 20. The account puts forward the important "law of retaliation" (*lex talionis*) embedded within it (see Chapter 14).

> Anyone who takes the life of a human being is to be put to death.
>
> Anyone who takes the life of someone's animal must make restitution—life for life.
>
> Anyone who injures their neighbor is to be injured in the same manner: *fracture for fracture, eye for eye, tooth for tooth*. The one who has inflicted the injury must suffer the same injury.
>
> Whoever kills an animal must make restitution,
>
> but whoever kills a human being is to be put to death. You are to have the same law for the foreigner and the native-born. I am Yahweh your God. (24:17–22, emphasis added)

The key notion of the law of retaliation ("fracture for fracture, eye for eye, tooth for tooth," 24:19b–20a) falls at the center of the mirror-imaging structure of the story: A (vv. 13–14); B (vv. 15–16); C (v. 17); D (v. 18); X (vv. 19–20); D (v. 21a); C (v. 21b); B (v. 22); A (v. 23) (see Fishbane, 101, n. 41; Milgrom, *Leviticus 23–27*, 2128–30). In the case of murder, the law of retaliation was followed literally (see Num 35:31). In many other cases, according to traditional Judaic thinking, monetary compensation and other forms of compensation were accepted (see Levine, 268–70). The point of the law is not to exact punishment but to limit it.

Second, the account of the blasphemer's execution highlights the deadly consequences that accompany disobeying the instructions for holiness. Both narratives within Leviticus feature the death of sinners. The first narrative of the death of Nadab and Abihu in chapter 10 clarifies the serious reality of the instructions for the sanctity of the tabernacle in the first half of the book. The second narrative of the blasphemer in chapter 24 accents, by its grave consequences, the teachings regarding holiness in the second half of Leviticus. Not every infraction in either half of the book will result in the death of the offender. These two stories, however, demonstrate the weighty call to holiness created by the new realities of Yahweh's glory dwelling with his people.

*What is the possible significance of people dying in both narratives within Leviticus?*

Leviticus 25 and 27 each present instructions concerning the year of Jubilee; thus, in this sense they frame chapter 26. Chapter 25 opens with regulations for the Sabbath year. That is, every seventh year was to be an agriculture Sabbath for the land. After every seven Sabbath years, on the fiftieth year, the people were to celebrate Jubilee. The year of Jubilee was for the liberation of land-owning debt slaves, the canceling of debts, and the return of land to the family to whom it was decreed.

The rationale for the third item is instructive: "The land must not be sold permanently, *because the land is mine* and you reside in my land as foreigners and strangers. Throughout the land that you hold as a possession, you must provide for the redemption of the land" (25:23–24, emphasis added). Jubilee became a symbol of the ideals that would characterize the messianic age to come (see Isa 61:1–3; Luke 4:17–21). Leviticus 27 closes the book by explaining various regulations regarding vows and tithes, as well as how making vows impacted the Jubilee regulations. Whereas vows to Yahweh were voluntary acts of devotion, tithing of everything—giving a tenth to God—was required because all that they had been given belonged to Yahweh (27:30).

The teaching of Leviticus 26 has been commonly referred to as blessings and curses. Although this chapter does not actually use the terms "blessings" and "curses," it maintains similarity to other contexts that do (e.g., Deut 27–28; see Levine, 275–77). The chapter begins with two verses of instruction before the blessings and judgments. These verses rehearse the second and fourth commands of the Ten Words: "[second] Do not make idols or set up an image or a sacred stone for yourselves, and do not place a carved stone in your land to bow down before it. I am Yahweh your God. [fourth] Observe my Sabbaths and have reverence for my sanctuary. I am Yahweh" (26:1–2).

This pattern is similar to Leviticus 19, which was framed by the first, second, fourth, and fifth commands (see Milgrom, *Leviticus 23–27*, 2275–76). (It is notable that both chapters 19 and 26 skip the third command concerning the name, especially in light of the narrative of the blasphemer at the end of chapter 24.)

There are several similarities between the promised blessings and judgments. Both the blessings and the judgments are set up in an "if . . . then" format. For example, the blessings begin, "If you follow my decrees and are careful to obey my commands, I will send you rain in its season, and the ground will yield its crops and the trees of the field their fruit," and so forth (26:3–4). Also, both lists have five units: *blessings*—(a) plenty (vv. 4–5), (b) peace in land (v. 6), (c) victory outside land (vv. 7–8), (d) abundant life (vv. 9–10), (e) God's presence in Israel (vv. 11–12); *judgments*—(a) illness, famine, defeat (vv. 14–17), (b) drought and poor harvests (vv. 18–20), (c) harmful animals (vv. 21–22), (d) war, pestilence, famine (vv. 23–26), (e) destruction and exile (vv. 27–39) (see Milgrom, *Leviticus 23–27*, 2286–90).

Additionally, both the blessings and the judgments end with mention of the redemption from Egypt: "I am Yahweh your God, *who brought you out of Egypt* so that you would no longer be slaves to the Egyptians; I broke the bars of your yoke and enabled you to walk with heads held high" (26:13) and "But for their sake I will remember the covenant with *their ancestors whom I brought out of Egypt* in the sight of the nations to be their God. I am Yahweh" (26:45, emphases added). The basis of the covenant relationship in these two verses remains the same even while the perspective shifts from the generation of conquest to that of the postexilic community.

"I broke the bars of your yoke and enabled you to walk with heads held high" (Lev 26:13).

*Shutterstock.com/ Gianni Dagli Orti*

The graphic metaphorical expression of walking with God—notably used of Enoch, Noah, and Abraham in Genesis—reciprocally frames the blessing section of this chapter. "*If by my laws you walk*, and my commands you keep, and observe them . . . *I will walk about in your midst*, I will be for you as a God, and you yourselves will be for me as a people" (26:3, 12 Fox, emphasis added). Moreover, the list of judgments in several places stated that if the people walked in opposition to God, then he would walk in opposition toward them (see 26:21, 23–24, 27–28, 40–41 Fox).

The series of terrifying curses of 26:14–39 are structured as graduated judgments, one building on another (emphasis added below; see Figure 19-I).

> *But if you will not listen to me* and carry out all these commands, and if you reject my decrees and abhor my laws and fail to carry out all my commands and so violate my covenant, *then I will do this to you. . . .* (26:14–16a)
>
> *If after all this you will not listen to me, I will punish you* for your sins seven times over. . . . (26:18)
>
> *If you remain hostile toward me and refuse to listen to me, I will multiply your afflictions* seven times over, as your sins deserve. . . . (26:21)
>
> *If in spite of these things you do not accept my correction but continue to be hostile toward me, I myself will be hostile toward you* and will afflict you for your sins seven times over. . . . (26:23–24)
>
> *If in spite of this you still do not listen to me* but continue to be hostile toward me, *then in my anger I will be hostile toward you*, and I myself will punish you for your sins seven times over. . . . (26:27–28)

**Figure 19-I:** Graduated Judgments of Leviticus 26

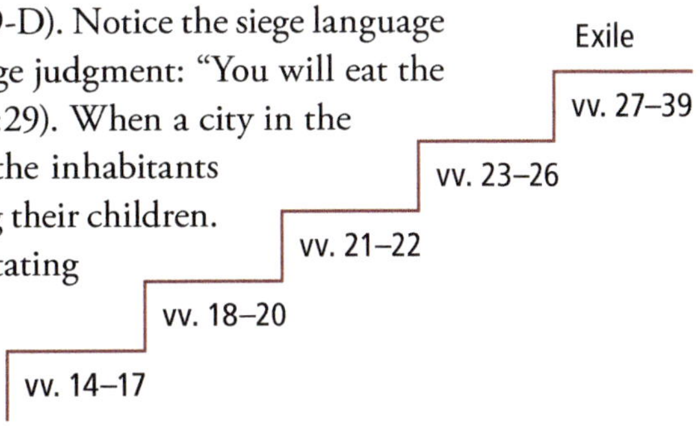

The fifth and final stage of judgment enumerated here is exile from the land of promise. The exile serves a double purpose: to punish Israel and to provide Sabbath years to the land that Israel had neglected (see Sidebar 19-D). Notice the siege language depicting doom on the hardened rebels in the fifth-stage judgment: "You will eat the flesh of your sons and the flesh of your daughters" (26:29). When a city in the ancient Near East was under siege, in order to starve the inhabitants into surrender, parents were sometimes reduced to eating their children. The last days of Jerusalem were represented with devastating poetic force: "With their own hands compassionate women have cooked their own children, who became their food when my people were destroyed" (Lam 4:10; cf. 2:20; Jer 19:9).

*What is the meaning of "graduated judgments"?*

The sequence of cumulative judgments terminating in exile is followed by a message of the hope of restoration (26:40–42). If the people confess their sin and the sin of their parents—corporate and transgenerational responsibility—and humble themselves before Yahweh, then he promises to remember his covenant to the Hebrew ancestors. The Septuagint translators understood the "humbled" heart as remorseful turnabout or repentance (see Wevers, 461). Note the parallel function of the ideas of confession and humility and their contrast to an uncircumcised heart.

> But *if they will confess* their sins and the sins of their ancestors—their unfaithfulness and their hostility toward me, which made me hostile toward them so that I sent them into the land of their enemies—*then when their uncircumcised hearts are humbled* and they pay for their sin, I will remember my covenant with Jacob and my covenant with Isaac and my covenant with Abraham, and I will remember the land. (26:40–42, emphasis added)

The later writings of the Hebrew Scriptures include several examples of those in exilic circumstance participating in this collective confession (see Ezra 9:3–15; Neh 1:4–11; 9:1–2; Dan 9:3–19; Additions to Esther 14:3–19, esp. vv. 6, 12; Baruch 1:15–3:8, esp. 3:5).

The significance of humility for walking with God, individually or within the covenantal community, cannot be overstated. Here confession and humility are necessary prerequisites for restoration of the covenant blessing. In more general terms, humility is basic to faith and love. That is, faith and love of God are functions of humility. First, the turning point in Judah's character was his self-humiliation (Gen 38:26). It was in this respect that David differed from Saul (see Another Look in Chapter 9). Second, if the humbled person is the opposite of one with an uncircumcised heart, then to have a circumcised heart is to be humbled. According to Deuteronomy, loving God is an effect of a circumcised heart (see Deut 30:6; the concept of heart circumcision is discussed further in Another Look below). Whereas humility is the antithesis of pride, pride is the opposite of faith (see Hab 2:4). The point in this immediate context is simply to notice the importance of the humble soul and humble people. Humility is perhaps the most basic level of new life.

*What is the significance of humility within the pentateuchal context?*

## ANOTHER LOOK

The important metaphorical idea of heart circumcision is first used in Leviticus 26. What is the meaning of this concept? The present discussion will try to answer this question in steps, beginning with the physical rite and moving through related metaphorical uses of the idea. Genesis 17 narrates the origin of circumcision as a physical sign of the covenant between God and Abraham:

> You shall *circumcise the flesh of your foreskins, and it shall be a sign of the covenant between me and you.* Throughout your generations every male among you shall be circumcised when he is eight days old, including the slave born in your house and the one bought with your money from any foreigner who is not of your offspring. Both the slave born in your house and the one bought with your money must be circumcised. So shall my covenant be in your flesh an everlasting covenant. *Any uncircumcised male who is not circumcised in the flesh of his foreskin shall be cut off from his people; he has broken my covenant.* (Gen 17:11–14 NRSVue, emphasis added)

For a male born into an Israelite family, the rite of circumcision was to be performed when he was eight days old (Lev 12:3). Circumcision was also required as a precondition of a marriage to an outsider (Gen 34:14–17) or to participate in the Passover (Exod 12:43–49). Circumcision was a basic Israelite feature to the extent that the Philistines were sometimes referred to derisively as "uncircumcised" (e.g., Judg 14:3; 1 Sam 14:6; 18:25)—a label that eventually came to be used equally of any gentile. In short, the identity of Israel is more than ethnicity or biological standing but includes the sign of the covenant.

The seriousness of this rite is demonstrated by the willingness of women to circumcise their sons even after Antiochus IV Epiphanes deemed it a capital crime during oppression in the Second Temple period (1 Maccabees 1:60–61; 2 Maccabees 6:10). The unusual story of Moses's encounter with God on the way to Egypt also illustrates the necessity of circumcision (Exod 4:24–26).

Circumcision functioned similarly to the way baptism later did for Christianity. Those who converted to either faith participated in the sign of identification. For those born within Jewish families, circumcision was given to the male child in infancy as a symbol of the parents' commitment to raise the child according to their faith. The same has been true of infant baptism in many segments of Christianity to the present day; other traditions practice infant "dedication" and believer's baptism. Circumcision, in the case of the next Israelite generation, was passive for the child. This last point will be important to appreciating the meaning of heart circumcision.

"Circumcise," "uncircumcised," and "foreskin" are sometimes used metaphorically in relation to other parts of the human body, such as the heart, ears, or lips. These terms could even be applied to fruit-bearing trees, as in Leviticus 19:23–25 (see the quotation earlier in this Chapter). The image of foreskin carried the idea of thickness, as in unfeeling or unresponsive. Hence, the organ is figuratively obstructed by a foreskin that inhibits or blocks proper functioning. Note Moses's description of his speech impediment: "Moshe spoke before YHWH, saying: 'Here, (if) the Children of Israel do not hearken to me, how will Pharaoh hearken to me?—and I am of *foreskinned lips*!'" (Exod 6:12 Fox, emphasis added; cf. 4:10; 6:30).

The idea of uncircumcised and circumcised is applied to the heart in several Torah contexts. The state of an uncircumcised heart is characterized in Leviticus 26:40–41 as lacking humility toward God (see Rashi, 3:423 [on Lev 26:41]). That is, there was a stubbornness that needed to be removed. Moses commanded, "So *circumcise the foreskin of your heart*, your neck you are not to keep-hard any more" (Deut 10:16 Fox, emphasis added). The notion of heart circumcision in Deuteronomy 10:16 can be attached with the command to love God in 10:12.

The connection between heart circumcision and loving God is made explicit in the next occurrence in Deuteronomy: "Yahweh your God *will circumcise your hearts and the hearts of your descendants, so that you may love him* with all your heart and with all your soul, and live" (30:6, emphasis added). In contrast to Deuteronomy 10:16, where the people are exhorted to circumcise their own hearts, 30:6 stipulates that Yahweh is the one who performs heart circumcision. Just as physical circumcision of the Hebrew male child symbolized the parental commitment to raise their child according to the covenant, so Yahweh's circumcision of the person's heart depicts his parental commitment to those he has changed.

*What is the symbolic meaning of heart circumcision?*

Other Hebrew Scriptures occasionally use circumcision/uncircumcision in a figurative sense regarding ears and hearts. Although the term "uncircumcised" is not used in Isaiah 6 or Psalm 119, each aptly portrays the people's condition that often prompted this imagery—"Their hearts are thick like fat" (Ps 119:70a NRSVue; see Isa 6:10; also see Carpenter and Grisanti 2:732–33). Jeremiah expressed his frustration at the inability of his listeners to hear him because of their uncircumcised ears. "To whom can I speak and give warning? Who will listen to me? Their ears are closed [uncircumcised] so they cannot hear. The word of Yahweh is offensive to them; they find no pleasure in it" (Jer 6:10). The state of uncircumcision renders the ears figuratively disabled or deaf to God's word.

For Jeremiah the need for heart circumcision and the people's lack of the same form a root problem. "*Circumcise yourselves to Yahweh, circumcise your hearts*, you people of Judah and inhabitants of Jerusalem, or my wrath will flare up and burn like fire because of the evil you have done—burn with no one to quench it" (4:4, emphasis added). Also, "'The days are coming,' declares Yahweh, 'when I will punish all *who are circumcised only in the flesh*—Egypt, Judah, Edom, Ammon, Moab and all who live in the wilderness in distant places. For all these nations are *really uncircumcised*, and even the whole house of Israel is *uncircumcised in heart*'" (9:25–26, emphasis added). The difference between external and internal circumcision is explicit here. Physical circumcision without the corresponding internal changed heart caused Israel to be regarded like other peoples under judgment (also see Ezek 44:4–10; cf. 11:19–20; 36:26–27).

Within the New Testament Stephen and Paul each make use of the idea of heart circumcision as one of the defining characteristics that distinguish between those that know only the old life versus those that enjoy the new. Stephen compares his opponents to the Israelites that rebelled with the golden calf:

> "But *our ancestors* refused to obey him. Instead, they *rejected him and in their hearts turned back to Egypt*. They told Aaron, 'Make us gods who will go before us. As for this fellow Moses who led us out of Egypt—we don't know what has happened to him!' That was the time they made an idol in the form of a calf. They brought sacrifices to it and reveled in what their own hands had made. . . . *You stiff-necked people! Your hearts and ears are still uncircumcised. You are just like your ancestors: You always resist the Holy Spirit*!" (Acts 7:39–41, 51, emphasis added)

Paul goes further than Jeremiah by regarding heart circumcision as essential but physical circumcision as not.

> Circumcision has value if you observe the law, but if you break the law, you have become as though you had not been circumcised. So then, if those who are not circumcised keep the law's requirements, will they not be regarded as though they were circumcised? The one who is not circumcised physically and yet obeys the law will condemn you who, even though you have the written code and circumcision, are a lawbreaker. A person is not a Jew who is only one outwardly, *nor is circumcision merely outward and physical*. No, a person is a Jew who is one inwardly; and *circumcision is circumcision of the heart*, by the Spirit, not by the written code. Such a person's praise is not from other people, but from God. (Rom 2:25–29, emphasis added)

In another place Paul and Timothy pointedly discuss how they understood the significance of internal circumcision, or the circumcision of Christ.

> *In him you were also circumcised with a circumcision* not performed by human hands. Your whole self ruled by the flesh was put off when *you were circumcised by Christ*, having been buried with him in baptism, in which you were also raised with him through your faith in the working of God, who raised him from the dead. When you *were dead in your sins and in the uncircumcision of your flesh*, God made you alive with Christ. He forgave us all our sins, having canceled the charge of our legal indebtedness, which stood against us and condemned us; he has taken it away, nailing it to the cross. (Col 2:11–14, emphasis added)

For Paul and Timothy, the effects of internal circumcision could be described as "putting off the body of the flesh," which, in ethical use of "flesh" (*sarx*), refers to human sinfulness or fallenness. The internal circumcision, or circumcision of the heart, therefore, is interpreted in the New Testament as that event or state that both begins and characterizes the new life, sometimes called regeneration. To be stiff-necked or stubborn or fat in the heart or uncircumcised in heart is to be rebellious or insensitive and disabled toward God. Conversely, to be circumcised in heart is to be made alive or healed by means of spiritual surgery performed by Yahweh. More specifically, the circumcision of the heart refers to a work of God that changes a person and establishes new life.

## INTERACTIVE WORKSHOP

### *Chapter Summary*

The holiness collection (Lev 17–26) instructs Israel in the personal holiness required of the community of Yahweh's people. Failure to listen to the instructions will bring judgment and eventually exile. Even still, Yahweh will remain faithful to his word.

### *Can You Explain the Key Terms?*

- blood
- circumcision of the heart
- ellipsis
- euphemism
- Jubilee
- nakedness
- personification
- Sabbath year

### *Challenge Questions*

1. What does it mean that "the life is in the blood" in Leviticus 17?
2. Select one of the literary characteristics of Leviticus 18 and explain its theological implication in this context.
3. What is the significance of the fact that both neighbors and residing foreigners are to be loved as oneself (see Lev 19)?
4. How did the holy calendar of Leviticus 23 affect the life of ordinary Hebrew people?
5. What is the meaning of "uncircumcised heart" (Lev 26:41)?

### *Advanced Questions*

1. Trace out examples of the "personification" of the land of promise in Leviticus 18–26 and explain the theological significance.
2. Why did God disallow persons with certain disabilities from serving him as priests (see Lev 21–22)?
3. What is the significance of the episode of the blasphemer in Leviticus 24? Why is it located where it is?
4. How does the logic of Sabbath years interrelate with the exile of the people?

*5. Define the meaning and theological significance of *ger* in Leviticus 19:33–34.

*6. Evaluate the Septuagint's translation of the Hebrew word for "humbled" (*kn'*) in Leviticus 26:41 with the Greek verb denoting "remorseful turnabout" or "repentance" (*entrepomai*).

## *Research Project Ideas*

Evaluate prohibitions against sexual capital crimes in Leviticus 18 and 20 (adultery, same-sex relations, and bestiality) in the light of ancient Near Eastern context and creational instruction (Longman, 207–65; Sklar, 187–91; Wenham, 359–63).

Examine the theme of the personification and defilement of the land in Leviticus 18–26.

Investigate the structure of Leviticus 17–27, especially focusing on chapter 24 (see Master, 415–24; Morales, 103–19, esp. 106–7).

Compare the structure and theological significance of the blessings and curses in Leviticus 26 and Deuteronomy 27–28.

## *The Next Step*


Auld, Graeme. "Leviticus at the Heart of the Pentateuch." Pages 40–51 in *Reading Leviticus: A Conversation with Mary Douglas*. Edited by John F. A. Sawyer. Journal for the Study of the Old Testament Supplement Series 227. Sheffield: Sheffield Academic, 1996.

Carpenter, Eugene, and Michael A. Grisanti. "כשׁה." Pages 732–33 in vol. 2 of *New International Dictionary of Old Testament Theology and Exegesis*. Edited by Willem A. VanGemeren. Grand Rapids: Zondervan Academic, 1997.

Chavel, Simeon. *Oracular Law and Priestly Historiography in the Torah*. Forschungen zum Alten Testament II 71. Tübingen: Mohr Siebeck, 2014.

Fishbane, Michael. *Biblical Interpretation in Ancient Israel*. Oxford: Clarendon, 1985.

Fuad, Chelcent. "Priestly Disability and Centralization of the Cult in the Holiness Code." *Journal for the Study of the Old Testament* 46.3 (2022): 291–305.

Harmon, Matthew and Gary Edward Schnittjer. *Seven Hermeneutical Choices to Study the Bible's Use of the Bible*. Grand Rapids: Zondervan Academic, forthcoming.

Hartley, John E. *Leviticus*. Word Biblical Commentary 4. Dallas: Word, 1992.

Johnson, Luke Timothy. "The Use of Leviticus 19 in the Letter of James." *Journal of Biblical Literature* 101 (1982): 391–401.

Knight, Douglas A. *Law, Power, and Justice in Ancient Israel*. Louisville: Westminster John Knox, 2011.

Levine, Baruch A. *Leviticus*. JPS Torah Commentary. Philadelphia: Jewish Publication Society, 1989.

Longman, Tremper, III. *Confronting Old Testament Controversies: Pressing Questions about Evolution, Sexuality, History, and Violence*. Grand Rapids: Baker Books, 2019.

Master, John. "The Placement of Chapter 24 in the Structure of the Book of Leviticus." *Bibliotheca Sacra* 159 (2002): 415–24.

Milgrom, Jacob. *Leviticus 17–22*. Anchor Bible 3A. New York: Doubleday, 2000.

———. *Leviticus 23–27*. Anchor Bible 3B. New York: Doubleday, 2001.

Miller, James E. "Sexual Offenses in Genesis." *Journal for the Study of the Old Testament* 25 (2000): 41–53.

Mohrmann, Doug C. "Making Sense of Sex: A Study of Leviticus 18." *Journal for the Study of the Old Testament* 29 (2004): 57–79.

Morales, L. Michael. "How the Dwelling Becomes a Tent of Meeting: A Theology of Leviticus." *Unio cum Christo* 5.1 (2015): 103–19.

Morrow, William S. *An Introduction to Biblical Law*. Grand Rapids: Eerdmans, 2017.

Noth, Martin. *Leviticus: A Commentary*. Translated by J. E. Anderson. Philadelphia: Westminster, 1965.

Rashi (Rabbi Shlomo Yitzhaki). *The Metsudah Chumash/Rashi*. 5 vols. Edited by Rabbi Avrohom Davis. New York: Ktav, 1998.

Rattray, Susan. "Marriage Rules, Kinship Terms and Family Structure in the Bible." Pages 537–42 in *Society of Biblical Literature 1987 Seminar Papers*. SBLSPS 26. Atlanta: Scholars Press, 1987.

Rhyder, Julia. "Sabbath and Sanctuary Cult in the Holiness Legislation: A Reassessment." *Journal of Biblical Literature* 138.4 (2019): 721–40.

Schnittjer, Gary Edward. "Going Vertical with Love Thy Neighbor: Exegetical Use of Scripture in Leviticus 19.18b." *Journal for the Study of the Old Testament* 47.1 (2022): 114–42.

———. *Old Testament Use of Old Testament*. Grand Rapids: Zondervan Academic, 2021.

Sklar, Jay. "The Prohibitions against Homosexual Sex in Leviticus 18:22 and 20:13: Are They Relevant Today?" *Bulletin for Biblical Research* 28.2 (2018): 165–98.

Stone, Mark Preston. "Don't Do What to Whom?: A Survey of Historical-Critical Scholarship on Leviticus 18.22 and 20.13." *Currents in Biblical Research* 20.3 (2022): 207–37.

Wenham, Gordon J. "The Old Testament Attitude to Homosexuality." *Expository Times* 102 (1991): 359–63.

Wevers, John William. *Notes on the Greek Text of Leviticus*. Atlanta: Scholars Press, 1997.

# *Numbers*

## IN THE WILDERNESS

יאר יהוה פניו אליך ויחנך

# 20 MACROVIEW OF NUMBERS

Boris Diakovsky/Shutterstock.com

## GETTING STARTED

### *Focus Question*

What is the structure of the Numbers narrative?

### *Look for These Terms*

- first generation
- second generation
- Tetrateuch
- wilderness

## AN OUTLINE

A. **The First Generation Prepares to Leave the Mountain (1:1–10:10)**
   1. Census of the first generation (1–4)
   2. Setting apart the people (5:1–10:10)

B. **The Wilderness (10:11–21:35)**
   1. The failure of the first generation (10:11–14:45)
   2. Laws and rebellion during the thirty-eight years in the wilderness (15–19)
   3. Failures of the second generation (20–21)

C. **The Second Generation Prepares to Enter the Land of Promise (22–36)**
   1. The threat from Moab (22–25)
   2. Census of the second generation (26)
   3. Review of the journey and preparation for possession of the land (27–36)

## A READING

The student of the Torah will likely find Numbers challenging. Variegated materials are interspersed, including censuses, strange laws, and obscure and (sometimes) choppy narratives. One interpreter says it seems like "a poorly organized junk room" (Sprinkle, 186). Within the Christian Bible, only Ezra-Nehemiah surpasses Numbers for its juxtaposed assortment of challenging narrative elements. The test for a wife suspected of infidelity in Numbers 5, for example, is perhaps the most bizarre ritual in the Torah. The story of the rebellion of Korah and his associates is difficult in those places where the details rub against one another. The account of Moses's striking the rock omits enough detail that it has created ambiguity for generations to wonder and debate about the exact nature of his sin.

Still, for all its challenges, Numbers offers readers many of the most vivid and graphic images of the Torah. Two men, Caleb and Joshua, stand alone courageously against the prevailing opinions of the sizable Israelite community—perhaps two million people. The earth opens its mouth to swallow up rebel leaders along with their families. Balaam, a foreign prophet for hire, is rebuked verbally (!) by his faithful donkey. Phinehas, the original zealot, drives his spear through the sexual organs of an Israelite man and his Moabite girlfriend while they are fornicating. The repetitive note that may, in the end, be most memorable is that of the people grumbling, grumbling, grumbling.

Whereas the Christian name for the book, "Numbers," highlights the censuses of the successive generations (chs. 1; 26), the traditional Judaic name provides the context for hearing this challenging and strange story—"In the wilderness."

The wilderness became a grand test. The rebellion against God's word reached its height at Kadesh, and then even greater heights with the insurrection of Korah and other leaders. It seemed as though the human revolution would prevail. When Israel faced its most formidable threats from Moab—external and internal—the word of God changed the course of the story.

Discerning the structure of this book is difficult. There are clues in the chronology and geography, time and space, of the book. The time-space structure will serve as a basis to consider the narrative and theology of the book.

Before considering the chronological peculiarities of Numbers itself, it is helpful to sketch out the general chronology of Exodus through Deuteronomy. The chronology of these books can be broadly attached to Moses, who was born in Exodus 2 and died at 120 years of age in Deuteronomy 34. Approximately eighty of these years elapse in Exodus 2; thus, Exodus 3 through the end of the Torah correspond to Moses's last forty years (see Exod 7:7; Acts 7:23, 30). It is perhaps obvious because of the uneven treatment of times within these forty years that the Torah is not a general history of these years but a story about certain events. Table 20-A presents the general chronology (also see Table 20-B as well as 12-A in Chapter 12).

Table 20-A leads to two observations. First, the largest blocks of text correspond to the events at Sinai and the plains of Moab—both locales include lengthy instruction (esp. Lev and Deut). Second, the longest period of time elapses in just five chapters. The case is even more extreme when it is noted that Numbers 15, 18, and 19 are law rather than narrative.

| Egypt to Sinai | at Sinai | to Kadesh | wandering in the wilderness | to the plains of Moab |
|---|---|---|---|---|
| Exod 12–18 | Exod 19–Num 10:10 | Num 10:11–14:45 | Num 15–19 | Num 20–Deut 34 |
| three months | about eleven months | about three months | thirty-eight years | seven months |

**Table 20-A:** General Chronology from Exodus to Deuteronomy

The point of the text-time ratio in the case of the thirty-eight years of wilderness wandering is theologically significant. Once the first generation of Israelites decisively rebel against God at Kadesh, their story is over. They disappear from the narrative. This observation hits still harder when the reader recognizes that the only events recorded from the thirty-eight "silent years" are the rebellion of Korah and his associates and its related aftermath, including the budding of Aaron's staff (Num 16–17). Does this imply that there is no memory of those who reject the word of God?

*What is the significance for Numbers of the general chronology of Exodus through Deuteronomy?*

The key chronological markers in Numbers itself can now be considered (see Table 20-B). The book of Numbers is not, strictly speaking, arranged in chronological order. Said differently, the census of the first generation (ch. 1) has been taken out of chronological sequence and placed at the head of the book (see Table 20-B). The storyteller may have foregrounded the generation that did not make it in order to invite the reader to think generationally. By raising the generation to the reader's consciousness from the beginning, the two generations can be compared at nearly every point. The important temporal divide in Numbers is the two generations—the one that died in the wilderness and the one that was preparing to enter the land of promise.

**Table 20-B:** Chronological Markers in Numbers

| | |
|---|---|
| Num 1:1 | first day, second month, second year |
| Num 7:1 (with Exod 40:17) | first day, first month, second year |
| Num 9:1–3 | fourteenth day, first month, second year |
| Num 10:11 | twentieth day, second month, second year |
| Num 20:28 (with 33:38) | first day, fifth month, fortieth year |

One innovative approach regards the book in two uneven sections headed by the censuses of the first and second generations in chapters 1 and 26, respectively (see Olson, 5–6). The logic is that because the census of the first generation was moved to the beginning, the census of the second generation must have been placed at the head of the second section of the book. This observation has much to commend it.

Elat at the Red Sea

*Boris Diakovsky/ Shutterstock.com*

The problem, however, is that the story of the second generation does not begin in chapter 26 but in chapter 20 (see Table 20-B). Therefore, the important generational categories function within another interpretive framework.

The dominant structure seems to correlate generational time with literal-symbolic space (see Childs, 190–201). The primary geographic spaces include Sinai, the wilderness, Egypt, Moab, and Canaan, which respectively signify something like meeting God, present testing, tempting fictive memories, physical and moral enemies, and future hope. These literal-symbolic spaces fit within the broad narrative structure of the first generation's preparation at the mountain for their journey to the land of promise (Num 1–10), temptations in the wilderness (chs. 10–21), and the second generation's preparation on the plains of Moab to enter the land of promise (chs. 22–36). Within these story units, many symbolic spaces can be plotted along the axes of the first and second generations. Reading the book in this manner provides an unexpected, if superficial, symmetry (see Table 20-C).

*What is the significance of the "time and space" or generational and geographical structure of the book of Numbers?*

| Sinai | Wilderness | | | Moab |
|---|---|---|---|---|
| first generation prepares for their journey | failures of the first generation | the rebel generation disappears into the wilderness | failures of the second generation | second generation prepares to enter the land of promise |
| 1:1–10:10 | 10:11–14:45 | 15–19 | 20–21 | 22–36 |

**Table 20-C:** The Geographical-Generational Macrostructure of Numbers

The surprising twist of the story comes in chapters 22–25, at the beginning of the last section, when first God, through the wicked prophet, and then Phinehas, the zealous priest, rescue the second generation of Israelites from severe threats. Without these providential interventions, the second generation might have met the same fate as their parents. Both threats—the external menace from a prophet bent on cursing Israel and the internal peril of Israel's rebellion with a high hand—were defeated by the word of God. Thus, the controlling structure of the book of Numbers is its story. The climactic turning point occurs when God, by his word, delivered the people from the twofold threat from Moab.

*What is the turning point of the Numbers story?*

Within the literal-symbolic spatial structure, the story develops according to generational categories that seem to invite some extraordinary comparisons (see Smith, 205–6; Another Look in Chapter 11). The Numbers narrative appears to create a double echo of the Exodus wilderness stories by the first and second generations, respectively. The reader can hear the double echo by comparing the two main Numbers travel and camp narratives with their prequels in Exodus (see Table 20-D). The three major travel and camp narratives are not the only journeys or encampments, for the people made forty stops (see Num 33); rather, they are the only fully narrated accounts (see Num 33 and Table 23-G in Chapter 23).

| Reed Sea to Sinai | Sinai | Sinai to Kadesh | Kadesh | Kadesh to Moab | Plains of Moab |
|---|---|---|---|---|---|
| Exod 13:17–19:1 | Exod 19:1–Num 10:10 | Num 10:11–12:16 | Num 13–19 | Num 20–21 | Num 22–36 |

**Table 20-D:** Three Primary Travel and Camp Narratives‡

‡Modified and adapted from Gordon J. Wenham, *Numbers*, Tyndale Old Testament Commentary. (Downers Grove, IL: InterVarsity Press, 1981), 18. Copyright © 1981 Gordon J. Wenham. Used by permission of InterVarsity Press.

The three major camp and travel narratives follow a predictable pattern. Many, but not all, of the events of the first generation in the Exodus wilderness stories are echoed, often in the same order, by both the first and the second generations in Numbers (see Tables 20-E and 20-F). Readers of Numbers often get the sense of having been there before. Indeed, we have! There are significant differences, but the overriding rhetorical-literary strategy of the storyteller is to develop the narrative in an interrelated manner. The repetitions are occasionally noted explicitly—for example, "This is what your ancestors did . . ." (Num 32:8a lit.). The extended echo effect provides clues to the meaning of the story.

In sum, the primary chronological aspect of Numbers appears to be the divide between the first generation and the second. The generational categories provide the substructure that runs through the dominant geographical framework of the narrative (see Table 20-C). The book opens with the first generation preparing for their journey in the shadow of Sinai. The book closes with the second generation camped on the plains of Moab, preparing for their invasion of the land of promise. In between are the stories of moral failure in the wilderness by both the first and second generations. By locating the literal-symbolic space of the story's mainframe along the axis of the two successive generations, the reader can interpret several significant things about God, his people, and the world.

First, the range of Yahweh's character is revealed within the story. He condescended by filling the dwelling with his glory and leading the people on their journey through the wilderness. The proximity of the people with their holy God requires a particular

| | Reed Sea to Sinai | Sinai to Kadesh | Kadesh to Moab |
|---|---|---|---|
| Led by cloud | Exod 13:21 | Num 10:11 (cf. 9:15–23) | — |
| Victory over enemies | 14 | — | Num 21:21–35 |
| Victory song | 15:1–18 | 10:35–36 | 21:14–15 |
| Miriam | 15:20–21 | 12 | 20:1 |
| People complain | 15:23–24 | 11:1 | 21:5 |
| Moses's intercession | 15:25 | 11:2 | 21:7 |
| Well | 15:27 | — | 21:16 |
| Manna and quail | 16 | 11:4–35 | — |
| Water from a rock | 17:1–7 | — | 20:2–13 |
| Victory over Amalek | 17:8–16 | — | 21:1–3 (cf. 14:45) |
| Jethro | 18:1–2 | 10:29–32 | — |

**Table 20-E:** Comparing the Three Major Journeys in the Wilderness‡

‡Adapted from Wenham, *Numbers*, 19. Copyright © 1981 Gordon J. Wenham. Used by permission of InterVarsity Press.

| | Sinai | Kadesh | Moab |
|---|---|---|---|
| Divine promises | Exod 19:5–6; 23:23–33 | Num 13:2 | Num 22–24 |
| Forty days | 24:18 | 13:25 | — |
| Rebellion | 32:1–8 | 14:1–10 | 25:1–3 |
| Moses's intercession | 32:11–13 | 14:13–19 | — |
| Judgment | 32:34 | 14:20–35 | 25:4 |
| Plague | 32:35 | 14:37 | 25:8–9 |
| Laws of sacrifice | 34:18–26; Lev 1–7 | 15:1–31 | 28–29 |
| Trial | Lev 24:10–23 | 15:32–36 | 27:1–11 |
| Judgment against priests or Levites | 10:1–3 | 16:1–35 | — |
| Atonement through priests or Levites | Exod 32:26–29 | 16:36–50 | 25:7–13 |
| Priestly prerogatives | Lev 6–7; 22 | 17–18 | 31:28–30; 35:1–8 |
| Impurity rules | 11–16 (cf. Num 9:6–14) | 19 | 31; 35:9–34 |
| Census | Num 1–4 | — | 26 |

**Table 20-F:** Comparing the Three Major Encampments in the Wilderness‡

‡Adapted from Wenham, *Numbers*, 20. Copyright © 1981 Gordon J. Wenham. Used by permission of InterVarsity Press.

physical arrangement of the tribal groups and careful adherence to his regulations for purity in the camp. The stories of Israel's repeated grumbling demonstrate the extent of Yahweh's patience, tolerating extraordinary unfaithfulness. Moses later reflects that Yahweh's patience and provision is akin to a parental role toward the people (Deut 1:31; 8:5). Although Yahweh is exceedingly patient, he is a righteous judge. The first generation crosses the line for the tenth time when they embrace the second report of the ten scouts—a fictionalized report—rather than trusting the word of God (Num 14:22; see Chapter 22). Yahweh reveals his grace to the second generation who may have been worse than their parents, preserving them by his word and his priest (Num 22–25). The second generation will enter the land promised to their ancestors.

*What does the book of Numbers say about God?*

Second, the character of the people is defined by an incurable addiction to sinfulness (see Sherwood, 105–10). Both generations were stiff-necked rebels. The first generation saw Yahweh provide for all of their physical needs in the wilderness. Yet when they faced the difficulties of the desert, they created new fictional memories in order to legitimize their rejection of God's instruction (see Chapter 22). They learned how far is too far when they decisively rejected God's will at Kadesh. The judgment matched the crime—they were afraid that they would die in the land that "devours those living in it" (13:32)—when they died in the wilderness that swallowed their rebellious leaders. Perhaps the most notable feature is what is not there, namely, that when they rejected the word of God, they disappeared from the story.

The story of the second generation is more remarkable and telling. They had never known any life except the wilderness, constantly sustained by the provision of Yahweh. They were after the kind of their parents, however, and emulated their faithless rebellion.

*What does the book of Numbers say about the people of God?*

Third, Numbers explains something about the wilderness or the external world. The wilderness was at one time both the physical realm of the historical Israelites who made the trek from Egypt to Canaan and representative of the challenges of all readers. The wilderness narratives demonstrate that the problem was never really from the wilderness, that is, from outside the people. Every time the people faced ordeals, Yahweh provided. Their problem, according to Deuteronomy, was never physical—they had bread and everything else they needed. The real problem was failing to embrace God's word. Moses interpreted that humans do not "live on bread alone but on every word that comes from the mouth of Yahweh" (Deut 8:3b). The people who lived in a "great and fear-inspiring" (v. 15 lit.) wilderness could have, and should have, trusted the word of their "great and fear-inspiring" God (Deut 10:17 lit.; cf. 4:34; 7:21).

*What is the significance of the wilderness in the book of Numbers?*

## ANOTHER LOOK

The collection of books from Genesis through Numbers is called the Tetrateuch, the four books. The four-scroll serial narrative functions as a story unit from the perspective of Deuteronomy. Although there is a real sense in which Deuteronomy completes the Torah, the Tetrateuch also has a sense of closure. Deuteronomy is, in large part, comprised of theological commentary on and contextual application of the tetrateuchal story. If Deuteronomy is to be better appreciated as a reading of the Torah story, it is first necessary to hear the closure of the Tetrateuch.

The Tetrateuch begins with the creation of the human world along with an explanation of how the chosen family of Abraham fits among the peoples of the earth. On the one side, all of the families of earth will be blessed through the chosen family, which eventually takes the name of Abraham's grandson. How exactly will the human families be blessed through Israel? Reading backwards from the Abrahamic covenant, it seems that his offspring of promise is the selfsame offspring that was divinely promised in the poem of judgment on the serpent in the garden. Perhaps Abraham's offspring will bless the families of the earth by defeating the revolution that started in the garden. Reading forward from the word of God to Abraham, it appears that *the* offspring will be the Judah-king who is to come in the last days and will rule the nations.

On the other side, the family of Abraham was chosen from among the families of the earth. Looking back through the primeval narrative, this means that he is a Shem representative and will rise above the line of Ham and his son Canaan. Noah himself pronounces the oath: "'Cursed be Canaan! The lowest of slaves will he be to his brothers.' He also said, 'Praise be to Yahweh, the God of Shem! May Canaan be the slave of Shem. May God extend Japheth's territory; may Japheth live in the tents of Shem, and may Canaan be the slave of Japheth'" (Gen 9:25–27). Looking ahead through the stories of the first generations of the chosen family, there are several other political casualties. The various peoples to fall outside of the chosen family include Ishmael, the sons of Lot (Ammon and Moab), and Esau. Moreover, the internal strife among the Israelite brotherhood also creates a pecking order among the tribal groups that bear the names of the sons of Jacob.

It is the intertribal and international expectations of Genesis into which the storyteller of Numbers chooses to situate his story. Numbers brings to fruition many of the latent social fractures initiated in Genesis. The Numbers narrative develops both the social configuration between the tribal groups of Israel and some of the international conflicts that the chosen family is destined to face, according to the beginning of its story in Genesis. The narrative segments of Numbers are largely occupied by showing the coming of age of the chosen nation according to the Genesis story. Numbers, in the main, plays off the social world of Genesis in reverse order (see Douglas, xiii-xiv, 98–101).

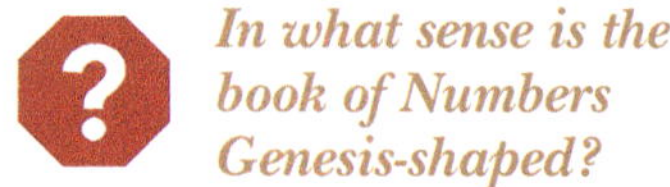

Table 20-G summarizes many instances that Numbers operates according to the social world of Genesis. The narrative world of Numbers is Genesis-shaped.

**Table 20-G:** Reverse-Order Commentaries in Numbers of Sibling Rivalry Themes of Genesis

| Numbers | | | Genesis |
|---|---|---|---|
| ch. 1 (cf. ch. 26) | The tribes took a military census to prepare to invade the land. | The tribal families of the brothers of Joseph will inherit the promised land. | 50:24; cf. 13:15, 17; 15:7, 8, 18; 26:3; 28:13; 35:12 |
| chs. 2; 3 | The camp was arranged around the tabernacle with the tribes of servant's sons and disgraced sons excluded from the privileged areas. | Some of Leah's sons were disqualified and cursed. | 49:3–7; cf. 34:25–30; 35:22 |
| chs. 2; 3; 7; 13–14; 26:65 | The tribe of Judah was the largest and was given the leading position for travel, worship, and camp. The Judah representative, Caleb, first believed God's word, along with the Ephraim representative, Joshua. | Judah had a change of heart and offered himself for his brother, which effectively ended the prolonged fraternal feud. His descendant would rule all nations in the last days. | chaps. 43–44; 49:8–12 |
| 20:14–21; 24:18 | The king of Edom refused Israel safe passage through their land. Balaam predicted Edom's doom. | God gave Rebekah an oracle concerning her fighting sons. Jacob and Esau quarreled over the birthright and the blessing. | 25:23, 27–34; chap. 27 |
| chs. 22–24; 25:1–5 | Balak hired Balaam to curse Israel, and the Moabite women tried to seduce Israel. | Lot's two youngest daughters rape him and conceive Moab and Ammon. | 19:30–38 |
| 21:1–3, 10–35; 31:1–12 | Israel defeated the Canaanite nations in the Transjordanian part of the promised land. | Noah cursed Canaan, son of Ham, as servant to the people of Shem, ancestor of the Hebrews. | 9:20–27 |

## INTERACTIVE WORKSHOP

### *Chapter Summary*

Numbers is structured according to its story. It develops around the generational and geographical segments and reaches its turning point and resolution when God delivers the people from both the external and internal threats of Moab by the power of his word.

## *Can You Explain the Key Terms?*

- first generation
- second generation
- Tetrateuch
- wilderness

## *Challenge Questions*

1. What is the significance of placing the census of the first generation in chapter 1 out of its chronological sequence?
2. What is the theological significance of each of the three major geographical sections of Numbers, namely, 1:1–10:10; 10:11–21:35; 22–36?
3. What aspects of the Balaam narrative (Num 22–24) and the Phinehas narrative (ch. 25) function as a turning point in the story?

## *Advanced Questions*

1. How should the Numbers wilderness narratives be read in relation to the Exodus wilderness narratives? Demonstrate the answer with a specific example.
2. Why is it theologically significant that the wilderness narratives of the second generation so often echo those of the first generation?

*3. How does the term "wilderness" (*midbar*) take on theological and symbolic significance within the Torah, especially within Numbers and Deuteronomy?

## *Research Project Ideas*

Evaluate the leading views of the structure of Numbers (chronological, geographical, generational).
Explain the placement and function of the legal sections within Numbers.
Compare Numbers to Genesis with a view to explaining the theological meaning of the relationship.

## *The Next Step*

Childs, Brevard S. *Introduction to the Old Testament as Scripture*. Philadelphia: Fortress, 1979.

Douglas, Mary. *In the Wilderness: The Doctrine of Defilement in the Book of Numbers*. New York: Oxford University Press, 2001.

Olson, Dennis T. *The Death of the Old and the Birth of the New: The Framework of the Book of Numbers and the Pentateuch*. Chico, CA: Scholars Press, 1985.

Sherwood, Stephen K. *Leviticus, Numbers, Deuteronomy*. Berit Olam: Studies in Hebrew Narrative and Poetry. Collegeville, MN: Liturgical, 2002.

Smith, Mark S. "Matters of Space and Time in Exodus and Numbers." Pages 182–207 in *Theological Exegesis: Essays in Honor of Brevard S. Childs*. Edited by Christopher Seitz and Kathryn Greene-McCreight. Grand Rapids: Eerdmans, 1999.

Sprinkle, Joe M. *Leviticus and Numbers*. Teach the Text. Grand Rapids: Baker Books, 2015.

Wenham, Gordon J. *Numbers: An Introduction and Commentary*. Tyndale Old Testament Commentaries. Downers Grove, IL: InterVarsity Press, 1981.

# 21 THE FIRST GENERATION AT SINAI

## *Numbers 1:1–10:10*

*Isaiah and Abby Cramer*

## GETTING STARTED

### *Focus Question*

How does the opening section of Numbers rely on Genesis, Exodus, and Leviticus?

### *Look for These Terms*

- census
- cloud
- large numbers
- Levites
- Nazirite
- official order
- priestly benediction

## AN OUTLINE

A. **Census of the First Generation (1–4)**
   1. The military census (1)
   2. The arrangement of the camp (2)
   3. The census and arrangement of the Levites (3–4)

B. **Setting Apart the People (5:1–10:10)**
   1. Regulations concerning holiness (5–6)
   2. The dedication of the dwelling (7)
   3. Regulations concerning the Levites (8)
   4. The Passover (9:1–14)
   5. The cloud (9:15–23)
   6. The silver trumpets (10:1–10)

## A READING

The first section of Numbers embodies a literary diversity that has made the book challenging to interpreters. As noted in the outline, these chapters contain censuses, narratives, and regulations, some of which are quite strange. The controlling factor that holds these seemingly diverse materials together is the symbolic significance of the geographical setting. The opening chapters of Numbers can be thought of as the preparation of the first generation of Israelites at the mountain of revelation.

The preparations at the mountain aim at the invasion of the land of promise, though they also include several other matters. The Levites were separated out from military responsibility to attend to the dwelling of God on behalf of the people. Moreover, the movement of the camp with the tabernacle through the wilderness would cause various ritual pollutions, creating the need for further regulations concerning ritual purity and worship. The institution of the tabernacle on the first Passover celebrated the memory of the community's identity as God's own people.

While it is difficult to make sense of some of the details, many matters form patterns that suggest rationale and meaning. The prominence of Judah and the ranking of the families of the Levites set the stage for some of the narrative events later in the book. The centrality of Yahweh's glory in the camp and his leading in the travels yield a three-dimensional picture of his rightful role in any community. These spatial ideals were expressed through the arrangement of the camp and the marching order. The Numbers story does not simply record facts but, by design, instructs readers.

Numbers begins with Yahweh's instructing Moses to take a military census. The rationale for the census was to enumerate the men for the army for the invasion of the promised land. "Take a census of the whole Israelite community by their clans and families, listing every man by name, one by one. You and Aaron are to count according to their divisions all the men in Israel who are twenty years old or more *and able to serve in the army*" (1:2–3, emphasis added). The census accounted for twelve tribes—Levi was excluded and Joseph's sons each formed a tribe.

God explained that the Levites were not counted because they had other responsibilities:

> Yahweh had said to Moses: "You must not count the tribe of Levi or include them in the census of the other Israelites. Instead, *appoint the Levites to be in charge of the tabernacle of the covenant law*—over all its furnishings and everything belonging to it. They are to carry the tabernacle and all its furnishings; they are to take care of it and encamp around it." (1:48–50, emphasis added)

The reason for the Levites' special duties was that Yahweh had delivered Israel from Egypt by striking down the firstborn of the Egyptians; therefore, Israel owed Yahweh every firstborn, human and animal. Yahweh took the Levites in place of the firstborn of the people.

> Yahweh also said to Moses, "I have taken the Levites from among the Israelites *in place of the first male offspring* of every Israelite woman. *The Levites are mine, for all the firstborn are mine.* When I struck down all the firstborn in Egypt, I set apart for myself every firstborn in Israel, whether man or animal. They are to be mine. I am Yahweh." (3:11–13, emphasis added; cf. 3:45; 8:14; Exod 13:2)

*Why was the tribe of Levi excluded from the military census?*

**Table 21-A:** Military Census of Numbers 1

| | |
|---|---|
| Reuben | 46,500 |
| Simeon | 59,300 |
| Gad | 45,650 |
| Judah | 74,600 |
| Issachar | 54,400 |
| Zebulun | 57,400 |
| Ephraim | 40,500 |
| Manasseh | 32,200 |
| Benjamin | 35,400 |
| Dan | 62,700 |
| Asher | 41,500 |
| Naphtali | 53,400 |
| **Total Militia** | **603,550** |

*What is the creational significance of Judah as the largest of the tribes?*

Moses and Aaron took the census tribe by tribe and calculated the totals together for a fighting force of more than six hundred thousand (see Table 21-A). The relationship of size and significance hints at the prominence of the tribes of Judah and "Joseph"—Ephraim and Manasseh are referred to in relation to Joseph (Num 1:32–35)—74,600 and 72,700, respectively. The size/significance issue is predicated on the idea that it is the Creator alone who grants life, an idea emphasized repeatedly in Genesis. Thus, the tribes of Judah and Joseph were larger because God had filled them with life.

Later in Numbers, it was Caleb and Joshua, representing Judah and Ephraim, who stood against the prevailing view of the ten other scouts and the people at large (cf. Another Look in Chapter 9). Moreover, when the nation split apart in Kings, it was Judah in the south and Ephraim in the north that took the leading roles of the two kingdoms. The census of the second generation in Numbers 26 runs along a similar line (see Table 23-D in Chapter 23).

The order of the census of the twelve tribes does not follow the list of tribal affiliations of assistants in Numbers 1:1–17, mothers of the tribe, or the "official order" (see Table 21-B). The official order refers to that by which they camped (2:1–31), gave offerings (7:12–83), and marched through the wilderness (10:13–28; on the seven lists of twelve tribes in Numbers, see Douglas, *Tears*, 20–21). These lists could also be compared to the different arrangements in the lists of the sons of Israel coming to Egypt in Genesis 46 and Exodus 1, and in the blessings by Jacob and Moses in Genesis 49 and Deuteronomy 33, respectively.

| Genesis 29; 30; 35 *Birth Order/Mother* | Numbers 1:1–17 *By Assistants* | Numbers 1:20–43 *First Census* | Numbers 2; 7; 10 *"Official Order"* | Numbers 26 *Second Census* |
|---|---|---|---|---|
| Reuben (Leah) | Reuben | Reuben | Judah | Reuben |
| Simeon (Leah) | Simeon | Simeon | Issachar | Simeon |
| Levi (Leah) | Judah | Gad | Zebulun | Gad |
| Judah (Leah) | Issachar | Judah | Reuben | Judah |
| Dan (Bilhah) | Zebulun | Issachar | Simeon | Issachar |
| Naphtali (Bilhah) | Ephraim | Zebulun | Gad | Zebulun |
| Gad (Zilpah) | Manasseh | Ephraim | Ephraim | Manasseh |
| Asher (Zilpah) | Benjamin | Manasseh | Manasseh | Ephraim |
| Issachar (Leah) | Dan | Benjamin | Benjamin | Benjamin |
| Zebulun (Leah) | Asher | Dan | Dan | Dan |
| Joseph (Rachel) | Gad | Asher | Asher | Asher |
| Benjamin (Rachel) | Naphtali | Naphtali | Naphtali | Naphtali |

**Table 21-B:** Comparing Lists of the Sons/Tribes of Israel

Numbers 2 presents the instructions for the arrangement of the wilderness encampment. The camp was laid out in relation to the idea of graduated sacred space in Leviticus and Exodus (see Table 17-A in Chapter 17). The tabernacle was in the center of the camp, surrounded in concentric circles by the Levites, the twelve tribes, and the wilderness. The east side was most important because the dwelling of God was approached from the east. Thus, the tribes of Judah and Levi were granted the favored positions. Table 21-C presents the layout of the encampment.

*What was the symbolic significance of the layout of the camp?*

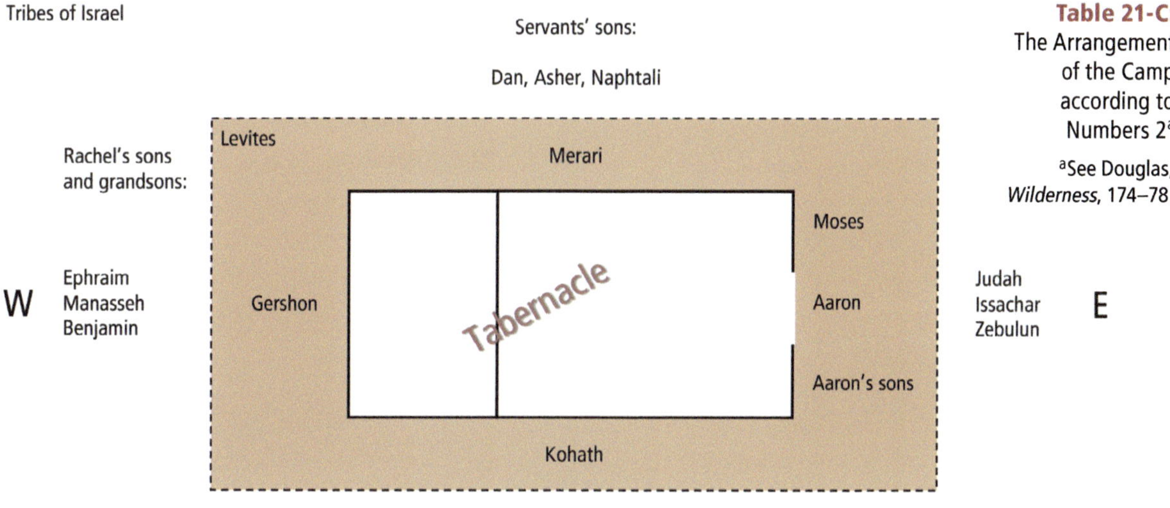


**Table 21-C:** The Arrangement of the Camp according to Numbers 2[a]

[a]See Douglas, *Wilderness*, 174–78.

Numbers 2 also divides and enumerates the four divisions of the twelve tribes. The Judah division of 186,400 camped to the east and led the march, the Reuben division of 151,450 camped to the south and followed the Judah division in the march, and the Ephraim division of 108,100 camped to the west and preceded the Dan division of 157,600. The ark led the entire march, and the dwelling, along with its furnishings, traveled in the middle between the Reuben and Ephraim divisions.

The camp arrangement and the marching order emphasize sacred space and the centrality of God. Moreover, the relationships between the tribes follows some of the logic of Genesis. Judah led the way and thus was first to face the threat from the nations and first with respect to approaching Yahweh's presence. Although Levi was not counted among the armed forces of Israel, they maintain their reputation as fighters across the Torah (see Gen 34; Exod 32; Num 25). The Levites' responsibilities, camped between the tabernacle and Israel's tribes, included protecting Israel from their greatest danger, namely, the holiness of Yahweh's glory.

Numbers 3–4 explain the duties of the families within the Levites. The family of Aaron was responsible for the priestly duties, and the Kohathites carried the tabernacle and its furnishings through the wilderness in accord with the instructions from the Aaronic clan. The differences between the levitical vocations set up the animosity behind the rebellion in Numbers 16–17.

Numbers is routinely punctuated by regulations that emphasize purity and worship. Numbers 5 opens with the effect of the tabernacle moving into the center of the encampment. All those with ritual impairment (see Lev 11–15) needed to get out (Num 5:1–4). They could not remain within the camp now that the holiness of Yahweh's glory had come to dwell in their midst.

The instruction regarding the wife suspected of adultery is perhaps the strangest regulation in the Bible. It addresses cases with insufficient evidence to convict the wife suspected of infidelity. This law makes provision to discover whether she was guilty or innocent. The method of making that determination sounds something like a magical potion and an oath. After she drank the bitter water—a concoction of holy water mixed with dust from the floor of the tabernacle and ink from a written oath—her "belly" would swell and her "thigh" drop if she had been unfaithful, thus preventing her from having other children. The belly and thigh may have been euphemistic for her reproductive organs. Some interpreters understand this passage as depicting an abortion as judgment for illegitimate pregnancy (see Levine, 201–5). It seems better to read the divine judgment as permanent infertility (cf. Gen 20:4, 17–18).

The Nazirite vow was generally a voluntary and temporary individual commitment to Yahweh by men or women. The case of Samson as a lifelong Nazirite by divine designation was unique (see Judg 13:7; 16:17). Samuel was a lifelong Nazirite according to certain traditions (e.g., 4QSam [1 Sam 1:22 in Abegg, 215]; also see 1 Sam 1:11).

No one other than Samson, however, in either the Hebrew or Greek Scriptures, is called a permanent Nazirite. Jesus was a Nazarene because he grew up in the town of Nazareth, but this has nothing to do with being a Nazirite (in spite of the fact that confusion about Matt 2:23 has led to pictures of Jesus with long hair). Nazirite vows were usually temporary, like those taken by and sponsored by the apostle Paul (see Acts 18:18; 21:23–24, 26). The Nazirite vow included not cutting one's hair, abstaining from wine and the fruit of the vine, and avoiding contact with dead bodies.

Tiny silver scrolls inscribed with some of the priestly blessing from Numbers 6:24–26. This is the oldest known scriptural inscription (late seventh century BCE). Discovered in a tomb on a hill overlooking the Hinnom Valley in Jerusalem.
*William Krewson*

The story of God's instruction for priestly benediction is included at the end of Numbers 6. The blessing itself is close to poetry along the continuum between narrative and poetry (see Sidebar 10-B in Chapter 10). The priestly blessing was a significant part of Israelite life. Many biblical passages allude to the language of the priestly blessing (see, e.g., Gen 43:29; Ruth 2:4; Pss 4:6; 67:1; 120–134 [see Liebreich, 33–36]; Jer 31:23; Mal 1:9). Also note the two silver plaques inscribed with the blessing—plaques dating to the seventh century BCE, found in 1980 in a tomb outside ancient Jerusalem on the western slope of the Hinnom Valley (Aḥituv, 49–55). These are the oldest fragments of Scripture yet discovered.

The account in Numbers 7 chronologically precedes the census of chapter 1 and following (see Table 20-B in Chapter 20). The dedication of the tabernacle continued for almost two weeks as each tribe presented offerings before the altar on successive days. The chapter is long, as the individual offering of each tribe, beginning with Judah, is recounted using a formula, emphasizing the importance of the dwelling and the ongoing importance of redemption from Egypt. The twelvefold account of the offerings is followed by a summary of the total gift of dedication.

This long chapter ends with Moses's entering the tent of meeting to speak with Yahweh. This context, along with Leviticus, continues to extend the narrative of setting up the dwelling in Exodus. It also demonstrates the progressive relationship of Moses and Yahweh (see Table 21-D). The idea that God's word proceeded from the presence in the most holy place suggests the great privilege and weighty responsibility for all who listen to the Torah of God.

*How does the holy space in the dwelling interrelate with the importance of God's word?*

**Table 21-D:** The Progressive Intimacy of Moses and Yahweh

| | |
|---|---|
| Exodus 40:34–35 | the glory of Yahweh preventing Moses from entering the tabernacle |
| Leviticus 1:1–2 | Yahweh speaking to Moses from the tabernacle |
| Numbers 7:89 | Yahweh speaking to Moses from the holy of holies |

The preparation to leave Mount Sinai closes with narrative reflection on the cloud above the dwelling and the trumpets of the priests. The cloud was unusual in several ways. For example, it perpetually hovered over the tabernacle and had a fiery appearance at night. According to the generalized narrative of the cloud (referring not to any particular occasion but simply the routine phenomena of the cloud), its movement directed the travels of the camp (Num 9:15–23; cf. Exod 13:21–22; 40:36–38). When the cloud lifted up and moved, the people broke camp and followed. Moreover, the trumpets of the priests signaled the people about the need to pack up and march. The priests also used the trumpets with varying signals when Israel went into battle, so that God would remember his people, and when the new moon festival began, so that the people could remember God.

Readers need to be patient when considering these opening chapters of Numbers. There are many details, some confusing in themselves, that are juxtaposed in a way that does not seem to fit neatly. It is more than geography, however, that holds these chapters together. In nearly every case, the materials that make up the first nine and a half chapters build on and connect with the first three books of the Torah.

Sinai wilderness
*© 1995 Phoenix Data Systems*

The interrelationship between and organization of the families of Israel reflects the logic of the sons of Jacob in Genesis. Moreover, the instruction concerning purity and the emphasis on the tabernacle create an interconnectivity between the preparations to leave the mountain and the preceding narratives of Exodus and Leviticus. It is not really a new story but a new venture for a people with a past. Their past includes both their redemption by Yahweh and their responsibility for worship and holiness because their God's glory, the Creator himself, dwells in the very center of their traveling home.

## ANOTHER LOOK

One of the challenges for readers of Numbers is the large number of Israelites recorded in it. According to the tallies from the censuses, there were about six hundred thousand men eligible for military service (see Table 21-A above and Table 23-D in Chapter 23). If women and children are added, the number is traditionally approximated at two million people (see Keil, 1:5). Among the reasons that some doubt these numbers are the problem of sustaining so many in the wilderness regions between Egypt and Canaan, the lack of corroborative archaeological evidence in the land of Israel for a military campaign of this size, and the tendency among various ancient societies to exaggerate the size of their populace.

First, it has never been a problem for faithful readers of Numbers to accept the large numbers because, whether larger or smaller, the survival of the people was accomplished by a series of supernatural acts as well as by the daily provision of manna.

Second, the problem of there being no corroborative archaeology is as true of the stories in Numbers as for (almost) all the events recorded in the Torah. Part of the problem is inherent to the field of archaeology. The ambiguity of archaeological evidence, in tandem with the necessary multiple, interrelated subhypotheses that must be assumed in order to entertain new guesses, has eroded much confidence in archaeology. The better archaeologists today tend to be more cautious than some of the over-optimists of former generations. Archaeological findings have told us many things, but few of these are certain "proof" of specific events. Thus, archaeological findings, or lack thereof, have not provided conclusive evidence either that the Israelite wilderness community must have been that large or that it could not have been that large.

Third, some have argued that the large numbers in the censuses of Numbers are an example of ancient narrative hyperbole (see Allen, 2:65–69; Sidebar 21-E). Was it considered a lie or generally understood as a form of political boasting when ancient Near Eastern societies exaggerated the numbers of things like populace? Reasonable arguments have been made both ways by critical and evangelical interpreters. Different passages point in different directions. The sizable nation was described,

Tel Jericho
*iStock.com/rparys*

"Your ancestors who went down into Egypt were seventy in all, and now Yahweh your God has made you *as numerous as the stars in the sky*" (Deut 10:22). Yet the Torah refers to the small size of Israel, "Yahweh did not set his affection on you and choose you because you were more numerous than other peoples, *for you were the fewest of all peoples*" (7:7, emphasis added in both cases).

## Sidebar 21-E: Large Numbers in Scripture

Dave,

Could you tell me the bottom line concerning your view on large numbers in the Old Testament?

*Gary*

Gary,

The largest numbers of the Old Testament are reflective of a common ancient Near Eastern literary device of numerical hyperbole. They are purposefully embellished in like literature to glorify their king. Glorifying the King of kings in the Old Testament, the numbers are larger and more frequent than any other ancient Near Eastern culture. We would expect them to be so.

*Dave*

These excerpts come from my personal correspondence. Dave Fouts has written several essays, from an evangelical perspective, on large numbers in the Scriptures.


Fouts, David. "Added Support for Reading '70 Men' in 1 Samuel iv 19. *Vetus Testamentum* 42 (1992): 394.

———. "Another Look at Large Numbers in Assyrian Royal Inscriptions." *Journal of Near Eastern Studies* 53 (1994): 205–11.

———. "A Defense of the Hyperbolic Interpretation of Large Numbers in Old Testament." *Journal of the Evangelical Theological Society* 40 (1997): 377–87.

———. "The Incredible Numbers of the Hebrew Kings." Pages 283–99 in *Giving the Sense: Understanding and Using the Old Testament Historical Texts*. Edited David M. Howard Jr. and Michael A. Grisanti. Grand Rapids: Kregel Academic & Professional, 2003.

Moreover, it is common to note things such as how small the city of Jericho was. (It took me ten minutes to walk at a casual pace around the entire ruins.) The apprentice who is seeking a theological reading of the narrative as Scripture needs to interpret the Torah story, in either case, in light of what the text says—in this case, a large fighting force of more than half a million (for more detail, see Schnittjer, 21-3).

## INTERACTIVE WORKSHOP

### *Chapter Summary*

Numbers begins with a military census of the Israelites to signal their preparation to take the land of promise. The census is followed by several short narratives and laws centered on the preparation of the community to leave the mountain. The opening section, in many ways, extends themes, laws, and narratives from the preceding books of the Torah.

### *Can You Explain the Key Terms?*

- census
- cloud
- large numbers
- Levites
- Nazirite
- official order
- priestly benediction

### *Challenge Questions*

1. How did the tribes prepare to leave the mountain for their trek to the land of promise in the opening chapters of Numbers?
2. How does Genesis inform some of the intramural tribal relations of Israel in the opening chapters of Numbers?
3. How does Numbers 1–9 extend instructions for ritual purity and worship from Exodus and Leviticus?
4. What new things do readers learn about the Levites in Numbers 1–9?
5. What is the function of the presence of Yahweh's glory among his people according to Numbers 9?

### *Advanced Questions*

1. In what ways do the census and lists of Numbers 1–4 use concepts and categories from Genesis?
2. What is the significance of expelling ritually impaired persons in Numbers 5:1–4?

*3. On what basis should one resolve discussions that *'eleph* means "contingent of troops" versus "thousand" (see Mendenhall, 52–61; Fouts, 381–82; also see Ashley, 66–70; Schnittjer, 21-3)?

### *Research Project Ideas*

Compare the relationship between Numbers and any preceding book of the Torah.

Explain, exegetically and theologically, the spatial significance of the camp and travel arrangements.

Evaluate the literal and hyperbolic views of the large numbers in Numbers (see Ashley, 66–70; Fouts, 377–87; also see Sidebar 21-E; Schnittjer, 21-3).

## *The Next Step*

Abegg, Martin, Jr., Peter Flint, and Eugene Ulrich. *The Dead Sea Scrolls Bible: The Oldest Known Bible Translated for the First Time into English.* San Francisco: HarperSanFrancisco, 1999.

Aḥituv, Shmuel. *Echoes form the Past: Hebrew and Cognate Inscriptions from the Biblical Period.* Jerusalem: Carta, 2008.

Allen, Ronald B. "Numbers." Pages 23–455 in vol. 2 of *Expositor's Bible Commentary.* Grand Rapid: Zondervan Academic, 2012.

Ashley, Timothy R. *The Book of Numbers.* New International Commentary on the Old Testament. Grand Rapids: Eerdmans, 1992.

Douglas, Mary. *In the Wilderness: The Doctrine of Defilement in the Book of Numbers.* New York: Oxford University Press, 1993, 2001.

———. *Jacob's Tears: The Priestly Work of Reconciliation.* New York: Oxford University Press, 2004.

Fouts, David. "A Defense of the Hyperbolic Interpretation of Large Numbers in Old Testament." *Journal of the Evangelical Theological Society* 40 (1997): 377–87.

Keil, C. F., and F. Delitzch. *Commentary of the Old Testament.* 10 vols. Reprint. Peabody, MA: Hendrickson, 1989.

Levine, Baruch A. *Numbers 1–20: A New Translation with Introduction and Commentary.* Anchor Bible 4. New York: Doubleday, 1993.

Liebreich, Leon J. "The Songs of Ascent and the Priestly Blessing." *Journal of Biblical Literature* 74 (1955): 33–36.

Mendenhall, G. "The Census Lists of Numbers 1 and 26." *Journal of Biblical Literature* 77.1 (1958): 52–66.

Schnittjer, Gary Edward. *Torah Story Video Lectures.* Grand Rapids: Zondervan Academic, 2017.

# 22 TWO GENERATIONS IN THE WILDERNESS

## *Numbers 10:11–21:35*

*Isaiah and Abby Cramer*

## GETTING STARTED

### *Focus Questions*

What was the problem with the first generation? Was the next generation any different?

### *Look for These Terms*

- Aaron's staff
- Anakites
- bad report
- Sheol
- temptation
- Transjordan

## AN OUTLINE

A. **The Failure of the First Generation (10:11–14:45)**
   1. Grumbling in the wilderness (10:11–12:16)
   2. Unbelief at Kadesh (13–14)

B. **The Thirty-Eight (Almost) Silent Years (15–19)**
   1. Various laws (15)
   2. The revolt of Israelite leaders (16–17)
   3. Levite responsibilities (18)
   4. The red heifer and other laws (19)

C. **Failures of the Second Generation (20–21)**
   1. The sin of Moses and Aaron (20:1–13)
   2. Edom refused passage for Israel (20:14–21)
   3. The death of Aaron (20:22–29)
   4. The fiery snake (21:1–9)
   5. Victories over the Transjordanian kingdoms (21:10–35)

## A READING

The major category of Numbers 10–21 is the threefold repetition of the failure of the leaders and the people in each of the three major sections outlined. The issue, repeated at both levels and at each stage along the way, is that the people rejected God's word (see Table 22-A). First, the people grumbled, as did Moses and Miriam and Aaron before the definitive unbelief of the first generation at Kadesh. Second, some of the leading families of Israel revolted against Moses and Aaron, as did the people. Both revolutions were judged severely. Third, Aaron and Moses failed irrevocably, and the people grumbled and were judged. The narrator makes explicit the sinfulness that led to moral failure at every level of the Israelite community, at every stage of the journey through the wilderness. How will God's word prevail over the human revolution boldly embraced by his people?

**Table 22-A:** The Threefold Account of Moral Failure in Numbers 10–21

| First Generation | Thirty-Eight Silent Years | Second Generation |
|---|---|---|
| grumbling of the people (11:4–10) | | grumbling of the people (20:1–5) |
| Moses, Miriam, and Aaron grumbled (11:11–15; 12:1–2) | revolt of Levite and other leading families (16:12–40) | the sin of Moses and Aaron (20:6–13) |
| unbelief of the people (14:1–4) | revolt of the people (16:41–50) | grumbling of the people (21:4–5) |
| Moses prays for the people (14:13–19) | Aaron stops the plague against the people with the incense censer (16:46–50) | Moses prays for the people and makes a fiery snake on a pole (21:7–9) |

The three sections of wilderness travel narrative are divided by two sections of laws (chs. 15 and 18–19; see Table 22-B). The placement of the sections of laws has a dual effect. In regard to the narratives, these laws divide the stories into the first generation, that is, the dying generation, and the second generation. The segmentation of the stories into separate sections invites the reader to make comparisons between them even while seeing them as separate episodes. Moreover, the effect on the law collections is to see them as inherently bound up with the people's story. The laws were a part of the historical context of Israel's wandering years.

*What are the significances of the law sections embedded within the narrative?*

**Table 22–B:** Story and Law in Numbers 10–21

| 10:11–14:45 | 15 | 16–17 | 18–19 | 20–21 |
|---|---|---|---|---|
| the first generation in the wilderness | laws for offerings and other regulations | rebellion against and reaffirmation of Aaron's leadership | laws concerning Levites, priests, and the red heifer | the second generation in the wilderness |

That Numbers 20 and following relate to the second generation is, on first reading, not apparent. The story sounds as though it is a continuation of the narrative of the selfsame people who have been complaining about their physical needs since entering the wilderness in Exodus 15. The continuity in character between the first and second generations is crucial for the meaning of Israel and humanity in the Torah. It is not until we get to Numbers 33:38, which reports that Aaron's death occurred in the fortieth year, that we realize the story in Numbers 20 is about the second generation (see Table 20-B in Chapter 20).

In other words, in first reading everything seems like one long account of the people's grumbling in the wilderness. Yet dating Aaron's death to the fortieth year forces readers to go back to Numbers 20 and consider it as the beginning of the story of the new generation. The second generation would not get out of the wilderness and into the land of promise if they have to be better than their parents. They are not. If they ever left the wilderness, it would be in spite of their fundamental commonality with the dead generation.

*What is the theological importance of the way Numbers 20 characterizes the second generation?*

The departure of the people from Mount Sinai started well enough, or so it seemed. One ominous foreshadowing is the reference to those Levites who would revolt. "Then the Kohathites set out, carrying the holy things" (10:21a). They had to carry the holy articles of the tabernacle and yet were not even allowed to look at them. These menial tasks as porters without privilege combined with the Aaronite clan telling them what to do set the stage for animosity.

The report of the beginning of the march from Sinai concludes with routines of the poem Moses spoke when the ark started and stopped. "Whenever the ark set out, Moses said, 'Rise up, Yahweh! May your enemies be scattered; may your foes flee before you.' Whenever it came to rest, he said, 'Return, Yahweh, to the countless thousands of Israel'" (10:35–36). A psalmist uses this poetic framework in a psalm that depicts God's procession from Sinai to Jerusalem.

Desert of Zin
*Earl Hagar*

May God arise, may his enemies be
scattered;
may his foes flee before him. . . .
The chariots of God are tens of thousands
and thousands of thousands;
the Lord has come from Sinai into
his sanctuary.
When you ascended on high,
you took many captives;
you received gifts from people,

even from the rebellious—
that you, Yahweh God, might dwell there.
(Ps 68:1, 17–18; cf. Eph 4:8)

Just as the people quickly began complaining after the Lord had delivered them from the Egyptian army at the sea, so also they began to grumble continuously after leaving the mountain of revelation. The problem with complaining, whether by the people or the leaders, was that Yahweh was listening.

> Now the people complained about their hardships **in the hearing of Yahweh**, and when he heard them his anger was aroused. Then fire from Yahweh burned among them and consumed some of the outskirts of the camp. (11:1)

> Miriam and Aaron began to talk against Moses because of his Cushite wife, for he had married a Cushite. "Has Yahweh spoken only through Moses?" they asked. "Hasn't he also spoken through us?" **And Yahweh heard this**. (12:1–2, emphasis added in both cases)

The terror produced by the fire of Yahweh at the outskirts of the encampment was not enough to dissuade the people from complaining, not for long anyway.

What started among the rabble quickly spread through the masses, and they again complained about the lack of meat (11:40). The reader has heard all this before in Exodus 16 and may wonder why they were still struggling with the same problems. The repetition foregrounds the habits of sinfulness that plague not only Israel but all of humankind. Their whining depicted what sounds like a creative use of memory: "If only we had meat to eat! We remember the fish we ate in Egypt at no cost—also the cucumbers, melons, leeks, onions and garlic" (11:4c–5). The people manipulated their memories of Egypt to suppress the slavery and focus on a picnic. The fictive element in their complaining will be discussed in relation to temptation theory in Another Look below.

The effect of the people's complaining included, among other things, Moses's complaining about the people. Moses blamed Yahweh. For example, in 11:11–12 he asked Yahweh:

> "*Why have you* brought this trouble on your servant? What have I done to displease you that *you put the burden* of all these people on me? Did I conceive all these people? Did I give them birth? *Why do you* tell me to carry them in my arms, as a nurse carries an infant, to the land you promised on oath to their ancestors?" (emphasis added)

Moses was worn out by people quick to forget Yahweh's provision and able to remember the supposed good life in Egypt. His weariness near the beginning of the trek may explain his susceptibility to the sin he and Aaron commit almost four decades later in Numbers 20.

Yahweh answered the complaint of the people and of Moses in parallel fashion (see Table 22-C). The answer to each seems at the same time to be what they asked for and judgment: Moses's authority was diminished and the people got piles of rotten meat—"until it comes out of your nostrils" (11:20). They were better off before Yahweh answered their prayers. Stated differently, they did not know what they were asking for. How often do people pray for the wrong thing? The problem, it seems, is their failure to gratefully trust in Yahweh for the provision he has given. The people and their leader here lacked faith (see 11:21–22). In each case the answer was the effect of his *ruah* ("spirit," "wind").

- **The people want meat (11:4–9)**
  - **Moses wants help (11:10–15)**
  - **The "spirit" (*ruah*) on Moses is put on the elders (11:16–30)**
- **The "wind" (*ruah*) brings quail from the sea that brings a plague (11:31–34)**

**Figure 22-C:** Yahweh Answers the Prayers of the People and Moses with Judgment

Aaron and Miriam followed suit and complained about Moses's leadership, because he had married a Cushite woman. The worldview regarding the nations was based on the Genesis story. Cush, like Canaan, was one of the sons of Ham (Gen 10:6–12). Cush's son Nimrod was associated with both Nineveh and Babylon, the capitals of the two kingdoms that later conquered the Northern and Southern Kingdoms of Israel. Yahweh judged Miriam, not Aaron, with a skin disease, but removed it after seven days. He affirmed Moses as his unique spokesperson. Yahweh said:

> Listen to my words:
>
> "When there is a prophet among you,
> I, Yahweh, reveal myself to them in visions,
> I speak to them in dreams.
> But this is not true of my servant Moses;
> he is faithful in all my house.
> *With him I speak face to face,*
> clearly and not in riddles;
> he sees the form of Yahweh.
> Why then were you not afraid
> to speak against my servant Moses?" (12:6–8, emphasis added)

The distinction between prophets who saw visions and Moses who talked with Yahweh face to face (lit. "mouth to mouth") speaks to the relationship between Torah itself and the other writings of the Hebrew Scriptures. The endorsement of Moses's role echoes Yahweh's special revelation to him at Sinai.

When the Israelites arrived in Kadesh, twelve scouts were sent into the land of promise, one from each of the tribes. The two who stand out, Caleb and Joshua, were from Judah and Ephraim, respectively. The tribal relations within Israel were still functioning in accord with the expectations of the Genesis narrative (see Another Look in Chapter 20). The scouts returned after forty days to the camp situated between the wilderness and the land of promise.

When the scouts returned bearing samples of the bounty of the land like a grape cluster that needed two people to carry it, they gave two different reports, each followed by a different response. The arrangement of their reports and the responses are instructive (see Table 22-D; on the literary interchange see Chapter 1). The first report by the twelve scouts was "factual" in that they emphasized the good land as well as the strong inhabitants. The report was followed by a recommendation from the scout of Judah. "Then Caleb silenced the people before Moses and said, 'We should go up and take possession of the land, for we can certainly do it'" (13:30).

**Table 22-D:** The Reports of the Scouts and the Responses

| | | | |
|---|---|---|---|
| 13:26–29 | the twelve scouts | factual report | the land is good and the people are strong |
| 13:30 | Caleb | faithful response | let's go into the land of promise |
| 13:31–33 | the ten scouts | mythologized report | the people are the mythic warriors of old and the land eats people |
| 14:1–4 | the people | unbelieving response | let's go back to Egypt |

Grapevines
*iStock.com/lenazap*

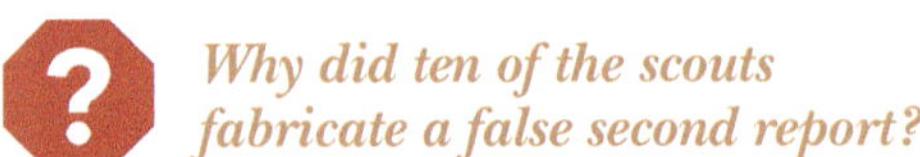
*Why did ten of the scouts fabricate a false second report?*

The other scouts, at least ten of them, disagreed with Caleb's bold recommendation and created a second report, a "bad report." In this context, the term for "bad report" (*dibbah*) appears to mean "false report" (see discussion of this term in Gen 37:2 in Chapter 9). This report intentionally distorted the facts as a kind of propaganda in order to dissuade the people against Caleb's recommended course of action (see Ashley, 243). It worked. The people embraced the mythologized report because they wanted a reason—an excuse, so it seems—to abandon their responsibility to invade the land.

The people wanted to believe a lie, and the ten scouts gave them what they wanted. The locust or grasshopper is the smallest ritually clean food in Leviticus. The scouts use grasshopper imagery as though Israel were a light snack for the Anakites. Notice both the logic and the mythological distortions in the second report.

> But the men who had gone up with [Caleb] said, "*We can't attack those people; they are stronger than we are.*" And they spread among the Israelites a *bad report* about the land they had explored. They said, "*The land we explored devours* those living in it. All the people we saw there are of great size. We saw *the Nephilim there (the descendants of Anak come from the Nephilim).* We seemed like grasshoppers in our own eyes, and we looked the same to them." (13:31–33, emphasis added)

Both of the false elements in the bad report immediately become theologically significant. First, the Israelites were afraid to enter the land that devours because they did not wish to die. Yahweh's judgment was for them to die in the wilderness over the next forty years, one for each day of scouting. Moreover, the wilderness, not Canaan, devoured the enemies of God's chosen leaders. The only narrative of the long years of wandering and death was the story of the rebels who were swallowed by the desert.

Second, the rebellious scouts insisted that the large-sized Anakites were descended from the legendary Nephilim—the children of the sons of God and daughters of humans wiped out by the flood (Gen 6:1–4). There could be no biological link between the Anakite people and the preflood peoples. Moreover, there is nothing in Genesis that even denotes that the Nephilim of old were physically large. "The Nephilim were on the earth in those days, and also after, when the sons of God came into the daughters of humans, and they bore children to them. Those were the heroes of old, persons of name" (6:4 lit.). The fact that they were heroes or warriors of old and persons of name says nothing at all about their physical size. The only good reason we, or the Septuagint translators, might have for insisting the Nephilim were giants is if we accept the scouts' myth and read it back into Genesis 6 (see Sidebar 6-B in Chapter 6). But why should a bad report be considered the basis for good interpretation?

Locusts or grasshoppers are the smallest edible ritually pure animal (Lev 11:22).

*Furiarossa/ Shutterstock.com*

The point at hand is that the gigantic Anakites needed to be faced by faith. Caleb had it and the people did not. The symbolic or theological category that this set up was the faith dimension of the special Israelites who faced giants. The only persons who ever led battles against giants, according to the Scriptures, were Moses, Joshua, Caleb, David, and their respective associates (see Table 22-E). Moses led Israel in victory over Anakite-like peoples. Thus, when Joshua and Caleb fought the Anakites, it not only extended their faith from Numbers 13–14 but also showed them as Moses-like.

Moreover, when David challenged the giant warrior of the Philistines, he is both contrasted to Israel's gigantic champion, Saul, and placed in the faith category with Moses, Joshua, and Caleb. Joshua defeated all of the remaining Anakites except those in three cities, including Gath, the hometown of Goliath.

When the people embraced the mythologized second report of the ten scouts, Moses and Aaron responded as they typically did to flagrant sin in these chapters of Numbers: They fell on their faces. Moses prayed to Yahweh on behalf of the Israelites asking him to forgive them. Moses based his prayer for forgiveness on two things: first, Yahweh's reputation before the Egyptians and Canaanites, and second, the revelation of Yahweh during the covenant renewal at Sinai. Table 22-F depicts parallels with Moses's previous intercession but also demonstrates an omission (wavy underlining and underlining refer to parallels; broken underlining refers to omission).

**Table 22-E:** The Giant-Fighters of Israel

| | |
|---|---|
| Moses | Deut 2:10–11; 3:11; Josh 12:4–6; 13:8–12 |
| Joshua | Josh 11:21–22 |
| Caleb | Josh 15:13–14; Judg 1:20 |
| David | 1 Sam 17; 2 Sam 21:18–22; 1 Chr 20:4–8 |

*What was the theological significance of the mythological second report of the ten scouts?*

In response to the people's sin and after Moses's intercession, Yahweh judged the people with death in the wilderness, except for Caleb and Joshua. These two alone, who had a different spirit from those who did not believe in God's word, would enjoy the beginning of the fulfillment of that word to the Hebrew ancestors. Although Moses did not base his prayer directly on the Abrahamic promise, Yahweh's answer revealed that he remembered (see 14:23–24, 30). The enduring power of the covenant is based on Yahweh's love (see Sakenfeld, 87–92).

The people wanted to believe the bad report so they could excuse themselves from trusting Yahweh. They said that they would rather die in the wilderness. Yahweh made the judgment fit the sin: They died in the wilderness, not immediately but over the next forty years. Yahweh judged them for the rebellion at Kadesh, but not simply for that. Rather, this climactic rebellion by those Israelites he had redeemed was merely the latest in a long list. Yahweh said that they had tested him ten times (14:22). Whether ten times is literal or figurative, the well-deserved judgment was withheld until now because of Yahweh's longsuffering patience (see Sidebar 22-G).

The regulations regarding the sacrifices in Numbers 15 come as a break after the end of the story of the first generation's journey to the land of promise (see Table 22-B). At the same time, these instructions are to be regarded as part of the narrated identity of the people. They qualify those given in Leviticus 1–7. A significant new element here is the teaching concerning "high-handed sin." "But *whoever acts with a high hand*, whether a native-born or a residing foreigner, blasphemes Yahweh, and shall be cut off from among the people. Because of having despised the word of Yahweh

**Table 22-F:** Comparing Moses's Advocacy for Israel at Sinai and Kadesh[a]

| Kadesh—Numbers 14 | Sinai—Exodus 32–34 |
|---|---|
| [Yahweh said:] "I will strike them down with a plague and destroy them, but I will make you into a nation greater and stronger than they." Moses said to Yahweh, "Then the Egyptians will hear about it! By your power you brought these people up from among them. And they will tell the inhabitants of this land about it. They have already heard that you, Yahweh, are with these people and that you, Yahweh, have been seen face-to-face, that your cloud stays over them, and that you go before them in a pillar of cloud by day and a pillar of fire by night. If you put all these people to death, leaving none alive, the nations who have heard this report about you will say, 'Yahweh was not able to bring these people into the land he promised them on oath, so he slaughtered them in the wilderness.' Now may the Lord's strength be displayed, just as you have declared: 'Yahweh is slow to anger, abounding in love and forgiving wickedness and rebellion. Yet he does not leave the guilty unpunished; he punishes the children for the sin of the parents to the third and fourth generation.' In accordance with your great love, forgive the sin of these people, just as you have pardoned them from the time they left Egypt until now." (14:12–19, v. 18 lit.) | [Yahweh said:] "Now leave me alone so that my anger may burn against them and that I may destroy them. Then I will make you into a great nation." But Moses sought the favor of Yahweh his God. "Yahweh," he said, "why should your anger burn against your people, whom you brought out of Egypt with great power and a mighty hand? Why should the Egyptians say, 'It was with evil intent that he brought them out, to kill them in the mountains and to wipe them off the face of the earth'? Turn from your fierce anger; relent and do not bring disaster on your people. Remember your servants Abraham, Isaac and Israel, to whom you swore by your own self: 'I will make your descendants as numerous as the stars in the sky and I will give your descendants all this land I promised them, and it will be their inheritance forever.'" (32:10–13)<br><br>And he passed in front of Moses, proclaiming, "Yahweh, Yahweh, the compassionate and gracious God, slow to anger, abounding in love and faithfulness, maintaining love to thousands, and forgiving wickedness, rebellion and sin. Yet he does not leave the guilty unpunished; he punishes the children and their children for the sin of the parents to the third and fourth generation." (34:6–7) |

[a]Deuteronomy 9 interprets the golden calf incident including what might be another version of this prayer or another prayer (9:25–29). I read the references to the grumbling and rebellion at Kadesh (9:22–24) as parenthetical remarks that demonstrate Israel's continued stubbornness. The prayer in Deuteronomy 9:25–29 may be attached to the golden calf incident by the repetition of the forty-day fast (9:18, 25; cf. Exod 34:28). But it must be remembered that Moses prayed often during this time, such as Exod 32:31–32 and 34:9.

and broken his commandment, such a person shall be utterly cut off and bear the guilt" (Num 15:30–31 lit., emphasis added). The meaning of "high hand" is defiant. Numbers 33:3 notes that Israel marched out of Egypt "with a high hand" (lit.) in full view while the Egyptians buried their dead sons. Thus, to sin with a high hand is to sin defiantly with no remorse or repentance (see discussion of the reparation offering in Chapter 17).

The instruction concerning high-handed sin is followed immediately by an example. A man gathered wood on the Sabbath in the sight of the Israelites—a capital offense (cf. Exod 35:2–3). The series of instructions close with the command regarding the tassels, visual reminders to obey God's instructions, that were to adorn the corners of garments. The tassels were, within the community of Yahweh's people, an ever present testimony to the binding power of Yahweh's word.

## Sidebar 22-G: "Ten Times"

After the unbelief of the people at Kadesh, Yahweh told Moses that the Israelites had disobeyed him and tested him "ten times" (Num 14:22). The use of ten times in the Torah sometimes is metaphorical, meaning many times or repeatedly or consistently (see Gen 31:7, 41). Traditional Judaic interpreters, however, read ten times in Numbers 14 as a literal number. The following table summarizes the rabbinic counting (see 'Arakin 15a in the Babylonian Talmud).

The Talmud's Counting of "Ten Times" the People Tested God (Num 14:22)

| | | The people complained (or rebelled): |
|---|---|---|
| 1 | Exod 14:11–12 | at the Sea |
| 2 | 15:24 | at Mara |
| 3 | 16:2–3 | at wilderness of Sin |
| 4 | 16:20 | about gathering the manna daily |
| 5 | 16:27 | about no manna on the Sabbath |
| 6 | 17:1–2 | at Rephidim |
| 7 | 32:1–6 | at Sinai |
| 8 | Num 11:1 | at Taberah |
| 9 | 11:4 | at Taberah regarding meat |
| 10 | 14:1–4 | at Kadesh |

The two questionable items are numbers four and five. The account of the problems with manna seem general when compared to the other narrated failures in the list. Still, the literal reading of ten times in the Talmudic tradition does not stretch the imagination too much.

The only view of the long years of wandering in the wilderness afforded to readers is the rebellion of Korah of Levi, with Dathan, Abiram, and On of Reuben and their compatriots, along with the related aftereffects. This one series of stories alone speaks to the thirty-eight years of journeys. The reason for the silence regarding the rest seems to be that when Israel rejected the word of Yahweh at Kadesh, their part in God's story ended. The protracted judgment of the unbelieving generation is outside the purview of readers, similar to the brief glimpse of the damning waters of God's wrath in Genesis 7 (see Chapter 6). The judgment of the rebel generation is not a spectacle for human inspection but a divine prerogative, one of the mysteries. The single view that readers have of the years of invisible wrath disturbs because of the method of destroying Korah and company: The wilderness devoured them. One of the myths the people chose to believe about the land of promise was, ironically, actually only true about the barren desert where they chose not to follow the word of God.

The rebels spoke a partial truth. Often blatant rebellion is couched in half truths. They said: "You have gone too far! *The whole community is holy, every one of them, and Yahweh is with them.* Why then do you set yourselves above Yahweh's assembly?" (16:3). Yahweh had said that Israel is a holy nation (Exod 19:6) and he promised to go with them (33:14). The rebels tried to use these truths for their own personal advantage and to reject Yahweh's will.

Korah, Dathan, and company were tired, on the one hand, of their menial tasks such as carrying the holy furniture of Yahweh's dwelling through the wilderness, and on the other (in their view) of Moses's and Aaron's place above the people. As usual, Moses immediately fell on his face (Num 16:4). The rebels met with Moses before the tabernacle, and Moses assured them that Yahweh would make his will clear. Moses said:

> "*But if Yahweh brings about something totally new, and the earth opens its mouth and swallows them*, with everything that belongs to them, and they go down alive into the realm of the dead, then you will know that these men have treated Yahweh with contempt."
>
> *As soon as he finished saying all this, the ground under them split apart and the earth opened its mouth and swallowed them* and their households, and all those associated with Korah, altogether with their possessions. They went down alive into the realm of the dead, with everything they owned; the earth closed over them, and they perished and were gone from the community. (16:30–33, emphases added)

This extraordinary damning of the rebels did not end the matter. Many in Israel sided with the rebels who had been forcibly relocated to Sheol—that is, the realm of the dead or the underworld or the grave. They resented the judgment and assembled against Moses. At that moment the glory appeared over the dwelling, and Moses and Aaron again fell on their faces (16:45). Yahweh sent a deadly plague among the friends of the revolution.

This narrative offers a powerful picture of the gracious place of the law in the redeemed community. Aaron "ran into the midst of the assembly. The plague had already started among the people, but Aaron offered the incense and made atonement for them. *He stood between the living and the dead*, and the plague stopped" (16:47–48, emphasis added). The priest of God standing between the living and the dead resembles Israel and the reader of the Torah in a certain sense. At the close of the Torah, Israel stands between the choice of life and death, and Moses commends "choose life" (Deut 30:19).

In the aftermath of the rebellions, Yahweh reaffirmed Aaron as his chosen leader among the Levites. It was his staff and only his that budded with almond blossoms. Aaron's staff was placed before the ark as a permanent warning to rebels. A copy of the Torah itself, according to Deuteronomy 31, was later placed before the ark also as a warning to rebels. The function of negative testimony (i.e., a word against sinners) is the terrible reality of the graciousness of God's word to his sinful people. Each of the items placed in and before the ark—the Ten Words, a jar of manna, Aaron's staff, and a copy of the Torah (Exod 16:33; Num 17:10; Deut 10:5; 31:26)—symbolized the primary dimensions of creation, namely, separation and life.

*What was the meaning of those things placed in and/or with the ark of the covenant?*

Almond blossoms

*iStock.com/ Emma Grimberg*

Numbers 18–19 presents ritual instructions that again serve to segment the preceding from the following narratives. The teaching in Numbers 18 begins by Yahweh reiterating that he chose Aaron and his family to bear the burden of holiness. Because holiness is dynamic—transferred by touch—the priests are set apart to bear the burden of holiness and guard the tabernacle to ensure that its holiness is not extended to the Levites or to the community putting them in jeopardy of divine wrath (Liss, 342; Milgrom, "Encroachment," 265). Yahweh repeats that he has gifted the Levites to serve the priests to guard the tabernacle (Num 18:1–7). All of this fits with the context since Yahweh wants to prevent his wrath from again striking down Israel (v. 5).

The instructions for and function of the red heifer offering are explained in Numbers 19. Many consider this among the most unusual teachings in the Torah. The purpose of the red heifer ritual was to extend the ritual clean/unclean regulations, especially regarding dead human bodies, from Leviticus 11–15. The seriousness of ritual cleansing by means of the holy water is accented by the fate of those who failed to receive this rite—they were to be cut off from Israel (19:13; see explanation of "cut off" in Chapter 17).

The story itself resumes in Numbers 20, but in the fortieth year of wilderness travels (see 20:28 with 33:38). The older generation was gone. This is now the story of their children, the younger generation. The chapter begins and ends with the death of Moses's siblings, Miriam and Aaron, respectively. In between the bracket of these two deaths are the accounts of the sin of Moses and Aaron and of Edom's refusal to grant passage to Israel.

The younger generation was so much like their parents that readers could not tell the difference if it were not for the dating later provided for the death of Aaron.

Traditional Mount Hor where Aaron died
*© 1995 Phoenix Data Systems*

The narrator depicts the second generation with complete continuity to the generation buried along the path that stretched back to Egypt.

> They quarreled with Moses and said, "If only we had died when our brothers fell dead before Yahweh! Why did you bring Yahweh's community into this wilderness, that we and our livestock should die here? **Why did you bring us up out of Egypt** to this terrible place? It has no grain or figs, grapevines or pomegranates. And there is no water to drink!" (Num 20:3–5, emphasis added)

> But the people were thirsty for water there, and they grumbled against Moses. They said, "**Why did you bring us up out of Egypt** to make us and our children and livestock die of thirst?" (Exod 17:3, emphasis added)

They complained because they were thirsty, so Moses and Aaron once again fell on their faces. The scene is familiar to Torah readers—too familiar. Readers have listened to the people complain across the chapters since God redeemed them from Egypt. It is easy to understand that Moses was tired of the complaining and tired of the complainers. If he was exasperated almost four decades before in Numbers 11, how much more so now?

What exactly was the sin of Moses? According to Moses it was the people's fault, something he repeats three times in Deuteronomy 1–4 (Deut 1:37; 3:26; 4:21; see Schnittjer, 113–15). According to the narrator of Numbers 20 and Yahweh in Deuteronomy 32, it was Moses's fault. In the latter reference Yahweh simply said he "broke faith" (32:51). The former reads: "But Yahweh said to Moses and Aaron, 'Because you did not trust in me enough to honor me as holy in the sight of the Israelites, you will not bring this community into the land I give them'" (Num 20:12; cf. 27:14). In what way did he break faith and dishonor Yahweh? Biblical readers have been debating this for thousands of years.

Several items in the story itself have given rise to various views of the sin of Moses.

> Yahweh said to Moses, "Take the staff, and you and your brother Aaron gather the assembly together. *Speak* to that rock before their eyes and it will pour out its water. You will bring water out of the rock for the community so they and their livestock can drink."
>
> So Moses took the staff from Yahweh's presence, just as he commanded him. He and Aaron gathered the assembly together in front of the rock and Moses said to them, "Listen, *you rebels*, must *we* bring you *water out of this rock?*" Then Moses raised his arm and *struck the rock twice with his staff.*" (20:7–11, emphasis added)

Here are some of the suggested options (see Milgrom, *Numbers*, 448–56):

- Moses struck the rock instead of speaking.
- Moses struck it twice, not once.
- Moses spoke to the people instead of the rock.
- Moses was angry at the people.
- Moses called the people "rebels," overstepping his present responsibility.
- Moses's question may have cast doubt on God's power.
- Moses may have actually doubted.
- Moses spoke *and* performed an action like an ordinary magician.
- Moses said "must *we* bring . . . ," taking too much credit on himself and Aaron.

Good arguments can be made for most of these readings. That so many can be based on the text (as well as others with no basis in the text) suggests that the story was composed with intentional ambiguity to hide the precise nature of Moses's sin from readers.

*What features of the account of Moses's and Aaron's sin have given rise to so many different interpretations of it?*

Why would the storyteller wish to hide answers from the reader? This phenomenon is, of course, not unique to this passage. Torah readers have similar kinds of challenges with the sins of Cain, the sons of God, Ham, and Aaron's sons. The accounts of the sins of Cain and Aaron's sons lack information, and the accounts of the sins of the sons of God, Ham, and Moses and Aaron have too much information (see Chapters 5, 6, 18). Something like this may be going on in later biblical passages as well. For example, what exactly is the sin of David in 2 Samuel 24? Moreover, the idea of what is left unsaid also invites readers to wonder and guess. The entire nature of biblical study supposes that it is an all-the-time preoccupation. We are told to be forever talking of God's word with the next generation (see Deut 6:6–9). Along with this, the understanding in biblical wisdom literature that the Scriptures are to be mined for treasure provides part of the reason for purposeful ambiguity (for other examples see Brown, 80–84).

Edom

*Isaiah and Abby Cramer*

In this case, as mentioned above, Numbers and Deuteronomy reflect on this event in more than one way. There is a right answer. But the right answer—God said Moses "broke faith"—is not so specific that it erases the conversation among readers.

To return to the question, why would the storyteller desire to keep the specific sin of Moses and Aaron from the reader? It seems like retaining ambiguity provides the space for readers to wrestle with and converse regarding the story itself. The Bible is designed to be studied and pondered and studied again. The biblical narrator did not want to frustrate readers per se but to create the need for careful study and ensure that the story will be discussed through the generations. In this sense, exegesis is a communal enterprise.

*What are possible reasons why the Bible sometimes leaves room for wondering and debate?*

Although Edom refused to let Israel pass through its land, Edom was not judged in the way that Moab and Ammon were for their attacks against Israel (see Num 24:17; Deut 23:3–6 and discussion in Chapter 27). Israel went the long way, around Edom. After the death of Aaron and victory against Arad, the people returned to what they did best—they complained.

They were hungry, they were thirsty, they did not like the manna, and they did not know why they needed to leave Egypt to begin with, unless it was to die in the desert.

Yahweh responded with snakes. After the people repented, Yahweh instructed Moses to make a "fiery snake" (lit., "fire" [*saraph*]) on a pole, and those who looked at it were healed. Messiah interpreted turning to the snake as an act of faith and the fiery snake on the pole as a symbol of himself (John 3:14–15; cf. 8:28; 12:32–33). The people kept the snake on the pole and eventually came to regard it with religious devotion worthy of God alone, until King Hezekiah destroyed it (2 Kgs 18:4; see Rosh Hashanah 3:8 in the Mishnah [1:691]).

The journey section of Numbers closes with accounts of the Israelite victories over the Transjordanian kingdoms of Sihon and Og, the peoples on "the other side of the Jordan River," that is, the east side (Deut 3:8 lit.). The commentary about these victories in Deuteronomy 2–3 is longer than the story itself in Numbers 21. The importance of defeating Sihon and Og can be explained in part by the place of these kingdoms according to Genesis. The Shemites, including Abraham's descendants, were to rule over the Canaanites, as Noah's only spoken word made clear (Gen 9:25–27). The Canaanites are comprised of several tribes or nations, including the Amorites (10:15–18). Moreover, God promised Abraham the lands of several nations, including that of the Amorites (15:21). The conquest of the kingdoms on the east of the Jordan River, then, is the beginning of the fulfillment of the promise of the land. A high point in Numbers is that "Israel settled in the land of the Amorites. . . . And they took possession of his [Og's] land" (Num 21:31, 35).

The story of the long travels in the wilderness tells of damning misery and undying faith in the power of God's word. The prevailing story line recounts the failure of the Israelites—the leaders and the people. At every stage they complained, looked back at Egypt with longing, looked ahead to the land of promise with dread,

Wadi Arnon marking the border between Moab and the Transjordanian kingdom of Sihon

*Isaiah and Abby Cramer.*

and failed to see Yahweh's grace in their everyday survival. The first generation rejected God's word and died in the wilderness. The younger generation appeared exactly like their parents. Readers cannot tell the difference between the older and younger generations without the narrator's help. The leaders, like the people, sinned at every stage along the way (see Table 22-A). The wickedness and unworthiness of the Israelites was total.

After forty years there was little hope. But there was hope. Two scouts would see the land. Two! Also, the Israelites defeated the kingdoms of the Transjordan. The greatest problems of the wilderness, however, lay ahead. Moab was bent on destroying the Israelites, one way or another, before they reached the land of promise.

## ANOTHER LOOK

Paul and Sosthenes used the wilderness stories of Exodus and Numbers as part of their teaching concerning temptation (see 1 Cor 10:13). The wilderness narratives instruct readers in overcoming enticements to sin. In addition to at least eight allusions to wilderness stories from Exodus and Numbers, Paul and Sosthenes said: "*Now these things occurred as examples to keep us* from setting our hearts on evil things as they did. . . . *These things happened to them as examples and were written down as warnings for us*" (1 Cor 10:6, 11; cf. Rom 15:4, emphasis added).

But how do these stories help gentile readers overcome temptations? How does hearing these stories provide part of the way out of temptation? The present discussion briefly works through temptation theory in line with the wilderness narratives of Exodus and Numbers. The categories of time and story come from Augustine (an important African church leader, 354–430 CE) to access the way that these narratives function as warnings to readers. These categories can help us hear what the stories say about the problem of temptation.

In his *Confessions*, Augustine tried to say something about eternity. In order to get at this, he contrasted eternity with time. I want to borrow these ideas, in a different way and for different purposes, on the meaning of time past, present, and future (see Ricoeur, 1:5–51). For Augustine the words past, present, and future as they are used in everyday language seem clear enough, but they do not and cannot actually denote three different kinds of time. "Who will tell me that there are not three times, past, present, and future, as we learnt when children and as we have taught children, but only the present, because the other two have no existence?" (11.17.22 [233]). He noted that past is always "no longer" and future is forever "not yet"; thus, if they exist, it can only be in the present (11.18.23 [233–34]).

Augustine's most significant contribution is where he located the three "times."

> It is inexact language to speak of three times—past, present, and future. Perhaps it would be exact to say: there are three times, a present of things past, a present of things present, a present of things to come. *In the soul* there are these three aspects of time, and I do not see them anywhere else. The present considering the past is *memory*, the present considering the present is *immediate awareness*, the present considering the future is *expectation*. (11.20.26 [235], emphasis added)

The past exists for Augustine in the present as memory and the future as expectation. He illustrated this by referring to a song (11.28.37 [243]). A given word does not, when we sing, sound like a word by itself, although we can only hear one moment at a time. Our minds naturally place the note and word within the context of the song; that is, our memory of the sounds and words that have come before and our expectation of what is to come create music and poetic lyrics. The same holds true for one's life or all of the human ages. We interpret the meaning of given events and moments in light of how we perceive that they fit with what has gone before and what we expect.

What do memory and expectation have to do with temptation? Everything—that's the point. There is nothing good or bad about a desert or fortified cities per se; rather, the mind is the context for temptation (see Figure 22-H). Thus, the fortified cities of Canaan may or may not be a temptation, depending on the memory and expectation of the individual and society. For Caleb and Joshua, the cities of Canaan provided an opportunity to embrace the power of God's word, but for the rest of the Israelites, they were the temptation that killed them. What was the difference? The way their minds accorded with, or distorted, the word of God.

**Figure 22-H:** The Mind as Context for Temptation—The General Framework

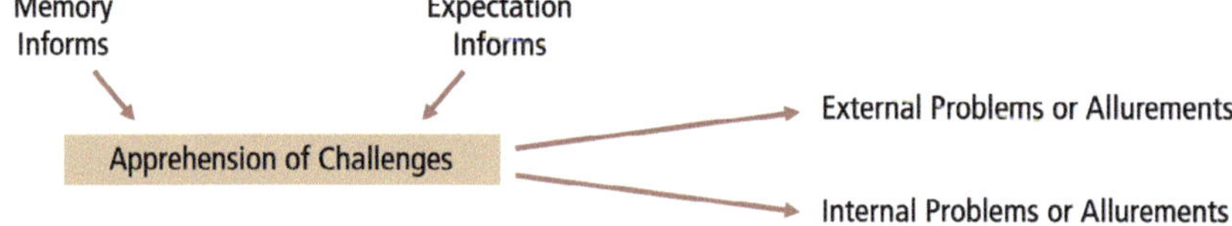


The Israelites faced problems. The apprehension of problems through experience, however we define it, is informed by memory and expectation. Remembering the past one way, such as "Yahweh did what he promised," may lead to faith. But remembering it differently, such as "Moses was deceiving us in order to kill us in the desert," breeds temptation. Thus the issue has little to do with the facts themselves but everything to do with the perception of circumstances (see Figure 22-I). This is why two people can respond differently in relation to the selfsame situation. The manipulation of one's own mind by fabricating memories can be called rationalization or self-deception. The purpose of inventing fictive memories, in the case of temptation, is to avoid or embrace given expectations—whether problems or allurements.

*What is the relationship of memory and expectation to faith and/or temptation?*

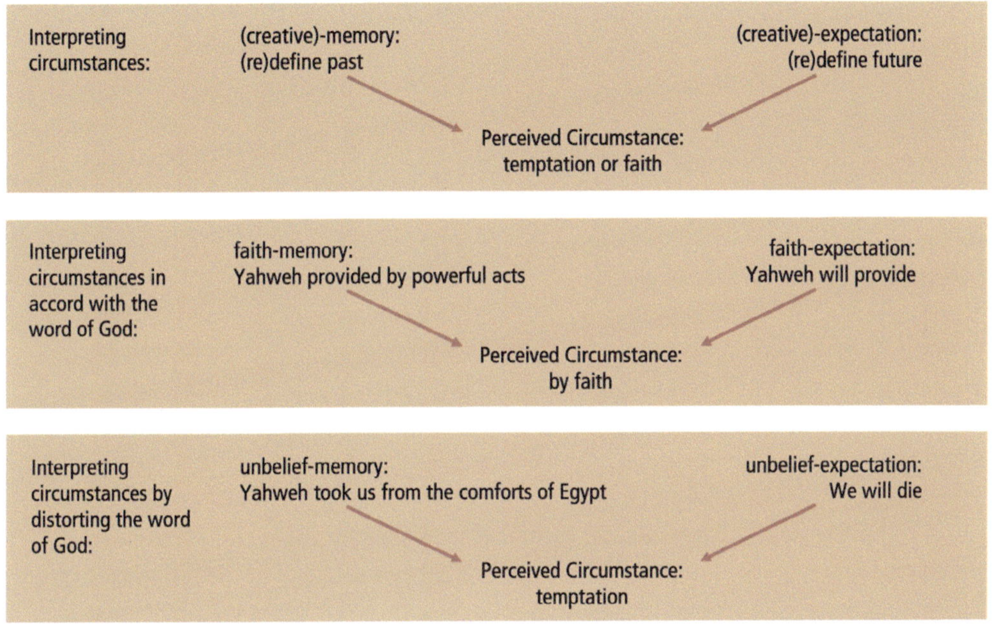


**Figure 22-I:** Faith and Temptation as a Function of Perception[a]

[a]Perceived circumstance may be things like hunger, thirst, or fortified cities in the land of promise.

When Israel redefined their past, it changed not only their identity but defied God's word concerning himself. He had acted because of his promise to the Hebrew ancestors. To deny his acts for Israel was to deny who he said he was. Notice in the following passages the manipulation of memory and expectation, self-deception, and, in other cases, the acceptance of Yahweh's testimony (some of these texts have been cited above; emphasis added in all cases).

> Moses said, "This is what Yahweh has commanded: 'Take an omer of manna and *keep it for the generations to come, so they can see the bread I gave you to eat in the wilderness* when I brought you out of Egypt.'" (Exod 16:32)

> The rabble with them began to crave other food, and again the Israelites started wailing and said, "If only we had meat to eat! *We remember* the fish we ate in Egypt at no cost—also the cucumbers, melons, leeks, onions and garlic. But now we have lost our appetite; we never see anything but this manna!" (Num 11:4–6)

All the Israelites grumbled . . . "If only we had died in Egypt! Or in this wilderness! Why is Yahweh bringing us to this land only to let us fall by the sword? Our wives and children will be taken as plunder. *Wouldn't it be better* for us to go back to Egypt?" . . .

[Joshua and Caleb said,] "Do not rebel against Yahweh. And do not be afraid of the people of the land, because we will devour them. Their protection is gone, but *Yahweh is with us*. Do not be afraid of them." (14:2–3, 9)

[Dathan and Abiram] said, "We will not come! Isn't it enough that *you have brought us up out of a land flowing with milk and honey to kill us in the wilderness?* And now you also want to lord it over us!" (16:12–13)

[At Kadesh] you grumbled in your tents and said, "*Yahweh hates us*; so he brought us out of Egypt to deliver us into the hands of the Amorites to destroy us." (Deut 1:27)

[Moses said,] "*Because he loved your ancestors and chose their descendants after them*, he brought you out of Egypt by his Presence and his great strength, to drive out before you nations greater and stronger than you and to bring you into their land to give it to you for your inheritance, as it is today." (4:37–38)

The wilderness narratives teach, as Paul and Sosthenes said, something about temptation. First, the identity of the people, along with their view of God, was tied to their collective memory. Second, when faced with challenges or allurements, the people frequently reinvented the past in order to change their direction and thus alter their

Oasis in wilderness
*Earl Hagar*

expected future. Complaining against Yahweh's will is an act of unbelief. Third, the antidote to temptation—as Paul and Sosthenes said, "he will provide a way out"—is bound up with faith, that is, to accord individual and collective memories and expectations with God's word.

## INTERACTIVE WORKSHOP

### *Chapter Summary*

The first generation of Israelites fell to temptation in the wilderness and definitively rebelled against God's word at Kadesh. The revolution effectively ended the story of the older generation. The second generation grew up in the desert and faced many of the same temptations as their parents. They failed also. The younger generation was as sinful as their parents.

### *Can You Explain the Key Terms?*

- Aaron's staff
- Anakites
- bad report
- Sheol
- temptation
- Transjordan

### *Challenge Questions*

1. What are the similarities and differences between the people and the leadership in Numbers 10–21 in terms of facing temptation?
2. What was the significance of the mythologized second report of the ten scouts in Numbers 13?
3. How is the story of the man gathering wood on the Sabbath in Numbers 15 an example of "high-handed sin"?
4. What was the importance of the red heifer regulation (Num 19) for the Israelites?
5. Why is it difficult to determine the specific sin of Moses and Aaron in Numbers 20?

### *Advanced Questions*

1. Compare the implied positive and negative narrative views of "prophesying" in Numbers 11 and 1 Samuel 10:9–13; 19:18–24, and explain the significance of the tension between the two.
2. How does the theological commentary in Deuteronomy 1 and 9 interpret the people's failure at Kadesh (Num 13–14)?
3. Make a comparison between the prayers of Moses in Exodus 32 and Numbers 14 (see Table 22-F). Why did the prayers have different effects within the two narrative contexts?
4. What is the narrative and theological function of the poems embedded in Numbers 21?
5. Explain the relationship between memory and identity and its role in the temptation narratives, with special attention to the different memories of Yahweh and the Israelites concerning what things were like in Egypt and the wilderness.

*6. What are the theological functions of *ruah* in Numbers 11?

*7. How should *saraph* be understood in Numbers 21:8 (NIV "snake"), and how might this be related to the idea of light mentioned in the context of the three "lifted up" passages in John 3:14–21; 8:21–28; 12:30–36?

## Research Project Ideas

Compare, literarily and theologically, the grumbling narratives in Numbers 11 and 20–21 with those in Exodus 15–17.

Compare, literarily and theologically, the rebellion at Kadesh (Num 13–14) with the rebellion with the golden calf (Exod 32), especially the function of Moses's intercession, within their narrative contexts.

Explain how the instructions of Numbers 18 fit into the book of Numbers.

Exegetically explain the sin of Moses within its narrative context (Num 20).

Synthesize the nature and function of prayer in Numbers 11–21.

## The Next Step


Ashley, Timothy R. *The Book of Numbers*. New International Commentary on the Old Testament. Grand Rapids: Eerdmans, 1993.

Augustine. *Confessions*. Edited and Translated by Henry Chadwick. Oxford World's Classics. New York: Oxford University Press, 1991.

Brown, Jeannine K. *Scripture as Communication: Introducing Biblical Hermeneutics*. 2nd ed. Grand Rapids: Baker Academic, 2021.

Liss, Hanna. "Ritual Purity and the Construction of Identity: The Literary Function of the Laws of Purity in the Book of Leviticus." Pages 329–54 in *The Books of Leviticus and Numbers*. Edited by Thomas Römer. Leuven: Uitgeverij Peeters, 2008.

Milgrom, Jacob. "Encroachment." Pages 264–65 in *The Interpreter's Dictionary of the Bible: Supplementary Volume*. Edited by Keith Crim. Nashville: Abingdon, 1976.

———. *Numbers*. JPS Torah Commentary. Philadelphia: Jewish Publication Society, 1989.

*The Oxford Annotated Mishnah*. Edited by Shaye J. D. Cohen, Robert Goldberg, and Hayim Lapin. 3 vols. New York: Oxford University Press, 2022.

Ricoeur, Paul. *Time and Narrative*. Translated by Kathleen McLaughlin and David Pellauer. 3 vols. Chicago: University of Chicago Press, 1984.

Sakenfeld, Katharine Doob. *Journeying with God: A Commentary on the Book of Numbers*. Grand Rapids: Eerdmans, 1995.

Schnittjer, Gary Edward. "Kadesh Infidelity of Deuteronomy 1 and Its Synoptic Implications." *Journal of the Evangelical Theological Society* 63.1 (2020): 95–120.

# 23 THE SECOND GENERATION ON THE PLAINS OF MOAB

*Numbers 22–36*

© William D. Mounce

## GETTING STARTED

### *Focus Question*

How did God deliver the second generation of wilderness Israelites from the perils of sin?

### *Look for These Terms*

- Balaam
- bless
- curse
- itinerary
- Phinehas
- zealous

## AN OUTLINE

A. **The Threat from Moab (22–25)**
   1. The external threat—the Balaam story (22–24)
   2. The internal threat—sin with the Moabites (25)

B. **Census of the Second Generation (26)**

C. **Review of the Journey and Preparation for Possession of the Land (27–36)**
   1. Inheritance of Zelophehad's daughters (27:1–11)
      2. The new leader for Israel (27:12–23)
      3. Regulations concerning offerings and vows (28–30)
      4. The war against Midian (31)
      5. The settlement of the Transjordan by two and a half tribes of Israel (32)
      6. A review of the wilderness itinerary (33)
      7. A preview of the land itself (34–35)
         a. Boundaries and allotments of the land (34)
         b. Special cities dispersed through the land (35)
            1. Levite towns described (35:1–5)
            2. Cities of refuge (35:6–34)
   8. Marriage restrictions for the inheritance of Zelophehad's daughters (36)

## A READING

When readers reach Numbers 22–25, they arrive at the defining moments of the book—the turning point of the story. The first generation fell to temptation and rejected the promise of Yahweh when they were encamped at the very threshold of the land he had given them. Now, after long years of growing up wandering, the younger generation has arrived at the edge of the land. They are like their parents in that they too have the bad habit of complaining and breaking faith. Yet, they have enjoyed victories over the Transjordanian kingdoms. The first-time reader may wonder: Will they too reject God's word like the older generation? Or will they overcome the addiction to unbelief they inherited from their parents? It seems as if it could go either way. In this precarious position, a grave new threat is born.

The scene shifts from the lifelong desert travelers to the enemy of Israel, Moab. In chapters 22–24, the Moabite king seeks to ruin Israel by hiring a despicable prophet—an evil prophet of Israel's God (!)—to curse them. This external threat failed because Yahweh's word ruined Balaam's conspiracies. The depraved prophet tried a second time to destroy Israel, this time from within. He helped launch a conspiracy with the Moabites and Midianites to incite Israel to debauchery and thus bring the wrath of God on themselves. The plan almost worked. One person, however, heard God's word and responded decisively to deliver Israel. The righteous zealot Phinehas saved the Israelites from themselves.

The word of God prevailed over both the external and internal threats conceived by the enemies of his people. The census of the second generation symbolized their readiness to enter the land of promise. After the census of chapter 26, the book concludes with the story of how the Israelites prepared to invade the land of promise. There was still at least one surprise in the narrative of the war against Midian in Numbers 31. Some in Israel were rebelling just as the older generation had at Kadesh. This time, however, God let them continue preparing for invasion. What was the difference? There was no difference in the people, for the younger generation was just like their parents (Schnittjer, "Kadesh," 108). If the people had to deserve to enter the land before actually doing so, then the wandering stories of the Torah would never end. The point is grace. Yahweh kept his promise (14:31; cf. Deut 1:31). Yahweh's people did invade the land, even though they did not deserve it.

*Why was the second generation of Israelites able to enter the land of promise?*

The Balaam narratives of Numbers 22–24 are remarkable for many reasons. For example, the shift of focus, from story and law concerning Israel to foregrounding an account of the enemies of God's people, is unique. Balaam himself was a prophet of Israel's God, Yahweh. Balaam is also known from the eight century BCE Tell Deir 'Alla' inscription of Succoth (Aḥituv, 438–39).

The fact that someone outside of Israel served Yahweh is not exceptional in itself. The distinctive feature here is that this prophet of Yahweh was evil and sought to harm Yahweh's people for the sake of greed. Also, the story of Balaam's donkey, the second talking animal in the Torah (cf. Gen 3), is noteworthy because the donkey admonishes and shames the prophet before readers through the ages. The point seems to be that Yahweh can make a donkey or an evil prophet speak his will. And, perhaps most importantly, the poetic oracles of Balaam become an enduring witness to the hope for the coming king whom later readers called the Messiah.

Balak, the king of Moab, resembles pharaoh in several respects. Both monarchs viewed Israel as a problem because they were too mighty or numerous (Exod 1:9; Num 22:6). Both kings conspired against Israel because Yahweh had blessed his people. The two rulers, however, used different strategies to oppose Israel. Whereas pharaoh used oppression and resisted the word from Yahweh's prophet, Balak wanted to get the help of a prophet of Yahweh.

Balak hired a mercenary prophet, Balaam, to curse Israel by Yahweh. The whole thing backfired on the Moabite king because the power of God's word was already on Israel, giving yet another example of the Numbers story being based on Genesis (see Table 20-G in Chapter 20). Balak's request stated:

"Then the Lord opened the donkey's mouth, and it said to Balaam, 'What have I done to you to make you beat me these three times?'" (Num 22:28).

*iStock.com/ GEFHunter*

> A people has come out of Egypt; they cover the face of the land and have settled next to me. Now come and *put a curse on these people*, because they are too powerful for me. Perhaps then I will be able to defeat them and drive them out of the land. For I know that *whoever you bless is blessed, and whoever you curse is cursed.* (Num 22:5b–6, emphasis added)

The king of Moab was right about one thing, namely, the power of Yahweh's word spoken by the prophet. But he failed to appreciate that Balaam was merely a messenger, not a composer, of the prophetic word he uttered.

Moreover, Balak did not realize that Israel could not be cursed because the curser would be cursed. Yahweh told Abraham, "I will bless those who bless you, and *whoever curses you I will curse*" (Gen 12:3a, emphasis added). Isaac's accidental and irrevocable blessing of Jacob confirmed the same thing (27:29). Because Israel was already under this word of Yahweh, Balak invited the curse of God on himself and the Moabites. Balaam concluded his third failed oracle thus, "May those who bless you be blessed *and those who curse you be cursed*" (Num 24:9b, emphasis added). We will return to these allusions to the ancestral promises below. For now the point is that the Moabite king damned himself by the word of God.

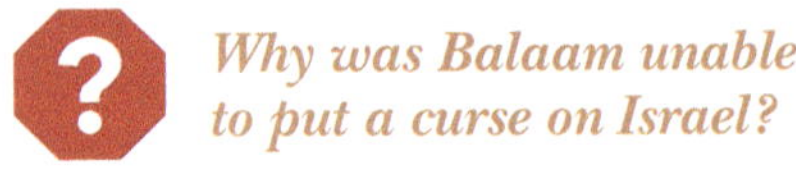

*Why was Balaam unable to put a curse on Israel?*

The importance of the Balaam narrative stems from his oracles as based on God's authoritative word. Even the way the narrative plays out reveals the decrease of Balak and the increase of Balaam (see Table 23-A). It is as though the political ruler recedes to make room for God's word to be heard.

**Table 23-A:** Balak's Diminishing Role and Balaam's Growing Esteem in the Series of Oracles[a]

[a] Table based on observations in Milgrom, 467–68.

| | Balak | Balaam |
|---|---|---|
| First oracle (23:7–10) | king of Moab (23:7) | passive instrument of Balak (23:7) |
| Second oracle (23:18–24) | son of Zippor (23:18) | giving orders to Balak (23:18) |
| Third and fourth oracles (24:3–9, 15–24) | not mentioned | confident mediator of God's word (24:4, 16) |

In this context, the plentiful references to Yahweh's speaking (i.e., to the prophet speaking God's word) not only strengthens the message but also makes an important theological point about prophets of Yahweh. Before reflecting on the theological point itself, it is worth taking note of the many explicit statements.

> [Balaam said], "I will report back to you *the answer Yahweh gives me.*" (22:8)
>
> But Balaam answered them, "Even if Balak gave me all the silver and gold in his palace, *I could not do anything great or small to go beyond the command of Yahweh my God.*" (22:18)
>
> That night God came to Balaam and said, "Since these men have come to summon you, go with them, but *do only what I tell you.*" (22:20)
>
> The angel of Yahweh said to Balaam, "Go with the men, but *speak only what I tell you.*" So Balaam went with Balak's officials. (22:35)
>
> "Well, I have come to you now," Balaam replied. "*But I can't say whatever I please. I must speak only what God puts in my mouth.*" (22:38)
>
> Then Balaam said to Balak, "Stay here beside your offering while I go aside. Perhaps Yahweh will come to meet with me. *Whatever he reveals to me I will tell you.*" . . .

> *Yahweh put a word in Balaam's mouth* and said, "Go back to Balak and give him this word." (23:3, 5)

> He [Balaam] answered, "*Must I not speak what Yahweh puts in my mouth?*" (23:12)

> Yahweh met with Balaam *and put a word in his mouth* and said, "Go back to Balak and give him this word." So he went to him and found him standing beside his offering, with the Moabite officials. Balak asked him, "*What did Yahweh say?*" (23:16–17)

> Balaam answered, "Did I not tell you *I must do whatever Yahweh says?*" (23:26)

> When Balaam looked out and saw Israel encamped tribe by tribe, *the Spirit of God came upon him and he uttered his message*: "The prophecy of Balaam son of Beor, the prophecy of one whose eye sees clearly, the prophecy of *one who hears the words of God, who sees a vision from the Almighty*, who falls prostrate, and whose eyes are opened." (24:2–4)

> Balaam answered Balak, "Did I not tell the messengers you sent me, 'Even if Balak gave me all of the silver and gold in his palace, *I could not do anything of my own accord, good or bad, to go beyond the command of Yahweh—and I must say only what Yahweh says*'?" (24:12–13, emphasis added in all cases)

At least one thing stands out: The prophet spoke the word of God.

Balaam, though evil, was a prophet of Yahweh. What does this mean? If the story of Balaam and his oracles from God were not in the Torah, readers could be tempted to associate, to one extent or another, the character of the messenger with the import of the message. God revealed his will to Noah, Abraham, Isaac, Rebekah, Jacob, Joseph, and especially Moses. Considering just Moses and Balaam will make the point since Moses seems to provide a model for the prophets of Israel and Judah.

God's word does not depend at all, in any way, on the prophet himself or herself —whether they are good or wicked. God's word utterly transcended Moses as much as Balaam. The prophet was a mere vessel or delivery person for his word. The basis of power and reason for hope was always and only that the word of the prophet is the word of Yahweh.

Balaam's oracles are of great importance for the theology of the Torah as a whole. Notice how Balaam's second and third oracles blend together the language of Yahweh's covenant with the Hebrew ancestors and the blessing of Judah (Table 23-B). By bringing these details together, Balaam's oracle identifies the expected rule of the Judah-king with the fulfillment of the Abrahamic covenant (cf. allusion to Gen 12:3 in Table 10-C in Chapter 10).

**Table 23-B:** Identifying the Blessing of the Hebrew Ancestors and the Expectation for the Judah-King in Balaam's Second and Third Oracles[a]

[a]Bold-red and broken underlining mark verbal parallels in Hebrew between Genesis and Numbers, and underlining marks verbal parallels between Balaam's second and third oracles. One of the terms for "curse" in Genesis 12:3 is not marked because it is a different word in Hebrew. Also, "lie down" in Gen 49:9 and Num 24:9 are unmarked because they are based on different Hebrew verbs with a similar meaning. This table is based on Schnittjer, "Blessing," 21–22.

| Genesis | Numbers |
|---|---|
| [Yahweh says to Abraham] "I shall bless those who bless you, but the one who curses you I shall curse, and all the families of the earth will be blessed by you." (Gen 12:3 lit.)<br><br>[Isaac says to Jacob] "May those who curse you be cursed and those who bless you be blessed." (27:29 lit.)<br><br>[Jacob says to Judah] "A young lion, Judah, from the prey you go up, **like a lion he crouches** and lies down, **and as a lioness—who dares rouse him**?" (49:9 lit.) | [In the second oracle Balaam says] God brings them out of Egypt, like horns of a wild ox. Surely there is no divination against Jacob, and no evil spells against Israel. It will be said of Jacob and Israel, "What God has done." Look, a people **like a lioness rising up, like a lion** they get themselves up and they will not lie down until they eat prey and drink the blood of the slain. (23:22–24 lit.)<br><br>[In the third oracle Balaam says] God brings him out of Egypt, like horns of a wild ox . . . **Like a lion he crouches** and lies down, **and as a lioness—who dares rouse him**? May those who bless you be blessed and those who curse you be cursed. (24:8a, 9 lit.) |

*Right:*
Lion from ancient city of Susa
*Robert C. Kashow*

*What biblical evidence shows that the Abrahamic covenant will be fulfilled by the rule of the Judah-king?*

The fourth oracle makes use of poetic imagery to dramatize the coming of the king. The mention of several specific nations helps us to look ahead to their fate in the David stories and the sermons of the prophets of Israel and Judah. Compare, for example, the most famous imagery with one of the victory reports of David as well as Isaiah's expectations about Moab blended with imagery of trampled to the dust from Genesis:

> So Yahweh God said to the serpent, "Because you have done this, "Cursed are you above all livestock and all wild animals! You will crawl on your belly and you will eat dust all the days of your life. And I will put enmity between you and the woman, and between your offspring and hers; he will crush your head, and you will strike his heel." (Gen 3:14–15)

> I see him, but not now,
> I gaze on him, but not near,
> A star will come out from Jacob,
> and a scepter will rise from Israel.
> He will crush the edges of Moab,
> and he will shatter all the sons of Sheth.
> *Edom will be conquered;*
> *Seir, his enemy, will be conquered,*
> but Israel will grow strong.
> A ruler will come out of Jacob
> and destroy the survivors of the city. (Num 24:17–19, v. 17 lit.)

> David also defeated the Moabites. He made them lie down on the ground and measured them off with a length of cord. Every two lengths of them were put to death, and the third length was allowed to live. So the Moabites became subject to David and brought tribute. . . . He put garrisons throughout Edom, and *all the Edomites became subject to David.* Yahweh gave David victory wherever he went. (2 Sam 8:2, 14)

> The hand of Yahweh will rest on this mountain; but Moab will be trampled in their land as straw is trampled down in the manure. They will stretch out their hands in it, as swimmers stretch out their hands to swim. God will bring down their pride despite the cleverness of their hands. He will bring down your high fortified walls and lay them low; he will bring them down to the ground, to the very dust. (Isa 25:10–12, emphases added to each quotation)

Second Samuel 8:2 refers to the humiliation of the Moabites as well as to their giving tribute to David. It seems as if the narrator may have wanted to reflect imagery from both Numbers 24 (specifically, Moab humbled; see Rashi 4:338 [on Num 24:17]) and Genesis 49 (namely, giving the Judah-king that which belongs to him—tribute; see discussion of Gen 49:10 in Another Look of Chapter 10; and see Schnittjer, "Blessing," 16–17, n. 3). Moreover, that "he will crush the edges of Moab" means that in Balaam's fourth oracle, Moab symbolized the seed of the serpent (cf. Gen 3:15; Jer 48:45). This imagery connects with the combination of expectations for the trampling of Moab to the dust in the end of Isaiah 25 (cf. Gen 3:14; Isa 65:25; Mic 7:17).

The story of Israel's sin and deliverance in Numbers 25 and the battle in chapter 31 should be read forward and backward and forward again, but for the sake of space I will summarize the backward or second reading and then read it forward (see discussion of first and second readings in Chapter 1). The broad connection between chapters 25 and 31 (the intervening chapters are census and law) can be seen by comparing Yahweh's twice-cited command to attack the Midianites: "*Yahweh said to Moses, 'Treat the Midianites as enemies and kill them*, because they treated you as enemies when they deceived you in the Peor incident'" (25:16–18a), and "*Yahweh said to Moses, 'Take vengeance on the Midianites* for the Israelites'" (31:1a, emphases added).

Scripture depicts Balaam as a shameful prophet (Sidebar 23-C). After Balaam failed to curse Israel, he did not give up. If he could not bring the curse of Yahweh on them from without, he determined to destroy them from within. Balaam devised a conspiracy with the enemies of Yahweh's chosen people, apparently a cooperative effort between Moab and Midian, to cause Israel to rebel against Yahweh's word. The idea, it seems, was to get the Israelites to damn themselves through sin against Yahweh. After the Israelites defeated the Midianites, Moses confronted the officers. "'Have you allowed all the women to live?' he asked them. '*They were the ones who followed Balaam's advice and enticed the Israelites to be unfaithful to Yahweh* in the Peor incident, so that a plague struck Yahweh's people'" (31:15–16, emphasis added). The women in question are Moabite women, perhaps religious prostitutes, and the daughter of one of the Midianite tribal chiefs (25:15–18; 31:8, 15–17; see Yamauchi, 218–19).

Balaam persuaded the enemies of Israel to ally together and attack God's people with temptation and sin:

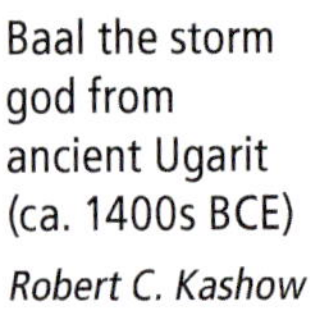

Baal the storm god from ancient Ugarit (ca. 1400s BCE)
*Robert C. Kashow*

> While Israel was staying in Shittim, *the men began to indulge in sexual immorality with Moabite women, who invited them to the sacrifices to their gods.* The people ate the sacrificial meal and bowed down before these gods. So Israel yoked themselves to the Baal of Peor. And Yahweh's anger burned against them. . . . *Then an Israelite man brought into the camp a Midianite woman right before the eyes of Moses and the whole assembly of Israel.* (Num 25:1–3, 6a, emphasis added)

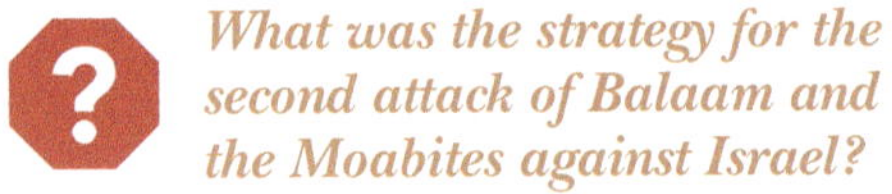

*What was the strategy for the second attack of Balaam and the Moabites against Israel?*

It almost worked. Balaam almost succeeded in getting the Israelites to invite Yahweh's wrath on themselves.

This rebellion of the younger generation with the Moabite and Midianite women and their gods surpassed the wickedness of the older generation. Yahweh immediately responded with a deadly plague that killed thousands. At the very moment when the defiance was at its height, symbolized by the high-handed sin of the Israelite who openly brought a Midianite

## Sidebar 23-C: Balaam as Prototype

The prophet Balaam is used as a prototypical wicked character by later biblical writers. They interpreted his sinful character in relation to the curses he tried to pronounce on Israel and for the lustful immorality he tried to instigate (see Num 31:15–16 with 25:1–6).

> They have left the straight way and wandered off to follow the way of Balaam son of Bezer, who loved the wages of wickedness. But he was rebuked for his wrongdoing by a donkey—an animal without speech—who spoke with a human voice and restrained the prophet's madness. (2 Pet 2:15–16)
>
> Woe to them! They have taken the way of Cain; they have rushed for profit into Balaam's error; they have been destroyed in Korah's rebellion. (Jude 11)
>
> Nevertheless, I have a few things against you: There are some among you who hold to the teaching of Balaam, who taught Balak to entice the Israelites to sin so that they ate food sacrificed to idols and committed sexual immorality. (Rev 2:14, emphases added in these texts)

to his tent for illicit sexual relations, grace intervened. One person listened to God's word. Phinehas, the grandson of Aaron, obeyed that word while everyone else seemed paralyzed watching the flagrant sin. He killed the bold sinners by spearing them through their sexual organs while in the act of fornicating. Fox, following others, sees the wordplay between her tent as a "private-chamber" (*qubbah*) and her lower abdomen as her "private-parts" (*qebah*) (see Num 25:8 Fox; cf. NET note). Notice the relation of God's word and the response of Phinehas.

> *Yahweh said to Moses, "Take all the leaders of these people, kill them and expose them in broad daylight before Yahweh, so that Yahweh's fierce anger may turn away from Israel."* So Moses said to Israel's judges, "Each of you must put to death those of your people who have yoked themselves to the Baal of Peor." Then an Israelite man brought into the campe a Midianite woman right before the eyes of Moses and the whole assembly of Israel while they were weeping at the entrance to the Tent of Meeting. *When Phinehas* son of Eleazar, the son of Aaron, the priest, *saw this, he left the assembly, took a spear in his hand, he came after the man of Israel into the private-chamber, and he thrust through the two of them, the man and the woman, in her private-parts,* and the plague was held-back from the Children of Israel. (25:4–8, v. 8 Fox, emphasis added)

Phinehas, one of the original zealots, saved Israel by obeying God's instruction. Yahweh rewarded the zealous priest with a covenant of peace (Num 25:11–13).

Balaam failed. The external threat had been ruined by the oracles bringing blessing to Israel and curse to their enemies. The internal threat, orchestrated by Balaam and embraced by many in Israel, was defeated by Phinehas's obedience to God's word. The difference between the first and second generation was not virtue or character. The younger generation evidenced great propensity for sin. The difference, the turning point of the entire book, was the grace of Yahweh prevailing according to his word.

The symbol that the younger generation would enter the land of promise is the census of the militia. The census of the second generation immediately follows the deliverance from the Moabite threats. This generation needed to prepare for the military campaign of the land of promise. This census, like the previous one, revealed the intramural tribal relations according to the Genesis worldview (see Table 23-D).

**Table 23-D:** Comparing the Military Censuses of Numbers 1 and 26

| First Generation in Numbers 1 | | Second Generation in Numbers 26 | |
|---|---|---|---|
| Reuben | 46,500 | Reuben | 43,730 |
| Simeon | 59,300 | Simeon | 22,200 |
| Gad | 45, 650 | Gad | 40,500 |
| Judah | 74,600 | Judah | 76,500 |
| Issachar | 54,400 | Issachar | 64,300 |
| Zebulun | 57,400 | Zebulun | 60,500 |
| Ephraim | 40,500 | Manasseh | 52,700 |
| Manasseh | 32,200 | Ephraim | 32,500 |
| Benjamin | 35,400 | Benjamin | 45,600 |
| Dan | 62,700 | Dan | 64,400 |
| Asher | 41,500 | Asher | 53,400 |
| Naphtali | 53,400 | Naphtali | 45,400 |
| **Total Fighting Force** | **603,550** | **Total Fighting Force** | **601,730** |

Just as with the first generation, the tribes of Judah and Joseph (i.e., Ephraim and Manasseh) were the two largest groups, with 72,700 and 85,200 respectively. In both chapters 1 and 26, the tribes of Ephraim and Manasseh are listed as the descendants of Joseph (1:32; 26:28, 37). The symbolic size significance of the leading tribes, in accord with Genesis theology that life is a gift from the Creator, parallels the arrangement of the encampment and the marching order from Numbers 1, 2, and 7 as well as the birthright and blessing in the sons of Jacob story in Genesis (see Chapters 9, 10, and 21). If the tribes are considered individually, Judah provided the largest fighting forces by far according to either census. The census itself signaled a shift in the Numbers story. The rest of the book is oriented toward the preparation of the new generation to enter the land Yahweh had promised to their ancestors.

The final unit of Numbers, the various laws and stories in chapters 27–36, is framed by the matter of the inheritance of Zelophehad's daughters (see Figure 23-E). The family of Zelophehad had no male heir, so it was determined that his daughters had the right to inherit the family land, just as a son would have. Both Numbers 27 and 36 demonstrate that law serves redemption, not the other way around, when the people petition Yahweh and he adjusts the legal standards (27:3–4; 36:2–5). The framing of this unit immediately after the second census signals that this section of Numbers serves as a literary unit of the preparation to enter the land of promise.

**Figure 23-E:** Literary Framing of Numbers 27–36

- Inheritance of Zelophehad's daughters (27:1–11)
    - Joshua to replace Moses (27:12–23)
    - Law and narrative of Israel's present (28–32)
    - A review of the wilderness journeys (33)
    - A preview of the land (34–35)
- Inheritance of Zelophehad's daughters (36)

The first element within the literary frame is the appointment of a leader to replace Moses (see Figure 23-E). Yahweh repeated his indictment against Moses and Aaron and invited Moses to climb a mountain and look at the land across the Jordan River before he died. Moses prayed for a new leader "so Yahweh's people will not be *like sheep without a shepherd*" (27:17b, emphasis added). The idea of a prophet like Moses as "shepherd" strengthens the well-rounded messianic imagery associated with Israel's shepherd made king, David. Moreover, Matthew interprets Messiah's ministry of compassion along the same lines. "When he saw the crowds, he had compassion on them, because they were harassed and helpless, *like sheep without a shepherd*" (Matt 9:36, emphasis added).

The appointment of Joshua to replace Moses is repeated in Deuteronomy 31, 32, and Joshua 1, and the invitation for Moses to ascend the mountain to see the land before he died appears at the end of Deuteronomy 32 (also see Deut 34). The journey was over. All that remained was to prepare the people to cross the river.

The laws in Numbers 28–30 supplement those in Leviticus. Chapters 28–29 summarize additional sacrifices for the feasts listed in the holy calendar of Leviticus 23, except Firstfruits (see Tables 19-G and 19-H in Chapter 19). Leviticus 23 focuses on individual laity for the worship festivals. Numbers 28–29 emphasizes the cumulative force of the sacrifices, moving from the daily, through the weekly and monthly, to those at the annual holy memorials. Numbers 30 provides further instruction regarding vows (cf. Lev 27). Specifically, the regulations are given for the exoneration of responsibility (i.e., the releasing from the commitment to a vow) when a daughter or wife made a vow against the will of her father or husband. The father or husband needed to consent to the woman's vow for it to be binding. These regulations demonstrate, among other things, the corporate view of religious devotion.

The narrative of the Israelites' assault and victory over the Midianites resumes in chapter 31 (see discussion above). After the defeat, all the Midianite captives were killed

**Map 23-F:** The Transjordan Tribal Regions

except for virgin females. Also, all of the spoils were passed through fire or water to make them ritually clean. Finally, Yahweh was given his portion.

The entire nation was again put in mortal jeopardy, this time by two and a half tribes. The tribes of Reuben, Gad, and half of Manasseh requested that they simply settle down in the Transjordanian region, which was already secured (see Num 21), rather than cross the Jordan River to assist the other tribes in the campaign against the Canaanites. This request demonstrates once more that the younger generation was as sinful as the older generation (Schnittjer, "Kadesh," 108).

> Moses said to the Gadites and Reubenites, "Should your fellow Israelites go to war while you sit here? Why do you discourage the Israelites from crossing over into the land Yahweh has given them? *This is what your ancestors did* when I sent them from Kadesh Barnea to look over the land . . . *And here you are, a brood of sinners, standing in the place of your ancestors* and making Yahweh even more angry with Israel. If you turn away from following him, he will again leave all this people in the wilderness, and you will be the cause of their destruction." (32:6–8, 14–15, vv. 8, 14 lit., emphasis added)

The comparison to the rebellion at Kadesh signifies that the second generation did not deserve to go into the land. Fortunately, the two and a half tribes repented. The second generation invaded the land of promise, not because they were worthy but even though they were unworthy. The book of Numbers, ultimately, is a story of grace for sinners.

*What is the significance of the comparison between the uprising of the two and a half Transjordanian tribes and the rebellion at Kadesh almost forty years earlier?*

Numbers 33–35 looks back and ahead. Chapter 33 reviews the entire journey from Egypt to the plains of Moab, including forty stops. The brief remarks in the itinerary-journal are similar to the relevant portions of the pentateuchal narrative (see Num 33:3 = Exod 14:8 and Num 33:37–39 = 20:22–29). Table 23-G compares the itinerary of Numbers 33 with the travel narratives elsewhere in the Torah. Scanning Table 23-G will reveal that the narratives in Exodus and Numbers present only selected events from Israel's wilderness years.

**Table 23-G:** Comparing the Travel Accounts of Torah

| Exodus and Numbers | Numbers 33 | Deuteronomy |
|---|---|---|
| Rameses (Exod 12:37) | Rameses | |
| Succoth (12:37) | Succoth | |
| Etham (13:20) | Etham | |
| Pi Hahiroth (14:2) | Pi Hahiroth | |
| Marah (15:23) | Marah | |
| Elim (15:27) | Elim | |
| | by Reeds Sea | |
| Desert of Sin (16:1) | Desert of Sin | |
| | Dophkah | |
| | Alush | |
| Rephidim/Massah and Meribah (17:1) | Rephidim | Massah (9:22) |
| Desert of Sinai (19:1) | Desert of Sinai | Horeb (1:19; 5:2) |
| Desert of Paran (Num 10:12) | | |
| Kibroth Hattaavah/Taberah (11:3, 34) | Kibroth Hattaavah | Kibroth Hattaavah, Taberah (9:22) |
| Hazeroth (11:35) | Hazeroth | |
| Desert of Paran/Kadesh (12:16; 13:26) | | Kadesh Barnea (1:19; 9:23) |
| | Rithmah | |
| | Rimmon Perez | |
| | Libnah | |
| | Rissah | |
| | Kehelathah | |
| | Mount Shepher | |
| | Haradah | |
| | Makheloth | |
| | Tahath | |
| | Terah | |
| | Mithcah | |
| | Hashmonah | |
| | Moseroth | (Moserah, 10:6) |
| | Bene Jaakan | wells of Bene Jaakan (10:6) |
| | Hor Haggidgad | (Gudgodah, 10:7) |
| | Jotbathah | Jotbathah (10:7) |

*(continued)*

| Exodus and Numbers | Numbers 33 | Deuteronomy |
|---|---|---|
| | Abronah | |
| | Ezion Geber | Ezion Geber (2:8) |
| Kadesh, Desert of Zin (20:1)/ Meribah (20:13) | Kadesh, Desert of Zin | |
| Mount Hor (20:22) | Mount Hor | Mount Hor (32:50)/(Moserah, 10:6) |
| | Zalmonah | |
| | Punon | |
| Oboth (21:10) | Oboth | |
| Iye Abarim (21:11) | Iye Abarim | |
| | Dibon Gad | |
| | Almon Diblathaim | |
| | Hills of Abarim | |
| Zered valley (21:12) | | Zered valley (2:13) |
| Arnon (21:13) | | Arnon (2:24) |
| Beer (21:16) | | |
| Mattanah (21:18) | | |
| Nahaliel (21:19) | | |
| Bamoth (21:19) | | |
| valley of Pisgah (21:20) | | Desert of Kedemoth (2:26) |
| Jahaz (21:23) | | Jahaz (2:32) |
| Jazer (21:32) | | |
| Edrei (21:33) | | Edrei (1:4; 3:1, 10) |
| Plains of Moab (22:1; 26:3) (Shittim 25:1) | Plains of Moab | Plains of Moab (1:5) |

Moreover, the reflections on these travels are not chronologically arranged in Deuteronomy. Beyond these comparisons, it is difficult to identify the location of many of the places, especially because of the continued uncertainty concerning the location of the sea crossing and Mount Sinai (see Sidebar 13-H in Chapter 13).

Numbers 34 presents the boundaries of the land of promise and explains how the land would be divided among the tribes. The actual land allotment is later narrated in Joshua 14–19. The tribe of Levi did not get a land allotment per se but received forty-eight towns spread throughout the land. Each Levite town was supposed to have

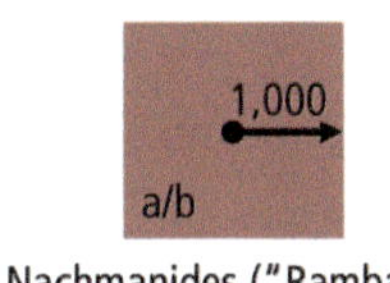

Nachmanides ("Ramban")

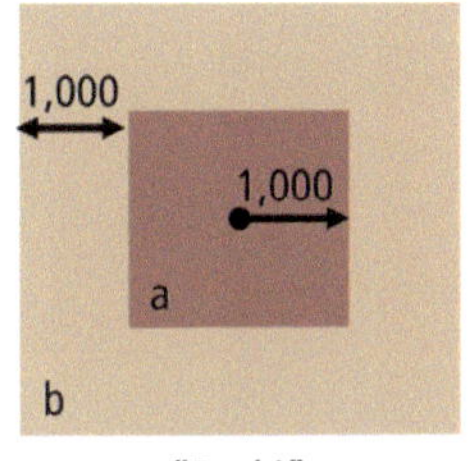

"Rashi"

2,000
1,000
a
b

Maimonides ("Rambam")

**Figure 23-H:** Traditional Judaic Views of the "Open Space" around Levite Towns (Num 35:4–5) a = open space; b = fields and vineyards; all measurements in cubits

open space around the outside for fields and vineyards, though the meaning of Numbers 35:4–5 is understood in various ways (see Figure 23-H, based on Scherman, 927; and see Rashi 4:465 [on Num 35:4]; Rashi's view is slightly preferred because it allows for the open space to expand if the town grows; also see Milgrom, 502–4). Of these, six were allocated as "cities of refuge," safe havens for persons involved in manslaughter or accidental killing.

The book of Numbers tells the story of the long travels of the Israelites through the wilderness. Why was the second generation allowed into the land? It had nothing to do with them. They were inclined to greater rebellion than their parents. The only answer is that Yahweh is gracious. His word provided a way. This book is the story of grace, surprising grace, that was there all along in the power of God's word.

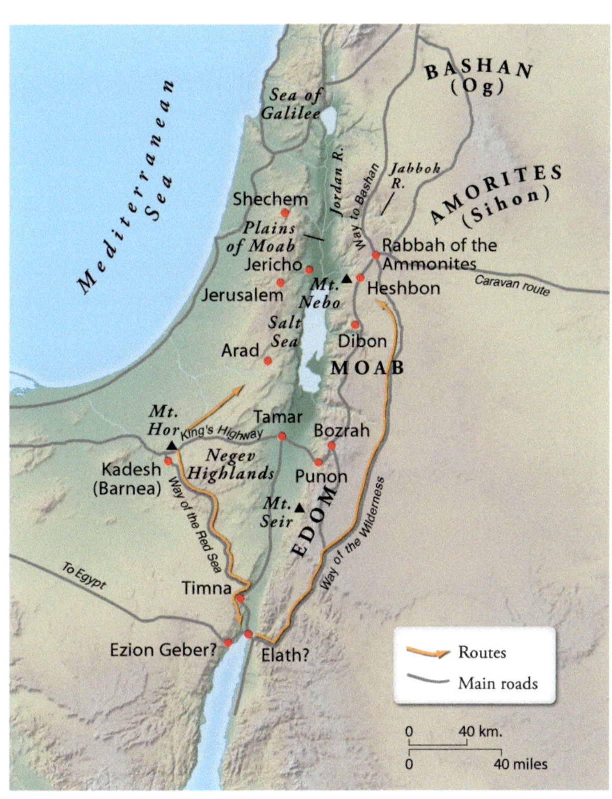


**Map 23-I:** The Geographical Setting of the Wilderness Journeys and the Transjordanian Military Campaigns

## ANOTHER LOOK

Phinehas is not the first zealot (though he is the first to be referred to as zealous). Four decades earlier, the Levites brought bloody retribution on thousands in Israel who had worshiped and immorally danced before the golden calf. Levi himself, along with his brother Simeon, had long before established his reputation as a sword-wielding vigilante when he helped avenge his sister's humiliation at Shechem by deceit and terror. The story of Phinehas, however, essentially sets out the paradigm for the zealot way, for those who wield the sword for God. Yahweh described him as "zealous" when he gave him a covenant of peace (Num 25:13).

David, in Psalm 69, sounds as if he belonged in the tradition of Phinehas, at least in the sense that the poem states "zeal for your house consumes me" (Ps 69:9; cf. vv. 24–26 = Num 25:16–17). Later the prophet Elijah, who had just overcome the prophets of Baal in a duel that ended in their slaughter, prayed, "I have been very zealous for Yahweh God Almighty" (1 Kgs 19:10a, 14a). Many aspects of the Elijah narrative echo the sounds of Psalm 69 (see Table 23-J). Even Elijah's protégé, Elisha, was chosen, in part, because he would be a prophet who killed for God (1 Kgs 19:17). Early Judaic writers observed the zealot tradition within the Hebrew Scriptures, especially in relation to Phinehas, David, and Elijah (see Sirach 45:23–25; 48:1–2; also see Kugel, 813–14).

| David | | Elijah |
|---|---|---|
| Ps 69:6–8 | the enemies of the psalmist and prophet | 1 Kgs 19:3–5 |
| 69:19–20 | the isolation and disdain of each | 19:10, 14 |
| 69:7 | covering the face | 19:13 |
| 69:13, 16 | "answer me . . . answer me" | 18:37 |

**Table 23-J:** Similarities between the Elijah Narratives and Psalm 69

The interplay between imagery associated with Phinehas may also be used in Malachi (see Zeron, 99). Note especially:

> "And you will know that I have sent you this warning so that my covenant with Levi may continue," says Yahweh Almighty. "*My covenant was with him, a covenant of life and peace*, and I gave them to him; this called for reverence and he revered me and stood in awe of my name. True instruction was in his mouth and nothing false was found on his lips. He walked with me in peace and uprightness, and turned many from sin." (Mal 2:4–6, emphasis added)

The mention of "true instruction" in this context may be compared to the mention of Levi teaching "your instruction" in Moses's blessing of Levi (Deut 33:10 lit.).

When Paul applied the term "zealous" to himself (it is also attributed to him in Acts), he was not classifying himself with the political activists known as zealots—Jewish political revolutionists seeking military uprising against Rome (some of whom were merely terrorists)—nor did he seem to be referring merely to an emotional-psychological assessment of his former religious devoutness.

> If someone else thinks they have reasons to put confident in the flesh, I have more: circumcised on the eighth day, of the people of Israel, of the tribe of Benjamin,

> a Hebrew of Hebrews; in regard to the law, a Pharisee; *as for zeal, persecuting the church*; as for righteousness based on the law, faultless. (Phil 3:4b–6)

> Then Paul said: "I am a Jew, born in Tarsus of Cilicia, but brought up in this city. I studied under Gamaliel and was thoroughly trained in the law of our ancestors. I was just as *zealous for God* as any of you are today. *I persecuted the followers of this Way* to their death, arresting both men and women and throwing them into prison, as the high priest and all the Council can themselves testify. I even obtained letters from them to their associates in Damascus, and went there to bring these people as prisoners to Jerusalem to be punished." (Acts 22:2c–5, emphasis added)

Paul was saying more than he was enthusiastic and less than he was seeking to overthrow Rome by force. Instead, he may have been aligning himself with the biblical tradition that stretched from Phinehas through David and Elijah.

## INTERACTIVE WORKSHOP

### *Chapter Summary*

The second generation faced their greatest challenge after they arrived on the plains of Moab. Yahweh delivered them from the threat of the Moabites, both external and internal, by the power of his word. After they were delivered, they prepared to enter the land of promise.

### *Can You Explain the Key Terms?*

- Balaam
- bless
- curse
- itinerary
- Phinehas
- zealous

### *Challenge Questions*

1. In what sense do the external threat of Numbers 22–24 and the internal threat of Numbers 25 mark the turning point of the book?
2. After Balaam failed to curse Israel, how did he continue to try to destroy them (include verse references to support your answer)?
3. What is the importance of Phinehas's act of obedience in Numbers 25?
4. What is the significance of the census of Numbers 26?
5. What are the social implications of the instruction concerning vows in Numbers 30?
6. What are the social implications of the ruling concerning Zelophehad's daughters (27:1–11; 36:1–13)?
7. What are the theological implications of the request of the two and a half tribes in Numbers 32 (see esp. vv. 1–15)?

## *Advanced Questions*

1. What are the possible problems with and solutions for evil prophets bringing forth the word of Yahweh? Compare 1 Kings 22:19–23 where God is said to have revealed lies to false prophets.
2. What is the significance of the prophetic expectations of Balaam that connect to promises to the Hebrew ancestors and the blessing of Judah in Genesis?
3. How did the reference to Moab in Numbers 24:17 get interpreted by Isaiah 25:10–12 and Jeremiah 48:45–46?
4. Why do Numbers 25:1 and 25:6 refer to Moabite *and* Midianite women?
5. Why are only forty stages included in the travel itinerary of Numbers 33, given the several other places mentioned elsewhere in the Torah (see Table 23-G)?
6. How should the geographical note regarding Aaron's death in Deuteronomy 10:6 be handled in light of Numbers 20:22–29; 33:37–39; and Deuteronomy 32:50?

*7. What is the symbolic theological significance of "zeal/zealous" (*qn'/qin'ah*) in light of its use in Numbers 25:11 and throughout the Hebrew Scriptures?

## *Research Project Ideas*

Compare Balaam's fourth oracle to the nations referred to in the primeval narrative (esp. Gen 9–11; Sailhamer 99–101).

Compare the treatment of the rebellion at Kadesh in Numbers 32:1–15 with the accounts in Numbers 13–14 and Deuteronomy 1:19–45 (Schnittjer, "Kadesh," 108).

Compare the travel itinerary of Numbers 33 with the geographical details in the parallel pentateuchal narratives (see Table 23-G).

## *The Next Step*


Aḥituv, Shmuel. *Echoes from the Past: Hebrew and Cognate Inscriptions from the Biblical Period.* Jerusalem: Carta, 2008.

Kugel, James L. *Traditions of the Bible: A Guide to the Bible As It Was at the Start of the Common Era.* Cambridge: Harvard University Press, 1998.

Milgrom, Jacob. *Numbers.* JPS Torah Commentary. Philadelphia: Jewish Publication Society, 1989.

Rashi (Rabbi Shlomo Yitzhaki). *The Metsudah Chumash/Rashi.* 5 vols. Ed. Rabbi Avrohom Davis. New York: Ktav, 1998.

Sailhamer, John. "Creation, Genesis 1–11, and the Canon." *Bulletin for Biblical Research* 10.1 (2000): 89–106.

Scherman, Nosson, ed. *The Chumash.* Brooklyn: Mesorah, 1994.

Schnittjer, Gary Edward. "The Blessing of Judah as Generative Expectation." *Bibliotheca Sacra* 177 (2020): 15–39.

———. "Kadesh Infidelity of Deuteronomy 1 and Its Synoptic Implications." *Journal of the Evangelical Theological Society* 63.1 (2020): 95–120.

Yamauchi, Edwin M. "Cultic Prostitution: A Case Study in Cultural Diffusion." Pages 211–22 in *Orient and Occident: Essays Presented to Cyrus H. Gordon on the Occasion of His Sixty-Fifth Birthday.* Edited by Harry A. Hoffner Jr. Neukirchener: Butzon & Berker, 1973.

Zeron, Alexander. "The Martyrdom of Phinehas-Elijah." *Journal of Biblical Literature* 98 (1979): 99–100.

# Deuteronomy

## THESE ARE THE WORDS

שמע ישראל יהוה אלהינו יהוה אחד

# 24 MACROVIEW OF DEUTERONOMY

A.D. Riddle/BiblePlaces.com

## GETTING STARTED

### *Focus Questions*

What are the key structural features of Deuteronomy? What are the literary signals the reader should notice to best hear this book?

### *Look for These Terms*

- the command
- headings
- Hittite suzerain-vassal treaty
- narrator
- next generation
- today
- transgenerational
- village economy
- voices
- you

## AN OUTLINE

A. **"These are the words" 1:1—the First Discourse (1:1–4:43)**

B. **"This is the torah" 4:44—the Second Discourse (4:44–28:68)**

1. "This is the torah"—the Ten Words (4:44–5:33)
2. "This is the command" 6:1—an exposition of the first word (6–11)
3. "These are the rules and the regulations" 12:1—an exposition of the other words (12–26)
4. The blessings and curses (27–28)

C. **"These are the words of the covenant" 29:1—the New Covenant and the Song of Moses (29–32)**

D. **"This is the blessing" 33:1—the Blessing and the Death of Moses (33–34)**

## A READING

The trick to reading Deuteronomy (traditionally known as "These Are the Words") is *knowing how* to hear what it is saying. It contains the words of life and death. How so? Some treatments of Deuteronomy reduce its theology to obey and be blessed or disobey and be cursed. Such a reduction is true, but it is not the whole truth.

Deuteronomy can be thought of as the story of the torah of God that Moses delivered to his people (see McConville, 36–38). The narrative refers to "the book of the torah" within it (Deut 31:26). Deuteronomy shares characteristics with sermon, covenant, and law collections. The similarities between the Mosaic covenant and ancient Hittite treaty forms require consideration.

Deuteronomy shares many elements in common with ancient Hittite suzerain-vassal (ruler-subject) treaties (second millennium BCE) as well as featuring some differences (see Table 14-H in Chapter 14; cf. Barré 6:655; Moskala and Masotti, 76–82; and on the curses of Deut 28 see Quick, 179–82). But such a suggestion raises a question: How would Moses or Israel be exposed to Hittite treaty forms?

Hittite copy of treaty between Hattušili and Rameses II (1259 BCE)

*BearFotos/ Shutterstock.com*

Johnston collates several findings to show that Moses and Israel were in the right place at the right time. In 1259 BCE the Hittite ruler Hattušili sent the Silver Treaty Tablet to Rameses II in Pi-Rameses. This is one of the very cities Israel worked on in their forced labor (Exod 1:11). Several versions of the treaty were read aloud publicly in Egypt as well as displayed at the temple of Amon in Karnak. A careful reading of Rameses's letters to Hattušili about public reading and public display of the treaty throughout Egypt, especially letter 3, suggests how Israel could have become aware of Hittite treaty form. Though the Hittite treaty form may have been known some other way, this evidence corresponds to the place Israel worked at the time of their redemption (Johnston, "What"; Johnston, "Writing," 93–99).

Some say Deuteronomy is a "sermon patterned after a treaty" (Grisanti 2:462–63). To speak of Deuteronomy as a sermon gets at the motivation running throughout the entire book. These different elements need to be summarized in a way that gets at how Deuteronomy works.

The purpose of the Deuteronomy story is to explain Torah. It explains Torah by means of motivation to encourage Yahweh's people to faith and obedience. Considering both of these elements can show how Deuteronomy works.

The narrator says of the entire book that "Moses began to explain the Torah"

(Deut 1:5 lit.). Although some interpreters try to limit "the Torah" to the laws in chapters 12–26, the evidence suggests it refers to the narratives, motivation, and laws. Just as Deuteronomy 1–4 are narratives at the opening of the book, the next section features a heading "this is the Torah Moses set before Israel" in 4:44 and then begins with story. The long section of motivation in chapters 6–11 that begins with Yahweh commanding Moses to teach Israel in 6:1 also includes stories. These headings (1:5; 4:44; and 6:1) and the stories that follow in each case demonstrate that Moses's explanation of the Torah in Deuteronomy includes narratives and law (see Schnittjer, "Kadesh," 104, n. 35). Torah shapes the identity of readers by story and command.

*What is included in the Torah Moses explains in Deuteronomy?*

The stories and laws of Deuteronomy are both infused with motivation. It may be helpful to illustrate the different kind of motive clauses typical of laws in Leviticus compared to laws of Deuteronomy. Notice the motive clauses in bold (see Schnittjer, *OT*, 87–88).

> Do not go over your vineyard a second time or pick up the grapes that have fallen. Leave them for the poor and the foreigner. **I am Yahweh your God**. (Lev 19:10)

> When you harvest the grapes in your vineyard, do not go over the vines again. Leave what remains for the foreigner, the fatherless and the widow. **Remember that you were slaves in Egypt. That is why I command you to do this**. (Deut 24:21–22)

Leviticus often grounds motivation for laws in the self-declaration of Yahweh's identity such as "I am Yahweh" or "I am Yahweh your God." Deuteronomy frequently motivates by grounding Israel's identity in the redemptive narrative (appearing sometimes in Exod and Lev). As noted above, "Remember that you were slaves in Egypt. That is why I command you to do this." This shows that redemption leads to obedience, not the other way around. An important example of redemption before law with motivation is located in the parental answer to the youthful question of the meaning of the commands in Deuteronomy 6:20–25. The student will do well to look for motivation interwoven throughout Deuteronomy.

*What kind of motivation does Moses use in Deuteronomy?*

The people stand on the threshold between two worlds. Moses delivers three speeches, looking back and looking ahead. The story ends with his death. The book, and thus the entire Torah, is an exilic and forward looking story. The narrated speeches are pulled between Yahweh's fulfillment of his word to the Hebrew ancestors and the sinfulness of the Israelites.

The use of headings in Deuteronomy signals its macrostructure (see Olson, 14–17). The four main sections begin with these headings: "These are the words" (1:1); "This is

Looking across the plains of Moab and the northern end of the Dead Sea toward Jericho
*A.D. Riddle/ BiblePlaces.com*

the torah" (4:44); "These are the terms of the covenant" (29:1); and "This is the blessing" (33:1). The important second section is the longest.

The first section ("These are the words") sets the speeches, the final words of Moses, on the plains of Moab between the wilderness and the land of promise, just beyond the Jordan River. This first discourse is largely a retrospective theological interpretation of the first four books of the Torah. It puts a new perspective on the Torah.

The second discourse ("This is the torah") contains the soul of the book and comprises several sections. The story of the Ten Words constitutes the first section. After a brief introduction, Deuteronomy 5 tells the story of the giving of the Ten Words as a covenant, surprisingly not to their parents "but with us, all of us who are alive here today" (5:3). This present-tense orientation ("today") is no mere word game to make the instruction vivid, although it does, but it provides one of the theological clues for reading the book. The story of the Ten Words is followed by the three other sections of the discourse that relate directly to it (see Figure 24-A). The story of the Ten Words unfolds with precedent-setting exposition.

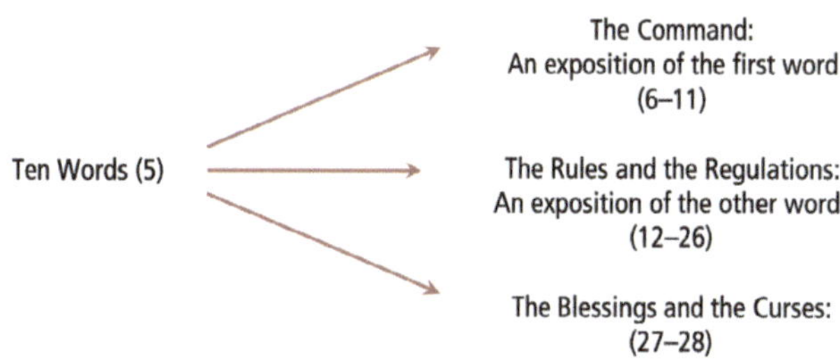


**Figure 24-A:** The Structure of the Second Discourse in Deuteronomy 5–28

The three sections that occupy Deuteronomy 6–11, 12–26, and 27–28 are the command, the rules and regulations (also known as the torah collection), and the blessings and the curses. Notice how these subheadings divide the discourse: "This is the command, the rules and the regulations" and "These are the rules and regulations" (6:1a; 12:1a lit.). The headings in 6:1 and 12:1 tell the reader that chapters 6–11 offer an exposition of the command, and chapters 12–26 an exposition of the rules and regulations. The command is an explanation of the first of the Ten Words: "Hear, O Israel: Yahweh our God, Yahweh is one. Love Yahweh your God with all your heart and with all your soul and with all your strength" (6:4–5). This command has been recognized universally as the great command to which all other commands are related. Deuteronomy 12–26 provides an exposition of the other words. The blessings and the curses (chs. 27–28) prescribe the consequences of listening to or rejecting the instruction.

The third section ("These are the words of the covenant," 29:1 lit.) explains the manner in which the covenant will shape the destiny of the people. This is not the Sinai covenant that Moses has been talking about all day (chs. 1–28) but rather a covenant "*in addition to* the covenant he had made with them at Horeb" (29:1, emphasis added). This new covenant situates the story of the Hebrew kingdom, the exile, and the anticipated restoration in relation to God's word. The new covenant, along with the blessings and curses of Leviticus 26 and Deuteronomy 27–28, provides the rationale for and ultimate ends of the people in God's plan. The language of the new covenant memorably lays out two paths that stretch before the listener/reader, namely, life and death. The reader faces the same kind of choice that Adam and Eve faced in the garden at the front end of the Torah—the tree of life or the tree of the knowing of good and evil, along with the life or death that the respective trees promised partakers. Moses explains that the new covenant places life and death before the listener. He urges Israel, with the heavens and earth as witnesses, to choose life.

The new covenant is followed by the passing of Moses's leadership to Joshua and to the Torah scroll, which in turn leads naturally to the Song of Moses. The song, which Moses received from Yahweh in some sense, poetically reflects across the Torah story as a whole, offering one of the most significant interpretations of the story ever written. It also includes expectation of the ultimate ends of God's people and humankind—ideals that, in later biblical revelation, developed into what have come to be called hell and heaven.

The final section ("This is the blessing," 33:1) formally resembles the closing of Genesis. Moses, like Jacob before his death, pronounces blessing on the families of Israel. The poetic blessing is followed by a brief account of Moses's death and the hope for the coming of a prophet like Moses. The hope expressed by the closing verses reaches back to Moses's prediction that a prophet like himself will one day rise. This prediction in Deuteronomy 18 is based, in turn, on the selection of Moses as mediator in the story of the Ten Words in chapter 5, which retells the story of Exodus 20. The creation of the nation in Exodus 19–20 echoes the sounds of creation in the opening of the Torah. The Torah ends as it began, awaiting the creative, life-giving power of God's word—this time, as before, through a new prophet like Moses.

Several distinctive features run across every section of Deuteronomy. First, the relationships of the major teachings, especially the covenant, the command, the word of God, and life, are of foremost importance in hearing Deuteronomy in the right manner.

It has often been noted (so often that it is almost a truism in some circles) that the essence of Deuteronomic theology can be understood as a covenant relationship that elaborates blessing for obedience and curses for disobedience. Is this reading of Deuteronomy correct? That depends. It depends on whether the obey-blessings and disobey-curses model is regarded as the entire affair or a part, albeit an important part, of a larger program for blessing and life. It is easy to agree that Deuteronomy teaches of specific and far-reaching consequences attached to its teachings—they are the blessings and curses. If, however, the book is effectively reduced to this principle of reward and retribution, it becomes a distortion of the instruction and an error.

Deuteronomy teaches the principle of covenantal reward and retribution within a larger understanding of the relationship between Yahweh and his people. Its teaching might be better summarized as "Love God in order to live and obey" (see Figure 24-B).

*Why is it too narrow to say that the theology of Deuteronomy is simply blessing for obedience and punishment for disobedience?*

circumcision of the heart ⟶ love God ⟶ (true) obedience ⟶ blessing and life

**Figure 24-B:** The Path to Blessing and Life according to Deuteronomy

The shorthand for the command is "love God" (6:4–9). This command is the basis of any true obedience and is thus basic to the kind of obedience that leads to life. Obedience that is not based on love for God is not obedience at all. It is hypocrisy. The command to love God is a cause of obedience, but it is also caused. It is the effect of the circumcision of the heart in the new covenant (30:6; see Another Look in Chapter 19). Therefore, while "love God" comes before the kind of obedience that brings life and blessing, something comes before loving God—a work of Yahweh in the heart. This instruction, according to the Torah itself, is "the word" that is near you (30:11–14), the word that brings life beyond physical life (8:3). The instruction of the Instruction—that is, the torah of the Torah—is the beginning of the gospel (see Chapter 28). This instruction is not too hard; it is in your mouth when you teach it—the Torah—to the next generation (see 6:6–9; 30:11, 14).

*What is the basis of true obedience?*

Second, Deuteronomy constantly addresses itself to "you." The second-person pronoun *you* in English can refer either to *you* personally or to *you* collectively as a group. In Deuteronomy the use of *you* is mixed between singular and plural throughout, indicating that personal responsibility and collective identity are closely bound together. Ancient authors commonly used grammatical interchange within their writings, as can be seen in ancient Hittite, Aramaic, and Hebrew documents (Schnittjer, "Say You," n. 5). Furthermore, the direct address in Deuteronomy to "you" takes on a timeless quality or, better, a present force to every reader in light of the many generations spoken to in the book.

Consider the elasticity across time of the reference of "you" in the following context:

> When all these blessings and curses I have set before *you* come upon *you* and *you* take them to heart wherever Yahweh your God disperses *you* among the nations, and when *you and your children* return to Yahweh your God and obey him with all *your* heart and with all *your* soul according to everything I command *you today*, then Yahweh *your* God will restore *your fortunes* and have compassion on *you* and gather *you* again from all the nations where he scattered *you*. Even if *you* have been banished to the most distant land under the heavens, from there Yahweh *your* God will gather *you* and bring *you* back. He will bring *you* to the land that belonged to *your ancestors*, and *you* will take possession of it. He will make *you* more prosperous and numerous than *your ancestors*. (30:1–5, emphasis added)

The rhetorical force of this context stretches the referentiality of "you" across centuries from the days of Moses to exile to return.

"You" refers to those listening to Moses "today" (see 5:1–3) and to the much later descendants who will one day realize the fullness of the promise on the other side of the exile. Moreover, the reference to "your ancestors," which typically refers either to the ancestors in Genesis or to the first generation of wilderness travelers, here refers to the people who will live between the conquest under Joshua through the fall of Jerusalem, including the original addressees standing before Moses. The book is written in a way that puts together original readers and later readers—across hundreds of years—to hear the selfsame message.

The point here concerns the context in which to read Deuteronomy. Specifically, this book defies interpretations that seek to relate the book merely to the second generation of wilderness travelers. If we take the use of "you" seriously, we should read the book as speaking directly to a transgenerational readership spanning the last days of Moses to the exile and beyond.

Third, the reader's application of Deuteronomy's instruction targets the next generation. In many, if not most, North American Christian contexts, participants define their religious devotion in terms related to their own personal lives. How we ourselves are doing religiously is not, according to Deuteronomy, an adequate measurement of how we are doing. The teachings of this book look toward the next generation. Readers are instructed to teach the commands to their children everywhere, all the time (6:6–9). This certainly applies to the reader's biological offspring. This notion also signifies the generation that follows more generally. If one wishes to measure the success of one's own or the community's religious devotion, the standard of measurement must be the generation that comes after. The next generation is, among other things, the target for devotion to Yahweh.

*How is the next generation related to one's own religious devotion?*

## ANOTHER LOOK

The authorship of Deuteronomy, at least the book as we now have it, has been much discussed, and rightly so. The book begins by talking about Moses in the third person, and it regularly returns to this reporting voice. The discourses themselves, however, largely refer to Moses in the first person. Within Deuteronomy 1–11 no other character speaks except Moses. All other voices are transmitted by Moses (Robson, 4). Moreover, Deuteronomy refers to Moses's writing the book (31:9, 24). On the surface, then, the book sounds as if it has three main voices: the reporting voice that here is called the "narrator" for ease of discussion; the voice of Moses; and the voice of Yahweh (another voice is Moses with the elders and the priests in Deut 27).

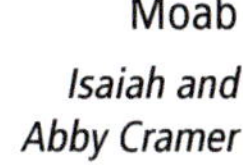

Moab
*Isaiah and Abby Cramer*

The reader who is a careful listener will quickly learn to hear the voices in Deuteronomy. Table 24-C presents Robert Polzin's list of the sixty-four verses he regards as the narrator's voice (Polzin, 29; also see Block, 392, n. 40). The verses are arranged according to the outline at the beginning of the chapter. The narrator's verses are often placed in parentheses, effectively setting them off from the rest of the text, in standard English translations such as the NIV and the NRSVue.

| The narrator's reporting context includes the following verses: |
|---|
| 1:1–5; 2:10–12, 20–23; 3:9, 11, 13b–14 |
| 4:41–5:1a; 10:6–9; 27:1a, 9a, 11 |
| 29:1;[a] 29:2a;[b] 31:1, 7a, 9–10a, 14a, 14c–16a, 22–23a, 24–25, 30; 32:44–45, 48 |
| 33:1; 34:1–4a, 5–12. |
| **The narrator reports God's words in direct discourse in the following verses:** |
| 31:14b, 16b–21, 23b; 32:49–52; 34:4b. |

**Table 24-C:** The Proposed Narrator of Deuteronomy

[a]Deut 29:1 in the English Bible is 28:69 in the Hebrew Bible.

[b]Deut 29:2a in the English Bible is 29:1a in the Hebrew Bible.

The narrator introduces all the material in Deuteronomy, including each of the discourses, and frequently inserts commentary to assist readers. That is, the narrator sounds as if he is at some distance from the time of Moses. The frequent updates the narrator provides put a natural distance between the final speeches of Moses and the hearing of those speeches by later Torah readers. Consider a few examples (emphases added).

> Horites used to live in Seir, but the descendants of Esau drove them out. They destroyed the Horites from before them and settled in their place, *just as Israel did in the land Yahweh gave them as a possession*. (2:12)

> Yahweh had done the same for the descendants of Esau, who lived in Seir, when he destroyed the Horites from before them. They drove them out and have lived in their place *to this day*. (2:22)

> Jair, a descendant of Manasseh, took the whole region of Argob as far as the border of the Geshurites and the Maacathites; it was named after him, so that *to this day* Bashan is called Havvoth Jair. (3:14)

The narrator explains things to the readership from a vantage point long after the conquest (as one can see from 2:12 cited above).

Should we accept the book at face value—Moses's speeches placed in the context of this book by the narrator? Or, is it not what it seems? Is the narrator's voice a literary device, used by Moses himself, to put distance and objectivity between himself and his own book? These two options can be refined further—and there are others—but this is enough for now. The preferred view here is to read Deuteronomy in a straightforward manner. Yahweh gave his word in many ways—in this case through Moses and through a later narrator. The narrator and Moses guide the reader.

*Why is the question of the "narrator" of Deuteronomy not directly related to the issues of authority or inspiration of the book?*

Important work on dating the contents of Deuteronomy comes from Sandra Richter. She synthesizes economic data in the main middle section of Deuteronomy (4:44–27:26) and collates this against a series of archaeological studies of the hill country of Israel. The dominant economics of the book do not point to a centralized government with king and temple but to rural village economy. This sets the economic profile of the teachings of Deuteronomy at a time before economics of king and temple reconfigured Israel with centralized economic structures (Richter, "Question" 2017, 23–50, esp. 47–50; Richter, "Question," 2020, 547–66, esp. 562–65; Richter, "What's?," 313–16). In this way, the economic profile of the teachings of Deuteronomy largely corresponds to taking the book in a straightforward manner.

The economic evidence compiled by Richter may be considered in the light of the possible mediation of the Hittite suzerain-vassal treaty form in Pi-Rameses in the mid-thirteenth century BCE as discussed in the opening of this Chapter (see Johnston, "What"; Johnston, "Writing," 71–99; cf. Table 14-H in Chapter 14). Both of these lines of evidence corroborate a straightforward reading of the text.

I invite the new apprentice of the Torah not to get too agitated by these matters.

They are important issues, especially for those who read the Scriptures as God's word. They are, however, not new. Critical and evangelical scholars alike have discussed these things for many years. Any reader, but particularly a believer, should be open and honest about what the biblical writings say. It has always been as it is now. I urge you to take your time and carefully read Deuteronomy for yourself. The goal is not to beat your theological opponents but to hear, really hear, the word of God.

## INTERACTIVE WORKSHOP

### *Chapter Summary*

Deuteronomy presents the last words of Moses as he spoke to the people of Israel on the plains of Moab. This book has several distinctive features that shape the way readers need to hear it, which include *the command* as foundational, the next generation as present responsibility, and special use of "you" and "today."

### *Can You Explain the Key Terms?*

- the command
- headings
- Hittite suzerain-vassal treaty
- narrator
- next generation
- today
- transgenerational
- village economy
- voices
- you

### *Challenge Questions*

1. How is Deuteronomy related to the rest of the Torah?
2. What are the major structural features of Deuteronomy?
3. What is the meaning of *the* command?
4. What is the significance of teaching the Torah to the next generation?

### *Advanced Questions*

1. What is the significance of the transgenerational use of "you" in Deuteronomy?
2. Whose voice represents the controlling ideological viewpoint of Deuteronomy? What are the issues in evaluating the significance of this question?
3. The "narrator" attempts to represent Moses as the great prophet, a spokesperson for God. What is the significance of passages that affirm the permanence of Moses's message when compared to the narrator's interpretations of these teachings (see texts in Table 24-C)? How can one approach Deuteronomy in light of Deuteronomy as interpretation—a putting in perspective—of the teachings of Moses and the command within the book not to add to it (see 4:2; 12:32)?

*4. What is the range of meaning of *torah* within the context of Deuteronomy?

## *Research Project Ideas*

Explain the function of the interchange between second-person singular and second-person plural throughout Deuteronomy (see Schnittjer, "Say You"; Grisanti, 2:486).

Evaluate the debates concerning the authorship and dating of Deuteronomy (see Block, 385–408; Richter, "Question" 2017, 23–50; Johnston, "What"; Johnston, "Writing," 71–99).

## *The Next Step*


Barré, Michael L. "Treaties in the ANE." Pages 653–56 in vol. 6 of *Anchor Bible Dictionary*. Edited by David Noel Freedman. New York: Doubleday, 1992.

Block, Daniel I. "Recovering the Voice of Moses: The Genesis of Deuteronomy." *Journal of the Evangelical Theological Society* 44.3 (2001): 385–408.

Grisanti, Michael A. "Deuteronomy." Pages 457–814 in vol. 2 of *Expositor's Bible Commentary*. Rev. ed. Grand Rapids: Zondervan Academic, 2012.

Johnston, Gordon. "What Biblical Scholars Should Know about Hittite Treaties." In *TORAH: Treaty, Law, and Ritual in the Hebrew Bible in Its Ancient Near Eastern Environment*. Edited by David C. Deuel et al. Bulletin for Biblical Research Supplement Series. University Park, PA: Pennsylvania State University Press, forthcoming [2023].

———. "The Writing/Reading/Hearing of the Stone Tablet Covenant in the Light of the Writing/Reading/Hearing of the Silver Tablet Treaty." Pages 71–99 in *Write That They May Read: Studies in Literacy and Textualization in the Ancient Near East and in the Hebrew Scripture, Essays in Honour of Professor Alan R. Millard*. Edited by Daniel I. Block. Eugene, OR: Pickwick, 2020.

McConville, J. G. *Deuteronomy*. Apollos Old Testament Commentary. Leicester: Apollos, 2002.

Moskala, Jiří and Felipe A. Masotti. "The Hittite Treaty Prologue Tradition and the Literary Structure of the Book of Deuteronomy." Pages 73–94 in *Exploring the Composition of the Pentateuch*. Edited by L. S. Baker, Jr., et al. University Park, PA: Eisenbrauns, 2020.

Olson, Dennis T. *Deuteronomy and the Death of Moses: A Theological Reading*. Minneapolis: Fortress, 1994.

Polzin, Robert. *Moses and the Deuteronomist: A Literary Study of the Deuteronomic History*. New York: Seabury, 1980.

Quick, Laura. *Deuteronomy 28 and the Aramaic Curse Tradition*. New York: Oxford University Press, 2018.

Richter, Sandra Lynn. "The Question of Provenance and the Economics of Deuteronomy." *Journal for the Study of the Old Testament* 42.1 (2017): 23–50.

———. "The Question of Provenance and the Economics of Deuteronomy: The Neo-Babylonian and Persian Periods." *Catholic Biblical Quarterly* 82 (2020): 547–66.

———. "What's Money Got to Do with It?: Economics and the Question of the Provenance of Deuteronomy in the Neo-Babylonian and Persian Periods." Pages 301–21 in *Paradigm Change in Pentateuchal Research*. Edited by Matthias Armgardt, Benjamin Kilchör, and Markus Zehnder. Beihefte zur Zeitschrift für Altorientalische und Biblische Rechtsgeschichte 22. Wiesbaden: Harrassowitz Verlag, 2019.

Robson, James E. *Deuteronomy 1–11*. Baylor Handbook on the Hebrew Bible. Waco: Baylor University Press, 2016.

Schnittjer, Gary Edward. "Kadesh Infidelity of Deuteronomy 1 and Its Synoptic Implications." *Journal of the Evangelical Theological Society* 63.1 (2020): 95–120.

———. *Old Testament Use of Old Testament*. Grand Rapids: Zondervan Academic, 2021.

———. "Say You, Say Ye: Individual and Collective Identity and Responsibility in Torah." *Center for Hebraic Thought* (2022) https://hebraicthought.org/individual-collective-identity-responsibility-torah/.

# 25 THE WORDS
## *Deuteronomy 1:1–4:43*



## GETTING STARTED

### *Focus Question*

In what ways does Moses's discourse in Deuteronomy 1–4 reinterpret the creation, exodus, and wilderness narratives?

### *Look for These Terms*

- as tall as the Anakites
- Horeb
- judges and elders
- motivation
- Rephaites
- your eyes (your hearing)

## AN OUTLINE

A. **Heading (1:1–5)**
B. **Retrospective—the journey from Horeb to Moab (1:6–3:29)**
  1. Resuming the journey (1:6–8)
  2. Shared leadership (1:9–18)
  3. The death of the old and the birth of the new (1:19–46)
  4. Israel among the nations (2:1–25)
  5. Remembering the victories over Sihon and Og (2:26–3:29)
C. **Exhortation to observe God's instruction (4:1–40)**
D. **The cities of refuge (4:41–43)**

## A READING

Deuteronomy opens with "These are the words"—the traditional name of the book—which serves as the heading both for the first discourse of Moses and for the entire book. The first five verses set up the book's story: Moses explains Torah. Moses proclaims his last words to the Israelites on the plains of Moab, the wilderness behind and the land of promise across the Jordan River. His first discourse is a commentary of sorts on the entire narrative of Genesis through Numbers—the Torah story that forms the basis of the covenant and the instructions that Moses delivers to the people.

The people stood on the threshold between the wilderness and Canaan. The narrator describes the path that has led to this moment in ironic dimensions. "(*It takes eleven days* to go from Horeb to Kadesh Barnea by the Mount Seir road.) *In the fortieth year* . . ." (1:2–3a, emphasis added). The parents and grandparents of these people had stood at another threshold to the same land listening to the report of the twelve scouts. That entry point was less than two weeks of travel distance from Mount Horeb, yet they are still outside the land four decades later. The eleven-day path that required a forty-year journey explains many aspects of the identity of the listeners within the story itself. Those listeners forty years of age and under have known only the wilderness. Egypt and Canaan are places they have heard of, places that have framed their homeless travels.

Mount Horeb (Mount Sinai)
*David Bivin/ BiblePlaces.com*

Moses begins his series of speeches by reflecting on what God said when it was time to leave Horeb (the mountain usually called Sinai in Exodus through Numbers is called Horeb in Deuteronomy). Yahweh called the people to lay claim to the land he had promised their ancestors. The land was theirs because of the power of his word to Abraham, Isaac, and Jacob.

Moses explains the leadership structure that was established at the time they departed from Mount Horeb. The event Moses refers to resembles the accounts in Exodus 18 and Numbers 11. At first blush they sound like two different stories about the same or similar things. There is no clear solution even after comparing details. Still, the context of Deuteronomy 1:9–18 invites readers to look back at these two events (see Table 25-A). Moses had something more in mind than a nostalgic walk down memory lane.

? *Why does the instruction concerning the appointment of judges serve as an invitation to reconsider the teachings of Exodus 18 and Numbers 11?*

If the account of establishing judges in Exodus 18 focused on how the law instructs and reforms the people, and if Numbers 11 indicted Moses and the people for complaining, the emphasis on judges in Deuteronomy 1 gets at something else. Moses underscores the need to protect the vulnerable party to ensure justice.

| Exodus 18 | Numbers 11 | Deuteronomy 1 |
|---|---|---|
| Moses complained to his father-in-law | Moses complained to God | Moses complained to the people |
| Jethro suggested appointing judges over thousands, hundreds, fifties, and tens | God distributed the spirit that was on Moses among the seventy elders | Moses suggested appointing judges and placed them over thousands, hundreds, fifties, and tens |
| at Sinai | at Kibroth Hattaavah ("Graves of Craving") | at Horeb |

**Table 25-A:** Three Accounts of Establishing Judges and/or Elders

> And I charged your judges at that time, "Hear the disputes between your people and judge fairly, whether the case is between two Israelites *or between an Israelite and a foreigner residing among you*. Do not show partiality in judging; *hear both small and great alike*. Do not be afraid of anyone, for judgment belongs to God. Bring me any case too hard for you, and I will hear it." (Deut 1:16–17, emphasis added)

Moses sets human judgment within the framework of divine justice when he says: "Do not be afraid of anyone, for judgment belongs to God." Moses begins his explanation of torah by emphasizing God's requirement of justice for all people.

"You shall appoint judges for each of your [city] gates" (Deut 16:18 lit.).

City gate of ancient Dan (mid-eighteenth century BCE).

The clash between the sinful people and the word of God comes to the fore through the latter half of Deuteronomy 1. The collision centers on the interpretive retelling of the rebellion of the first generation at Kadesh. This retelling focuses on the death of the old and birth of the new generation, with a twist.

Numbers 13–14 tells of the rebellion at Kadesh focusing on the people collectively in a rapid overview fashion. Part of the purpose of framing the rebellion as such in Numbers is explaining why the older generation was condemned to wander and die in the desert. But the retelling in Deuteronomy 1 leaves no room for anyone in Israel to blame their problems on mass hysteria.

Deuteronomy 1:19–45 focuses on individual responsibility and methodical premeditated revolution. The story does not focus on the crowds listening to the report of the scouts as in Numbers. Moses takes the congregation and readers into Israel's private quarters. "You grumbled in your tents and said, *'Yahweh hates us; so he brought us out of Egypt to deliver us into the hands of the Amorites to destroy us'*" (1:27, emphasis added). The attack of the people was directed at Yahweh's goodness. They accepted that he was powerful and had redeemed them from Egypt, but they reinterpreted his intentions as vindictive and destructive (the role of deceptive imagination is discussed in Another Look of Chapter 22).

If the people standing before Moses were looking for someone to blame, Moses removes the force of their argument by getting personal. He identifies the problem as an individual, methodical rebellion. Moses makes clear that lust for revolution against the will of Yahweh begins in the privacy of one's own tent (Schnittjer, "Kadesh," 105–15). The congregation before Moses and the readers of Deuteronomy need to be warned against private meditations that breed unfaithfulness (ibid., 120).

The surprise for us as readers is that Moses deflects from himself the blame for his own judgment. He claims, repeatedly, that he was forbidden from entering the land because of the people (see Another Look below).

Petra in Edom
*iStock.com/Aurelie1*

Deuteronomy 2 and 3 retell, from a different perspective, many of the events presented in Numbers 20–21 and 31–32 (see Tigay, 422–27). The arrangement of material is different, and some things appear in different chronological sequence. Some of the differences are in point of view. For example, whereas Numbers focused on Edom's refusal to let Israel travel through their land (Num 20:14–21), Moses's review in Deuteronomy emphasizes God's blessing on Israel and the need to remain at peace with the descendants of Esau (Deut 2:2–8).

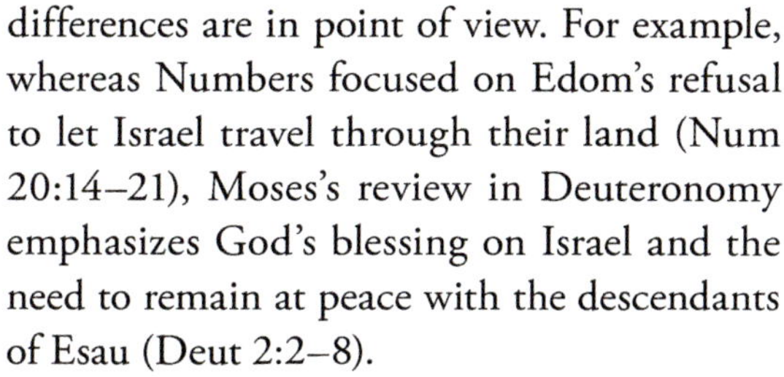

Red Sea at Elat (cf. Deut 2:1)
*iStock.com/miljko*

The focus on the other nations, especially the relatives of Israel, denotes how similar they are to Israel in many respects (see Mann, 30–33). Compare the parallels between the Moabites, Edomites, Israelites, and Ammonites relative to their respective lands.

> Then Yahweh said to me, "Do not harass the Moabites or provoke them to war, for I will not give you *any part of their land. I have given Ar to the descendants of Lot as a possession*." (The Emites used to live there—a people strong and numerous, and as tall as the Anakites. Like the Anakites, they too were considered Rephaites, but the Moabites called them Emites. Horites used to live in Seir, *but the descendants of Esau drove them out. They destroyed the Horites from before them and settled in their place, just as Israel did in the land Yahweh gave them as their possession*). (2:9–12)

> Yahweh said to me . . . "When you come to the Ammonites, do not harass them or provoke them to war, for I will not give you possession of *any land belonging to the Ammonites. I have given it as a possession to the descendants of Lot*." (That too was considered a land of the Rephaites, who used to live there; but the Ammonites called them Zamzummites. They were a people strong and numerous, and as tall as the Anakites. *Yahweh destroyed them from before the Ammonites*, who drove them out and settled in their place. *Yahweh had done the same for the descendants of Esau, who lived in Seir, when he destroyed the Horites from before them*. They drove them out and have lived in their place to this day.) (2:17, 19–22, emphasis added to both contexts)

Perhaps the parenthetical notations provided by the narrator can be thought of as the heightening of Edom, Moab, and Ammon and the diminishment of Israel's status to a certain degree.

The Ammonites and Moabites drove out the Rephaites. The Rephaites were large like the Anakites, and the large stature of the Anakites was a key factor in Israel's unbelief at Kadesh in Numbers 13–14 (see von Rad, 42–43). Israel needed to catch up to the Ammonites and Moabites in this sense. The only Israelites that the biblical text credits with defeating giant people were Moses, Joshua, Caleb, David, and their respective associates (see Table 22-E in Chapter 22). Is this a clue that Israel's God was with the hated enemies of Israel? How could they defeat Anakite-like people without faith? While the text invites these questions, they are not followed by answers. The implied questions are suggestive. Yahweh is the God of Israel and of the other nations. Moreover, it seems that Yahweh's special relationship with Abraham's descendants was in no way evidence that he had given up on other peoples, even the enemies of Israel.

*What are the possible significances of the focus on the Edomites, Moabites, and Ammonites in Deuteronomy 2 and 3?*

After the retrospective presentation in Deuteronomy 1–3, chapter 4 turns toward exhortation. This distinction does not mean that there are no further reflections; rather, the interpretations of the acts of Yahweh are of a different sort. The series of allusions to Yahweh's mighty acts are presented in a context overflowing with motivation. Nearly two-thirds of Moses's exhortation is motivation (see Table 25-B; cf. Chapter 24).

**Table 25-B:** Motivation and Retelling Mighty Actions in Deuteronomy 4[a]

| | | |
|---|---|---|
| **13 verses:** | Retrospective allusions to Yahweh's mighty works | Deut 4:10–12, 13, 14, 15, 32, 33, 34–35, 36, 37, 38 |
| **23 verses:** | Sermonic motivation | Deut 4:5–9, 16–31, 39–40 |

[a]Table based on Schnittjer, *OT*, 98.

Yahweh's people are unique because the acts of their God—creation, redemption, revelation, defeat of the Transjordanian kingdoms—are unique. Moses asked, "*What other nation* is so great as to have their gods near them the way Yahweh our God is near us whenever we pray to him? *And what other nation* is so great as to have such righteous decrees and laws as this body of laws I am setting before you today?" (4:7–8, emphasis added).

This motivation-filled challenge to the people presents allusions to events from Genesis through Numbers. One basis for the instruction to remain loyal to Yahweh alone is the historical event at Mount Horeb. Notice how the creational design from Genesis is enfolded into the revelation at the mountain:

> You saw no form of any kind the day Yahweh spoke to you at Horeb out of the fire. Therefore watch yourselves very carefully, so that you do not become corrupt and make for yourselves an idol, an image of any shape, whether *formed like a man or a woman, or like any animal on earth or any bird that flies in the air, or like any creature that moves along the ground or any fish in the waters below.* (4:15–18, emphasis added)

In the midst of this challenge based on Yahweh's actions, an incredible shift takes place. In one sense it is so subtle that some readers may not see it. Yet this context is among the most important in all Scripture regarding the power and function of the Scriptures. Note the merger of "the former days" and "you" hearing and seeing.

> *Ask now about the former days, long before your time*, from the day God created human beings on the earth; ask from one end of the heavens to the other. Has anything so great as this ever happened, or has anything like it ever been heard of? Has any other people *heard the voice of God speaking out of fire, as you have*, and lived? Has any god ever tried to take for himself one nation out of another nation, by testings, by signs and wonders, by war, by a mighty hand and an outstretched arm, or by great and awesome deeds, *like all the things Yahweh your God did for you in Egypt before your very eyes*? (4:32–34, emphasis added)

None of the people hearing this had been held responsible for what God had done for their parents. The older generation saw and heard these things. Although some listening to Moses were children during the exodus and revelation at Horeb, most of the congregation was born later in the desert.

But they really did "see" it and "hear" it. They saw and heard when they read or heard a witness to it. They saw it and heard it when their parents told them about it, or when they listened to the proclamation of the acts of Yahweh narrated in the Scriptures. One of the psalms interpreted it along this line: ". . . things we have heard and known, things our ancestors have told us" (Ps 78:3). To hear the story of what Yahweh has done—the Torah story—recreates it.

The extension of "you" to later generations who also saw and heard it for themselves heightens the point all the more.

*In what sense did the younger generation "see" and "hear" the revelation at the mountain?*

> *You were shown these things* so that you might know that Yahweh is God; besides him there is no other. From heaven *he made you hear his voice* to discipline you. On earth *he showed you his great fire, and you heard his words from out of the fire.* Because he loved your ancestors and chose their descendants after them, he brought you out of Egypt by his Presence and his great strength, to drive out before you nations greater and stronger than you and to bring you into their land *to give it to you for your inheritance, as it is today.* (4:35–38, emphasis added)

Those who saw and heard Yahweh's revelation were not only those who actually stood there but also those later generations who inherited the land after the conquest. How? To faithfully hear the Torah story is to hear and see what Yahweh has done.

This discourse is followed by a short narrative concerning the establishment of the three cities of refuge on the east side of the Jordan River (4:41–43). These cities provided safe haven for those who killed accidentally so that they could escape vigilante justice. The first three cities of refuge signified that Yahweh was beginning to fulfill his word. The short narrative also makes a break between exhortation based on the revelation at Horeb and the retelling of the remarkable event in Deuteronomy 5.

## ANOTHER LOOK

The opening discourse of Deuteronomy offers the reader another view of many things. Moses himself places an astounding spin on his judgment from God. He blames the people for the pronouncement that he could not enter the land. Showing that he means it, he repeats this accusation three times (emphases added).

> *Because of you Yahweh became angry with me* also and said, "You shall not enter it, either." (1:37)

> *But because of you Yahweh was angry with me* and would not listen to me. "That is enough," Yahweh said. "Do not speak to me anymore about this matter." (3:26)

> *Yahweh was angry with me because of you*, and he solemnly swore that I would not cross the Jordan and enter the good land Yahweh your God is giving you as your inheritance. I will die in this land; I will not cross the Jordan; but you are about to cross over and take possession of that good land. (4:21–22)

Readers may be surprised that Moses tells the people, "It is your fault." How can Moses blame the people? Does he really think that it is their fault that he was judged? On the surface, it appears to contradict the account of his sin. "But Yahweh said to Moses and Aaron, '*Because you did not trust in me* enough to honor me as holy in the sight of the Israelites, you will not bring this community into the land I give them'" (Num 20:12, emphasis added; see Chapter 22).

The attempt to shift blame by Moses may be one of the most difficult reinterpretations in Deuteronomy. It is not difficult because Moses gave a new interpretation of the rationale for his judgment, for there is much new material in the book. It is also not a problem, of itself, that Moses's new interpretation disagrees with the account of his sin in Numbers, because he could have been wrong or in denial. The problem is that Moses seems to disagree with the biblical narrative within the very book that presents him as the authoritative lawgiver. Moses said within the first discourse itself, for example:

> Now, Israel, hear the decrees and laws I am about to teach you. . . . *Do not add to what I command you and do not subtract from it*, but keep the commands of Yahweh your God that I give you. . . . See, I have taught you decrees and laws as Yahweh my God commanded me, so that you may follow them in the land you are entering to take possession of it. (4:1a, 2, 5, emphasis added; cf. 12:32)

Although the language of not adding and subtracting promotes obedience, it is grounded on the authority of Moses's presentation of the will of Yahweh. How are readers supposed to respond to the tension created by the blame game of the spokesperson of Yahweh?

Region of Moab

*Isaiah and Abby Cramer*

The discrepancy between Moses and the narrative in Numbers serves to place a twofold perspective on Moses and Torah. First, Moses was just a prophet, sinful like anyone else. Moses was a great prophet; there was no other prophet like him. He had a unique tolerance to sustain the presence of Yahweh, and they spoke like friends (Num 7:89; 12:6–8). Still, he was merely a human being representing Yahweh. The apparent disagreement about Moses's blame accentuates his humanity.

Second, it is the one whom Moses represents who provides the power of the word. In this sense, Yahweh is wholly other and transcends the prophets who deliver his word. It is easy for readers to see that the binding force of the word has nothing to do with the moral character of the wicked prophet Balaam. It is more difficult to see, but just as true, in the case of Moses. The fact that Moses was exceptional among Israel—performing wonders, talking to Yahweh, leading the people—did not add one thing to the power and grace of God's word. The power of the Torah has nothing to do with Moses. When Moses repeatedly tries to blame Israel for his sin, it shows readers his limits and shortcomings.

The psalmist deals with this same tension head-on. He brings together the interpretation of Moses's sin from the narrative in Numbers directly with Moses's claims in Deuteronomy: "They provoked him to anger by the waters of Meribah, so it went badly for Moses *on their account*, for they made his spirit bitter, *and he spoke rashly with his own mouth*" (Ps 106:32–33 lit., emphasis added). Instead of trying to smooth out the details, the psalmist underlines it by acknowledging that this went bad for Moses because of Israel but also because he spoke wrongly "with his own mouth" (see Schnittjer, "Kadesh," 116–17).

*How does the psalmist of Psalm 106 affirm both Moses blaming the people as well as the narrator blaming Moses?*

Anyone who reads the entire wilderness narrative can echo the sentiments of the psalmist. The people complained so extensively that it was a heavy burden for Moses to bear. The people wore out Moses, yes, but his sin was his responsibility. Toward the end of Deuteronomy, the narrator provides Yahweh's explanation of why Moses would die in the wilderness.

> This is *because both of you* [Moses and Aaron] *broke faith with me* in the presence of the Israelites at the waters of Meribah Kadesh in the Desert of Zin and *because you did not uphold my holiness* among the Israelites. Therefore, you will see the land only from a distance; you will not enter the land I am giving to the people of Israel. (Deut 32:51–52, emphasis added)

## INTERACTIVE WORKSHOP

### *Chapter Summary*

Deuteronomy opens with the story of Moses's first discourse on his last day. The people stand on the threshold between the wilderness and Canaan and listen to a new interpretation of many of the most significant events of the Torah narrative. This recounting of the past is not merely informational but presents the people with demands to serve God and him only, according to his instruction.

### *Can You Explain the Key Terms?*

- as tall as the Anakites
- Horeb
- judges and elders
- motivation
- Rephaites
- your eyes (your hearing)

### *Challenge Questions*

1. How does the setting in Deuteronomy 1:1–5 affect the meaning of the entire book?
2. What does Deuteronomy 1:19–45 emphasize about the rebellion at Kadesh in comparison to the account in Numbers 13–14 ?
3. Deuteronomy tends to emphasize the uniqueness of the people and yet diminish the significance of that uniqueness. What is the impact of comparing the teaching on the uniqueness of the people (e.g., 4:32–34; 7:6–8) with the teaching on the status of the descendants of Esau and Lot (e.g., 2:5, 9, 10–12, 19, 20–22; cf. 9:4–6)?
4. How do the "former days" relate to the "later days" (4:30, 32)?

## *Advanced Questions*

1. What is the emphasis of the interpretation of the appointment of judges in Deuteronomy 1:9–18 when compared to the narratives in Exodus 18 and Numbers 10–11?
2. What is the implication of comparing Moses's interpretation of his fate (1:37; 3:26; 4:21–22) and the narrator's and Yahweh's interpretation of the same (32:48–52; 34:1–5; cf. Num 20:12; 27:14)?
3. How does Moses use the narratives of Genesis and Exodus in Deuteronomy 4?
4. How does the metaphorical hearing and seeing of the acts of God in Scripture take precedence over eyewitness observation?

*5. What are the meanings of *huqim* and *mishpatim*, and how do they function together (see 4:1; 6:1; 12:1) in relation to *torah* within Deuteronomy?

## *Research Project Ideas*

Compare the details and chronology of the three accounts of the appointment of judges (Exod 18; Num 11; Deut 1:9–18).

Evaluate the different presentations of the rebellion at Kadesh in Numbers 13–14, Deuteronomy 1:19–45, and other interpretations of the same events elsewhere in Scripture (Num 32:8–14; Ps 106:24–26; Neh 9:17; see Schnittjer, "Kadesh," 105–20).

Compare the details of the battles and travels in Deuteronomy 2:24–3:20 and the parallels in Numbers (cf. Table 23-G in Chapter 23).

## *The Next Step*


Mann, Thomas W. *Deuteronomy.* Westminster Bible Companion. Louisville: Westminster John Knox, 1995.

Schnittjer, Gary Edward. "Kadesh Infidelity of Deuteronomy 1 and Its Synoptic Implications." *Journal of the Evangelical Theological Society* 63.1 (2020): 95–120.

———. *Old Testament Use of Old Testament.* Grand Rapids: Zondervan Academic, 2021.

Tigay, Jeffrey H. *Deuteronomy.* JPS Torah Commentary. Philadelphia: Jewish Publication Society, 1996.

von Rad, Gerhard. *Deuteronomy: A Commentary.* Old Testament Library. Philadelphia: Westminster, 1966.

# 26 THE TEN WORDS AND THE COMMAND

## *Deuteronomy 4:44–11:32*

*iStock.com/Algul*

## GETTING STARTED

### *Focus Questions*

What is the significance of retelling the story of the Ten Words? How is the command related to the Torah story?

### *Look for These Terms*

- the command
- next generation
- remember
- Ten Words
- today
- wisdom

## AN OUTLINE

A. **The Ten Words (4:44–5:33)**
   1. Heading (4:44–49)
   2. Prologue (5:1–5)
   3. The Decalogue (5:6–21)
   4. The mediator (5:22–33)

B. **The command (6–11)**
   1. Yahweh is one—love God and teach his word to the next generation (6:1–9)
   2. The danger of gifts (6:10–25)
   3. The danger of other gods (7:1–10:22)
      a. . . . military might (7:1–26)
      b. . . . wealth (8:1–20)
         (1) Observe the commandment so you may live (8:1)
            (a) Remember (8:2–10)
               (i) The wilderness journey of the past (8:2–6)
               (ii) The promised land of the future (8:7–10)
            (b) Do not forget (8:11–17)
               (i) The promised land of the future (8:11–14)

(ii) The wilderness journey of the past (8:15–17)

(2) Remember and live, forget and die (8:18–20)

c. . . . self-righteousness (9:1–10:11)

4. A catechism-style summary of what Yahweh expects (10:12–22)
5. Motivation to love God—life and death, blessing and curse (11:1–32)

## A READING

If there is a high point in Deuteronomy, it is chapters 5–11. These chapters present "the Torah" (4:44), that is to say, the Ten Words and *the* command. Much of the rest of the Hebrew Scriptures are built on the instruction found here. The story of God's word and the human rebellion against that word resound loudly in this context.

The second discourse opens with the narrative setting for the retelling of the Ten Words. But the story is *not* that of the previous generation receiving the Decalogue—literally "ten-words"—at the mountain forty years before. It is the story of when Yahweh made a covenant "with us at Horeb" (5:2). What? How can this be? The congregation standing before Moses and readers both know that the generation who committed themselves to obey the Ten Words in Exodus 20 are buried in the wilderness. Moses continues with sixfold clarity (emphases added):

> "**Not with our ancestors** did Yahweh cut this covenant [Ten Words],
> but with **us**,
> **us**,
> **those here today**,
> all of **us alive**.
> Yahweh spoke **to you face to face** out of the fire on the mountain."
> (5:3–4, lit.)

Moses uses a word game, but it is not a trick and it is not just metaphorical. The word game identified a relationship between the historic revelatory event at Mount Horeb and its reality to the generation standing before him and to the generations to come. The covenant was not with an individual generation of Israel, though it was, but to the living generation of Israelites. He spoke "to you face to face"—literally, really, by the proclamation of the revelation event in the biblical story and by their parents' testimony to it. The scriptural witness to it is, in fact, the very word of God—face to face, as it were (see Schnittjer, 113).

The covenant relationship was with the chosen community—the Hebrew nation—but it was new or renewed with the living generation of Israel. The force of the constant reacceptance of the covenant—today—is underlined by the renewal of the covenant by this generation (Deut 5 and 30), and again (Josh 5), and by the next generation as well (Josh 24).

The collective responsibility to the Ten Words does not erase personal responsibility. It does, however, explain and offer compelling rationale for the fall of Israel and Judah, even while some walked with God. Although individual persons embraced Yahweh and the covenant by faith (see 1 Kgs 19:18; Ps 44), Israel as a people rebelled against him (see 2 Kgs 17:7–23; 2 Chr 36:15–16). This evokes Abraham's question once again, "Will you sweep away the righteous with the wicked?" (Gen 18:23; cf. 20:4). The covenant responsibility was with Israel and extended across time continually. Every generation needs to embrace the covenant as a people.

*How did the Horeb covenant relate to the community and to individuals within the community?*

The retelling of the story of the Ten Words in Deuteronomy 5 generally follows the narrative of the same in Exodus 20. Table 26-A notes the main differences (new elements marked by red text, deleted or adjusted language marked by broken underlining, and rearranged material marked by underlining). The rationales for keeping the Sabbath as holy seem to differ most, at first. But upon reflection, they demonstrate deep-level continuity.

**Table 26-A:** A Comparison of the Ten Words in Exodus and Deuteronomy

| Exodus 20 | Deuteronomy 5 |
|---|---|
| I am Yahweh your God, who brought you out of Egypt, out of the land of slavery. You shall have no other gods before me. | I am Yahweh your God, who brought you out of Egypt, out of the land of slavery. You shall have no other gods before me. |
| You shall not make for yourself an image in the form of anything in heaven above or on the earth beneath or in the waters below. You shall not bow down to them or worship them; for I, Yahweh your God, am a jealous God, punishing the children for the sin of the parents to the third and fourth generation of those who hate me, but showing love to a thousand generations of those who love me and keep my commandments. | You shall not make for yourself an image in the form of anything in heaven above or on the earth beneath or in the waters below. You shall not bow down to them or worship them; for I, Yahweh your God, am a jealous God, punishing the children for the sin of the parents to the third and fourth generation of those who hate me, but showing love to a thousand generations of those who love me and keep my commandments. |
| You shall not misuse the name of Yahweh your God, for Yahweh will not hold anyone guiltless who misuses his name. | You shall not misuse the name of Yahweh your God, for Yahweh will not hold anyone guiltless who misuses his name. |

| Exodus 20 | Deuteronomy 5 |
| --- | --- |
| Remember the Sabbath day by keeping it holy. Six days you shall labor and do all your work, but the seventh day is a sabbath to Yahweh your God. On it you shall not do any work, neither you, nor your son or daughter, nor your male or female servant, nor your animals, nor any foreigner residing in your towns. For in six days Yahweh made the heavens and the earth, the sea, and all that is in them, but he rested on the seventh day. Therefore Yahweh blessed the Sabbath day and made it holy. | Observe the Sabbath day by keeping it holy, **as Yahweh your God has commanded you**. Six days you shall labor and do all your work, but the seventh day is a sabbath to Yahweh your God. On it you shall not do any work, neither you, nor your son or daughter, nor your male or female servant, **nor your ox, your donkey** or **any** of your animals, nor any foreigner residing in your towns, **so that your male and female servants may rest, as you do**. Remember **that you were slaves in Egypt and that Yahweh your God brought you out of there with a mighty hand and an outstretched arm**. Therefore Yahweh **your God has commanded you to observe** the Sabbath day. |
| Honor your father and your mother, so that you may live long in the land Yahweh your God is giving you. | Honor your father and your mother, **as Yahweh your God has commanded you**, so that you may live long **and that it may go well with you** in the land Yahweh your God is giving you. |
| You shall not murder. | You shall not murder. |
| You shall not commit adultery. | You shall not commit adultery. |
| You shall not steal. | You shall not steal. |
| You shall not give false testimony against your neighbor. | You shall not give false testimony against your neighbor. |
| You shall not covet your neighbor's house. You shall not covet your neighbor's wife, or his male or female servant, his ox or donkey, or anything that belongs to your neighbor. | You shall not covet your neighbor's wife. You shall not set your desire on your neighbor's house **or land**, his male or female servant, his ox or donkey, or anything that belongs to your neighbor. |

The Sabbath command in Exodus 20 is based on the creation of the heavens and the earth and in Deuteronomy 5 on the redemption of the nation. If the command in Exodus 20 spoke of the household not working, the retelling in Deuteronomy 5 calls for rest of the entire household, including servants.

The adjustment in the motivation for honoring parents gets at more than long life. Honoring parents is a starting point for a good life—"that it may go well with you."

The rearrangement and shifting of language in the prohibition against coveting elevates attention to the faithfulness necessary for the marriage covenant. This shift corresponds to the lesser penalties of acting on coveting anything else versus the death penalty for acting on lust after someone else's spouse (see Table 14-G in Chapter 14 and associated discussion).

We know there are ten commands because the Torah says there are ten (Exod 34:28; Deut 4:13; 10:4). But there are at least three different ways to count them (see Table 26-B). The Judaic, Roman Catholic/Lutheran, and Reformed traditions count the first two words in three different ways, and the Roman Catholic/Lutheran traditions count the last two in their own way (Block, 169–73; DeRouchie, 95–102).

**Table 26-B:** Traditional Ways of Counting Ten Words

| Judaic | Roman Catholic/Lutheran | Reformed |
|---|---|---|
| I am Yahweh your God | | |
| no other gods or images | no other gods or images | no other gods |
| | | no graven images |
| name command | name command | name command |
| Sabbath day | Sabbath day | Sabbath day |
| honor parents | honor parents | honor parents |
| do not kill | do not kill | do not kill |
| do not commit adultery | do not commit adultery | do not commit adultery |
| do not steal | do not steal | do not steal |
| do not give false witness | do not give false witness | do not give false witness |
| do not covet | do not covet neighbor's house | do not covet |
| | do not covet neighbor's wife and so on | |

How can there be different views of how to count the Decalogue? They differ at the more ambiguous places. The Judaic tradition counts the self-declaration of God himself as the first word, but it is not a command. The various Christian traditions regard that statement as a prologue or introduction and begin counting with the first command. Part of the reason for this is because Judaic and Christian traditions have called these verses the Ten Commandments. The Torah does not call the list the Ten Commandments but the Ten Words (Exod 34:28; Deut 4:13; 10:4). While this lends weight to the traditional Judaic view, it does not entirely remove the problem.

*Why does the Judaic tradition count the heading as the first command?*

There are difficulties with each of the traditional views. A slightly modified version of the Reformed view fits well within the context of Deuteronomy. "The command" in Deuteronomy 6:4–5 holds together a prologue statement about God himself with a command: "Hear O Israel, Yahweh our God, Yahweh is one. You shall love Yahweh your God . . ." (lit.). This aligns well with regarding the so-called prologue of the Ten Words as the heading of the first word rather than of the Ten Words as a whole. In this view, the first command is: "I am Yahweh your God, who brought you out of Egypt, out of the land of slavery. You shall have no other gods before me" (5:6–7). This helps associate who God is with the responsibility of his people to devote themselves to him exclusively. Josephus, the Jewish historian to the Romans in the first century CE, approaches the first commandment along these lines. He wrote, "The first command teaches us that there is but one God and that we ought to worship him only" (*Antiquities* 3.5.5).

The Ten Words call the people of God to righteousness. They also demonstrate the depth of the human revolution against Yahweh (see Sidebar 26-C).

## Sidebar 26-C: Selections from the Heidelberg Catechism

**Question 113.** What is God's will for you in the tenth commandment?
**Answer.** That not even the slightest thought or desire contrary to any one of God's commandments should ever arise in my heart. Rather, with all my heart I should always hate sin and take pleasure in whatever is right.

**Question 114.** But can those converted to God obey these commandments perfectly?
**Answer.** No. In this life even the holiest have only a small beginning of this obedience. Nevertheless, with all seriousness of purpose, they do begin to live according to all, not only some, of God's commandments.

**Question 115.** No one in this life can obey the Ten Commandments perfectly: why then does God want them preached so pointedly?
**Answer.** First, so that the longer we live the more we may come to know our sinfulness and the more eagerly look to Christ for forgiveness of sins and righteousness. Second, so that, while praying to God for the grace of the Holy Spirit, we may never stop striving to be renewed more and more after God's image, until after this life we reach our goal: perfection.

Translation from Christian Reformed Church in North America, 2004 (www.crcna.org).

"This is the command" heads Deuteronomy 6–11 (lit.; see Chapter 24). How should the opening line of the command be translated? Compare two ways to translate 6:4. Most translations go in one of these two directions (the divine name is used in place of "the Lord").

> Hear, O Israel: Yahweh our God, Yahweh is one. (NIV)
>
> Hear, O Israel: Yahweh is our God, Yahweh alone. (NRSVue)

iStock.com/tzahiV

iStock.com/Emma Grimberg

"When [Yahweh] your God brings you into the land . . . Filled with all kinds of good things you did not provide, wells you did not dig, and vineyards and olive groves you did not plant. . . " (Deut 6:10–11).

The word "is" is not in the Hebrew text, which says, "Hear O Israel, Yahweh our God, Yahweh one." This is not a problem because Hebrew does not require it. In translation we supply the "is" and place it where it should go based on context. In this case there are two places for "is," which point in different directions.

The first translation foregrounds the person of God himself, and the second the people's loyalty to God. Though both are acceptable, the placement of "is" in the first translation works a little better. Focusing on the person of Yahweh himself corresponds to frequent statements in the Torah, especially Leviticus—such as "I am Yahweh"—in sections giving commands (see Lev 19). Also, in Deuteronomy "Yahweh" and "our God" never occur as subject and complement but always as in the first translation above (see 1:6; 5:2; 6:20, 24, 25, and so on; also see Weinfeld, 337–38). Moreover, the Septuagint, an ancient Greek translation of the Hebrew Scriptures, supplied an "is" as in the first translation above to emphasize Yahweh's oneness (Wevers, 114).

The proclamation "Hear, O Israel, Yahweh our God, Yahweh is one" is the basis of the great command that naturally grows out of it.

> Now this is the command . . .
>
> Hear, O Israel, Yahweh our God, Yahweh is one.
>
> *You shall love Yahweh your God* with all your heart and with all your soul and with all your strength.
>
> *Keep these words* that I am commanding you today *in your heart. Recite them to your children* and talk about them when you are at home and when you are on the way, when you lie down and when you rise. Bind them as a sign on your hand, fix them as an emblem on your forehead, and write them on the doorposts of your house and on your gates. (Deut 6:1a, 4–9 lit., emphasis added)

The interrelationship of the passage binds it together with the fabric of creational reality itself. First, the command—love God—is rooted in the person of Yahweh God himself. It is because of who he is that love is required of every human being. He is one. He is God. The very fact of his divinity and oneness places the demand of devotion and loyalty to him on everyone.

The requirement to devote oneself to Yahweh relates to human design. Human beings are created in the image of God. Humans are designed to love him. The gospel, forged on the sacrifice of the Messiah, the very image of God, is the basis of obeying the first command. The power of the gospel begins to make us who we are supposed to be by creational intention. The command to love Yahweh, then, is a mandate for those in the image of God. It is the meaning of human life.

*In what senses is the great command creational?*

Second, the command is the first priority within the human situation. Israel and the human race they represent were to loyally devote themselves to Yahweh with everything. When the ancient Judaic scholar asked Messiah, "What is the first command?" he replied, "The first is: 'Hear, O Israel, the Lord our God, the Lord is one. Love the Lord your God with all your heart and with all your soul and with all your mind and with all your strength.' The second is: 'Love your neighbor as yourself'" (Mark 12:28–31a, lit.). If the first command is not right, then the second—to love others—is a hollow social nicety. Without the first command, life becomes selfish and phony. Thus, *the* command is the *first* command, creationally and in priority.

Third, the command defines the all-consuming focus of life. To love Yahweh is the first thing, and it is everything. It can be paraphrased thus, "Love Yahweh your God with everything you are, and teach his word to the next generation everywhere, all the time." The meaning of "love" here is something like loyalty and devotion. What it looks like includes teaching his word to the younger generation as a perpetual occupation.

Within a family structure, the next generation is our own children. More broadly, however, the next generation refers to those coming after us. Many devout North American Christians miss this understanding because of the tendency to extreme individualism in the prevailing culture. Our responsibility before God does not end with each of us considered alone. If we measure our obedience to the command, it necessarily includes instructing the generation that follows after. How the next generation is doing with God says a lot about how the older generation is doing with God.

*What is the place of instructing the next generation in obeying the great command?*

The reference to tying Scripture on foreheads and arms seems metaphorical (though literally wearing Scripture has been practiced in some Judaic traditions). God's instruction should be on our mind and in our heart (see 6:6b). The parallel passages in the Torah also sound metaphorical. "*This observance [the Passover] will be for you like a sign* on your hand and a reminder on your forehead that this law of Yahweh is to be on your lips" (Exod 13:9, emphasis added). "Fix these words of mine *in your hearts and minds*; tie them as symbols on your hands and bind them on your foreheads" (Deut 11:18, emphasis added). The metaphorical reading of this teaching by other portions of the Hebrew Scriptures, especially wisdom parallels, will be taken up in Another Look below (also see Propp, 423–25; Weinfeld, 341–43).

The command to love Yahweh is both an interpretation of the first word and a concise summary statement of the entire section (Deut 6–11). These chapters unfold out of and situate the meaning of the command (see Table 26-D). Each section previews Israel's future history in relation to how the nation will fail to obey the first command. The sections interweave interpretive review of the wilderness journeys, showing the continuity of Israel's sinfulness. Thus, the meaning of the command is explained within a storied context. These teachings are not limited to Israel's path but offer some of the most important teaching to anyone who desires to obey the command. It is no accident that each of the three passages Messiah quoted when he faced temptation came from these chapters (see 8:3; cf. 6:13, 16; Matt 4:1–11).

**Table 26-D:** A Selected Summary of Deuteronomy 6–11

| | | |
|---|---|---|
| 6:4–9 | The Command | |
| | 6:10–25 | The danger of enjoying the gifts of God |
| | 7 | The danger of military might |
| | 8 | The danger of prosperity |
| | 9–10 | The danger of self-righteousness |
| 11 | Summary of the Command | |

The first instruction concerning the meaning of the command within Israel's story is the warning about the danger of God's gifts. The dangerous gifts, in this case, are not just any gifts but acts of Yahweh's grace to his people. The problem has nothing to do with the gifts from God but has everything to do with the recipients of his kindness. The hazard of the gifts is that people will enjoy them and forget the giver. Gifts and each of the other dangers presented in these chapters reveal the problem of human rebellion against God's word. The gifts are treated in chronologically reverse order (see Table 26-E).

**Table 26-E:** Chronologically Reversed Order of Instructions in Deuteronomy 6:10–25

| | |
|---|---|
| 6:10–15 | Immediate future—the land |
| 6:16–19 | Immediate past—the wilderness provisions |
| 6:20–25 | The previous generation—deliverance from slavery |

The next generation must learn that redemption precedes obedience to Yahweh's will, not the other way around. Notice the critical logic:

> In the future, *when your son asks you, "What is the meaning of the stipulations, decrees and laws Yahweh our God has commanded you?" tell him:* "We were slaves of Pharaoh in Egypt, but Yahweh brought us out of Egypt with a mighty hand. Before our eyes Yahweh sent signs and wonders—great and terrible—on Egypt and Pharaoh and his whole household. But he brought us out from there to bring us in and give us the land that he promised on oath to our ancestors. *Yahweh commanded us to obey all these decrees and to fear Yahweh our God,* so that we might always prosper and be kept alive, as is the case today." (6:20–24)

The narrative framework of redemption explains the meaning of obedience to Yahweh's will.

"For Yahweh your God is bringing you into a good land—a land with brooks, streams, and deep springs gushing out into the valleys and hills; a land with wheat and barley, vines and fig trees, pomegranates, olive oil and honey . . ." (Deut 8:7–8). An olive press. *William Krewson*

The next three dangers—military might, wealth, and self-righteousness (see Table 26-D)—form a set. The relationship among them can be seen by the phrase "say to yourself" (emphases added):

> *You may say to yourselves,* "These nations are stronger than we are. How can we drive them out?" (7:17)

*Left:* Maternal and phallic Asherah household images *William Krewson*

> *You may say to yourself*, "My power and the strength of my hands have produced this wealth for me." (8:17)

> After Yahweh your God has driven them out before you, *do not say to yourself*, "Yahweh has brought me here to take possession of this land because of my righteousness." (9:4a, emphasis added to each)

This set of three teachings, including the self-conversations, seems to be followed in various contexts (see Isa 47:5–7, 8–9, 10–11; cf. Ps 10:3–4, 5–6, 10–13; Eccl 2:1; 3:17, 18; also see Olson, 52–53). This set of perils provides a virtual outline of Israel's downfall. Each should be considered briefly.

First, the danger of *military might* runs in two directions. The people could misjudge the reason for their being chosen by Yahweh or fail to trust him when faced with military challenge. In the case of the former problem, the theological explanation makes clear:

> Yahweh did not set his affection on you and choose you because you were more numerous than other peoples, for you were the fewest of all peoples. *But it was because Yahweh loved you and kept the oath he swore to your ancestors* that he brought you out with a mighty hand and redeemed you from the land of slavery, from the power of Pharaoh king of Egypt. (Deut 7:7–8, emphasis added)

Concerning the latter problem Moses said, "You may say to yourselves, 'These nations are stronger than we are. How can we drive them out?' But do not be afraid of them; *remember well what Yahweh your God did* to Pharaoh and to all Egypt" (7:17–18, emphasis added). In both cases, the antidote centers on placing the fears within the framework of the story of redemption.

Second, *financial security*, in terms of the good life, presents grave danger to those who would be loyal to Yahweh. Deuteronomy 8 says, repeats, and says again that the people must remember and must not forget the story of what he has done. He redeemed Israel from bondage and provided for them through the long, sparse wilderness years. The Torah story, the word of God itself, again offers decisive substance for the people's responsibility (see, e.g., 8:17–18). It describes the challenges and provides the solution within itself. The opening instruction captures the spirit of the larger context:

> Remember how Yahweh your God led you all the way in the wilderness these forty years, to humble and test you in order to know what was in your heart, whether or

> not you would keep his commands. He humbled you, causing you to hunger and then feeding you with manna, which neither you nor your ancestors had known, to teach you that man does not live on bread alone *but on every word that comes from the mouth of Yahweh*. (8:2–3, emphasis added)

The word of God is the foremost of life's essentials.

The problem with financial prosperity is not the prosperity itself. The peril is in forgetting—failing to place present prosperity in its rightful perspective. The story of the successful life cannot begin with the success itself. A rightful and necessary worldview, especially under the grave threat of affluence, is placing life within God's story. The opposite of beginning with the narrative of redemption is conceit. Notice the attitudinal reason for moral failure and its relationship to the Torah story.

> Be careful that you do not forget Yahweh your God, failing to observe his commands, his laws and his decrees that I am giving you this day. Otherwise, when you eat and are satisfied, when you build fine houses and settle down, and when your herds and flocks grow large and your silver and gold increase and all you have is multiplied, *then your heart will become proud and you will forget* Yahweh your God, who brought you out of Egypt, out of the land of slavery. He led you through the vast and dreadful wilderness, that thirsty and waterless land, with its venomous snakes and scorpions. He brought you water out of hard rock. (8:11–15, emphasis added)

Third, the danger of *self-righteousness* may be the gravest of all. The nature of the problem stems from misunderstanding the meaning of circumstances. Self-righteousness could cause Israel wrongly to connect the results of grace with their own merits. This context emphatically denies a works-based religion. The fulfillment of God's word is not rooted in human achievement. It is accomplished because Yahweh said it.

> After Yahweh your God has driven them out before you, do not say to yourself, "Yahweh has brought me here to take possession of this land *because of my righteousness*." *No, it is on account of the wickedness* of these nations that Yahweh is going to drive them out before you. *It is not because of your righteousness or your integrity* that you are going in to take possession of their land; but on account of the wickedness of these nations, Yahweh your God will drive them out before you, *to accomplish what he swore to your fathers, to Abraham, Isaac and Jacob*. Understand, then, that *it is not because of your righteousness* that Yahweh your God is giving you this good land to possess, *for you are a stiff-necked people*. (9:4–6, emphasis added)

True obedience has nothing to do with earning anything. The rightful interpretation of circumstance, whether good or otherwise, begins by recognizing the sinfulness of humankind. This is the beginning of the great command and the beginning of the gospel.

*What is the basis of true obedience?*

Deuteronomy 9 continues with a detailed retelling of Israel's sin with the golden calf. The rebellion at Sinai provided a template for explaining Israel's other sins in the wilderness and at Kadesh. It was something that they needed to "remember" and "never forget" (9:7).

Deuteronomy 10:12–22 appears to be a catechism of sorts—a religious or theological summary designed for youth to memorize. This passage summarizes the message of the entire Torah in a manner suitable for younger people or anyone to learn and recite. The passage is remarkably compact and comprehensive. Memorizing and reciting this Torah summary with the next generation would be itself a fulfillment of the command.

Harvesting olives
*iStock.com/tapuzina*

The exposition of the first command closes as it began. The tight framing effect provides a stable structure to this entire section of the book. The outer framework depicted in Figure 26-F can be situated around the content summarized in Table 26-D to show how these teachings fit together in a mutually interdependent manner.

When we assign relative importance to different passages within the Scriptures, are we saying something about the texts or ourselves? The torah collection—the rules and regulations of Deuteronomy 12–26—is widely regarded as the heart of Deuteronomy, and rightfully so. The biblical narratives and prophets that follow constantly work from that context. The torah collection, however, is subordinate to the basic reality of the first command. What good are the rules and the regulations without the command? If any sections of the Hebrew Scriptures should be worn in the personal Bible of a Christian, that section should be Deuteronomy 6–11.

**Figure 26-F:** The Outer Framework of Deuteronomy 6–11

| | |
|---|---|
| 6:1–3 | to remain in the land of promise |
| 6:4–9 | Hear, O Israel: Yahweh our God, Yahweh is one. **Love Yahweh your God with all your heart and with all your soul** and with all your strength. These commandments that I give you today are to be on your hearts. Impress them on your children. Talk about them when you sit at home and when you walk along the road, when you lie down and when you get up. *Tie them as symbols on your hands and bind them on your foreheads. Write them on the doorframes of your houses and on your gates.* |
| 11:13, 18–20 | So if you faithfully obey the commands I am giving you today—**to love Yahweh your God** and to serve him **with all your heart and with all your soul** . . . Fix these words of mine in your hearts and minds; *tie them as symbols on your hands and bind them on your foreheads.* Teach them to your children, talking about them when you sit at home and when you walk along the road, when you lie down and when you get up. *Write them on the doorframes of your houses and on your gates.* |
| 11:22–25 | to remain in the land of promise |

## ANOTHER LOOK

The creational shape of the first command to love God can be seen at the intersection of Torah and wisdom. The wisdom of Proverbs makes frequent use of the teaching from Deuteronomy 6:4–9 as well as from other sections of the book (see Fishbane, 284; Shipper, 59). The wisdom from the son of David is for his "son," the heir of the Davidic messiah's instruction, the reader (see Prov 1:1). The wisdom is "torah" that the reader should not forget (3:1). The parallels between wisdom and torah are exhibited most strongly in the need to instruct the next generation (see Table 26-G).

The life-giving power of torah and wisdom establishes the force of the mandate to instruct the up-and-coming generation. The difference between life and death rests on instructing the next generation in God's word. Just as God wrote the Ten Words on stone, parents are called to write wisdom on the tablets of the heart of the next generation (Prov 3:3; 7:3; Table 26-G).

*What do wisdom and torah share in common?*

If Deuteronomy talks about instructing the up and coming generation, Proverbs shows readers what the older generation needs to teach. Consider examples of wise instruction to the next generation that come after the allusions to the first command in Table 26–G.

> *Trust in Yahweh with all your heart* and lean not on your own understanding; in all your ways submit to him, and he will make your paths straight. (Prov 3:5–6)

| Deuteronomy 6 | Proverbs | | | |
|---|---|---|---|---|
| [6]These commandments that I give you today are to be on your hearts. | [3:1]My son, do not forget my torah, but guard my commands in your heart, | [3:21]My son, do not let wisdom and understanding out of your sight, keep sound judgment and discretion; | [6:20]My son, guard your father's command and do not forsake your mother's torah. | [7:1]My son, keep my words and store up my commands within you. [2]Keep my commands and you will live; keep my torahs as the apple of your eye. |
| [7]Impress them on your children. Talk about them when you sit at home and when you walk along the way, when you lie down and when you get up. | [2]for they will prolong your life many years and bring you peace and prosperity. | [23]Then you will walk on your way in safety, and your foot will not stumble. [24]When you lie down, you will not be afraid; when you lie down, your sleep will be sweet. | [22]When you walk, they will guide you; when you lie down, they will watch over you; when you awake, they will speak to you. [23]For this command is a lamp, this torah is a light, and correction and instruction are the way to life. | |
| [8]Tie them as symbols on your hands and bind them on your foreheads. [9]Write them on the doorframes of your houses and on your gates. | [3]Let love and faithfulness never leave you; tie them around your neck, write them on the tablet of your heart. | [22]they will be life for you, an ornament to grace your neck. | [21]Tie them always on your heart; fasten them around your neck. | [3]Tie them on your fingers; write them on the tablet of your heart. |

**Table 26-G:** Deuteronomy 6:6–9 and the Wisdom of Proverbs[a]

[a]Translation in table NIV with mild modifications to show verbal parallels in Hebrew. Emphases mark verbal parallels in Hebrew.

*For this command is a lamp, this teaching is a light*, and correction and instruction are the way to life, *keeping you from your neighbor's wife*, from the smooth talk of a wayward woman. *Do not lust in your heart after her beauty or let her captivate you with her eyes*. (6:23–25)

She [the temptress] took hold of him and kissed him and with a brazen face she said: "*Today I fulfilled my vows*, and I have food from my fellowship offering at home. So I came out to meet you; *I looked for you and have found you!* . . . My husband is not at home; he has gone on a long journey." . . . With persuasive words she led him astray; she seduced him with her smooth talk. All at once he followed her like an ox going to the slaughter, like a deer stepping into a noose. (7:13–15, 19, 21–22, emphases added)

The older generation teaches the younger to trust Yahweh and follow his paths (3:5–6). The older generation warns of the temptress who uses her religious devotion as a pickup line for illicit relations (7:14). Mixtures of some truth with an appealing evil appetite requires wisdom. Deuteronomy commands "thou shall not commit adultery" and "thou shall not covet thy neighbor's wife" (lit.). Proverbs offers wisdom to avoid the deceptive ways of the temptress.

To love Yahweh includes constant instruction of the next generation. Teaching the next generation to be loyal to Yahweh gets at where torah and wisdom intersect.

## INTERACTIVE WORKSHOP

### *Chapter Summary*

The Ten Words were not confined to the generation of Israel who originally received them, but they were to be renewed by Israel as a society in every living generation. The first command—including the oneness of Yahweh himself and the mandate to love him with everything we are and to proclaim his word everywhere, all the time, to the next generation—is explained in terms of the story of his great redemption.

### *Can You Explain the Key Terms?*

- the command
- next generation
- remember
- Ten Words
- today
- wisdom

### *Challenge Questions*

1. Why did Moses say that the covenant at Horeb was not with their parents but with the congregation before him (Deut 5:2–3)?
2. What are the major structural features of Deuteronomy 6–11?
3. Explain the significance of instructing the next generation.
4. How are "remember" and "do not forget" something more than simply mental activities in the context of Deuteronomy 6–11?

### *Advanced Questions*

1. Evaluate the main traditional views for counting the Ten Words and explain which one works best.
2. How does "the command" of Deuteronomy 6–11 relate to the "rules and regulations" in chapters 12–26?
3. What is the function of the Torah story within Deuteronomy 6:20–25?

*4. Evaluate the major translations of Deuteronomy 6:4 and offer your own translation, along with an explanation regarding the key issues.

## *Research Project Ideas*

Compare the two accounts of the Ten Words in Exodus 20 and Deuteronomy 5 and their narrative contexts.

Evaluate the literary and theological significance of the interpretation of the rebellion at Sinai in Deuteronomy 9 by comparing it to the account in Exodus 32–34 (see Hayes, 45–93).

Investigate how the great command was interpreted by Messiah or Paul.

Define the rationale behind Jesus's three quotations from Deuteronomy during his temptation.

## *The Next Step*


Block, Daniel I. *The Gospel according to Moses: Theological and Ethical Reflections on the Book of Deuteronomy.* Eugene, OR: Cascade, 2012.

DeRouchie, Jason S. "Counting the Ten: An Investigation into the Numbering of the Decalogue." Pages 93–125 in *For Our Good Always: Studies on the Message and Influence of Deuteronomy in Honor of Daniel I. Block.* Edited by Jason S. DeRouchie, Jason Gile, and Kenneth J. Turner. Winona Lake, IN: Eisenbrauns, 2013.

Fishbane, Michael. "Torah and Tradition." Pages 275–300 in *Tradition and Theology in the Old Testament.* Edited by Douglas A. Knight. Philadelphia: Fortress, 1977.

Hayes, Christine E. "Golden Calf Stories: The Relationship of Exodus 32 and Deuteronomy 9–10." Pages 45–93 in *The Idea of Biblical Interpretation: Essays in Honor of James L. Kugel.* Edited by Hindy Najman and Judith H. Newman. Journal for the Study of the Old Testament Supplement Series 83. Leiden: Brill, 2004.

Olson, Dennis T. *Deuteronomy and the Death of Moses: A Theological Reading.* Minneapolis: Fortress, 1994.

Propp, Willam H. C. *Exodus 1–18.* Anchor Bible 2. New York: Doubleday, 1999.

Schnittjer, Gary Edward. "Kadesh Infidelity of Deuteronomy 1 and Its Synoptic Implications." *Journal of the Evangelical Theological Society* 63.1 (2020): 95–120.

Shipper, Bernd U. "'Teach Them Diligently to Your Son!': The Book of Proverbs and Deuteronomy." Pages 21–34 in *Reading Proverbs Intertextually.* Edited by Katharine Dell and Will Kynes. Library of the Hebrew Bible/Old Testament Studies 629. New York: T&T Clark, 2019.

Weinfeld, Moshe. *Deuteronomy 1–11.* Anchor Bible 5. New York: Doubleday, 1991.

Wevers, John William. *Notes on the Greek Text of Deuteronomy.* Atlanta: Scholars Press, 1995.

# 27 THE RULES AND REGULATIONS

## *Deuteronomy 12–28*



## GETTING STARTED

### *Focus Questions*

What was the function of the rules and the regulations for Israel? How should they be interpreted?

### *Look for These Terms*

- assembly of Yahweh
- blessings and curses
- Canaanites
- Deuteronomistic narrative
- indecency
- Moabites and Ammonites
- the rules and regulations
- torah collection

## AN OUTLINE

A. **The Rules and Regulations (12–26)**
  1. Worship (12–13)
  2. Dietary regulations (14:1–21)
  3. Tithes and holy time (14:22–16:17)
  4. Leaders (16:18–18:22)
    a. Judges (16:18–17:13)
    b. Kings (17:14–20)
    c. Levitical priests (18:1–14)
    d. The prophet-like-Moses (18:15–22)
  5. Matters of life and death (19–21)
    a. Protection of innocent life—cities of refuge boundary markers, witness laws (19:1–21)
    b. Limits on killing in warfare (20:1–20)
    c. Limits in life, death, captivity, and the unloved—protection of the socially challenged (21:1–23)
  6. Boundaries (22:1–23:14)
    a. Forbidden mixing (22:1–12)
    b. Marital and sexual misconduct (22:13–30)

c. On exclusion from and conversion to the assembly (23:1–8)
d. Purity within the camp (23:9–14)
7. Miscellaneous regulation, often concerned with financial matters—interest, vows, crops, spouses, pledges, wages, poverty, levirate marriages (23:15–25:19)
8. Offerings (26:1–15)
9. Concluding summary (26:16–19)

B. **Blessings and Curses (27–28)**
1. Altar and curses at Mount Ebal and Mount Gerizim (27)
2. Blessings for obedience (28:1–14)
3. Curses for disobedience (28:15–68)

## A READING

The rules and regulations ("decrees and laws" NIV), commonly called the torah collection (Deut 12–26), offer the framework for the life of Israel in the land of promise. The instructions explain the way life was supposed to look for the society of chosen people who listen to God's word. The effect of obeying or disobeying God's teaching will lead to life and blessing or to death and curses. The torah collection provides the norm for measuring the rebellion of Israel.

The purpose of this chapter is not to explain every teaching in Deuteronomy 12–28. Rather, this chapter will offer interpretive guidelines and then illustrate, from selected passages, how to read these chapters in light of their interconnection with Israel's story. Some of the matters passed by here are treated in other contexts where these teachings occur in the Torah.

- On not eating blood (Deut 12), see Chapter 19.
- On worshiping other gods (Deut 13), see Chapters 14 and 19.
- On dietary regulations—clean and unclean animals (Deut 14), see Chapter 18.
- On Sabbath years (Deut 15) and the holy calendar (Deut 16), see Chapter 19.
- On judges (Deut 16–17) and cities of refuge (Deut 19), see Chapter 25.
- On the prophet like Moses (Deut 18), see Chapter 28.

That many of these items have been treated previously in the Torah demonstrates the character of Deuteronomy as Torah explained. Stated differently, Deuteronomy serves as a built-in commentary for reading the Torah.

The guidelines for reading the torah collection can be apprehended from within Deuteronomy and the larger biblical context. The key issue for understanding the torah collection, along with the blessings and curses within Deuteronomy itself, is its relationship to the first great command. The previous chapter described the framing effect around Deuteronomy 6–11 (see Figure 26-F). The torah collection exhibits similar literary framing (see Figure 27-A). The two major units (Deut 6–11 and 12–26) each end with blessings and curses (see 11:26–32; chs. 27–28).

**Figure 27-A:** The Outer Framework of Deuteronomy 12–26

| | |
|---|---|
| 11:26–32 | ceremony of the blessings and curses |
| 12:1 | These are the rules and regulations you must be careful to follow in the land that Yahweh, the God of your ancestors, has given you to possess—as long as you live in the land (lit.). |
| 26:16–19 | Yahweh your God commands you this day to follow these rules and regulations; carefully observe them with all your heart and with all your soul. You have declared this day that Yahweh is your God and that you will walk in obedience to him, that you will keep his decrees, commands and laws—that you will listen to him. And Yahweh has declared this day that you are his people, his treasured possession as he promised, and that you are to keep all his commands. He has declared that he will set you in praise, fame, and honor high above all the nations he has made and that you will be a people holy to Yahweh your God, as he promised. (v. 16 lit.; vv. 17–19 NIV) |
| 27–28 | the blessings and curses |

The torah collection as an instructional unit operates according to a relationship with the command. The great command is the basis for any true obedience. The torah collection, then, is subordinate to the command to be loyally devoted to Yahweh. Moreover, the two sections here (chs. 6–11 and 12–26) together maintain a relationship with the Ten Words (see Figure 27-B; also see Figure 24-A in Chapter 24). In a general sense the command expounds the first word, and the rules and regulations explain the covenant stipulations to Israel in the land of promise.

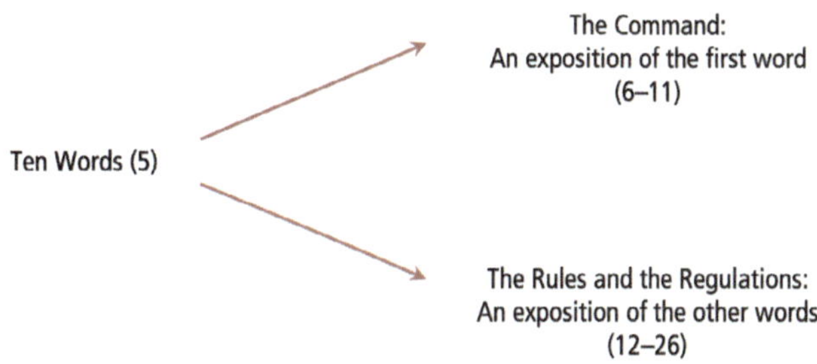


**Figure 27-B:** The Relationship of the Ten Words, the Command, and the Rules and Regulations

The biblical storytellers who narrated the rise and fall of the Hebrew kingdoms interpreted the meaning of that historical narrative in relation to these rules and regulations. The torah collection plays such a significant role in the four-part narrative that runs through Joshua, Judges, Samuel, and Kings that the serial narrative can be called the Deuteronomistic narrative.

*How do the rules and regulations fit within the context of Deuteronomy?*

The biblical writers believe that God's word effectively shapes and explains the meaning of the human world. Thus, when they tell stories, preach, write poetry, and present wisdom, their writings reflect this basic commitment. In the case of the Deuteronomistic narrative, the torah collection explains why Israel's history developed as it did.

*What is the relationship between the torah collection and the Deuteronomistic narrative?*

The close relationship between Israel's storyteller and Deuteronomy means that these writings can help with understanding how the torah collection works. The present Chapter will illustrate how these other biblical writings can shed light on the torah collection of Deuteronomy.

Several examples will illustrate how the interpretive guidelines operate, including centrality of worship, the law of the king, devoting the nations of Canaan, the law of the assembly, and the law of divorce. These laws have not been treated extensively elsewhere in this book. They are each, in different ways, significant in the torah collection itself but also for the entire Torah within its biblical setting. Finally, these examples present a crosssection of the types of law in the torah collection and the kinds of approaches needed to interpret them.

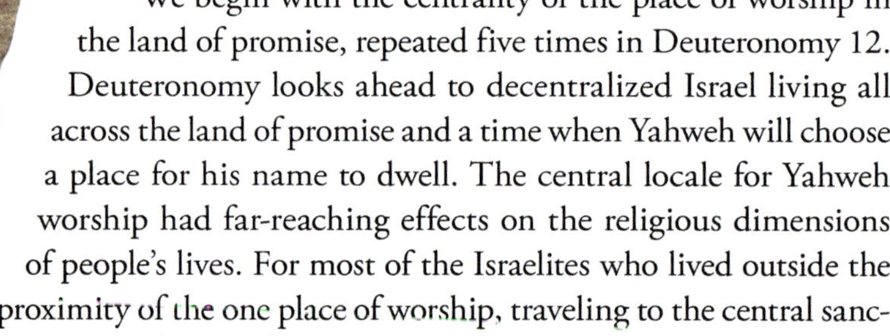

Four-horned altar found at tel Dan
*William Krewson*

We begin with the centrality of the place of worship in the land of promise, repeated five times in Deuteronomy 12. Deuteronomy looks ahead to decentralized Israel living all across the land of promise and a time when Yahweh will choose a place for his name to dwell. The central locale for Yahweh worship had far-reaching effects on the religious dimensions of people's lives. For most of the Israelites who lived outside the proximity of the one place of worship, traveling to the central sanctuary became an event that regularly punctuated their lives. In practical terms, vows, purification, and thanksgiving offerings were all situated around the three annual pilgrimage feasts (see Exod 23:14–17). But decentralized Israel not living near the shrine also changed day-to-day life of Israel. The in-between times had room for Sabbath, prayer, meditation on Torah, and looking forward to worship at the place of Yahweh's choosing.

The theological significance of the singular place of worship reflected the reality that Yahweh is one. Although later local synagogues and local congregations of Christians do not suggest polytheism (see Tigay, 461), the central sanctuary serving decentralized Israel signals an ideal of unity. This singularity is reinforced by the repetition of the place as a "dwelling for his name" (Deut 16:2, 6, 11 lit.). This centralized worship signifies that the nation of Israel, like their God, is one.

*How does the instruction for a central place of worship relate to monotheism?*

Under the kingship of David and his son Solomon, the place of worship was identified as Jerusalem. The establishment of the temple with the ark in the holy of holies signaled the height of Torah-shaped national life (Schnittjer, "Your House"). The division between the northern and southern kingdoms of Israel and Judah in the generation of Solomon's son included the building of rival places to worship for the northern kingdom. The first king of the north, Jeroboam, realized that if his subjects continued to worship in Jerusalem, the kingdom might be reunited. To prevent this, he built two golden calves, one at the northernmost region and the other at the southernmost region of his kingdom—in Dan and Bethel—to provide an alternative to worshiping in Jerusalem (see Map 27-D).

The beginning of the rival places of worship signaled the coming end of the northern kingdom of Israel. During the institution of these competing places of worship, Jeroboam stated his rationale and echoed the rebellion at Sinai.

> Aaron had said: "*These are your gods, Israel, who brought you up out of Egypt.*" (Exod 32:4)
>
> Jeroboam said: "It is too much for you to go up to Jerusalem. *Here are your gods, Israel, who brought you up out of Egypt*" (1 Kgs 12:28, emphases added).

Whereas the narrator of 1–2 Kings frequently used David as the standard of measurement for faithfulness, Jeroboam became the standard for rebellion against God (see Table 27-C). The storyteller repeated that each subsequent king of the north continued to sin after the manner of Jeroboam.

The story of Jeroboam, therefore, offers a dramatic theological counterpoint. Jeroboam is un-Davidic and acted in accord with the rebellion at Sinai (cf. Deut 9:12–17).

**Table 27-C:** Jeroboam and David as Measures for the Northern and Southern Kings, Respectively

| Jeroboam | David |
|---|---|
| every king of Israel followed the pattern of rebellion with the golden calf[a] | kings of Judah were often evaluated as either like or unlike David[b] |

[a]The narrator condemns nearly every king of Israel for following the sin of Jeroboam, son of Nebat: Nadab (1 Kgs 15:26); Baasha (15:34; 16:2, 7); Elah (16:13); Zimri (16:19); Tibni (n/a, splinter faction not able to sponsor the shrines); Omri (16:25–26); Ahab (16:31); Ahaziah (22:52); Jehoram/Joram (2 Kgs 3:3); Jehu (10:29, 31); Jehoahaz (13:2); Jehoash/Joash (13:11); Jeroboam II (14:24); Zechariah (15:9); Shallum (n/a, too short to sponsor shrines); Menahem (15:18); Pekahiah (15:24); and Pekah (15:28). And see summary statement in 2 Kgs 17:21–23. References on Jeroboam in note a from Schnittjer, *OT*, 203, n. 28.

[b]David walked in the statutes and ordinances of Yahweh (1 Kgs 3:14; cf. 9:4; 15:4–5). Later kings walked after the ways of David (Solomon, 3:3; Asa, 15:11; Hezekiah, 2 Kgs 18:3; Josiah, 22:2) or did not walk in the ways of David (Solomon, 1 Kgs 11:4, 6, 33; Jeroboam, 14:8; Abijam, 15:3; Amaziah, 2 Kgs 14:3; Ahaz, 16:2). References on David in note b from von Rad, 163.

David, who established Jerusalem as the place of worship, is the prototype of the person who humbled himself and repented from his sin in accord with Judah (1 Sam 13:14; 2 Sam 12:13; Ps 51; cf. Gen 38:26 and Another Look in Chapter 9). Jeroboam's rebellion is a narrative depiction of the human revolution against God's word.

In sum, the singular place of worship where Yahweh's name would dwell stems from the oneness of God and the solidarity of Israel. The downfall of God's people begins with division into rival kingdoms and rival places of worship.

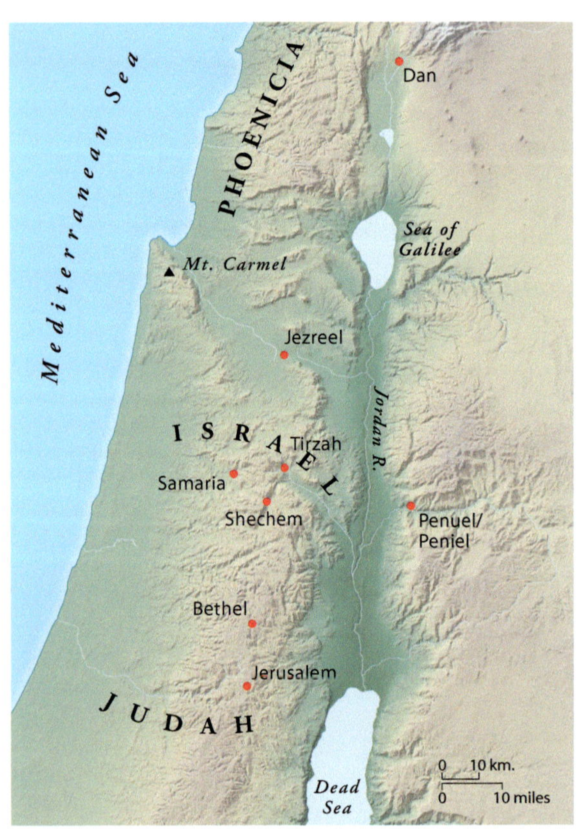


**Map 27-D:** The cities of Dan and Bethel effectively marked the northern and southern borders of the northern kingdom of Israel

The instructions for kings in Deuteronomy 17 need to be considered in general and then in connection to the downfall of the son of David. Was it God's will or was it against his will for Israel to have a human king? The way this question gets answered largely depends on which passages control the others. Many interpreters explain that Yahweh never really wanted Israel to have a king, that the instructions here for kings were a concession if they ever did select a king. The most explicit context to support this reading is 1 Samuel 8:6–7: "But when they said, 'Give us a king to lead us,' this displeased Samuel; so he prayed to Yahweh. And Yahweh told him: 'Listen to all that the people are saying to you; *it is not you they have rejected, but they have rejected me as their king*'" (emphasis added). The people rejected Yahweh.

Deuteronomy does not imply that there was anything wrong with having a human king, but it had to be the right person.

> When you enter the land Yahweh your God is giving you and have taken possession of it and settled in it, and you say, "Let us set a king over us like all the nations around us," be sure to appoint over you a king Yahweh your God chooses. He must be from among your fellow Israelites. Do not place a foreigner over you, one who is not an Israelite. (Deut 17:14–15)

The problem in 1 Samuel is not that the Israelites wanted a king but why they wanted one. They wanted a king because they had rejected Yahweh. They said, "We want a king over us. *Then we will be like all the nations*, with a king to lead us and to go out before us to fight our battles" (1 Sam 8:19b–20, emphasis added; cf. 10:19; 12:12–15).

While it was wrong to reject Yahweh and his rule, securing the right king had always been the plan. David said:

> Yet Yahweh, the God of Israel, chose me from my whole family to be king over Israel forever. *He chose Judah as leader*, and from the tribe of Judah he chose my family, and from my father's sons he was pleased to make me king over all Israel. Of all my sons—and Yahweh has given me many—*he has chosen my son Solomon to sit on the throne of the kingdom of Yahweh over Israel*. (1 Chr 28:4–5, emphasis added; cf. 29:23)

High place and altar (marked by frame) from the time of Jeroboam at tel Dan, used for worshiping a calf image of Israel's God



David's perspective that his son sits upon the throne of Yahweh's kingdom is built on the blessing of Judah in Genesis (Schnittjer, "Blessing," 32–34). The poetic expectations of Jacob/Israel on his deathbed called for a Judah-king one day (cf. Gen 49:8–12; see Chapter 10; Figure 27-E). Deuteronomy 17 explains who should be king and how he should rule.

→ David →

| The Torah story and premonarchical narratives anticipate a divinely appointed Judah-king | The prophets, sages, psalmists, and later narrators re-present David and Solomon as pictures of the coming king |
|---|---|

**Figure 27-E:** David as Focal-point of the Hebrew Scriptures

Solomon's story collided with the teachings of Deuteronomy 17 (Hays, 154–57; Schnittjer, "Composite"). Notice how the biblical narrator told Solomon's story against the Torah warning for the king's lifestyle (emphases added).

*In what ways do the Torah and later biblical narratives support the view that Yahweh intended Israel to have a human king of Yahweh's choosing?*

> *The king, moreover, must not acquire great numbers of horses for himself or make the people return to Egypt to get more of them*, for Yahweh has told you, "You are not to go back that way again." **He must not take many wives, or his heart will be led astray**. *He must not accumulate large amounts of silver and gold.* (Deut 17:16–17)

> *Solomon accumulated chariots and horses. . . . The king made silver as common in Jerusalem as stones. . . . Solomon's horses were imported from Egypt* and from Kue. . . .

> *King Solomon, however, loved many foreign women* besides Pharaoh's daughter—Moabites, Ammonites, Edomites, Sidionians and Hittites. They were from nations about which Yahweh had told the Israelites, "You must not intermarry with them, because they will surely turn your hearts after their gods." Nevertheless, **Solomon held fast to them in love**. . . . As Solomon grew old, his wives turned his heart after other gods, and his heart was not fully devoted to Yahweh his God, as the heart of David his father had been. (1 Kgs 10:26a, 27a, 28a; 11:1–2, 4)

The remarkable story of King Solomon's downfall echoes the sounds of the instruction from Deuteronomy 17. The king's problem was his success. Deuteronomy 8 had warned of the dangers of prosperity. Solomon is a classic example of the problem. Solomon and his kingdom, therefore, were not everything that had been hoped for. Solomon points beyond himself to a coming son of David, the Judah-king.

The instructions to kill the nations of Canaan cause great embarrassment. The situation has led some scholars to do a disservice to students by presenting different views but not taking a position themselves (Hofreiter, 240–62).

Modern Christians find the killing of civilians including women and children a hard teaching. Modern nations like the United States rarely resort to killing all civilians, such as by dropping atomic bombs on two cities of Japan toward the end of the Second World War. Anyone who served in the Pacific theater for the United States military could explain the importance of this decision. Such explanations do not make this action less challenging.

Although the difficult reality of God's extreme measures to protect Israel from rebellion cannot and should not be swept away, at least five lines of evidence can help put in perspective the law of devoting the nations of Canaan. Ignoring this evidence causes great confusion. The first line of evidence requires especially close attention.

First, devoting the nations of Canaan was Israel's idea and a decision that Yahweh accepted during a time of national crisis (see Greenberg, 11–12; Fishbane, 204–8). The first use of "devote" (*ḥrm*) in relation to warfare in Scripture appears in the opening of Numbers 21 (Num 21:2, 3 lit.). In the face of a crisis in the wilderness, Israel made a vow. The king of Arad had taken some Israelites captive (Num 21:1). Israel vowed to "devote" the people of Canaan if Yahweh granted Israel victory, which he did (21:2–3). Yahweh delivered the captives, and the people killed the captors and destroyed their towns. Although this vow might be thought to apply narrowly to this situation, it becomes institutionalized, so to speak, by being spliced into the law of conquest in Deuteronomy 7 and 20 (updating Exod 23:20–33).

Before focusing on how Israel's vow was integrated into the law of conquest, the meaning of the difficult term "devote" needs to be examined. In two cases the verb is used with "to Yahweh," signifying that the objects—material objects, animals, lands, humans—may not be redeemed, for they have been "devoted to Yahweh" (Lev 27:28; Mic 4:13). Starting here, some scholars define "devote" as "removal of something from human use" but not destroy. If "devoted" (*herem*) objects are destroyed, it is only "to make sure nobody can use it" (Walton and Walton, 170). But this qualification does not work in all warfare contexts of Scripture (Grisanti, 259; also see Longman, 172–76; Lynch, 135, n. 24). Deuteronomy 20:16–17 says, "do not leave alive anything that breathes, instead *you shall completely devote them*" (lit., emphasis added). Some contexts pair "smite" (*nkr*) with the sword and "devote" (*hrm*) and speak of leaving no survivors (Josh 10:28, 35, 37, 39 lit.). Other contexts with "devote" speak of "leaving no survivors" among "all who breathe" (10:40 lit.).

The inscription on the Mesha monument of ancient Moab (ca. 830 BCE) uses the equivalent term "devote" (*hrm*) in Moabite.

> Then Chemosh said to me [king Mesha], "Go, seize Nebo from Israel." So I went by night and I waged war against it from the break of dawn until midday. I seized it and I killed everyone—seven thousand m[e]n and boys and g[ir]ls and young women of marriageable age—because **I had devoted it** [*hḥrmth*] to Ashtar-Chemosh. Then I took from there th[e ves]sels of Yahweh and I dragged them before Chemosh (14b–18a, emphasis added; translation from Green, 104–5).

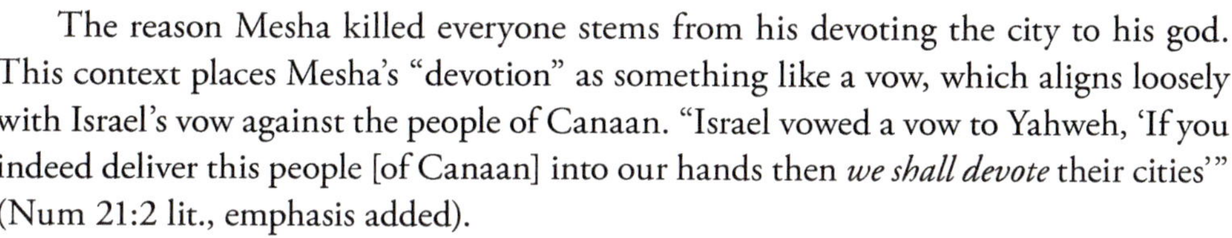

Mesha Inscription (ca. 830 BCE)



The reason Mesha killed everyone stems from his devoting the city to his god. This context places Mesha's "devotion" as something like a vow, which aligns loosely with Israel's vow against the people of Canaan. "Israel vowed a vow to Yahweh, 'If you indeed deliver this people [of Canaan] into our hands then *we shall devote* their cities'" (Num 21:2 lit., emphasis added).

The contested meaning of the verb and noun "devote"/"that which is devoted" (*hrm*/*herem*) do not inherently refer to killing or destruction but to "devotion of." This can include removal from common use to the deity and his priests, such as slavery in the case of the devotion of humans. The term can also function as "devote to destruction" in contexts of warfare where the devoted persons are removed from common use such as slavery, concubinage, or the like, by death.

The important issue for this law pivots on the introduction of the devotion of the peoples of Canaan by Israel, not Yahweh. Though Yahweh does not initiate devoting the nations of Canaan, he accepts Israel's vow and delivers the captives. Since Yahweh delivers the prisoners, this naturally sets a course to integrate the terms of the vow into the legal instructions regarding the invasion of the land of promise. In the previous versions of the instructions regarding the conquest, Yahweh speaks of "drive out" and "wipe out" used in parallel to "drive out." After the people made a vow, the language of "devote" them is added to the law (emphases added).

> My delegate will go ahead of you and bring you into the land of the Amorites, Hittites, Perizzites, Canaanites, Hivites and Jebusites, and *I will wipe them out*. . . . I will send the hornet ahead of you **to drive out** the Hivites, Canaanites and Hittites before you. (Exod 23:23, 28 lit.; cf. "drive out" in 23:29, 30, 31)

> Obey what I command you today. **I will drive out** before you the Amorites, Canaanites, Hittites, Perizzites, Hivites and Jebusites. (34:11 lit.)

> When Yahweh your God brings you into the land you are entering to possess and clears out before you many nations—the Hittites, Girgashites, Amorites, Canaanites, Perizzites, Hivites and Jebusites, seven nations larger and stronger than you—and when Yahweh your God has delivered them over to you and you **smite** them, then **you must completely devote them to destruction**. (Deut 7:1–2a lit.)

In sum of this point, in a time of national crisis Israel made a vow to devote the people of Canaan if Yahweh would deliver their captives. Yahweh fulfilled Israel's request and added devoting to the legal standards for invading the land of promise according to Israel's vow.

Second, the lead-in, "*When* Yahweh your God brings you into the land" (7:1, emphasis added; cf. 12:29) limits the application of this law. The law of devoting the nations of Canaan does not stand for all times in all places. It relates to a specific situation and comes with a near-future expiration date. Deuteronomy uses this exact phrase in 11:29 referring to a ceremony at Mount Gerizim and Mount Ebal that was actualized after defeating Ai (Josh 8:30–35). Similar phrases appear in Deuteronomy 17:14 referring to the appointment of an Israelite king and in 26:3 referring to when Yahweh chooses a place for his name to dwell. These events were actualized when Saul became king and when Solomon built the temple (1 Sam 12; 1 Kgs 5:4; 6:1). This helps explain why Solomon began to treat the remaining peoples of the nations of Canaan as though they were from nations far away after the temple was built (1 Kgs 9:20–21; cf. Deut 20:11; also see Schnittjer, *Old*, 198–99). Killing the peoples of the nations of Canaan is a temporary measure and applies only to the initial military invasion of the land of promise. This is confirmed by presumption of Israel's failure and the prohibition against intermarrying with the peoples of Canaan in the next verse (Deut 7:3).

Third, the rationale for devoting the nations of Canaan hinges on protection of Israel from worshiping their gods, which would incite Yahweh's anger.

> You must destroy them totally. Make no treaty with them, and show them no mercy. Do not intermarry with them. Do not give your daughters to their sons or take their daughters for your sons, *for they will turn your children away from following me to serve other gods*, and Yahweh's anger will burn against you and will quickly destroy you. (Deut 7:2b–4, emphasis added)

> However, in the cities of the nations Yahweh your God is giving you as an inheritance, do not leave alive anything that breathes. Completely destroy them—the Hittites, Amorites, Canaanites, Perizzites, Hivites and Jebusites—as Yahweh your God has commanded you. *Otherwise, they will teach you to follow all the detestable things they do in worshiping their gods, and you will sin against Yahweh your God.* (20:16–18, emphasis added)

The point of devoting the nations of Canaan has nothing to do with ethnicity but to protect Israel from temptation.

Fourth, the basis for judgment of the nations of Canaan is their rebellion, not race or ethnicity. In Yahweh's patience, he forewarned Abraham that the nations of Canaan would be judged for their iniquity (Gen 15:16). Moses assured Israel that occupying the land of promise has nothing to do with Israel's righteousness and everything to do with the wickedness of the nations of Canaan (Deut 9:4–6). In short, Moses claims that the nations of Canaan deserve this judgment. This does not mean that the nations of Canaan sinned more gravely than other peoples. Instead, as noted in the previous point, the wicked nations of Canaan were dangerous because of their close proximity to Israel. This leads to the next point.

Fifth, Yahweh does not treat Israel any differently than the nations of Canaan with respect to standards for inheriting the land of promise. Just as the land will vomit out the nations of Canaan that defile it, so too shall the land vomit out Israel (Lev 18:24–30; 20:22–23). Just as Yahweh uses the military invasion of Israel to bring judgment upon the nations of Canaan, the prophets of Israel and Judah proclaim that he uses the Mesopotamian war machines of Assyria and Babylon to bring Yahweh's judgment upon his own people. In a similar vein, the destruction that came upon the cities of the plain—Sodom, Gomorrah, Admah, and Zeboyim—shall fall upon Israel when they rebel (Deut 29:22–25). Yahweh uses the judgment upon the wicked nations who lived in the land before Israel as an analogy for how he shall treat Israel. As them, so Israel.

In sum of these five lines of evidence, devoting the nations of Canaan started with Israel, not Yahweh. The law of devoting the nations of Canaan held Israel to its vow. The law of devoting is a temporary measure with the purpose of protecting Israel from rebellion. In spite of Yahweh's patience, the nations of Canaan deserved judgment because of their rebellion. Yahweh brings his wrath upon Israel for its rebellion in the same manner he had used Israel to bring his judgment against the nations of Canaan.

Now that the lines of evidence have been investigated, we can briefly observe an example of how the law of devoting is handled in Joshua. The first story of Joshua shows readers that the law is not ethnic. The apostle Paul writes that "not all who are descended from Israel are Israel" (Rom 9:6). In like manner, the story of Rahab the prostitute demonstrates that not all descended from the Canaanites are Canaanites. Rahab turns in faith to the God of Israel. She said:

> We have heard how Yahweh dried up the water of the Red Sea for you when you came out of Egypt, and what you did to Sihon and Og, the two kings of the Amorites east of the Jordan, whom you completely destroyed. When we heard of it, our hearts melted in fear and everyone's courage failed because of you, *for Yahweh your God is God in heaven above and on the earth below.* (Josh 2:10–11, emphasis added)

Was it unlawful to spare Rahab and her family? Is this an example of the sinfulness of Israel (see discussion in Firth, 20–24)? No, just the opposite. The story of Rahab's faith is a narrative commentary on the meaning of Torah. The New Testament explains her faith side by side with the faith of Abraham (Jas 2:25).

This evidence does not take away the gravity of Yahweh's judgment against the nations of Canaan. At the same time, modern people, including well-meaning Christians, who draw a sharp contrast between a wrathful God of hate in the Old Testament versus a Messiah of love in the New Testament, badly distort both Yahweh's mercy and Messiah's demand for righteousness. The evidence in Torah promotes a view that differs from what many modern people say about Israel's God. The gospel of mercy and the need for faithful loyalty to Yahweh begin in Torah.

The beginning of Deuteronomy 23 explains who may and who may not enter the assembly of Yahweh. Notice the two kinds of foreigners and the rationale for exclusion.

> No one whose genitals have been crushed or cut off shall come into the assembly of Yahweh.
>
> No one born of illicit relations shall come into the assembly of Yahweh. Even to the tenth generation none of their descendants shall enter the assembly of Yahweh.
>
> No **Ammonite** or **Moabite** shall come into the assembly of Yahweh, even to the tenth generation none shall come into the assembly of Yahweh, ever. For they did not meet you with bread and water on the way when you were coming out from Egypt, and they hired Balaam son of Beor from Pethor in Mesopotamia to damn you. . . . Do not seek their welfare or their good at any time, ever. You shall not despise an **Edomite** for he is part of your family. You shall not despise an **Egyptian** for you

were guests in his land. Children born to them in the third generation may enter the assembly of Yahweh (Deut 23:1–4, 6–8 lit., emphasis added)

The two kinds of foreigners marked with emphasis are the concern here, but several contextual issues need to be addressed briefly.

What does it mean to be "born of illicit relations"? This difficult expression could mean a bastard (KJV)—one born out of wedlock—or, more broadly, the offspring of any forbidden relationship, such as those listed in Leviticus 18.

Inscription forbidding strangers to enter temple area from the days of the Second Temple



Is "the assembly of Yahweh" the place of worship (i.e., tabernacle or temple) or the nation of Israel? Some understand it as the place of worship since a deformed male organ eliminates one from priestly service (Lev 21:20; cf. Deut 23:1). However, the use of the law of the assembly elsewhere in Scripture applies it to citizenship in Israel (1 Kgs 11:1; Neh 13:1–3).

Did the injunction against Ammonites and Moabites refer only to males? Some have suggested this reading because of Ruth (cf., e.g., m. Yadamaim 4:4; b. Yebam 77a, 77b), but restoration leaders repeatedly say it applies to both genders (Ezra 9:12; Neh 10:30; 13:25; cf. 1 Kgs 11:1; Ruth and Neh 13 will be discussed below).

Should the "tenth generation" be taken literally? Both metaphorical and literal readings effectively mean the same thing in this context (compare Gen 31:7, 41; Num 14:22; also see Table 22-G in Chapter 22). No person will ever live long enough to see their tenth-generation descendant. Therefore, Ammonites and Moabites could never see their offspring enter the assembly of Yahweh. The paraphrase of Deuteronomy 23:3 in Nehemiah 13:1 interprets "tenth generation" as "never."

What is the significance of the "third generation"? Ordinarily an outsider would signify submission to the covenant of Yahweh by being circumcised and circumcising the males of their household. The sign of infant circumcision is passive to the individual, so the commitment to the covenant could not be demonstrated as real until the circumcised children grew up within the covenant and placed the mark of the covenant on their children. Thus, one's devotion to Yahweh's ways was demonstrated in the faith of one's grandchildren—the third generation. Note the relevance of the next generation in the great command of Deuteronomy 6 and for entry into the assembly of Yahweh (see Chapter 26).

*What is the significance of "third generation" concerning commitment to the covenant in Deuteronomy 23? What is the meaning of "tenth generation" in the same context?*

The previous paragraph says "ordinarily" because the four peoples in the law of the assembly—people of Ammon, Moab, Edom, and Egypt—practiced non-covenantal

circumcision (Jer 9:25–26). It was part of their culture. It seems that these four were selected to represent two kinds of others in the law of the assembly because they practiced circumcision and would not be able to take circumcision as a sign of turning in faith to the God of Israel. The law of the assembly demonstrates that it is not circumcision but the commitment to the covenant, which ordinarily would be symbolized by circumcision, that counts.

There were, then, at least two kinds of foreigners: those who could enter the assembly of Yahweh in three generations and those who could never enter. The context explains why the Edomites and Egyptians could enter the assembly of Yahweh in three generations and why the Moabites and Ammonites could not. The former were relatives (Esau's descendants) and Israel's "host," respectively. But Moabites and Ammonites were also relatives (descendants of Lot's sons/grandsons). Ammon and Moab were conceived by illicit relations, but that is not the rationale for exclusion given here. These nations were excluded because of their hostility against Israel in the wilderness (see Num 22–25). It is worse to bring God's curse on his people than to physically oppress them. Oppression and murder only drive someone out of this world, whereas damning and inciting to sin with false gods are attempts to drive someone out of the world to come (see Rashi, 5:272–73 [on Deut 23:8–9]; also see the threat from Moab in Chapter 23).

The teaching of two kinds of others in the law of the assembly in Deuteronomy 23 needs to be measured against related teachings in Scripture. These related teachings help make sense of the law of the assembly.

There are two kinds of others referred to in the teachings on the Passover in Exodus. The context tells of a "mixed crowd" that went up from Egypt (Exod 12:38 lit.). It is not clear what this means, but it may refer to Egyptians and other peoples who joined Israel when they departed from Egypt. In any case, circumcised residing foreigners were invited to participate in the Passover ceremonies while uncircumcised others were forbidden (cf. Konkel, 1:836–39).

> Yahweh said to Moses and Aaron, "These are the regulations for the Passover meal: No foreigner may eat it. Any slave you have bought may eat it *after you have circumcised him*, but a temporary resident or a hired worker may not eat it. . . . A foreigner residing among you who wants to celebrate Yahweh's Passover *must have all the males in his household circumcised*; then he may take part like one born in the land. *No uncircumcised male may eat it.* The same law applies both to the native-born and to the foreigner residing among you." (Exod 12:43–45, 48–49, emphasis added)

The two kinds of others in this context are distinguished based on their sign of commitment to the covenant of Yahweh without respect to genealogy or ethnicity.

What does it mean to be an Ammonite or Moabite? Better, what is the meaning of Deuteronomy 23:1–8, especially as it pertains to Ammonites and Moabites? Are they ethnic or symbolic designations? Isaiah 56 opens with a poetic commentary on this passage. Note the way these categories are interpreted toward temple worship and the community of faith—thus, toward the broader and narrower views of "assembly of Yahweh" mentioned above.

> Let no foreigner **who is bound to Yahweh** say, "Yahweh will surely exclude me from his people." And let no eunuch complain, "I am only a dry tree." For this is what Yahweh says: "To the eunuchs **who keep my Sabbaths, who choose what pleases me and hold fast to my covenant**—to them I will give within my temple and its walls a memorial and a name better than sons and daughters; I will give them an everlasting name that will endure forever. And foreigners **who bind themselves to Yahweh** to minister to him, to love the name of Yahweh, and to be his servants, all who keep the Sabbath without desecrating it and who hold fast to my covenant—these I will bring to my holy mountain and give them joy in my house of prayer. Their burnt offerings and sacrifices will be accepted on my altar; for my house will be called a house of prayer for all nations." (Isa 56:3–7, emphasis added)

Based on the interpretation of the law of the assembly in Isaiah 56, some interpreters think Isaiah has turned aside from the distinction between two kinds of others in Exodus 12 and Deuteronomy 23, accepting anyone. This view badly distorts the evidence. Elsewhere Isaiah alludes to the law of the assembly to exclude forbidden others. The prophet says: "Awake, awake, Zion, clothe yourself with strength! Put on your garments of splendor, Jerusalem, the holy city. **The uncircumcised and defiled will not enter you again**" (52:1, emphasis added). In this way Isaiah continues a commitment to two kinds of others: the uncircumcised and ritually defiled may never enter, but foreigners and eunuchs who bind themselves to Yahweh and his covenant are always welcome (56:3, 4, 6; Schnittjer, "Fall").

Nehemiah 13 narrates the troubles of the postexilic restoration assembly. It begins by telling the story of reading Deuteronomy 23 leading to a third spectacular mass divorce (cf. Ezra 10; Neh 9:2).

> On that day the Book of Moses was read aloud in the hearing of the people and there it was found written that no Ammonite or Moabite should ever be admitted into the assembly of God, because they had not met the Israelites with food and water but had hired Balaam to call a curse down on them. . . . When the people heard this law, **they excluded from Israel all who were of foreign descent**. (Neh 13:1–2a, 3, emphasis added)

Ancient Assyrian eunuch depicted as clean shaven
*Robert C. Kashow*

The restoration assembly did not interpret Ammonites and Moabites ethnically but applied this standard to any excluded others. Elsewhere the restoration assembly made clear that foreigners who turned from the pollutions of the peoples of the lands to the Torah of Yahweh were welcome to join the assembly (Ezra 6:21; Neh 10:28).

The meaning of the Ammonite and Moabite sort of other—the excluded other—is disclosed later in Nehemiah 13. The problem with their otherness is not ethnicity:

> Moreover, in those days I saw men of Judah who had married women from Ashdod, Ammon and Moab. **Half of their children spoke the language of Ashdod or the language of one of the other peoples, and did not know how to speak the language of Judah.** I rebuked them and called curses down on them. I beat some of the men and pulled out their hair. I made them take an oath in God's name and said: "You are not to give your daughters in marriage to their sons, nor are you to take their daughters in marriage for your sons or for yourselves. **Was it not because of marriages like these** that Solomon king of Israel sinned? Among the many nations there was no king like him. He was loved by his God, and God made him king over all Israel, but **even he was led into sin by foreign women**. (Neh 13:23–26, emphasis added)

The dilemma was not ethnic or genealogical but covenantal. Most important, relative to our concern with Deuteronomy, consider the way these people were raising their children. The path of faith revolves around training the next generation in God's instruction (Deut 6:6–9). Nehemiah physically abused these hapless rebels because they had married out, turning away from God. The evidence of their apostasy is that the children did not even know the language of God's people—a sign that they were not being raised according to his teachings (see Schnittjer, "Bad," 43–45).

*How did the problem of intermarriage with others in Nehemiah 13 relate to Deuteronomy's command to instruct the next generation in the teachings of Yahweh?*

The book of Ruth forces readers to interpret the Moabite aspect of Deuteronomy 23 in light of the story of David and the Davidic covenant. Throughout the Ruth story the title character is referred to as a Moabitess seven times, and her homeland is also mentioned seven times. One of Boaz's workers underlines the point when he says: "She is *the Moabitess* who came back from *Moab* with Naomi" (Ruth 2:6 lit., emphasis added). Readers get it: Ruth is a Moabitess from Moab. The identity of Ruth from a people excluded forever from the assembly of Yahweh prepares readers for the very last word of the story.

Ruth is the great-grandmother of David (4:17). If her family is excluded, David is excluded. If David is excluded, so too is the Davidic covenant and its hopes for a messiah.

But Ruth is not excluded. The law of the assembly forbids ever "seeking the welfare or good" of Moabites (Deut 23:6 lit.). But Boaz realizes that although Ruth was born a Moabitess, she has turned to Yahweh (Ruth 2:12). For this reason Boaz extends her the rights of gleaning open to included others (2:8; cf. Lev 19:9–10; Deut 24:19; and see Schnittjer, *Old*, 581–85, 589).

Ruth faithfully embraced Israel's God. She spoke an oath to her Israelite mother-in-law: "Your people will be my people and your God my God" (Ruth 1:16c). Boaz interpreted her commitment according to the Torah's language for people who belong to Yahweh: "May you be richly rewarded by Yahweh, the God of Israel, under whose wings you have come to take refuge" (2:12b). The maternal animal imagery is used to describe God's creative and redeeming acts in Gen 1:2, Exod 19:4, and Deut 32:10–12 (see Table 2-C in Chapter 2).

In the book of Ruth the meaning of this imagery is pushed further. Men like Boaz wore robes, and if they lifted the sides it looked like wings. When Ruth proposed marriage to Boaz, she said, "Spread your wing over me" (3:9b, lit.; cf. Keita and Dyk, 23). Ruth used a figure of speech with a double meaning. Deuteronomy 22:30 uses the expression "uncover the wings" to refer to conjugal relations (lit.; cf. Ezek 16:8). Boaz knew Ruth was not simply saying she was cold—he knew she was seeking marriage (Ruth 3:13). Notice how Ruth's proposal of marriage connects backward through Boaz's prayer to her own oath (see Table 27-F).

*What imagery does the book of Ruth use to depict the assimilation of a Moabite woman into Israel?*

| "Your God, my God" (1:16) | under Yahweh's wings (2:12) | under Boaz's wing (3:9) |
|---|---|---|
| commitment to God's people | adoptive parental protection | marital relationship |
| Ruth to Yahweh | Yahweh to Ruth | Ruth to Boaz and Boaz to Ruth |

**Table 27-F:** Parallel Imagery in the Book of Ruth

In sum, the opening part of Deuteronomy 23 concerns entry into and exclusion from the assembly of Yahweh. Ammonites and Moabites symbolized those who desired God's curse on his people as they had in Numbers 22–25. However, just as not all Israel is Israel (Rom 9:6), not all Moabites are Moabites. The book of Ruth reveals that Moabites could embrace Yahweh's covenant and assimilate into his people and bring forth the fruit of wisdom and righteousness. In this way Ruth the Moabitess became a matriarch in the line of Messiah.

*What is the meaning of Ammonite and Moabite in Deuteronomy 23?*

Examining the law of divorce can illustrate case law. The torah collection contains many case laws that require discovering the principle as precedent for kindred circumstances (see Chapter 14). Among the common denominators between these laws and those concerning other social relationships is the protection of the weak and vulnerable.

Polygamy, capturing a bride while at war, marriage to servants, and serial divorces were all permissible, but socially disadvantaged persons were protected in each case. In the case of a harem, the rights of all wives were defended, explicitly in the case of one who was unloved (Deut 21:15–17; cf. 21:10–14; 22:13–30).

Discussions about the meaning of these rules has stretched across the centuries. An ancient collection of commentaries on many laws, called the Mishnah, includes numerous debates among Judaic scholars (Pharisees) from around the time of Messiah (though it was not written down until 180 or 200 CE). Compare Deut 24:1 (which in its larger context refers to serial divorces and marriages) and the debate about the meaning of this teaching itself in the Mishnah (underlining shows different ways the bold phrase was interpreted):

> If a man marries a woman **and she does not find favor in his eyes because he finds anything indecent about her**, and he writes her a certificate of divorce. (24:1a lit.)

> The School of Shammai say: A man may not divorce his wife unless he has found unchastity in her, for it is written, "Because he hath found in her <u>indecency</u> in anything." And the school of Hillel say: [He may divorce her] even if she spoiled a dish for him, for it is written, "Because he hath found in her indecency <u>in anything</u>." R. Akiba says: Even if he found another fairer than she, for it is written, "And it shall be <u>if she find no favour in his eyes</u>." (Mishnah, Gittin 9:10, emphasis added [p. 321 Danby ed.])

The difference between these three interpretations of Deuteronomy 24:1 embedded in the Mishnah largely relates to which part of the verse was allowed to control the rest—note underlining and bold text above. Compare the three views above to the debate about this law between Messiah and some opposing scholars:

> Some Pharisees came to him to test him. They asked, "Is it lawful for a man to divorce his wife <u>for any and every reason</u>?" . . . Jesus replied, "Moses permitted you to divorce your wives because your hearts were hard. But it was not this way from the beginning. I tell you that anyone who divorces his wife, <u>except for sexual immorality</u>, and marries another woman commits adultery." (Matt 19:3, 8–9, emphasis added)

The religious scholars used an interpretation something like that of Hillel. Messiah explained both the creational context that takes precedence over the teaching itself—a concession for the hard-hearted—and the meaning of the difficult term "indecency" (the Hebrew term *'ervah* is used in the expression *'ervat davar* only in Deut 24:1 and of human excrement in 23:14), which he interpreted as "sexual immorality" (*porneia* in Greek).

Messiah's new torah eliminates polygamy and makes explicit that both male and female marriage partners must be faithful to their marriage vows (contra the traditional Judaic interpretation that only females, not males, can commit adultery, see Freundel, 285). Messiah frames the law in a typical male-oriented manner and says that any man who divorces his wife without cause of sexual infidelity and remarries commits adultery, since (apparently) the first marriage still binds him before God. The punchline relative to the question of polygamy: If a person commits adultery by remarrying after a socially legal but theologically immoral divorce because there is no sexual infidelity (Matt 19:9), then how much more is it adultery to marry another when the person is still legally married to the first spouse (Wenham, 144)? By inference, therefore, Messiah's new torah regarding divorce eliminates any potential moral grounds for polygamy and concubinage.

*How did Messiah's teaching on Deuteronomy 24:1 in Matthew 19:9 eliminate the practices of polygamy and concubinage?*

The larger implications of Messiah's interpretation of Deuteronomy 24:1 can be seen in relation to his followers' response to the debate. Here, as elsewhere, they favored the interpretation of the religious scholars but consented, with reservation, to the view of their master. "The disciples said to him, 'If this is the situation between a husband and wife, it is better not to marry'" (Matt 19:10). They liked the rules better according to the religious leaders.

Why? They realized, apparently, that Messiah's torah protected married women who faced significant social disadvantages in the previous divorce practices. The disciples may have recognized that they were "stuck" with their wives who had just been granted a large measure of freedom and position within the marriage bond. For Messiah, divorce was only permitted in the case of the hard-hearted for sexual unfaithfulness. He accented the permanence of the marriage covenant according to its creational shape. Notice how Messiah explains Deuteronomy in the line with Genesis:

> Some Pharisees came to him to test him. They asked, "Is it lawful for a man to divorce his wife for any and every reason?" **[Deut 24:1]** "Haven't you read," he replied, "that at the beginning the Creator 'made them male and female,' **[Gen 1:27]** and said, 'For this reason a man will leave his father and mother and be united to his wife, and the two will become one flesh' **[Gen 2:24]**?" (Matt 19:3–5)

*Why did Messiah's disciples like the religious leaders' reading of Deuteronomy 24:1?*

Messiah interpreted the teaching on divorce in line with the spirit of many other regulations in this section of Deuteronomy—to provide protection and justice to the socially disadvantaged.

These five examples of how to read the torah collection demonstrate several guidelines for work on other laws in this section of Deuteronomy. First, the reader must be sensitive to context. The immediate context often offers clues for difficult passages. Also, the larger context of the entire torah collection situates it in relationship to the great command, the basis of any meaningful obedience. Moreover, the torah collection functioned as rules and regulations for Israel in the land of promise.

Second, the Bible is the best commentary on the Bible. Readers should recognize that the biblical writings themselves contain the most important interpretations of the laws and narrative of the Torah. If the apprentice of Torah desires to know the limitations and possibilities of the meaning of regulations, she or he needs to learn to hear the conversations on the teachings within the biblical writings themselves.

Third, mastering biblical contexts, like the torah collection, requires patience and humility. The nature of biblical study may seem at odds with the value placed on "practical" and "straightforward" talk in North American culture. My students have often asked things like: "Why doesn't the Bible just say it clearly?" or "How come it takes so much effort to figure out what the Scriptures mean?" These are good questions. The biblical poets and sages are among those who reflected on the profound and, at times, dense nature of the biblical writings. They thought that Torah held treasures to be discovered and cherished (Ps 119:18, 148). The very nature of the Scriptures insist that studying them be a continual, everyday preoccupation of those who love God.

Deuteronomy speaks of continual Scripture study and rehearsal of commands by families (Deut 6:7; 11:19), sharing narratives with the next generation (6:20–25), and measuring the instruction of prophets against the commands (13:2–3). Civil rulers are expected to study Torah every day (17:19). The people should gather and Torah shall be written on a monument at a special ceremony (27:3, 8). Men, women, children, and residing foreigners gather for public Torah reading (31:12). The Torah is placed with the ark as a witness against the people (31:26). The Levities are charged to teach the Torah to Israel (33:10). Reading and study of Scripture individually may be a good place to start. But Deuteronomy pictures much more—godly society devoted to Scripture study in all areas of life.

Still, some people try too hard or in the wrong way. They may offer an interpretation from too small or too big a frame of reference. Most of us have had to endure interpretive fanatics presenting their overreadings with too much zeal and overconfidence, without allowing for the complexities and realities of the scriptural instruction. This does not mean we should say nothing or that we have to be specialists to say anything—not at all. Rather, the excellent apprentice will say something in the right spirit, asking many questions, reading the larger biblical conversation, and remaining patient for greater understanding. God's word invites readers to hear the explanation of the human situation and commands them to teach his word to the next generation, everywhere, all the time.

## ANOTHER LOOK

The rules and regulations—the torah collection—is preceded by the ceremony for the blessings and curses and followed by the blessings and curses themselves (see Figure 27-A). The blessings and curses were the results for the nation of obeying or disobeying the torah collection. They start with an ironic expression that "all these blessings *will come on* you" (28:2, emphasis added). The term for "come on you" often signals an enemy predator overtaking (Harmon, 33). The great Davidic psalm 23 closes similarly with a different term: "Goodness and mercy *will chase* me all of the days of my life" (Ps 23:6 lit.). The context also frames the curses with sickening language. The horrific curses would eventually drive the rebel people to act against all sense.

> Because of the suffering that your enemy will inflict on you during the siege, *you will eat the fruit of the womb, the flesh of the sons and daughters* Yahweh your God has given you. Even the most gentle and sensitive man among you will have no compassion on his own brother or the wife he loves or his surviving children, *and he will not give to one of them any of the flesh of his children that he is eating.* It will be all he has left because of the suffering your enemy will inflict on you during the siege of all your cities. The most gentle and sensitive woman among you—so sensitive and gentle that she would not venture to touch the ground with the sole of her foot—will begrudge the husband she loves and her own son or daughter *the afterbirth from her womb and the children she bears. For in her dire need she intends to eat them secretly* because of the suffering your enemy will inflict on you during the siege of your cities. (Deut 28:53–57, emphasis added)

In certain respects the blessings and curses resemble those in Leviticus 26, though the form is distinct. The curses in both contexts far outweigh the blessings. This may have something to do with the certainty of rebellion against the Torah predicted in Deuteronomy 31. The curses in general can be summarized thus: "'Cursed is anyone who does not uphold the words of this torah by carrying them out.' Then all the people shall say, 'Amen!'" (Deut 27:26; cf. Gal 3:10).

The covenantal nature of the blessings and curses and their attachment to the torah collection can be seen in the introductory setting of Deuteronomy 27. Moses and the elders describe a monument with the law written on it that the people must place on Mount Ebal to demonstrate themselves bound to the covenant. This monument relates to the ceremony the people are to participate in, according to the closing of Deuteronomy 11. They are to recite the blessings from Mount Gerizim and the curses from Mount Ebal. The story of the fulfillment of these teachings is found in Joshua 8, following Israel's defeat of the cities of Jericho and Ai.

"When you have crossed the Jordan, these tribes shall stand on Mount Gerizim to bless the people: Simeon, Levi, Judah, Issachar, Joseph and Benjamin. And these tribes shall stand on Mount Ebal to pronounce curses: Reuben, Gad, Asher, Zebulun, Dan and Naphtali" (Deut 27:12–13).

Shechem is between Mount Gerizim (left) and Mount Ebal (right). *Todd Bolen/ BiblePlaces.com*

It is important not to reduce the cause-and-effect relationship of obey/bless, disobey/curse to rigid, mechanistic thinking. The first command, to love Yahweh with all of one's being, is a prerequisite of any true obedience. The legal standards for obedience do not seek mindless compliance. The instructions for righteousness provide a pathway for faithful devotion within the context of a covenantal relationship. Those who love Yahweh seek to follow his will (Deut 7:9).

Joining the assembly of Yahweh was open to the most cursed of the nations. As discussed above, not all Canaanites are Canaanites and not all Moabites are Moabites. The difference between them turned on how they relate to Yahweh. Rahab and Ruth each acknowledged God as God and embraced the story of what he had done—the word of God—as the beginning of loyalty and devotion to him. More than examples of entry into the assembly, Rahab and Ruth became part of the larger story of the coming of the Messiah, part of his ancestral lineage within the tribe of Judah (Matt 1:5). Messiah came from God to a family of sinners including Canaanites, Moabites, and Israelites. His human family makes an important statement on the scope of his mission. He is the Messiah for the cursed, the outcast, the sinner—humankind at large.

## INTERACTIVE WORKSHOP

### *Chapter Summary*

The rules and regulations, also known as the torah collection, are the collection of laws that bound the nation of Israel in the land of promise. Biblical storytellers interpreted the covenant relationship established by the torah collection. To apprehend the meaning of the rules and regulations requires listening to the conversation between the torah collection and the biblical commentaries on it. The covenant relationship established by the torah collection, moreover, bound Israel to the blessings and curses attached to it.

## *Can You Explain the Key Terms?*

- assembly of Yahweh
- blessings and curses
- Canaanites
- Deuteronomistic narrative
- indecency
- Moabites and Ammonites
- the rules and regulations
- torah collection

## *Challenge Questions*

1. What is the relationship between the Ten Words (Deut 5), the command (chs. 6–11), the rules and the regulations (chs. 12–26), and the blessings and curses (chs. 27–28)?
2. How does the torah collection (Deut 12–26) function in the context of the covenant relationship set out in Deuteronomy?
3. How did the law concerning the centrality of worship reflect on Israel's God?
4. Why would assimilation into Israel not reach its end for three generations?

## *Advanced Questions*

1. How does the torah collection to Israel in the land function in relation to the universal effect of the great command?
2. What lines of evidence explain the rationale for the law of devoting the nations of Canaan in Deuteronomy 7 and 20?
3. What are the specific ways in which the regulations concerning marriage and rape in Deuteronomy 22:13–30 protect the socially disadvantaged?

*4. What are the leading views of the meaning of *mamzer* (Deut 23:2[3]), and how should it be translated?

*5. What does the use of *'ervat davar* in Deuteronomy 23:14[15] tell us about its significance in 24:1? Evaluate the possibility and implication of the use of the Greek term *porneia* in Matthew 19:9 to interpret the Hebrew expression *'ervat davar* in Deuteronomy 24:1.

## *Research Project Ideas*

Explain the effects of the instruction of central worship on decentralized Israel in the land of promise (see Schnittjer, *Old*, 111–19).

Compare the structure and content of the dietary regulations in Deuteronomy 14 and Leviticus 11 (see Table 18-D and source cited there).

Evaluate the protections against sexual predators and violence in Deuteronomy 22:22–29 (see Lynch, 191–200).

Investigate—historically, theologically, and exegetically—the reading of Deuteronomy 23 in 4QFlorilegium/4Q174 1.3–4 (note the way that Amos 9:11 is used by 4QFlor/4Q174 1.12 in an opposite manner than by James, who applied it to uncircumcised gentiles in Acts 15:16–18).

Compare the instructions for and the story of the ceremonies and monument on Mount Ebal and Mount Gerizim (Deut 11; 27; Josh 8).

## *The Next Step*


Firth, David G. *Including the Stranger: Foreigners in the Former Prophets.* Downers Grove, IL: IVP Academic, 2019.

Fishbane, Michael. *Biblical Interpretation in Ancient Israel.* New York: Clarendon, 1985.

Freundel, Barry. *Contemporary Orthodox Judaism's Response to Modernity.* New York: Ktav, 2004.

Green, Douglas J. *"I Undertook Great Works": The Ideology of Domestic Achievements in West Semitic Royal Inscriptions.* Forschungen zum Alten Testamentum 2/41. Tübingen: Mohr Siebeck, 2010.

Greenberg, Moshe. "Ḥerem." Pages 10–13 in vol. 9 of *Encyclopedia Judaica.* 2d ed. Edited by F. Skolnik. Farmington Hills, MI: Thomson Gale, 2007.

Grisanti, Michael A. Review of *The Lost World of Israelite Conquest* by John H. Walton and J. Harvey Walton. *Master's Seminary Journal* 29.2 (2018): 257–60.

Harmon, Matthew S. *Rebels and Exiles: A Biblical Theology of Sin and Restoration.* Essential Studies in Biblical Theology. Downers Grove, IL: IVP Academic, 2020.

Hays, J. Daniel. "Has the Narrator Come to Praise Solomon or Bury Him?: Narrative Subtlety in 1 Kings 1–11." *Journal for the Study of the Old Testament* 28.2 (2003): 149–74.

Hofreiter, Christian. "Genocide in Deuteronomy and Christian Interpretation." Pages 240–62 in *Interpreting Deuteronomy: Issues and Approaches.* Edited by David G. Firth and Philip S. Johnson. Downers Grove, IL: IVP Academic, 2012.

Keita, Schadrac, and Janet W. Dyk. "The Scene at the Threshing Floor: Suggestive Readings and Intercultural Considerations on Ruth 3." *Bible Translator* 57 (2006): 17–32.

Konkel, A. H. "גור." Pages 836–39 in vol. 1 of *New International Dictionary of Old Testament Theology and Exegesis.* Edited by Willem A. VanGemeren. Grand Rapids: Zondervan Academic, 1997.

Longman, Tremper, III. *Confronting Old Testament Controversies: Pressing Questions about Evolution, Sexuality, History, and Violence.* Grand Rapids: Baker Books, 2019.

Lynch, Matthew J. *Flood and Fury: Old Testament Violence and the Shalom of God.* Downers Grove, IL: IVP Academic, 2023.

———. *Portraying Violence in the Hebrew Bible: A Literary and Cultural Study.* Cambridge: Cambridge University Press, 2021.

*The Mishnah.* Edited and translated by Herbert Danby. New York: Oxford University Press, 1933.

Rashi (Rabbi Shlomo Yitzhaki). *The Metsudah Chumash/Rashi.* 5 vols. Edited by Rabbi Avrohom Davis. New York: Ktav, 1998.

Schnittjer, Gary E. "The Bad Ending of Ezra-Nehemiah." *Bibliotheca Sacra* 173 (2016): 32–56.

———. "The Blessing of Judah as Generative Expectation." *Bibliotheca Sacra* 177 (2020): 15–39.

———. "The Fall and Rise of Lady Zion." *Cateclesia Forum* (2021). https://cateclesia.com/2021/08/02/the-fall-and-rise-of-lady-zion/

———. *Old Testament Use of Old Testament.* Grand Rapids: Zondervan Academic, 2021.

———. "An Overview of Composite Citations in the Hebrew Bible: with a Case Study from 1 Kings 11:1–4." In *Composite Allusions in Antiquity.* Edited by Sean A. Adams and Seth M. Ehorn. Library of New Testament Studies. London: Bloomsbury, forthcoming.

———. "Your House Is My House: Exegetical Intersection within the Davidic Promise." *Bibliotheca Sacra* (forthcoming).

Tigay, Jeffrey H. *Deuteronomy.* JPS Torah Commentary. Philadelphia: Jewish Publication Society, 1996.

von Rad, Gerhard. *From Genesis to Chronicles: Explorations in Old Testament Theology.* Edited by K. C. Hanson. Translated by E. W. Trueman Dicken. Minneapolis: Fortress, 2005.

Walton, John H. and J. Harvey Walton. *The Lost World of Israelite Conquest: Covenant, Retribution, and the Fate of the Canaanites.* Downers Grove, IL: IVP Academic, 2017.

Wenham, Gordon J. *Story as Torah: Reading Old Testament Narrative Ethically.* Grand Rapids: Baker Academic, 2000.

# 28 A VIEW OF THE OTHER SIDE

## *Deuteronomy 29–34*

*iStock.com/ArtistAllen*

## GETTING STARTED

### *Focus Question*

What does it mean that the Torah ends by looking across to the other side?

### *Look for These Terms*

- the book of the Torah
- heaven and earth
- life and death
- new covenant
- other side
- prophet like Moses
- realm of the dead (*sheol*)

## OUTLINE

A. **New covenant (29–30)**
B. **Moses to be replaced by Joshua and the Torah (31)**
C. **Song of Moses (32)**
D. **Blessing of Moses (33)**
E. **Death of Moses (34)**

## A READING

The view from the end of Deuteronomy is a view of "the other side." The end of the Torah story does not signify that the story is finished—it looks forward to the rest of the story. The narrative as a whole functions as a prologue for the story that is about to begin. The Five Books of Moses are serial narratives, each with a beginning and ending; but in a real sense, together they begin a larger narrative series, the biblical story. The view from the end is a view of the next beginning.

The act of looking toward the other side of the Jordan River—which readers behold with Moses—carries with it many far-reaching elements. Each of the five points in the outline can be metaphorically expressed in terms of the other side (see Table 28-A). At the same time, the dramatic forward looking posture of these closing chapters seems entirely bound up with the story that has gone before. The beyond-the-ending vision of the ending stems from the Torah story that has led up to this point. This culmination of the story re-situates the narrative itself in its entirety. The Torah, it turns out, is the beginning of the story. The other side of the Jordan and all that it means only makes sense in the light of the path to the plains of Moab—from the garden to the river.

*In what sense does Deuteronomy look ahead? And in what sense does it look back?*

| | A view of . . . |
|---|---|
| New covenant (29–30) | the other side of Israel's history in exile |
| Moses to be replaced by Joshua and Torah (31) | Israelite leadership on the other side of the Jordan |
| Song of Moses (32) | the other side of time—the last days |
| Blessing of Moses (33) | tribal life on the other side of the Jordan |
| Death of Moses (34) | the other side of the Jordan |

**Table 28-A:** A View of the Other Side in Deuteronomy 29–34

The five parts of the ending of Deuteronomy can be read backward and forward. In each case, emphasis falls on God's word and the human rebellion against his word.

The new covenant looks back at the older covenant—including both versions of the Ten Words to both generations (Exod 20; Deut 5)—and surpasses it, even before the completion of the Torah story in which it is presented. Moses says this covenant is "in addition to" the covenant at Horeb that he has been explaining all day (29:1). The people have not even begun to live under the covenant that will shape their lives in the land of promise before it is already seen as a thing of the past. It is effectively a relic before it begins. A new covenant is needed.

The new covenant also intentionally reaches beyond the people's dwelling in the land of promise to a time when they will again be in exile and long to return to the land (Deut 30:1–6; cf. discussion of "you" in Chapter 24). They look so far ahead that they already need to look back to the land once again, yet they have not yet been there in the first place.

Future generations will see the curses and judgments that have fallen on the land of promise and God's people. It will be like Sodom and Gomorrah (29:22–28). The terrifying acts of God in the Torah story offer a template for the judgment to come. The wickedness of the people is expected to reach the heights of ancient sinners from the days of Abraham. Even Lot, the father of the Ammonites and Moabites, escaped the destruction of these cities.

Moab plateau
*© Glowimages/ Designpics*

The generation of Israelites to come will not escape. They are invited to imagine looking back at the future, after their rebellion against the covenant. "Therefore Yahweh's anger burned against this land, so that he brought on it all the curses written in this book. In furious anger and in great wrath Yahweh uprooted them from their land and thrust them into another land, as it is now" (Deut 29:27–28).

Is it all in vain? Is Yahweh redeeming Israel and giving his covenant to them only to initiate certain failure? Yes and no. The judgment of Israel is inevitable. They will rebel against the commands and promises of God until they receive the full measure of his wrath. Yet, Torah does not end in a word of death. The hope of every generation of Yahweh's people is that one day Yahweh will "restore their fortunes." He will bring them back again. The God of Israel promises that on the other side of their well-deserved captivity he will gather them up and bring them back. The cause-and-effect relationship of the manner by which God's word will prevail over the rebellious and stubborn hearts of his people is spelled out: "*Yahweh your God will circumcise your hearts* and the hearts of your descendants, *so that you may love him* with all your heart and with all your soul, and live" (30:6, emphasis added; see Figure 28-B).

**Figure 28-B:** Path to Obedience and Life in Deuteronomy 30:6

circumcision of the heart ⟶ love God ⟶ life

God's word will prevail over the rebellion against it. The success is rooted in his power and grace. Yahweh will act on the hearts of his people to accomplish what nothing within the human world can. The symbolic force of this hope starts with Yahweh's ownership as father (see Another Look in Chapter 19). The act of circumcision is passive for the child. It signifies his parents' will for him. Moreover, the sign of the covenant on the human body denotes the commitment to instruct the up-and-coming generation in the word of God. The people need Yahweh to teach them what they had seen with their eyes but failed to apprehend (29:2–4).

Jeremiah advances the new covenant by a classic statement. "I will put my torah in their minds and write it on their hearts. I will be their God, and they will be my people" (Jer 31:33b). Jeremiah's sermonic oracle refers to active not passive knowledge. Because God's word must come to pass, writing the torah on the mind and heart of his people is a figural way of saying he will change who they are. As Deuteronomy 30:6 says, they will love him with their all and will obey the great command. Israel will, finally, live life in accord with the design of humankind. Moreover, in a new sense Yahweh will be their covenantal Father.

The new covenant, though set beyond the exile, carries immediate force—it is for "today" (30:11). The people are invited to choose life. The already and not-yet dimensions of the new covenant cannot be taken as mere rhetorical flare. "See, I set before you *today* life and prosperity, death and destruction. . . . *This day* I call the heavens and the earth as witnesses against you that I have set before you life and death, blessings and curses. Now choose life, so that you and your children may live" (30:15, 19, emphasis added).

What does it mean that it is not out of their reach (30:11–14)? The answer, or at least a partial answer, runs along two lines. To obey the command requires an act of God—a miracle. The human rebellion can only be overcome by divine grace. The new life needed for obedience to God's will has always been the effect of his grace. The work of God is here expressed as an act of Yahweh in the heart (30:6). The other matter is the individual and community dimensions. The new covenant promises life and blessing to all Israel. For now, however, not all Israel is Israel (see Rom 9:6; Bruno, Compton, and McFadden, 122–37).

The new covenant, however it is understood, is "already" in some sense though "not yet" for that aspect concerning the other side of the exile. "Now what I am commanding you today is not too difficult for you or beyond your reach" (30:11). Where is it? "The word is very near you; it is in your mouth and in your heart so you may obey it" (30:14). The word is in their mouths when they read Torah, recite it, and teach it everywhere, all the time, to the next generation (6:6–7; 11:18–19). The word that brings life is the Torah story.

*What points toward the present force of the new covenant teaching within Deuteronomy?*

The approaching death of Moses signals the need for a replacement. Deuteronomy 31 offers a view of his replacements for life on the other side of the Jordan River. Moses is to be replaced by Joshua and a book, the Torah scroll. The chapter moves back and forth in interchange between the two, demonstrating, among other things, the enduring place of the Torah of Moses in the life of the people (see Table 28-C). Moses is, in this sense, unique among the prophets of Yahweh. The prophets' poetic oracles and other sermons must all, somehow or other, fit within the framework of the Torah.

**Table 28-C:** Interchange Structure of Deuteronomy 31

| |
|---|
| Moses summons Joshua (vv. 1–8) |
| Torah to be read to the people (vv. 9–13) |
| Yahweh summons Moses to call Joshua (vv. 14–15) |
| The Song of Moses will bear witness against the rebellion of the people (vv. 16–22) |
| Yahweh commissions Joshua (v. 23) |
| Torah will bear witness against the people when they rebel (vv. 24–29) |

The commission of Joshua here follows his selection in Numbers 27. At this juncture Yahweh promises never to leave him or forsake him. Joshua is a prophet like Moses in the sense that Yahweh is with him. He, like Moses, becomes a pointer toward one who will come.

The "book of the Torah," within this context, may refer to the torah collection (Deut 12–26) or to the entire second discourse (4:44–28:68)—"this is the torah" (4:44)—or perhaps the entire book of Deuteronomy. In its present form, however, it effectively includes the entire Torah. In any case, the Torah scroll testifies against the sinfulness of the people.

The heavens and the earth of the Negev

*iStock.com/ Vladimir1965*

After Moses finished writing in a book the words of this torah from beginning to end, he gave this command to the Levites who carried the ark of the covenant of Yahweh: "Take this Book of the Torah and place it beside the ark of the covenant of Yahweh your God. **There it will remain as a witness against you.** For I know how rebellious and stiff-necked you are. If you have been rebellious against Yahweh while I am still alive and with you, how much more will you rebel after I die! Assemble before me all the elders of your tribes and all your officials, so that I can speak these words in their hearing and call the **heavens and the earth to testify against them**. For I know that after my death you are sure to become utterly corrupt and to turn from the way I have commanded you. In days to come, disaster will fall upon you because you will do evil in the sight of Yahweh and arouse his anger by what your hands have made." (Deut 31:24–29, emphasis added)

*What was the function of the Torah for sinners?*

The written Torah joins the heavens and the earth for their parallel functions. Both are the effect of God's word and both symbolically testify against the human rebels. More significant, perhaps, is that it is placed with the ark. Placing a copy of a treaty or covenant before a god is attested in ancient Hittite treaties (see Treaty between Suppiluliuma I of Hatti [14th cent. BCE] and Shattiwaza of Mittanni, 6A §13 in Beckman, 46; Carpenter, 1:515).

Placing the Torah scroll with the ark establishes connections. At the beginning of the Torah story, the winged sphinxes and flaming sword stood guard, preventing anyone from entering the garden. The tree of life was sealed off from humanity. At the end of the Torah, it is the Torah itself that is placed outside of reach. It is guarded by the winged sphinxes on the veil that enclosed the holy of holies. The book that presented Israel with the choice between life and death and the tree that granted life are each in a realm beyond human reach, protected by the guardians of Yahweh. Yet Torah is not out of reach. To read the Torah and teach it to the next generation brings the storied world of God's word—his holy revelation that brings life—into the mouths of readers.

*In what ways is the Torah scroll before the ark similar to the tree of life?*

The Song of Moses looks backward to the beginning of humankind and the creation of Israel and looks ahead to the "last days" (Deut 31:29 lit.). The last days were referred to earlier in the blessing of the sons of Jacob, the oracles of Balaam, and in the first discourse of Deuteronomy (Gen 49:1; Num 24:14; Deut 4:30). This song, by its placement and by its content, offers a sense of closure to the Five Books of Moses. It is the fourth major poetic section of the Pentateuch—the blessing of the sons of Jacob, the Song of the Sea, the oracles of Balaam, and the Song of Moses—each placed after major narrative sections (see Table 10-A in Chapter 10).

The Song of Moses has a profound effect on the rest of the Bible. The song's scope includes all of time, and its powerful poetic imagery establishes embryonic ideals that later become known as heaven and hell. Notice the language of the fires of the underworld or realm of the dead (*sheol*): "For a fire will be kindled by my wrath, one that burns down to the realm of the dead (*sheol*) below. It will devour the earth and its harvests and set afire the foundations of the mountains" (Deut 32:22). Many biblical writers draw heavily on its poetic interpretation of the Torah narrative. For readers familiar with the word pictures and poetic inclinations of the Davidic psalms, like the protective wings (32:11; Pss 17:8; 63:7), it is a good guess that the Song of Moses was a favorite song of the psalmist. The preachers and letter writers like Isaiah and Paul drew on the song's imagery in various places (see Deut 32:1//Isa 1:2; Deut 32:35//Rom 12:19; Another Look below).

The blessing of Moses offers a poetic view of tribal life on the other side of the Jordan River. The general fact of this blessing to the tribes resembles Jacob's blessing to his sons on his deathbed. At the same time, there are several similar poetic phrases in the Balaam oracles and the blessing of Moses. One of the more difficult issues to explain is why Simeon is not included. Two ideas that seem to work and are not mutually exclusive concern the locale of the tribe of Simeon in the land and the judgment included in the blessing of Jacob. The small tribe of Simeon resided within Judah and may have been absorbed into the larger tribe (Map 28-D). Note also, "Simeon and Levi . . . I will scatter them in Jacob and disperse them in Israel" (Gen 49:5a, 7b). Perhaps this is fulfilled in the sense that Levi was given to God and placed in cities throughout Israel, and Simeon was swallowed up by Judah (though the tribe of Simeon could be identified at least as late as the days of Josiah, 2 Chr 34:6). Thus, omitting Simeon from the blessing of Moses may be fulfilling the last words of Jacob regarding Simeon, at least in a symbolic sense. The reason, however, may be something else now lost to us.

**Map 28-D:** Was the tribe of Simeon absorbed into the tribe of Judah?

Deuteronomy closes with the death and burial of Moses and the expectation for the coming of a prophet like Moses. The general shape of the ending is reminiscent of Genesis (see Table 28-E). The last thing Moses sees is the land of promise as it unfolds on the other side of the Dead Sea across from Mount Nebo (just south of the plains of Moab). The ending looks back to the land God promised to Abraham, Isaac, and Jacob and looks back on the life of Moses, while Israel mourns for thirty days. It also looks ahead to the same things: the land of promise and the coming of a prophet like Moses.

**Table 28-E:** A General Comparison of the Closing of Genesis and Deuteronomy

| Genesis | Deuteronomy |
|---|---|
| blessing of the twelve sons of Jacob (49) | blessing of the twelve tribes of Israel (33) |
| death and burial of Israel (50) | death and burial of Moses (34) |

The expectation for the coming prophet like Moses closes Deuteronomy and the entire Torah by situating this expectation into the indefinite future of the book, making it contemporary through the kingdom, the exile, and beyond:

> Since then, *no prophet has risen in Israel like Moses, whom Yahweh knew face to face, who did all those signs and wonders* Yahweh sent him to do in Egypt—to Pharaoh and to all his officials and to his whole land. For no one has ever shown the mighty power or performed the awesome deeds that Moses did in the sight of all Israel. (Deut 34:10–12, emphasis added)

The prophet expected to come one day is depicted by three Torah-pictures of Moses (see Table 28-F). To look for the future promises of Yahweh, one has to study the story of what he has done.

The expectation for the coming prophet is drawn from three main contexts, each one further back within the Torah. The expectation for a prophet like Moses is first reported in Deuteronomy 18. Moses himself said, "Yahweh your God will raise up for you *a prophet like me* from among you, from your fellow Israelites. You must listen to him"

View of the promised land from Mount Nebo
*iStock.com/ArtistAllen*

| Deuteronomy 34 | Background |
|---|---|
| "prophet like Moses" (v. 10) | promised in Deuteronomy 18 (which looks back to Deut 5, which looks back to Exod 20) |
| "whom Yahweh knew face to face" (v. 10) | narrative of the routine of revelation in Exodus 33:7–11 (cf. Num 7:89; 12:6–8) |
| "who did all the signs and wonders in Egypt" (v. 11) | confrontations with pharaoh in Exodus 5–15 |

**Table 28-F:** Background for the "Prophet like Moses" Imagery

(18:15, emphasis added). The basis of this expectation is rooted in the historic event at Mount Horeb (see Table 28-G; bold and underlining mark parallels and wavy underlining marks the new element). The interpretation of the revelatory event at the mountain by Yahweh gave rise to this expectation. Thus, the past revelation of God's word creates the necessary coming of a new mediator.

| Story of the revelatory event at the mountain | Retelling the story of the revelatory event at the mountain | Expected prophet based on the revelatory event at the mountain |
|---|---|---|
| When the people saw the thunder and lightning and heard the trumpet and saw the mountain in smoke, they trembled with fear. They stayed at a distance and said to Moses, "Speak to us yourself and we will listen. **But do not have God speak to us or we will die**." (Exod 20:18–19) | When you heard the voice out of the darkness, while the mountain was ablaze with fire, all the leaders of your tribes and your elders came to me. . . . "**But now, why should we die? This great fire will consume us, and we will die if we hear the voice of Yahweh our God any longer.**" . . . Yahweh heard you when you spoke to me, and Yahweh said to me, "I have heard what this people said to you. Everything they said was good." (Deut 5:23, 25, 28) | For this is what you asked of Yahweh your God at Horeb on the day of the assembly when you said, "**Let us not hear the voice of Yahweh our God nor see this great fire anymore, or we will die.**" Yahweh said to me: "What they say is good. I will raise up for them a prophet like you from among their fellow Israelites, and I will put my words in his mouth. He will tell them everything I command him." (Deut 18:16–18) |

**Table 28-G:** The Origin of the Expectation for a Prophet like Moses

The Torah story, therefore, is not merely an account of what has happened. The narrated acts of Yahweh themselves create the future hope that will bring his word to pass. The future-creating nature of the Torah narrative is apprehended by Israel's preachers. The prophets envision a future according to the scriptural past. They speak of new heavens and new earth, days like Noah's, new exodus, the coming of a king, new covenant, and so forth. What Yahweh has done provides the shape and meaning of what he will do.

*How did the historic event of God's revelation at Horeb establish the biblical expectation for a prophet like Moses?*

The prophet like Moses will know God "face to face."

Jacob proclaimed that he had seen God face to face after his encounter at the Jabbok (Gen 32:30). The revelation at Mount Horeb was described as Israel's seeing God face to face (Deut 5:4). Neither of these come close to what it meant for Moses to see God face to face. One of the normal routines in the wilderness was Moses's conversing with God in the tent of meeting—"Yahweh would speak to Moses face to face, as one speaks to a friend" (Exod 33:11a; cf. Num 7:89). The categorical distinction between Moses and other prophets, even important ones like Aaron and Miriam, was made clear by God during their bout of grumbling in the wilderness. He said:

> When there is a prophet among you, I, Yahweh, reveal myself to them in visions, I speak to them in dreams. But this is not true of my servant Moses; he is faithful in all my house. *With him I speak mouth to mouth, clearly and not in riddles; he sees the form of Yahweh.* Why then were you not afraid to speak against my servant Moses? (Num 12:6b–8, v. 8 lit., emphasis added)

The prophet like Moses will perform signs and wonders, like the fear-inspiring acts against Egypt. The cosmic terrors, mediated from the Creator through his servant Moses, offer a view of the power of the coming prophet. The story of terrifying judgments against the rebel Egyptians becomes a vault of apocalyptic imagery that the biblical visionaries use to describe the coming day of judgment (see Another Look in Chapter 13).

Genesis ends with the promise of the Judah-king who would come in the last days to rule the nations. Deuteronomy, and thus the Torah story, closes with the narrator's stated expectation for a prophet like Moses, one who will know God and wield his power in accord with Moses himself. The Torah's promises reach into and beyond the world of the reader. The Torah-shaped king and prophet will return.

## ANOTHER LOOK

The last section of Deuteronomy is frequently used by later Scripture writers. Three brief examples can illustrate the importance of the last part of Deuteronomy.

First, the Elijah and Messiah narratives echo the sounds of the prophet-like-Moses imagery. Elijah's signs and his unusual experience on Mount Horeb give him a Moses-like story (see Isbell, 160–62). Yahweh sent a wind, earthquake, and fire, but he was not in them. When Elijah heard the "gentle whisper," he covered his face and went into the cave (1 Kgs 19:11–14). There are several similarities between this incident and the revelation of God to Moses. God covered Moses's face with his hand and placed him in the cleft of the rock on the same mountain (Exod 33:21–23). The narratives of

Messiah have many echoes from the accounts of Moses and Elijah. His transfiguration on a mountain is all the more reminiscent of the revelations to Moses and Elijah because they were both there (Matt 17:1–13//Mark 9:2–13//Luke 9:28–36). Messiah unveils what he normally veils.

Second, although he never directly quoted it, Paul's Athenian-friendly speech depicts a worldview that applies imagery that seems to be based on the Song of Moses (see Table 28-H). Most of the parallels are at the conceptual level, but there are several terms that are common between Acts 17 and the Septuagintal translation of Deuteronomy 32. The only direct quotations in the speech are from ancient Greek poets. This does not make it a secular speech. What is usually overlooked is that, while Paul's speech was packaged for the worldly Athenians, he based his message on a theological framework from the Torah.

The point of departure for Paul's speech is the monument "to an unknown god," whom he identifies as the one and only God. This possible echo of the Song of Moses is ironic because it inverts the reference to "unknown gods" that Israel wrongly worshiped in the desert (see Table 28-H). Moreover, Paul uses language similar to Deuteronomy 32 to refer to the Creator's relationship with humankind and his providential will over the nations.

**Table 28-H:** Similarities between Paul's Speech to the Athenians and the Song of Moses

| Acts 17 | Deuteronomy 32 |
|---|---|
| (All the Athenians and the foreigners who lived there spent their time doing nothing but talking about and listening to the latest ideas.) Paul . . . said: "People of Athens! I see that in every way you are very religious. For as I walked around and looked carefully at your objects of worship, I even found an altar with this inscription: **'To an unknown god.'** So you are ignorant of the very thing you worship—and this is what I am going to proclaim to you. . . . And he is not served by human hands, as if he needed anything. Rather, he himself gives everyone life and breath and everything else. From one man he made all the nations, that they should inhabit the whole earth; and he marked out their appointed times in history and the boundaries of their lands. . . . "Therefore since we are God's offspring, we should not think that the divine being is like gold or silver or stone—an image made by human design and skill. In the past God overlooked such ignorance, but now he commands all people everywhere to repent. **For he has set a day when he will judge the world with justice** by the man he has appointed. He has given proof of this to everyone by raising him from the dead." (Acts 17:21–22a, 23b, 25–26, 29–31) | They sacrificed to false gods, which are not God—**gods they had not known**, gods that recently appeared, gods your ancestors did not fear. (Deut 32:17)<br><br>When the Most High gave the nations their inheritance, when he divided all mankind, he set up boundaries for the peoples according to the number of the sons of Israel. (32:8)<br><br>They are corrupt and not his children; to their shame they are a warped and crooked generation. Is this the way you repay Yahweh, you foolish and unwise people? Is he not your Father, your Creator, who made you and formed you? (32:5–6)<br><br>"It is mine to avenge; I will repay. In due time their foot will slip; **their day of disaster is near** and their doom rushes upon them." . . . He will say: "Now where are their gods, the rock they took refuge in. . . . See now that I myself am he! There is no god besides me. I put to death and I bring to life, I have wounded and I will heal, and no one can deliver out of my hand." (32:35, 37, 39) |

Athens, the Areopagus (Mars Hill), where Paul gave his speech in Acts 17

*iStock.com/IgorDymov*

He also uses the concept of ultimate judgment to press his point. Paul goes on to connect the Song-of-Moses-shaped discourse to the resurrection of the Messiah. Thus, when Paul wants to connect with his biblically illiterate listeners, he does not cite chapter and verse, but he still bases his message on Scripture.

*How does Paul connect the worldview of the Song of Moses with the gospel in his message to the people of Athens?*

Third, the letter to the Romans offers a powerful reading of the teaching in Deuteronomy 30. The meaning of the teaching on the new covenant has significant overlap with the gospel. The Torah is not the gospel but the beginning of the gospel, reaching its apex in its teaching of the new covenant. Paul notes the relationship between the Torah's instruction on the new covenant and the gospel of Messiah (see Table 28-I; also see Hays, *Echoes*, 77–83; Hays, *Conversion*, 85–100).

**Table 28-I:** A Comparison of Deuteronomy 30 and Romans 10

| Torah | Romans 10 |
| --- | --- |
| Keep my decrees and laws, for the person who obeys them will live by them. I am Yahweh. (Lev 18:5)<br><br>Now what I am commanding you today is not too difficult for you or beyond your reach. It is not up in heaven, so that you have to ask, "Who will ascend into heaven to get it and proclaim it to us so we may obey it?" Nor is it beyond the sea, so that you have to ask, "Who will cross the sea to get it and proclaim it to us so we may obey it?" No, **the word is very near you; it is in your mouth and in your heart** so you may obey it. See, I set before you today life and prosperity, death and destruction. (Deut 30:11–15) | Moses writes this about the righteousness that is by the law: "The person who does these things will live by them." But the righteousness that is by faith says: "Do not say in your heart, 'Who will ascend into heaven?'" (that is, to bring Christ down) "or 'Who will descend into the deep?'" (that is, to bring Christ up from the dead). But what does it say? "**The word is near you; it is in your mouth and in your heart**," that is, the message concerning faith that we proclaim: If you declare with your mouth, "Jesus is Lord," and believe in your heart that God raised him from the dead, you will be saved. (Rom 10:5–9, emphases added) |

Paul's use of "law" (from Lev 18:5) and "faith" (related to the word or command of Deut 30) seems to refer to contrary ideals. Moses and Paul, however, are in agreement. Neither Moses nor Paul think people will obey God's commands. They both think that the Torah reveals the rebellion of Israel and humankind (see Deut 31:26–27; Rom 3:19–20). The meaning of Leviticus 18:5 is true for all to whom it applies: The one who obeys the law will live by it. The Five Books of Moses and Romans agree that it is true in principle but is a fictional or hypothetical category in the context of sinful humankind. No one obeys. Torah damns sinners.

Though likely not ancient Golgotha, this hill outside Jerusalem resembles a skull.

*iStock.com/ paul fisher*

If Torah condemns, how can it speak life? Is it not the word that gives life? Of course! If Moses and Paul are both talking about the life-giving word "in your mouth," the Torah for the former and the gospel for the latter, then is it a word of death or of life? Yes and yes. The Torah as a collection of laws, according to Moses and Paul, demonstrates the sin and rebellion of Israel and of humanity in general. It speaks death. But that is not all.

Torah as the beginning of God's story—from the garden to the Skull—speaks the good news to all who have ears to hear. The Torah story, which has a beginning and an ending, is not a world unto itself. Deuteronomy closes, as does Genesis, with a view of the other side, a view that stretches to Golgotha and beyond.

Torah is the beginning of the story that reaches its height in the teaching, death, and resurrection of Messiah. The Torah story is the beginning of the gospel story. Paul says it this way, "Messiah is *the culmination of the Torah* so that there may be righteousness for everyone who believes" (Rom 10:4 lit., emphasis added; see Sanders, 48–51; Hays, *Echoes*, 75–77). The gospel does not remove the need for the Torah story; it enlarges it. The story that the Torah begins finds its completion and goal in the gospel.

*What is the relationship between the Torah and the gospel?*

## INTERACTIVE WORKSHOP

### *Chapter Summary*

The closing chapters of Deuteronomy look back, but only in order to look forward. The view of the other side of the Jordan River carries with it the devastating reality that the people will break the covenant and be exiled from the land. Yet there is hope. The expectations include the new covenant that God will establish with Israel and the coming prophet like Moses.

## *Can You Explain the Key Terms?*

- the book of the Torah
- heaven and earth
- life and death
- new covenant
- other side
- prophet like Moses
- realm of the dead (*sheol*)

## *Challenge Questions*

1. Why did there need to be another covenant (Deut 29:1)?
2. How does the Song of Moses (Deut 32) relate to the biblical narrative of the Torah?
3. What are the leading aspects of the future according to the Song of Moses?
4. What are the similarities and differences between the blessing of Moses (Deut 33) and the blessing of Jacob (Gen 49)?

## *Advanced Questions*

1. How is the expectation for the prophet like Moses related to God's revelation at Mount Horeb?
2. What are the differences and similarities between the endings of each of the Five Books of Moses?
3. What is the significance of the relationship between Joshua 1:1–9 and Deuteronomy 31:1–8?

*4. What is the theological significance of the differences in grammatical construction between "circumcise your heart" in Deuteronomy 10:16 and "he will circumcise your heart" in 30:6?

## *Research Project Ideas*

Compare, exegetically and theologically, the new covenant in Deuteronomy 29–30, Jeremiah 31, and the letter to the Hebrews.

Define the significance of, and any pentateuchal literary relationships between, the items placed in or in front of the ark.

Compare, literarily and/or theologically, the opening chapters of Genesis and the closing chapters of Deuteronomy.

## *The Next Step*


Beckman, Gary. *Hittite Diplomatic Texts*. 2nd ed. Edited by Harry A. Hoffner Jr. Atlanta: Scholars Press, 1999.

Bruno, Chris, Jared Compton, and Kevin McFadden. *Biblical Theology According to the Apostles: How the Earliest Christians Told the Story of Israel*. New Studies in Biblical Theology 52. Downers Grove, IL: IVP Academic, 2020.

Carpenter, Eugene E. "Deuteronomy." Pages 418–547 in vol. 1 of *Zondervan Illustrated Bible Backgrounds Commentary*. Grand Rapids: Zondervan Academic, 2009.

Hays, Richard B. *Echoes of Scripture in the Letters of Paul*. New Haven: Yale University Press, 1989.

———. *The Conversion of the Imagination: Paul as Interpreter of Israel's Scripture*. Grand Rapids: Eerdmans, 2005.

Isbell, Charles David. *The Function of Exodus Motifs in Biblical Narratives: Theological Didactic Drama*. Studies in the Bible and Early Christianity 52. Lewiston, NY: Edwin Mellen, 2002.

Sanders, James A. *Canon as Paradigm: From Sacred Story to Sacred Text*. Philadelphia: Fortress, 1987.

# 29 REINTRODUCING THE TORAH

*Paul Venning*

## GETTING STARTED

### *Focus Questions*

What is the Torah story? How does the Torah fit together with the rest of the Hebrew Scriptures? How does the Torah function within the entire Christian Bible?

### *Look for These Terms*

- Deuteronomistic narrative
- exile
- Former Prophets
- Latter Prophets
- Primary Narrative
- Tanak
- Writings

## THE TORAH STORY

The Five Books of Moses are at the same time the word of God and the beginning of that word, and they tell the story of the beginning of God's word. Each book—Genesis, Exodus, Leviticus, Numbers, Deuteronomy—is a book, but not unto itself. The five books fit together in a coherent and unified narrative series. The serial story begins with God's speaking creation and ends with the hope for the prophet like Moses who will one day bring God's word to his people. The five-part story moves from the garden to the river, just across from the land of promise (see Figure 29-A).

**Figure 29-A:** The Torah Story from the Garden to the River

The serial story begins with the gift of the garden as the home for the new human society. The young society rebelled against the word of God—against the wisdom, order, and life of his word—and was sentenced to death. The sin they embraced brought death, namely, separation from creational life in all its dimensions. The rebels were expelled to the east of the garden into a world that was suddenly conflicted—creational yet cursed, life yet death. The people themselves became the parents of conflicted peoples—in the image of God and yet in lifelong rebellion against the God in whose image they were made.

Sunrise over Maasai Mara, Africa—an echo of the beauty of Eden
*iStock.com/Rixipix*

The tension within creation and the conflicted human race gives birth to the question that impels Torah's story: *How will the word of God prevail over the human rebellion?* The revolution runs across the generations. Eventually everyone is only sinful all the time. God poured out the flood waters of his wrath against the rebellious people and killed everyone except one family, whom he delivered to start over. The new beginning turned out just like the previous one: The peoples grew up in sinfulness and opposition to God's word.

*How does the beginning of the Torah shape its plotline?*

The story takes a surprising turn when Yahweh calls Abraham. He gave him a new word, but not entirely new, to carry forward his creational intention. Yahweh chose Abraham to be the recipient and vehicle of his grace to all families of the earth. He was granted land, the promise of offspring, and blessing. Why did Yahweh grant his word to Abraham? The answer to that question, whatever it is, is one of the hidden things that belongs to God alone. What the reader knows is that Yahweh called Abraham—just because he called him.

Abraham's family, Israel as it turns out, is characterized by the human problem of sin, but God gave his word of hope to them. The chosen people looked forward to the hope for a ruler to one day come from one of their own families. The Judah-king will rule the nations in the last days. Such was the hope of the family even as they were removed from their land to Egypt.

The Egyptians turned against Israel, who cried out to their God. He heard them and remembered his word to their ancestors. God called Moses from a burning bush and revealed himself. He is the I am, Yahweh. God, through his servant Moses, delivered his people and brought them through the wilderness. He gave them life and revelation. Israel, however, rebelled against God's word even as his glory dwelt among them and led them through the treacherous wilderness.

Old Torah scroll opened to Genesis 12

*Scroll of William Krewson used by permission. Photograph by Gary Edward Schnittjer.*

The story closes on the east side of the Jordan River. The people listened to God's word and looked to the land he had promised. The Torah story ends the way it began. The people had before them a choice between death and life—both effects of God's word. They were ready for a new beginning.

The Torah, then, does not finally resolve the human problem. The question remains: How will the word of God overcome the human rebellion? The way to answer the question is bound up within the Torah story. The solution remains in the future of the story. The forward looking serial narrative, therefore, is the beginning of the gospel story. The question of God's word and humankind's rebellion against it continues through the rest of the Scriptures.

*How does the ending of the Torah shape its plotline?*

The "Genesis-shaped" features of Exodus through Deuteronomy provide another clue to the meaning of the Torah story. Each subsequent book of the Torah reflects in different ways the Genesis story. Exodus narrates the creation of the nation based on God's word to the Hebrew ancestors. Moreover, the tabernacle symbolically reflects the creation narrative. Leviticus extends the emphasis on the sacred space of the tabernacle, demonstrating the holiness of the Creator. Numbers explains the interrelationship of the tribes of Israel and the nation's place among the nations according to the relational patterns established in Genesis. Deuteronomy offers a new beginning, setting before the people life and death—a setting with parallels to the garden (also see Block, 133–58).

*In what sense are the latter four books of the Pentateuch Genesis-shaped?*

Are Exodus through Deuteronomy Genesis-shaped or is Genesis Torah-shaped? In either case, the Torah narratives demonstrate significant interdependence and interrelationship. The Torah story as it stands invites readers to think creationally. These tendencies extend into and throughout the Hebrew Scriptures.

## THE TORAH AND THE HEBREW SCRIPTURES

The Torah has a most significant place in the Christian Bible as a whole. But before that can be seen, its place within the Hebrew Scriptures needs to be discerned. The Torah (Genesis, Exodus, Leviticus, Numbers, Deuteronomy) and the Deuteronomistic narrative (Joshua, Judges, Samuel, Kings) together comprise the nine-book serial narrative called the Primary Narrative (see Freedman, 5–6; Alexander, 183). The Primary Narrative presents the story of God's word and his people set in universal context, from the creation of the heavens and the earth to the fall of the city of Jerusalem, the capital of Judah's ancient kingdom. The Torah story is the beginning of the Primary Narrative, a story that begins and ends with the exile of the rebels against God's word (see Figure 29-B). The Primary Narrative continues what the Torah began, namely, searching for the answer to this question: How will God's word prevail over the human rebellion against it?

**Figure 29-B:** Exilic Framing of the Primary Narrative

The Primary Narrative provides the story that serves as the theological framework for the rest of Israel's Scriptures. The remaining writings of Israel's Scriptures—prophetic, narrative, poetic, wisdom, visionary—are in very different ways theological commentary on the Primary Narrative. The Hebrew Scriptures as a whole, therefore, constitute the biblical conversation with the story of God's word and the human rebellion. The specific shape of the conversation, at least in its broadest outlines, can be foregrounded by looking at the Hebrew Scriptures the way the New Testament writers did, as the Torah, Prophets, and Writings.

? *What is the place of the Primary Narrative in the conversation among the books of the Hebrew Scriptures?*

Judaic traditions came to refer to their Scriptures as the Torah, Prophets, and Writings—later called the Tanak, based on the first letter of each word in Hebrew: *Torah*, *Nevi'im* (Prophets), *Ketuvim* (Writings)—the same Scriptures that Protestant Christians call the Old Testament (see Table 29-C). The scrolls were kept in this arrangement in ancient synagogues. The Protestant arrangement of the Hebrew Scriptures apparently follow the Septuagint and Vulgate, the common Greek and Latin translations of these Scriptures (though the Septuagint and Vulgate have additional writings known as the Apocrypha or Deuterocanonical Writings).

| **Judaic arrangement of the Tanak** | | | | |
|---|---|---|---|---|
| *Torah* | *Prophets* | | *Writings* | |
| Genesis<br>Exodus<br>Leviticus<br>Numbers<br>Deuteronomy | (Former Prophets)<br>Joshua<br>Judges<br>Samuel<br>Kings | (Latter Prophets)<br>Isaiah<br>Jeremiah<br>Ezekiel<br>The Twelve | Psalms<br>Job<br>Proverbs<br>Ruth<br>Song of Songs<br>Ecclesiastes | Lamentations<br>Esther<br>Daniel<br>Ezra-Nehemiah<br>Chronicles |

| **Protestant arrangement of the Old Testament** | | | | |
|---|---|---|---|---|
| *(Historical)* | | *(Poetic/Wisdom)* | *(Prophetic)* | |
| Genesis<br>Exodus<br>Leviticus<br>Numbers<br>Deuteronomy | Joshua<br>Judges<br>Ruth<br>1, 2 Samuel<br>1, 2 Kings<br>1, 2 Chronicles<br>Ezra<br>Nehemiah<br>Esther | Job<br>Psalms<br>Proverbs<br>Ecclesiastes<br>Song of Songs | Isaiah<br>Jeremiah<br>Lamentations<br>Ezekiel<br>Daniel | Hosea<br>Joel<br>Amos<br>Obadiah<br>Jonah<br>Micah<br>Nahum<br>Habakkuk<br>Zephaniah<br>Haggai<br>Zechariah<br>Malachi |

**Table 29-C:** Arrangement of the Hebrew Scriptures by Judaic and Protestant Traditions

The arrangements do not change the meaning of the individual books, but they do reflect the different viewpoints of the arrangers concerning the books (sort of like meta-commentaries). The order of the scrolls within the Prophets and the Writings sections of the Tanak are not entirely fixed in the days of Messiah, but the Torah, Prophets, and Writings structure is widespread. The arrangement of the Protestant Old Testament reflects its commitment to chronology and genre, with each genre-based collection ordered chronologically in general.

*How do the different arrangements of the books of the Hebrew Scriptures within the Tanak and Old Testament reflect the general concerns of the arrangers?*

In both arrangements, the leading concerns of the books that converse with the Primary Narrative are the kingdom, exile, and return. Table 29-D summarizes how these three themes dominate in the Latter Prophets and the Writings. The main point of the present discussion is the place of the Torah, which will be addressed in light of this summary.

**Table 29-D:** Kingdom, Exile, Return in the Latter Prophets and Writings

| | |
|---|---|
| Isaiah, Jeremiah, Ezekiel, the Twelve | kingdom, exile, return |
| Psalms | kingdom, exile, return |
| Job | (fear of God, loss, return) |
| Proverbs, Ruth, Song of Songs, Ecclesiastes, Lamentations, Esther, Daniel, Ezra-Nehemiah | kingdom, exile, return |
| Chronicles | kingdom, exile, (return) |

*Isaiah, Jeremiah, Ezekiel,* and the *Twelve Prophets* present stylized anthologies of the prophets' sermons and poetic oracles, each arranged roughly around kingdom, exile, and return.

*Psalms* is arranged into five books (I = 1–41; II = 42–72; III = 73–89; IV = 90–106; V = 107–150). These five books, in broad terms, emphasize the themes of kingdom (Books I and II), exile (Books III and IV), and return (Book V).

*Job* may be an exception, unless it is read at two levels. On the surface, the dialogical poetic narrative interacts with the problem of the righteous who suffer. On a second level, Job's story can be viewed as a parable of sorts on the problem of the exile and the prospect of hope for the faithful remnant who were swept away with the wicked. At this second level, the logic of the book runs along the lines of Psalm 44.

*Proverbs, Ruth,* and *Song of Songs* present wisdom, narrative, and poetry broadly oriented around David and Solomon.

*Ecclesiastes, Lamentations, Esther,* and *Daniel* offer exilic poetry and narrative.

*Ezra-Nehemiah* presents a narrative of the return to the land and the faltering restoration in the early Second Temple period.

*Chronicles* begins with Adam and ends with an edict to return to the land to rebuild the temple. It focuses on the Davidic kingdom and its support of the temple.

If the writings of the Hebrew Scriptures carry on a conversation with the Primary Narrative and are largely oriented around kingdom, exile, and return, then the element that stands out is the first section of the Primary Narrative, namely, the Torah story. The fact that the Hebrew Scriptures deal with kingdom, exile, and return does not mean that they are not concerned with Torah. Just the opposite is true. The conversation among the scrolls about kingdom, exile, and return is all about the meaning of these things in light of the Torah.

Again and again biblical authors make connections with Torah. A tiny fraction of the biblical interconnections with Torah were discussed in the Another Look sections of the preceding Chapters. Detailed interaction with hundreds of places biblical authors interpreted specific Torah contexts can be found elsewhere (see lists in Schnittjer, chs. 1–5).

The Torah, especially its expectation of kingdom, exile, and return, establishes the basis for the biblical interpretation of the meaning of kingdom, exile, and return. The reality of the fall of the Hebrew kingdoms pushes a question to the foreground in many ways: How will God's word finally prevail over the human rebellion?

*What is the place of the Torah in relation to the Hebrew Scriptures' focus on the kingdom, exile, and return?*

The various biblical writings try to explain the meaning of kingdom, exile, and return in the light of Torah. The basis of the conversation is that God's word will not and cannot fail. He speaks, and it must come to pass. The past as explained in the Primary Narrative propels the faithful reader to look forward to what Yahweh will do. The biblical past, as told in the Torah and Deuteronomistic narrative, insists on a future that includes the fulfillment of God's word. Yahweh gave his word to Abraham, Balaam, Moses, and David. The biblical writers look for the coming of the Judah-king, the star of Jacob, the coming of the prophet like Moses, and the return of the son of David. They expect God's word to prevail over sinfulness and death. The fall of the city of God and the exile create expectations for a new beginning. The Torah itself fully expects the collapse of the Hebrew kingdoms and exile, especially in Leviticus 26 and Deuteronomy 27–31.

The Creator spoke. The human race, even the chosen people, rebels. But the story is not over. The Torah is just the beginning. The conversation among the writings of the Hebrew Scriptures presses the question in various directions. How will God's word prevail? The New Testament takes up the conversation and provides the story's answer.

## THE TORAH AND THE ENTIRE CHRISTIAN BIBLE

What is the Torah and who is it for? In his interaction with Genesis 1:1, Rashi, the well-known Judaic commentator of the eleventh century CE, quotes an ancient rabbi who had said the Torah could have begun with Exodus 12:1—"This month is to be for you the first month, the first month of your year"—because it is the first command to Israel (see 1:1). The logic behind such a statement is that the function of the Torah is to give commands—613 commands, 248 positive and 365 prohibitions according to traditional Judaic reckoning—and that it is for the nation of Israel. The Torah houses commands, and many of these teachings are for Israel. The commands to Israel, however, are set within a broader framework.

The New Testament provides several summary reflections on the Torah. I will limit attention to two predominant readings. First, the Torah explains human sinfulness:

> Now we know that *the Torah is good* if anyone uses it the way it should be used. Knowing this, that *the Torah does not exist for a righteous person, but for the torah-less and defiant*, the irreligious and sinful, the unholy and unclean, father-killers and mother-killers, human-killers, sex-seekers, those who practice same-sex relations, human-stealers, liars, deceivers, and any other such thing which opposes wholesome teaching; according to the good news of the blessed God, which he committed to me." (1 Tim 1:8–11, lit., emphasis added; see discussion of this passage in Another Look of Chapter 2)

The Torah is good, as long as it is used according to its design, namely, to reveal the sinfulness of humans. Similar views on the function of the Torah are expressed in Romans 3:19–20 and 7:12–13.

*According to Paul, what is the "good" function of the Torah?*

Second, the Torah points toward Messiah. Jesus spoke against some of his opponents:

> You study the Scriptures diligently because you think that in them you have eternal life. *These are the very Scriptures that testify about me*, yet you refuse to come to me to have life. . . . But do not think I will accuse you before the Father. Your accuser is Moses, on whom your hopes are set. If you believed Moses, you would believe me, *for he wrote about me*. But since you do not believe what he wrote, how are you going to believe what I say?" (John 5:39–40, 45–47; emphasis added)

Messiah's opponents are looking for the right thing (life) in the right place (the Scriptures), but, according to Messiah, they missed what the Scriptures are saying. He taught that the Torah leads to the Messiah. The same thing is taught in many other contexts (see, e.g., Luke 16:31; 24:26–27, 45–46; Acts 24:14; 26:22–23).

*What is the relationship between the Torah and messianic expectations?*

The New Testament states that reading Torah rightly means hearing it explain sin as the human problem and seeing how it points to Messiah. How can these things be? Or, as asked above, what is the Torah and who is it for?

The Torah is the beginning of *the story*. It is God's word for all of humankind. The plotline of the redemptive story, which can best be stated in the form of a question because of the nature of serial narratives, is: *How will the word of God prevail over the human rebellion?* The story, even when it is largely focused on Israel, is the human story. The descendants of Abraham were chosen to, among other things, bring blessing to all nations. Moreover, the chosen nation was to be a kingdom of priests to the families of the entire earth.

The word of God prevails in the Messiah. "*Messiah is the culmination of the Torah* so that there may be righteousness for everyone who believes" (Rom 10:4, lit., emphasis added; see third point of Another Look in Chapter 28). Stated differently, the redemptive narrative initiated in the Torah comes to its highpoint in the Gospels.

After the Primary Narrative, the four Gospels along with the Acts of the Apostles are the next installments of the serial narrative that reaches back to creation. All the writings of the Bible fit into the narrative framework of the Primary Narrative and its sequel, the Gospels. The letters of the New Testament engage in conversation with the Hebrew Scriptures. They are not merely commentaries on the Scriptures but rather explain them in light of the Messiah's teaching, death, and resurrection. Faith in Messiah showed the New Testament authors how to interpret Israel's Scriptures, and those Scriptures explain the meaning of Messiah. Faith in Jesus the Messiah transforms the way we read Israel's Scriptures as the beginning of the gospel story (similarly see Childs, 726).

*How did the New Testament writers approach the relationship between the Hebrew Scriptures and the Messiah?*

The Messiah did not come with his mighty delegates to rule by power. The celestial delegates were restrained even as their Lord faced his own death (Matt 26:53–54). The story of Messiah accords with the stories of Judah's humiliation and the humble confession of Judah's descendant David. While Messiah was like Judah and David in their self-humiliations, he did what they did not and could not do.

This ancient empty garden tomb outside Jerusalem provides a place for Christians to reflect on the resurrection of Messiah.



The Torah story is not opposed to the gospel, nor is it the gospel. The Torah story is the beginning of the gospel story. The story that begins in Eden reaches its

### What is the relationship between the Torah story and the gospel?

"They will beat their swords into plowshares" (Isa 2:4).

A chair of guns made after the civil war in Mozambique in 1992 to symbolize peace in the Transforming Arms into Ploughshares Project

*Jon Cooper*

height on the Skull. "Messiah died for our sins according to the Scriptures . . . he was buried . . . [and] was raised on the third day according to the Scriptures" (1 Cor 15:3b–4).

How will the word of God overcome the human rebellion? The deadly effects of sin have already been vanquished in the Messiah's humiliation and death. But the end is not yet. Genesis ends with the expectation for the coming of the Judah-king in the last days. The Torah ends with a view of the other side of the Jordan River, looking forward to a prophet like Moses. The prophets spoke of a day when swords will be beaten into plowshares. The New Testament, likewise, looks forward. We wait for the return of the king, in accord with the Torah story, the beginning of the gospel.

## INTERACTIVE WORKSHOP

### Chapter Summary

The Torah story can be summarized in the form of a question: How will the word of God conquer the human rebellion? The other writings of the Old Testament engage in lively interpretive conversation with the Torah story in relation to the kingdom, the exile, and the return. The result is an abiding expectation for the coming of the Judah-king. The New Testament presents Jesus as the long-expected Messiah who conquers sin by his teaching, death, and resurrection. The Torah, then, is the beginning of the gospel.

### Can You Explain the Key Terms?

- Deuteronomistic narrative
- exile
- Former Prophets
- Latter Prophets
- Primary Narrative
- Tanak
- Writings

### Challenge Questions

1. In what ways is the Torah Genesis-shaped?
2. How does the Torah function within the Primary Narrative?
3. What is the relationship between the Torah and the gospel?

## *Advanced Questions*

1. How does the Primary Narrative function as the framework for the interpretive conversation of the other books of the Hebrew Scriptures?
2. How do the New Testament writings join with, and yet expand on, the ongoing biblical conversation with the story that begins in the Torah?

## *Research Project Ideas*

Explain the relationship between the Torah and the Deuteronomistic narrative.

Explain the "conversation" between one book of the Hebrew Scriptures and the Primary Narrative.

Explain the relationship of the Torah and the gospel.

## *The Next Step*


Alexander, T. Desmond. "Royal Expectations in Genesis to Kings: Their Importance for Biblical Theology." *Tyndale Bulletin* 49 (1998): 191–212.

Block, Daniel I. "In the Tradition of Moses: The Conceptual and Stylistic Imprint of Deuteronomy on the Patriarchal Narratives." Pages 133–58 in *Exploring the Composition of the Pentateuch*. Edited by L. S. Baker Jr. et al. University Park, PA: Eisenbrauns, 2020.

Childs, Brevard S. *Biblical Theology of the Old and New Testaments: Theological Reflection on the Christian Bible*. Minneapolis: Fortress, 1992.

Freedman, David Noel. *The Unity of the Bible*. Ann Arbor: University of Michigan Press, 1991.

Rashi (Rabbi Shlomo Yitzhaki). *The Metsudah Chumash/Rashi*. 5 vols. Edited by Rabbi Avrohom Davis. New York: Ktav, 1998.

Schnittjer, Gary Edward. *Old Testament Use of Old Testament*. Grand Rapids: Zondervan Academic, 2021.

# A NOTE ON THE SECOND EDITION

I am humbled by and grateful for the warm reception of *Torah Story*. The second edition is long overdue. The primary reason for the delay relates to other projects that I needed to complete. This note on the second edition is mainly directed to professors who are familiar with the previous edition of *Torah Story*.

What has *not* changed? The thesis, argument, and interpretive angle remains the same, even though all has been extensively refined. The Chapters of both editions follow the same natural transitions in the Torah itself. In that sense, adopting the second edition can be somewhat seamless. The pedagogical elements at the beginning and end of the Chapters follow the same structure even though many elements have been upgraded.

What has changed in the study of Torah since the first edition came out? A lot. This provided an opportunity for a large number of updates. My own continued research on connections within the Bible also helped me to carefully evaluate and adjust the biblical interconnections featured throughout this book.

What has changed within the textbook? A lot. Here is a list of the main elements that are new in the second edition.

- Updating citations based on new research throughout
- Presentation of new evidence for the covenant shape of Exodus 20–24 and Deuteronomy (see Chapters 14 and 24)
- Extensive revisions to Chapters 14 (Exod 15–24), 15 (Exod 25–40), and 25 (Deut 1–4)
- Chapter 1 completely re-written with a couple of elements from the first edition added back in
- All other Chapters revised and updated medium to lightly, including many new elements
- Streamlining the entire book by trimming more than 27,000 words
- Many dozens of new images
- Images of the so-called Tower of Babel relief (by permission) and the four-horned altar discovered at Shilo (by permission)

- Updating interior design
- Full updating and expansion of professor's resources available at no cost in TextbookPlus at ZondervanAcademic.com
- *Workbook* (available separately)
- American Stories and the Torah Story activities moved to TextbookPlus

Though most of the items listed above are transparent, it may be worth explaining a couple. Many textbooks seem to get thicker with each revision simply adding more. But with massive changes in academic delivery and a new generation of students coming of age, I decided to trim the second edition. It is still a full-size textbook—many students will likely complain that it is too long. The second edition is approximately 27,000 fewer words. This was due mostly to tightening up everything even while retaining detailed attention to everything that needs it. This reduction, along with a tighter design, translates into an overall reduction of more than sixty pages.

Chapter 1 has been completely re-written (with a couple of elements retained and added back in). I do not repent of Chapter 1 in the first edition. It always makes me smile when students or professors who use the textbook refer to some of the Chapter's distinct language. No one has complained. But students have changed. The sort of students targeted by Chapter 1 in the first edition have been coming into the classroom less and less in recent years. The second edition's Chapter 1 seeks to introduce an apprenticeship on Torah in a more direct manner with less jargon suited to a newer generation of students.

It remains a pleasure to study and learn with students who wrestle with Torah's call to Yahweh's redemptive will. It is my hope that the second edition of *Torah Story* will help students accept the invitation of an apprenticeship on Torah.

# CREDITS

NJPS is used to indicate Scripture quotations from the Jewish Publication Society Bible. The Jewish Bible: Torah, Nevi'im, Kethuvim. Copyright © 1985 by The Jewish Publication Society. Used by permission. All rights reserved.

Scripture quotations marked by Fox refer to Everett Fox, *The Five Books of Moses*, vol. 1, Schocken Bible (New York: Schocken, 1983, 1986, 1990, 1995).

# ACKNOWLEDGMENTS

Thanks be to the Lord for Torah as well as for the strength and mercy needed for this project in its second edition.

I express my gratitude to Cairn University and its Divinity School. I am grateful for their funding my participation in several academic societies and conferences, an annual book budget, as well as covering the cost of the indexes. Thank you to the president and the provost's office for supporting research that benefits students.

The dean of the Divinity School, Keith Plummer, fosters a spirit of comradery and values research. I have enjoyed favorable course schedules, frequent relief from committee responsibilities, and funding for research assistants. I am grateful to Keith for offering critical feedback on some very subtle and sensitive areas of interpretation.

I was humbled by and grateful for the invitation to present research toward the second edition to the School of Divinity faculty. I benefitted from their warm reception, encouragement, and lively feedback.

Thank you to my research assistants Matthew Wilson, Paul Velamparampil, and Kimberly Ellis for helping create new professors' materials for the second edition. I am grateful to several research assistants, who did much scanning and many trips to the library—always with good cheer. Thank you to Caroline Master, Hannah Conger, Rachel Hevalow, and Lauren Raab. For assistance with the *Workbook*, thank you to Caroline Master, Briana Borowski, Courtney Bottge, Katie Colabella, Bobby Larew, and Cai Matthews. I have also benefitted by administrative assistance from Laurie Handzlik and Katrina Selby.

I owe special thanks to Carmen Joy Imes. Carmen took time away from her own research to read a new version of Chapter 1 and offer critical and student-oriented feedback. She said she wished there was a way to visually depict the slowing down of narrative time in Genesis 12–21 which led to making Figure 1-B. Carmen also graciously tested an early draft of the *Workbook* with her Torah students. The critical feedback from Carmen and her students were invaluable. Carmen also graciously provided me a pre-publication copy of her *Being God's Image*.

Thank you to my students for dynamic and spirited engagement with Torah in the classroom and elsewhere. It remains a joy to spend my days with students who seek to understand and obey the redemptive will of God in the Scriptures. Special thanks go to my spring 2020 Pentateuch sections. They worked through an early version of the *Workbook* in its entirety and provided weekly feedback. Their unrestrained critical evaluation led to many concrete improvements.

I am grateful to Todd Williams for visiting my Pentateuch class for many years to share his expertise on butchering large game animals. This has been a great help in interpreting the sacrifices in Leviticus.

Thank you to Mark Sanders for feedback on two particularly challenging paragraphs.

I owe a great debt of gratitude to Barbara Arnold. She has looked up every verse reference in the second edition of the textbook along with its *Workbook* looking for errors. Barbara has also offered many other kinds of suggestions.

Thank you to Gordon Johnston for providing me with a prepublication copy of his essay on Hittite treaties. I am grateful to Matthew Lynch for sharing a prepublication copy of his book *Flood and Fury* with me. Thank you to Danny Hays for letting me use a prepublication copy of his book on the Pentateuch.

I am grateful to those who generously provided images that are used in the second edition: Jess Belani, John Cooper, Isaiah and Abby Cramer, Donald Cruz, Earl Hagar, Robert C. Kashow, William Krewson, Matthew Parks, SSG Randy Welchel. I express my gratitude to Michael C. Luddeni and Scott Stripling for permission to use images of the four-horned altar of Shiloh and to Andrew George for permission to use an image of his drawing of the Tower of Babel stele. Credits for all images appear ad loc.

I am grateful to several authors and publishers that granted permission to use tables, figures, and poems. These credits for permissions appear ad loc.

Thank you to Jenny Moo for producing the indexes and discovering many typos.

I here express my gratitude to Nancy Erickson at Zondervan Academic. Nancy's expertise with exegesis of the Hebrew Bible complements her excellence as an editor. Nancy never forgets student readers. This project has benefitted by Nancy's plentiful feedback and suggestions. Nancy seamlessly navigated this project through many production complications. She remains encouraging and patient along with quick responses to emails. For all of this I say thank you.

Thank you to Kait Lamphere for the interior design and to Jeanine Strock for visual editing. It was encouraging that Jeanine began by reading the book. This helped toward finding, securing, and presenting the right kind of images in the right ways. Kait and Jeanine both went extra miles to develop a streamlined format in a way that visually supports student learning. They did not merely try to get it done. They tackled many small details working to make sure it was done well. I am grateful to Matthew Miller for patience going through extra rounds with the cover as well as for other help with marketing. I remain grateful for the warmth and professionalism of Zondervan Academic.

It needs to be said that any errors are my responsibility.

I am grateful to my wife Cheri. This project would have been impossible without Cheri. She put me through my graduate studies making that my full-time vocation for those years. All of my teaching and writing projects, including this one, benefit from those years of study. Cheri made it possible to do the research and writing needed for the second edition of this project. In addition she proofread the manuscript detecting a large number of errors as well as offering many suggestions for improvement. For all of this and more I here express my gratitude.

# INDEX OF SCRIPTURE AND OTHER ANCIENT LITERATURE

## Old Testament

### Genesis

## Exodus

## Leviticus

## Numbers

## Deuteronomy

## Joshua



## Judges



## Ruth



## 1 Samuel



## 2 Samuel



## 1 Kings

## 2 Kings



## 1 Chronicles



## 2 Chronicles



## Ezra



## Nehemiah



## Esther



## Job



## Psalms

# INDEX OF SUBJECTS AND AUTHORS

# INDEX OF FIGURES, MAPS, SIDEBARS, AND TABLES

# Torah Story Workbook

*Gary Edward Schnittjer*

This workbook accompanies Gary Edward Schnittjer's *Torah Story*. Following the textbook's structure, it offers chapter-by-chapter guided exercises designed to support the students learning experience and enhance their comprehension of the Pentateuch.

Working knowledge of the Bible's first five books is essential for every serious student of the Scriptures. *Torah Story* by Gary Edward Schnittjer emphasizes the content of the text itself, moving beyond debating dates and theories of authorship into understanding how these key books of the Bible help us understand the story of salvation.

*Available in stores and online!*